COGNITIVE BEHAVIOR THERAPY WITH OLDER ADULTS

About the Authors

Kristen Hilliard Sorocco, PhD, is an Assistant Professor of Research in the Donald W. Reynolds Department of Geriatric Medicine at the University of Oklahoma Health Sciences Center and a Geropsychologist for the Community Living Center at the VA Medical Center, Oklahoma City, OK. Dr. Sorocco received her PhD in clinical psychology and a certificate in gerontology from Oklahoma State University. She completed her clinical internship in California at the Palo Alto Veterans Affairs Health Care System. During her internship year, she received specialized training in geropsychology. She completed her postdoctoral training in biological psychology through the Department of Psychiatry and Behavioral Sciences at the University of Oklahoma Health Sciences Center. Dr. Sorocco is a chapter author in several books, including the *Handbook of Obesity Intervention for the Lifespan; Psychopathology: Contemporary Issues, Theory, and Research* (2nd ed.); and *Cognitive Behavioral Therapy with Ethnically Diverse Populations.* She has written articles on cognitive behavioral therapy (CBT) with older adults in professional journals, such as *The Clinical Gerontologist, Clinical Psychology Review, Journal of Clinical Geropsychology, The Gerontologist, American Journal of Geriatric Psychiatry,* and *Professional Psychology: Research and Practice.* Dr. Sorocco is also an active member of the Association for Behavioral and Cognitive Therapies, having served as past membership chair and current co-leader of the Aging Behavioral and Cognitive Therapy Special Interest Group.

Sean Lauderdale, PhD, is an Associate Professor of Psychology and Counseling at Pittsburg State University. He is also the Director of Pittsburg State University's Center for Human Services' Older Adult Screening and Intervention Services (OASIS), which provides psychological screening and assessment services specifically tailored for older adults. His work appears in many professional journals including *The Gerontologist, Clinical Gerontologist, Journal of Geriatric Psychiatry and Neurology,* and *American Journal of Alzheimer's Disease and Other Dementias.* Dr. Lauderdale has been an invited reviewer for the *Clinical Gerontologist, Psychosomatics,* and *Therapy.*

COGNITIVE BEHAVIOR THERAPY WITH OLDER ADULTS

Innovations Across Care Settings

Kristen Hilliard Sorocco, PhD
Sean Lauderdale, PhD

SPRINGER PUBLISHING COMPANY
NEW YORK

Springer Publishing Company, LLC
11 West 42nd Street
New York, NY 10036
www.springerpub.com

Acquisitions Editor: Sheri W. Sussman
Senior Production Editor: Diane Davis
Cover Design: David Levy
Composition: Absolute Service, Inc.; Teresa Exley, Project Manager

ISBN: 978-0-8261-0619-3
E-book ISBN: 978-0-8261-0620-9
11 12 13 14 15/ 5 4 3 2 1

The author and the publisher of this work have made every effort to use sources believed to be reliable to provide information that is accurate and compatible with the standards generally accepted at the time of publication. Because medical science is continually advancing, our knowledge base continues to expand. Therefore, as new information becomes available, changes in procedures become necessary. We recommend that the reader always consult current research and specific institutional policies before perform-ing any clinical procedure. The author and publisher shall not be liable for any special, consequential, or exemplary damages resulting, in whole or in part, from the readers' use of, or reliance on, the information contained in this book. The publisher has no responsibility for the persistence or accuracy of URLs for external or third-party Internet Web sites referred to in this publication and does not guarantee that any content on such Web sites is, or will remain, accurate or appropriate.

Library of Congress Cataloging-in-Publication Data

Sorocco, Kristen Hilliard.
  Cognitive behavior therapy with older adults : innovations across care settings / Kristen Hilliard Sorocco, Sean Lauderdale.
     p. ; cm.
  Includes bibliographical references and index.
  ISBN 978-0-8261-0619-3 (alk. paper) — ISBN 978-0-8261-0620-9 (e-book)
  1. Cognitive therapy. 2. Psychotherapy for older people. 3. Mental illness—Treatment. I. Lauderdale, Sean. II. Title.
  [DNLM: 1. Cognitive Therapy—methods. 2. Aged. 3. Mental Disorders—therapy. WM 425.5.C6]
  RC489.C63S67 2011
  616.89'142—dc22
                                              2011002643

Printed in the United States of America by Hamilton Printing Company.

Contents

Part I: Cognitive Behavior Therapy and Common Mental Health Problems Among Older Adults

MOOD DISORDERS

ANXIETY DISORDERS

IMPLEMENTING CBT FOR CAREGIVERS

Contributors

Kristi L. Bratkovich, PhD
University of Oklahoma Health Sciences Center
Oklahoma City VAMC
Oklahoma City, OK

Gregory K. Brown, PhD
Department of Psychiatry
University of Pennsylvania
Philadelphia, PA

Rebecca P. Cameron, PhD
California State University, Sacramento
Sacramento, CA

Jennifer S. Cheavens, PhD
The Ohio State University
Columbus, OH

Suzie Chen, PhD
VA Long Beach Healthcare System
Long Beach, CA

Colleen Clemency, PhD
Edith Nourse Rogers Memorial Veterans Hospital
Bedford, MA

Joan M. Cook, PhD
Yale University School of Medicine and National Center for PTSD
New Haven, CT

Jacquelynn N. Copeland, MA
University of Alabama at Birmingham
Birmingham, AL

Jeffrey A. Cully, PhD
Michael E. DeBakey Veterans Affairs Medical Center
Baylor College of Medicine South Central Mental Illness Research,
    Education, and Clinical Center
Houston Center for Quality of Care and Utilization Studies
Houston, TX

Natalie D. Dautovich, PhD
Department of Aging and Mental Health Disparities
Florida Mental Health Institute
University of South Florida
Tampa, FL

John P. Dennis, PhD
Department of Psychiatry
University of Pennsylvania
Philadelphia, PA

Laura E. Dreer, PhD
Assistant Professor and Director of Psychological and
   Neuropsychological Services
Department of Ophthalmology
University of Alabama at Birmingham
Birmingham, AL

Leilani Feliciano, PhD
Department of Psychology
University of Colorado at Colorado Springs
Colorado Springs, CO

Sarah S. Fraley, PhD
VA Long Beach Healthcare System
Long Beach, CA

Sharon Morgillo Freeman, PhD, PMHCNS-BC, CARN-AP
Associate Faculty
Purdue University
Fort Wayne, IN

Dolores Gallagher-Thompson, PhD, ABPP
Director, Stanford Geriatric Education Center and
Professor of Research, Department of Psychiatry and Behavioral Sciences
Stanford University School of Medicine
Certified Cognitive Therapist, Specialist in Geropsychology
Palo Alto, CA

Zvi D. Gellis, PhD
Hartford Geriatric Social Work Faculty Scholar
Associate Professor and Director, Center for Mental Health and Aging
School of Social Policy and Practice
University of Pennsylvania
Philadelphia, PA

Gali Goldwaser, PhD
Independent Practice
San Marcos, CA

Amber M. Gum, PhD
Department of Aging and Mental Health Disparities
Florida Mental Health Institute
University of South Florida
Tampa, FL

John Paul Jameson, PhD
Michael E. DeBakey Veterans Affairs Medical Center
Baylor College of Medicine South Central Mental Illness Research,
    Education, and Clinical Center
Houston Center for Quality of Care and Utilization Studies
Houston, TX

Bradley E. Karlin, PhD
Erickson School of Aging Studies
University of Maryland, Baltimore County, Baltimore, MD
Office of Mental Health Services
U.S. Department of Veterans Affairs Central Office
Washington, DC

Larry Lemos, RN, MSN, MHA, GCNS-BC
VA Long Beach Healthcare System
Long Beach, CA

Sharon Lewis , RN, PhD, FAAN
Research Professor, Castella Distinguished Professor
School of Nursing
University of Texas Health Sciences Center at San Antonio
San Antonio, TX

Julie Loebach Wetherell, PhD
VA San Diego Healthcare System and
University of California, San Diego
San Diego, CA

Jocelyn McGee, PhD
Office of Mental Health Services
Psychotherapy and Psychogeriatrics Section
Veterans Health Administration and
    Department of Psychiatry and Human Behavior
University of Mississippi Medical Center
Jackson, MS

Linda R. Mona, PhD
VA Long Beach Healthcare System
Long Beach, CA

Denise Miner-Williams, RN, PhD, CHPN
Research Assistant Professor, School of Nursing
University of Texas Health Sciences Center at San Antonio
GREC Educator, Researcher
South Texas Veterans Healthcare System
San Antonio, TX

Arthur M. Nezu, PhD, ABPP
Drexel University
Philadelphia, PA

Monica M. Parkins, BA
Pacific Graduate School of Psychology
Palo Alto, CA

Andrew J. Petkus, MA
San Diego State University/University of California
San Diego Joint Doctoral Program in Clinical Psychology
San Diego, CA

Robert Reiser, PhD
Pacific Graduate School of Psychology
Palo Alto University
Palo Alto, CA

Shilpa Reddy, MA
Pacific Graduate School of Psychology
Palo Alto, CA

Joshua L. Ruberg, PhD
VA San Diego Healthcare System
San Diego, CA

Daniel L. Segal, PhD
Department of Psychology
University of Colorado at Colorado Springs
Colorado Springs, CO

Heather M. Sones
San Diego State University/University of California
San Diego Joint Doctoral Program in Clinical Psychology
San Diego, CA

Maggie L. Syme, PhD
VA Boston Healthcare System
Boston, MA

Larry W. Thompson, PhD
Professor Emeritus, Department of Medicine
Stanford University School of Medicine
Stanford, CA

Steven R. Thorp, PhD
The Center of Excellence for Stress and Mental Health
VA San Diego Healthcare System
University of California, San Diego
San Diego, CA

Christina L. Vair, MA
Department of Psychology
University of Colorado at Colorado Springs
Colorado Springs, CO

Dina O. Wirick, MS
VA Long Beach Healthcare System
Long Beach, CA

Foreword

This book contains an excellent selection of chapters designed to introduce the reader to the field of clinical gerontology: the application of psychological and developmental theories and practices to diagnosis and treatment of mental health problems of later life. This field is attracting more attention on the national level now that Medicare has recognized that mental health services can be given by various providers— such as licensed clinical social workers, licensed psychologists, clinical nurse practitioners, and board-certified psychiatrists—can be reimbursed. Until relatively recently, the lack of government-sponsored reimbursement was a significant barrier to older adults seeking care for their problems. Recent legislation has emphasized parity among providers of both standard health care and mental health care, so in the future, it is anticipated that more individual providers will become Medicare-eligible, and more older adults will take advantage of their mental health benefits under the law. Given this context, there is a substantial need for information about just what the common mental health problems of later life are, and what effective ways to treat them have been developed. In this book the editors have brought together, in one volume, chapters that address many of these needs.

Part I discusses the use of various forms of psychosocial interventions (emphasizing cognitive behavioral therapy, CBT) for treating common problems such as depression (both unipolar and bipolar), generalized anxiety disorder, and PTSD. The book is enriched by the inclusion of several other chapters that are not commonly found including a detailed discussion of how to assess suicidal risk in older adults, and how to use CBT to help the person become less suicidal. This is an innovative feature of this volume and one that has great relevance to clinical practice. The chapters in Part II discuss innovations in treating late-life mental health problems in a variety of settings, including primary care, hospice, and the patient's home. An informative chapter on the VA Health Care System as a major provider of mental health care to older veterans is also included. As in the first section, the flexibility and breadth of application of CBT are emphasized, and the reader is strongly encouraged to incorporate this approach into his/her every-day practice—regardless of where it takes place.

Several other features of this book are worth noting: first, it is clearly written and easy to follow; second, the chapters are written by practitioners and clinical researchers from a variety of disciplines, including nursing, social work, cognitive rehabilitation, and psychology (which adds to the breadth and depth of topics being discussed); third, each chapter includes clinical case examples that bring the information "to life" and finally, various forms and other self-help tools are included, making it easier for busy practitioners to incorporate these methods into their practice.

In short, this book is strongly recommended as a textbook on the graduate level in courses containing content on mental health and aging. It provides a fine introduction to the field and gives a strong overview of what is currently known—and not known—regarding the disorders the editors chose to focus on. It definitely fills a gap in the field at the present time. The writing is clear, and the information is tremendously valuable for students from a wide variety of disciplines who are planning to develop a career in the mental health care of older adults.

Dolores Gallagher-Thompson, PhD, ABPP
Director, Stanford Geriatric Education Center
Professor of Research, Department of Psychiatry and Behavioral Sciences
Stanford University School of Medicine
Certified Cognitive Therapist, Specialist in Geropsychology
Palo Alto, CA

Preface

This book was designed to be a one-stop shop for all practitioners of mental health disciplines, including nursing, medicine, psychology, and social work, who provide care to older adults. The contributing authors of this book represent various disciplines, including nursing, social work, and psychology, and bring expertise from various health care settings. The primary goal of the book is to provide an overview of cognitive behavioral therapy (CBT) and evidence-based practices specifically designed for older adults. The book begins with an introduction that provides an overview on CBT and adaptations that need to be made when working with older adults.

Following the Introduction, the book is divided into two parts. Part I focuses on the most prevalent mental health issues among older adults, including mood and anxiety disorders, dementia, and sexual dysfunction. Each of these chapters provides an overview on the epidemiology, diagnosis, and assessment procedures specific to the common mental health disorders among older adults. Useful assessment tools are identified, described, and guidelines for administration are highlighted. Evidence-based practices concerning the treatment of common mental health issues among older adults are reviewed, with a heavy emphasis on CBT.

Part II of this book highlights innovations in the use of CBT across health care settings such as primary care, cognitive rehabilitation, hospice and palliative care, home-based interventions, and the VA Health Care System. Implementation issues and necessary adaptations to CBT are discussed by the contributing authors. For example, the flexibility of CBT allows for briefer sessions in fast-paced clinics such as primary care, and tips for talking with medical providers are highlighted. Furthermore, the cognitive rehabilitation section discusses adaptations to CBT that need to be made based on the region of the brain impacted by a cognitive impairment. Insights provided are critical to the dissemination of evidence-based practices among the diverse settings that serve older adults.

Incorporated into each chapter are the following:

1. Case examples to illustrate how to implement cognitive–behavioral skills and therapies to treat common disorders; and
2. Tools to assist mental health providers to integrate cognitive–behavioral skills and therapies within various health care settings designed to address the needs of older adults.

Contributing authors have included practice friendly tools, such as a five-column thought record, a pocket card on suicide risk assessment with older adults, and an assessment note template for working with older adults in primary care. A complete toolkit, comprised of clinician and educational tools, can be copied from the Appendix sections of the book or can be downloaded with the code provided by the publisher to the buyer at the time of purchase.

The partnership for this book began when the editors were geropsychology interns at the Palo Alto Veterans Administration Health Care System. Drs. Lauderdale and Sorocco continued their collaboration following internship and co-lead the Aging Behavioral and Cognitive Therapy Special Interest Group within the Association for Behavioral and Cognitive Therapies. Being the editors, it is their hope that readers find this book a useful tool for both everyday practice as well as for training of future mental health care providers.

Acknowledgments

As the next generation of cognitive behavioral therapists working with older adults, there are many individuals who are responsible for getting us to this point in our careers. We would like to acknowledge our mentors, including Dolores Gallagher-Thompson, PhD; Gayle Iwamasa, PhD; David Freed, PhD; and Antonette Zeiss, PhD. The Association for Behavioral and Cognitive Therapies (ABCT) has provided us with a professional home throughout our career development, for which we are truly grateful. The guidance from our mentors and involvement in ABCT has led to our collaboration with the contributing authors. A special gratitude goes to our contributing authors for their time, dedication, and expertise, without whom this book would not be possible. We are truly honored to work with such a dedicated and inspiring group of clinicians, researchers, and educators.

We would like to express our sincere appreciation to Springer Publishing Company for the opportunity to provide the field with this innovative book. Without the perseverance and support of Sheri W. Sussman, Senior Vice President, Editorial, this book would not have been born. We'd like to recognize and thank Kristi Bratkovich, PhD, for assisting with the final submission of the book. The production editor and staff took our words and turned it into an amazing final product.

Major endeavors, such as this book, are only feasible with the support of institutions, colleagues, and families. We would like to thank our affiliated institutions and colleagues for the opportunity to engage in a work for which we truly have a passion. Our settings provide us with the opportunity to collaborate with and learn from older adults and their families, which in turn allows the field to grow. Finally, we'd like to express our appreciation to our families who have sacrificed their time with us, to enable us to dedicate the time necessary to complete this book. We also are grateful to our families for reminding us of the importance of finding balance between our personal and professional lives.

COGNITIVE BEHAVIOR THERAPY WITH OLDER ADULTS

1

Cognitive Behavioral Therapy With Older Adults

Bradley E. Karlin

Cognitive behavioral therapy (CBT) is a brief, structured psychotherapy that focuses on the key roles that cognitions and behaviors have in the onset and maintenance of mental illness. CBT has been shown to be effective in treating a wide range of mental disorders, including depression, anxiety, bipolar disorder, substance use disorders, eating disorders, insomnia, and personality disorders (e.g., Butler, Chapman, Forman, & Beck, 2006). In addition, recent research has also shown CBT to be efficacious in treating symptoms of schizophrenia (Beck & Rector, 2005), with additional research currently underway. CBT has also been shown to be at least as efficacious as medication for moderate-to-severe major depression (e.g., DeRubeis et al., 2005). For many patients, a combination of CBT and medication has shown to be more effective than either treatment alone (e.g., DeRubeis et al.). CBT has also been shown to have enduring effects that often far outlast the completion of treatment (e.g., Hollon, Stewart, & Strunk, 2006).

Over the last several decades, there has been significant research examining the efficacy of CBT with older adults, specifically. This research has consistently shown that CBT is efficacious with older individuals. Much of this research has focused on the use of CBT for treating depression in older adults (e.g., Pinquart & Sörensen, 2001; Scogin, Welsh, Hanson, Stump, & Coates, 2005), although there has been increasing research in recent years documenting the efficacy of CBT for the treatment of late-life anxiety (Barrowclough et al., 2001; Stanley et al., 2003), insomnia, and pain (Morin, Colecchi, Stone, Sood, & Brink, 1999; Vitiello, Rybarczyk, Von Korff, & Stepanski, 2009). In general, older adults can benefit from CBT to approximately the same degree as younger adults. Specific adaptations to the therapy strategies and process can maximize treatment gains with older clients, although the core ingredients of CBT remain the same when working with older adults. This chapter provides an overview of CBT, identifying the theoretical foundations and core therapy processes and strategies, along with important considerations and modifications for adapting CBT to, and maximizing outcomes with, older clients. Particular emphasis is placed on the application of CBT for depression with older adults. Readers interested in a more detailed discussion of CBT for depression are referred to a therapist manual and specific protocol we have developed for veterans and military Servicemembers (Wenzel, Brown, & Karlin, 2011).

THEORETICAL FOUNDATIONS OF COGNITIVE BEHAVIORAL THERAPY

The backbone of CBT is the integration of cognitive theory and behavioral theory. According to cognitive theory, how we think about or interpret situations affect our mood and behaviors. It is our beliefs and perceptions of events—not the events themselves—that lead us to feel the way we do in a given situation (Beck, 1967). The notion that our thoughts or beliefs mediate the relationship between a situation (or "activating event") and our emotional or behavioral response is often referred to as the "ABC" model, where "A" refers to *activating event*, "B" refers to the *belief* or interpretation of the activating event, and "C" refers to the *consequent emotional, physiological, and/or behavioral response*. This is presented diagrammatically in Figure 1.1.

Because it is the meaning that we ascribe to situations or encounters that contribute to how we feel about a situation, two people in the same situation may have different emotional reactions. For example, consider Elena and Fred who work on a team together in an advertising firm. Elena and Fred, 67 and 69 years of age, respectively, are employed as marketing consultants and recently completed a proposal for a new advertising campaign, which they submitted to their supervisor for review. After reviewing the proposal, their boss sent Elena and Fred an e-mail message stating, "This looks okay; let's meet tomorrow to discuss some ideas further" (Activating event). In response to this message, Elena immediately had the thought, "She hates it; I can't do this job, and others are starting to figure this out" (Belief). Consequently,

Activating Event (Situation)	⇒	Belief (Thought/Interpretation)	⇒	Consequence (Emotional, Physiological, and/or Behavioral Response)

FIGURE 1.1   ABC Model

she feels great disappointment and dreads the meeting tomorrow, and the next day she calls in sick (Consequent emotion and behavior). The type of sudden, negative thought that Elena had in this example is called an "automatic thought" in CBT. An "automatic thought" is a sudden thought, often unrecognized by an individual, that leads to a negative emotional or behavioral response. Unlike Elena, however, Fred reacts to his boss's e-mail message with the thought, "I'm glad she thinks this is a reasonable first draft; it would be good to discuss this further tomorrow" (Belief). This leaves him with feelings of contentment and curiosity (Consequent emotion).

What accounts for the different interpretations individuals may have to a common event, and why some individuals may have one or more automatic thoughts in response to a situation whereas another individual in the same situation will not? In the previous example, why is it that Elena had the interpretation that she did, whereas Fred had a much more neutral interpretation of the same e-mail message from their boss? According to cognitive theory, individuals develop cognitive schemas that affect how they evaluate and make meaning of internal and external stimuli. Schemas are influenced by experiences and help to organize the massive amount of incoming information with which individuals are presented and need to process. Schemas can be thought of as filters or lenses through which we perceive situations.

Schemas serve a necessary organizing function for dealing with abundant amounts of information. However, some individuals may develop depressive or anxious schemas that lead to overly negative, pessimistic, or fearful views about oneself, the world, or the future. In essence, these individuals perceive incoming information through "colored" or distorted lenses. This distorted information processing may lead to overly extreme interpretations, as well as a tendency to focus on negative pieces of information and to minimize or ignore positive information.

Furthermore, schemas bring about core beliefs individuals have about themselves, the world, and the future. These core beliefs make up a central belief system of an individual. Core beliefs typically lay dormant in the background until activated by stressful and context-relevant events. When activated, the core belief(s) affect how events are interpreted and give rise to automatic thoughts that are consistent with them. Examples of negative core beliefs are "I am unlovable" and "I am unworthy." These specific core beliefs and their associated schema are usually the result of early childhood experiences of abandonment, neglect, or severe criticism. Elena had the core belief, "I am incompetent", related to years of being told and learning that she would and could not accomplish tasks on her own and that she needed to be reliant on others for help. Earlier in her life, Elena was infrequently given the opportunity to engage in independent tasks, much like how her mother was treated by her father. Following from her core beliefs of incompetency, she interpreted her boss's e-mail message to mean that she failed at her assignment.

Significantly, individuals often engage in specific compensatory strategies in an effort to help cope with the difficult core belief, although these attempts at coping ultimately serve to maintain and strengthen the core belief. Such compensatory strategies include behaviors that support the belief (maintaining behaviors), behaviors that try to invalidate the core belief (opposing behaviors), and behaviors that are designed to avoid activation of the core belief (avoidance behaviors). Elena displayed avoidance behavior by calling in sick the following day to avoid further activation of her core belief of incompetency. She also frequently avoided volunteering for assignments and preferred group tasks where she felt she could rely on the superior skills of others. Elena also has the core belief "People don't like me." To compensate, she often tries hard to please others, including not standing up for herself so that others will not dislike her.

Individuals who harbor maladaptive core beliefs and automatic thoughts are highly vulnerable to developing depressive and anxiety disorders. Conversely, depressed and anxious patients commonly harbor negative core beliefs and rigid and extreme automatic thoughts. Furthermore, individuals with depression tend to have an internal attributional style in which they excessively attribute blame to internal (versus external) factors. Cognitive behavioral therapists work closely with patients to develop more realistic and flexible thinking styles and information processing, including learning how to identify, challenge, and modify maladaptive automatic thoughts and core beliefs. This process is discussed in further detail later in this chapter in the section "Cognitive Strategies."

The process of identifying and changing maladaptive cognitions and thinking patterns is only one core component of CBT. The other key focus in CBT is on changing maladaptive behaviors. According to Lewinsohn's behavioral model of depression, depression is the result of limited meaningful engagement with, and response-contingent positive reinforcement from, the environment (Lewinsohn, Sullivan, & Grosscup, 1980). Individuals who are depressed often engage in few activities that provide a sense of pleasure and/or mastery. This leads to a vicious cycle, as the more depressed they become, the less they pursue enjoyable or rewarding activities and interactions, which further maintains and exacerbates depression and related symptoms.

Low rates of response-contingent positive reinforcement may be caused by few available positive reinforcers in an individual's environment, lack of skills to take advantage of positive reinforcers, or reduced strength of the positive reinforcers (Lewinsohn et al., 1980). Moreover, for some older individuals, late life can present particular challenges at one or more of these levels. As individuals age and their environments change, previously available reinforcers may no longer be available. For example, friends or relatives may relocate or pass away, physical surroundings may change, or health or physical status may mean that older adults can no longer engage in certain previously enjoyable activities, or at least not in the same way. For example, cognitive impairment caused by stroke or dementia may render previous hobbies like crossword puzzles or reading more difficult; they may also expose or inflame vulnerabilities the individuals were previously able to compensate for. These aging-related changes notwithstanding, older adults can derive significant meaning from their environment, and it is not normative for older individuals to lack any positive reinforcers. Rather, the key is adapting to changes one might experience in late life and incorporate what is meaningful into one's life to match the individual's present lifestyle.

Although the main focus of Lewinsohn's behavioral model of depression is on the lack of response-contingent positive reinforcement, it also provides that depression can result from a high rate of aversive experiences, such as when (a) there are many punishers in patients' lives, (b) patients lack coping skills for dealing with adversity, or (c) the impact of aversive events is heightened. Accordingly, another behavioral strategy in CBT is to help patients to develop effective problem-solving strategies and social skills to minimize the negative impact of and overcome adverse events. Loss and other changes relatively common in late life fit well with this component of Lewinsohn's model. That said, it is worth noting that many older adults develop significant coping abilities from their years of experience and wisdom that can be harnessed in CBT.

Behavioral theory also has an important role in accounting for and treating anxiety in CBT. Anxiety may result from experiencing an uncontrollable or unpredictable traumatic event, watching others having a traumatic experience or reacting with fear, or by learning from others that certain things are dangerous or should be avoided (Mineka & Zinbarg, 2006). Anxiety is maintained or exacerbated when individuals avoid thoughts or contact with stimuli associated with the anxiety. Not all individuals, however, develop an anxiety disorder after experiencing a traumatic life event. Genetic vulnerability, personality factors (e.g., neuroticism, inability to tolerate uncertainty), and environmental factors (e.g., early childhood environments with limited, previous experiences with the feared stimulus) increase the risk of developing significant anxiety responses. Moreover, what follows a stressful or traumatic life event can influence the likelihood of subsequent onset of anxiety. Later experience of anxiety is more likely to occur when the individual is unable to escape the event, when the traumatic event is followed by another highly stressful or traumatic event shortly thereafter, when an individual learns after a highly stressful event that the event was more dangerous than he or she originally perceived it to be, and when an individual mentally rehearses the stressful or traumatic event (Mineka & Zinbarg).

In CBT, cognitive theory and behavioral theory are blended to provide a more sophisticated understanding of clients' problems and to develop a comprehensive treatment approach than would be provided by singly focusing on each component separately. This integration of cognitive theory and behavioral theory forms the cognitive behavioral model. Beyond their individual effects, the interaction of cognitions and behaviors contributes significantly to the onset and maintenance of mental disorders. Thoughts affect behaviors and behaviors affect thoughts in a highly interactive and cyclical fashion. In this way, the integrated cognitive behavioral model is greater than the sum of its individual parts. For example, patients who are depressed often have cognitions, such as thoughts of self-doubt or pessimism, that contribute to behaviors (e.g., inactivity) that maintain and often exacerbate the depression by strengthening or confirming the very cognitions that led to the maladaptive behavior. In the case of Elena, who has long been battling depression, she has limited her involvement in activities that may activate, or be inconsistent with, her core belief of incompetence. This avoidance has also prevented her from disproving this belief and receiving satisfaction from engaging in activities of pleasure and mastery. Thus, it is essential to break the vicious thought–belief cycle. When individuals learn how to change extreme cognitions, they come to do things differently; and, when individuals do things differently (e.g., engage in rewarding activities), the self-defeating thoughts are weakened and new self-affirming thoughts and beliefs are strengthened. With depressed patients, particularly severely depressed patients, it is typically best to initially focus on instilling some behavior change, which may quickly provide some relief, increase energy, and instill confidence in the therapeutic process, before extensively working on changing entrenched thoughts with a particular client.

Before implementing CBT, it is essential for the therapist to recognize the constellation of (interacting) components that contribute to the individual's current problems. This is done through the *case conceptualization* process (Persons, 2006). Case conceptualization is an essential component of CBT, which is often not incorporated in purely psychoeducational and skills-based cognitive-behavioral approaches. Case conceptualization is often an especially important component of CBT when working with older clients because this can allow for aging-related factors (e.g., loss, physical decline, changes in appearance) that may play a contributing role in the onset or maintenance of psychological symptoms to be identified and addressed in therapy. For example, Elena's thoughts of incompetence have been strengthened by recent health problems and occasional forgetfulness she experiences. These experiences, and her interpretations of these experiences, may be a focus of therapy.

In the case conceptualization process, therapists generate hypotheses about cognitive, emotional, behavioral, and situational factors, including early childhood experiences, as well as later-life experiences, that contribute to, maintain, and exacerbate a client's problems. For example, early childhood experiences (e.g., parental divorce, abuse, neglect) may lead to the formation of particular core beliefs, as well as intermediate beliefs and compensatory strategies, that affect cognitive, emotional, and/or behavioral reactions to situations or circumstances in the patient's present life. These hypotheses are generated by applying cognitive behavioral theory to an understanding of the patient obtained by the therapist through information gathered during an initial interview with the client and from other available sources. As new information is gathered over the course of treatment and specific hypotheses are validated or disconfirmed, the case conceptualization is modified accordingly. A diagram, such as the one presented in Figure 1.2, can be helpful for piecing together the components of the case conceptualization and for illustrating the relationships between key past events, core beliefs, intermediate beliefs (i.e., conditional rules and assumptions), and compensatory strategies as they relate to a specific client (Beck, 1995). The form also allows for identifying key situations, automatic thoughts and their associated meanings, emotions, and behaviors in a client's current life that fit within the overarching conceptual framework.

MOTIVATIONAL ENHANCEMENT AND TREATMENT SOCIALIZATION

After the initial case conceptualization is developed, the therapist identifies specific cognitive and behavioral strategies to incorporate

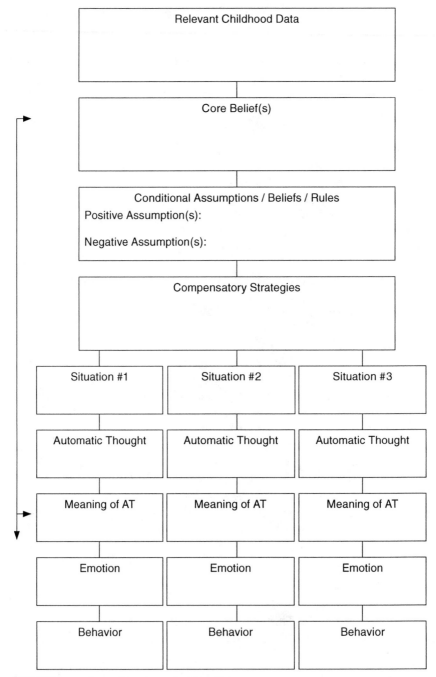

FIGURE 1.2 Case Conceptualization Diagram

Source: Adapted from Beck, J. S. (1995). *Cognitive therapy: Basics and beyond.* New York: Guilford.

into treatment. However, before implementing these strategies, it is important to assess for and, if necessary, enhance motivation for treatment. This is especially important with older adults who infrequently use mental health services and are often especially unaccustomed to psychotherapy (Karlin & Duffy, 2004; Karlin, Duffy, & Gleaves, 2008). Further, some older clients may attend therapy for external reasons, such as persuasion by a child, spouse, or primary care physician. Accordingly, assessing older clients' readiness to change is highly recommended at the outset of treatment.

To assess an older client's motivation for therapy and readiness to change, it is important to inquire about the client's reasons for seeking treatment, attitudes and expectations for therapy, past experiences in psychotherapy, and potential obstacles to attending and participating in treatment. Potential obstacles may include, but are not limited to, transportation factors, financial issues, lifestyle factors (e.g., disorganization, crises), and/or physical issues (e.g., decreased energy, sensory impairment, pain). The therapist should brainstorm with the client ways to overcome identified obstacles.

If an older client expresses limited motivation for therapy, nondirective motivational enhancement approaches, akin to motivational interviewing, are recommended. The goal of motivational enhancement is to help the client recognize through his or her own eyes how therapy may be relevant and useful to him or her. As part of the process, the therapist may ask the client to identify areas of his or her life that he or she would like to change and the benefits of participating in therapy to achieve those changes. The therapist then works with the client to develop specific measurable short-term goals. If a client remains ambivalent to participate in therapy, the therapist may consider suggesting a "trial," whereby the client agrees to commit to a limited number of sessions, after which time the therapist and client agree to assess how treatment is going and whether therapy should continue. It is recommended that this be a minimum of four sessions to allow for sufficient exposure to the treatment.

Following the motivational enhancement process, the therapist should educate the client about the structure and process of CBT to ensure that the client has accurate expectations of his or her role and responsibilities in treatment, the therapist's role and responsibilities in treatment, and of how treatment will proceed. Socializing clients to CBT is especially important with older individuals, given that older clients are often unfamiliar with the treatment. Moreover, the active, change-oriented focus of CBT may be different from more medically oriented interventions that older individuals are often more accustomed to, which typically assign a more passive (sick) role to the patient. Older adults may also be unfamiliar with homework, which is a core component to CBT. Some older clients may also not identify with the concept of homework. With some older clients, it may be preferable to use the term "practice."

Topics to cover in socializing the client to treatment include (a) structure, length, and frequency of sessions; (b) rationale for regular attendance, homework, and full participation; (c) goals of CBT and how they relate to the client's goals and problems; (d) roles and responsibilities of the client and therapist; (e) research on the effectiveness of CBT; (f) personal experiences of the effectiveness of CBT with past (older) clients; and (g) the relationship between thoughts and emotions.

In the next section, specific cognitive and behavioral strategies in CBT are reviewed. However, before implementing cognitive or behavioral strategies, it is strongly recommended that therapists conduct a suicide risk assessment when working with older clients. This typically occurs as part of or immediately following the initial clinical interview. Suicide risk assessments should also be conducted, as needed, *throughout* therapy. Although a full discussion of the suicide risk assessment is beyond the scope of this chapter, clinicians should consider conducting a suicide risk assessment following a recent suicide attempt; report of new or increased severity or frequency of suicide ideation, intent, or plan; threat or other behavior indicating imminent risk; questionable impulse control; sudden positive or negative change in clinical presentation; no positive clinical change or worsening of symptoms during treatment; or a significant loss or other significant life stressor. Furthermore, a suicide risk assessment should be conducted when a client endorses a 1 or higher on the suicide item of the *Beck Depression Inventory*, or on a similar item of another clinical measure a client may routinely complete as part of treatment. Clinicians should also take into account risk and protective factors for suicide when conducting a suicide risk assessment. For clients for whom there is concern about imminent danger to them or others, appropriate actions and steps should be taken. These may include hospitalization, other treatment (possibly in addition to ongoing CBT), and/or the development of a safety plan (Stanley, Brown, Karlin, Kemp, & VonBergen, 2008).

Behavioral Strategies

Behavioral strategies in CBT for depression are designed to promote engagement in activities that provide pleasure and a sense of mastery. As mentioned earlier, a secondary benefit of such behavioral change is the impact that self-promoting behaviors have on cognitions, including thoughts about oneself, the world, and the future. Given that depressed clients often have limited energy and become caught in the depressive thought–behavior cycle described earlier, behavioral strategies are often implemented before cognitive strategies to activate patients and engage them in treatment.

Activity Monitoring

Activity monitoring is a process by which the client monitors how he or she is making use of his or her time. Patients with depression often have a low baseline level of engagement in activities that provide them with sense of pleasure, meaning, or accomplishment. As part of activity monitoring, clients record the activities they engage in as they occur throughout the day. In addition to recording the activity, patients are also asked to rate the degree of pleasure (P) and mastery (M), each on a scale of 0 to 10, with 10 indicating maximal pleasure and mastery, as well as their overall mood for the day on a scale of 10 to 0 with 10 being the most depressed the client could imagine being, and 0 being not depressed at all. A form, such as the one included in Figure 1.3, is typically used for making these recordings throughout the week. (Note: An enlarged version of this form is recommended for use with older adults.)

Clients are asked to bring the completed activity monitoring form to the next session for review together with the therapist. It can be most effective to review the form sitting alongside the client. The therapist should use questions to guide discussion and enhance clients' understanding of the types and frequency of activities they engage in and the association between their mood and their behaviors. This exercise can also help clients identify activities they enjoy, if they have engaged in enjoyable activities. It can be useful to ask clients "Were there times when you experienced pleasure?" or "What kinds of activities gave you pleasure?" Higher ratings of pleasure, mastery, and mood should be given greatest attention.

After reviewing her activity monitoring form, Elena made two key discoveries: (a) she spends a great deal of time sitting on the couch watching television (which she rated as providing very low levels of pleasure and mastery), and (b) when she goes out of the house, even just to sit on her front porch, she feels better.

Activity Scheduling

Baseline activity data gathered through the activity monitoring process can help to inform the next behavioral exercise—activity scheduling. Activity scheduling is a process by which the client and therapist work together in a structured manner to identify and schedule throughout the week specific activities that provide the client with a sense of pleasure

Activity Monitoring Form							
	Monday	Tuesday	Wednesday	Thursday	Friday	Saturday	Sunday
7–8 am							
8–9 am							
9–10 am							
10–11 am							
11am–12							
12–1 pm							
1–2 pm							
2–3 pm							
3–4 pm							
4–5 pm							
5–6 pm							
6–7 pm							
7–8 pm							
8–9 pm							
9–10 pm							
10–11 pm							
11 pm–12							
12–1am							
1–2 am							
2–3 am							
3–4 am							
4–5 am							
5–6 am							
6–7 am							
Overall mood (0–10) 10 = Most depressed							

FIGURE 1.3 Activity Monitoring Form
Note: For each time frame, use **P** to indicate degree of pleasure and **M** to indicate degree of mastery or accomplishment.
0 = No pleasure/No accomplishment; 10 = Greatest pleasure/Accomplishment

and/or accomplishment. Some such activities may have become apparent during the activity monitoring process. However, many depressed clients may have difficulty identifying pleasant or rewarding activities. This is sometimes even more common with older clients because it may have been some time since they have engaged in certain activities, and they may have few pleasant activities in their behavioral repertoire. If this is the case, the therapist can ask the client what he or she previously enjoyed when he or she was happier. In addition, activity checklists that list a wide range of activities that individuals may find enjoyable can be provided to clients. These checklists are often very useful and they do not rely on memory, which can be quite fallible and can often neglect very small behaviors (e.g., taking a bath, eating an ice cream cone) that can make a difference on one's mood, especially highly depressed individuals who have not engaged in such activities for some time. One commonly used checklist of pleasant activities in CBT is the Pleasant Events Schedule (PES; MacPhillamy & Lewinsohn, 1982). An adapted version of the PES, known as the California Older Person's Pleasant Events Schedule (COPPES; Rider, Gallagher-Thompson, & Thompson, 2004), that includes more age-relevant activities for older individuals and takes less time to complete has been developed. The COPPES includes 66 age-appropriate and mood-related items, with activities organized into the following five domains: socializing, relaxing, contemplating, being effective, and doing. Examples of items on the COPPES are listening to the birds sing, helping someone, meditating, and working on a community project. The COPPES and accompanying manual can be downloaded free of charge at http://oafc.stanford.edu/coppes.html. In addition, a version of the PES for individuals with Alzheimer's disease (Pleasant Events Schedule-AD) has also been developed (Teri & Logsdon, 1991). A version of the PE is also available for use with nursing home residents (Pleasant Events Schedule-NH; Meeks, Shah, & Ramsey, 2009)

When introducing activity checklists with older clients, it is recommended to complete a few items in session to begin the process stimulate interest on the part of the client. It can also provide an opportunity for the client to ask questions about the task or the rationale behind it.

Some older clients may not engage in previously enjoyable activities because of age-related changes (e.g., physical decline, sensory impairment) and, more specifically, what clients believe these changes mean. This author has experienced this relatively frequently in depressed older clients; in many cases, the no longer engaged-in activity involves an activity that was once quite meaningful to the client and may have been a significant part of their self-identity.

1. **A**ssess types of activities in which the patient used to engage.
2. **A**cquire information and knowledge about patient's physical functioning and medical condition.
3. **A**ssess actual versus perceived level of physical ability relative to areas of interest.
4. **A**dapt previously engaged-in pleasant activity to patient's current level of functioning.

FIGURE 1.4   The 4-A Approach to Activity Scheduling With Older Clients

This author has developed the following 4-A approach (see Figure 1.4) for such situations (Karlin, 2008):

1. **A**ssess the types of activities in which the patient used to engage. Have the patient describe the experience in detail, and listen carefully to the patient's description of the activity. Also watch for important nonverbal cues (e.g., tone, pace, and volume of speech; facial expressions; posture) that may indicate interest or pleasure.
2. **A**cquire information and knowledge about the patient's physical functioning and medical condition.
3. **A**ssess actual versus perceived level of physical ability relative to the areas of interest. Some patients may have extreme or overly pessimistic beliefs about their abilities that are incongruent with their actual abilities, either because of lack of information or understanding or because of the negative cognitive bias of depression. For example, some patients may hold beliefs such as, "I don't feel well enough to do anything," "I'm too tired," or "There's no one left of my old friends to play cards or go out with" and subsequently fully abandon activities that they once enjoyed.
4. **A**dapt previously engaged-in pleasant activity to patient's current level of functioning. After identifying one or more activities that previously provided significant meaning to the patient, the therapist, with creativity, can adapt the activity to fit the patient's current life. In so doing, the therapist can enable the patient to reconnect with the meaning of the activity, even though the specific relationship with the activity may now be different. The overall goal is to identify the significant thematic area(s) for the client (e.g., baseball, gardening, teaching) and adapt the activity to fit the client's current abilities, while staying within the same thematic area.

The 4-A approach was used very effectively with Robert, a 76-year-old homebound client who was in the moderate stage of Alzheimer's disease and several other medical and physical conditions. Robert had significant difficulty in identifying activities that he found enjoyable.

He spent most of his hours and days sitting in his rocking chair in front of the television. On multiple occasions during previous sessions, Robert had made mention of his experiences growing up in New York (where this author/therapist author also grew up), and how he frequently went to the horse track and bet a few dollars on the thoroughbreds. His affect brightened and his voice became more robust as he would talk about the days visiting "the track." Robert now lived in a highly suburban city in Utah where he had great difficulty getting around and had no access to a horse track. However, this therapist learned that his local newspaper published the list of horses to race that day at the major horse tracks, along with the results of the previous day's races. After discovering this, Robert and I worked to develop an approximation of his previously enjoyable activity of going to the horse track in which Robert would select the horses he thought would win, which he would match up against the results in the next day's newspaper. Robert found great pleasure (and often mastery) in this exercise. This also brought him positive anticipation as he looked forward to the race results in the newspaper the next day. Beyond the activity itself, it became apparent that this exercise harnessed meaning from his earlier life with which he was now more deeply connected.

Once the therapist and client have identified pleasant or meaningful activities, they begin the process of planning activities that the client commits to engage in during the week at specific times. An activity scheduling form is used to schedule specific activities on specific days and times. The activity scheduling form looks very similar to the activity monitoring form, although the activity scheduling form lists specific activities that the client commits to engage in during the coming week. Like the activity monitoring form, the activity scheduling form includes a place for the client to record his or her overall mood for the day on a scale of 10 to 0, with 10 being the most depressed the client could imagine being, and 0 being not depressed at all. For some older clients, it may be difficult to schedule every hour of their day. In these instances, a simplified version of the activity scheduling form may also be used. This may also be useful early on when beginning activity scheduling. An excerpt from a simplified activity scheduling form used with Elena is presented in Figure 1.5.

As clients implement the activity schedule, they continue to monitor their activities and mood. With their own behavioral data, they can usually come to quickly recognize a close relationship between the nature and frequency of activities they engage in and their mood. Therapists can use Socratic questioning to help clients see this relationship.

Activity Scheduling Form							
	Days						
Pleasurable Activities	Monday	Tuesday	Wednesday	Thursday	Friday	Saturday	Sunday
1. Read magazine (*Reader's Digest, Home & Gardens*)	✓		✓		✓	✓	
2. Listen to music	✓		✓		✓		✓
3. Call Sandy (or Kathy)		✓				✓	
4. Get frozen yogurt waffle cone				✓			✓
5. Watch a movie		✓		✓		✓	✓
Total number of events	2	2	2	2	2	3	3
Overall mood (0–10)	8	6	7	4	5	3	4

FIGURE 1.5   Simplified Activity Scheduling Form

When beginning this process of activity scheduling with older clients, it is important to be specific and to start with activities that can be easily achieved. This can help to activate clients and build behavioral momentum and confidence. Furthermore, small activities (e.g., shaving, eating a good meal) can have a significant impact on depressed clients who may engage in few, if any, self-promoting or rewarding behaviors. Behavioral activation is a simplified approach to activity scheduling that can be particularly useful with older clients, particularly older clients who are more significantly depressed or who are experiencing executive functioning difficulties. In behavioral activation, the client identifies one or two activities he or she believes may improve his or her mood within a short period. The therapist encourages the client's participation in just the one or two activities, without adding additional activities or expectations. The goal is to get the client activated and break the chain of inactivity. Once initially activated in this manner, the client is usually more likely to carry out a more sophisticated behavioral plan.

Another specific behavioral technique that is often very useful with older clients with more significant levels of depression or with executive functioning or organizational difficulties is graded task assignment. Graded task assignment involves simplifying behavioral tasks into smaller component parts. Graded task assignment was used with Ruth, an 81-year-old widow who had suffered a stroke and was receiving CBT for major depression. Ruth felt overwhelmed by her depression and diminished cognitive ability resulting from the stroke. After talking with her therapist and completing the COPPES, she identified volunteering as something she wanted to engage in. Because Ruth was previously a nurse and teacher, this seemed like a good fit for her, but this seemed too overwhelming to make happen. Therefore, she and her therapist broke this down into more easily smaller tasks throughout the week: On Monday, Ruth would call the Jewish Community Center Volunteer Line to request a list of volunteer positions and the volunteer application; on Wednesday and Thursday, Ruth would review the list of volunteer activities and identify one or more activities of interest to her; on Friday, Ruth would complete the top portion (identifying information section) only of the application; on Saturday, she would complete the rest of the application.

Finally, behavioral anxiety management techniques can be very useful for promoting psychological and physical relaxation with older clients. Breathing exercises, including breathing retraining (use of diaphragmatic breathing) and meditative breathing, require little modification for use with older individuals. It is important, however, to assess for any breathing difficulty or related medical condition (e.g., severe asthma, chronic obstructive pulmonary disease) before beginning breathing exercises. Furthermore, clients should be instructed not to breathe too rapidly because this can lead to lightheadedness.

Progressive muscle relaxation (PMR), which involves the systematic tensing and relaxing of muscles throughout the body, is another effective anxiety management technique commonly used in CBT. However, PMR is not recommended for clients who have arthritis or physical pain (e.g., joint or knee pain). An alternative to traditional PMR for use with older clients is imaginal PMR, whereby the client *imagines* the tensing and relaxing of specific muscles, rather than physically engaging in the exercises. In fact, imaginal PMR has been shown to be as effective as traditional physical PMR (Crist & Rickard, 1993; Scogin, Rickard, Keith, Wilson, & McElreath, 1992).

Cognitive Strategies

Cognitive strategies in CBT focus directly on the "C" in CBT, although given the reciprocal relationship between cognitions and behaviors, cognitive strategies can also help promote behavioral change, especially when cognitions impede self-promoting behaviors. Cognitive interventions are designed to promote more accurate and flexible information processing through a process of "cognitive restructuring," or the restructuring or changing of rigid and extreme thoughts and beliefs.

Recognizing Automatic Thoughts

Cognitive work in CBT typically begins with helping the patient to recognize the link between his or her thoughts and emotions, behaviors, and physiological responses (the "A–B–C" relationship discussed in the section "Theoretical Foundations of CBT" earlier in this chapter). This key principle is often very new to older clients. Imagery exercises can be used to help demonstrate this relationship. This author will often ask clients to first think of an unpleasant event in their life and then to report their emotion(s) and the intensity thereof. Next, clients are asked to replace the thoughts of the unpleasant event by thinking about a very happy or pleasant time in their life and to report the emotions that they feel at that moment. This exercise is often a powerful demonstration of the impact of thoughts. After introducing the relationship between thoughts and emotions, the therapist typically educates the client about automatic thoughts. The therapist typically asks clients to describe situations where there was an identifiable shift in mood. As clients provide this description, the therapist uses questioning to identify the cognitions at work. This process of using questioning to promote understanding is known as "guided discovery." A question the therapist might ask the client to help identify the automatic thought(s) is, "What was running through your mind just then?" If the patient has difficulty identifying the thought, the therapist may help to guide the client by asking, "Might you have been thinking _____ or _____?"

After learning about automatic thoughts and their role in producing emotions, clients are then introduced to the three-column thought record for recording the emotion (and intensity on a 0 to 100 scale), the related thought, and the specific situation or event that immediately precipitated the shift in emotion. The three-column thought record is displayed in Figure 1.6.

It is recommended that the therapist begin completing the three-column thought record in session with older clients to ensure understanding and get the process started. Events from that day or earlier in the week can be used for the initial entries. With some older clients, it can be helpful for the therapist to record the first couple of entries, sitting alongside the client with the thought record in hand. If the client comprehends the exercise and is agreeable, the client can be asked to

Date	Situation	Emotion	Thought
	What event led to a shift in emotion?	What emotion(s) did you experience? (Rate intensity on a 0–100 scale)	What thoughts or images ran through your mind? What did the situation mean to you?

FIGURE 1.6   Three-Column Thought Record

monitor his or her thoughts and complete the three-column thought record as practice between sessions.

Evaluating and Changing Automatic Thoughts
Socratic questioning is the core skill employed by the therapist in helping clients to evaluate their automatic thoughts. Specifically, the therapist asks questions that enable accurate and more complete examination of the thought and the situation. However, with older clients in particular, it is important not to directly challenge the validity of the thought or to take a highly directive stance in the evaluation process because this may feel insulting, disrespectful, or dismissing. Further, the more the client draws the conclusion, the more likely it is that he or she is going to believe in it. Thus, rather than serve as a teacher, the therapist's role here is to serve as a *guide*, helping the client to engage in the necessary process to perform his or her own examination. Specific questions the therapist can ask to help the client examine his or her automatic thoughts are the following:

- What evidence supports that thought? What evidence does not support that thought?
- Could there be any other explanations of the situation?
- If the worst thing were to happen, how bad would that be?
- What would you tell a friend if he or she were in the same situation?

Additional questions can be found in Beck (1995).

An extension of the three-column thought record is used to help clients evaluate their thoughts. This is known as the five-column thought record. The five-column thought record adds two additional columns to its more basic three-column counterpart. In addition to situation, emotion, and thought, the five-column thought record has a column for clients to record an alternative response to the situation after evaluating the automatic thought. In the fifth column, clients record the outcome resulting from the alternative response (e.g., reduction in intensity of initial emotion, new emotion, new behavioral response). The outcome could also be an adaptive behavioral response that the patient initiates because of the more balanced alternative response. An example of the five-column thought record is presented in Figure 1.7.

With repeated practice, clients become increasingly more adept at identifying, challenging, and changing their automatic thoughts. As they see the rigidity or bias in their automatic thoughts and develop more balanced responses, they come to experience important emotional changes. In some instances, clients may develop reasonable alternative responses that do not lead to a reduction or change in the emotional

Date	Situation	Emotion	Thought	Alternative Response	Outcome
	What event led to a shift in emotion?	What emotion(s) did you experience? (Rate intensity on a 0–100 scale)	What thoughts or images ran through your mind? What did the situation mean to you?	Use the questions to evaluate the automatic thought and construct a more balanced thought.	Re-rate the intensity of the emotion you listed in column 2 or list a new emotion you are experiencing. Describe what you will do differently as a result of the alternative response.

FIGURE 1.7 Five-Column Thought Record

response. This may be because the client does not truly believe the alternative response or because there are other more significant automatic thoughts that are not identified and evaluated.

Coping Cards

Use of coping cards is another technique for challenging and changing automatic thoughts. The coping card can be a very useful supplement to the five-column thought record or as an alternative tool for older clients who may have difficulty learning or regularly using the five-column thought record. Coping cards are often better suited and are recommended for older clients with some degree of cognitive impairment or who prefer more simplified approaches. Coping cards capitalize on recognition memory, which is typically more enduring than recall memory. A coping card consists of an index card or similar card in which a common automatic thought (or core belief, which can also be used for challenging) for a particular client is written on one side and an alternative response is placed on the opposite side of the card. Coping cards are simple and concrete, and they have the advantage of being easy to carry around and can be accessed in any situation. Moreover, in addition to their use for facilitating cognitive restructuring, coping cards can also be used for listing or providing reminders of behavioral coping strategies that older clients can engage in for managing specific situations or experiences.

Core Belief Identification and Modification

In addition to identifying and changing automatic thoughts, cognitive behavioral therapists can also work with older clients to identify and change core beliefs. This typically occurs later in therapy, after the therapist has developed a case conceptualization and cognitive restructuring at the level of automatic thoughts has progressed. Although a detailed examination of core belief modification is beyond the scope of this chapter, a brief review of how therapists can identify and change core beliefs is provided here.

Core beliefs are often identified during Socratic questioning during discussion of situations of acute stress when core beliefs are typically activated from their dormant state. Therapists may begin to make hypotheses about possible types of core beliefs as clients describe critical negative events in their lives and their reactions to these experiences. Therapists may solicit feedback on these hypotheses at appropriate opportunities. It is often best to do this when the core belief is most accessible—that is, when the emotional experience is being discussed or occurs in session. In such situations, core beliefs may also be articulated as automatic thoughts. Other means of identifying core beliefs include, but are not limited to, identifying themes across automatic thoughts or core beliefs, completing a core belief questionnaire, and employing the downward arrow technique (Burns, 1999), whereby therapist repeatedly asks the client, "What does this mean to you?" (or similar question). This occurs following identification of a key automatic thought. A key time to use this technique is when the severity of the emotional reaction on the part of the client does not fit with the content of the automatic thought. This typically suggests that there may be more than the automatic thought itself that is contributing to the client's reaction.

Once identified, a core belief may be selected for focusing on during therapy. Often, the therapist and client begin working on the client's most strongly held or central core belief. A core beliefs worksheet or thought record may be used to evaluate the thought similar to how automatic thoughts are evaluated (Beck, 1995). Therapists may also put the core belief down on paper and use Socratic questioning to evaluate the validity of the belief. This may also include continuous shaping of the core belief until it changes its meaning. This chipping away at core beliefs is often more likely than is clients fully letting go of them, given their enduring and formative nature. However, sometimes, just the act of separating the core belief from the client, with whom it has long been fused, so that the client can more objectively visualize and consider it can yield progress.

Adjustments to the Therapy Process With Older Clients

In addition to important considerations in and adaptations to the implementation of cognitive and behavioral strategies already identified, there are several adjustments to the therapy process that can maximize engagement and CBT outcomes when working with older clients. These adjustments are summarized as follows:

1. *Slow general pace.* Because of the reduction in the speed of information processing and increased reaction time with aging, it is often useful to slow the general pace of therapy with older clients.
2. *Speak slower and clearly.* Because of the changes in auditory perception with aging, it is important that the therapist speak slowly (though naturally) and that the pronunciation be clear, so that older clients do not miss or misinterpret information conveyed by the therapist. Moreover, many older adults may consider it to be impolite or may be embarrassed to ask the therapist to speak louder or more clearly.

3. *Use multiple modalities ("say it, write it, show it").* It is often very useful to present material in multiple modalities to older clients to facilitate and reinforce learning. Using a white board or flip chart and printed materials with large print can be helpful.
4. *Incorporate greater structure, as appropriate.* Incorporating greater structure can be very useful with some older clients. This includes writing down the session agenda on a white board or flip chart and notating as the session progresses where on the agenda the therapist and client are. This can be helpful in keeping the client in parallel with the therapist.
5. *Minimize "storytelling" and redirect.* Some older clients may think of therapy as being their time to discuss whatever is on their mind. Providing visual and verbal cues and redirecting clients, as necessary, can help keep the client focused on the session content and goals.
6. *Encourage note taking by the client, if desired.* Note taking may help the client to remember key information from session, although excessive note taking can be counterproductive.
7. *Provide examples and role-play demonstrations when appropriate.* Examples and role-play demonstrations can help make concrete and more easily understandable new or more complex topics and principles. Examples and role-play demonstrations can also be valuable prior to homework or practice exercises outside of session that the client will be engaging in for the first time.
8. *Begin homework or practice in session.* Beginning practice or homework in session allows the client the opportunity to ask additional questions and enables the therapist to see if the client understands the task or exercise.
9. *Provide and elicit more summaries.* Therapist summary statements can help older clients make important connections in session and can reinforce or promote deeper learning. Periodically requesting summaries from older clients can also be valuable for seeing what clients have understood or interpreted from the discussion. This can provide valuable feedback to the therapist to slow down or present information in a different way.
10. *Provide a folder or binder for organizing notes and materials.* If the client does not have access to one, it is recommended to provide a folder or binder to promote organization.
11. *Regularly incorporate bridge from previous session and assist client with this, if necessary.* The bridge from the previous session is a standard part of the CBT session structure, in which the therapist asks the client what he or she learned from or found especially helpful about the previous session. The goal is to link sessions to ensure

seamless flow and continuity. This is an especially useful exercise with older clients. Questions that the therapist may ask include, "What did we cover in the previous session that you found helpful?" or "What stood out for you about our last session?" If the client has difficulty recalling content or discoveries from the previous session, the therapist may help the client by mentioning two key pieces of information from the previous session and asking the client which, if any, he or she found helpful.

12. *Lengthen course of therapy.* Slowing the pace of therapy, increasing the use of multiple modalities, and incorporating more summaries often necessitate that therapy be extended by a few extra sessions for the full therapy protocol to be implemented. This also allows for some time for review of gains and information covered at the end of therapy. Furthermore, as noted earlier, it may sometimes be beneficial to shorten the length of therapy sessions. When this occurs, there may not be sufficient time to cover all material in each individual session.

Therapeutic Relationship

The therapeutic relationship is a critical, and sometimes underrecognized, component of CBT. The strength of the therapeutic relationship moderates the success of cognitive and behavioral strategies used with clients. In this author's experience, without a truly collaborative therapeutic relationship, cognitive and behavioral strategies will virtually always fall flat. This is especially true with older clients for whom CBT is often very new and unfamiliar and who often value respect. Therefore, CBT therapists should devote important attention to developing (and maintaining) a strong therapeutic relationship with older clients. At the outset of therapy with older clients, it is important to show respect and empathy and to listen carefully and actively. It can also be beneficial early on to demonstrate competence and expertise on aging issues, which can often increase older clients' confidence in and identification with the therapist.

Furthermore, attention to "transference" and "countertransference" issues is important in establishing and maintaining a collaborative and productive relationship with older clients. Older clients may knowingly or unknowingly associate a younger therapist with a child or grandchild, which could undermine the authority of the therapist and inhibit progress of the client inside or outside of session. Conversely, younger therapists may implicitly or explicitly behave toward older clients as they would toward a grandparent or older relative.

This may include being overly passive or providing too little structure or direction to the therapy process. Therefore, it is important for therapists to be attuned to how they and their clients perceive and behave toward each other during the course of therapy. Scogin (2000) provides additional suggestions and information on developing the therapeutic alliance with older adults.

To assess the strength of the therapeutic relationship, the therapist may take note of relevant, nonverbal cues (e.g., posture, speech, level of attention), although we find that often the most useful way to assess the strength or degree of collaboration of the therapeutic alliance is to inquire about it. One way to do this is by administering a measure of the therapeutic relationship. This is often especially useful with older clients who initially may feel more comfortable reporting on the therapeutic relationship by completing a questionnaire. A brief measure that we recommend incorporating as part of CBT for depression and have included in our CBT for depression protocol (Wenzel et al., 2010) for administration at the end of sessions 1, 4, 7, and 11 is the *Working Alliance Inventory–Short Revised* (WAI-SR; Hatcher & Gillaspy, 2006), an abbreviated version of the *Working Alliance Inventory* (Horvath & Greenberg, 1989). The WAI-SR contains 12 items that measures (a) agreement on the treatment goals, (b) agreement on how to achieve the goals, and (c) development of a personal bond between patient and the therapist. After the client completes the WAI-SR (or similar measure), the therapist can review and briefly discuss the client's responses, if the client agrees. Clients usually find the structure of a brief therapeutic alliance measure helpful for organizing discussion on the therapeutic relationship and, more generally, on how therapy is going. In our experience, this feedback provides very useful information on how the client is perceiving therapy and on whether any midcourse adjustments may need to be made. Moreover, the solicitation of feedback sends the message to clients that the therapist cares about and values their feedback.

Special Issues With Termination

Finally, there are important issues and considerations that CBT therapists should be aware of with respect to terminating therapy with older clients. In light of the role that loss often plays in late life, it is important for therapists to attend to the meaning that loss of the therapist may have to the client. Asking clients whether they have thought about what it will be like (or, directly, what it means) for therapy and regular meetings to end can help provide the therapist with insight along these lines. Furthermore, some older adults give themselves less credit for changes in therapy than they deserve. Therefore, reinforcing attributions that the client is the agent of change and that self-change can and will continue after termination of the therapy can help to promote confidence and internal locus of control.

Lastly, tapering of therapy sessions so that sessions occur less frequently toward the end of therapy may help clients adjust to termination. "Booster" sessions (i.e., one or few sessions scheduled some time, often 3 to 6 months, following the termination of therapy) are also often valuable with older clients because they provide an opportunity for the therapist and client to discuss how the client is doing at a later time and to review how therapy skills that the client used may be used to address or to head off to new or reemerging issues. Booster sessions can also provide the older client with something to look forward to at the time of termination of therapy. Of course, clients should be encouraged to call the therapist (or take other appropriate action) if the client's condition should worsen and additional treatment is needed.

CONCLUSION

CBT is an effective psychotherapy for late-life depression. The theoretical and applied components of CBT are often very well suited to depressed older individuals. In light of mounting evidence demonstrating CBT to be effective for late-life mental health and behavioral health conditions beyond depression, and increases in the accessibility of psychotherapy in the years ahead because of forthcoming changes in Medicare and private insurance (Karlin & Humphreys, 2007), CBT very well may soon be an increasingly prominent psychological treatment for older adults. Although CBT with older adults works in much the same way as it does with younger individuals, specific considerations and adaptations to CBT strategies and the therapy process with older clients can significantly enhance engagement, adherence, and outcomes.

Finally, for CBT clinicians who practice with older adults, the experience is often extremely rewarding. Older adults have extensive experience, personal resources, and wisdom to draw on that can make CBT a very dynamic, creative, and meaningful experience for therapist and client alike.

REFERENCES

Barrowclough, C., King, P., Colville, J., Russell, E., Burns, A. S, & Tarrier, N. (2001). A randomized trial of the effectiveness of cognitive-behavioral therapy and supportive counseling for anxiety symptoms in older adults. *Journal of Consulting and Clinical Psychology, 69*(5), 756–762.

Beck, A. T. (1967). *Depression: Causes and treatment.* Philadelphia, PA: University of Pennsylvania Press.

Beck, J. S. (1995). *Cognitive therapy: Basics and beyond.* New York: Guilford.

Beck, A. T., & Rector, N. (2005). Cognitive approaches to schizophrenia: Theory and therapy. *Annual Review of Clinical Psychology, 1,* 577–606.

Burns, D. D. (1999). *Feeling good: The new mood therapy* (revised). New York, NY: Penguin Group.

Butler, A. C., Chapman, J. E., Forman, E. M., & Beck, A. T. (2006). The empirical status of cognitive-behavioral therapy: A review of meta-analyses. *Clinical Psychology Review, 26,* 17–31.

Crist, D. A., & Rickard, H. C. (1993). A "fair" comparison of progressive and imaginal relaxation. *Perceptual and Motor Skills, 76*(2), 691–700.

DeRubeis, R. J., Hollon, S. D., Amsterdam, J. D., Shelton, R. C., Young, P. R., Salomon, R. M., et al. (2005). Cognitive therapy vs. medications in the treatment of moderate to severe depression. *Archives of General Psychiatry, 62*(4), 409–416.

Hatcher, R.L., & Gillaspy, J.A. (2006). Development and validation of a revised short version of the Working Alliance Inventory. *Psychotherapy Research, 16,* 12–25.

Hollon, S. D., Stewart, M. O., & Strunk, D. (2006). Enduring effects for cognitive behavior therapy in the treatment of depression and anxiety. *Annual Review of Psychology, 57,* 285–315.

Horvath, A. O., & Greenberg, L. S. (1989). Development and validation of the Working Alliance Inventory. *Journal of Counseling Psychology, 36,* 223–233.

Karlin, B. E. (2008). Delivering cognitive behavioral therapy to patients in later life. Workshop presented at the University of Michigan Medical School Continuing Medical Education Conference on Geriatrics, Ann Arbor, MI.

Karlin, B. E., & Duffy, M. (2004). Geriatric mental health policy: Impact on service delivery and directions for effecting change. *Professional Psychology: Research and Practice, 35,* 509–519.

Karlin, B. E., Duffy, M., & Gleaves, D. H. (2008). Patterns and predictors of mental health service use and mental illness among older and younger adults in the United States. *Psychological Services, 5,* 275–294.

Karlin, B. E., & Humphreys, K. (2007). Improving Medicare coverage of psychological services for older Americans. *American Psychologist, 62*(7), 637–649.

Lewinsohn, P. M., Sullivan, J. M., & Grosscup, S. J. (1980). Changing reinforcing events: An approach to the treatment of depression. *Psychotherapy: Theory, Research and Practice, 47,* 322–334.

MacPhillamy, D. J., & Lewinsohn, P. M. (1982). The Pleasant Events Schedule: Studies on reliability, validity, and scale intercorrelations. *Journal of Consulting and Clinical Psychology, 50,* 363–380.

Meeks, S., Shah, S. N., & Ramsey, S. K. (2009). The Pleasant Events Schedule - nursing home version: A useful tool for behavioral interventions in long-term care. *Aging and Mental Health, 13,* 445-255.

Mineka, S., & Zinbarg, R. (2006). A contemporary learning theory perspective on the etiology of anxiety disorders: It's not what you thought it was. *American Psychologist, 61,* 10–26.

Morin, C. M., Colecchi, C., Stone, J., Sood, R., & Brink, D. (1999). Behavioral and pharmacological therapies for late-life insomnia: A randomized controlled trial. *Journal of the American Medical Association, 281*(11), 991–999.

Persons, J. B. (2006). Case formulation-driven psychotherapy. *Clinical Psychology: Science and Practice, 13,* 167–170.

Pinquart, M., & Sörensen, S. (2001). How effective are psychotherapeutic and other psychosocial interventions with older adults? A meta-analysis. *Journal of Mental Health and Aging, 7,* 207–243.

Rider, K. L., Gallagher-Thompson, D., & Thompson, L. W. (2004). California Older Person's Pleasant Events Schedule: Manual. Available at: http://oafc.stanford.edu/coppes_files/Manual2.pdf.

Scogin, F. (2000). *The first session with seniors: A step-by-step guide.* San Francisco, CA: Jossey Bass.

Scogin, F., Rickard, H. C., Keith, S., Wilson, J., & McElreath, L. (1992). Progressive and imaginal relaxation training for elderly persons with subjective anxiety. *Psychology and Aging, 7*(3), 419–424.

Scogin, F., Welsh, D., Hanson, A., Stump, J., & Coates, A. (2005). Evidence-based psychotherapies for depression in older adults. *Clinical Psychology: Science and Practice, 12,* 222–237.

Stanley, B., Brown, G. K., Karlin, B. E., Kemp, J. E., & VonBergen, H. A. (2008). *Safety plan treatment manual to reduce suicide risk: Veteran version.* Washington, DC: U.S. Department of Veterans Affairs.

Stanley, M. A., Beck, J. G., Novy, D. M., Averill, P. M., Swann, A. C., Diefenbach, G. J., et al. (2003). Cognitive-behavioral treatment of late-life generalized anxiety disorder. *Journal of Consulting and Clinical Psychology, 71,* 309–319.

Teri L., & Logsdon, R. G. (1991). Identifying pleasant activities for Alzheimer's disease patients: The pleasant events schedule-AD. *Gerontologist, 31,* 124–127.

Vitiello, M. V., Rybarczyk, B., Von Korff, M., & Stepanski, E. J. (2009). Cognitive behavioral therapy for insomnia improves sleep and decreases pain in older adults with co-morbid insomnia and osteoarthritis. *Journal of Clinical Sleep Medicine, 5*(4), 355–362.

Wenzel, A., Brown, G. K., & Karlin, B. E. (2010). *Cognitive behavioral therapy for depressed veterans.* Washington, DC: U. S. Department of Veterans Affairs.

I

Cognitive Behavior Therapy and Common Mental Health Problems Among Older Adults

2

Major Depressive Disorder

Leilani Feliciano, Daniel L. Segal, and
Christina L. Vair

Major depression is a common and debilitating mental disorder that affects many older adults. In this chapter, we first provide an overview of the criteria for major depressive disorder (MDD) and its symptom presentation in older adults, discuss the course and prognosis of the disorder, and address its epidemiology. The latter half of the chapter focuses on assessment and treatment of MDD using a cognitive-behavioral therapy (CBT) framework and any necessary modifications needed to successfully conduct CBT with older people.

DEFINITION OF MAJOR DEPRESSION AND
LATER-LIFE PRESENTATION

According to the *Diagnostic and Statistical Manual of Mental Disorders*, 4th Edition, Text Revision (*DSM-IV-TR*; American Psychiatric Association [APA], 2000), MDD is classified within the broad category of mood disorders as a condition in which the most salient characteristic is a disruption in subjective mood that is substantially different from the person's normal mood state. Mood disturbances can be of a depressive nature, a manic nature, or sometimes a combination of both experiences that shift from one to the other. Besides MDD, other unipolar depressive disorders include dysthymia and depressive disorder not otherwise specified (NOS), whereas mood disorders characterized by various combinations of depressive symptoms and manic symptoms include cyclothymia, bipolar I disorder, bipolar II disorder, and bipolar disorder NOS.

MDD is arguably the most severe of the unipolar depressive disorders that affect older adults. Specifically, MDD is diagnosed only in the presence of at least one *major depressive episode,* in which the person experiences at least five of the following nine symptoms (including at least the first or second listed symptom) that are present for most of the day, nearly every day of the week over at least a 2-week period.

■ Dysphoric, sad, or depressed mood
■ Diminished capacity for enjoyment or interest in usual activities (commonly called anhedonia)
■ Significant weight loss or gain, or a decrease or increase in appetite
■ Sleep disturbance, for example, too much or too little sleep
■ Observable psychomotor agitation or retardation
■ Fatigue or decreased energy
■ Feelings of worthlessness or excessive or inappropriate guilt
■ Decreased ability to think, concentrate, or make decisions
■ Recurrent thoughts of death, suicidal ideation, plans, or attempts

The cluster of depressive symptoms must be severe enough to interfere with the person's ability to function in daily life (e.g., negatively impacting the person's social, educational, or occupational performance) or cause significant distress to the person. To qualify for a diagnosis of MDD, the person must not have ever met criteria for a manic episode, hypomanic episode, or cyclothymic disorder, and the symptoms must not be attributable to a current medical condition, substance use, or normal bereavement although this last criterion is slated to be changed in DSM-V. (APA, 2000).

Although depression is not a natural consequence of aging, it is one of the most common mental health disorders experienced by older adults. There appear to be some consistent differences in the presentation of depressed older adults compared to depressed younger adults, with depressed older adults showing less affective symptoms (e.g., feelings of sadness or guilt) and less reported suicidal ideation but more cognitive symptoms (e.g., complaints about memory, executive function deficits), somatic symptoms in the absence of a medical cause (e.g., fatigue, joint pain, sleep disruption, psychomotor retardation, weight loss, and loss of appetite), and loss of interest in activities and living (see recent reviews by Fiske & O'Riley, 2008; Fiske, Wetherell & Gatz, 2009). A significant problem with the current DSM diagnostic criteria for MDD is that many of the somatic symptoms of the disorder (e.g., weight loss or gain, sleep disturbance, fatigue, poor concentration) may be endorsed by physically ill but not depressed older adults.

COURSE AND PROGNOSIS OF
MAJOR DEPRESSIVE DISORDER

Qualifying Severity

In the diagnosis of MDD, the disorder is characterized by the severity of the presenting symptoms. MDD can be qualified by the clinician as mild, moderate, or severe. The severity qualifier is given based on (a) the number of symptoms reported or evidenced, and (b) the level of disability experienced by the person with MDD. In MDD with a *mild qualifier*, the affected person would generally present with only the minimum number of symptoms to qualify for the diagnosis and would report significant distress from the symptoms. However, the person would still be able to manage social, educational, or occupational tasks but with some difficulty and increased effort. In contrast, a person with MDD who has a *severe qualifier* would present with several symptoms in addition to what is needed to qualify for diagnosis and would report significant distress from these symptoms. In severe MDD, the person's symptoms would significantly interfere with the ability to function in social, educational, and occupational arenas. A person with MDD of *moderate* severity would have symptoms that would fall in between mild and severe, demonstrating more symptoms than those with a mild qualifier, but not enough symptomatology to merit a severe qualifier. Similarly, the affected person would also exhibit substantial difficulty in maintaining social, educational, or occupational pursuits.

Qualifying Chronicity

The chronicity of the mood disorder is usually specified in terms of the number and length of the depressive episode. An episode would be labeled as *single* if this was the first depressive episode experienced and would be identified as *chronic* if the duration exceeds 2 years.

These same qualifiers are used regardless of the age of the affected individual. An additional qualifier related to the *age of onset* of the specific disorder is particularly useful in terms of understanding depression in older adults, including aspects such as the potential etiology and prognosis. This qualifier is discussed in the next subsection.

Onset Qualifiers

For older adults who are experiencing their first major depressive episode, this has been collectively referred to in the literature as *late-life depression*. There is some debate as to when the age of late onset would begin, with some researchers identifying it as after the age of 60 (Brodaty et al., 2001) and others reporting it as occurring in the mid-30s (Klein et al., 1999).

Late-life depression has long been recognized as having poor prognosis and higher morbidity and mortality (Alexopoulos, Young, Abrams, Meyers, & Shamoian, 1989) and greater disability (Alexopoulos et al., 1996) than early-onset depression. More recent research has indicated that individuals with late-life depression are more likely to have comorbid cognitive impairments, particularly attention and executive function (Rapp et al., 2005), and may be more likely to transition to dementia (Schweitzer, Tuckwell, O'Brien, & Ames, 2002). In addition, a subset of individuals with late-life depression may have concomitant neurological disorders related to specific structural changes in the brain and vascular risk factors (Alexopoulos & Kelly, 2009). However, late-life depression is also associated with fewer recurrent episodes, and is less often comorbid with personality disorders and substance abuse disorders relative to early-onset depression (Klein et al., 1999).

Factors that Result in Better Chances of Recovery

Researchers in the field of psychology have begun to identify variables that can predict better course and outcome, but there is still a great deal of uncertainty (i.e., mixed results across studies). As with many other mental disorders, some of the factors that can lead to optimal recovery include the availability of resources such as social (family or friend support), economic (financial resources or strategies to minimize financial stressors), access to health care services (mental and physical), and personal factors (e.g., high self-efficacy, help-seeking behaviors, adaptive personality factors such as low *neuroticism* and high *openness* to new experiences). In contrast, the presence of comorbid personality disorder complicates the treatment of MDD in older adults, as well as most other clinical disorders (see Segal, Coolidge, & Rosowsky, 2006).

Effects of Major Depressive Disorder on Quality of Life

There are many studies that outline the detrimental effects of MDD on the quality of life of older adults, their families, and society. These are highlighted in the following:

■ Familial/social (e.g., decreased quality of life and increased burden on family members, high costs to society in terms of loss of productivity

and negative impacts on the health care system, which absorbs the cost of increased health care visits and treatment for related chronic illnesses)
- Medical (e.g., associated with increased health service usage, bidirectional relationship with many health problems leading to excess disability or exacerbation of symptoms)
- Cognitive (e.g., exacerbates decline)
- Financial (e.g., missed work—although less likely to impact the old and old-old groups, out-of-pocket costs associated with increased health service usage and associated treatments can tax already limited and/or fixed incomes)
- Mortality (i.e., associated with increased mortality)

Common Comorbidities

Of all other mental health disorders, anxiety is more likely to co-occur with MDD. Whether this represents a difficulty with the diagnostic system (e.g., overlapping criteria) or whether anxiety is a personality characteristic that increases the risk of developing depressive symptoms, thus serving as a risk factor for depression (Wetherell, Gatz, & Pedersen, 2001), the rates of comorbid anxiety and depression are significantly high, approaching 48% (Beekman et al., 2000). Comorbid anxiety symptoms in older adults with MDD lead to poor social functioning, increased suicidality, and poor prognosis (Lenze et al., 2000).

In terms of physical disorders, MDD is highly correlated with risk factors for certain medical illnesses. The research underscores that MDD is often comorbid with vascular diseases including diabetes, stroke, and cardiovascular disease. MDD is also commonly associated with insomnia, chronic pain, hypothyroidism, vascular dementia, Alzheimer's disease, and cancer. Elevated rates of MDD are also found in postsurgery patients, individuals with sensory impairment (e.g., visual impairment), and those with alcohol abuse.

EPIDEMIOLOGY

Prevalence Rates of Major Depressive Disorder in Older Adults

Two of the most commonly used strategies for examining patterns of disorders in a given population is to examine the rates of disorder either as occurring within the past year (1-year prevalence rates) or at anytime within the person's lifetime (lifetime prevalence rates). The following prevalence rates are drawn from the recent literature reviews by Fiske, Wetherell, and Gatz (2009) and Blazer (2003) and from studies using large representative older adult samples including Gum, King-Kallimanis, and Kohn (2009) and Steffens, Fisher, Langa, Potter, and Plassman (2009).

The prevalence of MDD varies depending on the specific population sampled. For example, in general community samples, older adults typically exhibit lower rates of diagnosable MDD compared to the general population, with lifetime prevalence rates ranging up to 10.9% despite the fact that living longer affords more years in which MDD could develop (Hasin, Goodwin, Stinson, & Grant, 2005). These data may suggest that older adults are more resilient as they are able to fend off developing a clinical depression despite many of the challenges associated with aging (Segal, Qualls, & Smyer, 2011). Alternative explanations for the lower levels of MDD in older adults may include selective mortality rates for persons with MDD, differences in retrospective recollections of depressive episodes, and/or weaknesses in the current diagnostic system used to capture the diagnoses in older persons.

Prevalence rates for MDD are much higher in older persons in institutional settings (i.e., long-term care settings; Blazer, 2003), hospital settings (i.e., medical inpatient and primary care settings; Djernes, 2006), and hospice and other palliative care settings (Akechi et al., 2004). The interested reader is referred to Feliciano and Areán (2008) for more detailed review of prevalence of depressive disorders in specific settings in the general adult population.

There are few differences in prevalence rates by race or ethnicity noted in older adults with MDD (Fiske et al., 2009). Some studies suggest that rates of MDD may be higher in older Hispanic women, particularly in those with comorbid diabetes (Black, 1999) than in non-Hispanic White men and women (Swenson, Baxter, Shetterly, Scarbro, Hamman, 2000). There is some evidence to suggest that rates may be lower in African American older adults (Gum et al., 2009).

Etiology

Investigations into the causality of MDD have led to much debate within the field. The current consensus is that depressive disorders are multifaceted and most likely result from biopsychosocial factors

(Kendler, Thornton, & Prescott, 2001; O'Keane, 2000). See Feliciano and Areán (2008) or Segal et al. (2011) for a thorough review of etiological concerns.

Risk and Protective Factors

Biological, psychological, and social factors have all been identified as either serving to increase vulnerability to developing MDD or to protect against its development.

Environment/Social Factors Versus Genetics
There is general support in the literature that older adults with late-onset depression have different risk factors than older adults with early-onset depression (occurring before the age of 20 years). Fiske and colleagues report that genetics are more likely to be relevant in early-onset depression because of the tendency for greater familial incidence. Environmental factors related to chronic stress either can lead to an increased vulnerability or can be protective over time. Chronic financial problems, chronic illness, and caregiving have all been shown to have negative effects on mental health, and depression in particular in adults and older adults. Social support, on the other hand, has been identified to have positive and protective effects against the negative impact of chronic stress (George, 1994).

Certain environments can promote the development of depression. For example, institutionalization is a substantial risk factor for depression. Risk can be inferred from the high frequency of nursing home residents who are clinically depressed, with estimates ranging from 14% to 42% (see review by Fiske et al., 2009). Institutionalization alone can certainly be iatrogenic, in addition to the risks produced by physical illnesses (described in more detail later in this chapter). This process is likely related to an interaction of factors including increased disability caused by physical illness, isolation, decreased engagement in meaningful activities, external locus of control (e.g., a reduced sense of control), and increased dependency on others. Given the high prevalence of depression in institutional settings, leaders in the field of geriatrics have recommended standards of care that include regular and routine screening of depression in long-term care settings (American Geriatrics Society and American Association for Geriatric Psychiatry, 2003). Despite this endorsement, appropriate assessment and treatment of MDD among long-term care residents remain poor.

Protective factors against developing MDD are currently under investigation and include both psychological and social factors (e.g., emotion regulation, resilience, being married, size and quality of social support network). Hendrie et al. (2006), in their review of longitudinal studies of cognitive and emotional health, discuss results that implicate several groups of variables that emerge as protective including having resources (cognitive, physical, emotional, and economic), adaptive life experience (ability to use psychological strategies and social resources effectively) and self-efficacy, and the role of meaningful engagement. A thorough review of this topic is beyond the scope of this chapter, but interested readers are directed to Fiske et al. (2009) for an excellent and concise review.

Medical/Physical Factors

Given the higher prevalence of MDD with comorbid medical conditions, it may be of no surprise that medical and physical disorders represent significant risk factors for developing depression. Physical illness is a major risk factor for depression in older adults. As noted earlier, medical populations report a substantially higher rate of MDD (12 times the rate that appears in community-dwelling older adults; Lichtenberg, 1998). Indeed, it has been noted by some that "the greater the medical burden, the higher the risk of depression" (Alexopoulos, 2005, p. 1962). Depression associated with medical and/or physical problems can result from two pathways: (a) a psychological reaction to a recent medical diagnosis, increased disability, or pain; or (b) the illness or its treatment could increase the affected person's vulnerability to developing depression. In the latter case, medical conditions such as abnormalities in thyroid function, cardiovascular diseases, and neurological/cognitive disorders all have been found to lead to increased risk for development of MDD.

Hypothyroidism has been found to be consistently linked to depression and impairments in cognitive function in adults. However, a recent review of the literature has demonstrated that older adults may be more susceptible to impairments in thyroid function that are subthreshold (i.e., subclinical hypothyroidism), and the prevalence increases with age (Davis, Stern, & Flashman, 2003). Abnormalities in thyroid functioning may serve as a risk factor for the development of depression, cardiovascular disease, and dementia in older adults.

An emerging body of literature has identified an important connection between cardiovascular disease and depression in older adults. Termed the "vascular depression hypothesis," this theory suggests that cardiovascular disease can serve as a risk factor or can precipitate a depressive episode in many older adults with concomitant neurological disorders (Alexopoulos et al., 1997). This hypothesis is supported by the high prevalence of depression in older adults with coronary artery disease, hypertension, diabetes, and myocardial infarction.

Related to this issue is the observation that late-life depression is often associated with greater cognitive impairments, especially executive function deficits such as planning and organization. Older adults with late-onset depression are also more likely to subsequently transition to dementia. This seems to be particularly true for those with accompanying mild cognitive impairment with observed conversion rates reported to be about 21% (Gabryelewicz et al., 2007).

Gender/Ethnic/Cultural/Racial Factors

As previously mentioned, there is less variability in prevalence rates by race or ethnicity in older samples than in younger samples. However, some differences have been noted including that older African Americans are less likely to report the presence of any mood disorder (Gum et al., 2009) and thus have a smaller odds ratio than Whites. Currently, the reason for the discrepancy is unclear but may be related to reporting, assessment issues, and discrepancy in access to health care.

ASSESSMENT

Accurate and thorough assessment of older clients and their context is a hallmark of the CBT model. An emphasis on comprehensive assessment is an important part of the gerontological and clinical geropsychological traditions as well, given the typically complex nature of problems experienced by older adults who need mental health services (Segal et al., 2011). In this section, we first describe several screening measures for MDD symptoms among older adults and next we describe some interviewing approaches to diagnose MDD.

Screening Measures

Screening measures for MDD are useful for identifying those who may need further assessment, quantifying clinical levels or severity of depression, and measuring progress toward treatment goals, but they should not be used to diagnose as a stand-alone procedure. Several brief and well-validated depression screening instruments are readily available for clinical and research use with older adults. We begin this discussion with a measure designed specifically for older adults and then review several measures that were not developed specifically for older adults but have some psychometric support for their use with older adults. For more extensive reviews, the interested reader is referred to Edelstein et al. (2008); Edelstein and Segal (2011); Fairchild and Scogin (2008); and Karel, Ogland-Hand, Gatz, and Unützer, (2002).

Geriatric Depression Scale

The Geriatric Depression Scale (GDS; Yesavage et al., 1983) was designed specifically to assess depression in older adults and, as such, has clearly become the most widely used screening scale for older adults. It includes 30 self-report items rated on a simple dichotomous Yes/No response format, and all of the items have content and face validity for appropriate usage with older adults. Most individuals can complete the GDS in less than 10 minutes. The GDS focuses on cognitive and behavioral aspects of depression, whereas somatic items are generally excluded. This was intentionally done to prevent the possible spurious elevation in GDS scores obtained by medically ill but not depressed older adults.

For 20 of the 30 items, the answer "yes" indicates depression. In the remaining 10 items, the answer "no" indicates depression. The total GDS score consists of the sum of all items endorsed with the depressive response and thus can range from 0 to 30. Recommended cutoffs for the GDS include 0–10 for minimal to mild depression, 11–20 for mild to moderate depression, and 21–30 for severe depression. Psychometric support for the GDS is good across a diverse range of older adult populations including psychiatric patients, medically ill outpatients, hospitalized older adults, nursing home residents, and individuals with mild-to-moderate dementia (for more specific data, see Edelstein & Segal, 2011; Marty, Pepin, June, & Segal, 2011). Notably, a 15-item short version of the GDS is available and has been well validated as a screening measure (Sheikh & Yesavage, 1986). The original GDS and the 15-item short form are in the public domain and can be accessed at: http://www.stanford.edu/~yesavage/GDS.html. Translations of the GDS in more than 30 languages are also available on the Web site. For convenience, the full GDS is provided in Table 2.1.

TABLE 2.1 Original Geriatric Depression Scale and Scoring

Choose the Best Answer for How You Felt Over the Past Week:		
1. Are you basically satisfied with your life?	Yes	<u>No</u>
2. Have you dropped many of your activities and interests?	<u>Yes</u>	No
3. Do you feel that your life is empty?	<u>Yes</u>	No
4. Do you often get bored?	<u>Yes</u>	No
5. Are you hopeful about the future?	Yes	<u>No</u>
6. Are you bothered by thoughts you can't get out of your head?	<u>Yes</u>	No
7. Are you in good spirits most of the time?	Yes	<u>No</u>
8. Are you afraid that something bad is going to happen to you?	<u>Yes</u>	No
9. Do you feel happy most of the time?	Yes	<u>No</u>
10. Do you often feel helpless?	<u>Yes</u>	No
11. Do you often get restless and fidgety?	<u>Yes</u>	No
12. Do you prefer to stay at home, rather than going out and doing new things?	<u>Yes</u>	No
13. Do you frequently worry about the future?	<u>Yes</u>	No
14. Do you feel you have more problems with memory than most?	<u>Yes</u>	No
15. Do you think it is wonderful to be alive now?	Yes	<u>No</u>
16. Do you often feel downhearted and blue?	<u>Yes</u>	No
17. Do you feel pretty worthless the way you are now?	<u>Yes</u>	No
18. Do you worry a lot about the past?	<u>Yes</u>	No
19. Do you find life very exciting?	Yes	<u>No</u>
20. Is it hard for you to get started on new projects?	<u>Yes</u>	No
21. Do you feel full of energy?	Yes	<u>No</u>
22. Do you feel that your situation is hopeless?	<u>Yes</u>	No
23. Do you think that most people are better off than you are?	<u>Yes</u>	No
24. Do you frequently get upset over little things?	<u>Yes</u>	No
25. Do you frequently feel like crying?	<u>Yes</u>	No
26. Do you have trouble concentrating?	<u>Yes</u>	No
27. Do you enjoy getting up in the morning?	Yes	<u>No</u>
28. Do you prefer to avoid social gatherings?	<u>Yes</u>	No
29. Is it easy for you to make decisions?	Yes	<u>No</u>
30. Is your mind as clear as it used to be?	Yes	<u>No</u>

Note. Assign one point for each of the underlined answers, indicating the depressive response.

A potential drawback to the GDS is its limited validity for use with some ethnically diverse older adults (Mui, Burnette, & Chen, 2001), although literature in this area is emerging. For example, the GDS has shown to be a satisfactory screening tool in Chinese older adults (Boey & Chiu, 1998), Portuguese older adults (Pocinho, Farate, Dias, Lee, & Yesavage, 2009), Iranian older adults (Malakouti, Fatollahi, Mirabzadeh, Salavati, & Zandi, 2006), and Japanese American older adults (Iwamasa, Hilliard, & Kost, 1998). Results from a study comparing Korean and American older adults indicated that the short version of the GDS had good reliability with both groups, but the underlying factor structure differed (Jang, Small, & Haley, 2001).

Center for Epidemiologic Studies Depression Scale

The Center for Epidemiologic Studies Depression Scale (CES-D; Radloff, 1977) consists of 20 self-report items that assess depressive symptoms experienced over the past week. Each item is rated on a 4-point Likert-type scale ranging from 0 (rarely/none) to 3 (most of the time). Traditionally, a total score is calculated by adding the ratings for all items. The possible range of total scores is from 0 to 60, with higher scores reflecting greater levels of depression. A common cutoff score for depression is 16 or higher. The CES-D was developed primarily as a research instrument for studies with adolescents and adults, although it has been used successfully with community-dwelling older adults, older medical inpatients, and depressed older adults (see Edelstein & Segal, 2011) because of its relatively low emphasis on somatic symptoms. A 10-item short form of the CES-D is also available and it has reasonable psychometric support for use with older adults.

Beck Depression Inventory—Second Edition

The Beck Depression Inventory–Second Edition (BDI-II; Beck, Steer, & Brown, 1996) is a 21-item self-report questionnaire that is widely used for screening adults. Each item describes a specific manifestation of depressive symptoms, and the respondent reads four evaluative statements and indicates his or her current severity level for that item. Thirteen items assess psychological symptoms of depression whereas eight items assess somatic symptoms. Potential scores range from 0 to 63, with higher scores corresponding to higher levels of depression. According to the BDI-II manual, scores of 0–13 denote minimal depression, scores of 14–19 indicate mild depression, scores of 20–28 signify moderate depression, and scores of 29–63 denote severe depression.

The main criticisms of the BDI-II are that it has many somatic items, which may not be reflective of depression in older adults and that the response format is not as simple as the other popular self-report measures, a particular detriment when working with individuals with cognitive impairment. These potential limitations not withstanding, recent studies reported excellent psychometric properties of the BDI-II among community-dwelling older adults (Segal, Coolidge, Cahill, & O'Riley, 2008) and depressed older psychiatric inpatients (Steer, Rissmiller, & Beck, 2000), suggesting that the BDI-II has adequate support for its use with older adults.

Cornell Scale for Depression in Dementia

The Cornell Scale for Depression in Dementia (CSDD; Alexopoulos, Abrams, Young, & Shamoian, 1988) is unique in that it is designed for use with individuals with cognitive impairment and it is completed by the clinician in conjunction with another person with sufficient knowledge of the identified patient (e.g., administered directly to a caregiver, spouse, or significant other). For its 19 items, depressive symptoms are evaluated on a 3-point rating scale (0 = absent, 1 = mild or intermittent, and 2 = severe), with higher scores indicating greater severity of depression. Total scores range from 0 to 38. The CSDD has adequate inter-rater reliability (kappa = 0.67), good internal consistency (0.84), and concurrent validity with other screening measures of depression (Kørner et al., 2006). The CSDD is the measure of choice for the screening of depression in individuals with dementia.

Despite the popularity of the self-report instruments described previously, it should be noted that a definitive diagnosis of MDD (or any psychological disorder for that matter) should never be made on the basis of self-report inventories alone, which can be subject to response biases (e.g., social desirability) and generally can be easily faked. In practice, a two-step process is typical whereby elevated self-reported scores on the screening instrument are followed up by a clinical or structured interview to confirm presence or absence of the disorder.

The Clinical Interview and Structured and Semistructured Interviews

In contrast to screening measures, interviews are more useful for determining contextual and historical variables that aid in the formal diagnosis of MDD. The clinical interview is the most common method of assessing depression in everyday practice, typically in unstructured format. During the interview, the clinician gathers information about the person's current symptoms of depression, including a history of the depression and attempts at coping with the depression. Other topics are typically pursued to place the experiences with depression in the context of overall functioning, including an in-depth personal history; mental health history (including interventions); medical, marital, family, social, and work history; current living conditions; and a mental status examination.

Collateral interviews with concerned family members or caregivers are a common and usually informative component of the depression assessment. Sometimes, collateral interviews reveal information about the patient's symptoms and functioning that was not presented in the initial interview with the patient. In one of our cases, for example, the wife of the patient revealed that the patient had recently been threatening to kill himself and possibly others, although he denied suicidal and homicidal ideation upon initial questioning. Any discrepancies should be gently explored in further interviews with the patient. Other advantages to collateral interviews are that they can be used to secure cooperation with the treatment plan from important individuals in the patient's network and collateral interviews may make clear the need for couples or family therapy interventions. Strategies to incorporate significant others into client care are discussed later.

To facilitate rapport in the clinical interview, clinicians should clearly explain the purposes and procedures of the interview, address any concerns the person may have about the evaluation, and be especially flexible when engaging older persons and their family members (Segal, Coolidge, & Hersen, 1998). Being generous with warmth, support, and reassurance (when needed) also helps with rapport especially for the evaluation of MDD, which can be particularly stigmatizing for some older adults. During the interview, it is important for clinicians to screen for cognitive disorders to rule out cognitive impairments that could be mimicking some or all of the depressive symptoms.

Structured and semistructured interviews are especially useful for determining reliable and valid diagnoses for a host of mental disorders, including MDD. In general, these types of interviews provide increased clinical accuracy by structuring questions to elicit details about frequency and intensity of symptoms (Segal & Coolidge, 2007). Full administration of a structured or semistructured interview typically takes more than 1 hour, which can pose a problem for some older clients. Examples of structured interviews that are commonly used for clinical research and training include the *Diagnostic Interview Schedule for DSM-IV* (DIS-IV; Robins et al., 2000) and the *Structured Clinical Interview for DSM-IV-TR Axis I Disorders* (SCID; First, Spitzer, Gibbon, & Williams, 2002). Each of these has been demonstrated to be useful for older adults. The DIS-IV is a fully structured interview that requires limited training on the part of the interviewer but also has a rigid format that does not permit deviations. As such, for clinical purposes, we recommend the SCID, which is a semistructured interview and can be flexibly used by mental health professionals.

The SCID is considered a state-of-the-art semistructured clinical interview based on the *DSM-IV* and has been used in hundreds of studies worldwide. The SCID fully assesses the criteria for mood disorders and contains sections designed to differentiate depressive and bipolar episodes and to differentiate mood symptoms induced by substances or medical illness. The format of items includes standard questions, qualifying questions, and optional probe questions to clarify diagnostic criteria. The SCID is available in two formats: The Clinician Version (SCID-CV) and the Research Version (SCID-RV). The SCID-RV may be used with the SCID-CV and supplements the interview with focus given to additional diagnoses and specifiers.

Reliability studies overall indicate good to excellent reliability for current diagnoses, moderate test–retest reliability, moderate concurrent validity, and moderate convergent validity in diverse adult populations (for a comprehensive review, see Rogers, 2001). Two studies specifically examining reliability of the MDD diagnosis among older adults provided strong psychometric support for the SCID. The first study (Segal, Hersen, Van Hasselt, Kabacoff, & Roth, 1993), which included 33 older psychiatric inpatients and outpatients, indicated a solid reliability estimate (kappa) for MDD (47% base rate, kappa = 0.70). The second study (Segal, Kabacoff, Hersen, Van Hasselt, & Ryan, 1995) included older psychiatric outpatients exclusively ($N = 40$), and the results similarly showed substantial diagnostic agreement for the general mood disorder category (60% base rate, kappa = 0.79) and for MDD (58% base rate, kappa = 0.90). In our experience, many older persons respond particularly well to semistructured interviews like the SCID because they like the comprehensive nature of the assessment and extended time with the interviewer. However, adequate rapport should be established and the interview procedure should be carefully explained before beginning the interview.

The Impact of Medical Illness, Medications, and Substance Abuse

It is critically important for clinicians working with older adults to understand that medical conditions and medications are particularly likely to affect psychological functioning. Thus, assessment of MDD in older adults must include a careful medical and pharmacological evaluation. A listing of medical conditions and medications that are known to produce depressive symptoms is presented in Table 2.2. As can be seen in the table, many illnesses and medications cause depressive symptoms so a full assessment in this area is critical. We typically advise our patients to bring to the interview a list of their current medications including dosing options. We also typically ask patients to sign a release so we can communicate with their medical providers, especially the primary care physician.

In addition to a full assessment of medical problems and medications, clinicians working with depressed older adults must also rule out substance abuse as a potential cause of the depression or as a maintaining factor in the depression. Substance abuse assessment among older adults is particularly challenging because some older adults do not openly and truthfully disclose their substance use. Alcohol is the most commonly abused psychoactive substance among older adults who have relatively lower rates of illicit drug use compared to younger adults (Johnson-Greene & Inscore, 2005; see Dautovich & Gum in this volume for a comprehensive review of depression and psychiatric

TABLE 2.2   Medical Conditions and Medications Associated With Major Depressive Disorder Among Adults and Older Adults

Medical Conditions
Cancers Pancreatic, breast, lung, colonic, and ovarian carcinoma; lymphoma and undetected cerebral metastasis
Coronary Artery Disease Hypertension, myocardial infarction, coronary artery bypass surgery, congestive heart failure
Metabolic Disturbances Diabetes mellitus, hypothyroidism or hyperthyroidism, hypercortisolism, hyperparathyroidism, Addison's disease, autoimmune thyroiditis
Neurologic Disorders Cerebrovascular accidents, Alzheimer's disease, Parkinson's disease, amyotrophic lateral sclerosis, multiple sclerosis, Binswanger's disease
Other Conditions Chronic obstructive pulmonary disease, rheumatoid arthritis, deafness, chronic pain, sexual dysfunction, renal dialysis, chronic constipation
Medications anesthetics, analgesics (used to relive pain), anticholinergics, anticonvulsants (e.g., carbamazepine), antihypertensives (used to relieve high blood pressure), anti-Parkinson medications, antiulcer medications, cardiac medications (e.g., digitalis, calcium channel blockers), psychotropic medications (e.g., antidepressants, benzodiazepines), muscle relaxants, steroids, sulfonamides

Source: Adapted from the American Psychiatric Association, 2000.

comorbidity in older adults). Obviously, medical conditions, medications, and substance abuse must be ruled out as significant etiological factors of the depression before initiation of CBT interventions.

Impact of Race, Culture, and Ethnicity

According to Feliciano and Gum (2010), the impact of cultural, ethnic, and racial factors on the assessment of older adults is noteworthy. Specifically, the authors indicate that cultural factors influence how individuals conceptualize and thus report their mood symptoms. For example, there is some evidence that Hispanic American adults tend to emphasize somatic symptoms more so than emotional or mood-related symptoms, and also are less likely to distinguish between mood and somatic symptoms. Similarly, older adults may report more somatic symptoms or anhedonia and less affective symptoms (Gallo & Rabins, 1999). Appreciation of culture-based reporting practices will affect our ability to accurately assess mood symptoms in older adult and minority populations.

Assessment of Pleasant Events

As we describe more fully later in this chapter. clinicians working from the CBT model are interested in the client's participation in pleasant and unpleasant events, which can relate to fluctuations in the client's mood symptoms. As such, clinicians commonly assess the frequency of participation in such events as a precursor to behavioral activation interventions. An excellent example of an elder-specific measure is the California Older Person's Pleasant Events Schedule (COPPES; Rider, Gallagher-Thompson, & Thompson, 2004), which contains 66 activities commonly enjoyed by older adults. On this scale, the respondent rates each activity on two dimensions: how often the activity occurred in the past month; and how pleasant, rewarding, or enjoyable the activity was (or would have been if completed). The 66 items are grouped into 5 subscales, which are included in the following list and include a sample item from each subscale:

1. *Socializing.* Sample item: Being with someone I love.
2. *Relaxing.* Sample item: Listening to music.
3. *Contemplating.* Sample item: Thinking about pleasant memories.
4. *Being Effective.* Sample item: Completing a difficult task.
5. *Doing Things.* Sample item: Doing volunteer work.

The COPPES and a computerized scoring program are available from http://oafc.stanford.edu/coppes.html

Besides the COPPES, Teri and Lewinsohn (1982) provided a Pleasant Events Schedule that has been widely used with older adults, and more recently, Meeks, Shah, and Ramsey (2009) developed the Pleasant Events Schedule–Nursing Home (PES-NH), which includes 30 items that cover the content of daily activities available in nursing homes.

Regardless if formal measures are used or if a more individualized approach is used, we encourage flexibility in assessing pleasant events. Laidlaw, Thompson, Dick-Siskin, and Gallagher-Thompson (2003) astutely said that "Anything that a person likes to do is a pleasant event" (p. 57). Indeed, pleasant events do not need to be major activities. Rather, many older adults derive enjoyment from smaller activities (e.g., reading from a novel, taking a brisk walk, petting a cat), and activities like these can and should be part of the assessment.

TREATMENT STRATEGIES

The effectiveness of psychological interventions for depression in older adults is well established, and several types of psychotherapy meet the standard for an evidence-based intervention (Mackin & Areán, 2005; Scogin & McElreath, 1994). These psychosocial interventions include behavioral therapy, cognitive-behavioral therapy, problem-solving therapy, cognitive bibliotherapy, brief psychodynamic therapy, and life review therapy (see review by Scogin, Welsh, Hanson, Stump, & Coates, 2005). Of these approaches, CBT is the most widely researched.

Overview of Efficacy of Cognitive-Behavioral Therapy for Major Depressive Disorder with Older Adults

CBT is an active and directive evidence-based practice that has demonstrated efficacy in working with various older adults (Scogin & Yon, 2006), including older adults who are cognitively impaired (Laidlaw et al., 2003). The theoretical underpinnings for CBT are based on the premise that the combination of negative affect and emotional distress, in conjunction with maladaptive processing, lower the rates of participation in rewarding activities, perpetuating a cycle of decreased mood, increased apathy, decreased motivation, isolation, and reduction in pleasurable activities (Laidlaw et al., 2003).

A diminishing sense of mastery over the environment coupled with increasing dependence on others can precipitate increased isolation and social withdrawal in older adults, impacting overall well-being (Kasl-Godley & Gatz, 2000).

In a recent review of psychosocial therapies for older adults with late-life depression, Mackin and Areán (2005) examined the available treatment literature from 1840 to 2005. Using the Chambless and Hollon (1998) criteria for empirically supported treatments, the authors identified only 17 studies that met all criteria including having a minimum of 30 participants per active treatment cell in the study and a comparison condition (which must be either the standard of care, care as usual, or a wait-list control). Of these studies, 10 examined CBT in older adults with diagnoses of major depressive disorder, minor depression, or dysthymia. Overall, the results indicated that CBT was superior to usual care, wait-list control, and pill-placebo. In addition, for several studies reviewed, treatment gains were maintained for up to 1 year posttreatment (Koder, Brodaty, & Anstey, 1996; Thompson, Coon, Gallagher-Thompson, Sommer, & Koin, 2001).

In another study, Pinquart, Duberstein, and Lyness (2007) conducted a meta-analysis examining the effects of psychosocial interventions on clinical depression in older adults. The authors examined 57 controlled studies and found large effect sizes in support of CBT with older adults with depressive symptoms ($d = 1.26$), and smaller but substantial effect sizes for those studies that only used older adults with diagnosis of MDD ($d = 0.76$).

Several studies have evaluated the efficacy of using CBT in older adult samples with varying degrees of cognitive impairment, typically in relation to comorbid disorders such as anxiety and depression (Koder, 1998; Teri & Gallagher-Thompson, 1991). However, outside of mood disturbances, CBT strategies have also been investigated in relation to enhancing quality of life and increasing active, positive coping in individuals experiencing cognitive decline (Kasl-Godley & Gatz, 2000). Of note, the focus of CBT interventions in cognitively impaired populations is not to improve cognitive skills and memory function per se but rather to enhance the areas of cognition that are preserved as well as to develop adaptive beliefs about memory decline and improve overall well-being (Clare & Woods, 2004; Kasl-Godley & Gatz, 2000), which could also indirectly impact mood symptoms.

Together, these studies indicate that CBT has been found to meet the criteria for an evidenced-based treatment for older adults with depression.

Cognitive-Behavioral Therapy for Older Adults

Overview of Session Goals

CBT with older adults in many respects is the same as CBT with younger people. CBT for depression is a time-limited therapy with the overarching goal to reduce depressive symptoms. CBT interventions are often cited as being particularly well suited to aging populations because of the "here-and-now" focus on identifying needs and interventions, the focus on skill enhancement and practice, and the structured and organized nature of sessions (Laidlaw et al., 2003). Older clients are taught the relationship between thoughts, behaviors, and mood to help them gain a better understanding of the factors that affect depression. Throughout the process, clients are taught skills that are useful in managing their depressive symptoms. The goals of sessions can be summarized as follows:

■ *Early sessions* of CBT typically focus on gathering important history including the reasons the client is seeking treatment at this particular time, mental health history including any prior experience with therapy, client expectations for therapy, and then socializing the client to the process of CBT to develop a working therapeutic alliance. At the outset of the therapeutic relationship, a critical undertaking is to collaboratively establish goals for treatment. Establishing realistic goals is critical, which may warrant providing psychoeducation tailored to the client's understanding, while also normalizing the situation that brought the client into treatment. Throughout treatment, goals should be approached in a manner that consistently encourages and supports the client's personal resources in an attempt to maximize functioning (Kasl-Godley & Gatz, 2000).

   During these early sessions, therapists need to observe for and attend to any sensory deficits the older adult clients may have. Approximately 14% of community-dwelling older adults have some type of sensory deficit and the prevalence increases with age (e.g., 35% in those aged 85 and older; Waldrop & Stern, 2003). In addition, any concerns that the older client may have about therapy or the ability to complete therapy (i.e., potential barriers) should be assessed and addressed in a collaborative fashion during this time. Interventions such as relaxation techniques can be integrated into early sessions to help the client learn to better manage distress and decrease mood disturbances that can further negatively impact overall well-being and cognitive capacity.

■ *Middle sessions* typically focus on education and skill development. Clients learn about depression, its prevalence, and common causes. Clients are taught the CBT framework including the interrelationship of thoughts, behavior, and mood. Specifically, clients are taught about the factors that affect depression (i.e., how their thoughts, behaviors, and engagement with others affect their mood, and the relationship between physical health and mood) and how positive change in any one of these areas affects the other areas. During these sessions, clients are taught to identify maladaptive thought patterns and their antecedents, attending to the specific negative/harmful thoughts and positive/helpful thoughts that they may have about a particular situation as well as examining the consequences of these patterns of thinking. Therapists and clients collaboratively identify adaptive beliefs and the negative automatic thoughts that the client would like to replace, helping the client to build a perception of control over performance, and thus restructuring cognitions. Middle and later sessions typically also target skills practice and integration of other behavioral interventions (e.g., homework and in vivo assignments). Skills practice generally takes the form of in-session practice but also includes homework assignments that the client completes between sessions. Homework assignments help facilitate generalization of skills learned within session to the older client's everyday life. For example, clients are taught how to challenge negative thoughts in session by (a) examining the evidence for or against this thought being true, (b) come up with some simple interventions to evaluate the evidence that the client will be able to try on his or her own (e.g., if the client believes that he or she is not going to enjoy an event at the senior center, have him or her actually go with an open mind and evaluate the reality), and (c) substitute more realistic thoughts (e.g., I might actually enjoy the event. Maybe I could try it rather than trying to predict what it might be like). Other skills taught might include breaking down large or more complex tasks into smaller, more manageable chunks, and then reinforcing one's self for achieving each step. This set of skills model some problem solving and setting clear goals and allows the person to contact positive outcomes. In addition, tracking mood symptoms is typically taught to demonstrate variability in mood from day to day and to highlight connections between mood and other events (e.g., pain or engagement in activity). According to behavioral models, affected individuals engage in lower rates of activities (behavior) and thus receive lower levels of positive reinforcement (Laidlaw et al., 2003; Zarit & Zarit, 2007). Thus, the client feels depressed and so he or she

withdraws from others, which provides less contact with reinforc-
ing/pleasurable outcomes and leads to the client feeling even worse;
thus maintaining the depression. Increasing and tracking engagement in pleasant events assist in breaking the negative downward
spiral by getting the clients to be more active in their own treatment
and thus in their own lives. Lastly, initial efforts are made to prepare
for and address termination.

■ *Later sessions* generally target identifying potential barriers to task
completion and problem-solving solutions. Attention is given to
assessing the client's support network and either maintaining this
network at its current level or working to increase the size and
strength of the support system. Assessment of interpersonal relationships, role changes (e.g., retirement, caregiving status), or transitions (e.g., grief or loss) that might impact depression need to occur
during these sessions. If there is relationship conflict or struggles
that exist in developing healthy relationships, skills training in the
form of assertiveness training, listening skills, or setting limits may
also be necessary. The following five steps to problem solving may
be helpful here:

1. Identifying problems,
2. Brainstorming possible strategies to address these factors,
3. Encouraging evaluation,
4. Choice of possible solutions, and
5. Trial of the chosen option.

These five steps can help to empower older adults and increase a sense
of mastery (see Gellis and Nezu in this volume for a comprehensive
overview of problem-solving therapy). In addition to these skills,
emphasis is placed on recognizing when symptoms may reoccur
or worsen so that the client might get support earlier (e.g., relapse
prevention). Identifying additional physical health problems that
could affect depression (e.g., sleep difficulty, pain) and address them as
needed (e.g., teaching relaxation skills, increasing good sleep hygiene)
may also occur in these later sessions. Sessions may be spaced several weeks apart during the late phase of treatment, allowing the client
time to independently use the skills that have been developed during
treatment, actively exploring areas that remain problematic while still
having the support of the therapist. Lastly, efforts are made to review
success, problem solve any new or remaining barriers, and complete
the termination process.

Specific Discussion Points

Psychoeducation

Psychological treatment has changed dramatically over the last century. Older adults are more likely to have had a history in which the predominant psychotherapeutic treatment available when they were younger was psychoanalysis and shared generational beliefs that only "crazy people" saw a "shrink." The media has assisted in perpetuating this psychotherapeutic stereotype, portraying therapy in which the person lies on a couch and talks aloud to a seemingly univolved therapist who sits in a chair behind the person. Given this context of misinformation, older adults may need substantial education about the process of therapy, the role expectations of client and therapist, as well as the specific structure of CBT. In addition, many older adults adhere to stereotypic beliefs or have attitudes about their cohort that can interfere with treatment effectiveness (Knight, 2004; Laidlaw et al., 2003). Thus, older people may require information regarding what mental health services are and how psychotherapy is not equivalent to inpatient care or having a severe mental illness. In addition, therapists will need to dispel common myths and educate the older client that depression is not a natural consequence of aging and that although depression is often a common response to grief, loss, disability, and role transitions (e.g., retirement), it is treatable at any age/life stage. Laidlaw et al. (2003) suggest that therapists can encourage openness and change in belief systems and attitudes through discussion of shared beliefs of the individual's cohort, with emphasis on the fact that these beliefs would no longer be endorsed in today's society, given improvements in our understanding of mental health.

Attention should be given to assessing barriers to engagement and completion of therapy. For example, it is not uncommon for older clients to have transportation barriers (e.g., they no longer drive because of visual decline or have financial limitations that affect access to transportation; Coon & Gallagher-Thompson, 2002). Further, given the current state of the economy, some older clients may still work, serve as caregivers for spouses or grandchildren, and thus have limited available time to pursue homework assignments, learn new materials, or attend weekly sessions. Other older clients may have a disability that prevents regular attendance in sessions, or may experience a physical or cognitive decline during the course of treatment that prevents them from attending sessions. For these reasons, therapists working with older populations will need to maintain an openness regarding the therapeutic frame in early sessions and continuously attend to potential barriers to completion of the prescribed therapy (Areán & Feliciano, 2008).

Termination

Through the process of therapy, the older client will have learned about depression and new strategies to cope and manage mood and psychosocial stressors. By the end of therapy, some older adults may feel anxious about their ability to remember and use these new skills independently. CBT therapists need to ensure that older clients feel competent enough to manage these new skills independently. Areán and Feliciano (2008) note that this process requires attention in early treatment sessions to ensure that the client understands the expectation that these new skills will need to be mastered and used independent of the therapist. Therapists should work to ensure that older clients are able to use the worksheets (e.g., thought records) effectively so as to facilitate continued usage of these tools after the prescribed course of therapy has come to an end (i.e., to facilitate maintenance of skills and treatment gains).

Modifications

In general, CBT for depression in older populations is quite similar to CBT for depression in younger populations, with a few modifications. As previously stated, in the early sessions, there is a psychoeducational component to introduce the client to the CB theory of depression and provide an explanation of how the process of therapy works. There is also a focus on the here and now, introducing maladaptive thoughts and challenging negativistic thinking; engagement in behavioral activation strategies; and introducing other skills-based training as necessary (e.g., the client could benefit based on his or her particular situation) including social skills training, stress, anxiety or time management, and/or problem solving. Modifications to CBT, if necessary, are centered around age-related changes in cognitive functions that may challenge the client's ability to learn and attend to new material; accounting for any sensory or other physical disabilities; adjusting the therapeutic frame to allow for disability and the numerous demands that older people have on their time and energy; and a consideration of both developmental processes and cohort beliefs. Thus, the content of CBT will not change, but rather the means by which it is presented should be adjusted to meet the needs of the older client. Table 2.3 summarizes some suggestions for modifications depending on the age-related challenge in using specific CBT strategies. Specific examples of modifications that may be needed in relation to cognitive impairment are addressed in the following case example of CBT with a client demonstrating cognitive impairment.

TABLE 2.3   Late-Life Adaptations for Cognitive-Behavioral Therapy

Age-Related Challenge	Cognitive-Behavioral Therapy Process	Adaptation
Disability, time constraints, instrumental barriers	The therapeutic frame, frequency of visits	Modality change (e.g., home/telephone-based therapy); increasing the number of visits, shortening the length of visits, and/or incorporating frequent breaks; case management
Learning novel concepts	Overall knowledge acquisition	Tie new information to overlearned and contextual information
Verbal recall	Thought records, differentiating thought from feeling	Simplify terms and provide forms, avoid jargon
Perceptual speed	Homework, adherence, session time	Increase number of sessions, simplify homework; schedule time for homework; telephone support
Attention and focus	Structured tasks, information gathering, weighing the evidence	Redirection, use handouts
Working memory	Learning new skills	Cue and review, multimodal presentation
Isolation	Termination	Early fading, relapse prevention, booster sessions

Source: Adapted from Areán & Feliciano, 2008.

CASE STUDY

Mrs. Jones, a 64-year-old European American woman who came to treatment with mild cognitive impairment, which was evidenced on neuropsychological testing, as well as MDD. A CBT-oriented framework modified to encourage Mrs. Jones' strengths and to accommodate areas of cognition that were compromised was used throughout the course of treatment. The early phase of treatment was dedicated to developing a supportive structure for Mrs. Jones to examine her cognitions and emotions related to her diagnosis of cognitive impairment and the long-term implications of the cognitive impairment, as well as to discuss and appreciate her mood disturbance. Attention was given to normalizing Mrs. Jones' grieving the loss of her cognitive abilities and discussing that although her cognitive impairment was not reversible, her depression could be treated and improved. Interventions such as relaxation techniques were used to help Mrs. Jones learn to better manage distress and decrease her mood disturbances that further negatively impacted her cognitive capacity. We engaged in exploration of her negative automatic thoughts, considering together adaptive beliefs that support her perception of control over her mood disturbance as well as her memory impairment. Given her memory impairment, Mrs. Jones was provided with handouts to facilitate remembering the content of her sessions and external cueing to complete the homework activities accomplished using cue cards and other visual prompts. Additionally, sessions were audiotaped and provided to Mrs. Jones as another resource for her to review material in between sessions. As treatment progressed, and she was willing, Mrs. Jones' daughter, whom she resided with, was invited into session to learn skills to actively support her mother. Given a report of family discord earlier in treatment, inviting Mrs. Jones' daughter to participate in treatment provided a supportive environment for both parties to discuss and consider current and past patterns of interaction that were affecting their well-being. Additionally, Mrs. Jones' daughter was able to learn strategies to help structure her mother's environment to maximize Mrs. Jones' functional abilities, as well as helping to reinforce Mrs. Jones' adaptive behaviors and engage in active problem solving around any problematic behaviors.

Laidlaw and McAlpine (2008) warn against assuming that modifications need to be made based on age (in a sense, ageism) and emphasize assessing the particular needs of older clients. The authors suggest that CBT with older adults may be different from CBT in younger population in several different ways:

1. The need to incorporate a "comprehensive conceptualization framework" that takes into account developmental stages,
2. The need to develop an understanding about the different time frames in which older adults may operate,
3. The need to balance achieving goals with teaching strategies to assist with coping with losses,
4. The need to place a focus on maintenance of current skill level and education rather than potential causes in treatment sessions,
5. The need to develop an understanding of potential differences between the generation of the client and that of the therapist (i.e., cohort differences), and
6. The assessment of the fit between this model of therapy and the client.

Strategies to Incorporate Others Who Support the Client

Considering the social and familial context of an older adult is imperative when undertaking a therapeutic relationship (Knight, 2006). Identifying significant others in the lives of older clients can benefit the
therapeutic relationship by helping identify additional stressors (e.g.,
caregiving roles) and by targeting additional resources for the client's
treatment. Collaborating with the client to determine whether he or
she feels comfortable engaging the family member as part of therapy
would need to be investigated, and the roles of each participant in the
treatment would need to be negotiated before bringing another person
into the therapeutic context. In the case of caregiving, older adults who
are physically or cognitively compromised may have care provided by
family members or close friends, or the older adult may be acting as a
caregiver for a loved one.

In the case of a cognitively compromised older adult receiving
care from a familial caregiver, several studies have been undertaken
that target treatment for decreasing depression in dementia involving both the care recipient and the caregiver. Teri, Logsdon, Uomoto,
and McCurry (1997) used behavioral treatments with both cognitively
impaired older adults suffering from depression and the caregiver of the
older adult, with the caregiver integrated into the treatment as an active
agent of change. Findings indicated that both the older adults and their
caregivers benefited from the dyadic interventions and demonstrated
decreased depressive symptoms. Developing an understanding of the
significant others in the lives of older adults increases the effectiveness
of treatment as it provides a fuller picture of the client's world.

Discussion of Combining Cognitive-Behavioral Therapy with Psychopharmacological Treatment

Therapy outcome studies examining pharmacological and psychosocial interventions find that pharmacotherapy and psychotherapy of
various types are approximately equally effective, with efficacy rates
of between 50% and 70% of older adults with MDD within 12–20 sessions (Agency for Health Care Policy and Research, 1993). Pinquart et al.
(2007) in their meta-analysis comparing psychological and pharmacological interventions for depression reported that effect sizes might favor
psychotherapy.

In outcome studies that examine a combination of both CBT and psychopharmacological treatments, the results indicate that the combination

of the two therapies is slightly better than either one alone. In a study by Thompson et al. (2001), CBT was compared with an antidepressant (desipramine) and a combination of CBT and desipramine in older adults with MDD. Results indicated that both CBT and the combination therapy were more effective in treating depression symptoms than using desipramine alone, and the combination therapy had slightly better outcomes than CBT alone. Zarit and Zarit (2007) suggest that the combined treatment is particularly well suited to older clients who have a history of recurrent depression and have previously responded well to treatment with antidepressants and those clients whose depression is severe. The rationale behind this suggestion is thought to be the effects on mood that occur quickly after starting the medication (secondary to either placebo or the medication), which can then allow the therapist to engage them with the CB material. These immediate improvements in mood can be encouraging to the client and thus may potentially prevent premature dropout. The drawbacks of combined therapy approach include the likelihood of negative side effects and the possibility of drug–drug interactions. However, in a CBT framework, the therapist is likely to have frequent contact (and a well-developed relationship) with the client that these side effects can be reported before they become too problematic. The CBT therapist can facilitate discussion with the older client's physician to address the older client's concerns (Zarit & Zarit, 2007). Zarit and Zarit provide helpful suggestions for how to work with combined treatment and a brief overview of the available antidepressant medications.

SUMMARY

Aging can be conceptualized as a multidimensional experience, a series of transitions that is influenced by both the individual and collective experience. For many older adults, aging can be a time for rediscovering self and exploring new learning experiences without the encumbrance of work responsibilities or raising children. However, for others, it is a time of changing roles within society and family, declining medical health status and cognitive impairment, experiencing grief and loss, all of which contributes to development of depression and results in a decrease in quality of life. However, we have substantial evidence that late-life depression is treatable. We have discussed several reasons why CBT may be particularly well suited as a treatment to work with older adults with depression including its emphasis on psychoeducation, focus on the present, application of techniques to everyday life situations, and its ability to address issues of loss in later life. CBT has substantial empirical support, has shown efficacy in addressing late-life depression, and can offer a source of hope to those older adults in need.

REFERENCES

Agency for Health Care Policy and Research. (1993). *Depression guideline panel. Depression in primary care: Volume 2. Treatment of major depression. Clinical practice guideline, Number 5* (AHCPR Publication No. 93-0551). Rockville, MD: U.S. Department of Health and Human Services, Public Health Service, Agency for Health Care Policy and Research.

Akechi, T., Okuyama, T., Sugawara, Y., Nakano, T., Shima, Y., & Uchitomi, Y. (2004). Major depression, adjustment disorders, and post-traumatic stress disorder in terminally ill cancer patients: Associated and predictive factors. *Journal of Clinical Oncology, 22*(10), 1957–1965.

Alexopoulos, G. S. (2005). Depression in the elderly. *Lancet, 365*(9475), 1961–1970.

Alexopoulos, G. S., Meyers, B. S., Young, R. C., Campbell, S., Silbersweig, D., Charlson, M. (1997). 'Vascular depression' hypothesis. *Archives of General Psychiatry, 54*(10), 915–922.

Alexopoulos, G. S., Abrams, R. C., Young, R. C., & Shamoian, C. A. (1988). Cornell Scale for Depression in Dementia. *Biological Psychiatry, 23*(3), 271–284.

Alexopoulos, G. S., & Kelly, R. E., Jr. (2009). Research advances in geriatric depression. *World Psychiatry, 8*(3), 140–149.

Alexopoulos, G. S., Vrontou, C., Kakuma, T., Meyers, B. S., Young, R. C., Klausner, E., et al. (1996). Disability in geriatric depression. *American Journal of Geriatric Psychiatry, 153*(7), 877–885.

Alexopoulos, G. S., Young, R. C., Abrams, R. C., Meyers, B., & Shamoian, C. A. (1989). Chronicity and relapse in geriatric depression. *Biological Psychiatry, 26*(6), 551–564.

American Geriatrics Society, & American Association for Geriatric Psychiatry. (2003). Consensus statement on improving the quality of mental health care in U.S. nursing homes: Management of depression and behavioral symptoms associated with dementia. *Journal of the American Geriatrics Society, 51*(9), 1287–1298.

American Psychiatric Association. (2000). *Diagnostic and statistical manual of mental disorders* (4th ed., text rev.). Washington, DC: Author.

Areán, P.A., & Feliciano, L. (2008). Older adults. In M. A. Whisman (Ed.), Adapting cognitive therapy for depression (pp. 417–438). New York, NY: The Guilford Press.

Beck, A. T., Steer, R. A., & Brown, G. K. (1996). *Manual for the Beck Depression Inventory-II.* San Antonio, TX: Psychological Corporation.

Beekman, A. T., de Beurs, E., van Balkom, A. J., Deeg, D. J., van Dyck, R., van Tilburg, W. (2000). Anxiety and depression in later life: Co-occurrence and communality of risk factors. *American Journal of Psychiatry, 157*(1), 89–95.

Black, S. A. (1999). Increased health burden associated with comorbid depression in older diabetic Mexican Americans: Results from the Hispanic Established Population for Epidemiologic Study of the Elderly survey. *Diabetes Care, 22*(1), 56–64.

Blazer, D. G. (2003). Depression in later life: Review and commentary. *Journals of Gerontology: Series A: Biological Sciences and Medical Sciences, 58*(3), 249–265.

Boey, K. W., & Chiu, H. F. K. (1998). Assessing psychological well-being of the old-old: A comparative study of GDS-15 and GHQ-12. *Clinical Gerontologist, 19*, 65–75.

Brodaty, H., Luscombe, G., Parker, G., Wilhelm, K., Hickie, I., Austin, M. P., et al. (2001). Early and late onset depression in old age: Different aetiologies, same phenomenology. *Journal of Affective Disorders, 66*(2–3), 225–236.

Chambless, D. L., & Hollon, S. D. (1998). Defining empirically supported therapies. *Journal of Consulting and Clinical Psychology, 66*(1), 7–18.

Clare, L., & Woods, R. T. (2004). Cognitive training and cognitive rehabilitation for people with early-stage Alzheimer's disease: A review. *Neuropsychological Rehabilitation, 14*, 385–401.

Coon, D. W., & Gallagher-Thompson, D. (2002). Encouraging homework completion among older adults in therapy. *Journal of Clinical Psychology, 58*(5), 549–563.

Davis, J. D., Stern, R. A., & Flashman, L. A., (2003). Cognitive and neuropsychiatric aspects of subclinical hypothyroidism: significance in the elderly. *Current Psychiatry Reports, 5*(5), 384–390.

Djernes, J. K. (2006). Prevalence and predictors of depression in populations of elderly: A review. *Acta Psychiatrica Scandinavica, 113*(5), 372–387.

Edelstein, B. A., & Segal, D. L. (2011). Assessment of emotional and personality disorders in older adults. In K. W. Schaie & B. G. Knight (Eds.), *Handbook of the psychology aging* (7th ed.) (pp. 325–337). New York, NY: Academic Press.

Edelstein, B. A., Woodhead, E. L., Segal, D. L., Heisel, M. J., Bower, E. H., Lowery, A. J., et al. (2008). Older adult psychological assessment: Current instrument status and related considerations. *Clinical Gerontologist, 31*(3), 1–35.

Fairchild, K., & Scogin, F. (2008). Assessment and treatment of depression. In K. Laidlaw & B. G. Knight (Eds.), *Handbook of emotional disorders in later life: Assessment and treatment* (pp. 213–231). New York, NY: Oxford University Press.

Feliciano, L, & Areán, P. A. (2007). Mood disorders: Depressive disorders. In M. Hersen, S. M. Turner, & D. C. Beidel (Eds.), *Adult psychopathology and diagnosis* (5th ed., pp. 286–316). Hoboken, NJ: John Wiley & Sons, Inc.

Feliciano, L., & Gum, A. M. (2010). Mood disorders. In M. Hersen & D. L. Segal (Eds.), *Diagnostic interviewing* (4th ed., pp. 153–176). New York, NY: Springer Publishing Company.

First, M. B., Spitzer, R. L., Gibbon, M., & Williams, J. B. W. (2002). *Structured clinical interview for DSM-IV-TR Axis I Disorders, Research Version, Patient Edition (SCID-I/P)*. New York, NY: Biometrics Research, New York State Psychiatric Institute.

Fiske, A., & O'Riley, A. A. (2008). Depression in late life. In J. Hunsley & E. J. Marsh (Eds.), *A guide to assessments that work* (pp. 138–157). New York, NY: Oxford University Press.

Fiske, A., Wetherell, J. L., & Gatz, M. (2009). Depression in older adults. *Annual Review of Clinical Psychology, 5*, 363–389.

Gabryelewicz, T., Styczynska, M., Luczywek, E., Barczak, A., Pfeffer, A., Androsiuk, W., et al., (2007). The rate of conversion of mild cognitive impairment to dementia: Predictive role of depression. *International Journal of Geriatric Psychiatry, 22*(6), 563–567.

Gallo, J. J., & Rabins, P. V. (1999). Depression without sadness: alternative presentations of depression in late life. *American Family Physician, 60*(3), 820–826.

George, L. K. (1994). Social factors and depression in late life. In L. S. Schneider, C. F. Reynolds, B. D. Lebowitz, & A. J. Friedhoff (Eds.), *Diagnosis and treatment of depression in late life: Results of the NIH consensus development conference* (pp. 131– 53). Washington, DC: American Psychiatric Press.

Gum, A. M., King-Kallimanis, B., & Kohn, R. (2009). Prevalence of mood, anxiety, and substance-abuse disorders for older Americans in the national comorbidity survey-replication. *American Journal of Geriatric Psychiatry, 17*(9), 769–781.

Hasin, D. S., Goodwin, R. D., Stinson, F. S., & Grant, B. F. (2005). Epidemiology of major depressive disorder: Results from the National Epidemiologic Survey on Alcoholism and Related Conditions. *Archives of General Psychiatry, 62*(10), 1097–1106.

Hendrie, H. C., Albert, M. S., Butters, M. A., Gao, S., Knopman, D. S., Launer, L. J., et al. (2006). The NIH Cognitive and Emotional Health Project Report of the Critical Evaluation Study Committee. *Alzheimer's & Dementia, 2*(1), 12–32.

Iwamasa, G. Y., Hilliard, K. M., & Kost, C. R. (1998). The Geriatric Depression Scale and Japanese American older adults. *Clinical Gerontologist, 19,* 13–24.

Jang, Y., Small, B. J., & Haley, W. E. (2001). Cross-cultural comparability of the Geriatric Depression Scale: Comparison between older Koreans and older Americans. *Aging & Mental Health, 5*(1), 31–37.

Johnson-Greene, D., & Inscore, A. B. (2005). Substance abuse in older adults. In S. S. Bush & T. A. Martin (Eds.), *Geriatric neuropsychology: Practice essentials* (pp. 429–451). New York, NY: Taylor & Francis.

Karel, M. J., Ogland-Hand, S., Gatz, M., & Unützer, J. (2002). *Assessing and treating late-life depression: A casebook and resource guide.* New York, NY: Basic Books.

Kasl-Godley, J., & Gatz, M. (2000). Psychosocial interventions for individuals with dementia: An integration of theory, therapy, and a clinical understanding of dementia. *Clinical Psychology Review, 20*(6), 755–782.

Kendler, K. S., Thornton, L. M., & Prescott, C. A. (2001). Gender differences in the rates of exposure to stressful life events and sensitivity to their depressogenic effects. *The American Journal of Psychiatry, 158*(4), 587–593.

Klein, D. N., Schatzberg, A. F., McCullough, J. P., Keller, M. B., Dowling, F., Goodman, D., et al. (1999). Early- versus late-onset dysthymic disorder: Comparison in out-patients with superimposed major depressive episodes. *Journal of Affective Disorders, 52*(1–3), 187–196.

Knight, B. G. (2004). *Psychotherapy with older adults* (3rd ed.). Thousand Oaks, CA: Sage Publications.

Knight, B. G. (2006). Unique aspects of psychotherapy with older adults. In S. H. Qualls & B. G. Knight (Eds.), *Psychotherapy for depression in older adults* (pp. 3–28). Hoboken, NJ: John Wiley & Sons, Inc.

Koder, D. A. (1998). Treatment of anxiety in the cognitively impaired elderly: Can cognitive-behavior therapy help? *International Psychogeriatrics, 10*(2), 173–182.

Koder, D. A., Brodaty, H., & Anstey, K. J. (1996). Cognitive therapy for depression in the elderly. *International Journal of Geriatric Psychiatry, 11,* 97–107.

Børner, A., Lauritzen, L., Abelskov, K., Gulmann, N., Brodersen, A. M., Wedervang-Jensen, T. et al. (2006). The Geriatric Depression Scale and the Cornell Scale for Depression in Dementia. A validity study. *Nordic Journal of Psychiatry, 60*(5), 360–364.

Laidlaw, K., & McAlpine, S. (2008). Cognitive behavior therapy: How is it different with older people? *Journal of Rational-Emotive Therapy, 26,* 250–262.

Laidlaw, K., Thompson, L. W., Dick-Siskin, L., & Gallagher-Thompson, D. (2003). *Cognitive behaviour therapy with older people.* New York, NY: John Wiley & Sons, Inc.

Lenze, E. J., Mulsant, B. H., Shear, M. K., Schulberg, H. C., Dew, M. A., Begley, A. E., et al. (2000). Comorbid anxiety disorders in depressed elderly patients. *American Journal of Psychiatry, 157*(5), 722–728.

Lichtenberg, P. A. (1998). Cost-effective geriatric neuropsychology. In P. E. Hartman-Stein (Ed.), *Innovative behavioral healthcare for older adults: A guidebook for changing times* (pp. 79–102). San Francisco, CA: Jossey-Bass.

Mackin, R. S., & Areán, P. A. (2005). Evidence-based psychotherapeutic interventions for geriatric depression. *Psychiatric Clinics of North America, 28*(4), 805–820.

Malakouti, S. K., Fatollahi, P., Mirabzadeh, A., Salavati, M., & Zandi, T. (2006). Reliability, validity, and factor structure of the GDS-15 in Iranian elderly. *International Journal of Geriatric Psychiatry, 21*(6), 588–593.

Marty, M. A., Pepin, R., June, A., & Segal, D. L. (2011). Geriatric depression scale. In M. Abou-Saleh, C. Katona, & A. Kumar (Eds.), *Principles and practice of geriatric psychiatry* (3rd ed.) (pp. 152–156). New York, NY: John Wiley & Sons, Inc.

Meeks, S., Shah, S. N., & Ramsey, S. K. (2009). The Pleasant Events Schedule—nursing home version: A useful tool for behavioral interventions in long-term care. *Aging & Mental Health, 13*(3), 445–455.

Mui, A. C., Burnette, D., & Chen, L. M. (2001). Cross-cultural assessment of geriatric depression: A review of the CES-D and the GDS. *Journal of Mental Health and Aging, 7*(1), 137–164.

O'Keane, V. (2000). Evolving model of depression as an expression of multiple interacting risk factors. *British Journal of Psychiatry, 177,* 482–483.

Pinquart, M., Duberstein, P. R., Lyness, J. M. (2007). Effects of psychotherapy and other behavioral interventions on clinically depressed older adults: A meta-analysis. *Aging & Mental Health, 11*(6), 645–657.

Pocinho, M. T. S., Farate, C., Dias, C. A., Lee, T. T., & Yesavage, J. A. (2009). Clinical and psychometric validation of the Geriatric Depression Scale (GDS) for Portuguese elders. *Clinical Gerontologist, 32,* 223–236.

Radloff, L. S. (1977). The CES-D scale: A self-report depression scale for research in the general population. *Applied Psychological Measurement, 1,* 385–401.

Rapp, M. A., Dahlman, K., Sano, M., Grossman, H. T., Haroutunian, V., & Gorman, J. M. (2005). Neuropsychological differences between late-onset and recurrent geriatric major depression. *American Journal of Psychiatry, 162*(4), 691–698.

Rider, K. L., Gallagher-Thompson, D., & Thompson, L. W. (2004). *California older person's pleasant events schedule: Manual.* Retrieved February 18, 2010, from http://oafc.stanford.edu/coppes_files/Manual2.pdf

Robins, L. N., Cottler, L. B., Bucholz, K. K., Compton, W. M., North, C. S., & Rourke, K. (2000). *Diagnostic Interview Schedule for DSM-IV (DIS-IV).* St. Louis, MO: Washington University School of Medicine.

Rogers, R. (2001). *Handbook of diagnostic and structured interviewing.* New York, NY: Guilford Press.

Schweitzer, I., Tuckwell, V., O'Brien, J., & Ames, D. (2002). Is late onset depression a prodome to dementia? *International Journal of Geriatic Psychiatry, 17*(11), 997–1005.

Scogin, F., & McElreath, L. (1994). Efficacy of psychosocial treatments for geriatric depression: A quantitative review. *Journal of Consulting and Clinical Psychology, 62*(1), 69–74.

Scogin, F., Welsh, D., Hanson, A., Stump, J., & Coates, A. (2005). Evidence-based psychotherapies for depression in older adults. *Clinical Psychology: Science and Practice, 12*, 222–237.

Scogin, F., & Yon, A. (2006). Evidence-based psychological treatment with older adults. In S. H. Qualls & B. G. Knight (Eds.) *Psychotherapy for depression in older adults* (pp. 157–176). Hoboken, NJ: John Wiley & Sons, Inc.

Segal, D. L., & Coolidge, F. L. (2007). Structured and semi-structured interviews for differential diagnosis: Issues and applications. In M. Hersen, S. M. Turner, & D. C. Beidel (Eds.), *Adult psychopathology and diagnosis* (5th ed., pp. 78–100). New York, NY: John Wiley & Sons, Inc.

Segal, D. L., Coolidge, F. L., Cahill, B. S., & O'Riley, A. A. (2008). Psychometric properties of the Beck Depression Inventory II (BDI-II) among community-dwelling older adults. *Behavior Modification, 32*(1), 3–20.

Segal, D. L., Coolidge, F. L., & Hersen, M. (1998). Psychological testing of older people. In I. H. Nordhus, G. R. VandenBos, S. Berg, & P. Fromholt (Eds.), *Clinical geropsychology* (pp. 231–257). Washington, DC: American Psychological Association.

Segal, D. L., Coolidge, F. L., & Rosowsky, E. (2006). *Personality disorders and older adults: Diagnosis, assessment, and treatment.* Hoboken, NJ: John Wiley & Sons, Inc.

Segal, D. L., Hersen, M., Van Hasselt, V. B., Kabacoff, R. I., & Roth, L. (1993). Reliability of diagnoses in older psychiatric patients using the structured clinical interview for DSM-III-R. *Journal of Psychopathology and Behavioral Assessment, 15*, 347–356.

Segal, D. L., Kabacoff, R. I., Hersen, M., Van Hasselt, V. B., & Ryan, C. F. (1995). Update on the reliability of diagnosis in older psychiatric outpatients using the Structured Clinical Interview for DSM-III-R. *Journal of Clinical Geropsychology, 1*, 313–321.

Segal, D. L., Qualls, S. H., & Smyer, M. A. (2011). *Aging and mental health* (2nd edition). Hoboken, NJ: John Wiley & Sons, Inc.

Sheikh, J. I., & Yesavage, J. A. (1986). Geriatric Depression Scale (GDS): Recent evidence and development of a shorter version. *Clinical Gerontologist, 5*, 165–173.

Steer, R. A., Rissmiller, D. J., & Beck, A. T. (2000). Use of the Beck Depression Inventory-II with depressed geriatric inpatients. *Behaviour Research and Therapy, 38*(3), 311–318.

Steffens, D. C., Fisher, G. G., Langa, K. M., Potter, G. G., & Plassman, B. L. (2009). Prevalence of depression among older Americans: The Aging, Demographics and Memory Study. *International Psychogeriatrics, 21*(5), 879–888.

Swenson, C. J., Baxter, J., Shetterly, S. M., Scarbro, S. L., Hamman, R. F. (2000). Depressive symptoms in Hispanic and non-Hispanic White rural elderly: The San Luis Valley Health and Aging Study. *American Journal of Epidemiology, 152*(11), 1048–1055.

Teri, L., & Gallagher-Thompson, D. (1991). Cognitive-behavioral interventions for treatment of depression in Alzheimer's patients. *The Gerontologist, 31*(3), 413–416.

Teri, L., & Lewinsohn, P. M. (1982). Modification of the Pleasant and Unpleasant Events Schedules for use with the elderly. *Journal of Consulting and Clinical Psychology, 50*(3), 444–445.

Teri, L., Logsdon, R. G., Uomoto, J., & McCurry, S. M. (1997). Behavioral treatment of depression in dementia patients: A controlled clinical trial. *Journals of Gerontology: Series B: Psychological Sciences and Social Sciences, 52*(4), P159–166.

Thompson, L. W., Coon, D. W., Gallagher-Thompson, D., Sommer, B. R., & Koin, D. (2001). Comparison of desipramine and cognitive/behavioral therapy in the treatment of elderly outpatients with mild-to-moderate depression. *The American Journal of Geriatric Psychiatry, 9*(3), 225–240.

Waldrop, J., & Stern, S. M. (2003). *Disability status: 2000, Census 2000 brief.* Washington, DC: U.S. Government Printing Office.

Wetherell, J. L., Gatz, M., & Pedersen, N. L. (2001). A longitudinal analysis of anxiety and depressive symptoms. *Psychology and Aging, 16*(2), 187–195.

Yesavage, J. A., Brink, T. L., Rose, T. L., Lum, O., Huang, V., Adey, M. B., et al. (1983). Development and validation of a geriatric depression screening scale: A preliminary report. *Journal of Psychiatric Research, 17*(1), 37–49.

Zarit, S. H., & Zarit, J. M. (2007). *Mental disorders in older adults* (2nd ed.). New York, NY: Guilford Press.

3

Psychosocial Treatment of Bipolar Disorder in Older Adults

Robert Reiser, Shilpa Reddy, Monica M. Parkins,
Larry W. Thompson, and Dolores Gallagher-Thompson

Bipolar disorder is ranked among the top 10 disabling illnesses in the world (World Health Organization, 2004). Bipolar disorder is typically characterized by lifelong mood instability where most individuals have residual symptoms with an equal likelihood of recovery or a chronic unremitting course. Symptomatic recovery does not generally translate to functional recovery (Tohen et al., 2003). Episodes occur in the form of marked mood instability with substantial social and occupational impairment (Ng et al., 2008).

As the population continues to age, health and health care delivery for elderly persons become an increasingly significant issue (Jeste et al., 1999). As of 2008, individuals older than 65 accounted for 12.8% of the U.S. population or about one in every eight Americans, and this is expected to grow to 19% of the population by 2030 (Administration on Aging, 2008). The aging trend in U.S. demographics and the serious and chronic nature of bipolar disorder should place bipolar disorder as a high priority for health care researchers and clinicians (Jeste et al.). The advocacy group, Depression and Bipolar Support Alliance, in a consensus statement, reported an important gap in the literature on late-life bipolar disorder and highlighted a need for research on the diagnosis and treatment in this area (Charney et al., 2003).

In general, the over 65-year-age group tends to have a lower prevalence of mood disorders (Gum, King-Kallimanis, & Kohn, 2009). Community samples suggest that the lifetime prevalence of bipolar disorder ranges from 0.4% to 1.6% for bipolar I disorder in the general population (American Psychiatric Association [APA], 2000). The National Comorbidity Survey-Replication (NCS-R) reported lifetime prevalence rates of 0.04% to 0.05% in the over 65-year-age group (Ng et al., 2008). Depp and Jeste (2004) in their comprehensive review of late-life bipolar disorder suggest community prevalence rates to be between 0.1%

and 0.5%. However, with the increasing aging of the population, the absolute number will likely increase in the coming years (Jeste et al., 1999) and, currently, older adults still represent about 8% to 10% of all inpatient psychiatric cases (Depp & Jeste, 2004).

Bipolar disorder typically involves cyclical and periodic mood swings alternating between manic, hypomanic or mixed, and depressive states. Symptoms of mania include the presence of an elevated, expansive, or irritable mood combined with at least three of the following: unusually high self-esteem; a decreased need for sleep; pressured speech or excessive talkativeness; flight of ideas; increased distractibility; increased goal-directed activities or psychomotor movement; and seeking out/engaging in pleasurable but high-risk activities. The current classification system recognizes two main types of bipolar disorder, typically referred to as primary bipolar disorder, or bipolar disorder I, and secondary bipolar disorder, or bipolar disorder II. Bipolar disorder I requires that the individual has had at least one manic or mixed episode that has lasted 1 week in length (APA, 2000). Episodes lasting less than a week but at least 4 days are considered hypomanic and are characteristic of bipolar disorder II, unless substantial impairment requiring hospitalization is present. Episodes that meet concurrent criteria for both a manic and major depressive episodes for a period of 1 week are considered mixed episodes.

Older adults with bipolar disorder face several additional challenges including the likelihood of increased cognitive impairment, declines in health-related quality of life, and a high risk of suicide (Depp, Davis, Mittal, Patterson, & Jeste, 2006; Depp et al., 2007). Although older adults already have an elevated risk of suicide (Depp & Jeste, 2004), bipolar disorder is one of the diseases associated with the highest suicide risk in older adults (Kales, 2007).

Bipolar disorder, in general, tends to be highly comorbid with other disorders, with up to 65% of bipolar patients having at least one comorbid disorder within their lifetime, the most common being substance abuse and anxiety disorders (McElroy et al., 2001). Compared to young and middle-aged adults with bipolar disorder, older adults are less likely to have a substance abuse disorder (Depp et al., 2005; Kilbourne et al., 2005) and more likely to have some type of cognitive disorder (Depp et al., 2005). Recent studies suggest that anywhere from 50% to 60% of bipolar patients have some form of cognitive impairment (Depp et al., 2007). Cognitive dysfunction usually manifests as impairment in executive function, memory, and/or processing speed (Bearden et al., 2006; Depp et al., 2007; Gildengers et al., 2004; Young, Murphy, Heo, Schulberg, & Alexopoulos, 2006). These cognitive symptoms persist even while patients are in euthymic states (Gildengers et al., 2004; Martino et al., 2008), and appear to worsen as individuals age (Depp et al., 2007).

Comorbidities associated with bipolar disorder in late life include physical illnesses as well as psychological disorders (Goldstein, Herrmann, & Shulman, 2006; Kales, 2007; Sajatovic & Kales, 2006). Concurrent medical illness has also been found to complicate course and prognosis of illness (Beyer, Kuchibhatla, Gersing, & Krishnan, 2005). Beyer et al. (2005) also found that 70% of adult outpatients with bipolar disorder had at least one significant comorbid medical illness by age 70. Among the most common medical complications are cardio-vascular illness and diabetes (Benedetti et al., 2008; Cassidy, Ahearn, & Carroll, 1999).

The current diagnostic system may not accurately capture symptom presentation of bipolar disorder in older adults. Early and late onset appear to be two distinct subtypes, a finding that should be addressed in the upcoming *Diagnostic and Statistical Manual of Mental Disorders* (DSM-V; Moorhead & Young, 2003; Sajatovic, Bingham, Campbell, & Fletcher, 2005; Sajatovic, Blow, Ignacio, & Kales, 2005; Shürhoff et al., 2000). Gender differences in prevalence rates of late-life bipolar disorder have been reported in the literature. In a review of 17 studies, Depp and Jeste (2004) reported aggregate data suggesting that the ratio of older adult women to older adult men with a bipolar diagnosis is 2:1.

Although the typical age of onset for developing bipolar disorder is in the 20s, a significant number of individuals do not experience their first manic episode until their 50s (APA, 2000). Most studies classify late-onset bipolar disorder accordingly as occurring at or after age 50. Sajatovic, Blow, Ignacio, and Kales (2005) found that 29% of older adults receiving outpatient care for bipolar disorder were classified as late-onset. Late-onset bipolar disorder appears to be more common in women (Sajatovic, Bingham, Campbell, & Fletcher, 2005). There appear to be some significant differences in late versus early-onset bipolar disorder, with late-onset being related more directly to cerebral organic factors (Almeida & Fenner, 2002) and less to genetic or familial influences (Moorhead & Young, 2003). Patients with late-onset bipolar disorder are at increased risk of vascular illness that may contribute in part to the manifestation of the disorder (Cassidy & Carroll, 2002). Patients with early-onset bipolar disorder, on the other hand, tend to have more family members with an affective disorder, with genetic influence apparently playing a larger role. Moreover, early-onset bipolar disorder is typically more severe, with more psychotic features and mixed episodes (Shürhoff et al., 2000). Late versus early-onset groups were not found to differ concerning medical comorbidity, substance abuse, or average stay during periods of hospitalization (Sajatovic, Bingham, et al., 2005).

ASSESSMENT

General Guidelines

In the United States, specific practice guidelines detailing clinical assessment strategies for patients with bipolar disorder have not been updated since the 2002 revision of the APA's (2002) guidelines. In a general review of the assessment and treatment of bipolar disorders, Ketter (2010) recommends a comprehensive assessment including careful review of the chief complaint, history of current illness, psychiatric, and medical and family history using collateral information from a significant other to distinguish bipolar depression from the more common presentation of a major depressive disorder. Patients in the depressed phase of the illness often have difficulty recalling prior periods of hypomania or mania, and a careful review of periods of both improved and impaired function can help identify periods of mood elevation (Ketter, 2010). The National Institute for Health and Clinical Excellence (NICE, 2006) offers the following general guidelines for assessment of bipolar disorder:

- Take a full history including family history, a review of all previous episodes and any symptoms between episodes.
- Assess the patient's symptom profile, triggers to previous episodes, social and personal functioning, comorbidities including substance misuse and anxiety, risk, physical health, and current psychosocial stressors.
- Obtain where possible, and within the bounds of confidentiality, a corroborative history from a family member or carer.
- Consider using formal criteria, including self-rating scales such as the Mood Disorder Questionnaire. (pp. 14–15)

In addition, the following consideration is given when assessing older patients for a bipolar diagnosis:

> Symptoms may be due to underlying organic conditions, such as hypothyroidism, cerebrovascular insults and other neurological disorders (for example, dementia), particularly in people with late-onset bipolar disorder (older than 40 years). (p. 15)

Clinical Interview

Older adults with bipolar disorder often present a complex clinical picture with comorbid general medical, neurological, and psychiatric illnesses and, therefore, a comprehensive biopsychosocial assessment involving patient interview, interview with significant others, and the use of selected standardized assessments are indicated. Older adults with bipolar disorder have an elevated risk of suicide; therefore, it is particularly important to assess suicide risk in the initial interview. The clinical interview will need to include a detailed history of any prior suicide attempts, self-harming behavior, family history, and other risk factors for suicide. Because of high-risk behaviors associated with periods of hypomania and mania, the clinician will want to assess for a prior history in which the patient exhibited poor judgment or took unwarranted risks (e.g., misused substances, extravagant spending, poor social judgment) to manage these risks appropriately. It will be especially important to take note of prior psychiatric history, including a review of any illness-related hospitalizations or periods of significant impairment.

Use of Standardized Rating Scales

The Mood Disorder Questionnaire (Hirschfeld et al., 2000) is a general screening instrument that can be considered as a useful screener for bipolar disorder in a general psychiatric outpatient population. However, the assessor must be aware of a high rate of false positives for this instrument. For depression, several self-report measures appear to have adequate reliability and validity for use with identifying depression in an older adult population including the Beck Depression Scale-II (Segal, Coolidge, Cahill, & O'Riley, 2008), the Geriatric Rating Scale (Yesavage et al., 1983), and the Center for Epidemiologic Studies Depression Scale (CES-D; Radloff, 1977). In terms of clinician-rated scales, the Hamilton Rating Scale for Depression (HAM-D; Williams, 1988) is recognized as a standard instrument for assessing severity of depression, but the appropriate use of this instrument requires significant training.

For assessing mania, we could locate only one brief self-report scale, the Altman Self-Rating Mania Scale (ASRM; Altman, Hedecker, Peterson, & Davis, 1997), without established data for older adults. Commonly used clinician-rated scales include the Bech-Rafaelsen Mania Scale (Bech, 2002; Bech, Baastrup, de Bleeker, & Ropert, 2001) and the Young Mania Rating Scale (YMRS; Young, Biggs, Ziegler, & Meyer, 1978). Both of the latter scales require significant interviewer training.

TREATMENT

In the past 15 years, psychosocial interventions for the treatment of bipolar disorder including cognitive behavioral therapy (CBT) and psychoeducational interventions have become increasingly accepted as important adjuncts to pharmacotherapy. The growing importance of psychosocial treatments for bipolar disorder is reflected in the fact that psychosocial treatments are now routinely recommended in several national guidelines for the treatment of bipolar disorder. This represents a tremendous reevaluation of the role of psychosocial treatments that previously were barely given consideration as adjunctive treatments to pharmacotherapy.

It should be noted that there is still some degree of variation in recommendations by region, locality, and nationality, and many of the key randomized controlled trials (RCTs) for bipolar disorder have been located outside of the United States. For example, in the *2002 APA Practice Guidelines for the Treatment of Patients with Bipolar Disorder* (APA, 2004), psychological treatments were reviewed in slightly less than four pages, given the following relatively lukewarm recommendation:

> Nevertheless, the weight of the evidence suggests that patients with bipolar disorder are likely to gain some benefit during the maintenance phase from a concomitant psychosocial intervention, including psychotherapy, that addresses illness management, (i.e., adherence, lifestyle changes, and early detection of prodromal symptoms) and interpersonal difficulties. (p. 586)

In addition, the Society of Clinical Psychology (Division 12 of the American Psychological Association), which promulgates empirically supported treatments, rates treatment of bipolar disorder for depression and mania as having "modest research support," indicating a "probably efficacious treatment" that falls below the accepted standard for a fully empirically supported treatment, but makes the following comment:

> It is important to note that there are many manuals of cognitive therapy for bipolar disorder, including group and individual approaches. Of these, the findings based on the manual by D. Lam and others have been particularly positive, as have those from the one-year report of the Systematic Treatment Enhancement Program for bipolar disorder. (STEP; Miklowitz et al., 2007)

Currently, several sets of national guidelines that rely strongly on examination of empirical evidence of treatment effectiveness have incorporated psychosocial treatments for bipolar disorder into their

TABLE 3.1   National Institute for Health and Clinical Excellence Guidelines for Bipolar Disorder

Individual structured psychological interventions should be considered for people with bipolar disorder who are relatively stable, but may be experiencing mild-to-moderate affective symptoms. The therapy should be *in addition to* prophylactic medication and should normally:

- Last at least 16 sessions (more than 6–9 months)
- Include psychoeducation about the illness, and the importance of regular daily routine and sleep and concordance with medication
- Enhance general coping strategies
- Include monitoring mood, detection of early warnings, and strategies to prevent progression into full-blown episodes

Source: Taken from *NICE National Clinical Practice Guideline Number 38* (NICE, 2006, p. 373).

recommendations for clinical practice. For example, NICE in its published guidelines for bipolar disorder in 2006 (see Table 3.1; NICE, 2006) devoted almost 50 pages to the psychological management of bipolar disorder and made numerous recommendations regarding optimizing psychosocial treatments including the following: psychoeducation; mood monitoring of symptoms, including triggers and early warning or prodromal signs; stabilizing sleep–wake cycles and activity levels; detection of early warning signs; and development of coping strategies to limit the progression into full-blown episodes.

Additional recommendations were made supporting both family-based interventions and motivational interventions for harmful drug and alcohol misuse (NICE, 2006, p. 373). The NICE guidelines note that many psychological treatments that have demonstrated effectiveness contain similar elements including the following elements listed in Table 3.2.

The Scottish Intercollegiate Guidelines Network (SIGN; 2005) that develops evidence-based clinical practice guidelines for the National Health Service in Scotland has incorporated a discussion of psychosocial interventions including CBT, interpersonal and social rhythm therapy

TABLE 3.2   Summary of Common Elements of Effective Psychological Therapies for Bipolar Disorder

- Psychoeducation about the illness
- Promoting medication adherence
- Promotion of regular daily routine and sleep
- Monitoring mood, detection of early warnings, and strategy to prevent early stages from developing into full-blown episodes
- General coping strategies including problem-solving techniques

Source: Taken from *NICE National Clinical Practice Guideline Number 38* (NICE, 2006, p. 357).

(IPSRT), behavioral family therapy, and group psychoeducation in its review of treatment guidelines for maintenance treatments for bipolar disorder. Interventions incorporating early-warning-signs-monitoring training to help patients identify early signs of illness and develop action plans to limit risk of an acute episode are given the second highest rating in terms of empirical evidence (a score of "1+" for well-conducted meta-analyses, systematic reviews of RCTs, or RCTs with a low risk of bias). In addition, group psychoeducation, behavioral family therapy, and IPSRT also receive a "1+" score. Finally, the guidelines note significant areas of overlap in these treatments including developing treatment adherence, helping clients become aware of illness, monitoring of early warning signs, social rhythm monitoring (regularizing sleep–wake cycles), and concluding with the recommendation that these treatments should be made available to all patients in addition to pharmacological maintenance, especially if sustained remission cannot be achieved with medication alone. (SIGN, 2005, pp. 16–17)

The Canadian national treatment guidelines for bipolar disorder also conclude:

> Adjunctive psychosocial therapies should be considered early in the course of illness to improve medication adherence, identify prodromes of relapse, decrease residual symptoms (particularly depressive) and suicidal behaviour, and help move patients towards a comprehensive functional recovery. (Yatham et al., 2006, p. 10)

There is now relative agreement about the effectiveness of CBT in general as a collateral treatment for individuals with bipolar disorder. The importance of collateral psychosocial treatments is highlighted by relatively high rates of nonadherence to pharmacological treatment, which is estimated to be between 40% and 50%, as well as rates of relapse estimated at 50% at 1 year after treatment is initiated (Perry, Tarrier, Morriss, McCarthy, & Limb, 1999). Clearly, pharmacological treatment alone is not sufficient to fully address issues of nonadherence and relapse prevention.

WHAT DO WE KNOW ABOUT COGNITIVE THERAPY FOR OLDER ADULTS WITH BIPOLAR DISORDER?

Although we can have strong confidence in CBT as an approach to bipolar disorder in a general population, unfortunately, there is an absolute dearth of empirical evidence from controlled randomized clinical trials to support the psychosocial treatment of older adults with bipolar disorder. This situation has not improved since 2007 when McBride and Bauer (2007) summarized the situation as follows:

> What is known specifically about psychosocial interventions for aging individuals with bipolar disorder? In short, very little. To our knowledge, there are no published studies of psychosocial treatments targeted toward older individuals with this illness. (p. 95)

Part of the problem is certainly the lack of treatment and research focus on the older adult population in part because of continuing barriers and stigma that limits the availability of effective treatments. This is probably compounded by the difficulty in recruiting for large clinical trials in the older adult population because of the problems related to demographics (declining population) and problem recruiting eligible subjects willing to participate (Knight, 2004). Much of the available clinical data is in the form of case reports and uncontrolled studies. Guidelines typically do not address specifically the needs of older adults. There is, however, a robust literature supporting the effectiveness of CBT for older adults with unipolar depression (see Laidlaw, Thompson, Gallagher-Thompson, & Dick-Siskin, [2003] for a summary).

For older adults, case studies have been reported (Nguyen, Truong, Marquett, Feit, & Reiser, 2006) that provide support for the use of cognitive behavioral treatment procedures used in a group format. McBride and Bauer (2007) in their review of psychosocial treatments for older adults discuss several cases that benefitted from a group psychoeducational approach that shares many common elements with CBT. Furthermore, a post hoc analysis of older adult outcomes in a controlled trial of CBT with bipolar disorder suggests that older adults do not drop out any more frequently and demonstrate improvements in terms of symptoms of depression and mania over treatment as usual controls in a standardized cognitive behavioral intervention using mood monitoring, detection of early warning signs, and development of coping plans to minimize severe episodes of mania and depression (Reiser & Thompson, 2005, unpublished data).

The primary goals of a bipolar disorder treatment program should include the following key components: teaching patients to monitor mood and detect prodromes of illness, helping patients maintain consistent activity levels, identifying helpful cognitive and behavioral interventions to stabilize mood, improving treatment adherence, improving psychosocial functioning, and assisting patients in developing specific coping plans to prevent or minimize relapses (Basco & Rush, 1996; Lam, Jones, Hayward, & Bright, 1999).

The treatment program may be conceptualized as a four-phase model with an understanding that the support and maintenance phase is likely to be extended through booster sessions, self-help groups, and periodic monitoring. The four-phase model concept is as follows:

Phase I: Engagement and socialization to model
Phase II: Skill development (mood monitoring, identifying triggers, early warning signs, coping plan development)
Phase III: Rehearsal and relapse prevention training
Phase IV: Support and maintenance

MONITORING MOOD AND DETECTING PRODROMES OR EARLY WARNING SIGNS

Detecting early warning signs appears to be a robust intervention that is cited in multiple guidelines including the NICE (2006) guidelines on bipolar disorder. Lam et al. (1999) developed the earliest treatment manual that addressed the importance of identifying prodromes of illness (see Table 3.3). By questioning patients separately about key manic and depressive symptoms associated with past episodes, it is possible to develop a unique relapse signature for each patient. Warning signs or early prodromes of illness are developed through a collaborative questioning process (Socratic questioning) and are written down on 3×5 cards for easy reference. Warning signs are then prioritized by identifying the most salient warning signs of illness. These signs then become a part of a monitoring process in which the patient routinely monitors of mood and activity state changes to determine if there is an incipient episode. The goal is to identify serious warning signs early on while actions can still be taken to reduce the likelihood of a severe episode. A sample list of warning signs can be found in Table 3.4.

TABLE 3.3   Key Treatment Objectives of Cognitive Behavioral Therapy for Bipolar Disorder

■ Develop a collaborative working relationship.
■ Psychoeducation on the diathesis-stress model with a focus on helping patients learn problem-solving skills to manage stress.
■ Develop specific cognitive behavioral skills for coping with prodromes including monitoring for prodromes, developing coping strategies, and altering behavior.
■ Assist patients in maintaining stable routines and getting adequate amounts of sleep.
■ Help patients address long-term vulnerabilities (such as excessive goal-driven behavior) to reduce future episodes.

Source: Adapted from Lam et al. (1999).

TABLE 3.4   Early Warning Signs of Mania (Client Example)

■ Increased special meaning to small things
■ Feeling too good—cannot slow down
■ Racing thoughts
■ Religious fantasies
■ Feeling being a part of a grand scheme
■ Disturbed/decreased sleep (< 4 hours)

HELPING PATIENTS MAINTAIN CONSISTENT ACTIVITY LEVELS (REGULARIZE SLEEP–WAKE CYCLES)

Another key behavioral goal in the treatment of bipolar disorder is to help patients manage activity level and sleep–wake cycles to promote a stable routine. Disruptions in routines have been shown to be associated with triggering unstable mood especially hypomania and mania. Mood and activity state monitoring has been demonstrated to be quite feasible even for patients who are rather seriously ill and experiencing episodes of mania and depression. Frank et al. (1997) used a 17-item paper and pencil assessment of daily events (the Social Rhythm Metric [SRM]) over a 10-week period with *acutely* ill bipolar I patients and reported that only 8.6% of these patients were excluded from the original group for noncompliance. In addition, Post et al. (2003) provide extremely compelling empirical evidence that patients can reliably monitor their mood despite serious fluctuations in functioning and level of impairment. Activity and sleep patterns can be effectively monitored either by using a specific instrument, such as the SRM developed by Frank et al. (1997), or by a simple activity schedule listing hours of the day and days of the week in a blocked fashion. The goal is to have the patient identify patterns of behavior that disrupt sleep–wake cycles, which then lead to destabilization of mood.

DEVELOPING COPING STRATEGIES AND A COPING PLAN TO PREVENT SEVERE EPISODES

A central intervention in the treatment of bipolar disorder is the development of individualized coping plans with the goal of minimizing the progression of episodes to avoid severe destabilizing episodes of depression and mania. Coping plans should very simple and translatable onto a 3 × 5 card for quick and easy reference. A sample coping plan for mania is identified in Table 3.5.

TABLE 3.5   Developing Coping Strategies—Mania

■ Telling significant other
■ Call doctor
■ Increase medication
Triggers
■ Feeling overwhelmed
■ Increased stress
■ Environmental changes

MAINTENANCE AND RELAPSE PREVENTION PHASE

A key goal in any care program for a chronic recurring illness will be the need to assist the patient in identifying warning signs and reducing the risk of future relapse. There is limited evidence of the effectiveness of treatment during acute episodes. However, maintenance of wellness and relapse prevention should be an ongoing focus of treatment as soon as the acute depressive or manic episode has remitted and the patient is sufficiently stable for ongoing outpatient care. Samples of a relapse prevention plan are outlined in Tables 3.4 and 3.5. Typically, patients should develop written materials over the course of therapy, including 3 × 5 "coping cards" and a therapy notebook to document effective coping and relapse prevention plans.

ADAPTING COGNITIVE THERAPY TO OLDER ADULTS

How might we then consider adapting CBT for a general population to be more culturally competent for older adults? In a previous publication, Reiser et al. (2007) proposed a conceptual model for adapting CBT to an older adult population using a formulation and case conceptualization model initially developed by Laidlaw et al. (2003) and outlined in a treatment manual for treating depression in older adults by Laidlaw, Thompson, & Gallagher-Thompson (2004). This model takes into account five factors considered instrumental in the treatment of older adults: cohort beliefs, transition in role investments, intergenerational linkages, sociocultural context, and physical health (Reiser et al., 2007).

Older adults have a unique cultural and historical perspective that colors their perceptions of the meaning of their illness, medical and mental health treatment, roles and expectations related to being a patient, and working toward acceptable treatment goals

(Reiser et al., 2007). Furthermore, older adults have had to navigate multiple losses and life transitions, including the progressive impact of chronic medical conditions and comorbid medical illness related to the normal aging process:

> The role of *disruptions in social rhythms* [emphasis added] as posited by Malkoff-Schwartz et al. (2000) in inducing new episodes of illness applies uniquely to older adults in term of the loss of structure associated with retirement and changes in activity levels and consequent changes in sleep–wake routines." (Gallagher-Thompson, Steffen, & Thompson, 2008, p. 253)

Based on these considerations, it is likely that the practitioner should expect to make several specific modifications in standard CBT practices. In standard practice, CBT depends on the development of a collaborative working relationship between the practitioner and the client in which feedback is instrumental in guiding the course of therapy. Indeed, one of the key underlying interventions (Socratic questioning) depends on a nonauthoritarian, nondirective, and nonpersuasive mode in which the practitioner eschews giving advice. This collaborative and democratic model may not be well suited to typical cohort beliefs of older adults who might wish to view the doctor as the "expert" (more consistent with medicine and medical practitioners) and to assume an essentially passive role in psychotherapy. Thus, there is going to be a need to focus on treatment expectations early on and to gradually, in a stepwise manner, socialize older adults to accept a more balanced and democratic view of therapy in which they can be active participants.

ADAPTING COGNITIVE THERAPY TO OLDER ADULTS WITH COGNITIVE LIMITATIONS OR DEFICITS

A second important consideration is modifying the timing, pacing, and coverage of topics in a typical therapy session to simplify the therapy agenda and emphasize a style that maximizes cognitive processing across several modalities: using frequent capsule summaries; writing summaries of key points; using a white board to mark down the agenda and important "take-away" thoughts; and prompting the client to make use of therapy notebooks, 3 × 5 cards, and other written materials. Memory problems or limitations in recall can be addressed by making sure that key points including homework or important discoveries about problematic thoughts and behavior are summarized and written down.

Finally, the therapist may need to be attentive to any physical limitations experienced by older adults and limit tasks that require extensive writing or preparation of materials for homework assignments.

CASE VIGNETTE: MRS. GW: "I CAN'T DO ANYTHING"

Mrs. GW, who attends the first interview with her daughter, is an attractively dressed and well-groomed 66-year-old college-educated, divorced woman of Russian descent. She presents with severe depression with psychotic features (distressing images and disturbing thoughts), anhedonia, psychomotor retardation, withdrawal, social isolation, and hopelessness. She lives with her daughter, son-in-law, and two young grandchildren. Per client, the presenting problem is a pervasive feeling that she is unable to get motivated to do anything; she states, "I just can't do anything," "I am not up for any social life," "I just pace around the house all day." Her daughter comments, "Mom seems like she doesn't want to get well."

The patient reports a 30-year history of bipolar type II disorder mainly characterized by long periods of severe depression (first diagnosed post-age 50) with a serious suicide attempt in 1992 in which she took a potentially lethal dose of medication. Mrs. GW notes two hypomanic episodes in 2004 and 2005 lasting several months. She has been referred by her psychiatrist because of minimal improvement in key depressive symptoms, which have not resolved despite aggressive pharmacotherapy. She reports that she has been seeing her psychiatrist consistently and is adherent to her regimen of a mood stabilizer, antidepressant, as well as an antipsychotic medicine (Seroquel 400 mg). It is remarkable, but consistent with the stigma and barriers to treatment identified in the literature on psychotherapy with older adults, that despite her lethal suicide attempt, she has never had psychological treatment. At intake, she scores a 41 on the Beck Depression Inventory (BDI), indicating a severe level of depression characterized by cognitive symptoms such as extreme feelings of guilt, pessimism, and self-dislike; and behavioral symptoms such as withdrawal isolation, psychomotor retardation, anhedonia, agitation, and pacing.

She divorced her husband 2 years ago after an unhappy long-term marriage in which she felt bullied by her husband. She had been very actively involved in family business for more than 30 years. After she moved into her own apartment, her mood became increasingly unstable and depressed, especially over the past 2 years. Recently, she has moved in with her daughter because of concerns that she could not care for herself.

In the initial interviews, she demonstrated several potential resources and strengths. She is likeable, charming, and pleasant with a sense of humor; she appears quite intelligent, although she complains of compromised intellectual functioning and fears she is becoming demented (ruled out with cognitive testing); and, she maintained high levels of functioning in the past despite chronic depression. Finally, she has a good relationship with her family, especially her grandchildren and her older daughter who is very engaged in her treatment, coming in for multiple collateral visits especially at the beginning of therapy.

In the initial interview, Mrs. GW presents as an attractive-looking woman who is nicely dressed in a traditional style and carefully groomed but who speaks only at the prompting of her daughter in a hesitant slow fashion. When asked about what she is able to do in her daily life, she responds, "I can't do anything" very emphatically and states, "I am not motivated to start anything, I will *not* make an effort." She appears slow in her speech and response time and seems a bit confused but is able to comprehend key ideas quite effectively on questioning. Although she is likeable, she is passive and disengaged in the session and leaves most of the talking to her daughter.

The initial treatment plan involves the following main treatment strategies that prioritize work on her pervasive sense of hopelessness, helplessness, and passivity:

1. Target *hopelessness about therapy* and disengagement by instilling hope and developing a strong therapeutic alliance (and including daughter in therapy)
2. Target *hopeless and helpless cognitions* through cognitive restructuring and behavioral experiments
3. Target *inactivity, withdrawal, and social isolation* through behavioral activation
4. Target loss of pleasure through behavioral activation emphasizing increasing pleasant events

USE OF COGNITIVE TECHNIQUES TO REDUCE DEPRESSION

Cognitive therapy techniques, the mainstay of Beck et al. (1979) treatment approach, target unhelpful assumptions, expectations, and beliefs about the self, others, and the world. The goal of cognitive restructuring is to help the patient identify problematic beliefs and through a collaborative process of open-ended exploration, often referred to as guided discovery or Socratic questioning. In depression, there is a tendency to selectively attend to and process events that are associated with underlying beliefs about weaknesses, losses, and failures; conversely, in hypomania and mania, there is a tendency to selectively attend to positive outcomes and to ignore risks and potential negative consequences. Standard cognitive therapy techniques, although developed for patients with unipolar depression, appear to be effective with bipolar depression, but there is limited scientific evidence from clinical trials at this point.

Several of the prominent symptoms identified in the initial intake, notably hopelessness about therapy and a helpless sense of being nonfunctional, appeared to be important targets for cognitive therapy. Hopelessness would be an important initial target for therapy not only because of potential suicide risk (not a factor in this case), but also because ongoing hopelessness and pessimism will rapidly disrupt progress in treatment. In this case, an initial cognitive intervention was chosen with the goal of highlighting actual functional capabilities against the patient's perceptions of her abilities.

In the second session, Mrs. GW was seen with her daughter, and the focus of this session was to review her hopeless thoughts, mainly: "I am not motivated to start anything, I won't make an effort. I can't do anything." She insisted that these thoughts were completely accurate and valid and rated her level of belief at 100%. We then reviewed her activities over the past week in detail and asked Mrs. GW and her daughter to come up with any countering evidence regarding this belief. The patient kept insisting that she had been unable to do anything, which was then countered by her daughter reminding her of activities she had completed. These activities were then written down on a list (see Table 3.6), which was copied and given to her by her

TABLE 3.6 List of Countering Evidence: Activities Completed in the Past Week

- Folded clothes
- Put away dishes
- Made the bed
- Went clothes shopping
- Got nails done
- Got hair done at the beauty shop
- Took shower and cleaned up
- Showed eaten meals
- Read bedtime stories to the grandkids
- Made a list of activities for Dr. Reiser
- Helped in the kitchen making a salad
- Showed up for her appointment (with me)

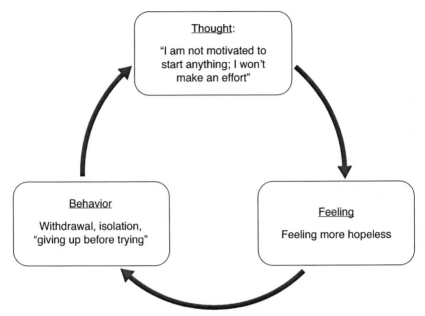

FIGURE 3.1   Identifying Unhelpful Cycles of Thinking–Feeling Behavior

daughter (because she felt too tired and fatigued at this point to write things down).

When prompted after reviewing the list, she was asked if she could describe any thoughts that she was having right now that were getting in the way of getting help. Mrs. GW was able to identify the following unhelpful thought that seemed pervasive in her thinking and responses: "I'm not motivated to start anything, I won't make an effort. I *can't* do anything!" At the end of the exercise (which took most of the session), her degree of conviction in this belief had fallen to about an 80% level of conviction (see Figure 3.1 and Table 3.7).

TABLE 3.7   Identifying More Helpful Cycles of Thinking–Feeling Behavior

- *Problematic Thought*: "I am not motivated to start anything; I won't make an effort. I *can't* do anything."
- *Countering Thought*: "If I am really motivated, I'll try to do the task."
- *Feeling*: Less hopeless
- *Behavior*: Reduced withdrawal, isolation, and "giving up."

USE OF BEHAVIORAL TECHNIQUES TO REDUCE DEPRESSION

We then designed a weekly activity schedule that contained all the elements on Mrs. GW's list of activities, as well as any other important activities that she felt *were important* and *that met her personal goals*. A major personal goal that emerged early in therapy was "feeling more useful; feeling like I am making an important contribution to the family." Specific activities were then targeted that would help her feel that she was meeting this goal. The therapy now focused on specific behavioral goals and tasks that were tracked and monitored weekly over several weeks using a standard activity schedule.

BEHAVIORAL STRATEGIES

In general, it appears that behavioral strategies are equally effective with bipolar depression as with unipolar depression, although solid empirical evidence from RCTs is not available. Behavioral activation is a key treatment strategy especially for depressed patients, such as Mrs. GW, who have a reduced level of activity, anhedonia, and difficulties or limitations in cognitive processing caused by either depression or cognitive impairments (Martell, Addis, & Jacobson, 2001). Behavioral activation is a simple technique for engaging the patient in a process of change that stimulates positive movement and hope. The goal of behavioral activation is to increase the frequency of positive experiences, to break patterns of avoidance and hopelessness, and to decrease the frequency of negative occurrences, if possible. It is also clear that depression can lead to increasingly aversive responses from significant others and that reversing this cycle can have positive interpersonal consequences.

> Although depressed affect and behavior initially may be maintained through positive reinforcement, depressed behavior ultimately may lead to aversive social consequences in the form of negative responses from significant others (Coyne, 1976). (cited in Hopko, Lejuez, Ruggiero, & Eifert, 2003, p. 701)

If it is not possible to avoid failures, problem-solving approaches can be used to discover barriers and possible solutions. For example,

Mrs. GW began avoiding going to regular appointments at the nail salon which had been a source of pleasure for her and contributed to her self-care and sense of self-worth. In order to help the client address this problem, the therapist used a modified thought record to explore her problematic thinking and how it lead to avoidance (see Figure 3.2). It appears that behavioral activation may produce symptom change regardless of whether the symptom change is mediated by cognitive change. It is clear in the cognitive behavioral model that the relationship between cognitions and behavior is a "two-way street" (Wright, Basco, & Thase, 2006, p. 21)

The therapist helps the client choose one or two actions that could make a difference in how he or she feels and then assists with working out a plan to carry out the activity. This may be introduced in the first session. It is important to approach the identification of possible new rewarding and meaningful activities in a collaborative way by brainstorming with the client: "What pleasurable activities did you used to do in the past that have been stopped or reduced?" "What did

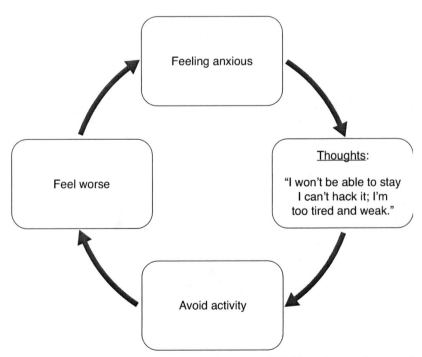

FIGURE 3.2   Sample Thought Record: Situation: "Thinking about going to nail salon"

TABLE 3.8 Sample Early Homework Assignment

1. Keep filling out your daily activity schedule.
2. Select three pleasant events and schedule them every week (*later assignment*: rate pleasure associated with this activity).
3. Ask family for help/express needs.
4. Notice one surprising new thing that you are doing.
5. Rate your level of anxiety, depression, and distress over psychotic thoughts on a 1–10 scale.

you do in the past when you were not so depressed?" "I wonder what kinds of things make you feel worse? For example, from what you told me, it seems that you often end up withdrawing and isolating. Does this seem to improve or worsen your depression?" The rationale for addressing behaviors that appear to be maintaining depression can be addressed specifically through exploration: "Is it possible that this withdrawal and isolation (oversleeping, staying alone in apartment, avoiding others, not taking calls) is contributing to your depression?" "What do you think you could do that would help you feel better? What has worked in the past?"

Typically, an activity-monitoring form or activity schedule is used to determine the current baseline of the patient's activities. It is important not to set initial goals unrealistically and follow the basic premise "Start where the patient is, not where you want him or her to be."

The therapist should incorporate information learned from the activity-monitoring form to make sure that initial goals are appropriate. Do not overlook simple yet pleasant activities (e.g. self-care/simple everyday pleasures). Have client write down these pleasant activities and assign them as homework (see Table 3.8). Use Socratic questioning to educate patient about behavioral model of depression, including the role of positive/negative reinforcement and the effect of depression on engagement in pleasant activities. It is useful to assess the potential impact of pleasant activity engagement on mood by asking, "How do you think this change could make you feel?"

COGNITIVE ASSESSMENT

Because of Mrs. GW's ongoing concerns about her cognitive ability and fear that she was experiencing symptoms of dementia, a referral was made to Larry W. Thompson, PhD. for a brief neuropsychological screening. Dr. Thompson's abbreviated report is as follows:

> She was administered the Cognistat as a screening instrument, followed by the California Verbal Learning Scale (short form) and select subtests of the WAIS-III. Her performance on the Cognistat was in the average range for 9 of the 11 subtests. Her score on the attention scale was in the mild impaired range, and her score on the construction subscale was in the mild to moderate impaired range. Detailed examination of her performance on the construction subscale suggested that she had difficulty in doing a visual search. Her performance on the picture description also suggested that she has some difficulty integrating visual components of a scene in order to form a meaningful interpretation. Other measures of verbal abstractions, learning and memory, social judgment and verbal comprehension all were well within the normal range. There was no evidence in this screening to suggest the presence of dementia.
>
> Her performance on the WAIS-III yielded a full scale IQ score of 106: her verbal scale score was 112 and the performance scale score was 98, indicating average intelligence and again, no evidence of dementia. Comparison of subtests offered further support for problems in attention and visual scanning, consistent with Cognistat data.
>
> The CVLT short form suggested that learning and memory functions were clearly intact. On the Delayed Memory her free recall score was 8 (of 9) words presented and all 9 words were correctly identified in the Recognition portion, with no intrusions or other errors.
>
> In summary, her intellectual problems are due to psychological distress, not degenerative dementia. Her slight impairments are consistent with marked anxiety and depression. The focal problem with visual scanning and integration is due to an accident earlier in life affecting her visual processing system.

SPECIAL ADAPTATIONS FOR COGNITIVE IMPAIRMENTS

Because of some apparent confusion and complaints about cognitive processing, all assignments and "key learnings" in therapy sessions were written down in a notebook, simplified sessions agendas were set, material in session was covered at a slow pace and often repeated, and the patient was asked to process material in session to test for retention and learning. Mood or symptom monitoring is always a key component of treating mood disorders including bipolar disorder. In this case, Mrs. GW was given a simplified monitoring form that listed key symptoms she had identified, including distressing thoughts, anxiety, and depression. Initially, her daughter was asked to help her with the form, tracking key problems or symptoms, as well as activity levels until she felt more comfortable doing it herself.

TREATMENT COURSE

Early in treatment, as Mrs. GW became slightly more active, she began to experience an increase in her negative thinking, and a theme of perfectionism and self-criticism emerged with the following types of thoughts: "I can't do anything," "They (others) are doing it better than me," "I can't pull it together," "I better not try, I might make a mistake," "I need to give up quickly on tasks (buttons, nylons, wrapping food, putting food away)."

To help her respond to some of her automatic negative thinking and to reinforce alternate responses, we developed several alternate responses through Socratic questioning and wrote these on a 3 × 5 cards: "Helpful thoughts when I worry about my cooking," "It's important to remember some past successes specifically," "Sometimes, my standards are too high and I beat myself up," "I tend to overgeneralize from one problem (a bad meal) to feeling that I am an unsuccessful person." Her homework assignment was to carry the card in her purse and refer to it periodically especially when these hypercritical thoughts came up during the week when she was doing chores (see Figure 3.2 and Table 3.9).

In midtreatment, around the fourth month in therapy, Mrs. GW's depression improved quite significantly with her BDI scores dropping from 41 to 21, a 50% or clinically significant improvement. Her self-rated reported distress from psychotic thinking was 8 → 0. In a collateral interview, her daughter noted that Mrs. GW was much more active in helping out with her grandchildren, cooking, and childcare, but was not taking many social risks in terms of engaging others outside her family. Her daughter reported feeling that her mother "*has plateaued.*" In the final stages of therapy, Mrs. GW experienced some rebound in her depression but maintained a significantly higher level of activity within the family system (total BDI score rebounded to 30 in the moderately to severely depressed range). There were only modest improvements in her overall level of social engagement. She also expressed continuing concerns about her cognitive processing, although neuropsychological testing revealed that she has no dementia or significant brain damage. It was felt that concerns about her intellectual functioning might

TABLE 3.9   Thought Record: "Negative Thoughts While Cooking"

Negative Automatic Thoughts	Feelings (Intensity Rating)	Possible Thinking Errors	More Helpful Thoughts
I hope this turns out good—what if it doesn't?	Anxious (50%) Worried (50%)	"I'm too hard on myself."	"Don't be so hard on yourself."
The recipe might not be good.	More depressed and discouraged	"I am generalizing."	"Don't have such high expectations."
I'm afraid it won't come out.	Hopeless		"Don't generalize from one specific problem."
It makes me feel that I am not a success in life.			
I am a good mother—I should be able to cook.			
I can't do anything right!			

be a symptom of her depression related to attention and concentration problems.

Unfortunately, after about 12 months of treatment, Mrs. GW had to be transferred to another psychologist because of insurance reimbursement issues. She has now been seen by this second psychologist over an 18-month period, for a total of 30 additional sessions (approximately every 2 weeks). During this interval, she has had one full-blown manic episode and two hypomanic episodes, although her depression has overall been improved. Her average BDI II scores over this period remained in the low 20s throughout.

The primary focus of this phase of her treatment has been on learning the warning signs of her manic episodes and learning more adaptive coping skills for managing herself at these times. It has been evident that prior to each one, she had excessive worry and very high anxiety about an upcoming event or interpersonal situation (e.g., granddaughter's wedding, where she was very fearful that she would not be dressed properly, or know the "right things" to say to other family members present [who might then realize how "sick" she really is]). An important trigger seems to be this combination of cognitive and physiological "warning signs" that she does not know how to deal with very effectively. She is learning to use several more adaptive coping skills such as questioning her "all-or-none" thinking and learning to challenge her negative beliefs about herself. However, she says (and daughter confirms) that once she is into this kind of mind-set, she is "wound up" and cannot seem to stop herself. Their immediate response has been to get her to her psychiatrist as quickly as possible for a medication adjustment, which has been very effective.

Fortunately, her psychiatrist is always available to his patients and generally could see her within a day or two of the onset of the episode. Then, when the manic episode is subsiding, the daughter works with her to try to get back on a regular schedule of activities. That has been a key intervention to help her stabilize: when she is eating at regular times every day, going to bed and getting up at regular times every day, and participating in scheduled activities (e.g., exercise classes or manicure appointments), she is much more emotionally stable and is much easier to live with. When her schedule becomes disrupted (e.g., family vacation), she has much more difficulty managing her mood shifts. Mrs. GW has slowly realized this and is much more cooperative now in setting up and sticking to a regular schedule each week. Her manic episodes have gotten less frequent (the first two were only 4 months apart; the last one occurred about 9 months later) and they are shorter in duration (3–4 weeks initially vs. 1–2 weeks for the most recent), and her depression, as measured by the BDI-II, remains at the mild-to-moderate level.

In many ways, although not achieving a perfect resolution of mood symptoms, this case is typical of the complexity of issues presented by older adults with bipolar disorder. Overall, the course of treatment, although complicated, provides support for the conclusion that ongoing cognitive behavioral treatment is effective in mood management for older adults. The presence of concentration and memory problems is common among older patients as noted previously and adds an additional challenge (for Mrs. GW, her daughter, and the therapist) for learning CBT techniques and using them effectively. It is our opinion that it is highly unlikely that there will ever be a formal "termination" of this client because of the fact that she continues to need significant reinforcement (from the current therapist and from her family) to remember to use what she has learned when she needs it the most.

SUMMARY

Unfortunately, given the state of clinical evidence at present, psychosocial treatments for older adults with bipolar disorder must largely be extrapolated from clinical trials for general populations. However, there is a significant evidence base for the effectiveness of CBT of depression in older adults (Laidlaw et al., 2003), and there is reasonable clinical evidence to conclude that many of the treatment strategies detailed in these studies can be equally effective for the treatment of bipolar depression. With some adaptation to the problems experienced by older adults, including medical comorbidity and neuropsychological deficits, as well as attending to the unique aspects of the older adult cohort, the clinician can be in a position to attend to the behavioral health needs of this growing, neglected, and increasingly important population.

REFERENCES

Administration on Aging. (2008). Retrieved March 6, 2010, from www.aoa.gov/AoARoot/Aging_Statistics/Profile/2009/4.aspx

Almeida, O. P., & Fenner, S. (2002). Bipolar disorder: Similarities and differences between patients with illness onset before and after 65 years of age. *International Psychogeriatrics, 14*(3), 311–322.

Altman, E. G., Hedeker, D., Peterson, J. L., & Davis, J. M. (1997). The Altman Self-Rating Mania Scale. *Biological Psychiatry, 42*(10), 948–955.

American Psychiatric Association. (2000). *Diagnostic and statistical manual of mental disorders* (4th ed.). Washington, DC: Author.

American Psychiatric Association (2002). *Practice guideline for the treatment of patients with bipolar disorder, second edition.* Retrieved March 6, 2010, from http://www.psychiatryonline.com/pracGuide/pracGuideChapToc_8.aspx

American Psychiatric Association. (2004). *Practice guidelines for the treatment of psychiatric disorders.* Arlington, VA: Author.

Basco, M. R., & Rush, A. J. (1996). *Cognitive-behavioral therapy for bipolar disorder.* New York, NY: Guilford Press.

Bearden, C. E., Glahn, D. C., Monkul, E. S., Barrett, J., Najt, P., Villarreal, V., et al. (2006). Patterns of memory impairment in bipolar disorder and unipolar major depression. *Psychiatry Research, 142*(2–3), 139–150.

Bech, P. (2002). The Bech-Rafaelsen Mania Scale in clinical trials of therapies for bipolar disorder: A 20-year review of its use as an outcome measure. *CNS Drugs, 16*(1), 47–63.

Bech, P., Baastrup, P. C., de Bleeker, E., & Ropert, R. (2001). Dimensionality, responsiveness, and standardization of the Bech-Rafaelsen Mania Scale in the ultra-short therapy with antipsychotics in patients with severe manic episodes. *Acta Psychiatrica Scandinavica, 104*(1), 25–30.

Beck, A. T., Rush, J. A., Shaw, B. F., & Emery, G. (1979). *Cognitive therapy of depression.* New York: Guilford Press.

Benedetti, A., Scarpellini, P., Casamassima, F., Lattanzi, L., Liberti, M., Musetti, L., et al. (2008). Bipolar disorder in late life: Clinical characteristics in a sample of older adults admitted for manic episode. *Clinical Practice and Epidemiology in Mental Health, 4*, 22.

Beyer, J., Kuchibhatla, M., Gersing, K., & Krishnan, K. R. (2005). Medical comorbidity in a bipolar outpatient clinical population. *Neuropsychopharmacology, 30*(2), 401–404.

Cassidy, F., Ahearn, E., & Carroll, B. J. (1999) Elevated frequency of diabetes mellitus in hospitalized manic-depressive patients. *The American Journal of Psychiatry, 156*(9), 1417–1420.

Cassidy, F., & Carroll, B. J. (2002). Vascular risk factors in late onset mania. *Psychological Medicine, 32*(2), 359–362.

Charney, D. S., Reynolds, C. F., III, Lewis, L., Lebowitz, B. D., Sunderland, T., Alexopoulos, G. S., et al. (2003). Depression and Bipolar Support Alliance consensus statement on the unmet needs in diagnosis and treatment of mood disorders in late life. *Archives of General Psychiatry, 60*(7), 664–672.

Colom F., & Vieta, E. (2006, May 20–25). *Efficacy of group psychoeducation in bipolar disorders: 5-year outcome.* Paper presented at New Research Abstracts, Annual Meeting of the American Psychiatric Association, Toronto, Ontario, Canada.

Colom, F., Vieta, E., Reinares, M., Martínez-Arán, A., Torrent, C., Goikolea, J. M., et al. (2003). Psychoeducation efficacy in bipolar disorders: Beyond compliance enhancement. *Journal of Clinical Psychiatry, 64*(9), 1101–1105.

Depp, C. A., Davis, C. E., Mittal, D., Patterson, T. L., & Jeste, D. V. (2006). Health-related quality of life and functioning of middle-aged and elderly adults with bipolar disorder. *Journal of Clinical Psychiatry, 67*(2), 215–221.

Depp, C. A., & Jeste, D. V. (2004). Bipolar disorder in older adults: A critical review. *Bipolar Disorders, 6*(5), 343–367.

Depp, C. A., & Lebowitz, B. D. (2007). Enhancing medication adherence: In older adults with bipolar disorder. *Psychiatry, 4*(6), 22–32.

Depp, C. A., Lindamer, L. A., Folsom, D. P., Gilmer, T., Hough, R. L., Garcia, P., et al. (2005). Differences in clinical features and mental health service use in bipolar disorder across the lifespan. *The American Journal of Geriatric Psychiatry, 13*(4), 290–298.

Depp, C. A., Moore, D. J., Sitzer, D., Palmer, B. W., Eyler, L. T., Roesch, S., et al. (2007). Neurocognitive impairment in middle-aged and older adults with bipolar disorder: Comparison to schizophrenia and normal comparison subjects. *Journal of Affective Disorders, 101*(1–3), 201–209.

Frank, E., Hlastala, S., Ritenour, A., Houck, P., Tu, X. M., Monk, T. H., et al. (1997). Inducing lifestyle regularity in recovering bipolar disorder patients: Results from the maintenance therapies in bipolar disorder protocol. *Biological Psychiatry, 41*(12), 1165–1173.

Frank E., Kupfer, D. J., Thase M. E., Mallinger, A. G., Swartz, H. A., Fagiolini, A. M., et al. (2005). Two-year outcomes for interpersonal and social rhythm therapy in individuals with bipolar I disorder. *Archives of General Psychiatry, 62*(9), 996–1004.

Gallagher-Thompson, D., Steffen, A. M., & Thompson, L. W. (Eds.). (2008). *Handbook of behavioral and cognitive therapies with older adults.* New York, NY: Springer.

Gildengers, A. G., Butters, M. A., Seligman, K., McShea, M., Miller, M. D., Mulsant, B. H., et al. (2004). Cognitive functioning in late-life bipolar disorder. *The American Journal of Psychiatry, 161*(4), 736–738.

Goldstein, B. I., Herrmann, N., & Shulman, K. I. (2006). Comorbidity in bipolar disorder among the elderly: Results from an epidemiological community sample. *The American Journal of Psychiatry, 163*(2), 319–321.

Gum, A. M., King-Kallimanis, B., & Kohn, R. (2009). Prevalence of mood, anxiety, and substance-abuse disorders for older Americans in the national comorbidity survey-replication. *The American Journal of Geriatric Psychiatry*, *17*(9), 769–781.

Hirschfeld, R. M., Williams, J. B., Spitzer, R. L., Calabrese, J. R., Flynn, L., Keck, P. E., Jr., et al. (2000). Development and validation of a screening instrument for bipolar spectrum disorder: The Mood Disorder Questionnaire. *The American Journal of Psychiatry*, *158*(11), 1873–1875.

Hopko, D. R., Lejuez, C. W., Ruggiero, K. J., & Eifert, G. H. (2003). Contemporary behavioral activation treatments for depression: Procedures, principles, and progress. *Clinical Psychology Review*, *23*(5), 699–717.

Jeste, D. V., Alexopoulos, G. S., Bartels, S. J., Cummings, J. L., Gallo, J. J., Gottlieb, G. L, et al. (1999). Consensus statement on the upcoming crisis in geriatric mental health: Research agenda for the next 2 decades. *Archives of General Psychiatry*, *56*(9), 848–853.

Kales, H. C. (2007). Medical comorbidity in late-life bipolar disorder. In M. Sajatovic & F. C. Blow (Eds.), *Bipolar disorder in later life* (pp. 162–181). Baltimore, MD: Johns Hopkins University Press.

Ketter, T. A. (Ed.). (2010). *Handbook of diagnosis and treatment of bipolar disorders.* Arlington, VA: American Psychiatric Publishing, Inc.

Kilbourne, A. M., Cornelius, J. R., Han, X., Haas, G. L., Salloum, I., Conigliaro, J., et al. (2005). General-medical conditions in older patients with serious mental illness. *The American Journal of Geriatric Psychiatry*, *13*(3), 250–254.

Knight, B. G. (2004). *Psychotherapy with older adults.* Thousand Oaks, CA: Sage Publications.

Laidlaw, K., Thompson, L. W., & Gallagher-Thompson, D. (2004). Comprehensive conceptualization of cognitive behaviour therapy for late life depression. *Behavioural and Cognitive Psychotherapy*, *32*, 389–399.

Laidlaw, K., Thompson, L. W., Gallagher-Thompson, D., & Dick-Siskin, L. (2003). *Cognitive behavior therapy with older people.* New York, NY: John Wiley & Sons, Inc.

Lam, D. H., Jones, S., Hayward, P., & Bright, J. A. (1999). *Cognitive therapy for bipolar disorder: Therapist's guide to concepts, methods and practices.* New York, NY: John Wiley & Sons, Inc.

Malkoff-Schwartz, S., Frank, E., Anderson, B. P., Hlastala, S. A., Luther, J. F., Sherrill, J. T., et al. (2000). Social rhythm disruption and stressful life events in the onset of bipolar and unipolar episodes. *Psychological Medicine*, *30*(5), 1005–1016.

Martell, C. R., Addis, M. E., & Jacobson, N. S. (2001). Depression in context: Strategies for guided action. NY: Norton

Martino, D. J., Igoa, A., Marengo, E., Scápola, M., Ais, E. D., & Strejilevich, S. A. (2008). Cognitive and motor features in elderly people with bipolar disorder. *Journal of Affective Disorders*, *105*(1–3), 291–295.

McBride, L., & Bauer, M. S. (2007). Psychosocial interventions for older adults with bipolar disorder. In M. Sajatovic & F. C. Blow (Eds.), *Bipolar disorder in later life.* Baltimore, MD: Johns Hopkins University Press.

McElroy, S. L., Altshuler, L. L., Suppes, T., Keck, P. E., Jr., Frye, M. A., Denicoff, K. D., et al. (2001). Axis I psychiatric comorbidity and its relationship to historical illness variables in 288 patients with bipolar disorder. *The American Journal of Psychiatry*, *158*(3), 420–426.

Miklowitz, D. J., Otto, M. W., Frank, E., Reilly-Harrington, N. A., Kogan, J. N., Sachs, G. S., et al. (2007). Intensive psychosocial intervention enhances functioning in patients with bipolar depression: Results from a 9-month randomized controlled trial. *The American Journal of Psychiatry, 164*(9), 1340–1347.

Moorhead, S. R., & Young, A. H. (2003). Evidence for a late onset bipolar-I disorder sub-group from 50 years. *Journal of Affective Disorders, 73*(3), 271–277.

National Institute for Health and Clinical Excellence. (2006) *Bipolar disorder: The management of bipolar disorder in adults, children and adolescents, in primary and secondary care.* London, United Kingdom: Author.

Ng, B., Camacho, A., Lara, D. R., Brunstein, M. G., Pinto, O. C., & Akiskal, H. S. (2008). A case series on the hypothesized connection between dementia and bipolar spectrum disorders: Bipolar type VI? *Journal of Affective Disorders, 107*(1–3), 307–315.

Nguyen, T., Truong, D., Marquett, R., Feit, A., & Reiser, R. (2006). Older adults can respond well to cognitive behavioral therapy. *Clinical Gerontology, 30*, 103–110.

Perry, A., Tarrier, N., Morriss, R., McCarthy, E., & Limb, K. (1999). Randomised controlled trial of efficacy of teaching patients with bipolar disorder to identify early symptoms of relapse and obtain treatment. *British Medical Journal, 318*(7177), 149–153.

Post, R. M., Leverich, G. S., Altshuler, L. L., Frye, M. A., Suppes, T. M., Keck, P. E., Jr., et al. (2003). An overview of recent findings of the Stanley Foundation Bipolar Network (Part I). *Bipolar Disorders, 5*(5), 310–319.

Radloff, L. (1977). The CES-D scale: A self-report depression scale for research in the general population. *Applied Psychological Measures, 1*, 385–401.

Reiser, R. P., & Thompson, L. W. (2005). Unpublished raw data.

Reiser, R. P., & Thompson, L. W. (2005). *Bipolar disorder.* Cambridge, MA: Hogrefe & Huber.

Reiser, R., Truong, D., Nguyen, T., Marquett, R., Feit, A., Wachsmuth, W., et al. (2007). Bipolar disorder and older adults. In D. Gallagher-Thompson, A. Steffen, S. Eperstein, & L. W. Thompson (Eds.), *Handbook of cognitive behavioral therapy for the elderly* (pp. 249–263). New York, NY: Springer.

Sajatovic, M., Bingham, C. R., Campbell, E. A., & Fletcher, D. F. (2005). Bipolar disorder in older adult inpatients. *The Journal of Nervous and Mental Disease, 193*(6), 417–419.

Sajatovic, M., Blow, F. C., Ignacio, R. V., & Kales, H. C. (2004). Age-related modifiers of clinical presentation and health service use among veterans with bipolar disorder. *Psychiatric Services, 55*(9), 1014–1021.

Sajatovic, M., Blow, F. C., Ignacio, R. V., & Kales, H. C. (2005). New-onset bipolar disorder in later life. *The American Journal of Geriatric Psychiatry, 13*(4), 282–289.

Sajatovic, M., & Kales, H. C. (2006). Diagnosis and management of bipolar disorder with comorbid anxiety in the elderly. *The Journal of Clinical Psychiatry, 67*(Suppl. 1), 21–27.

Scottish Intercollegiate Guidelines Network. (2005). *Bipolar affective disorder: A national clinical guideline.* Edinburgh, United Kingdom: Author.

Segal, D. L., Coolidge, F. L., Cahill, B. S., & O'Riley, A. A. (2008). Psychometric properties of the Beck Depression Inventory II (BDI-II) among community-dwelling older adults. *Behavior Modification, 32*, 3–20.

Shürhoff, F., Bellivier, F., Jouvent, R., Mouren-Siméoni, M. C., Bouvard, M., Allilaire, J. F., et al. (2000). Early and late onset bipolar disorders: Two different forms of manic-depressive illness? *Journal of Affective Disorders, 58*(3), 215–221.

Tohen, M., Zarate, C. A., Jr., Hennen, J., Khalsa, H. M., Strakowski, S., Gebre-Medhin, P., et al. (2003). The McLean-Harvard First-Episode Mania Study: Prediction of recovery and first recurrence. *The American Journal of Psychiatry, 160*(12), 2099–2107.

Williams, J. B. (1988). A structured interview guide for the Hamilton Depression Rating Scale. *Archives of General Psychiatry, 45*(8), 742–747.

World Health Organization. *The global burden of disease: 2004 update.* Retrieved on March 6, 2010, from http://www.who.int/healthinfo/global_burden_disease/ GBD_report_2004update_part3.pdf

Wright, J. H., Basco, M. R., Thase, M. E. (2006). Learning cognitive-behavior therapy: An illustrated guide. Washington, DC: American Psychiatric Press.

Yatham, L. N., Kennedy, S. H., O'Donovan, C., Parikh, S. V., MacQueen, G., McIntyre, R. S., et al. (2006). Canadian Network for Mood and Anxiety Treatments (CANMAT) guidelines for the management of patients with bipolar disorder: Update 2007. *Bipolar Disorders, 8*(6), 721–739.

Yesavage, J. A., Brink, T. L., Rose, T. L., Lum, O., Huang, V., Adey, M., et al. (1983). Development and validation of a geriatric depression screening scale: A preliminary report. *Journal of Psychiatric Research, 17*(1), 37–49.

Young, R. C., Biggs, J. T., Zielger, V. E., & Meyer, D. A. (1978). A rating scale for mania: Reliability, validity and sensitivity. *British Journal of Psychiatry, 133,* 429–435.

Young, R. C., & Falk, J. R. (1989). Age, manic psychopathology, and treatment response. *International Journal of Geriatric Psychiatry, 4,* 73–78.

Young, R. C., Murphy, C. F., Heo, M., Schulberg, H. C., & Alexopoulos, G. S. (2006). Cognitive impairment in bipolar disorder in old age: Literature review and findings in manic patients. *Journal of Affective Disorders, 92*(1), 125–131.

RESOURCES

Basco, M. R. (2006). *The bipolar workbook: Tools for controlling your mood swings.* New York, NY: Guilford Press.

Basco, M. R., & Rush, A. J. (1996). *Cognitive-behavioral therapy for bipolar disorder.* New York, NY: Guilford Press.

Gallagher-Thompson, D. (2010). *Treating late life depression: A cognitive-behavioral therapy approach, therapist guide.* New York, NY: Oxford University Press.

Gallagher-Thompson, D., Steffen, A. M., & Thompson, L. W. (Eds.). (2008). *Handbook of behavioral and cognitive therapies with older adults.* New York, NY: Springer Publishing Company.

Laidlaw, K., Thompson, L. W., Gallagher-Thompson, D., & Dick-Siskin, L. (2003). *Cognitive behavior therapy with older people.* New York, NY: John Wiley & Sons, Inc.

Lam, D., Jones, S., Hayward, P., & Bright, J. A. (1999). *Cognitive therapy for bipolar disorder: Therapist's guide to concepts, methods, and practices.* New York, NY: John Wiley & Sons, Inc.

Reiser, R. P., & Thompson, L. W. (2005). *Bipolar disorder.* Cambridge, MA: Hogrefe & Huber.

Thompson, L. W. (2010). *Treating late life depression: A cognitive-behavioral therapy approach, workbook (treatments that work).* New York, NY: Oxford University Press.

4

Suicidal Older Adults: Suicide Risk Assessments, Safety Planning, and Cognitive Behavioral Therapy

John P. Dennis and Gregory K. Brown

This chapter will describe the public health significance of suicide in older adults and present a review of the risk factors and protective factors for late-life suicide supported in the literature. Subsequently, procedures for conducting risk assessments with suicidal older adults will be presented with an emphasis on distinguishing between low- and high-suicide risk. This chapter will conclude with a description of a novel cognitive behavioral intervention for treating suicidal older adults.

PUBLIC HEALTH SIGNIFICANCE

Aggregate international data published by the World Health Organization (WHO) indicates that older adults represent the most at-risk age group for suicide in most countries (WHO, 2010). Moreover, global suicide rates continue to increase with age among older adults. Consistent with these findings, older adults living in the United States (U.S.) are disproportionately likely to die by suicide relative to younger cohorts (Centers for Disease Control and Prevention [CDC], 2010). They attempt suicide less than younger cohorts but complete suicide more frequently (Chan, Draper, & Banerjee, 2007; De Leo et al., 2001). There are an estimated four suicide attempts for every completed suicide in adults age 65 or older compared to 100 to 200 suicide attempts per completed suicide across other age groups (Goldsmith, Pellman, Kleinman, & Bunney, 2002). More than 5,000 adults 65 years of age or older died annually by suicide in the U.S. between 1999 and 2005 (CDC, 2010). Although the rate of late-life suicide has been declining in the U.S. in the past decade (Fiske, Wetherell, & Gatz, 2009), a substantial increase in the raw number of late-life suicides is expected as the older adult population is projected to increase dramatically over the next 15 years (Cukrowicz et al., 2009).

EPIDEMIOLOGICAL RESEARCH

Demographic Risk Factors

Men complete suicide an estimated three to four times more than women across age groups in most countries and cultures (Kung, Hoyert, Xu, & Murphy, 2008). The discrepancy in suicide rates across gender increases from middle (ages 40–60) to late adulthood in the U.S., where men account for an estimated 76% and 85% of suicides, respectively (CDC, 2010). Significant racial and ethnic differences also emerge in the suicide prevalence rates in late life. The following suicide prevalence rates per 100,000 were reported for suicides that occurred between 2002 and 2006 for the U.S. general population compared to adults aged 65 or older, respectively: non-Hispanic Whites = 13.9 versus 15.8; American Indian and Alaska Natives = 15.1 versus 13.0[1]; non-Hispanic Blacks = 5.0 versus 5.0; Hispanics = 4.9 versus 7.9; and Asian and Pacific Islanders = 5.7 versus 10.6 (CDC, 2010). Overall, non-Hispanic Whites and American Indian and Alaska Natives have the highest suicide risk across the life span among racial/ethnic groups.

Risk Factors for Suicide Common Between Younger and Older Adults

There is significant overlap among risk factors for suicide in younger and older adults. In addition to race/ethnicity and gender, the following diagnostic variables appear to increase suicide risk in younger and older adults: (a) one or more psychiatric disorder, particularly an affective disorder (Beautrais et al., 1996; Bertolote, Fleischmann, De Leo, & Wasserman, 2003); (b) presence of an affective disorder comorbid with panic attacks, severe anxiety, diminished concentration, global insomnia, or anhedonia (Fawcett et al., 1990; Hall, Platt, & Hall, 1999); (c) alcohol abuse and/or other substance abuse (CDC, 2010); (d) diagnosis of

---

[1]The female prevalence rate for suicide among American Indian and Alaska Native adults aged 65 or older from 2002 to 2006 was not reported by the CDC and, therefore, the 13.0 per 100,000 rate reported here reflects suicides only in males from this age group.

one or more medical illnesses (Kleespies, 2009; Levenson & Bostwick, 2005); (e) lower socioeconomic status (Beautrais, 2001); (f) financial hardship (Brown, Beck, Steer, & Grisham, 2000); (g) divorced, separated, or widowed status (Kposowa, 2000; Stroebe, Stroebe, & Abakoumkin, 2005); (h) social isolation (for a review, see Trout, 1980); and (i) incarceration (Fisk et al., 2009).

The following psychiatric history variables have also been found to increase suicide risk in younger and older adults: (a) family history of suicide (Cheng, Chen, Chen, & Jenkins, 2000; Moscicki, 2001); (b) exposure to suicidal behavior of others (Fisk et al., 2009); (c) history of physical and/or sexual abuse (Anderson, Tiro, Price, Bender, & Kaslow, 2002; Joiner et al., 2007); and (d) family history of mental illness or substance abuse (Fisk et al., 2009; Moscicki, 2001). Additionally, the following psychological variables have been found to increase suicide risk regardless of age: (a) hopelessness (Beck, Steer, Kovacs, & Garrison, 1985; McMillan, Gilbody, Beresford, & Neilly, 2007); (b) agitation/acute anxiety (Busch, Fawcett, & Jacobs, 2003); (c) abrupt clinical change in psychiatric health status (Slaby, 1998); (d) suicidal ideation (Krupinski et al., 1998); (e) suicidal intent (Harriss & Hawton, 2005; Harriss, Hawton, & Zahl, 2005); (f) problem-solving deficits (Dixon, Heppner, & Anderson, 1991; Priester & Clum, 1993; Rudd, Rajab, & Dahm, 1994); and (g) perceived burden to others (Joiner et al., 2002).

Risk Factors for Suicide Unique to Older Adults

Diagnostic Risk Factors
There are also significant differences with regard to risk factors for suicide in older and younger adults. Older adults who commit suicide are more likely than younger adults to have major depression (Conwell & Brent, 1995), with an estimated 85% of older adults who commit suicide meeting criteria for this diagnosis. Moreover, depression tends to be expressed uniquely in later life because older adults are less likely to endorse affective symptoms than younger adults and more likely to display cognitive changes, somatic symptoms, and loss of interest (Fiske et al., 2009). In general, the presence of any psychiatric illness increases the risk for suicide among older adults, with some findings indicating suicide risk is 44 to 113 times higher for older adults meeting criteria for at least one psychiatric disorder (Conwell & Thompson, 2008).

Some researchers have attributed the association between increasing age and risk for suicide in the U.S. to age-related increases in comorbid medical illnesses and the lethality of suicide attempts (Conwell, Duberstein, & Caine, 2002). It has been estimated that older adults with medical illnesses have a 1.5 to 4 times higher risk for suicide than older adults without medical illnesses, with this risk increasing as the number of medical illnesses increases (Conwell & Thompson, 2008). Despite substantial comorbidity between medical and mental illness (Kleespies, 2009), research has indicated that both contribute independently to suicide risk (Druss & Pincus, 2000). The extent of their individual contributions, however, is not clear at present (Wenzel, Brown, & Beck, 2009).

Sleep disturbance, which is often associated with both medical and mental disorders, is associated with suicidal cognitions and behaviors in later life (Ayalon, Mackin, Arean, Chen, & McDonel Herr, 2007). Preliminary research also indicates that older adults who attempt suicide display more impairment on frontal executive tasks relative to nonattempters (King et al., 2000). Moreover, older adults with a history of multiple suicide attempts tend to display more subcortical gray matter hyperintensities on magnetic resonance imaging (MRI) than depressed older adults without a history of previous suicide attempts. The association between dementia and risk for late-life suicide is uncertain at present with research supporting both positive and negative correlations (for a review, see Haw, Harwood, & Hawton, 2009).

Precipitating Risk Factors
Suicide attempts are generally more lethal in later life (Conwell et al., 2002; Dombrovski, Szanto, & Reynolds, 2005). Although self-poisoning is the most common method of suicide across age groups in most countries (Shah, 2007; WHO, 2010), firearms are used in an estimated two thirds of all suicides in the United States (CDC, 2010). Moreover, older adults more frequently use firearms to commit suicide than younger adults. The association between owning a firearm and suicide risk in later life may not be straightforward. Research has indicated that owning a firearm by itself may not necessarily increase suicide risk, particularly if the firearm is a rifle as opposed to a handgun (Conwell & Thompson, 2008). In contrast, having acquired a firearm within the past week does increase suicide risk for older adults, as does keeping a firearm loaded and/or storing a firearm in an unlocked location.

The recent occurrence of a significant life event stressor (within 1 to 2 years) and/or chronic stress is associated with greater suicide risk across the life span (Bongar, 2002). Life event stressors most often associated with late-life suicide are associated with aging and include bereavement (particularly in the first year after a death), financial stressors associated with retirement and living on reduced means, family discord and loss of social security, and social and psychological effects related to medical illness and pain (Conwell & Thompson,

2008; Kleespies, 2009; Wenzel et al., 2009). It has been hypothesized that life event stressors increase suicide risk across age groups via their association with psychological variables such as hopelessness, loneliness, and complicated grief (Szanto et al., 2006; Wenzel et al.).

Suicide-Relevant Cognitions
Hopelessness appears to be a strong predictor of suicidal ideation (Uncapher, Gallagher-Thompson, Osgood, & Bonger, 1998) and completed suicide (Rifai, George, Stack, Mann, & Reynolds, 1994; Ross, Bernstein, Trent, Henderson, & Paganini-Hill, 1990) in older adults. A popular hypothesis is that experiencing a significant life event stressor increases vulnerability to hopelessness, which in turn, increases vulnerability to suicidal thoughts and behavior (Beck, Kovacs, & Weissman, 1975; Britton et al., 2008; Wenzel et al., 2009). Based on a meta-analysis of the literature, hopelessness has been estimated to increase suicide risk at least threefold across age groups, with stable levels of hopelessness that persist over time serving as even stronger predictors of suicidal acts (McMillan, et al., 2007). Moreover, research has indicated that hopelessness may be a stronger predictor of suicide than severity of depressive symptoms across age groups (Beck et al., 1985).

Suicidal ideation appears to be another strong risk factor for late-life suicide. In one of the few prospective studies to investigate this association, Brown, Bruce, and Pearson (2001) demonstrated that older adults that obtained a score greater than zero on the Scale for Suicide Ideation (SSI) (Beck, Kovacs, & Weissman, 1979) were 15 times more likely to make future suicide attempts than those who obtained a zero, which indicated the absence of suicidal ideation. Suicide ideation may be a particularly strong risk factor among older adults who use home health care services (Rowe, Conwell, Schulberg, & Bruce, 2006).

Significant associations have been demonstrated between greater late-life suicide risk and the experience of loneliness and/or complicated grief,[2] particularly in the first 12 months after an interpersonal loss (Heikkinen & Lönnqvist, 1995; Szanto et al., 2006; Waern, Rubenowitz, & Wilhelmson, 2003). Significant associations have also been identified between risk for late-life suicide and certain personality

---

[2]As described by Szanto, Prigerson, Houck, and Reynolds (1997, p. 195), complicated grief is a syndrome distinct from bereavement and is defined as follows:

> Posttraumatic stress disorder-like symptoms such as intrusive thoughts about the deceased, avoidance of reminders of the deceased, feelings of bitterness and shock over the death, and survivor guilt, as well as attachment disturbance-like symptoms such as lack of acceptance of the death, persistent searching, longing for the lost person, and symptoms of identification. . . . (e.g., pain in the same parts of the body as that experienced by the deceased just prior to his or her death).

traits including impulsivity and aggressiveness (Mann, Waternaux, Haasm, & Malone, 1999; Oquendo et al., 2004), high neuroticism and low openness to experience (Duberstein et al., 2000), and obsessional and anxious traits and/or traits indicative of hostility or a rigid independent style (for a review, see Conwell & Thompson, 2008).

Relative to younger adults, older adults who attempt suicide display stronger suicidal intent and more planning of suicidal behavior (Conwell et al., 1998; Hawton & Harriss, 2006), are less likely to verbalize suicidal thoughts to others, have higher rates of death ideation, and are less likely to report new incidents of suicide attempts (Kuo, Gallo, & Tien, 2001). Moreover, the subsequent risk for suicide after an initial suicide attempt is extremely high in older adults (De Leo et al., 2001; Hawton & Harriss). Across age groups, repeat suicide attempts are most common in the first 3 months after an initial suicide attempt (Roy, 1998). It has long been recognized that suicide risk substantially increases across age groups following discharge from a psychiatric hospital (Simon, 1988). Of significance, up to 40% of older adults who died by suicide had disclosed suicidal ideation/intent to a health professional in the year prior to their death, whereas 75% had disclosed suicidal ideation/intent to a family member or acquaintance (Waern, Beskow, Runeson, & Skoog, 1999). Moreover, an estimated 70% of adults age 55 or older had visited a primary care provider within 1 month of their suicides (Luoma, Martin, & Pearson, 2002).

Protective Factors
Social support is generally considered to be one of the most reliable protective factors against suicide across the life span (Heikkinen, Isometsa, Marttunen, Aro, & Lönnqvist, 1995; Rowe et al., 2006). Older adults appear less likely to endorse suicidal ideation if they have larger social networks, more frequent contact with friends or relatives, more close friends and relatives and at least one confidante, and are satisfied with their level of social support (for a review, see Rowe et al., 2006). Other research has indicated that perceived social support decreases the risk for suicidal ideation among older adults but the size of the social network, instrumental support, and social interaction patterns did not. Having a sense of belonging, which was defined as feeling valued by others and integrated within the community, has been found to reduce the impact of depression on suicidal ideation (McLaren, Gomez, Bailey, & Van Der Horst, 2007). Agency, which refers to traits such as assertiveness, competitiveness, and independence, has also been found to buffer the effect of depression on suicidal ideation, particularly for men (Hobbs & McLaren, 2009). Research has identified that endorsing more wishes to live than wishes to die and having positive expectations about the future and one's coping ability are protective fac-

tors against suicide (Brown, Steer, Henriques, & Beck, 2005). Having a fear of death, dying, or suicide appears to be an additional protective factor for suicide across the life span (Joiner, 2005).

Summary of Epidemiological Research

Most research establishing risk factors and protective factors for late-life suicide are the result of cross-sectional or psychological autopsy studies.[3] As indicated previously, multiple subgroups of older adults at risk for suicide have been identified. The ability to use this information to identify specific individuals most prone to future suicidal behavior is extremely limited because most known risk factors are either fixed demographic variables or relatively common among both suicidal and nonsuicidal older adults. For example, although a diagnosis of depression is among the most significant risk factors for late-life suicide and suicide across age groups (Wenzel et al., 2009), only 4% of those who obtain inpatient psychiatric treatment for depression will ultimately die by suicide (Bostwick & Pankratz, 2000). To more effectively identify particular individuals at risk for suicide, which is the ideal for suicide prevention research, prospective research and treatment outcome research is critical. The appearance of this type of research has recently begun to increase in the literature.

ASSESSMENT OF SUICIDE RISK IN OLDER ADULTS

The American Psychological Association (APA) recommends that health professionals conduct comprehensive suicide risk assessments with all patients suspected to be at risk for suicide (APA, 2003). This risk assessment should be conducted in initial sessions with new patients, when an increase in suicide risk is suspected during treatment, and when an abrupt clinical change (positive or negative) is observed. Despite the fact that older adults constitute the most at-risk demographic group for suicide in most countries (WHO, 2010), many health professionals fail to conduct even the most basic risk assessments when treating this population.

Assessing suicide risk can be daunting for health professionals, given that procedures for doing are often not always readily available. Specific

---

[3]A psychological autopsy study involves an in-depth interview conducted with people who knew the subject and an analysis of data surrounding the suicide in an attempt to establish the reasons for the suicidal behavior.

guidelines for assessing suicide risk in older adults are even rarer. This oversight in the literature is beginning to be addressed because guidelines have now been developed for assessing suicide risk in the general population (Kleespies, 2009; Rudd, Joiner, & Rajab, 2001; Wenzel et al., 2009) and in older adults in primary care settings in the context of intervention research (Brown et al., 2001). The purpose of this section is to build upon these guidelines to provide more comprehensive coverage of the unique issues that health professionals should consider when assessing late-life risk in any outpatient setting. Guidelines for evaluating late-life risk during crisis calls or in emergency departments will vary, given the unique obstacles and resources present in those settings (APA, 2003).

Structure of Suicide Risk Assessments

General guidelines for conducting suicide risk assessments recommend including assessment of current clinical status, suicide-relevant variables, recent activating events, mental and medical treatment history, and protective factors (Kleespies, 2009; Rudd et al., 2001; Wenzel et al., 2009). The purpose of any suicide risk assessment should be to determine the most appropriate level of care needed for patients (inpatient versus outpatient) and to identify risk factors modifiable with treatment. The process of obtaining accurate assessments of suicide risk in older adults is often more challenging than with younger adults. A significant reason for this is that older adults are often less likely to self-disclose suicidal thoughts or behaviors to others (Conwell et al., 1998; Hawton & Harriss, 2006; Kuo et al., 2001). Moreover, health professionals often overestimate the ability of older adults to openly discuss such intimate topics as suicide or depression.

Establishing Rapport

To promote rapport building, it is recommended that health professionals preface all risk assessments with an explanation that the questions about to be asked may be stressful to think about or may evoke memories of distressing issues or events (Kleespies, 2009; Wenzel et al., 2009). It is also helpful to convey that risk assessments are part of standard care and to explain how the assessment can be expected to benefit the patient (protecting safety, treatment planning, etc.). The latter is often most significant to older patients, who are frequently uncertain about the purpose of the risk assessment.

   An assessment of the older adult's ability and motivation to disclose accurate information should be considered when deciding how much time to devote to rapport building and socializing the older adult to the risk assessment. A good place to start is to ascertain the referral source. Older adults who present for routine medical check-ups or because of pressure from others may be more guarded about discussing topics related to suicide. It may be particularly challenging to obtain accurate information about risk from older adults who are highly motivated to portray themselves as mentally healthy. Obtaining collateral information about the patient's functioning from sources such as family, friends, agencies, and other treatment providers should be routine when working with older adults, but is crucial in these instances.

Another way to strengthen rapport with older adults is to gradually socialize them to the risk assessment process via proceeding from more general inquiries about mood, functioning, and future outlook to more focused questions about suicidal thoughts and behaviors. Thorough assessment of the patient's medical and mental health treatment histories can aid the health professional in determining how familiar and comfortable the older adult might be with such questioning. Inquiring about the older adult's satisfaction level with past treatment can also be valuable. For older adults who initially appear resistant to questions about mental health issues and suicide, spending more time up-front empathetically listening to and validating their concerns will often strengthen the therapeutic alliance and, in turn, lessen this resistance.

Assessing Current Clinical Status

The strategies for developing rapport discussed previously will aid in the assessment of current clinical status. Clinical observation of behavior is also particularly useful when assessing older adults. Answers to the following questions can be significant: Has a caretaker accompanied the patient to the appointment? If so, is this caretaker the one describing the presenting problem? Does the older adult appear well groomed and well nourished? Are disabilities, medical conditions, or difficulty with speech or comprehension evident? Are there signs of bruising or other bodily injuries? Careful clinical judgment must be exercised when interpreting these observations. Noticeable malnourishment and bruising may be indicative of elder abuse, intentional self-harm, or inadequacy of self-care. Comprehension difficulties and tangential speech may represent signs of dementia or of hearing impairment. Follow-up inquiries are necessary to determine the significance of behavioral observations. Direct inquiries about elder abuse and hearing impairment should be included in every risk assessment.

When assessing current clinical status, it is also important to inquire whether older adults have experienced any recent changes in functioning or are currently receiving treatment or medication for any medical or mental disorders. Treatment histories should be also obtained. When possible, collateral information about these and all aspects of the risk assessment should be obtained. Obtaining multiple perspectives about current functioning is invaluable because older adults may underreport impairment for reasons such as pride, suspiciousness about how this information may be used, or to decrease the perceived burden on their families or treatment providers.

Assessing Risk Factors for Suicide

Table 4.1[4] provides a summary of most of the known risk factors and protective factors for suicide in older adults. Qualitative distinctions between lower and higher suicide risk are provided for all risk and protective factors. Objective measures that can be used to distinguish lower and higher risk are also listed where available. The absence or presence of each risk factor and protective factor should be assessed when evaluating late-life suicide risk. Careful assessment of suicidal cognitions and behaviors is critical because the absence or presence of these risk factors should be considered when determining appropriate levels of care (inpatient or outpatient treatment). Direct inquiries about suicidal cognitions and behaviors are necessary. Because this can be quite stressful for older adults, clinical judgment should be exercised to normalize the concerns about life and death being endorsed without diminishing the importance attributed to these concerns.

Supplementing direct inquiries of suicide risk with more objective measures of risk is also recommended (APA, 2003). A comprehensive battery of more than 30 measures assessing risk factors for suicide in the general population has been described elsewhere (Raue et al., 2001). Table 4.2 provides a list of measures that have adequate to good reliability and validity for assessing suicide risk in older adults. When possible, both clinician-administered and self-report measures of suicide risk should be used because some older adults may be more willing to disclose suicidal thoughts or behaviors via one method versus the other.

---

[4]Table 4.1 is a significant enhancement of the table of suicidal risk factors first reported in Brown et al. (2001).

TABLE 4.1   Risk Factors and Protective Factors for Suicide in Older Adults

	Lower Risk	Higher Risk
Risk Factors		
Previous Suicide Attempt	More than 3 months since last attempt	Less than 3 months since last attempt; regrets surviving a previous attempt
Psychiatric Hospitalization	More than 1 year since discharge	Less than 1 year since discharge
Hopelessness	Few positive expectations about future or future oriented goals	No positive expectations about future; stable hopelessness; more reasons for living indicated than reasons for dying **Objective Measurement:** BHS Total > 8; BDI-II #2 $= 3$
Suicidal Ideation	Death ideation/passive wish to die; no intent or plan **Objective Measurement:** SSI-C Item #2 $>$ SSI-C Item #1 $= 2$; BDI-II Item 9 $= 1$; SCID MDE Item #9 (ideation)	Active wish to die; suicide intent or plan; recently disclosed to health professional or family member **Objective Measurement:** SSI-C #4 or #5 or #12 > 0; BDI-II #9 > 1; S
Loneliness/ Bereavement	More than 12 months since interpersonal loss	Less than 12 months since interpersonal loss
Complicated Grief	More than 12 months since interpersonal loss	Less than 12 months since interpersonal loss **Objective Measurement:** ICG $= > 24$
Access to lethal method	No immediate access to method described in suicide plan; firearm is a rifle; bullets are kept separate from firearm; firearm is stored in locked location	Made preparations to kill oneself; immediate access to method described in suicide plan; purchased firearm in last week (firearm is a handgun); firearm is kept loaded; firearm is stored in unlocked location **Objective Measurement:** SSI-C #13 $= 2$
Recent Occurrence of Significant Life Stressor	Interpersonal loss; financial stressors associated with retirement or living on reduced means; family discord; sudden change in mental or medical health status	When hopelessness, suicidal ideation, loneliness/bereavement, and complicated grief accompany the life event stressors listed in the preceding column

(Continued)

TABLE 4.1 Risk Factors and Protective Factors for Suicide in Older Adults *(Continued)*

	Lower Risk	Higher Risk
Problem solving deficits	Mildly impaired problem solving abilities	Moderate to severely impaired problem solving abilities not attributable to dementia **Objective Measurement:** Social Problem Solving Inventory
Diagnosis of Mental Illness	Mild depressive episode; only one mental illness	Moderate to severe depressive episode*; depressive episode comorbid panic attacks, severe anxiety, global insomnia, alcohol and/or substance abuse, or anhedonia; more than one mental illness; abrupt clinical change in psychiatric health ***Objective Measurement:** HRSD total > 15; BDI-II total > 19
Diagnosis of Medical Illness	One medical illness with no or minimal impact to social and occupational functioning; without chronic pain	More than one medical illness; chronic pain; mild cognitive impairment; significant interference with social and/or occupational functioning
Psychiatric History Variables	Family history of suicide, mental illness, or substance abuse; exposure to suicidal behavior of others; history of physical or sexual abuse	History positive for multiple variables in preceding column
Demographic Risk Factors	Male gender; 60 or older; non-Hispanic white, American Indian, or Alaska native	Age 85 or older; presence of multiple demographic factors from the previous column;
Protective Factors		
Social Support	High perceived social support; at least one intimate confidante; family live in the area; supportive neighbors	Low perceived social support; no intimate confidantes
Reasons for Living	Multiple reasons for living endorsed; **Objective Measurement:** RFL-OA = higher scores (no cutoff score available)	Few or no reasons to live endorsed
Sense of Belonging	Feels valued by others and integrated into the community	Social isolation; feels neglected by or a burden to others

(Continued)

TABLE 4.1   Risk Factors and Protective Factors for Suicide in Older Adults *(Continued)*

	Lower Risk	Higher Risk
Religious background (particularly for non-Hispanic Black women)	Actively participates in religious activities	No participation in religious activities
Personality	Assertive; competitive, & independent	Hostile or rigid independent style; high neuroticism; low openness to experience; impulsive; obsessive and anxious
Mental Health Treatment	Currently obtaining treatment from a health professional for a diagnosable affective disorder	Not currently obtaining treatment from a health professional for a diagnosable affective disorder

Note: BDI-II, Beck Depression Inventory – 2nd Edition; BHS, Beck Hopelessness Scale; HRSD, Hamilton Psychiatric Rating Scale – Depression; ICG, Inventory of Complicated Grief; RFL-OA, Reasons for Living – Older Adult Version; SCID MDE, Structured Clinical Interview for DSM-IV; SSI-C, Scale for Suicidal Ideation – Current.

Distinguishing Between Low and High Risk

As indicated, qualitative and objective distinctions are provided in Table 4.1 to help health professionals distinguish lower and higher suicide risk in older adults. Unfortunately, there is no set rule to determine which older adults are most at risk for suicide. Although suicidal thoughts, hopelessness, and immediate access to lethal means appear to be three of the strongest risk factors for suicide in older adults

TABLE 4.2   Measures for Assessing Suicide Risk in Older Adults

Measure	Reference
Beck Depression Inventory—Second Edition	Beck, Steer, & Brown (1996)
Beck Hopelessness Scale	Beck & Steer (1993)
Hamilton Psychiatric Rating Scale— Depression	Hamilton (1960)
Inventory of Complicated Grief	Prigerson et al. (1995)
Reasons for Living – Older Adult Version	Britton et al. (2008)
Structured Clinical Interview for DSM-IV	First, Spitzer, Gibbon, & Williams (1995)
Scale for Suicidal Ideation	Beck et al. (1979)

(Wenzel et al., 2009), the overall level of suicide risk generally increases with the addition of each new risk factor. Consequently, an older adult who denies suicidal thoughts but endorses several other risk factors for suicide may have a similar or even greater risk for suicide than an older adult who endorses suicidal thoughts. Moreover, protective factors endorsed by older adults may counterbalance risk factors.

The duration, frequency, and intensity of any suicidal thoughts endorsed by older adults should be accessed. Clinical judgment should be exercised to quantify whether suicide intent, if present, is *weak*, *moderate*, or *strong*. Suicide intent in those with a plan for suicide or those who have been taking actions toward that plan (recently purchasing a handgun, stockpiling pills, etc.) should be considered most severe. It is common for suicidal older adults to make more prolonged plans for suicide such as discontinuing essential medications (insulin, heart medications, etc.) or refusing to maintain proper nutrition. Clinical judgment and direct inquiries should be used to determine whether older adults have made any such preparations. Moreover, the presence of any recent or past suicide attempts, interrupted attempts, or aborted attempts should also be assessed.

Older adults who do not endorse suicide risk factors currently supported in the literature may still be at risk for suicide for at least three reasons. First, multiple risk factors for late-life suicide have yet to be discovered. Second, multiple factors can make it challenging to obtain an accurate assessment of suicide risk in older adults (as discussed earlier). Third, suicidal schemas associated with past suicidal thoughts and behaviors that are now dormant in older adults may quickly be reactivated in response to either acute or chronic life event stress (for a review of this theory, see Wenzel et al., 2009).

Final Determination of Suicide Risk

After careful consideration of all information obtained during the suicide risk assessment with an older adult, sound clinical judgment should be exercised to make a final determination of overall suicide risk. This judgment should be based on professional experience, knowledge of empirically supported risk factors, the clinical presentation of the patient, and information obtained from collateral sources familiar with the patient (Brown et al., 2001; Wenzel et al., 2009). It is recommended that risk be quantified as *low, moderate,* or *imminent.* To accomplish this, the severity or weight of each risk factor should be considered, as should the extent that some risk factors may be counterbalanced by protective factors. The subjective level of distress that individual risk factors cause should be considered, although clinical judgment is necessary to evaluate the accuracy of any self-reports of distress. Brown et al. (2001) and Wenzel et al. (2009) have published templates that health professionals can use to determine whether imminent risk is present in suicidal patients. These templates provide structured guidelines for ensuring that comprehensive clinical reasoning is being used when determining level of suicide risk.

Safety Planning and Treatment Referrals

The purpose of conducting suicide risk assessments with older adults is to determine the appropriate level of care needed to ensure their safety. Older adults determined to have an imminent risk for suicide should be referred for inpatient psychiatric treatment. Many older adults determined to have a low or moderate suicide risk can be referred for outpatient treatment to reduce suicide risk after the necessary safety planning has been conducted. Safety planning is an innovative and brief treatment that was designed to be delivered in an emergency department as a stand-alone intervention (Stanley & Brown, 2010). The purpose of safety planning is to help suicidal older adults develop a written, prioritized list of coping strategies and sources of support that they can use to alleviate a suicidal crisis. Safety plans are brief, easy-to-read documents that are developed collaboratively with patients and include a hierarchically arranged list of coping strategies for (a) recognizing warning signs that precede the suicidal crisis, (b) identifying coping strategies that can be used without contacting another person, (c) contacting friends or family members, and (d) contacting mental health professionals or agencies (Stanley & Brown). Should the patient encounter a suicidal crisis, he or she is instructed to proceed through each step of the safety plan until the suicidal crisis has been resolved. Comprehensive instructions for developing safety plans with patients are provided by Wenzel et al. (2009).

AVAILABLE TREATMENTS FOR SUICIDAL OLDER ADULTS

Given the strong associations between depression, suicide ideation, and completed suicide, most suicide prevention treatments have been based on the idea that effectively treating depression will subsequently reduce suicide ideation and risk for suicide. There is a paucity of randomized controlled trials (RCTs), which are the gold standard for evaluating the efficacy and effectiveness of interventions, that have been conducted to examine the validity of this strategy for late-life suicide prevention.

The *Prevention of Suicide in Primary Care Elderly: Collaborative Trial* (PROSPECT; Bruce et al., 2004) and the *Improving Mood: Promoting Access to Collaborative Treatment* (IMPACT; Unützer et al., 2006) are two exceptions. Suicide ideation in older adults was reduced in both studies by using a collaborative care model to treat depression in a primary care setting. Preliminary findings from an open clinical trial have indicated that interpersonal psychotherapy can also be effective in reducing suicide ideation and death ideation in older adults (Heisel, Duberstein, Talbot, King, & Tu, 2009). It remains unclear if reducing suicide ideation in this study or the PROSPECT or IMPACT studies subsequently reduced the number of completed suicides for older adults.

RCTs demonstrating that any intervention is effective in preventing suicide are lacking in the literature (Wenzel et al., 2009). This is well recognized in the field and is typically attributed to ethical complications associated with conducting suicide prevention research and low base rates of suicidal behavior (Kleespies et al., 2009). It appears that the CBT protocol for suicidal patients developed by Brown, Ten Have, et al. (2005) was one of the first psychotherapy interventions demonstrated in an RCT to have effectiveness for decreasing suicidal behavior in a younger adult population. In their research, their 10-week CBT protocol was compared to usual care (UC) for reducing the frequency of repeat suicide attempts in a population of 120 adults who were recruited from medical or psychiatric emergency departments immediately following a suicide attempt. At the 18-month follow-up assessment, the CBT group was approximately 50% less likely to have made a repeat suicide attempt than those in the UC group.

The CBT protocol for suicidal patients was designed to reduce the frequency of repeat suicide attempts in adults who recently attempted suicide (Brown, Ten Have, et al., 2005). This focus is problematic for older adults because older adults attempt suicide much less frequently than younger adults and are more likely to complete suicide during initial attempts (Chan et al., 2007; De Leo et al., 2001). To address these challenges, the CBT protocol for suicidal patients was specifically adapted for use with older adults (Brown, Brown, Bhar, & Beck, 2008; Wenzel et al., 2009).

A COGNITIVE BEHAVIORAL THERAPY PROTOCOL FOR SUICIDAL OLDER ADULTS WITH CASE EXAMPLE

General Cognitive Model of Suicidal Acts

According to the cognitive model of suicidal acts (Wenzel et al., 2009), there are four main components that interact to produce suicidal acts: dispositional vulnerability factors, stress, cognitive processes associated with psychiatric disturbance, and cognitive processes associated with suicidal acts. Dispositional vulnerability factors constitute any risk factors (demographic variables, psychiatric history variables, psychological variables, etc.) that make individuals more susceptible to the activation of maladaptive schemas associated with psychiatric disturbance when encountering increasing stress. As the maladaptive schemas become activated, they influence the development of maladaptive cognitions, emotions, behavior, and heightened physiological reactivity. Consequently, the state of distress created by this process, which is often associated with an Axis I mental disorder, creates additional dispositional vulnerability factors that perpetuate this maladaptive cycle. As more stress is encountered, more maladaptive schemas are activated and more severe maladaptive cognitions, emotions, and behaviors develop. If this maladaptive cycle continues to intensify without interruption, hopelessness and other forms of defeatist thinking (negative views about the self, others, and the future) that are characteristic of maladaptive schemas for suicide are likely to develop. When individuals begin to feel powerless to stop or reverse this increasingly distressing negative feedback loop, a state of learned helplessness develops and they begin considering suicide as a potential solution.

General Overview of Cognitive Behavioral Therapy for Suicide

As for CBT with other disorders, the general cognitive model of psychiatric disturbance (Beck, Rush, Shaw, & Emery, 1979) provides the foundation for both the CBT protocol for suicidal younger adults and the adapted CBT protocol for suicidal older adults. Unlike most psychotherapies for suicide that attempt to decrease suicide risk by treating depression or other Axis I disorders, CBT for suicide targets the thoughts, feelings, and emotions directly associated with suicidal behaviors irrespective of psychiatric diagnoses. The latter becomes the focus of treatment only after patients demonstrate significant reductions in suicide risk, as evidenced by suicide risk assessments. Despite significant overlap between the cognitions, emotions, and behaviors associated with suicidal acts and Axis I disorders, Brown, Ten Have, et al. (2005) have hypothesized that using CBT skills and techniques to target the former is the most effective and immediate strategy for helping patients develop hope and problem solving to reduce suicide risk.

The underlying structure of the original CBT protocol for suicidal younger adults (Brown, Ten Have, et al., 2005) and the adapted protocol for suicidal older adults (Brown et al., 2008; Wenzel et al., 2009) is the same. The major difference is that the protocol for suicidal older adults specifies a process for teaching CBT skills and techniques that is more appropriate for older adults given the cognitive, physical, and sensory limitations that they often have. Available guidelines for adapting *standard* CBT for older adults were followed (Areán & Feliciano, 2008; Gallagher-Thompson & Thompson, 2010). A second difference is that the CBT protocol for suicidal older adults incorporates an increased focus on addressing the specific risk factors for late-life suicide, which include beliefs of worthlessness, uselessness, inadequacy, helplessness, or being a burden to others that are frequently related to experiences such as declining health, interpersonal conflict or loss, financial difficulties, and retirement (Wenzel et al., 2009).

Three Phases of the Cognitive Behavioral Therapy Protocol for Suicidal Older Adults Treatment

The CBT protocol for suicidal older adults was developed to be a brief 12-week intervention. It was not structured to be a session-by-session treatment manual because clinical work with suicidal older adults often requires great flexibility with regard to which skills and techniques are used in any given session. Rather, the protocol is structured according to core components that should be covered in the three phases of treatment: *early, intermediate,* and *later* phases. General goals include increasing hope and reasons for living, improving social resources, problem-solving skills, and adherence to medical regimens, and relapse prevention.

Early Phase of Treatment
The seven components covered during the early phase of treatment are the following:

1. Obtaining informed consent
2. Actively engaging the patient in treatment
3. Completing a comprehensive suicide risk assessment
4. Developing a safety plan
5. Conveying a sense of hope
6. Developing a cognitive case conceptualization
7. Engaging in treatment planning

The first two components are part of standard CBT. The next three components should be standard components for most treatments for suicidal patients, regardless of theoretic orientation. The guidelines described previously for conducting comprehensive risk assessments and safety planning should be followed with an additional emphasis on identifying the components of the older adult's suicidal schemas. Identifying the specific automatic thoughts, images, cognitive styles, moods, and behaviors that compose these schemas will enable more effective safety plans to be developed and will aid with the final two components of the early phase of treatment—the cognitive case conceptualization of the patient's suicide risk and treatment planning.

The cognitive case conceptualization of the older adult's suicide risk serves as the impetus for treatment planning. It provides the foundation through which all cognitions, suicide-related emotions, behaviors, and physiological reactions can be explained through the cognitive theory. To develop accurate cognitive case conceptualizations of risk, a time line is developed of the older adult's most recent suicidal crisis. Information from the comprehensive suicide risk assessment is integrated with this time line to develop an understanding of what recently activated the older adult's suicidal schema and what would be likely to reactivate it in the future. Next, treatment goals and strategies to obtain these goals are collaboratively set. This concludes the early phase of treatment.

CASE EXAMPLE

Mr. W is a 64-year-old married non-Hispanic Black male with three adult children who was referred by his counselor because of increasing suicidal thoughts ideation. Consultation with this counselor revealed that Mr. W had been receiving intermittent supportive counseling twice monthly for the past 15 months for depression and posttraumatic stress disorder (PTSD) related to past combat trauma. He reportedly had been experiencing passive suicide ideation for the past 10 years. The frequency and intensity of his suicidal thoughts had been increasing since his retirement from the post office 15 months ago, and he began endorsing a suicide plan without intent (overdosing on his insulin medication) in the last month. Mr. W had denied a history of any suicide attempts or any inpatient psychiatric hospitalizations.

Mr. W was administered the Beck Hopelessness Scale (BHS), Beck Depression Inventory–Second Edition (BDI-II), and Scale for Suicidal Ideation (SSI) at intake and obtained scores of 19, 41, and 13, respectively, indicating high levels of hopelessness, depression severity, and suicide ideation. He reported that he was currently taking an antidepressant as prescribed for depression by his psychiatrist. When asked about his most recent suicidal crisis, Mr. W described that he had an argument with his wife 2 days prior after she was critical of him for leaving a clothes hanger on the floor. He stayed in his bedroom alone for several hours after the argument, during which time he reportedly began feeling worthless and having the thoughts *I'm not doing anything in my life* and *I'm better off dead*. Mr. W clarified that such a suicidal crisis occurred 2 to 3 times weekly.

Further assessment revealed that the following maladaptive cycle triggered each of Mr. W's suicidal crises: he perceives criticism from others and loses his temper → he experiences feelings of guilt and depression → he isolates himself and neglects household responsibilities → he becomes more self-critical. As this pattern repeats, Mr. W begins to feel worthless and hopeless, which subsequently triggers suicidal thoughts. Mr. W's risk assessment revealed additional suicide risk factors including multiple medical conditions (diabetes, anemia, and emphysema), low perceived social support, insomnia, problem-solving deficits, feelings of loneliness and of being a burden to his family, and a lack of a sense of belonging. His protective factors against suicide included his strong religious beliefs, perceived responsibility for helping to raise one of his grandchildren, and having access to local medical and mental health services in his community.

To obtain a collateral understanding of his functioning, Mr. W's wife was consulted with his consent. Contrary to his self-report, she indicated that Mr. W had made a serious suicide attempt 2 years ago (overdosed on insulin). She expressed significant concern that he might make another attempt. She described that he was extremely inactive and depressed, no longer went to church, refused to socialize with others, often had angry outbursts, and spent most of his days alone in his bedroom.

Mr. W was determined to be at *moderate* risk for suicide but appropriate for outpatient CBT for suicide. The following safety plan was set up with Mr. W: (a) warning signs included thoughts such as *I'm better off dead* and *I'm not doing anything in my life* and feelings of worthlessness and hopelessness; (b) coping strategies included doing household chores, reading the newspaper, and staying out of his bedroom; (c) nonprofessional contacts he agreed to call for support were his wife or his friend Joe (for small talk); (d) professional contacts he agreed to contact for support were his CBT therapist via pager or the National Suicide Prevention Crisis Hotline. Mr. W agreed to keep a copy of this safety plan in his wallet. After establishing a safety plan, treatment planning was conducted. Mr. W identified his treatment goals as regaining ambition for life, learning to manage his temper, having more positive thoughts, and feeling more useful.

Intermediate Phase of Treatment

Clinicians must continue to assess suicide risk and treatment compliance throughout all phases of treatment. Safety plans should be reviewed during each session and revised frequently as new risk factors are identified and new coping skills are learned. During the intermediate phase of treatment, the primary focus is teaching suicidal older adults behavioral, affective, and cognitive coping strategies to deactivate suicidal schemas. Behavioral strategies include increasing pleasurable activities, improving social resources, and increasing compliance with other services. Affective coping skills include physical self-soothing, cognitive self-soothing, and sensory self-soothing. Cognitive strategies include modifying core beliefs, identifying reasons for living, developing coping cards, enhancing problem-solving skills, and reducing impulsivity. Detailed explanations of the strategies frequently used in the intermediate phase of treatment have been described by Wenzel et al. (2009).

> Mr. W's compliance with therapy appointments was initially problematic because of reported fatigue. Over multiple sessions, he was taught ways to improve his sleep hygiene and to cope more effectively with his trauma-related nightmares. Additionally, thought-challenging techniques helped him realize that he became more lethargic after missing appointments but more energized when after attending them. Gradually, his compliance with therapy appointments improved. To increase his positive thoughts and to combat feelings of uselessness, daily activity scheduling was used throughout treatment. As Mr. W began scheduling daily chores and pleasant activities, he slowly increased his contributions around the house (e.g., sweeping property, watering lawn, doing dishes) and to the care of his 8-year-old grandson (walking him to and from school, helping out with homework, etc.). Subsequently, he felt more useful and less guilty about scheduling pleasant activities such as going to his grandson's baseball games and attending regular church services.
>
> Mr. W's tendency for ruminative self-criticism, particularly in response to losing his temper with his wife, was also problematic. Assertiveness training was used to help him communicate his feelings more effectively to his wife, particularly in response to criticism he perceived from her. Mr. W's wife attended one session with him so that he could practice these skills in session. An additional treatment focus was to help Mr. W challenge the accuracy of his internal self-criticism. As he gradually became more proficient in doing so, he realized that he often lacked evidence to support his self-criticism.

A review of Mr. W's work history revealed that he was proud of his hard work and ability to solve daily problems on the job. He learned to identify similarities between the skills and strategies he used to succeed professionally and those he could use to address his current problems. Mr. W gradually began facilitating a more active problem-solving approach in his daily life, and consequently, he ultimately started to experience a resulting sense of empowerment and hope about his future.

Later Phase of Treatment

As indicated, regular assessments of suicide risk and revisions to safety plans are continued in the later phase of treatment. The primary tasks in the later phase of treatment are reviewing and consolidating skills, developing and practicing a relapse prevention protocol, reviewing progress toward treatment goals, and engaging in additional treatment planning. To promote the consolidation of skills, the following relapse prevention protocol is conducted. Clinicians help older adults recreate a past suicidal crisis in vivo during the session to prime as many thoughts, images, and feelings associated with this prior suicidal crisis. Older adults are asked to describe the newly acquired skills that they would now use to stay safe and to defuse this suicidal crisis. After successfully accomplishing this and in a subsequent session, older adults are asked to imagine a future suicidal crisis that could occur in the same manner. Again, they are asked to describe the skills that they would use to stay safe and to defuse this suicidal crisis. Older adults are debriefed after each guided imagery relapse prevention exercise.

Subsequently, the older adult's progress toward treatment goals is reviewed and additional treatment planning is conducted. If clinical judgment indicates that the older adult's suicidal schema has been deactivated and the older adult is no longer experiencing suicide ideation, treatment is terminated after a treatment referral has been made for any remaining problems that are causing the patient distress. However, if the older adult continues to endorse suicide ideation at this point, the necessary components of the two earlier phases of treatment are repeated (evaluating the accuracy of the case conceptualization, revising safety plans, teaching additional coping skills, etc.) until this ideation remits.

After Mr. W began using several of the skills he learned in the intermediate phase of treatment and he became more hopeful about his future, his intake scores of the BHS (19), BDI-II (41), and SSI (13) decreased to a 2, 8, and 0, respectively, indicating minimal hopelessness and depression, and no current suicide ideation. As his suicide ideation had remitted, the relapse prevention protocol was conducted.

Two imaginal exposure exercises were conducted. First, Mr. W was asked to imagine the events that led up to his most serious suicidal crisis—his suicide attempt 2 years ago. Second, he was asked to imagine events that could potentially lead to a future suicidal crisis. In both instances, Mr. W described the new skills and strategies that he would now use to successfully resolve the suicidal crisis (cognitive restructuring to combat self-criticism, distraction through household chores, expressing his emotions to his wife, etc.). After successfully completing each in vivo exposure, Mr. W's safety plan was adjusted to reflect his new approach to resolving suicidal crises. Next, his progress toward his treatment goals was reviewed and additional treatment goals were discussed. At the conclusion of treatment, Mr. W was referred to a local mental health clinic for weekly outpatient therapy for PTSD and depression because he was not satisfied with the intermittent counseling sessions he had been receiving.

CONCLUSION

Older adults have a higher risk for suicide than any other age group in most countries throughout the world. Research has identified numerous risk factors and protective factors for late-life suicide, and comprehensive guidelines for assessing suicide risk in older adults are now available. There continues to be a paucity of research supporting the effectiveness of treatments for preventing suicide. One treatment that appears promising is the innovative CBT protocol for suicidal older adults (Wenzel et al., 2009) that was described in this chapter.

REFERENCES

American Psychological Association. (2003). *Practice guideline for the assessment and treatment of patients with suicidal behaviors.* Washington, DC: Author.

Anderson, P. L., Tiro, J. A., Price, A. W., Bender, M. A., & Kaslow, N. J. (2002). Additive impact of childhood emotional, physical, and sexual abuse on suicide attempts among low-income African American women. *Suicide & Life-Threatening Behavior, 32*(2), 131–138.

Areán, P. A., & Feliciano, L. (2008). Older adults. In M. Whisman (Ed.), *Adapting cognitive therapy for depression* (pp. 417–438). New York, NY: Guildford Press.

Ayalon, L., Mackin, S., Arean, P. A., Chen, H., & McDonel Herr, E. C. (2007). The role of cognitive functioning and distress in suicidal ideation in older adults. *Journal of the American Geriatrics Society, 55*(7), 1090–1094.

Beautrais, A. L. (2001). Suicides and serious suicide attempts: Two populations or one. *Psychological Medicine, 31*, 837–845.

Beautrais, A. L., Joyce, P. R., Mulder, R. T., Fergusson, D. M., Deavoll, B. J., & Nightingale, S. K. (1996). Prevalence and comorbidity of mental disorders in persons making serious suicide attempts: A case-control study. *American Journal of Psychiatry, 153*, 1009–1014.

Beck, A. T., Kovacs, M., & Weissman, A. (1975). Hopelessness and suicidal behavior: An overview. *Journal of the American Medical Association, 234*(11), 1146–1149.

Beck, A. T., Kovacs, M., & Weissman, A. (1979). Assessment of suicidal intention: The Scale for Suicide Ideation. *Journal of Consulting and Clinical Psychology, 47*(2), 343–352.

Beck, A. T., Rush, A. J., Shaw, B. F., & Emery, G. (1979). *Cognitive therapy of depression.* New York, NY: Guilford Press.

Beck, A. T., & Steer, R. A. (1993). *Manual for the Beck Hopelessness Scale.* San Antonio, TX: The Psychological Corporation.

Beck, A. T., Steer, R. A., & Brown, G. K. (1996). *The Beck Depression Inventory–Second Edition.* San Antonio, TX: The Psychological Corporation.

Beck, A. T., Steer, R. A., Kovacs, M., & Garrison, B. (1985). Hopelessness and eventual suicide: A 10-year prospective study of patients hospitalized with uicidal ideation. *American Journal of Psychiatry, 142*, 559–563.

Bertolote, J. M., Fleischmann, A., De Leo, D., & Wasserman, D. (2003). Suicide and mental disorders: Do we know enough? *British Journal of Psychiatry, 183*, 382–383.

Bongar, B. (2002). *The suicidal patient: Clinical and legal standards of care* (2nd ed.). Washington, DC: American Psychological Association.

Bostwick, J. M., & Pankratz, V. S. (2000). Affective disorders and suicide risk: A reexamination. *American Journal of Psychiatry, 157*, 1925–1932.

Britton, P. C., Duberstein, P. R., Conner, K. R., Heisel, M., Hirsch, J. K., & Conwell, Y. (2008). Reasons for living, hopelessness, and suicide ideation among depressed adults 50 years or older. *American Journal of Geriatric Psychiatry, 16*, 736–741.

Brown, G. K., Beck, A. T., Steer, R. A., & Grisham, J. R. (2000). Risk factors for suicide in psychiatric outpatients: A 20-year prospective study. *Journal of Consulting and Clinical Psychology, 68*(3), 371–377.

Brown, G. K., Brown, L., Bhar, S., & Beck, A. T. (2008). Cognitive therapy for suicidal older adults. In D. Gallagher-Thompson, A. Steffen, & L. Thompson (Eds.), *Handbook of behavioral and cognitive therapies with older adults* (pp. 135–170). New York, NY: Springer.

Brown, G. K., Bruce, M. L., & Pearson, J. L. (2001). High-risk management guidelines for elderly suicidal patients in primary care settings. *International Journal of Geriatric Psychiatry, 16*, 593–601.

Brown, G. K., Steer, R. A., Henriques, G. R., & Beck, A. T. (2005). The internal struggle between the wish to die and the wish to live: A risk factor for suicide. *Journal of Consulting and Clinical Psychology, 162*, 1977–1979.

Brown, G. K., Ten Have, T., Henriques, G. R., Xie, S. X., Hollander, J. E., & Beck, A. T. (2005). Cognitive therapy for the prevention of suicide attempts: A randomized controlled trial. *Journal of the American Medical Association, 294*, 563–570.

Bruce, M. L., Ten Have, T. R., Reynolds, C. F., III, Katz, I. I., Schulberg, H. C., Mulsant, B. H., et al. (2004). Reducing suicidal ideation and depressive symptoms in depressed older primary care patients: A randomized controlled trial. *Journal of the American Medical Association, 291*, 1081–1091.

Busch, K. A., Fawcett, J., & Jacobs, D. G. (2003). Clinical correlates of inpatient suicide. *Journal of Clinical Psychiatry, 64*, 14–19.

Centers for Disease Control and Prevention. (2010). *Web-Based Injury Statistics Query and Reporting System (WISQARS)*. Centers for Disease Control and Prevention, National Center for Injury and Prevention Control. Retrieved January 24, 2010, from http://www.cdc.gov/ncicp/wisqars

Chan, J., Draper, B., & Banerjee, S. (2007). Deliberate self-harm in older adults: A review of the literature from 1995 to 2004. *International Journal of Geriatric Psychiatry, 22,* 720–732.

Cheng, A. T. A., Chen, T. H. H., Chen, C-C., & Jenkins, R. (2000). Psychosocial and psychiatric risk factors for suicide: Case-control psychological autopsy study. *British Journal of Psychiatry, 177,* 360–365.

Conwell, Y., & Brent, D. (1995). Suicide and aging I: Patterns of psychiatric diagnosis. *International Psychogeriatrics, 7,* 149–164.

Conwell, Y., Dubertstein, P. R., & Caine, E. D. (2002). Risk factors for suicide in later life. *Biological Psychiatry, 52,* 193–204.

Conwell, Y., Duberstein, P. R., Cox, C., Herrmann, J. H., Forbes, N. T., & Caine, E. D. (1998). Age differences in behaviors leading to completed suicide. *American Journal of Geriatric Psychiatry, 6,* 122–126.

Conwell, Y., & Thompson, C. (2008). Suicidal behavior in elders. *Psychiatric Clinics of North America, 31,* 333–356.

Cukrowicz, K. C., Duberstein, P. R., Vannoy, S. D., Lynch, T. R., McQuoid, D. R., & Steffens, D. C. (2009). Course of suicide ideation and predictors of change in depressed older adults. *Journal of Affective Disorders, 113,* 30–36.

De Leo, D., Padoani, W., Scocco, P., Lie, D., Bille-Brahe, U., Arensman, E., et al. (2001). Attempted and completed suicide in older subjects: Results from the WHO/EURO multicentre study of suicidal behaviour. *International Journal of Geriatric Psychiatry, 16,* 300–310.

Dixon, W. A., Heppner, P. P., & Anderson, W. P. (1991). Problem-solving appraisal, stress, hopelessness, and suicide ideation in a college population. *Journal of Counseling Psychology, 38*(1), 51–56.

Dombrovski, A. Y., Szanto, K., & Reynolds, C. F. (2005). Epidemiology and risk factors for suicide in the elderly: 10-year update. *Aging Health, 1,* 135–145.

Druss, B., & Pincus, H. (2000). Suicidal ideation and suicide attempts in general medical illnesses. *Archives of Internal Medicine, 160,* 1522–1526.

Duberstein, P. R., Conwell, Y., Seidlitz, L., Denning, D. G., Cox, C., & Caine, E. D. (2000). Personality traits and suicidal behavior and ideation in depressed inpatients 50 years of age and older. *Journals of Gerontology Series B: Psychological Sciences & Social Sciences, 55,* P18–P26.

Fawcett, J., Scheftner, W. A., Fogg, L., Clark, D. C., Young, M. A., Hedeker, D., et al. (1990). Time-related predictors of suicide in major affective disorder. *American Journal of Psychiatry, 147,* 1189–1194.

First, M. B., Spitzer, R. L, Gibbon, M., & Williams, J. B. W. (1995). *Structured clinical interview for DSM-IV. Axis I disorder with psychotic screen.* New York, NY: Biometric Research Unit, New York Psychiatric Institute.

Fiske, A., Wetherell, J. L., & Gatz, M. (2009). Depression in older adults. *Annual Review of Clinical Psychology, 5,* 363–389.

Gallagher-Thompson, D., Steffen, A. M., & Thompson, L. W. (2008). *Handbook of behavioral and cognitive therapies with older adults.* New York, NY: Springer.

Gallagher-Thompson, & Thompson, L. W. (2010). *Treating late-life depression: A cognitive-behavioral therapy approach.* New York, NY: Oxford University Press.

Goldsmith, S. K., Pellman, T. C., Kleinman, A. M., & Bunney, W. E. (2002). *Reducing suicide: A national imperative*. Washington, DC: National Academy Press.

Hall, R. C. W., Platt, D. E., & Hall, R. C. W. (1999). Suicide risk assessment: A review of risk factors for suicide in 100 patients who made severe suicide attempts. *Psychosomatics, 40*, 18–27.

Hamilton, M. (1960). A rating scale for depression. *Journal of Neurology and Neurosurgical Psychiatry, 23*, 56–61.

Harriss, L., & Hawton, K. (2005). Suicidal intent in deliberate self-harm and the risk of suicide: The predictive power of the Suicide Intent Scale. *Journal of Affective Disorders, 86*(2–3), 225–233.

Harriss, L., Hawton, K., & Zahl, D. (2005). The value of measuring suicidal intent in the assessment of deliberate self-harm patients. *British Journal of Psychiatry, 186*, 60–66.

Haw, C., Harwood, D., & Hawton, K. (2009). Dementia and suicidal behavior: A review of the literature. *International Psychogeriatrics, 21*(3), 440–453.

Hawton, K., & Harriss, L. (2006). Deliberate self-harm in people aged 60 years and over: Characteristics and outcome of a 20-year cohort. *International Journal of Geriatric Psychiatry, 21*, 572–581.

Heikkinen, M. E., Isometsa, E. T., Marttunen, M. J., Aro, H. M., & Lönnqvist, J. K. (1995). Social factors in suicide. *British Journal of Psychiatry, 167*, 747–753.

Heikkinen, M. E., & Lönnqvist, J. K. (1995). Recent life events in elderly suicide: A nationwide study in Finland. *International Psychogeriatrics, 7*, 287–300.

Heisel, M. J., Duberstein, P. R., Talbot, N. L., King, D. A., & Tu, X. M. (2009). Adapting interpersonal psychotherapy for older adults at risk for suicide: Preliminary findings. *Professional Psychology: Research and Practice, 40*(2), 156–164.

Hobbs, M., & McLaren, S. (2009). The interrelations of agency, depression, and suicidal ideation among older adults. *Suicide and Life-Threatening Behavior, 39*(2), 161–171.

Joiner, T. E. (2005). *Why people die by suicide*. Cambridge, MA: Harvard University Press.

Joiner, T. E., Pettit, J. W., Walker, R. L., Voelz, Z. R., Cruz, J., & Rudd, M. D. (2002). Perceived burdensomeness and suicidality: Two studies on the suicide notes of those attempting and those completing suicide. *Journal of Social and Clinical Psychology, 21*, 531–545.

Joiner, T. E., Sachs-Ericsson, N. J., Wingate, L. R., Brown, J. S., Anestis, M. D., Selby, E. A. (2007). Childhood physical and sexual abuse and lifetime number of suicide attempts: A persistent and theoretically important relationship. *Behaviour Research and Therapy, 45*(3), 539–547.

King, D. A., Conwell, Y., Cox, C., Henderson, R. E., Denning, D. G., & Caine, E. D. (2000). A neuropsychological comparison of depressed suicide attempters and nonattempters. *Journal of Neuropsychiatry and Clinical Neurosciences, 12*(1), 64–70.

Kleespies, P. M. (2009). Behavioral emergencies: An evidence-based resource for evaluating and managing risk of suicide, violence, and victimization. Washington, DC: American Psychological Association.

Kposowa, A. J. (2000). Marital status and suicide in the National Longitudinal Mortality Study. *Journal of Epidemiology and Community Health, 54*(4), 254–261.

Krupinski, M., Fischer, A., Grohmann, R., Engel, R., Hollweg, M., & Möller, H. J. (1998). Risk factors for suicides of inpatients with depressive psychoses. *European Archives of Psychiatry and Clinical Neuroscience, 248*(3), 141–147.

Kung, H-S, Hoyert, D. L., Xu, J., & Murphy, S. L. (2008). *Deaths: Final data for 2005.* National Vital Statistics Reports. Vol. 56 (10). Hyattsville, MD: National Center for Health Statistics. Retrieved from http://www.cdc.gov/nchs/data/nvsr/nvsr56/nvsr56_10.pdf

Kuo, W., Gallo, J. J., & Tien, A. Y. (2001). Incidence of suicide ideation and attempts in adults: The 13-year follow-up of a community sample in Baltimore, Maryland. *Psychological Medicine, 31,* 1181–1191.

Levenson, J. L., & Bostwisk, J. M. (2005). Suicidality in the medically ill. *Primary Psychiatry, 12*(3), 16–18.

Luoma, J. B., Martin, C. E., & Pearson, J. L. (2002). Contact with mental health and primary care providers before suicide: A review of the evidence. *American Journal of Psychiatry, 159,* 909–916.

Mann, J. J., Waternaux, C., Haasm, G. L., & Malone, K. M. (1999). Toward a clinical model of suicidal behavior in psychiatric patients. *American Journal of Psychiatry, 156,* 181–189.

McLaren, S., Gomez, R., Bailey, M., & Van Der Horst, R. K. (2007). The association of depression and sense of belonging with suicidal ideation among older adults: Applicability of resiliency models. *Suicide and Life-Threatening Behavior, 37*(1), 89–102.

McMillan, D., Gilbody, S., Beresford, E., & Neilly, L. (2007). Can we predict suicide and non-fatal self-harm with the Beck Hopelessness Scale? A meta-analysis. *Psychological Medicine, 37,* 769–778.

Moscicki, E. K. (2001). Epidemiology of completed and attempted suicide: Toward a framework for prevention. *Clinical Neuroscience Research, 1,* 310–323.

Oquendo, M. A., Harkavy, F. J., Grunebaum, M. F., Burke, A., Silver, J. M., & Mann, J. J. (2004). Suicidal behavior and mild traumatic brain injury in major depression. *Journal of Nervous and Mental Disease, 192*(6), 430–434.

Priester, M. J., & Clum, G. A. (1993). The problem-solving diathesis in depression, hopelessness, and suicide ideation: A longitudinal analysis. *Journal of Psychopathology and Behavioral Assessment, 15*(3), 239–255.

Prigerson, H. G., Maciejewski, P. K., Reynolds, C. F., Bierhals, A. J., Newsom, J. T., Fasiczka, A., et al. (1995). Inventory of complicated grief: A scale to measure maladaptive symptoms of loss. *Psychiatry Research, 59*(1–2), 65–79.

Raue, P. J., Alexopoulos, G. S., Bruce, M. L., Klimstra, S., Mulsant, B. H., & Gallo, J. J. (2001). The systematic assessment of depressed elderly primary care patients. *International Journal of Psychiatry, 16*(6), 560–569.

Rifai, A. H., George, C. J., Stack, J. A., Mann, J. J., & Reynolds, C. F. (1994). Hopelessness continues to distinguish suicide attempters after acute treatment of major depression in later-life. *American Journal of Psychiatry, 151,* 1687–1690.

Ross, R. K., Bernstein, L., Trent, L., Henderson, B. E., & Paganini-Hill, A. (1990). A prospective study of risk factors for traumatic deaths in the retirement community. *Preventive Medicine, 19,* 323–334.

Rowe, J. L., Conwell, Y., Schulberg, H. C., & Bruce, M. L. (2006). Social support and suicidal ideation in older adults using home healthcare services. *American Journal of Geriatric Psychiatry, 14,* 758–766.

Roy, A. (1998). Suicide. In H. I. Kaplan & B. J. Sadock (Eds.), *Synopsis of psychiatry* (8th ed., pp. 867–872). Baltimore, MD: Lippincott Williams & Wilkins.

Rudd, M. D., Joiner, T., & Rajab, M. H. (2001). *Treating suicidal behavior: An effective, time-limited approach.* New York, NY: Guilford Press.

Rudd, M. D., Rajab, M. H., & Dahm, P. F. (1994). Problem-solving appraisal in suicide ideators and attempters. *American Journal of Orthopsychiatry, 64*(1), 136–149.

Shah, A. K., & MacKenzie, S. (2007). Disorders of ageing across cultures. In D. Bhugra & K. Bhui (Eds.), *Textbook of cultural psychiatry* (pp. 323–344). Cambridge, United Kingdom: Cambridge University Press.

Simon, R. I. (1988). *Concise guide to clinical psychiatry and the law.* Washington, DC: American Psychiatric Press.

Slaby, A. E. (1998). Outpatient management of suicidal patients. In B. Bongar, A. L. Berman, R. W. Maris, M. M. Silverman, E. A. Harris, & W. L. Packman (Eds.), *Risk management with suicidal patients* (pp. 34–64). New York, NY: Guilford Press.

Stanley, B., & Brown, G. K. (2010). *Safety planning: A brief intervention to mitigate suicide risk.* Manuscript submitted for publication.

Stroebe, M., Stroebe, W., & Abakoumkin, G. (2005). The broken heart: Suicidal ideation in bereavement. *American Journal of Psychiatry, 162*(11), 2178–2180.

Szanto, K., Prigerson, H. G., Houck, P. R., & Reynolds, C. F. (1997). Suicidal ideation in elderly bereaved: The role of complicated grief. *Suicide and Life Threatening Behavior, 27*, 194–207.

Szanto, K., Shear, M. K., Houck, P. R., Reynolds, C. F., Frank, E., Caroff, K., et al. (2006). Indirect self-destructive behavior and overt suicidality in patients with complicated grief. *Journal of Clinical Psychiatry, 67*, 233–239.

Trout, D. L. (1980). The role of social isolation in suicide. *Suicide and Life-Threatening Behavior, 10*(1), 10–23.

Uncapher, H., Gallagher-Thompson, D., Osgood, N. J., & Bonger, B. (1998). Hopelessness and suicide ideation in older adults. *Gerontologist, 38*, 62–70.

Unützer, J., Tang, L. Q., Oishi, S., Katon, W., Williams, J. W., Hunkeler, E., et al. (2006). Reducing suicidal ideation in depressed older primary care patients. *Journal of the American Geriatrics Society, 54*, 1550–1556.

Waern, M., Beskow, J., Runeson, B., & Skoog, I. (1999). Suicidal feelings in the last year of life in elderly people who commit suicide. *Lancet, 354*, 917–918.

Waern, M., Rubenowitz, E., & Wilhelmson, K. (2003). Predictors of suicide in the old elderly. *Gerontology, 49*, 328–334.

Wenzel, A., Brown, G. K., & Beck, A. T. (2009). Cognitive therapy for suicidal older adults. In *Cognitive therapy for suicidal patients: Scientific and clinical applications.* Washington, DC: American Psychological Association.

World Health Organization. (2010). *Mental health: Suicide prevention.* World Health Organization Web site. Retrieved January 23, 2010, from http://www.who.int/mental_health/prevention/suicide/suicideprevent/en/index.html

ADDITIONAL RESOURCES

Detailed instructions for developing safety plans with older adults and for using the previously mentioned CBT protocol with suicidal older adults are provided in the books *Handbook of Behavioral and Cognitive Therapies with Older Adults* (Gallagher-Thompson, Steffen, & Thompson, 2008) and *Cognitive Therapy for Suicidal Patients* (Wenzel et al., 2009). Brown et al. (2001) has published templates that health professionals can use to determine whether imminent risk is present in suicidal patients.

APPENDIX

Pocket Card Summarizing Information That Can Be Useful for Health Professionals When Conducting Suicide Risk Assessments With Older Adults in Outpatient Settings

Steps for Conducting Suicide Risk Assessments[1]
1. Assess current clinical status.
2. Assess suicide-relevant variables.
3. Assess recent activating events.
4. Assess mental and medical treatment histories.
5. Assess protective factors.
6. Identify risk factors modifiable with treatment.
7. Determine the most appropriate level of care needed to maintain safety.

Necessary Components Included in Safety Plans With Older Adults[2]
1. Warning signs that precede the suicidal crisis
2. Coping strategies that can be used without contacting another person
3. List of friends or family members that can be contacted for social support
4. List of mental health professionals or agencies that can be contacted

Tips for Developing Rapport With Older Adults During Suicide Risk Assessments (RAs)
1. Assess for presence of any hearing or comprehension problems.
2. Explain that questions asked may be stressful.
3. Convey that RAs are part of standard care.
4. Explain the benefits of the RA.
a. Promotes patient's safety
b. Aids with treatment planning
5. Assess ability and motivation to disclose accurate information.
a. Ascertain the referral source
6. Obtain collateral information about the patient's functioning.
a. Consult with doctors, family, friends, caretakers, etc.
7. Proceed from more general questions about mood, functioning and future outlook to more focused questions about suicidal thoughts and behaviors.
8. Assess medical and mental health treatment histories.
a. Level of satisfaction with past treatment?
9. For more resistant patients, spend more time up-front empathically listening to and validating concerns.

Sources: [1]Kleespies, 2009; Rudd et al., 2001; Wenzel et al., 2009.
[2]Stanley and Brown, 2010

5

Cognitive Behavioral Therapy for Late-Life Depression and Comorbid Psychiatric Conditions

Natalie D. Dautovich and Amber M. Gum

Older adults rarely experience one mental disorder without additional mental or substance-related disorders or at least subthreshold symptoms. Unfortunately, little research has studied cognitive behavioral therapy (CBT) for comorbid conditions, and no CBT manuals have been deemed "evidence-based" for specific comorbidities. Of the existing research, most has focused on older adults with depressive disorders and comorbid conditions, including anxiety, sleep, personality, or alcohol or other substance disorder. In general, these comorbidities tend to result in poorer prognosis and treatment response to CBT when compared to depression alone.

For four categories of comorbid conditions (anxiety, sleep, personality, alcohol/substance misuse), we review the available evidence regarding prevalence and assessment, treatment course, and then we discuss clinical implications for using CBT. Please see other chapters in this volume for discussion of assessment and CBT approaches for individual disorders.

ANXIETY DISORDERS

Prevalence and Assessment

According to the most recent study using nationally representative data in the United States (King-Kallimanis, Gum, & Kohn, 2009), the comorbidity of depressive and anxiety disorders in older adults is high. Of adults aged 65 and older diagnosed with major depressive disorder (MDD), the most common comorbid anxiety disorders were social phobia (25.0%), specific phobia (16.7%), panic disorder (12.3%), and generalized anxiety disorder (GAD; 11.8%). GAD comorbidity dramatically increased to 24.1% when the exclusion criterion that GAD does not occur exclusively during a major depressive episode was removed, indicating that many depressed older adults have concurrent GAD-like symptoms. For adults of all ages with MDD or dysthymia, risk factors for a comorbid anxiety disorder were lower education, being not married, and having one or more disabilities. Older adults were not more or less likely to have a comorbid anxiety disorder compared to younger adults. Among the older adults with both lifetime depressive and anxiety disorders, the anxiety disorder most often preceded the depressive disorder (77.6%).

In addition to assessing comorbid anxiety disorders, it is important to assess depressive and anxiety symptoms using scales of symptom severity, given the high rate of subthreshold symptoms comorbid with the other type of disorder. In a national epidemiological study in England and Wales, for older adults with a depressive disorder, 17.1% had an anxiety disorder but an additional 60.1% had subthreshold anxiety symptoms. Likewise, of those with an anxiety disorder, 65.6% had a depressive disorder and an additional 30% had subthreshold depressive symptoms (Kvaal et al., 2008).

Such high rates of comorbidity, particularly for subthreshold symptoms, have led to questions regarding the distinction between depressive and anxiety disorders. Although there is significant overlap in symptom presentation and risk factors, the current perspective is that these remain distinct categories of psychopathology, supported by empirical research using factor analysis (Cook, Orvaschel, Simco, Hersen, & Joiner, 2004; Teachman, Siedlecki, & Magee, 2007; Watson, 2005; Wetherell, Gatz, & Pedersen, 2001). Moreover, the onset of depression, anxiety, or mixed anxiety and depression appear to have distinct risk factors. For example, in one prospective 9-year study, widowhood was the strongest risk factor for depression, other recent life events for anxiety, and several risk factors overlapped for mixed depression and anxiety (Vink et al., 2009). Comorbidity is also associated with greater severity of symptoms, disability, and suicide risk (Cassidy, Lauderdale, & Sheikh, 2005).

Course

As we have summarized elsewhere (Gum & Cheavens, 2008), the current research on CBT for late-life depressive or anxiety disorders suggests the following two patterns:

1. In treating one disorder, the other type of symptom improves on average; and

2. Participants with comorbidity at the beginning of treatment seem to improve more slowly or retain more residual symptoms at the end of a standard trial of CBT, compared to those with only one disorder.

For example, in a recent randomized clinical trial (RCT) of CBT for late-life GAD in primary care compared to enhanced usual care, Stanley et al. (2009) reported improvements in worry severity, depressive symptoms, and general mental health. The CBT protocol used was comprehensive, including relaxation, cognitive restructuring, exposure, problem-solving skills training, and behavioral sleep management. On the other hand, in a small RCT of clinical case management or group CBT for low-income depressed older adults, we reported that those with comorbid anxiety remained more severely depressed at the end of treatment with similar patterns across treatment groups (Gum, Areán, & Bostrom, 2007). Furthermore, effects for comorbid symptoms may differ according to the specific CBT protocol used and the patient population; for example, a recent study of problem-solving therapy (PST) delivered in-home for frail older adults with subthreshold depression and cardiovascular disease demonstrated improvements in depressive symptoms but not anxiety (Gellis & Bruce, 2010).

In summary, comorbidity appears to complicate CBT treatment for late-life depression, although research has yet to explicate the effects for specific anxiety disorders, CBT protocols, or older adult populations. The best approach according to current evidence is the application of existing evidence-based CBT protocols for late-life depression or anxiety disorders. Questions regarding treatment strategy then center on issues such as whether to focus on one type of disorder or both, and sequencing of the focus (e.g., treat the depression or anxiety first?).

Treatment Considerations

Collaborative treatment planning, psychoeducation, and ongoing treatment monitoring are particularly critical for older adults with comorbid depression and anxiety. In general, we would recommend that the clinician educate the client about the CBT model and its relation to both depressive and anxiety symptoms, and then develop an individualized treatment plan. How does the client perceive the depressive and anxiety symptoms to be related? Does one contribute to the other? Are there behavior patterns, personality characteristics, health behaviors, or common thinking patterns that contribute to both? For example, we have worked with clients who have developed social anxiety related to certain health conditions (e.g., hearing impairment, incontinence), which then contributes to withdrawal from social activities, leading to loneliness and depression. Addressing the social anxiety and isolation in relation to the health condition (e.g., problem-solving strategies for minimizing risk of odor or soiling due to incontinence, improving communication strategies to accommodate hearing loss) and unhelpful thinking patterns related to the health condition can lead to increased socialization, thereby reducing depression. When working with clients experiencing comorbid depression and anxiety, the clinician should educate the client that treatment might take longer and that the clinician will reevaluate progress intermittently to determine which symptoms are improving and which symptoms should remain a focus of treatment. This education may help the client have realistic treatment expectations and not become discouraged if treatment progress is slow.

The same stressor can contribute to both symptoms of depression and anxiety, such as loss of a loved one or medical illness, and addressing unhelpful thinking patterns or problem-solving styles regarding this stressor may alleviate both types of symptoms simultaneously. For example, an older depressed woman had experienced the death of a male romantic partner of about a year approximately 6 months prior to beginning therapy. She was not just saddened by his death but also distressed by comments made by other women at a senior center (e.g., "It's so sad that [name] died, how are you dealing with it?"). She also had social anxiety symptoms (but did not meet criteria for social anxiety disorder), particularly with regard to confrontation and conflict. Therefore, she had begun to avoid the senior center, which worsened her depression and sense of loneliness. The client prioritized the problem of the women's comments at the senior center, and we applied the following strategies from PST (D'Zurilla & Nezu, 2004): defining the problem and her thoughts about it, brainstorming solutions, and developing and then implementing a plan of action. The client developed a specific plan to confront the women (i.e., when she would go to the senior center next, what she would say, to whom, and how she would respond to possible reactions they might have), and we role-played this conversation in session. She implemented the plan, and the women were very apologetic and understanding, stating that they were trying to be sympathetic. The client began attending the senior center more frequently again, and she continued to address other interpersonal problems by asserting herself, such as with her physician and adult children. Therefore, this intervention reduced her loneliness and depressed mood as well as anxiety regarding her social skills.

Although no studies have evaluated the optimal sequencing of treatment targets, it has recently been recommended that the clinician begin by focusing treatment on depressive symptoms first, and then attend to residual anxiety after depressive symptoms improve (Wetherell, 2010). This general treatment strategy was recommended for four reasons:

1. Reduce suicidal risk which is higher with depression;
2. Effect sizes of CBT for late-life depression are higher than for current approaches for anxiety (Wetherell, Lenze, & Stanley, 2005);
3. Improvements in depression may increase motivation to address anxiety; and
4. Some treatment strategies for anxiety are unpleasant and may be better tolerated if depressed mood has improved.

For example, increasing pleasant activities may quickly improve depressed mood, whereas increasing exposure behaviors may negatively impact anxiety as well as depressed mood, potentially even leading to treatment dropout. Once depressive symptoms improve, the clinician should reevaluate anxiety symptoms and apply CBT strategies appropriate to the residual anxiety symptoms and behaviors.

SLEEP DISORDERS

Prevalence and Assessment

Sleep disturbances increase with age and, consequently, can be an important issue to consider when treating older adults. In addition to being prevalent among older adults, sleep disturbances are commonly comorbid with psychiatric conditions such as depression. The prevalence of insomnia in older adults varies depending on the methodology used to assess the sleep disturbances. In a study of community-dwelling older adults, 57% reported some type of sleeping difficulty (Foley et al., 1995). Whereas various sleep disorders show an increased prevalence with age, insomnia is the most common (Mellinger, Balter, & Uhlenhuth, 1985). Within the general adult population, insomnia accompanied by daytime impairment (e.g., fatigue, irritability, or difficulties with attention or concentration) has been reported by 10% of the population (Ohayon, 2002). Prevalence rates increase with age and range from 30% to 60% when insomnia is identified without daytime impairment (Foley et al.; Mellinger et al.) and from 12% to 25% when both the insomnia complaint and daytime impairment are present (American Psychiatric Association [APA], 2000; Bliwise, King, Harris, & Haskell, 1992). Similar to rates among younger adults, the rates for insomnia are higher among older women than men (Ohayon).

Changes in the structure of sleep (known as sleep architecture) and the patterning of the sleep–wake response occur with age; these changes are important to understand for assessment and diagnosis of sleep disturbance comorbid with depression. A commonly held belief is that sleep becomes progressively worse with age. In fact, although there are age-related changes in sleep architecture, most changes in sleep are not due to age per se, but rather a result of various medical and psychiatric comorbidities that become increasingly prevalent with age (Ohayon, Carskadon, Guilleminault, & Vitiello, 2004). In addition, most of the changes in sleep patterns appear to occur during the younger to middle-aged years. In a meta-analytic study of sleep across the life span, the bulk of changes in sleep were found to occur between the ages of 19 and 60 with fewer changes seen after age 60. Changes that do occur with age (sometimes beginning as early as young adulthood) include an increasing amount of time spent in the lighter stages (1 and 2) of sleep (Ohayon et al.), more time spent awake (Ohayon et al.), and an advancing of the circadian rhythm (i.e., become sleepier earlier; Monk, 2005). Older adults may have lowered expectations for their sleep and assume that poor sleep is a natural consequence of aging. Therefore, it may fall to the clinician to initiate a conversation and assessment of sleep with older clients.

Multiple systems exist for diagnosing insomnia including the *Diagnostic and Statistical Manual of Mental Disorders Fourth Edition* (*DSM-IV*; APA, 2000), the *International Classification of Diseases* (World Health Organization [WHO], 2004), and the *International Classification of Sleep Disorders* (American Academy of Sleep Medicine [AASM], 2005). Despite the existence of multiple diagnostic systems, researchers have found that the current systems for diagnosing insomnia are not sufficient (Lichstein, Durrence, Taylor, Bush, & Riedel, 2003) and, as a result, have developed specific criteria requiring sleep onset latency (time to fall asleep) or wake time after sleep onset (time spent awake during the night) of (a) at least 31 minutes, (b) occurring at least 3 nights per week, and (c) occurring for at least 6 months. Lichstein et al. (2003) also recommended the use of specific cut-off points on questionnaires to assess for daytime impairment, such as the Epworth Sleepiness Scale (Johns, 1991), Insomnia Impact Scale (Hoelscher, Ware, & Bond, 1993), Fatigue Severity Scale (Krupp, LaRocca, Muir-Nash, & Steinberg, 1989), Beck Depression Inventory (Beck & Steer, 1996), and the Stait-Trait Anxiety Inventory (Spielberger, Gorsuch, Lushene, Vagg, & Jacobs, 1983).

Given the subjective nature of insomnia, the primary assessment tool is a sleep diary. A sleep diary is a daily self-report measurement that requires individuals to document specific information regarding their previous night's sleep (e.g., bedtime, number of minutes spent awake; see Table 5.1). Typically, clients complete the sleep diary over a 2-week period to provide an overview of their sleep. In addition to sleep

TABLE 5.1 Example of a Sleep Diary

	Example	Days						
	Tues 3/18/2010	1	2	3	4	5	6	7
Nap (yesterday)	80 minutes							
Bedtime (last night)	10:35							
Time to Fall Asleep	40 minutes							
Number of Times You Awoke	4 times							
Time Spent Awake (after first falling asleep)	85 minutes							
Final Wake-up Time	6:45							
Time You Got Out of Bed	7:15							
Quality Rating (1–5) 1 (very poor), 2 (poor), 3 (fair), 4 (good), 5 (excellent)	2							

Source: From "Psychological Treatment of Late-Life Insomnia" by K. L. Lichstein, B. W. Riedel, and M. K. Means, 1999, in R. Schulz, G. Maddox, and P. Lawton (Eds.), *Annual Review of Gerontology and Geriatrics: Vol. 18. Focus on Interventions Research with Older Adults.* (pp. 74–110). New York, NY: Springer Publishing Company.

diaries, the clinician would conduct a thorough clinical interview. The clinician manual by Perlis, Jungquist, Smith, and Posner (2005) provides a thorough overview of both the assessment and treatment of insomnia. In addition to collecting a medical and psychiatric history, the clinician would assess for other sleep disorders, pain, current health status, level of daytime sleepiness and fatigue, and evaluate the sleep environment (Perlis et al., 2005).

Although insomnia can exist as a primary disorder, it commonly co-occurs with psychiatric disorders about 40% of the time (Roth & Roehrs, 2003). Depression is the psychiatric condition most likely to co-occur with insomnia, with prevalence estimates for those diagnosed with insomnia experiencing comorbid depression as high as 61% (Ohayon & Roth, 2003). Historically, insomnia was viewed as a symptom of depression—a secondary disorder that would resolve once the depression was treated. More recently, insomnia has been recognized both as a disorder in its own right (e.g., diagnosis of primary insomnia) and, when co-occurring with other disorders, as "comorbid" rather than "secondary" to other disorders. In fact, in 2005, the National Institutes of Health (NIH) released a State-of-the-Science Conference statement urging the treatment of insomnia that occurs with other disorders (NIH, 2005). When assessing for insomnia comorbid with depression, it can be helpful to consider when the onset of the sleep disturbance occurs (e.g., with or shortly following the onset of depressed mood), and if the course of the insomnia remits and resurfaces in relation to the depressive episodes (Roth, 2009).

Course

The use of the "comorbid" terminology in place of "secondary" to describe insomnia that co-occurs with another disorder is necessary given the complexity of the relationship. It is often unclear if the depression plays a causal role, is a consequence of the insomnia, or whether the two disorders are comorbid, perhaps originating from a third independent cause. According to the *Diagnostic and Statistical Manual of Mental Disorders Fourth Edition Text Revision* (*DSM-IV-TR*), insomnia is considered comorbid with depression (identified as "insomnia related to another mental disorder") if (a) there is a temporal relationship between the two disorders (i.e., either the depression or insomnia precedes or follows the other disorder or they overlap), and (b) the insomnia disturbance is sufficiently severe to warrant separate clinical attention (APA, 2000).

Researchers have attempted to delineate the complex relationship between depression and insomnia. Research has shown that insomnia can *increase the risk for developing depression,* such that older adults with persistent insomnia are 1.8 to 3.5 times more likely to develop depression (Pigeon et al., 2008). Similarly, whereas a meta-analytic study found bereavement to be the strongest predictor of late-life depression (odds ratio [OR] = 3.3), sleep disturbance was the second strongest predictor (OR = 2.6; Cole & Dendukuri, 2003). Another study reported that insomnia symptoms worsened as older individuals with recurrent MDD experienced the onset of a new depressive episode (Perlis et al., 2006). Other research has demonstrated that the experience of *depression increases the risk for developing insomnia* (Morgan & Clarke, 1997) and best predicts sleep disturbance compared to health complaints, medication use, and level of functioning (Quan et al., 2005). Clients diagnosed with MDD by a physician were 2.6 times more likely to develop mild insomnia and 8.2 times as likely to develop severe insomnia (Katz & McHorney, 1998). Finally, the *presence of insomnia has been found to perpetuate depression.* Older individuals with persistent insomnia were 1.8 to 3.5 times more likely to remain depressed compared to clients without insomnia (Pigeon et al.). Untreated insomnia has also been associated with worse depressive symptoms (Buysse et al., 1999; Carney, Segal, Edinger, & Krystal, 2007) and increased risk for suicide (Ağargün, Kara, & Solmaz, 1997).

Although insomnia could initially develop in response to a depressive episode, it can become a chronic condition once the depression remits. According to the behavioral model of insomnia (or the 3P model) first presented by Spielman, Caruso, and Glovinsky (1987), insomnia can develop in response to both predisposing and precipitating factors and can be maintained because of perpetuating factors (Spielman, Caruso, et al.). Predisposing factors refer to biopsychosocial characteristics that could predispose an individual for developing insomnia (e.g., hyperarousal, tendency to ruminate). Precipitating factors are acute occurrences that interact with an individual's predisposing characteristics to produce transient difficulties in sleeping. For example, an individual could experience a significant loss, change in lifestyle, or another medical or psychiatric condition that disrupts his or her current sleeping patterns. Perpetuating factors involve the maladaptive strategies that individuals engage in when experiencing transient insomnia. For example, an individual may spend excessive time in bed, nap during the day, or drink alcohol before bed. Consequently, whereas insomnia may develop in response to another disorder (e.g., depression), insomnia can be perpetuated because of maladaptive behaviors and continue to require treatment in the absence of the comorbid illness. A case example will illustrate this point.

Treatment Considerations

Research has shown that CBT is effective for the treatment of insomnia in older adults (Irwin, Cole, & Nicassio, 2006; Morin, Colecchi, Stone, Sood, & Brink, 1999) and effective in the treatment of insomnia that is comorbid with depression (Carney et al., 2007; Lichstein, Riedel, Wilson, Lester, & Aguillard, 2001). The addition of CBT-I to treatment with antidepressants for an adult population resulted in greater remission of both the insomnia and depressive symptoms compared to treatment of the depression alone (Manber et al., 2008). Treatment time generally ranges from 4 to 8 weeks with sessions ranging in length from 30 to 90 minutes (Perlis et al., 2005). Training in CBT for insomnia (CBT-I) is available through programs in behavioral sleep medicine.

Many CBT-I components exist (see Table 5.2). Treatments can be delivered as single treatments or as part of a multicomponent treatment package. Substantial evidence supports the use of nonpharmacological interventions for the treatment of insomnia, but there is less evidence of the superiority of one treatment type over another because few treatment comparison studies have been conducted. In 2006, AASM released a report detailing the evidential support for the psychological and behavioral treatment of insomnia. AASM gave the highest recommendation to relaxation training, stimulus control, and CBT-I. Sleep restriction, multicomponent therapy without cognitive therapy (CT), paradoxical intention, and biofeedback received the next highest level of recommendation. Sleep hygiene, imagery training, and CT did not receive a recommendation because of insufficient evidence.

Although no algorithms exist to guide the clinician in treating depression that is comorbid with insomnia, we can extrapolate general guidelines from the research. Previously, the treatment of insomnia comorbid with another psychiatric condition has focused on treating the psychiatric condition first, with the hope that the insomnia would resolve as a result (Stepanski, Rybarczyk, Lopez, & Stevens, 2003). However, this approach is ineffective as demonstrated by research showing that treating the depression alone (either pharmacologically or through CBT; Carney et al., 2007) results in residual insomnia. Furthermore, untreated insomnia has negative outcomes for the client in that it can (a) increase the risk for developing future depressive episodes (Ford & Kamerow, 1989), (b) perpetuate the current depressive episode (Buysse et al., 1999; Carney et al.; Perlis et al., 2006), and (c) exacerbate the symptoms of depression (e.g., irritability, difficulty concentrating, memory impairment). Therefore, a general guideline for treating depression comorbid with insomnia is to *address and treat the insomnia complaint*. Significant improvement in sleep disturbance has been seen in older adults when the insomnia that is comorbid with depression is treated (Lichstein, Wilson, & Johnson, 2000).

A second general guideline for the treatment of depression comorbid with insomnia is *if the sleep disturbance is distressing or salient for the client, treat the insomnia either first or concurrently with the depression.* To date, there is a lack of empirical support for the sequencing of interventions for depression comorbid with insomnia. As mentioned earlier, insomnia can exacerbate the symptoms seen in depression for older adults. Therefore, addressing the sleep of older adults could

TABLE 5.2   Nonpharmacological Treatments for Insomnia

Treatment Component	Explanation
Sleep Education	▪ Involves education about the processes and variability of sleep. For example, explaining that not everyone requires 8 hours of sleep and that sleep needs change with age (e.g., infants require more sleep than adults).
Sleep Hygiene	▪ Designed to eliminate sleep-interfering behaviors such as napping during the day, irregular bed/wake times, use of sleep-interfering substances (caffeine, alcohol, nicotine), heavy meals late in the day, and activities in the bedroom other than sleep (or sex).
	▪ Additional recommendations include engaging in regular exercise and creating a comfortable bed environment that is free of noise and light and has a comfortable temperature (Perlis et al., 2005).
Relaxation*	▪ Use of relaxation strategies to reduce the mental/physical tension that can accompany insomnia. Clients are encouraged to treat relaxation as an activity that requires practice by engaging in it during the day. Relaxation can be used prior to sleep and during the night when the client wakes up and does not fall back asleep.
	▪ Typical strategies include progressive muscle relaxation, autogenic training, imagery, and meditation (Perlis et al., 2005).
	▪ Passive muscle relaxation may provide a less physically demanding alternative for some older adults.
Stimulus Control*	▪ Designed to reduce the conditioned arousal associated with being in the bed or bedroom (Bootzin, 1972). Clients are instructed to eliminate activities from the bedroom that are not associated with sleep (e.g., television, reading, talking on the phone, paperwork, worrying). If the client does not fall asleep within 15–20 minutes, he or she has to leave the bedroom and engage in a relaxing activity, returning to bed once he or she begins to feel sleepy. The client will leave the bedroom whenever he or she is unable to sleep for 15–20 minutes (including during the night).
	▪ Importantly, stimulus control is contraindicated for those clients experiencing mania, a seizure disorder, parasomnias, or who are at risk for falls (Perlis et al., 2005).

(Continued)

TABLE 5.2 Nonpharmacological Treatments for Insomnia *(Continued)*

Treatment Component	Explanation
Sleep Restriction/Sleep Compression	■ To reduce the amount of time spent awake while in the bedroom, clients are given a "sleep prescription," which is the amount of time they should spend in bed calculated from their average total sleep time over the 2 weeks they completed the sleep diary. A regular bed and wake time is coordinated with the client.
	■ After another week of completing the sleep diary, using the sleep prescription, the "sleep efficiency" is calculated. Sleep efficiency is a ratio of the time spent sleeping divided by the time spent in bed multiplied by 100 (generates a percentage). Based on the sleep efficiency (the goal is greater than 85% for older adults), the amount of time spent in bed is titrated up or down (Spielman, Saskin, & Thorpy, 1987).
	■ Sleep restriction is effective in (a) reducing the association between being in bed and being awake and (b) creating a slight sleep debt that allows the client to fall asleep more easily the following night.
	■ Importantly, sleep restriction is contraindicated for clients with a history of mania, obstructive sleep apnea, seizure disorder, parasomnias, or those who are at risk for falls (Perlis et al., 2005).
	■ Sleep compression is a more moderate alternative to sleep restriction. Instead of setting the sleep prescription based on the amount of time spent in bed, the sleep compression is a gradual reduction of the amount of time spent in bed (e.g., subtracting 15 minutes each week until the goal of 85% sleep efficiency is met).
Cognitive Therapy	■ Cognitive therapy models for insomnia have been proposed by Morin (1993) and Harvey (2002). The goals of cognitive therapy are to reduce or restructure cognitive distortions that are specific to insomnia (e.g., "If I don't get enough sleep, I won't be able to function tomorrow"; Morin, 1993). Additionally, cognitive therapy may involve addressing safety behaviors that contribute to insomnia (e.g., missing work because of poor sleep), encouraging time for constructive worry, and using imagery techniques (Harvey, 2002).
CBT-I (multicomponent sleep treatment)*	■ Multicomponent CBT for insomnia typically consists of some of the components introduced earlier (e.g., sleep education, sleep hygiene, stimulus control, and sleep restriction) combined with cognitive therapy if warranted (e.g., clients who are worried about their sleep or have intrusive thoughts or worries; Perlis et al., 2005).

Note. CBT = cognitive behavioral therapy.
*Received the highest level of recommendation from the American Academy of Sleep Medicine based on empirical evidence for the treatments' efficacy.

lead to decreased daytime impairment, which, in turn, could lead to increased activation by improving daytime functioning. Additionally, depending on the client, insomnia can be addressed effectively in brief interventions (McCrae, Dautovich, & Dzierzewski, in press). Therefore, significant improvement in the quality of life could be implemented in a relatively short period, which could be reinforcing for the client and help the client implement depression treatment strategies, such as behavioral activation or problem solving.

Other treatment considerations for a clinician treating depression comorbid with insomnia in older adults are medication and alcohol. First, several medications are known to cause sleep difficulties in older adults (Ancoli-Israel & Cooke, 2005). Additionally, older adults may take sedating medications that could promote daytime napping, which, in turn, will disrupt nighttime sleep (Ancoli-Israel & Cooke). Older adults could avoid the sleep-disrupting effects of medication by consulting with their physician to adjust the dosage or timing of medication use (Ancoli-Israel & Cooke). In addition to medication use, older adults experiencing sleep disturbance may drink alcohol before bed in the hope of creating a relaxing or sedating effect. Although alcohol can initially have relaxing effects, promoting sleep, it can create rebound insomnia with awakenings later on during the night.

To illustrate application of these guidelines, we present an example of an older man with chronic insomnia and clinically significant depressive and anxiety symptoms. Mr. B was a 68-year-old retired male referred to therapy for treatment of dysthymia. Mr. B had retired from his job as a manufacturing specialist 5 years earlier. Mr. B described his former boss as "demeaning" and reported experiencing severe anxiety and depressed mood while working. He first experienced disrupted sleep when his former boss first began belittling him in front of other coworkers. He reported feeling anxious during the day and exhausted upon returning to home. Once home, he stated that he barely had energy to make meals or clean his house. He reported watching TV while using the Internet on his laptop in bed and then turning off the light around 8:30 p.m. Once in the dark, he would lie awake for hours, ruminating about interactions he had with his boss during the day. He reported finally falling asleep around 3 a.m. and awaking by 6 a.m. Once awake, he would feel so exhausted that he would lie in bed until 9 a.m. and, consequently, was often late to work. Since retiring, Mr. B reported a decrease in his anxiety but continued to experience sleeplessness, daytime fatigue, lack of motivation, depressed mood, and poor self-esteem. Although Mr. B's presenting complaint was "feeling down," he reported feeling too exhausted to follow treatment recommendations for improving his mood.

Following the 3P model of insomnia (Spielman, Caruso, et al., 1987), Mr. B's predisposing characteristics included a tendency toward ruminating and worrying. The precipitating factor for Mr. B's sleeplessness was the interpersonal conflict with his former boss, resulting in increased anxiety and depressed mood. The perpetuating factors that led to the development of the chronic insomnia included spending excessive time in bed, ruminating and worrying in bed, and decreased daytime activities. Consequently, although the acute stressor of his job was no longer present, Mr. B still experienced sleeplessness because of the maladaptive strategies he used to compensate for his sleep loss.

Treatment began with Mr. B keeping a sleep diary, which he would then bring to weekly treatment sessions. CBT-I was used with a focus on the sleep hygiene, stimulus control, relaxation strategies, sleep restriction, and CT components. In terms of sleep hygiene, it was important for Mr. B to reduce the sleep-interfering behaviors he was engaging in while in bed—namely, watching TV, using his laptop, and lying awake ruminating. For the stimulus control intervention, Mr. B was encouraged to leave the room when he was awake longer than 15 to 20 minutes. Mr. B reported having no motivation to get out of bed so we created a relaxing environment just outside of his room where he could sit in a recliner with a comforter until he became sleepy. Various relaxation exercises were tried until he found an audio tape that was effective. Mr. B's sleep diary revealed that although he was spending 12.5 hours in bed, he was only sleeping on average for 3 hours. Consequently, we restricted his sleep to 5 hours (standard recommendations suggest restricting for no less than 5 hours). CT enabled him to develop skills for restructuring his worrisome thoughts. As a result, the association between Mr. B being in the bedroom and feeling alert was decreased. Mr. B was no longer spending more than 12 hours in bed and the 5 hours of sleep he did receive was more restorative. After Mr. B's sleep efficiency improved, he reported having more energy for daytime activities. The next stage of treatment focused on increasing his activity level during the day with the goal of improving his self-esteem and mood, using standard cognitive-behavioral strategies for depression.

PERSONALITY DISORDERS

Prevalence and Assessment

Older adults diagnosed with depression have a greater likelihood of being diagnosed with a personality disorder (PD) compared to those without depression. The prevalence rates of a PD comorbid with depression vary, ranging from 31.2% (Devanand et al., 2000) to 61% (Molinari

& Marmion, 1995). Cluster C PDs (e.g., avoidant, dependent, obsessive-compulsive; Morse, Pilkonis, Houck, Frank, & Reynolds, 2005) and obsessive-compulsive and avoidant PD, in particular (Devanand et al.), are the most common PDs found in outpatient samples. Correlates of PD in depressed older adults include an earlier onset for the first experience of depression (Devanand et al.; Morse et al.), greater number of prior depressive episodes (Morse et al.), lower socioeconomic status (Devanand et al.), and higher rates of inpatient admissions (Rao, 2003).

An important consideration when assessing for depression comorbid with PDs is inherent biases in diagnostic tools. Many of the criteria used to assess for PDs do not have face validity for older adults (Agronin & Maletta, 2000), and measurement bias could account for the lower prevalence of PDs in older versus younger adults (Balsis, Woods, Gleason, & Oltmanns, 2007). A recent study demonstrated that up to 29% of *DSM-IV* criteria for PDs were endorsed differently by older adults compared to younger adults, even when both groups had the same level of pathology (Balsis, Gleason, Woods, & Oltmanns, 2007). For example, the *DSM-IV-TR* (APA, 2000) diagnostic criteria for schizoid PD ask if the person "has little, if any, interest in having sexual experiences with another person" (p. 641). For an older adult, a decreased desire for sexual relations could be due to many reasons other than an underlying PD. The differential responses to diagnostic items also lead to significantly different diagnoses of PDs for older versus younger adults (Balsis, Woods, et al.). Comparing individuals with equivalent pathology, Balsis et al. (2007) found that older adults were more likely to be diagnosed with obsessive-compulsive and schizoid PDs and less likely to receive diagnoses of avoidant and dependent PD. Younger adults and older adults had a similar likelihood of receiving diagnoses for histrionic and paranoid PDs. The implications of these findings for clinicians are that the current prevalence rates for PDs in older adults may be inaccurate because of measurement bias. Furthermore, diagnostic criteria used to assess for PD in older adults are not age-neutral and may actually overdiagnose or underdiagnose PD in this age group depending on the disorder being assessed.

Course

Depression comorbid with PDs in older adults is associated with several negative outcomes including longer treatment duration, greater likelihood of nonresponse, greater impairment in functioning, and poorer treatment response. Cluster C PDs comorbid with depression were associated with a longer treatment response time and a greater likelihood of nonresponse in continuation or maintenance phases of treatment (Agronin, 1999; Bearden, Lavelle, Buysse, Karp, & Frank, 1996; Morse et al., 2005). Individuals with cluster C (Abrams, Spielman, Alexopoulos, & Klausner, 1998) or cluster B (Abrams, Alexopoulos, Spielman, Klausner, & Kakuma, 2001) PDs comorbid with depression were more likely to have persistently impaired functioning following an acute depressive episode. In fact, PDs exerted the greatest effect on functioning when residual depressive symptoms remained. These results suggest that older adults with subsyndromal depression and PDs may be particularly susceptible to impaired functioning (Abrams et al., 1998) compared to individuals with acute levels of depression. Finally, adults with cluster C PDs comorbid with depression were found to have higher depression scores following treatment compared to those with a sole diagnosis of depression (Viinamaki et al., 2002).

Depression and PDs could interact in several different ways. One possibility is that individuals with cluster C PDs may experience prolonged depression due to a tendency to exaggerate obstacles to performing tasks either due to fear or due to an alternative motivation resulting from the PD (Abrams et al., 1998). Additionally, older adults with PDs may experience increased distress due to a lifetime of accumulated interpersonal conflicts and other losses due to rigid behaviors resulting from the PD and, consequently, may develop depression (Lynch et al., 2007). Finally, PDs may prove particularly disruptive to older adults by decreasing their ability to adapt to age-related changes and losses in relationships and lifestyle (Lynch et al.).

Treatment Considerations

In general, emerging research suggests that psychotherapy can be effective for treating individuals with comorbid PDs and depression. There is encouraging evidence that older adults with comorbid disorders can be retained in treatment (Gum et al., 2007) and that improvements made in response to CT can be maintained (Fournier et al., 2008). Importantly, one small study showed that older adults with comorbidity had increasing symptoms in the initial period following treatment with group CBT or clinical case management. These results suggest that these individuals with comorbid depression and PDs should receive careful monitoring of treatment response and residual symptoms and may benefit from longer treatment periods or "booster sessions" to restore treatment effects (Gum et al.).

Recently, treatments that have previously targeted other disorders have been adapted for use for late-life depression comorbid with PD. The first of these treatments is dialectical behavior therapy (DBT), which was originally developed to treat individuals with borderline personality disorder (BPD; Linehan, 1993). Lynch and Cheavens have adapted DBT for use with older adults with PDs (Cheavens & Lynch, 2008; Lynch & Cheavens, in press). The adapted DBT is designed to treat individuals diagnosed with paranoid PD, obsessive-compulsive PD, avoidant PD, non-BPD, anorexia nervosa, and chronic depression (Lynch & Cheavens, 2008). The authors describe these individuals as "overcontrolled, emotionally constricted, closed to new experience, perfectionistic, cognitive-behaviorally rigid, and highly risk-averse" (Lynch & Cheavens, 2008, pp. 154–155). Consequently, the DBT adaptation emphasized openness and flexibility to new experiences and the reduction of rigid thinking and corresponding behavior (Lynch & Cheavens, 2008). Lynch et al. (2007) tested the new adaptation with older adults with depression and found that treatment with medication and DBT resulted in significantly more clients reaching remission at a 6-month follow-up period compared to medication alone. A follow-up study extended the treatment approach to older adults with comorbid depression and PD (Lynch et al., 2007). Results indicated that treatment with both medication and DBT resulted in remission by the end of treatment, whereas the medication-alone group had symptom remission only by follow-up (Lynch et al., 2007).

Although not conducted with older adults, research with a general adult sample suggests that CT affects depression and comorbid PD through specific mechanisms. In an RCT of antidepressant medication plus either CT or interpersonal therapy (IPT) for comorbid depression and PD, both treatments were successful in terms of the rates of remission, improvement of global psychopathology, improvement of social and occupational functioning, and in reduction of depressive symptoms (Bellino, Zizza, Rinaldi, & Bogetto, 2007). Interestingly, CT appeared better at reducing anxious symptoms and improving subjective perception of psychological functioning, whereas IPT showed superior improvements in social functioning and interpersonal relationships. Therefore, choice of treatment for older adults with depression and PD may depend on the client's treatment priorities or most salient symptoms.

ALCOHOL AND SUBSTANCE MISUSE DISORDERS

Prevalence and Assessment

Alcohol is the substance most commonly abused by older adults with a small proportion abusing other substances (Blixen, McDougall, & Suen, 1997). Given that mood and loneliness are often triggers for drinking behavior in older adults (Schonfeld & Dupree, 1991), it is not surprising that depression is often comorbid with alcohol use in older adults. Prevalence rates for alcohol abuse comorbid with a depressive disorder vary depending on the setting. For older adults admitted to an inpatient facility, the rates of comorbidity range from 11% to 27% (Blixen et al., 1997; Oslin, Katz, Edell, & Ten Have, 2000). A study of community-dwelling older adults reported a prevalence rate of 13.3% (Grant & Harford, 1995). Regardless of the setting, depressed older adults have a greater likelihood of having an alcohol disorder compared to nondepressed older adults. Those who are depressed were found to be three to four times more likely to use alcohol than nondepressed older adults (Devanand, 2002; Grant & Harford, 1995). Alcohol abuse comorbid with depression is also associated with serious negative outcomes for older adults, including suicidality (59% higher; Cook, Winokur, Garvey, & Beach, 1991; Cornelius et al., 1995) and suicide attempts (Blixen et al., 1997).

The assessment of depression comorbid with alcohol abuse in older adults can be problematic because of decreased opportunities for detection, the masking of alcohol abuse or depression by symptoms of the other disorder, and the invalidity of diagnostic criteria for older adults (discussed later in this chapter). In terms of detection, older adults are less likely to be identified as problem drinkers because they may have fewer interactions with a family member, employer, school, or law enforcement official that could lead to the detection of problem drinking (Center for Substance Abuse Treatment [CSAT], 1998). In addition, the very nature of comorbidity with depression may make alcohol abuse difficult to detect because the warning signs may be masked or confused with other depressive symptoms (e.g., daytime fatigue, difficulty concentrating, hypersomnia; CSAT).

The Substance Abuse and Mental Health Services Administration (SAMHSA) has guidelines for treating substance abuse in older adults (*Treatment Improvement [TIP] #26*) and for treating co-occurring disorders (*TIP #42*). According to *TIP #26*, older adults should be screened or rescreened for substance abuse difficulties when (a) certain physical conditions are present (see Table 5.3), and (b) the older person is undergoing major life changes or transitions such as menopause, "empty nest," retirement, or caregiving. The *TIP #26* document also provides "warning signs" that an older adult may be abusing alcohol or prescription medication (e.g., displaying detailed knowledge about a specific drug, involved in minor traffic accidents, or displaying bruises, burns, or fractures).

If an older adult presents with "warning signs" or exhibits any of the physical conditions or major life changes warranting a screen, there are screening measures that are specifically validated for use with older adults. The CAGE questionnaire (see Figure 5.1; Ewing,

TABLE 5.3   Physical Symptom Screening Triggers

- Sleep complaints; observable changes in sleeping patterns; unusual fatigue, malaise, or daytime drowsiness; apparent sedation (e.g., a formerly punctual older adult begins oversleeping and is not ready when the senior center van arrives for pickup)
- Cognitive impairment, memory or concentration disturbances, disorientation or confusion (e.g., family members have difficulty following an older adult's conversation, the older adult is no longer able to participate in the weekly bridge game or track the plot on daily soap operas)
- Seizures, malnutrition, muscle wasting
- Liver function abnormalities
- Persistent irritability (without obvious cause) and altered mood, depression, or anxiety
- Unexplained complaints about chronic pain or other somatic complaints
- Incontinence, urinary retention, difficulty urinating
- Poor hygiene and self-neglect
- Unusual restlessness and agitation
- Complaints of blurred vision or dry mouth
- Unexplained nausea and vomiting or gastrointestinal distress
- Changes in eating habits
- Slurred speech
- Tremor, motor uncoordination, shuffling gait
- Frequent falls and unexplained bruising

Source. From "Substance Abuse Among Older Adults. Treatment Improvement Protocol (TIP) Series 26" by the Center for Substance Abuse Treatment, 1998.

1984) is most effective for identifying more serious problem drinkers and for identifying male rather than female heavy drinkers (*TIP #26*). The Michigan Alcoholism Screening Test-Geriatric Version (MAST-G; Blow et al., 1992) was developed specifically for use with older adults (see Figure 5.2). For older adults who are members of ethnic minority groups, the Alcohol Use Disorders Identification Test (AUDIT; Babor, de la Fuente, Saunders, & Grant, 1992) can be helpful because it has

1. Have you ever felt you should **cut down** on your drinking?
2. Have people **annoyed** you by criticizing your drinking?
3. Have you ever felt bad or **guilty** about your drinking?
4. Have you ever had a drink first thing in the morning to steady your nerves or to get rid of a hangover (**eye opener**)?

Scoring: Item responses on the CAGE are scored 0 for "no" and 1 for "yes" answers, with a higher score an indication of alcohol problems. A total score of 2 or greater is considered clinically significant.

FIGURE 5.1   The CAGE Questionnaire
Source: From "Detecting Alcoholism–the CAGE Questionnaire" by J. A. Ewing, 1984, *Journal of the American Medical Association, 252*(14), 1905–1907.

1. After drinking have you ever noticed an increase in your heart rate or beating in your chest?	YES	NO
2. When talking with others, do you ever underestimate how much you actually drink?	YES	NO
3. Does alcohol make you sleepy so that you often fall asleep in your chair?	YES	NO
4. After a few drinks, have you sometimes not eaten or been able to skip a meal because you didn't feel hungry?	YES	NO
5. Does having a few drinks help decrease your shakiness or tremors?	YES	NO
6. Does alcohol sometimes make it hard for you to remember parts of the day or night?	YES	NO
7. Do you have rules for yourself that you won't drink before a certain time of the day?	YES	NO
8. Have you lost interest in hobbies or activities you used to enjoy?	YES	NO
9. When you wake up in the morning, do you ever have trouble remembering part of the night before?	YES	NO
10. Does having a drink help you sleep?	YES	NO
11. Do you hide your alcohol bottles from family members?	YES	NO
12. After a social gathering, have you ever felt embarrassed because you drank too much?	YES	NO
13. Have you ever been concerned that drinking might be harmful to your health?	YES	NO
14. Do you like to end an evening with a nightcap?	YES	NO
15. Did you find your drinking increased after someone close to you died?	YES	NO
16. In general, would you prefer to have a few drinks at home rather than go out to social events?	YES	NO
17. Are you drinking more now than in the past?	YES	NO
18. Do you usually take a drink to relax or calm your nerves?	YES	NO
19. Do you drink to take your mind off your problems?	YES	NO
20. Have you ever increased your drinking after experiencing a loss in your life?	YES	NO
21. Do you sometimes drive when you have had too much to drink?	YES	NO
22. Has a doctor or nurse ever said they were worried or concerned about your drinking?	YES	NO
23. Have you ever made rules to manage your drinking?	YES	NO
24. When you feel lonely, does having a drink help?	YES	NO

Scoring: Five or more "yes" responses are indicative of an alcohol problem.
For further information, contact Frederic C. Blow, Ph.D., at University of Michigan Alcohol Research Center, 400 E. Eisenhower Parkway, Suite A, Ann Arbor, MI 48108; (734) 998-7952.

FIGURE 5.2 The Michigan Alcoholism Screening Test—Geriatric Version (MAST-G)

Source: From "The Michigan Alcoholism Screening Test – Geriatric Version (MAST-G): A new elderly-specific screening instrument", 1992, *Alcoholism: Clinical and Experimental Research, 16*.

been validated cross-culturally although not specifically for use with older adults (CSAT, 1998).

Following a positive screen for substance abuse, the clinician should follow up with a thorough assessment. Importantly, diagnostic criteria such as from the *DSM-IV-TR* may not be relevant for older adults. For example, maladaptive functioning for an older adult may not involve impaired occupational or work activities but rather could present as impairment in maintaining a home, participating in social activities, and managing finances (CSAT, 1998). The *TIP #26* presents additional information on applying the *DSM-IV-TR* diagnostic criteria to older adults.

The Substance Abuse Profile for the Elderly (SAPE) is a structured interview included in a CBT manual created by Dupree and Schonfeld (2005) for the treatment of substance abuse in older adults. The SAPE assessment provides information on an individual's history and characteristics related to drinking as well as information that can be used for a behavior chain analysis (see the treatment section later in this chapter). When comparing both current and past substance use history, Reifman and Welte (2001) showed that prior alcohol use (e.g., between ages 20–40) was a better predictor of current depressive state than even current alcohol use. The authors hypothesized that a longer history of alcohol use can result in cumulative effects on physiology or result in regret over alcohol-induced former life problems (Reifman & Welte, 2001). Therefore, it would be beneficial for clinicians to assess both prior and current substance abuse.

Course

The comorbidity of alcohol abuse and depression has implications for treatment. Research has shown that poorer depression treatment outcomes are seen when individuals engage in heavy drinking during treatment (Oslin, 2005) and when individuals have a history of alcohol abuse (Cook et al., 1991). Alcohol abuse may also indirectly negatively impact treatment for depression. For example, older heavy drinkers were two times less likely to have social support compared to nondrinkers (Kirchner et al., 2007). Social networks play an important role in the recovery from both substance abuse and depression. When a substance abuse disorder is comorbid with depression, the individual may already be experiencing depleted social support and, consequently, may require targeted interventions focused on building social networks. Additionally, alcohol use could inhibit treatment effectiveness by leading to poor compliance with treatment recommendations for depression (Oslin, 2000).

Treatment Considerations

There is a lack of research examining the effectiveness of treatments for depression comorbid with alcohol abuse in older adults. Although no studies specifically examined CBT for comorbid diagnoses, one study combined pharmacological treatment and compliance-enhancement therapy, which included some behavioral components such as psychoeducation and collaborative treatment planning, and direct advice regarding drinking and problem solving (Oslin, 2005). In addition to the compliance-enhancement therapy, participants received both medication for depression and alcohol dependence (sertraline and naltrexone) or just the medication for depression and a placebo (sertraline). The authors reported that 42% of all participants (those who received the pharmacological treatment for depression alone or both the depression and alcohol treatment) showed a remission in depression without a relapse to heavy drinking. Interestingly, there were no significantly better improvements in depression or alcohol use for the group receiving the combined treatment compared to the group receiving only the treatment for depression.

Another study compared a similar treatment approach with a focus on the endurance of treatment effects (Gopalakrishnan, Ross, O'Brien, & Oslin, 2009). The older adults received compliance-enhancement therapy and sertraline (for depression) and naltrexone (for alcohol use). Participants were divided into three groups: full responders (showed remission from depression and alcohol abuse), partial responders (showed remission from either depression or alcohol use), and nonresponders (showed no remission from either depression or alcohol use). Interestingly, there was a differential effect for depression versus alcohol outcomes. The full responders maintained significant improvement from depression at the 6- but not the 12-month follow-up but maintained improvements in alcohol use for both the 6- and the 12-month periods. Therefore, the best endurance of remission from depression and alcohol use was seen for individuals who showed remission in both depression and alcohol use during treatment. Improvements were not maintained for the depression outcomes suggesting that depression treatment may require longer follow-up.

SAMHSA's CSAT provides a CBT model of treatment in the free manual *Substance Abuse Relapse Prevention for Older Adults: A Group Treatment Approach* (Dupree & Schonfeld, 2005). This intervention focuses on reducing substance use behavior and mood-related triggers for substance use; therefore, it has relevance for older clients with depression as well as substance misuse. This brief intervention approach has been found to reduce substance misuse as well as depressive symptoms for older adults with identified substance misuse issues, although it has not been tested specifically for older adults with comorbid diagnoses (Schonfeld et al., 2010). This approach is consistent with a movement in the alcohol treatment field away from a focus on abstinence toward a focus on harm reduction (Fleming, 2002). The treatment manual provides information on 16 weekly group sessions that comprise the three stages of the model:

1. Behavioral analysis of each individual's drinking behavior resulting in the creation of a behavioral chain
2. Teaching the individual to identify his or her own high-risk situations for drinking
3. Teaching the individual the skills to prevent relapse

The first step of the treatment identifies the antecedents and consequences to drinking (Dupree, Schonfeld, Dearborn-Harshman, & Lynn, 2008). Using the SAPE assessment (described previously), the clinician identifies situations, thoughts, feelings, cues, and urges that precede a drink and the short- and long-term consequences for the client. During the second stage of treatment, the client is taught how to recognize antecedents, behaviors, and consequences (A-B-Cs) in general and specific to his or her own situation. The client also completes a weekly "alcohol self-monitor log" to track current A-B-Cs. The third stage of treatment involves teaching the skills necessary to prevent relapse. Example modules include managing social pressure (at home and alone), thoughts and negative emotions, anxiety and tension, how to manage anxiety and tension, and how to manage anger and frustration. Importantly, many of the skills learned in the modules would be effective for treating depressive symptoms. For example, clients are instructed how to identify negative self-talk, introduced to the thought-stopping techniques, and taught cognitive restructuring and problem-solving skills.

There is a lack of research on how best to integrate interventions for depression comorbid with alcohol use. On one hand, it is likely that alcohol could serve as a long-standing maladaptive coping mechanism for dealing with depression. Therefore, by first developing adaptive coping skills for managing the depression, the client could increase the likelihood that he or she will become less reliant on alcohol to cope. Conversely, addressing alcohol abuse a priori may be necessary when pharmacological interventions are warranted for depression. Given that alcohol consumption can prevent antidepressant medication from working effectively (CSAT, 1998), it may be necessary to reduce alcohol consumption to enable the full effects of a pharmacological treatment. The timing of interventions may also depend on the stage of recovery for the client. For example, significant depressive symptoms are a common reaction after detoxification and should be addressed prior to beginning further substance abuse treatment (CSAT).

The role of hope in therapy with individuals with depression comorbid with alcohol abuse is important, given that these individuals may experience demoralization and despair as a result of the challenges of two disorders (CSAT, 2005). An additional issue to be mindful of when working with an older adult with depression comorbid with alcohol abuse is to be aware of and address negative reactions toward the client. For example, the therapist may experience feelings of anger, being used, unhelpfulness, or "burnout" in reaction to the client's substance use and maladaptive coping mechanisms (CSAT, 2005).

CONCLUSIONS AND FUTURE DIRECTIONS

In summary, psychiatric comorbidity in depressed older adults can complicate assessment, diagnosis, and CBT interventions, although current CBT approaches show promise in reducing depressive and comorbid symptoms. These complications require careful diagnostic and symptom severity assessment, collaborative treatment planning with the client, ongoing treatment monitoring, and adjustment of the focus of CBT interventions as needed. For anxiety, it may be most beneficial to focus CBT on depressive symptoms first to enhance mood and behavioral activation before addressing residual symptoms of anxiety. For sleep, it is critical to address distressing or salient sleep concerns using one or more components of CBT-I concurrent with depressive symptoms and not assume that the sleep will improve as mood improves. For PDs, the most promising approach includes adapted DBT that emphasizes flexibility in thinking and behavior patterns. Finally, for alcohol misuse, a CBT manual specifically for older adults that targets substance misuse as well as mood and anxiety triggers is available.

Both the diagnosis and treatment of comorbidities in older adults may change dramatically in the coming years. At the time of this writing, workgroups are developing revisions in preparation for the fifth edition of the *DSM*. *DSM-V* is likely to retain the general categories of mood, anxiety, sleep, personality, and substance disorders described here, although specific criteria may be modified. Independently of the *DSM* revisions and outside of gerontology, researchers are also beginning to consider more novel conceptualizations of comorbid disorders and treatment approaches that transcend current diagnostic categories. For example, Barlow et al. have proposed a dimensional classification, noting that three dimensions underlie various mood and anxiety disorders: negative affect, positive affect, and autonomic arousal. These disorders are characterized by common mechanisms of cognitive distortions and avoidance of cognitions, behaviors, and emotions. Thus, they have developed and are conducting research on a "unified, transdiagnostic approach to emotional disorders that considers these commonalities and distills common therapeutic procedures across evidence-based protocols . . . restructuring maladaptive cognitive appraisals, changing action tendencies associated with the disordered emotion, preventing emotional avoidance, and using emotional exposure procedures" (Brown & Barlow, 2009, p. 267).

In a recent special issue of the *Journal of Cognitive Therapy,* several researchers discussed issues in transdiagnostic conceptualization and intervention strategies (Taylor & Clark, 2009). Common processes across a range of disorders include elevated self-focused attention, avoidance behavior, thought suppression, and rumination (Mansell, Harvey, Watkins, & Shafran, 2009); these processes then become the focus of an individualized treatment approach applicable across various diagnoses (McEvoy, Nathan, & Norton, 2009). In a small number of studies, transdiagnostic CBT interventions demonstrated promising outcomes compared to wait-list control groups and showed similar effect sizes as diagnostic-specific protocols (McEvoy et al., 2009). Although this research is in the early stage, it suggests that we may look forward to a future with a more focused CBT conceptualization and intervention strategies that simultaneously target a wide range of symptoms currently characterized as comorbid.

REFERENCES

Abrams, R. C., Alexopoulos, G. S., Spielman, L. A., Klausner, E., & Kakuma, T. (2001). Personality disorder symptoms predict declines in global functioning and quality of life in elderly depressed patients. *American Journal of Geriatric Psychiatry, 9*(1), 67–71.

Abrams, R. C., Spielman, L. A., Alexopoulos, G. S., & Klausner, E. (1998). Personality disorder symptoms and functioning in elderly depressed patients. *American Journal of Geriatric Psychiatry, 6*(1), 24–30.

Ağargün, M. Y., Kara, H., & Solmaz, M. (1997). Sleep disturbances and suicidal behavior in patients with major depression. *Journal of Clinical Psychiatry, 58*(6), 249–251.

Agronin, M. E. (1999). Mental health practice in geriatric health care settings. *Gerontologist, 39*(4), 489–492.

Agronin, M. E., & Maletta, G. (2000). Personality disorders in late life. Understanding and overcoming the gap in research. *American Journal of Geriatric Psychiatry, 8*(1), 4–18.

American Academy of Sleep Medicine. (2005). *The international classification of sleep disorders : Diagnostic and coding manual* (2nd ed.). Westchester, IL.: Author.

American Psychiatric Association (2000). *Diagnostic and statistical manual of mental disorders* (4th ed.). Washington, DC: Author.

Ancoli-Israel, S., & Cooke, J. R. (2005). Prevalence and comorbidity of insomnia and effect on functioning in elderly populations. *Journal of the American Geriatrics Society, 53*(7), S264–S271.

Babor, T. F., de la Fuente, J. R., Saunders, J. B., & Grant, M. (1992). *AUDIT: The Alcohol Use Disorders Identification Test: Guidelines for its use in primary health care.* Geneva, Switzerland: World Health Organization.

Balsis, S., Gleason, M. E. J., Woods, C. M., & Oltmanns, T. F. (2007). An item response theory analysis of DSM-IV personality disorder criteria across younger and older age groups. *Psychology and Aging, 22*(1), 171–185.

Balsis, S., Woods, C. M., Gleason, M. E. J., & Oltmanns, T. F. (2007). Overdiagnosis and underdiagnosis of personality disorders in older adults. *American Journal of Geriatric Psychiatry, 15*(9), 742–753.

Bearden, C., Lavelle, N., Buysse, D., Karp, J. F., & Frank, E. (1996). Personality pathology and time to remission in depressed outpatients treated with interpersonal psychotherapy. *Journal of Personality Disorders, 10*(2), 164–173.

Beck, A. T., & Steer, R. A. (1996). *BDI-II, Beck depression inventory: Manual* (2nd ed.). San Antonio, TX: Psychological Corp.

Bellino, S., Zizza, M., Rinaldi, C., & Bogetto, F. (2007). Combined therapy of major depression with concomitant borderline personality disorder: Comparison of interpersonal and cognitive psychotherapy. *Canadian Journal of Psychiatry-Revue Canadienne De Psychiatrie, 52*(11), 718–725.

Bliwise, D. L., King, A. C., Harris, R. B., & Haskell, W. L. (1992). Prevalence of self-reported poor sleep in a healthy population aged 50–65. *Social Science & Medicine, 34*(1), 49–55.

Blixen, C. E., McDougall, G. J., & Suen, L. J. (1997). Dual diagnosis in elders discharged from a psychiatric hospital. *International Journal of Geriatric Psychiatry, 12*(3), 307–313.

Blow, F. C., Brower, K. J., Schulenberg, J. E., Demo-Dananberg, L. M., Young, J. P., & Beresford, T. P. (1992). The Michigan Alcoholism Screening Test—Geriatric Version (MAST-G): A new elderly-specific screening instrument. *Alcoholism: Clinical and Experimental Research, 16.*

Bootzin, R. R. (1972). *A stimulus control treatment for insomnia.* Paper presented at the Proceedings of the 90th Annual Convention of the American Psychological Association, Washington, DC.

Brown, T. A., & Barlow, D. H. (2009). A proposal for a dimensional classification system based on the shared features of the DSM-IV anxiety and mood disorders: Implications for assessment and treatment. *Psychological Assessment, 21*(3), 256–271.

Buysse, D. J., Tu, X. M., Cherry, C. R., Begley, A. E., Kowalski, J., Kupfer, D. J., et al. (1999). Pretreatment REM sleep and subjective sleep quality distinguish depressed psychotherapy remitters and nonremitters. *Biological Psychiatry, 45*(2), 205–213.

Carney, C. E., Segal, Z. V., Edinger, J. D., & Krystal, A. D. (2007). A comparison of rates of residual insomnia symptoms following pharmacotherapy or cognitive-behavioral therapy for major depressive disorder. *Journal of Clinical Psychiatry, 68*(2), 254–260.

Cassidy, E. L., Lauderdale, S., & Sheikh, J. I. (2005). Mixed anxiety and depression in older adults: Clinical characteristics and management. *Journal of Geriatric Psychiatry and Neurology, 18*(2), 83–88.

Center for Substance Abuse Treatment. (1998). *Substance abuse among older adults. Treatment Improvement Protocol. (TIP) Series 26* (DHHS Publication No. [SMA] 01-3496). Rockville, MD: Department of Health and Human Services, Substance Abuse and Mental Health Administration.

Center for Substance Abuse Treatment. (2005). *Substance abuse treatment for persons with co-occurring disorders. Treatment Improvement Protocol (TIP) Series 42* (DHHS Publication No. [SMA] 05-3922). Rockville, MD: Substance Abuse and Mental Health Services Administration.

Cheavens, J. C., & Lynch, T. R. (2008). Dialectical behavior therapy for personality disorders in older adults. In D. Gallagher-Thompson, A. Steffen, & L. Thompson (Eds.), *Handbook of behavioral and cognitive therapies with older adults.* New York, NY: Springer.

Cole, M. G., & Dendukuri, N. (2003). Risk factors for depression among elderly community subjects: A systematic review and meta-analysis. *American Journal of Psychiatry, 160*(6), 1147–1156.

Cook, B. L., Winokur, G., Garvey, M. J., & Beach, V. (1991). Depression and previous alcoholism in the elderly. *British Journal of Psychiatry, 158,* 72–75.

Cook, J. M., Orvaschel, H., Simco, E., Hersen, M., & Joiner, T. (2004). A test of the tripartite model of depression and anxiety in older adult psychiatric outpatients. *Psychology and Aging, 19*(3), 444–451.

Cornelius, J. R., Salloum, I. M., Mezzich, J., Cornelius, M. D., Fabrega, H., Jr, Ehler, J. G., et al. (1995). Disproportionate suicidality in patients with comorbid major depression and alcoholism. *American Journal of Psychiatry, 152*(3), 358–364.

Devanand, D. P. (2002). Comorbid psychiatric disorders in late life depression. *Biological Psychiatry, 52*(3), 236–242.

Devanand, D. P., Turret, N., Moody, B. J., Fitzsimons, L., Peyser, S., Mickle, K., et al. (2000). Personality disorders in elderly patients with dysthymic disorder. *American Journal of Geriatric Psychiatry, 8*(3), 188–195.

Dupree and Schonfeld, 2005. *Substance abuse relapse prevention: A group treatment approach for older adults.* Rockville, MD: Substance Abuse and Mental Health Services Administration.

Dupree, L. W., Schonfeld, L., Dearborn-Harshman, K. O., & Lynn, N. (2008). A relapse prevention model for older alcohol abusers. In D. Gallagher-Thompson, A. Steffen, & L. W. Thompson (Eds.), *Handbook of behavioral and cognitive therapies with older adults* (pp. 61–75). New York, NY: Springer.

D'Zurilla, T. J., & Nezu, A. M. (2004). *Problem-solving therapy: A positive approach to clinical intervention* (3rd ed.). New York, NY: Springer Publishing Company.

Ewing, J. A. (1984). Detecting alcoholism: The CAGE questionnaire. *Journal of the American Medical Association, 252*(14), 1905–1907.

Fleming, M. (Ed.). (2002). *Identification and treatment of alcohol use disorders in the elderly.* New York, NY: Springer.

Foley, D. J., Monjan, A. A., Brown, S. L., Simonsick, E. M., Wallace, R. B., & Blazer, D. G. (1995). Sleep complaints among elderly persons: An epidemiologic study of 3 communities. *Sleep, 18*(6), 425–432.

Ford, D. E., & Kamerow, D. B. (1989). Epidemiologic study of sleep disturbances and psychiatric disorders: An opportunity for prevention. *Journal of the American Medical Association, 262*(11), 1479–1484.

Fournier, J. C., DeRubeis, R. J., Shelton, R. C., Gallop, R., Amsterdam, J. D., & Hollon, S. D. (2008). Antidepressant medications v. cognitive therapy in people with depression with or without personality disorder. *British Journal of Psychiatry, 192*(2), 124–129.

Gellis, Z. D., & Bruce, M. L. (2010). Problem solving therapy for subthreshold depression in home healthcare patients with cardiovascular disease. *American Journal of Geriatric Psychiatry, 18*(6), 464–474.

Gopalakrishnan, R., Ross, J., O'Brien, C., & Oslin, D. (2009). Course of late-life depression with alcoholism following combination therapy. *Journal of Studies on Alcohol and Drugs, 70*(2), 237–241.

Grant, B. F., & Harford, T. C. (1995). Comorbidity between DSM-IV alcohol use disorders and major depression: Results of a national survey. *Drug and Alcohol Dependence, 39*(3), 197–206.

Gum, A. M., Areán, P. A., & Bostrom, A. (2007). Low-income depressed older adults with psychiatric comorbidity: Secondary analyses of response to psychotherapy and case management. *International Journal of Geriatric Psychiatry, 22*(2), 124–130.

Gum, A. M., & Cheavens, J. S. (2008). Psychiatric comorbidity and depression in older adults. *Current Psychiatry Reports, 10,* 23–29.

Harvey, A. (2002). A cognitive model of insomnia. *Behavior Research and Therapy, 40*(8), 869–893.

Hoelscher, T. J., Ware, J. C., & Bond, T. (1993). Initial validation of the Insomnia Impact Scale. *Sleep Research, 22,* 149.

Irwin, M. R., Cole, J. C., & Nicassio, P. M. (2006). Comparative meta-analysis of behavioral interventions for insomnia and their efficacy in middle-aged adults and in older adults 55+ years of age. *Health Psychology, 25*(1), 3–14.

Johns, M. W. (1991). A new method for measuring daytime sleepiness: The Epworth Sleepiness Scale. *Sleep, 14*(6), 540–545.

Katz, D. A., & McHorney, C. A. (1998). Clinical correlates of insomnia in patients with chronic illness. *Archives of Internal Medicine, 158*(10), 1099–1107.

King-Kallimanis, B. L., Gum, A. M., & Kohn, R. (2009). Comorbidity of depressive and anxiety disorders for older Americans in the national comorbidity survey-replication. *American Journal of Geriatric Psychiatry, 17*(9), 782–792.

Kirchner, J. E., Zubritsky, C., Cody, M., Coakley, E., Chen, H. T., Ware, J. H., et al. (2007). Alcohol consumption among older adults in primary care. *Journal of General Internal Medicine, 22*(1), 92–97.

Krupp, L. B., LaRocca, N. G., Muir-Nash, J., & Steinberg, A. D. (1989). The fatigue severity scale. Application to patients with multiple sclerosis and systemic lupus erythematosus. *Archives of Neurology, 46*(10), 1121–1123.

Kvaal, K., McDougall, F. A., Brayne, C., Matthews, F. E., Dewey, M. E., & MRC CFAS. (2008). Co-occurrence of anxiety and depressive disorders in a community sample of older people: Results from the MRC CFAS (Medical Research Council Cognitive Function and Ageing Study). *International Journal of Geriatric Psychiatry, 23*(3), 229–237.

Lichstein, K. L., Durrence, H. H., Taylor, D. J., Bush, A. J., & Riedel, B. W. (2003). Quantitative criteria for insomnia. *Behaviour Research and Therapy, 41*(4), 427–445.

Lichstein, K. L., Riedel, B. W., Wilson, N. M., Lester, K. W., & Aguillard, R. N. (2001). Relaxation and sleep compression for late-life insomnia: A placebo-controlled trial. *Journal of Consulting and Clinical Psychology, 69*(2), 227–239.

Lichstein, K. L., Wilson, N. M., & Johnson, C. T. (2000). Psychological treatment of secondary insomnia. *Psychology and Aging, 15*(2), 232–240.

Linehan, M. M. (1993). *Cognitive-behavioral treatment of borderline personality disorder.* New York, NY: Guilford Press.

Lynch, T. R., & Cheavens, J. S. (2008). Dialectical behavior therapy for comorbid personality disorders. *Journal of Clinical Psychology, 64*(2), 154–167.

Lynch, T. R., & Cheavens, J. S. (in press). Dialectical behavior therapy for depression with comorbid personality disorder: An extension of standard DBT with a special emphasis on the treatment of older adults. In L. A. Dimeff & K. Koerner (Eds.), *Real world adaptations of DBT.* New York, NY: Guilford Press.

Lynch, T. R., Cheavens, J. S., Cukrowicz, K. C., Thorp, S. R., Bronner, L., & Beyer, J. (2007). Treatment of older adults with co-morbid personality disorder and depression: A dialectical behavior therapy approach. *International Journal of Geriatric Psychiatry, 22*(2), 131–143.

Manber, R., Edinger, J. D., Gress, J. L., Pedro-Salcedo, M. G. S., Kuo, T. F., & Kalista, T. (2008). Cognitive behavioral therapy for insomnia enhances depression outcome in patients with comorbid major depressive disorder and insomnia. *Sleep, 31*(4), 489–495.

Mansell, W., Harvey, A., Watkins, E., & Shafran, R. (2009). Conceptual foundations of the transdiagnostic approach to CBT. *Journal of Cognitive Psychotherapy, 23*(1), 6–19.

McCrae, C. S., Dautovich, N. D., & Dzierzewski, J. M. (in press). Short-term and group approaches. In M. J. Sateia & D. Buysse (Eds.), *Insomnia: Diagnosis and treatment.* New York, NY: Informa Healthcare USA, Inc.

McEvoy, P. M., Nathan, P., & Norton, P. J. (2009). Efficacy of transdiagnostic treatments: A review of published outcome studies and future research directions. *Journal of Cognitive Psychotherapy, 23*(1), 20–33.

Mellinger, G. D., Balter, M. B., & Uhlenhuth, E. H. (1985). Insomnia and its treatment: Prevalence and correlates. *Archives of General Psychiatry, 42*(3), 225–232.

Molinari, V., & Marmion, J. (1995). Relationship between affective disorders and Axis II diagnoses in geropsychiatric patients. *Journal of Geriatric Psychiatry and Neurology, 8*(1), 61–64.

Monk, T. H. (2005). Aging human circadian rhythms: Conventional wisdom may not always be right. *Journal of Biological Rhythms, 20*(4), 366–374.

Morgan, K., & Clarke, D. (1997). Risk factors for late-life insomnia in a representative general practice sample. *British Journal of General Practice, 47*(416), 166–169.

Morin, C. M. (1993). *Insomnia: Psychological assessment and management.* New York, NY: Guilford Press.

Morin, C. M., Colecchi, C., Stone, J., Sood, R., & Brink, D. (1999). Behavioral and pharmacological therapies for late-life insomnia: A randomized controlled trial. *Journal of the American Medical Association, 281*(11), 991–999.

Morse, J. Q., Pilkonis, P. A., Houck, P. R., Frank, E., & Reynolds, C. F., III. (2005). Impact of cluster C personality disorders on outcomes of acute and maintenance treatment in late-life depression. *American Journal of Geriatric Psychiatry, 13*(9), 808–814.

National Institutes of Health. (2005). National Institutes of Health State of the Science Conference statement on Manifestations and Management of Chronic Insomnia in Adults, June 13–15, 2005. *Sleep, 28*(9), 1049–1057.

Ohayon, M. M. (2002). Epidemiology of insomnia: What we know and what we still need to learn. *Sleep Medicine Reviews, 6*(2), 97–111.

Ohayon, M. M., Carskadon, M. A., Guilleminault, C., & Vitiello, M. V. (2004). Meta-analysis of quantitative sleep parameters from childhood to old age in healthy individuals: Developing normative sleep values across the human lifespan. *Sleep, 27*(7), 1255–1273.

Ohayon, M. M., & Roth, T. (2003). Place of chronic insomnia in the course of depressive and anxiety disorders. *Journal of Psychiatric Research, 37*(1), 9–15.

Oslin, D. W. (2000). Alcohol use in late life: Disability and comorbidity. *Journal of Geriatric Psychiatry and Neurology, 13*(3), 134–140.

Oslin, D. W. (2005). Treatment of late-life depression complicated by alcohol dependence. *American Journal of Geriatric Psychiatry, 13*(6), 491–500.

Oslin, D. W., Katz, I. R., Edell, W. S., & Ten Have, T. R. (2000). Effects of alcohol consumption on the treatment of depression among elderly patients. *American Journal of Geriatric Psychiatry, 8*(3), 215–220.

Perlis, M. L., Jungquist, C. R., Smith, M. T., & Posner, D. (2005). *Cognitive behavioral treatment of insomnia. A session-by-session guide.* New York, NY: Springer.

Perlis, M. L., Smith, L. J., Lyness, J., Matteson, S. R., Pigeon, W. R., Jungquist, C. R., et al. (2006). Insomnia as a risk factor for onset of depression in the elderly. *Behavioral Sleep Medicine, 4*(2), 104–113.

Pigeon, W. R., Hegel, M., Unutzer, J., Fan, M. Y., Sateia, M. J., Lyness, J. M., et al. (2008). Is insomnia a perpetuating factor for late-life depression in the IMPACT cohort? *Sleep, 31*(4), 481–488.

Quan, S. F., Katz, R., Olson, J., Bonekat, W., Enright, P. L., Young, T., et al. (2005). Factors associated with incidence and persistence of symptoms of disturbed sleep in an elderly cohort: The cardiovascular health study. *American Journal of the Medical Sciences, 329*(4), 163–172.

Rao, R. (2003). Does personality disorder influence the likelihood of in-patient admission in late-life depression? *International Journal of Geriatric Psychiatry, 18*(10), 960–961.

Reifman, A., & Welte, J. W. (2001). Depressive symptoms in the elderly: Differences by adult drinking history. *Journal of Applied Gerontology, 20*(3), 322–337.

Roth, T. (2009). Comorbid insomnia: Current directions and future challenges. *The American Journal of Managed Care, 15*(1), S6–S13.

Roth, T., & Roehrs, T. (2003). Insomnia: Epidemiology, characteristics, and consequences. *Clinical Cornerstone, 5*(3), 5–15.

Schonfeld, L., & Dupree, L. W. (1991). Antecedents of drinking for early-onset and late-onset elderly alcohol abusers. *Journal of Studies on Alcohol, 52*(6), 587–592.

Schonfeld, L., King-Kallimanis, B., Duchene, D. M., Etheridge, R. L., Herrera, J. R., Barry, K. L., et al. (2010). The Florida BRITE Project: Screening and brief intervention for substance misuse in older adults. *American Journal of Public Health, 100*(1), 108–114.

Spielberger, C. D., Gorsuch, R. L., Lushene, R., Vagg, P. R., & Jacobs, G. A. (1983). *Stait-Trait Anxiety Inventory, Form Y.* Palo Alto, CA: Consulting Psychologists Press.

Spielman, A. J., Caruso, L., & Glovinsky, P. (1987). A behavioral perspective on insomnia treatment. *Psychiatric Clinics of North America, 10*(4), 541–553.

Spielman, A. J., Saskin, P., & Thorpy, M. J. (1987). Treatment of chronic insomnia by restriction of time in bed. *Sleep, 10*(1), 45–56.

Stanley, M. A., Wilson, N. L., Novy, D. M., Rhoades, H. M., Wagener, P. D., Greisinger, A. J., et al. (2009). Cognitive behavior therapy for generalized anxiety disorder among older adults in primary care: A randomized clinical trial. *Journal of the American Medical Association, 301*(14), 1460–1467.

Stepanski, E., Rybarczyk, B., Lopez, M., & Stevens, S. (2003). Assessment and treatment of sleep disorders in older adults: A review for rehabilitation psychologists. *Rehabilitation Psychology, 48*(1), 23–36.

Taylor, S., & Clark, D. A. (2009). Transdiagnostic cognitive-behavioral treatments for mood and anxiety disorders: Introduction to the special issue. *Journal of Cognitive Psychotherapy, 23*(1), 3–5.

Teachman, B. A., Siedlecki, K. L., & Magee, J. C. (2007). Aging and symptoms of anxiety and depression: Structural invariance of the tripartite model. *Psychology and Aging, 22*(1), 160–170.

Viinamaki, H., Hintikka, J., Honkalampi, K., Koivumaa-Honkanen, H., Kuisma, S., Antikainen, R., et al. (2002). Cluster C personality disorder impedes alleviation of symptoms in major depression. *Journal of Affective Disorders, 71*(1–3), 35–41.

Vink, D., Aartsen, M. J., Comijs, H. C., Heymans, M. W., Penninx, B. W. J. H., Stek, M. L., Deeg, D. J. H., & Beekman, A. T. F. (2009). Onset of anxiety and depression in the aging population: comparison of risk factors in a 9-year prospective study. *American Journal of Geriatric Psychiatry, 17*(8), 642-652.

Watson, D. (2005). Rethinking the mood and anxiety disorders: A quantitative hierarchical model for DSM-V. *Journal of Abnormal Psychology, 114*(4), 522–536.

Wetherell, J. L. (2010). *Dimensional care: Psychosocial interventions and multidisciplinary collaboration.* Paper presented at the ann ual meeting of the American Association of Geriatric Psychiatry, Savannah, GA.

Wetherell, J. L., Gatz, M., & Pedersen, N. L. (2001). A longitudinal analysis of anxiety and depressive symptoms. *Psychology & Aging, 16*(2), 187–195.

Wetherell, J. L., Lenze, E. J., & Stanley, M. A. (2005). Evidence-based treatment of geriatric anxiety disorders. *Psychiatric Clinics of North America, 28*(4), 871–896, ix.

World Health Organization. (2004). *International statistical classification of diseases and related health problems* (10th revision, 2nd ed.). Geneva, Switzerland: World Health Organization.

6

Generalized Anxiety Disorder Among Older Adults

Julie Loebach Wetherell, Joshua Ruberg, and Andrew J. Petkus

SYMPTOMS AND DIAGNOSTIC CRITERIA

According to the *Diagnostic and Statistical Manual of Mental Disorders, 4th edition, Text Revision* (*DSM-IV-TR*) criteria, the cardinal symptom of generalized anxiety disorder (GAD) is excessive and hard-to-control worry and anxiety about multiple problems or life domains (American Psychiatric Association [APA], 2000). The worry must be present most days over a 6-month period or longer. In addition, the anxiety and worry must be accompanied by at least three of six of the following associated symptoms:

1. Feeling restless, keyed up, or on edge;
2. Fatigue;
3. Trouble concentrating;
4. Feeling irritable;
5. Muscle tension; and
6. Insomnia or restless sleep.

Hierarchical rules preclude assigning the diagnosis when it occurs exclusively during the course of a mood disorder such as major depression or dysthymia, posttraumatic stress disorder, a psychotic disorder, or a pervasive developmental disorder (e.g., autism). Significant changes have been proposed for *DSM-V*, including renaming the condition "generalized worry disorder," shortening the duration criterion to 3 months, and including behavioral manifestations such as avoidance and procrastination (Andrews et al., 2010).

SYMPTOM PRESENTATION IN OLDER ADULTS

Overall, the presentation of GAD in older adults does not appear to differ substantially from that observed in younger people (Nuevo et al., 2008). As could be expected, worries about health problems, family, finances, and minor matters predominate in late life, whereas work, school, or social concerns are much less common (Diefenbach, Stanley, & Beck, 2001; Doucet, Ladouceur, Freeston, & Dugas, 1998; Hunt, Wisocki, & Yanko, 2003). One investigation comparing older adults with and without GAD found that older adults with the disorder were more likely to worry about themselves, whereas both groups reported worries about spouses, family members, and current events (Wetherell, Le Roux, & Gatz, 2003).

The most common symptoms among older adults with GAD, in addition to worry, appear to be restlessness and fatigue; frequency and perceived uncontrollability of worry, insomnia, and muscle tension best distinguish between patients with GAD, those with subsyndromal symptoms, and those with nonanxious controls (Wetherell et al., 2003). Little research has been conducted on behavioral correlates of geriatric GAD, although some evidence suggests that avoidance coping may be associated with poorer response to treatment and long-term outcomes (Ayers, Petkus, Liu, Patterson, & Wetherell, 2010; Wetherell et al., 2009).

Older adults may report trouble concentrating as memory problems, but some research suggests that older patients with GAD do not report trouble concentrating at higher rates than those without anxiety symptoms (Wetherell et al., 2003). However, some evidence does suggest a bi-directional relationship between cognitive impairment and anxiety in older adults (Beaudreau & O'Hara, 2008). Older adults with GAD do appear to exhibit poorer performance in working memory, immediate and delayed recall, and executive functions (Caudle et al., 2007; Mantella et al., 2007).

Course and Prognosis

Although GAD is an often chronic condition that may onset in early life and persist through old age, several studies have suggested that about half of older adults with GAD experience onset of the disorder in late life (Chou, 2009; Le Roux, Gatz, & Wetherell, 2005; Lenze, Mulsant, Mohlman et al., 2005). Although the symptoms of GAD do not differ depending on the age of onset, older adults who experience onset early in life may experience a higher rate of comorbid anxiety disorders, whereas individuals with a late-life onset of symptoms may report poorer health-related quality of life and functional limitations (Chou, 2009; Le Roux et al., 2005). Regardless of the time of onset of GAD, the disorder tends to be chronic and is unlikely to remit without treatment.

Late-life GAD is associated with impairment in a broad range of areas, including social and family role functioning, financial burden, and engagement in daily activities. Compared to older adults with no psychiatric diagnoses, older adults with GAD report greater disability, more frequent health care utilization, and lower health-related quality of life, with levels of impairment similar to those reported by depressed older adults (Bourland et al., 2000; De Beurs et al., 1999; Porensky et al., 2009; Wetherell et al., 2004). Although GAD often co-occurs with other psychiatric disorders, older adults with a diagnosis of GAD alone were found to experience similar levels of impairment to older adults diagnosed with GAD and one or more other Axis I disorders, indicating that GAD alone is a sufficient cause of significant decrements in quality of life across multiple domains (Porensky et al., 2009; Wetherell et al., 2004).

Epidemiology and Risk Factors

Anxiety disorders in general are common in older adults. Recent epidemiological data have indicated that anxiety disorders in late life are almost three times as prevalent (7.0% 12-month prevalence) as are mood disorders (2.6% 12-month prevalence; Gum, King-Kallimanis, & Kohn, 2009). Several recent epidemiological studies from around the world have estimated the prevalence of GAD at 1.2% to 7.3% in community-dwelling older adults (Beekman et al., 1998; Gum et al., 2009; Schoevers, Beekman, Deeg, Jonker, & van Tilburg, 2003; Trollor, Anderson, Sachdev, Brodaty, & Andrews, 2007). However, the epidemiologic assessment of anxiety disorders in later life is a considerable challenge given the comorbidity of anxiety disorder symptoms with symptoms of other psychiatric and medical disorders, as well as the fact that a significant number of older adults live in long-term or residential care and do not participate in epidemiologic studies. For these reasons, the prevalence of GAD in older individuals could potentially be even higher than the estimates provided in the published literature.

Moreover, to date, little is known about the prevalence of GAD in ethnic minority populations because most participants in the published epidemiological studies are Whites. However, several recent studies have indicated that the prevalence of GAD appears to be lower among older African Americans (Ford et al., 2007) and higher among Puerto Ricans (Tolin, Robison, Gaztambide, & Blank, 2005), relative to Whites.

The prevalence of GAD is significantly higher in medical settings than in community settings (Bryant, Jackson, & Ames, 2008).

Prevalence estimates of anxiety disorders among patients with chronic obstructive pulmonary disease (COPD) range from 10% to 19% in patients with stable disease, 9.3% to 58% in individuals recovering from a recent acute exacerbation, and 50% to 75% in those with severe disease (Maurer et al., 2008; Solano, Gomes, & Higginson, 2006). GAD in particular is a common comorbidity with several medical conditions; in a study of patients with confirmed coronary heart disease, 18.7% met criteria for GAD (Todaro, Shen, Raffa, Tilkemeier, & Niaura, 2007), whereas GAD was also diagnosed in 20.6% of a sample of recent stroke patients and in 15% of patients with Alzheimer's disease (Leppavuori, Pohjasvaara, Vataja, Kaste, & Erkinjuntti, 2003; Starkstein, Jorge, Petracca, & Robinson, 2007).

GAD often co-occurs with major depressive disorder (MDD), leading to some controversy regarding whether GAD should be given as a separate diagnosis in depressed older adults (Lenze et al., 2000; Schoevers et al., 2003). However, a study of the lifetime course of GAD and MDD in older adults indicated that symptoms of MDD waxed and waned in multiple recurrent episodes, whereas symptoms of GAD were typically long-lasting and represented a single chronic episode, even in those individuals who had a history of both disorders (Lenze et al., 2000). Thus, GAD in the older adults appears to be a unique disorder that warrants its own diagnostic category.

To date, specific risk factors for the development of GAD in older adults have not been determined. However, risk factors for the development of anxiety disorders in general among older persons include female gender, "neurotic personality," early life stress, and chronic disability in self or spouse (Vink, Aartsen, & Schoevers, 2008). Research uncovering neurobiological risk factors for late-life, or late-onset, anxiety has not yet been done.

Assessment

Other people are less likely to recognize anxiety than are younger adults (Wetherell, Petkus, et al., 2009). Frequently, older adults with GAD have never been diagnosed or treated and may have a conceptualization of the problem as something other than an anxiety disorder. Moreover, *DSM* terminology may have different meanings or feel stigmatizing to the patient. Thus, a geriatric-sensitive assessment process is necessary to make an accurate diagnosis while maintaining rapport and developing a therapeutic alliance with the patient.

Many older patients with GAD downplay their symptoms and may use different words to describe them. Thus, it is necessary to get a thorough qualitative description of the behavior, symptom, or problem the patient is experiencing. Many older adults resist the term *anxiety, fear,* or even *worry. Concern* is often the preferred term, although some older adults use idiosyncratic words or phrases (e.g., "dither," "I can't turn my mind off"). It is counterproductive to insist that the patient adopt *DSM* terminology; using the patients' own words or descriptive phrases is preferable. Whatever it is labeled, older patients with GAD will describe a perseverative and threat-oriented thought process that a clinician can identify as worry.

Older adults often use different words to describe symptom severity as well. Our patients rarely endorse words like "excessive" or "uncontrollable" when describing their problem. Rather than phrasing questions this way, ask whether the patient experiences the symptom "more than most people your age" or ask, "Do your doctor, friends, or family think you (worry, fret, etc.) too much?" Some diagnostic interviews for GAD ask whether the patient has been feeling "particularly" worried or anxious during the past 6 months. For patients who have been experiencing anxiety for decades, the answer to this question is typically "no." Ask about the symptoms first, and then ask about the time frame or duration to avoid overlooking chronic worry. It is not uncommon for patients to deny that their worries are difficult to control when asked about this directly. Instead, have the patients describe what they do to control their worries. When queried, patients often describe extensive efforts to manage the worry (e.g., overinvolving themselves in activities). These strategies to control worry typically provide only temporary distraction but not long-term relief and may have negative short-term (e.g., fatigue) and long-term consequences (e.g., a person who relies on activity outside of the home as a coping strategy may decompensate after quitting driving).

As noted earlier, GAD often occurs in the context of physical illness; thus, it is important to distinguish symptoms related to anxiety from those of disease or medications. Nonphysician mental health providers should collect as much objective data as possible about comorbid medical illnesses. Information such as illnesses the patients have been diagnosed with, medications they are currently taking, and a detailed description of the physical symptoms they are experiencing should be gathered. A release from the patient to discuss this information with a physician should be sought, and the physician should be consulted to evaluate the excessiveness of the reported symptomatology in light of the patient's medical status.

Depression is often comorbid with GAD and has a similar presentation in many respects. Getting a description of the patient's mood is important to distinguish the two conditions. Again, it is helpful to use the patients' words (blue, "blah," etc.) instead of insisting on the word "depression." Older depressed patients sometimes present with "depression without sadness" that is characterized more by anhedonia and loss of interest, along with vegetative symptoms such as loss of appetite (Gallo & Rabins, 1999). Thus, it is usually instructive to find out if the patient has lost interest in doing hobbies and other activities that he or she used to enjoy.

Several instruments, including the Penn State Worry Questionnaire (PSWQ; Meyer, Miller, Metzger, & Borkovec, 1990) and its short form (PSWQ-A; Hopko et al., 2003), Geriatric Anxiety Inventory (GAI; Pachana et al., 2007), GAD-7 (Spitzer, Kroenke, Williams, & Löwe, 2006), Hamilton Anxiety Rating Scale (HARS; Hamilton, 1959), and Generalized Anxiety Disorder Severity Scale (GADSS; Shear, Belnap, Mazumdar, Houck, & Rollman, 2006), may be useful in assessing GAD symptoms in older adults. The HARS and GADSS are interview-based assessments not commonly used in clinical practice. Copies of the PSWQ, GAI, and GAD-7 are provided in Appendix A to C in this chapter.

The PSWQ (16 items) and PSWQ-A (8 items) are self-report instruments that assess worry severity. Both use a 5-point Likert scale with each item scored 1, "not at all typical of me" to 5, "very typical of me," resulting in a possible score of 16 to 80 on the full scale and 8 to 40 on the short form. Some older adults have difficulty with the Likert scale, and the short form was designed specifically for use with older adults in part because the full scale includes reverse-scored items that are often problematic for older people. A cut-score of 50 on the PSWQ and 22 on the PSWQ-A represent clinically significant worry in older individuals, and improvement of 9 points on the full PSWQ signifies significant improvement of symptoms (Stanley et al., 2003, 2009).

The GAI is a recently developed 20-item self-report instrument designed specifically to assess common symptoms of anxiety in older adults. Its yes/no format may make it particularly appropriate for patients who have difficulty with Likert scales. A score of 9 or greater indicates a possible anxiety disorder, with scores of 11 or greater suggesting GAD (Diefenbach, Tolin, Meunier, & Gilliam, 2009; Pachana et al., 2007).

The GAD-7 is a 7-item self-report questionnaire that is scored based on the duration of each symptom over the past week (0, "not at all," 1, "several days," 2, "more than half the days," and 3, "nearly every day"), with scores of 10 or more indicating possible GAD (Spitzer et al., 2006).

Other commonly used instruments for late-life anxiety include the Beck Anxiety Inventory (BAI; Beck, Epstein, Brown, & Steer, 1988) and the State-Trait Anxiety Inventory (STAI; Spielberger, 1983). The BAI has been used with older adults, but its many somatic items can lead to false-positive results when used with medical patients (Wetherell & Areán, 1997; Wetherell & Gatz, 2005). Although the STAI is the oldest and most well-established self-reported anxiety measure, some evidence suggests that it may not be as reliable as are other scales in older patients with GAD (Stanley, Novy, Bourland, Beck, & Averill, 2001).

If time is of the essence, it may be helpful to administer one scale that captures both anxiety and depressive symptoms. These include the Brief Symptom Inventory-18 (BSI-18; Derogatis, 2000) and the Hospital Anxiety and Depression Scale (HADS; Zigmond & Snaith, 1983). The BSI-18 includes three subscales measuring anxiety, depression, and somatic symptoms. The HADS is a 14-item scale with two subscales measuring anxiety and depression; it does not include somatic symptoms that can be confounded with anxiety in older adults or the medically ill. The HADS may be superior to the BSI-18 in detecting GAD in older medical patients (Wetherell, Birchler, Ramsdell, & Unützer, 2007).

Treatment

Although some evidence suggests that CBT is effective for late-life GAD, recent studies suggest that efficacy is modest, even when compared to minimal contact control conditions (Hendriks, Oude Voshaar, Keijsers, Hoogduin, & van Balkom, 2008; Stanley et al., 2009; Wetherell, Ayers, et al., 2009). Furthermore, other data suggest that medications may be more effective than CBT for this condition (Pinquart & Duberstein, 2007; Schuurmans et al., 2006; Schuurmans et al., 2009). Many older adults, however, prefer psychotherapeutic treatment to pharmacotherapy due to side effects, a desire to limit the number of drugs taken, or other factors (Gum et al., 2006; Metge, Grymonpre, Dahl, & Yogendran, 2005). Among psychotherapeutic approaches, relaxation training alone appears to deliver the same benefit as the full CBT package (Thorp et al., 2009). Therefore, based on the currently available evidence, we recommend a treatment strategy consisting of psychoeducation and relaxation training, followed by motivational interviewing (MI) to encourage a medication trial for those who do not obtain sufficient benefit from relaxation alone, and support for the patient and communication with the prescribing physician during the first few months of medication use to manage concerns about medications or side effects. Movement from one phase to another should be driven by patient readiness; therefore, the number of sessions devoted to each phase should be taken as suggestions only. A description of the goals and contents of such a protocol follows.

Phase I: Introduction and Psychoeducation (1–2 Sessions)

Obviously, a good therapeutic relationship is the foundation for any effective treatment. The therapist should therefore devote a substantial amount of time during the first session to get to know the patient and his or her situation. In addition to building rapport, the therapist should assess anxiety and worry symptoms as well as the impact these problems are having on the person's life. The patient should also be administered with whatever questionnaire the therapist intends to use during the course of treatment to measure progress.

Because psychotherapy works better for geriatric depression than for geriatric anxiety, and because the CBT components differ across these disorders, it is important to find out the patient's most pressing current problem. If the patient has both depression and GAD, the depression should be treated first because depressed patients are at higher risk of suicide, may lack motivation to practice relaxation skills, and may be more likely to prematurely drop out of treatment for anxiety (Allgulander & Lavori, 1993; Schuurmans et al., 2006; Swales et al., 1996).

Patients' past experiences with treatment should also be explored. It is important to find out information about psychotherapy and past and current pharmacotherapy (e.g., name of drug[s], dose). Therapists may need to inquire directly about the specific components of past psychotherapy, such as "Did the therapist give you at-home assignments like listening to tapes or writing down your anxiety symptoms?" "Did the therapist spend most of each session just being a sympathetic listener?" For both medications and talk therapy, the therapist should inquire about duration of treatment and helpful/unhelpful aspects.

As part of the psychoeducation process, the following information should be conveyed to older patients with GAD:

1. Unproductive, disruptive, or distressing worry and anxiety (use whatever term or phrase the patient endorses) may be related to another problem (e.g., patient's or partner's health) but also constitutes a problem in its own right. Furthermore, reductions in worry or anxiety may actually facilitate coping with the patient's other problems.
2. Chronic worry and anxiety has a detrimental effect on health and possibly cognition. Therefore, treatment is important. Patients should be commended for seeking help as a means to improve their health and well-being.

3. Problematic worry and anxiety can be successfully treated, even if they are long-standing or accompanying a major life problem.
4. Common anxiety symptoms in addition to worry include restlessness, muscle tension, sleep problems, fatigue, trouble concentrating, and irritability. Find out what symptoms the patient has experienced and get examples from the past week or two. For many patients, it is not necessary to provide any more information about GAD than that.
5. Patients may be confused about the distinction between depression and anxiety. Keep it simple: Depression is characterized by feeling sad or being uninterested in things, whereas anxiety is mostly characterized by worry, restlessness, and muscle tension. As noted previously, patients who endorse depression or both constellations of symptoms should be treated for depression rather than GAD.
6. Some patients, particularly those who have familiarity with psychodynamic approaches, may want to understand the origins of their anxiety. We recommend that therapists tell such patients that although some biological and environmental risk factors have been identified, no one can know exactly what causes anxiety in any particular person. The good news is that treatment works regardless.

Patients should also be introduced to the fundamentals of the treatment, which may contrast with other type(s) of therapy the patient has received in the past. These include the following:

1. Therapy is time-limited; although the number of sessions is flexible, the patient will likely not be seeing the therapist for more than a few months.
2. Sessions are structured and will focus on teaching the patient relaxation skills to manage anxiety. A brief description of the relaxation exercises, including a demonstration of diaphragmatic breathing if time permits, is helpful.
3. At-home practice is required; let the patient know that the more consistently people practice, the more they benefit (Wetherell et al., 2005).
4. Regular assessment is necessary to get an objective measure of progress.

Finally, although it is appropriate to provide psychotherapy in the absence of medications to older patients with GAD because some will benefit, we believe that ethical conduct requires informed consent for any treatment. Therefore, we recommend that providers tell older patients at the outset of treatment that an appropriate, closely monitored, and tailored course of pharmacotherapy may be more effective than behavioral treatment for their condition, and that this option may be discussed again depending on the outcome of the psychotherapy.

If a supportive family member or caregiver is available, this person should be strongly encouraged to accompany the patient to the second or third session. Older patients with GAD often report family problems, so it is important to ensure that the family member selected is not a major source of stress (Ayers et al., 2010). We have found that including friends or more distant relatives is not as helpful unless they live with the patient. It is better to forego a family session than to include someone who will be of only limited assistance (or an outright obstacle).

Start the family session by asking the patient to summarize the educational material from the previous session(s) for his or her support person, with the therapist filling in any gaps. Next, have the support person describe any of the patient's anxiety symptoms that he or she has observed, as well as the impact these symptoms have on the patient's functioning or the family as a whole. It can be helpful for the therapist to lead both patient and support person in a brief imagery exercise to demonstrate what therapy will entail. Finally, the patient and support person should agree on ways the latter can help the former participate in therapy (e.g., answering the phone or taking young children out of the house to provide quiet, uninterrupted time for daily practice; listening to tapes along with the patient). For some patients, reminders to practice are annoying rather than helpful, so it is important to ensure that any support offered is in fact supportive.

Phase II: Relaxation Training (4–8 Sessions)
Most patients will readily accept the rationale for and potential helpfulness of relaxation training in treating anxiety. Some patients may already have experience with some relaxation techniques (e.g., yoga or meditation). Patients should be encouraged to continue or return to any exercises they have found helpful for worry or tension. Patients who have tried some form of relaxation in the past and have not found it helpful can be encouraged to continue with the therapy anyway, because different techniques work for different people, and the therapist may be able to point out and help overcome factors that were problematic in the past.

The primary point to highlight is that relaxation is a skill requiring practice. At the outset, the patient will need 30 minutes of uninterrupted time every day to perform the exercises; eventually, this will diminish as the focus turns to integrating relaxation into daily life. The therapist should discuss any potential barriers to practice from the outset and help the patient problem-solve to make a plan to avoid or overcome them.

Many relaxation techniques are helpful in reducing anxiety, including listening to soothing music or commercially prepared tapes of nature sounds. Davis, Eshelman, McKay, and Fanning (2008) describe various options for self-help and therapist-guided strategies. We highlight three in this chapter: diaphragmatic breathing, progressive muscle relaxation (PMR), and imagery. Scripts for PMR and imagery are included in Appendix D and E at the end of this chapter.

We strongly recommend providing patients with a recording, which can be made in session, to facilitate at-home practice of PMR and imagery. We have used both cassette tapes and prerecorded CDs. The advantage of the former is that they can be created in session using the therapist's own voice; the patient's positive associations with the therapist will facilitate relaxation during at-home practice. We keep extra battery-operated cassette and CD players for patients to borrow. We do not use digital voice recorders because they are too expensive to lend. Therapists and patients should feel free to be creative; we had one patient with a hearing impairment who played the tapes in his car, where he could recline and turn up the volume without disturbing anyone else.

Diaphragmatic Breathing. Psychoeducation about the role of breathing in maintaining or reducing anxiety is often helpful. The basic message is that anxiety is often associated with breathing more quickly than is helpful, which produces more anxiety symptoms. This can be a subtle process, so patients may not recognize it. It is helpful to assess the patient's breathing style by having him or her place one hand on the chest while breathing normally. Count out loud, one number per second, during inhalation and exhalation to determine the breathing rate.

Because deep breathing may actually increase the tendency to hyperventilate, the emphasis should be on (a) slowing the breath and (b) spending more time exhaling than inhaling. This is most easily done by counting as the patient inhales and exhales approximately 10 times. In addition, patients should think a word like "calm," "relax," or "peace" as they exhale. For at-home practice, patients should find a comfortable and quiet place and plan to spend at least 15 minutes at a time, twice a day. As they develop their breathing skill, they should gradually increase the count until it reaches at least 4 seconds for inhalation and 5 seconds for exhalation.

Progressive Muscle Relaxation. Patients should be told that this relaxation technique has two components: one physical and one mental. Physically, PMR reduces muscle tension through the process of systematically flexing and releasing different muscle groups. Tensing the muscles first helps relax them, because it is normal for muscles to relax after being tensed. The mental component of PMR involves paying attention to the sensations of tension and relaxation. This can teach attentional focus and help patients identify when they are tense versus relaxed at an earlier stage of the process, enabling them to enlist coping resources.

We recommend a 12-muscle group exercise for the first week or two, reduced to 4 muscle groups over the following week. The 4 groups should include those in which the patient typically experiences the most tension (often the jaw or shoulders). After practicing with 4 groups, patients should be trained to relax all muscles at once, again in conjunction with the word "calm" or "relax" (i.e., cue-controlled relaxation).

Ideally, patients should perform the exercise with all parts of their body supported (i.e., in a recliner, not a regular chair). Patients should only tense their muscles enough to notice the difference from relaxation and should not be straining. The tension is held for about 10 seconds, followed by a sudden release and 20 seconds of relaxation. Patients with arthritis or injuries can skip the tension period and just focus on relaxing their muscles.

Patients should be instructed to concentrate on what they are experiencing and feeling in their body, particularly the contrast between tension and relaxation. As with other meditation exercises, it is normal for minds to wander, and if patients notice this, they should simply bring their attention back to the sensations of tension or relaxation.

Imagery. This relaxation technique consists of constructing a pleasant image in the mind, which can be real or imagined. To maximize benefits, it is important for patients to employ all five senses when constructing an image. You can use the script in Appendix E, or ask the patient to describe in detail an image or scene that he or she finds pleasant, then use those details to guide the patient while he or she reclines with eyes closed (e.g., "You are sitting on the beach. You feel the warm sun on your arms and the soft sand under your feet. You hear a seagull overhead. You feel completely relaxed and at peace.") This process should take at least 10 minutes, with pauses.

With any relaxation technique, patients should start by practicing for at least 2 weeks in a quiet, undisturbed setting. We recommend having patients try all three exercises; in our experience, patients typically find at least one helpful. PMR will take longer to learn than the others. After trying all of them, patients are encouraged to focus on what works best. After one of the skills is learned in a peaceful setting, it should be tried for at least a few days in nonstressful but active situations (e.g., standing in the grocery check-out line). After that, patients should try the skill in more stressful situations.

Monitoring the level of tension before and after each at-home practice session may be helpful to demonstrate improvement and increase motivation. Moreover, patients who are required to document at-home practice in writing are more likely to engage in it consistently. Patients should also complete a formal assessment tool weekly or every 2 weeks in session. The overall goal of treatment is a clinically significant response according to whatever measure is being used (e.g., a score of less than 22 on the brief PSWQ or less than 10 on the GAD-7). Each time the measure is administered, share the information with the patient and discuss remaining symptoms and inconsistencies in reporting (i.e., the patient may report symptomatic improvement in the absence of change on the objective measure). We have found that older adults with GAD often wish to please therapists and therefore may be reluctant to admit when treatment is not helping. In most cases, we therefore weigh the objective assessment slightly more heavily than the patient's subjective evaluation.

During the fourth session of relaxation training, discuss the patient's progress so far. If the patient is satisfied with the level of improvement, it may be appropriate to terminate treatment at this point. A patient who reports substantial improvement in the presence of high levels of objectively measured anxiety, however, should be gently challenged and encouraged to think about what changes would be required to decrease scores, examining individual items if necessary, and also to stay the course for another few sessions.

Termination may be appropriate at this point if treatment has been successful. In addition to the general termination tasks of saying goodbye and showing appreciation for the patient's hard work, termination from relaxation training should focus on maintenance of gains by continuing daily practice, discussing anxiety-provoking situations that may arise in the future, and determining how the patient will recognize if he or she is slipping back into anxiety and what he or she will do if so. Termination, including this type of relapse prevention work, may take one or two sessions.

If the patient is not satisfied with the level of improvement at session 4, the patient and therapist should collaborate to uncover contributing factors (e.g., not practicing often enough or long enough) and work together to overcome them. Progress should be reviewed again at sessions 6 and 8.

If the patient has not responded after eight sessions of relaxation training, it is not likely that additional sessions will be helpful. Although it is possible to begin other psychotherapeutic approaches at this point (for example, a mindfulness-based approach such as Acceptance and Commitment Therapy may offer some benefit; Wetherell, Afari et al., in press), as discussed earlier, there is no evidence that any are more efficacious than relaxation. At this point, therefore, the therapist should move into Phase III and reopen a discussion about medications.

Phase III: Motivational Interviewing to Encourage Medication Use (1–4 Sessions)

Perhaps the biggest hurdle to overcome in this phase of treatment is the therapist's own reluctance to encourage the use of medication. We agree that it would be optimal if CBT for late-life GAD were as effective as are medications (and frankly are puzzled about why it is not, given its success in treating depression in all age groups and anxiety in younger adults). The existing evidence, however, suggests that this is not the case. Therapists are encouraged to weigh the effects of untreated anxiety in their analysis of the costs and benefits of medications for patients who do not respond to relaxation training.

The combination of medication and CBT is not without controversy, particularly in the anxiety disorders (Foa, Franklin, & Moser, 2002; Westra & Stewart, 1998). For example, pharmacotherapy might interfere with the development of self-efficacy or the successful challenging of catastrophic beliefs during psychotherapy, individuals treated with medications may be less motivated to engage in psychotherapy, and psychotherapy in the context of medications may result in state-dependent learning that does not persist when the medication is discontinued (Barlow, Gorman, Shear, & Woods, 2000; Raffa et al., 2008). We believe that when monotherapy is inadequate, however, combination treatments involving selective serotonin reuptake inhibitor (SSRI) medications and psychotherapy may be more effective, because antidepressants and CBT have different mechanisms and may be able to treat different components of the illness (Arce, Simmons, Lovero, Stein, & Paulus, 2008; McNally, 2007).

Relatively, little research has been conducted on combinations of psychotherapy and pharmacotherapy for GAD. A team of researchers at Columbia University led by Laszlo Papp is currently investigating the effectiveness of the general approach described in this chapter: CBT followed by antidepressant medications for older patients with GAD who do not respond to psychotherapy alone. Our team is examining the efficacy of CBT with older patients with GAD who are already taking SSRIs to see whether adding psychotherapy can boost response and lower the risk of relapse after medication is discontinued. The final results of these trials are not yet available, but preliminary data from the latter suggest that CBT may be an effective augmentation to medications but may not be adequate to maintain response in the absence of medications (Wetherell, Stoddard et al., in press).

For patients who are open to using medication, including those who are currently taking a medication that is ineffective or has undesirable side effects, Phase III of this protocol may not be necessary. Older adults with GAD are very often reluctant to take medications, however, including psychotropics. Although no data are available on the topic, many in the field believe, based on clinical experience, that this reluctance is greater among those with GAD than among those with depression. This makes sense, because both worry about the potential negative consequences of medication and hypervigilance to somatic sensations that can be interpreted as deleterious medication effects are associated with anxiety.

MI is described in Miller and Rollnick (2002). MI is based on the principle that ambivalence is normal when people are considering behavior change. The goal of MI is to increase motivation by resolving ambivalence in the direction of change. The core principles of MI are expressing empathy without judgment, developing the discrepancy between the patient's values or goals and current behaviors, rolling with rather than challenging resistance, and supporting self-efficacy.

As always, specific MI techniques depend on the patient's current stage of readiness for change, which can fluctuate across sessions. If the patient is in *precontemplation* (i.e., not willing to take medications for anxiety), the therapist should provide information that may be helpful in leading patients to consider this possibility. This can include information about the patient's own level of anxiety (e.g., "based on the questions you've been answering, you worry much more than most people your age"), the health consequences of untreated worry and anxiety (e.g., higher risk of developing heart disease, possibly higher risk of premature death; Kubzansky, Kawachi, Weiss, & Sparrow, 1998; van Hout et al., 2004), and the health benefits of treatment (e.g., for GAD patients with hypertension, anxiolytic medication can help normalize blood pressure; Lenze et al., 2009). It may be useful to hold another family session to promote sharing about the consequences of the worry and anxiety to both the older person and the family. Additional information about the variety, safety, and efficacy of currently available medications may also be helpful, particularly if the patient has had a bad experience with medications in the past. If after 2 to 3 sessions of MI the patient remains in Precontemplation, however, it is best to terminate treatment, leaving open the possibility of future work when the patient is ready.

The second stage of change, *contemplation*, occurs when the patient is considering pharmacotherapy but is not ready to commit. This stage is characterized by a high degree of ambivalence. The goal of this stage is to increase the salience of the desirable aspects of trying a medication (e.g., better sleep) and decrease the salience of the undesirable aspects (e.g., by reframing medication use as a proactive step toward better health rather than a sign of weakness). It is often helpful to have the patient engage in a decisional balance exercise in which he or she lists the pros and cons of taking an anxiolytic. Therapists should encourage expression of both advantages and disadvantages.

In the *preparation* stage, the patient intends to try a medication but has not yet started. The therapist can encourage the patient to make an appointment with the doctor to discuss various medication options or obtain a prescription as part of this phase.

Ideally, patients will reach the *action* phase, in which they begin taking a medication, and the *maintenance* phase, in which they remain on it long enough to obtain beneficial effects. At this point, it is appropriate to move to Phase IV of the intervention. With patients who enter the *relapse* phase (i.e., become nonadherent to the medication), the therapist may need to return to Phase III strategies.

Phase IV: Support During the First Months of Medication Use (4–6 Sessions Over 1–3 Months, Plus Phone Check-Ins and Contact With the Prescribing Physician)

Benzodiazepines are frequently prescribed for older adults, but long-term use of these medications can carry substantial risks, including falls, disability, and cognitive decline (Benítez et al., 2008; Gray et al., 2006; Pariente et al., 2008; Wright et al., 2009). SSRI and serotonin-norepinephrine reuptake inhibitor (SNRI) medications are considered the treatments of choice for older patients with GAD (Katz, Reynolds, Alexopoulos, & Hackett, 2002; Lenze, Mulsant, Shear et al., 2005, Lenze et al., 2009). Rates of nonadherence may be as high as 60% in clinical practice, however, probably because prescribers in both primary care and specialty mental health do not have the resources to offer close monitoring and support (Wetherell & Unützer, 2003). Therapists can fill this important void.

Obviously, working with a patient around medication issues involves working with the prescribing physician. This can be daunting for therapists who are not psychiatrists. In our experience, however, most doctors are pleased to have another provider involved in their patients' care. Moreover, collaborative care models in which a nonphysician care manager (social worker, psychologist, or nurse) works with a primary care physician to provide algorithm-guided pharmacotherapy are effective in treating anxiety (Roy-Byrne et al., 2005, 2010) and geriatric depression (Unützer et al., 2002).

A therapist can be particularly helpful by providing close follow-up, which a busy physician may not have time to do. We recommend that therapists call patients 1 day and approximately 4 days after they start the medication, with an in-person visit 1 week later. If the medication is started on a Friday, we recommend calling on Saturday. Some patients may require weekly in-person visits for the first month; others may be satisfied with telephone check-ins for some or all of those sessions. At all contacts, the therapist should administer the same scale that was used during relaxation training, as well as inquire about side effects. The latter information should be relayed to the doctor promptly with a request that he or she telephone the patient. Even if the patient has no questions or concerns, the therapist should contact the prescriber after 4 weeks to provide information about the patient's progress. If the patient has not yet experienced significant improvement, the therapist should inquire about the advisability of a dose increase. This should be repeated monthly until the patient achieves response.

Although physicians should be informed about side effects, therapists can play an important role in educating patients and helping them manage bothersome symptoms. Patients should be informed that it usually takes at least 6 weeks to achieve a full response to SSRIs, so patience is encouraged (Lenze et al., 2009). Therapists should get familiar with the most common side effects of the medication the patient is taking. For SSRIs, these include drowsiness and gastrointestinal (GI) distress. These are typically temporary, not incapacitating, and can be addressed with short-term measures (e.g., Imodium for diarrhea) or changes in the way the patient takes the drug (e.g., with a meal for GI problems; at night for drowsiness). Patients can also be encouraged to engage in their relaxation skills to deal with unpleasant or worrisome sensations.

Some patients with GAD report sudden and dramatic onset of symptoms that are not plausibly related to the medication. Others attribute to the medication symptoms of anxiety that they experienced before starting the drug. We find that challenging these misattributions is counterproductive and instead recommend reassurance and a higher level of support in the form of more frequent calls or visits. One or more calls from the prescribing physician may also help encourage "staying the course."

Questions we have found helpful regarding side effects include "How bad is it right now?" Often patients indicate that it is not so bad at the moment, which may demonstrate to the patient that the problem may be quite manageable much of the time. Another helpful question is, "Is it incapacitating?" Almost always, patients report that it is not. We encourage patients to call either us or the physician, 24/7, if they continue to have concerns or questions. They almost never do, but knowing that someone is available at any time can be very reassuring to an anxious older person.

Our experience suggests that patients require more support when starting the medication than when a dose is increased, but this may not be the case for all patients.

Some patients may already be taking a medication that is not entirely effective. These patients will likely not require the level or type of support needed for a patient who is reluctant to take any medications at all. Patients can be encouraged to discuss the possibility of a dose increase or a switch in medications with the prescriber. The patient may experience a temporary exacerbation of symptoms while a dose is changed or a new medication is started; patients should be notified of this possibility in advance, and therapists should provide close monitoring (including inquiries about suicidal ideation) and support.

CONCLUSION

GAD is common, chronic, and detrimental among older adults. Unfortunately, currently available psychotherapeutic treatments, including CBT, appear to be less effective than are medications for this condition. Relaxation training is a relatively brief and easy to administer behavioral intervention that may provide relief for some older adults with GAD. For those who do not respond to relaxation, the most helpful psychotherapeutic intervention may be MI to encourage a medication trial, followed by intensive support until medication response is achieved. In the long term, additional research on nonpharmacological treatments for geriatric GAD is sorely needed.

REFERENCES

Allgulander, C., & Lavori, P. W. (1993). Causes of death among 936 elderly patients with 'pure' anxiety neurosis in Stockholm County, Sweden, and in patients with depressive neurosis or both diagnoses. *Comprehensive Psychiatry*, 34(5), 299–302.

American Psychiatric Association. (2000). *Diagnostic and statistical manual of mental disorders* (4th ed.). Washington, DC: American Psychiatric Press.

Andrews, G., Hobbs, M. J., Borkovec, T. D., Beesdo, K., Craske, M. G., Heimberg, R. G., et al. (2010). Generalized worry disorder: A review of DSM-IV generalized anxiety disorder and options for DSM-V. *Depression and Anxiety*, 27(2), 134–147. DOI: 10.1002/da.20658.

Arce, E., Simmons, A. N., Lovero, K. L., Stein, M B., & Paulus, M. P. (2008). Escitalopram effects on insula and amygdala BOLD activation during emotional processing. *Psychopharmacology (Berl)*, 196(4), 661–672.

Ayers, C. R., Petkus, A., Liu, L., Patterson, T. L., & Wetherell, J. L. (2010). Negative life events and avoidant coping are associated with poorer long-term outcome in older adults treated for generalized anxiety disorder. *Journal of Experimental Psychopathology, 1,* 146–154.

Barlow, D. H., Gorman, J. M., Shear, M. R., & Woods, S. W. (2000). Cognitive-behavioral therapy, imipramine, or their combination for panic disorder: A randomized controlled trial. *Journal of the American Medical Association, 283*(19), 2529–2536.

Beaudreau, S., & O'Hara, R. (2008). Late-life anxiety and cognitive impairment: A review. *American Journal of Geriatric Psychiatry, 16,* 790–803.

Beck, A. T., Epstein, N., Brown, G., & Steer, R. A. (1988). An inventory for measuring clinical anxiety: Psychometric properties. *Journal of Consulting and Clinical Psychology, 56,* 893–897.

Beekman, A. T., Bremmer, M. A., Deeg, D. J., van Balkom, A. J., Smit, J. H., de Beurs, E., et al. (1998). Anxiety disorders in later life: A report from the Longitudinal Aging Study Amsterdam. *International Journal of Geriatric Psychiatry, 13*(10), 717–726.

Benítez, C. I., Smith, K., Vasile, R. G., Rende, R., Edelen, M. O., & Keller M. B. (2008). Use of benzodiazepines and selective serotonin reuptake inhibitors in middle-aged and older adults with anxiety disorders: A longitudinal and prospective study. *American Jounal of Geriatric Psychiatry, 16,* 5–13.

Bourland, S. L., Stanley, M. A., Snyder, A. G., Novy, D. M., Beck, J. G., & Averill, P. M. (2000). Quality of life in older adults with generalized anxiety disorder. *Aging and Mental Health, 4,* 315–323.

Bryant, C., Jackson, H., & Ames, D. (2008). The prevalence of anxiety in older adults: Methodological issues and a review of the literature. *Journal of Affective Disorders, 109,* 233–250.

Caudle, D. C., Senior, A. C., Wetherell, J. L., Rhoades, H. M., Beck, J. G., Kunik, M. E., et al. (2007). Cognitive errors, symptom severity, and response to CBT in older adults with generalized anxiety disorder. *American Journal of Geriatric Psychiatry, 15*(8), 680–689.

Chou, K. L. (2009). Age at onset of generalized anxiety disorder in older adults. *American Journal of Geriatric Psychiatry, 17*(6), 455–464.

Davis, M., Eshelman, E. R., McKay, M., & Fanning, P. (2008). *The relaxation and stress reduction workbook* (6th ed.). Oakland, CA: New Harbinger Press.

de Beurs, E., Beekman, A. T., van Balkom, A. J., Deeg, D. J., van Dyck, R., & van Tilburg, W. (1999). Consequences of anxiety in older persons: its effect on disability, well-being and use of health services. *Psychological Medicine, 29,* 583–593.

Derogatis, L. R. (2000). *BSI-18: Administration, scoring and procedures Manual.* Minneapolis, MN: National Computer Systems.

Diefenbach, G. J., Stanley, M. A., & Beck, J. G. (2001). Worry content reported by older adults with and without generalized anxiety disorder. *Aging and Mental Health, 5,* 269–274.

Diefenbach, G. J., Tolin, D. F., Meunier, S. A., & Gilliam, C. M. (2009). Assessment of anxiety in older home care recipients. *Gerontologist, 49*(2), 141–153.

Doucet, C., Ladouceur, R., Freeston, M., & Dugas, M. (1998). Worry themes and the tendency to worry in older adults. *Canadian Journal on Aging, 17,* 361–371.

Foa, E. B., Franklin, M. E., & Moser, J. (2002). Context in the clinic: How well do cognitive-behavioral therapies and medications work in combination? *Biological Psychiatry, 52,* 987–997.

Ford, B. C., Bullard, K. M., Taylor, R. J., Toler, A. K., Neighbors, H. W., & Jackson, J. S. (2007). Lifetime and 12-month prevalence of Diagnostic and Statistical Manual of Mental Disorders, Fourth Edition disorders among older African Americans: Findings from the National Survey of American Life. *American Journal of Geriatric Psychiatry, 15,* 652–659.

Gallo, J. J., & Rabins, P. V. (1999). Depression without sadness: Alternative presentations of depression in late life. *American Family Physician, 60*(3), 820–826.

Gray, S. L., LaCroix, A. Z., Hanlon, J. T., Penninx, B. W., Blough, D. K., Leveille, S. G., et al. (2006). Benzodiazepine use and physical disability in community-dwelling older adults. *Journal of the American Geriatric Society, 54*(2), 224–230.

Gum, A. M., Areán, P. A., Hunkeler, E., Tang, L., Katon, W., Hitchcock, P., et al. (2006). Depression treatment preferences in older primary care patients. *Gerontologist, 46*(1), 14–22.

Gum, A. M., King-Kallimanis, B., & Kohn, R. (2009). Prevalence of mood, anxiety, and substance-abuse disorders for older Americans in the national comorbidity survey-replication. *American Journal of Geriatric Psychiatry, 17,* 769–781.

Hamilton M. (1959). The assessment of anxiety states by rating. *British Journal of Medical Psychology, 32*(1), 50–55.

Hendriks, G. J., Oude Voshaar, R. C., Keijsers, G. P., Hoogduin, C. A., & van Balkom, A. J. (2008). Cognitive-behavioural therapy for late-life anxiety disorders: A systematic review and meta-analysis. *Acta Psychiatrica Scandinavica, 117*(6), 403–411.

Hopko, D. R., Stanley, M. A., Reas, D. L., Wetherell, J. L., Beck, J. G., Novy, D. M., et al. (2003). Assessing worry in older adults: Confirmatory factor analysis of the Penn State Worry Questionnaire and psychometric properties of an abbreviated model. *Psychological Assessment, 15*(2), 173–183.

Hunt, S., Wisocki, P., & Yanko, J. (2003). Worry and use of coping strategies among older and younger adults. *Journal of Anxiety Disorders, 17,* 547–560.

Katz, I. R., Reynolds, C. F., III, Alexopoulos, G. S., & Hackett, D. (2002). Venlafaxine ER as a treatment for generalized anxiety disorder in older adults: Pooled analysis of five randomized placebo-controlled clinical trials. *Journal of the American Geriatric Society, 50*(1), 18–25.

Kubzansky, L. D., Kawachi, L., Weiss, S. T., & Sparrow, D. (1998) Anxiety and coronary heart disease: A synthesis of epidemiological, psychological, and experimental evidence. *Annals of Behavioral Medicine, 20*(2), 47–58.

Lenze, E. J., Mulsant, B. H., Mohlman, J., Shear, M. K., Dew, M. A., Schulz, R., et al. (2005). Generalized anxiety disorder in late life: Lifetime course and comorbidity with major depressive disorder. *American Journal of Geriatric Psychiatry, 13*(1), 77–80.

Lenze, E. J., Mulsant, B. H., Shear, M. K., Dew, M. A., Miller, M. D., Pollock, B. G., et al. (2005). Efficacy and tolerability of citalopram in the treatment of late-life anxiety disorders: Results from an 8-week randomized, placebo-controlled trial. *American Journal Psychiatry, 162*(1), 146–150.

Lenze, E. J., Mulsant, B. H., Shear, M. K., Schulberg, H. C., Dew, M. A., Begley, A. E., et al. (2000). Comorbid anxiety disorders in depressed elderly patients. *American Journal of Psychiatry, 157*(5), 722–728.

Lenze, E. J., Rollman, B. L., Shear, M. K., Dew, M. A., Pollock, B. G., Ciliberti, C., et al. (2009). Escitalopram for older adults with generalized anxiety disorder: A randomized controlled trial. *Journal of the American Medical Association, 301*(3), 295–303.

Leppavuori, A., Pohjasvaara, T., Vataja, R., Kaste, M., & Erkinjuntti, T. (2003). Generalized anxiety disorders three to four months after ischemic stroke. *Cerebrovascular Diseases, 16*(3), 257–264.

Le Roux, H., Gatz, M., & Wetherell, J. L. (2005). Age at onset of generalized anxiety disorder in older adults. *American Journal of Geriatric Psychiatry, 13*, 23–30.

Mantella, R. C., Butters, M. A., Dew, M. A., Mulsant, B. H., Begley, A. E., Tracey, B., et al. (2007). Cognitive impairment in late-life generalized anxiety disorder. *American Journal Geriatric Psychiatry, 15*, 673–679.

Maurer, J., Rebbapragada, V., Borson, S., Goldstein, R., Kunik, M. E., Yohannes, A. M, et al. (2008). Anxiety and depression in COPD: Current understanding, unanswered questions, and research needs. *Chest, 134*, 43S–56S.

McNally, R. J. (2007). Mechanisms of exposure therapy: How neuroscience can improve psychological treatments for anxiety disorders. *Clinical Psychology Review, 27*, 750–759.

Metge, C., Grymonpre, R., Dahl, M., & Yogendran, M. (2005). Pharmaceutical use among older adults: Using administrative data to examine medication-related issues. *Canadian Journal on Aging, 24*, 81–95.

Meyer, T. J., Miller, M. L., Metzger, R. L., & Borkovec, T. D. (1990). Development and validation of the Penn State Worry Questionnaire. *Behavior Research and Therapy, 28*, 487–495.

Miller, W. R., & Rollnick, S. (2002). *Motivational interviewing: Preparing people for change* (2nd ed.). New York, NY: Guilford Press.

Nuevo, R., Ruiz, M., Izal, M., Montorio, I., Losada, A., & Márquez-González, M. (2008). A comparison of the factorial structure of DSM-IV criteria for generalized anxiety disorder between younger and older adults. *Journal of Psychopathology and Behavioral Assessment, 30*, 252–260.

Pachana, N. A., Byrne, G. J., Siddle, H., Koloski, N., Harley, E., & Arnold, E. (2007). Development and validation of the geriatric anxiety inventory. *International Psychogeriatrics, 19*, 103–114.

Pariente, A., Dartigues, J. F., Benichou, J., Letenneur, L, Moore, N, & Fourrier-Réglat, A. (2008). Benzodiazepines and injurious falls in community-dwelling elders. *Drugs Aging, 25*, 61–70.

Pinquart, M., & Duberstein, P. R. (2007). Treatment of anxiety disorders in older adults: A meta-analytic comparison of behavioral and pharmacological interventions. *American Journal of Geriatric Psychiatry, 15*, 639–651.

Porensky, E. K., Dew, M. A., Karp, J. F., Skidmore, E., Rollman, B. L., Shear, M. K., et al. (2009). The burden of late-life generalized anxiety disorder: Effects on disability, health-related quality of life, and healthcare utilization. *American Journal of Geriatric Psychiatry, 17*, 473–482.

Raffa, S. D., Stoddard, J. A., White, K. S., Barlow, D. H., Gorman, J. M., Shear, M. K., et al. (2008). Relapse following combined treatment discontinuation in a placebo-controlled trial for panic disorder. *Journal of Nervous and Mental Disease, 196,* 548–555.

Roy-Byrne, P. P., Craske, M. G., Stein, M. B., Sullivan, G., Bystritsky, A., Katon, W., et al. (2005). A randomized effectiveness trial of cognitive-behavioral therapy and medication for primary care panic disorder. *Archives of General Psychiatry, 62,* 290–298.

Roy-Byrne, P., Craske, M. G., Sullivan, G., Rose, R. D., Edlund, M. J., Lang, A. J., Bystritsky, A., Welch, S. S., Chavira, D. A., Golinelli, D., Campbell-Sills, L., Sherbourne, C. D., & Stein, M. B. (2010). Delivery of evidence-based treatment for multiple anxiety disorders in primary care: a randomized controlled trial. *JAMA, 303,* 1921–1928.

Schoevers, R. A., Beekman, A. T., Deeg, D. J., Jonker, C., & van Tilburg, W. (2003). Comorbidity and risk-patterns of depression, generalised anxiety disorder and mixed anxiety-depression in later life: Results from the AMSTEL study. *International Journal of Geriatric Psychiatry, 18,* 994–1001.

Schuurmans, J., Comijs, H., Emmelkamp, P. M., Gundy, C. M., Weijnen, I., van den Hout, M., et al. (2006). A randomized, controlled trial of the effectiveness of cognitive-behavioral therapy and sertraline versus a waitlist control group for anxiety disorders in older adults. *American Journal Geriatric Psychiatry, 14,* 255–263.

Schuurmans, J., Comijs, H., Emmelkamp, P. M., Weijnen, I. J., van den Hout, M., & van Dyck, R. (2009). Long-term effectiveness and prediction of treatment outcome in cognitive behavioral therapy and sertraline for late-life anxiety disorders. *International Psychogeriatrics, 21,* 1148–1159.

Shear, K., Belnap, B. H., Mazumdar, S., Houck, P., & Rollman, B. L. (2006). Generalized anxiety disorder severity scale (GADSS): A preliminary validation study. *Depression and Anxiety, 23,* 77–82.

Solano, J. P., Gomes, B., & Higginson, I. J. (2006). A comparison of symptom prevalence in far advanced cancer, AIDS, heart disease, chronic obstructive pulmonary disease and renal disease. *Journal of Pain and Symptom Management, 31,* 58–69.

Spielberger, C. D. (1983). *Manual for the State-Trait Anxiety Inventory, Form Y.* Palo Alto, CA: Consulting Psychologists Press.

Spitzer, R. L., Kroenke, K., Williams, J. B., & Löwe, B. (2006). A brief measure for assessing generalized anxiety disorder: The GAD-7. *Archives of Internal Medicine, 166,* 1092–1097.

Stanley, M. A., Diefenbach, G. J., Hopko, D. R., Novy, D., Kunik, M. E., Wilson, N., et al. (2003). The nature of generalized anxiety in older primary care patients: Preliminary findings. *Journal of Psychopathology and Behavioral Assessment, 25,* 273–280.

Stanley, M. A., Novy, D. M., Bourland, S. L., Beck, J. G., & Averill, P. M. (2001). Assessing older adults with generalized anxiety: A replication and extension. *Behaviour Research and Therapy, 39,* 221–235.

Stanley, M. A., Wilson, N. L., Novy, D. M., Rhoades, H. M., Wagener, P. D., Greisinger, A. J., et al. (2009). Cognitive behavior therapy for generalized anxiety disorder among older adults in primary care: A randomized clinical trial. *Journal of the American Medical Association, 301,* 1460–1467.

Starkstein, S. E., Jorge, R., Petracca, G., & Robinson, R. G. (2007). The construct of generalized anxiety disorder in Alzheimer disease. *American Journal of Geriatric Psychiatry, 15,* 42–49.

Swales, P.J., Solfvin, J. F., & Sheikh, J. I. (1996). Cognitive-behavioral therapy in older panic disorder patients. *American Journal of Geriatric Psychiatry, 4*, 46–60.

Thorp, S. R., Ayers, C. R., Nuevo, R., Stoddard, J. E., Sorrell, J. T., & Wetherell, J. L. (2009). Meta-analysis comparing different behavioral treatments for late-life anxiety. *American Journal of Geriatric Psychiatry, 17*, 105–115.

Todaro, J. F., Shen, B. J., Raffa, S. D., Tilkemeier, P. L., & Niaura, R. (2007). Prevalence of anxiety disorders in men and women with established coronary heart disease. *Journal of Cardiopulmonary Rehabilitation and Prevention, 27*, 86–91.

Tolin, D. F., Robison, J. T., Gaztambide, S., & Blank, K. (2005). Anxiety disorders in older Puerto Rican primary care patients. *American Journal of Geriatric Psychiatry, 13*, 150–156.

Trollor, J. N., Anderson, T. M., Sachdev, P. S., Brodaty, H., & Andrews, G. (2007). Prevalence of mental disorders in the elderly: The Australian National Mental Health and Well-Being Survey. *American Journal of Geriatric Psychiatry, 15*, 455–466.

Unützer, J., Katon, W., Callahan, C. M., Williams, J. W., Jr., Hunkeler, E., Harpole, L., et al. (2002). Collaborative care management of late-life depression in the primary care setting: A randomized controlled trial. *Journal of the American Medical Association, 288*, 2836–2845.

van Hout, H. P., Beekman, A. T., de Beurs, E., Comijs, H., van Marwijk, H., de Haan, M., et al. (2004). Anxiety and the risk of death in older men and women. *British Journal of Psychiatry, 185*, 399–404.

Vink, D., Aartsen, M. J., & Schoevers, R. A. (2008). Risk factors for anxiety and depression in the elderly: A review. *Journal of Affective Disorders, 106*, 29–44.

Westra, H. A., & Stewart, S. H. (1998). Cognitive behavioural therapy and pharmacotherapy: Complementary or contradictory approaches to the treatment of anxiety? *Clinical Psychology Review, 18*, 307–340.

Wetherell, J. L., Afari, N., Ayers, C. R., Stoddard, J. A., Ruberg, J., Sorrell, J. T., Liu, L., Petkus, A. J., Thorp, S. R., Kraft, A., & Patterson, T. L. (in press). Acceptance and commitment therapy for generalized anxiety disorder in older adults: A preliminary report. *Behavior Therapy.*

Wetherell, J. L., & Areán, P. A. (1997). Psychometric evaluation of the Beck Anxiety Inventory with older medical patients. *Psychological Assessment, 9*, 136–144.

Wetherell, J. L., Ayers, C. R., Sorrell, J. T., Thorp, S. R., Nuevo, R., Belding, W., et al. (2009). Modular psychotherapy for anxiety in older primary care patients. *American Journal of Geriatric Psychiatry, 17*, 483–492.

Wetherell, J. L., Birchler, G. D., Ramsdell, J., & Unützer, J. (2007). Screening for generalized anxiety disorder in geriatric primary care patients. *International Journal of Geriatric Psychiatry, 22*, 115–123.

Wetherell, J. L., & Gatz, M. (2005). The Beck anxiety inventory in older adults with generalized anxiety disorder. *Journal of Psychopathology and Behavioral Assessment, 27*, 17–24.

Wetherell, J. L., Hopko, D. R., Diefenbach, G. J., Averill, P. M., Beck, J. G., Craske, M. G., et al. (2005). Cognitive-behavioral therapy for late-life generalized anxiety disorder: Who gets better? *Behavior Therapy, 36*, 147–156.

Wetherell, J. L., Le Roux, H., & Gatz, M. (2003). DSM-IV criteria for generalized anxiety disorder in older adults: Distinguishing the worried from the well. *Psychology and Aging, 18*, 622–627.

Wetherell, J. L., Petkus, A. J., McChesney, K., Stein, M. B., Judd, P. H., Rockwell, E., et al. (2009). Older adults are less accurate than younger adults at identifying symptoms of anxiety and depression. *Journal of Nervous and Mental Disease, 197,* 623–626.

Wetherell, J. L., Stoddard, J. A., White, K. S., Kornblith, S. J., Nguyen, H., Andreescu, C., Zisook, S., & Lenze, E. J. (in press). Antidepressant medication with modular CBT for geriatric generalized anxiety disorder: A pilot study. *International Journal of Geriatric Psychiatry.*

Wetherell, J. L., Thorp, S. R., Patterson, T. L., Golshan, S., Jeste, D. V., & Gatz, M. (2004). Quality of life in geriatric generalized anxiety disorder: A preliminary investigation. *Journal of Psychiatric Research, 38,* 305–312.

Wetherell, J. L., & Unützer, J. (2003). Adherence to treatment for geriatric depression and anxiety. *CNS Spectrums, 8* (3), 48–59.

Wright, R. M., Roumani, Y. F., Boudreau, R., Newman, A. B., Ruby, C. M., Studenski, S. A., et al. (2009). Effect of central nervous system medication use on decline in cognition in community-dwelling older adults: Findings from the health, aging and body composition study. *Journal of the American Geriatric Society, 57,* 243–250.

Zigmond, A. S., & Snaith, R. P. (1983). The hospital anxiety and depression scale. *Acta Psychiatrica Scandinavica, 67,* 361–370.

APPENDIX A

GERIATRIC ANXIETY INVENTORY

Read each statement and circle the best response for you, even if neither is perfect.

1.	I worry a lot of the time.	YES	NO
2.	I find it difficult to make a decision.	YES	NO
3.	I often feel jumpy.	YES	NO
4.	I find it hard to relax.	YES	NO
5.	I often cannot enjoy things because of my worries.	YES	NO
6.	Little things bother me a lot.	YES	NO
7.	I often feel like I have butterflies in my stomach.	YES	NO
8.	I think of myself as a worrier.	YES	NO
9.	I can't help worrying about even trivial things.	YES	NO
10.	I often feel nervous.	YES	NO
11.	My own thoughts often make me anxious.	YES	NO
12.	I get an upset stomach due to my worrying.	YES	NO
13.	I think of myself as a nervous person.	YES	NO
14.	I always anticipate the worst will happen.	YES	NO
15.	I often feel shaky inside.	YES	NO
16.	I think that my worries interfere with my life.	YES	NO
17.	My worries often overwhelm me.	YES	NO
18.	I sometimes feel a great knot in my stomach.	YES	NO
19.	I miss out on things because I worry too much.	YES	NO
20.	I often feel upset.	YES	NO

APPENDIX B

PENN STATE WORRY QUESTIONNAIRE AND ABBREVIATED PENN STATE WORRY QUESTIONNAIRE

Please select the answer that best fits you.

	Strongly Disagree	Disagree	Neither Agree nor Disagree	Agree	Strongly Agree
1. If I do not have enough time to do everything, I do not worry about it.	1	2	3	4	5
*2. My worries overwhelm me.	1	2	3	4	5
3. I do not tend to worry about things.	1	2	3	4	5
*4. Many situations make me worry.	1	2	3	4	5
5. I know I should not worry about things, but I just cannot help it.	1	2	3	4	5
*6. When I am under pressure, I worry a lot.	1	2	3	4	5
*7. I am always worrying about something.	1	2	3	4	5
8. I find it easy to dismiss worrisome thoughts.	1	2	3	4	5

	Strongly Disagree	Disagree	Neither Agree nor Disagree	Agree	Strongly Agree
*9. As soon as I finish one task, I start to worry about everything else I must do.	1	2	3	4	5
10. I never worry about anything.	1	2	3	4	5
11. When there is nothing more I can do about a concern, I do not worry about it any more.	1	2	3	4	5
*12. I have been a worrier all my life.	1	2	3	4	5
*13. I notice that I have been worrying about things.	1	2	3	4	5
14. Once I start worrying, I cannot stop.	1	2	3	4	5
15. I worry all the time.	1	2	3	4	5
16. I worry about projects until they are done.	1	2	3	4	5

Note. * indicates PSWQ-A items. Items 1, 3, 8, 10, and 11 are reversed scored

APPENDIX C

GENERALIZED ANXIETY DISORDER-7

Over the last 2 weeks, how often have you been bothered by the following problems?

	Not at All	Several Days	More Than Half the Days	Nearly Every Day
1. Feeling nervous, anxious, or on edge?	0	1	2	3
2. Not being able to stop or control worrying?	0	1	2	3
3. Worrying too much about different things?	0	1	2	3
4. Trouble relaxing?	0	1	2	3
5. Being so restless that it is hard to sit still?	0	1	2	3
6. Being easily annoyed or irritable?	0	1	2	3
7. Feeling afraid as if something awful might happen?	0	1	2	3

APPENDIX D

PROGRESSIVE MUSCLE RELAXATION SCRIPT

In a moment, I will instruct you to tense a specific area of your body. Only tense the muscles enough to notice the difference from relaxation; you should *not* be straining or tightening them more than a little bit. You want to hold that tension for about 10 seconds, then release it and focus on the area, for about 20 seconds, until I instruct you to tense again. Pay attention to the difference between how your muscles feel when they are tense and when they are relaxed.

Now, get into a comfortable position and take a few slow deep breaths. Watch me and do the exercises just like I do. We'll start with your feet and work your way up.

1. Build up the tension in your lower legs by flexing your feet and pointing your toes toward your upper body. Feel the tension as it spreads through your feet, your ankles, your shins, and your calf muscles. Feel the tension spreading down the back of the leg and into the foot, under the foot, and around the toes. Focus on that part of your body for 10 seconds. . . . Now release the leg tension. . . . Let your legs relax heavily onto the floor. Feel the difference in the muscles as they relax. Feel the release from tension, the sense of comfort, and the warmth and heaviness of relaxation. Relax the muscles for 20 seconds.

2. First, build up the tension in your upper legs by pulling your knees together and lifting your legs off the chair. Focus on the tightness through your upper legs. Feel the pulling sensations from your top down and notice the tension in your legs. Focus on that part of your body for 10 seconds. . . . Now, release the tension and let your legs drop heavily down onto the floor. Let the tension disappear. Focus on the feeling of relaxation. Feel the difference in your legs. Focus on the feeling of comfort for 20 seconds.

3. Now, build up the tension in your stomach by pulling your stomach in toward the spine. Feel the tension. Feel the tightness and focus on that part of your body for 10 seconds. . . . Now, let the stomach go—let it go further and further. Feel the sense of warmth circulating across your stomach. Feel the comfort of relaxation (20 seconds).

4. Now, build up the tension around your chest by taking a deep breath and holding it. Your chest is expanded and the muscles are stretched around your chest—feel the tension around your front and your back. Hold your breath (10 seconds). . . . Now, slowly let the air escape and breathe normally, letting the air flow in and out smoothly and easily. Feel the difference as the muscles relax in comparison to the tension (20 seconds).

5. Build up the tension in your lower arms by making fists with your hands and pulling up on the wrists. If your nails are long, press your fingers against your palms to make fists. Feel the tension through your lower arms, wrists, fingers, knuckles, and hands. Focus on the tension—notice the sensations of pulling and of tightness. Hold the tension for 10 seconds. . . . Now, release the tension and let your hands and lower arms relax onto your lap, with palms facing down. Focus your attention onto the sensations of warmth in your hands and arms. Feel the release from tension. Relax the muscles for 20 seconds. . . .

6. Now, build up the tension in your upper arms by pulling the arms back and in toward your sides. Feel the tension in the back of the arms, radiating up into your shoulders and back. Focus on the sensations of tension. Hold the tension for 10 seconds. . . . Now, release the arms and let them relax heavily down. Focus on your upper arms and feel the difference compared to the tension. Your arms feel heavy, warm, and relaxed. Relax for 20 seconds.

7. Moving up to your shoulders, imagine your shoulders are on strings being pulled up toward your ears. Feel the tension around your shoulders, radiating down into your back and up into your neck and the back of your head. Focus on that part of your body. Describe the sensations to yourself. Focus (10 seconds) . . . and then let the shoulders droop down. Let them droop further and further, feeling very relaxed. Feel the sense of relaxation around your neck and shoulders. Focus on the comfort of relaxation (20 seconds).

8. Build up the tension around your neck by pressing the back of your neck backward and pulling your chin down toward your chest. Feel the tightness around the back of the neck spreading up into your head. Focus on the tension (10 seconds). . . . Now release, letting your head rest heavily against the bed or chair. Nothing is holding it up except for the support behind. Focus on the relaxation and feel the difference from the tension (20 seconds).

9. Build up the tension around your mouth and jaw and throat by clenching your teeth and forcing the corners of your mouth back into a forced smile. Hold the tension. Feel the tightness and

describe the sensations to yourself (10 seconds). . . . And now, release the tension, letting your mouth drop open and the muscles around the throat and jaw relax. Focus on the difference in the sensations in that part of your body (20 seconds). . . .

10. Now, build up the tension around your eyes by squeezing your eyes together for a few seconds (10 seconds) . . . and releasing. Let the tension disappear from around your eyes. Feel the difference as the muscles relax (20 seconds). . . .

11. Now, build up the tension across the lower forehead by frowning, pulling your eyebrows down and toward the center. Feel the tension across your forehead and the top of your head. Focus on the tension for 10 seconds . . . and then release, smoothing out the wrinkles and letting your forehead relax. Feel the difference (20 seconds). . . .

12. Finally, build up the tension across the upper forehead by raising your eyebrows up as high as you can. Feel the wrinkling and the pulling sensations across your forehead and the top of your head. Hold the tension (10 seconds) . . . and then relax, letting your eyebrows rest down and the tension leave. Focus on the sensations of relaxation and feel the difference compared to the tension (20 seconds).

Now, your whole body is feeling relaxed and comfortable. As I count from one to five, feel yourself becoming even more relaxed. . . . One, letting all the tension leave your body. Two, sinking further and further into relaxation. Three, feeling more and more relaxed. Four, feeling very relaxed. Five, deeply relaxed. Now, as you spend a few minutes in this relaxed state, think about your breathing. Feel the cool air as you breathe in and the warm air as you breathe out. Your breathing is slow and regular. And every time you breathe out, think to yourself the word "relax" . . . "relax" . . . "relax." Feeling comfortable and relaxed (2 minutes). . . . Now, as I count backward from five to one, gradually feel yourself becoming more alert and awake. Five, feeling more awake. Four, coming out of the relaxation. Three, feeling more alert. Two, opening your eyes. One, sitting up and coming back to session.

APPENDIX E

IMAGERY SCRIPT

In front of you is a path to your special place. Walk slowly to your special place. As you walk, you notice that you are becoming calmer and less tense; you have left your worry and anxiety behind. The temperature is very comfortable. Look around. Feel yourself becoming more relaxed. What do you see? Notice how everything looks, where things are. *(pause)* What do you hear? *(pause)* Is there anything in front of you? *(pause)* Go ahead and reach out and touch it. Notice how it feels in your hand. You are feeling safe and calm, there's nothing that concerns you.

You have reached your special place. What's under your feet? How does it feel? Take a few more steps. Look around. What's above you? *(pause)* Do you hear anything? *(pause)* Do you hear anything else? *(pause)* Look around again. *(pause)* Go ahead and touch what's in front of you. Notice the texture. *(pause)* Now, look around again. Look as far as you can see. *(pause)* What do you see? *(pause)* Can you hear anything? Do you smell anything? Taste anything?

Sit or lie down in your special place. You are very calm, very relaxed. Pay attention to what you see, hear, feel, taste, and smell. Stay here for a while, knowing that you are safe, comfortable, and relaxed. (3–5 minutes)

Memorize the sights, sounds, feelings, tastes, and smells of this place. You can return here to relax any time you like. Now stand up, and walk back on the same path as before. Slowly open your eyes as you reach the end of your path. Remember that you can go back any time you want to.

7

Posttraumatic Stress Disorder Among Older Adults

Steven R. Thorp, Heather M. Sones, and Joan M. Cook

Posttraumatic stress disorder (PTSD) is the fourth most common psychiatric disorder in the United States, and is considered a major public health problem because of the high rates of associated disability (Davidson, 2000; Keane & Barlow, 2002; Zatzick, 2003). Among adults in the general population, PTSD has been linked to psychiatric and physical comorbidity (Brady, 1997; Kessler, Sonnega, Bromet, Hughes, & Nelson, 1995; Otis, Keane, & Kerns, 2003), dissociation (Bremner et al., 1992), substance use disorders (Chilcoat & Breslau, 1998), disruptions in social and occupational functioning (Thorp & Stein, 2005, 2008), reduction in quality of life (Warshaw et al., 1993), diminished social support (Davidson, Hughes, Blazer, & George, 1991), hospitalization (Solomon & Davidson, 1997), and mortality (Johnson, Fontana, Lubin, Corn, & Rosenheck, 2004).

The most recent *Diagnostic and Statistical Manual of Mental Disorders* (*DSM*) definition of PTSD (American Psychiatric Association [APA], 2000) dictates that to meet diagnostic criteria, individuals must (a) experience, witness, or learn about an event that involved actual or threatened death or injury to themselves or others, and respond with intense fear, helplessness, or horror; (b) "reexperience" the event in one or more ways (e.g., repeated, disturbing memories, thoughts, or vivid images); (c) persistently avoid stimuli associated with the traumatic event (e.g., talking about the event, or being in situations that cue memories) and/or demonstrate numbing of responsiveness (e.g., reduced ability to experience love or joy); (d) demonstrate persistent increased arousal that has emerged since the traumatic event (e.g., trouble sleeping, feeling irritable or angry, feeling "on guard" and "jumpy"); and (e) demonstrate functional impairment or clinically significant distress from symptoms for more than 1 month.

The population in the United States and other industrialized countries is growing older. Worldwide, the proportion of adults aged 65 or older will more than double from 2009 to 2050 (U.S. Census Bureau, 2009). There is also a greater proportion of women among older adults, and women are known to be at greater risk for developing PTSD (Davidson, 2000). Although compared to the general adult population there is relatively less known about PTSD in older adults, the changing age demographic will likely translate to an increased need for better understanding of PTSD in older individuals.

The purpose of this chapter is to briefly summarize the literature on the epidemiology, phenomenology, course, risk factors, assessment, and treatment of PTSD in older adults. It is important to note that most of the empirical literature on PTSD in older adults comes primarily from one of two groups: those who experienced trauma earlier in life during military combat/captivity (namely, World War II and the Korean Conflict) or the Holocaust; and those who experienced trauma later in life, namely, in natural and man-made disaster (for reviews, see Averill & Beck, 2000; Cook & Elmore, 2009). There is much less known about PTSD in older women and minority groups, and about the effects of interpersonal violence and crime victimization (including physical and sexual assault, rape, elder abuse) and terrorism in older adults.

EPIDEMIOLOGY OF TRAUMATIC EXPOSURE AND POSTTRAUMATIC STRESS DISORDER

Estimates of lifetime exposure to traumatic events among community samples of older adults range between 69% and 86% (Bramsen & van der Ploeg, 1999; Norris, 1992; Schnurr, Spiro, Aldwin, & Stukel, 1998), which is similar to rates reported by younger and middle-aged adults (Norris). The lifetime prevalence rate for PTSD in the general adult population is approximately 8% (Kessler et al., 1995). Until recently, most epidemiological investigations did not include any older adults or sufficient numbers of older adults on whom estimates could be established. Additionally, studies on prevalence rates in older adults typically focused on one particular event (i.e., combat, Holocaust, natural disaster), relied on nonrandom or convenience samples, and grouped all older adults into one age category (Cook & Niederehe, 2007). However, in the past few years, several large epidemiological studies using representative samples have examined the prevalence of traumatic exposure and rates of PTSD in older adults (Creamer & Parslow, 2008; De Vries & Olff, 2009; Kessler et al., 2005; Spitzer et al., 2008).

In one of the largest epidemiological investigations of psychiatric disorders in the United States, the National Comorbidity Survey-Replication, lifetime prevalence of PTSD in adults aged 60 or older was 2.5%, significantly lower than in other age groups (Kessler et al., 2005). In a large national survey of Australian community-residing adults, 12-month PTSD prevalence rates generally decreased across age cohorts, with a rate of 0.2% among those aged 65 or older (Creamer & Parslow, 2008). Similarly, in a national representative sample of adults residing in the Netherlands, De Vries and Olff (2009) found that there was a steady decrease in lifetime prevalence of PTSD with age, with a rate of 2.7% in those aged over 65. Only one large population-based survey of individuals, residing in Germany, indicated that lifetime and current PTSD prevalence rates did not differ among young, middle-aged, and older adults, with lifetime and current PTSD rates in older individuals at 3.1% and 1.5%, respectively (Spitzer et al., 2008). Although these investigations represent a significant advancement in the field, it is important to note that there are still limitations, particularly the exclusion of the least healthy and perhaps most vulnerable older adults, those who are physically or emotionally impaired, homebound, or long-term care residents (Cook & Elmore, 2009).

A large scale investigation that examined rates of PTSD in Vietnam theater veterans is particularly important to note given its increasing relevance to the literature on aging trauma survivors. In the largest study of prevalence rates of PTSD in combat veterans (Kulka et al., 1990), 30% of male veterans met criteria for lifetime PTSD, and 15% met criteria for current PTSD (more than a decade after the Vietnam war had ended). The fact that nearly half a million Vietnam veterans are approaching older adulthood with PTSD underscores the importance of studying PTSD in late life, particularly in populations with high rates of trauma (e.g., veterans, refugees).

Although, as previously noted, rates of syndromal PTSD are lower in older as opposed to younger adults, there is little investigation on partial or subsyndromal PTSD in this population. One exception is the population-based epidemiological study of PTSD in older adults in the Netherlands (Van Zelst, de Beurs, Beekman, Deeg, & van Dyck, 2003b). There was a 6-month prevalence rate of 0.9% for full syndromal PTSD; however, 13.1% met criteria for subsyndromal PTSD. Notably, subsyndromal PTSD was assessed by the SRIP, which is known to underestimate true PTSD symptoms (Van Zelst, de Beurs, Beekman, Deeg, & van Dyck, 2003a). This suggests that older adults may experience significant posttraumatic stress symptoms, and attending only to syndromal PTSD may neglect important problems in this population. Lack of recognition or acknowledgment of subsyndromal PTSD symptoms can have serious consequences for older adults and can dictate the effectiveness, efficiency, and cost of treatments (Averill & Beck, 2000). In addition, there are other long-term psychological effects of traumatic exposure that are in need of further investigation in older adult populations, particularly depression (e.g., Cook, Areán, Schnurr, & Sheikh, 2001).

Trauma exposure and PTSD have been described as "hidden variables" and "silent problems" in older adults because they are often neglected by clinicians, researchers, and older adults themselves (Hyer, Summers, Braswell, & Boyd, 1995; Nichols & Czirr, 1986; Spiro, Schnurr, & Aldwin, 1994). This may arise because PTSD is a relatively new and evolving psychiatric disorder. Because PTSD did not enter the official diagnostic nomenclature until 1980, individuals who likely met criteria for PTSD in prior years (e.g., veterans of World War II, the Korean Conflict, and the Vietnam War) were not diagnosed during or soon after the traumatic event. In addition, retrospective estimates of PTSD are likely biased by deficits in recall and by avoidance of thinking about or talking about the traumatic events, which is a diagnostic hallmark of the disorder. There is also increased mortality among individuals with PTSD relative to those who do not meet diagnostic criteria (Johnson et al., 2004), so those who may have died as a direct result of traumatic events or subsequent complications are not counted in prevalence estimates.

Several additional factors can also influence the ability to gain an accurate estimate of the prevalence of PTSD in older adults. Older adults may be more willing to disclose somatic complaints than mental health concerns. This may make PTSD particularly difficult to identify in older individuals, especially if the professional with whom they are working does not evaluate the individual's trauma history. Furthermore, older adults are less likely to report trauma or accurately interpret events in their lives as traumatic (Acierno et al., 2002), and may underreport mental health problems associated with negative events (Hankin, Abueg, Gallagher-Thompson, & Laws, 1996; Lasoski, 1986). These problems may be compounded when assessing PTSD, because trauma victims who develop PTSD seek help less often than individuals with other emotional problems (Kimerling & Calhoun, 1994; Norris, Kaniasty, & Scheer, 1990). Elderly ex-prisoners-of-war (POWs), for example, are believed to underreport psychiatric symptoms partly due to a hesitancy to complain, as well as a suspicion about institutions after war and repatriation experiences (Kluznik, Speed, Van Valkenberg, & Magraw, 1986; Lipton & Shaffer, 1986, 1988).

PHENOMENOLOGY

There is some evidence to suggest that PTSD may be experienced or expressed differently in older as opposed to younger adults (Rodgers, Norman, Thorp, Lebeck, & Lang, 2005). For example, older adults who experience trauma in late life appear to demonstrate higher levels of avoidance, more sleep problems, more crying spells, and more hyperarousal symptoms than middle-aged or younger adults (Goenjian et al., 1994; Hagstrom, 1995). When comparing older and younger male veterans, Frueh et al. (2004) found that older veterans had lower overall levels of PTSD symptoms, particularly within the arousal and avoidance/numbing clusters. However, there were no significant differences between age groups on reexperiencing symptoms or on depressive or dissociative symptoms.

It is suspected that older adults with PTSD or trauma-related pathology report somatic complaints more often than complaints about psychiatric symptoms. For example, when compared to their younger counterparts, older adults may be more likely to report problems with appetite, sleep, or cognitive problems than subjective problems with mood (Reynolds & Kupfer, 1999). In preparations for *DSM-V*, considerations of older adults with PTSD may influence how symptoms are described. However, despite some disparities in symptom presentation between older and younger adults, there is not enough evidence to warrant a unique set of diagnostic criteria for late-life PTSD.

COURSE AND PROGNOSIS OF POSTTRAUMATIC STRESS DISORDER

Most scientific investigations of older adult trauma survivors are cross-sectional, and few studies on young or middle-aged adult trauma survivors have longitudinally followed individuals into older adulthood. However, it does appear that if left untreated, PTSD is persistent and follows an episodic course (Ronis et al., 1996). Indeed, more than a third of people with PTSD fail to recover over many years (Kessler et al., 1995). For example, Summers, Hyer, Boyd, and Boudewyns (1996) found that half of the veterans in their sample had avoidant or hyperarousal symptoms of PTSD even 50 years after the initial traumatic event. Additionally, a study of Holocaust survivors found that 48% met criteria for current PTSD decades after the trauma (Yehuda, Kahana, Southwick, & Giller, 1994).

Only one investigation thus far obtained retrospective and longitudinal data indicating that older former POWs (mean age 76 years) showed an immediate onset and gradual decline of PTSD symptoms after the war, followed by a return of higher PTSD symptom levels in later life (Port, Engdahl, & Frazier, 2001). It is possible that the exacerbation of symptoms in later life may be caused by increased cognitive impairment, more social isolation, or decrements in health status. Indeed, it has been argued that age-related decreases in attention, working memory, explicit memory, and prospective memory may result in the recurrence of PTSD in late life (Floyd, Rice, & Black, 2002). It has been suggested that the neurodegeneration of memory pathways from dementias (e.g., Alzheimer's disease, vascular dementia, alcohol-related dementia) could result in the reexpression of PTSD symptoms (Mittal, Torres, Abashidze, & Jimerson, 2001). It is also possible that individuals can suppress PTSD symptoms via high levels of activity (e.g., working multiple jobs or carrying out demanding family duties) until disease, injury, or personal loss results in diminished activity and the reemergence of severe PTSD symptoms (Lipton & Shaffer, 1988).

Although there have been many clinical reports of late-onset PTSD, primarily in male combat veterans (for review, see Hiskey, Luckie, Davies, & Brewin, 2008), this phenomenon has rarely been empirically examined. In a systematic review of delayed-onset PTSD in heterogeneous samples including older adults, Andrews, Brewin, Philpott, and Stewart (2008) found that although delayed-onset PTSD is empirically verified, it is rare in the absence of any prior symptoms. Thus, delayed-onset PTSD is more likely subthreshold PTSD that worsens over time (Andrews et al.) and may be more accurately conceptualized as delayed recognition (Pary, Turns, & Tobias, 1986).

ASSOCIATED PSYCHIATRIC AND PHYSICAL COMORBIDITY

PTSD has very high rates of psychiatric comorbidity (Brown, Campbell, Lehman, Grisham, & Mancil, 2001). Kessler et al. (1995) found that 88% of men and 79% of women with PTSD had a lifetime history of at least one other psychiatric disorder. Among the most common comorbid psychiatric disorders are major depression, generalized anxiety disorder, panic disorder, substance abuse, personality disorders, and dissociative disorders. Although younger adults with histories of anxiety or affective disorders appear to be much more likely to develop chronic PTSD than those without such histories (Breslau & Davis, 1992), PTSD often precedes comorbid affective or substance use disorders (Kessler et al.). Among older adults, PTSD has been associated with major depression, other anxiety disorders, and substance and alcohol abuse (Averill & Beck, 2000).

PTSD has also been linked to various health problems among older adults. The nature of this association is often unclear. Early trauma histories may contribute to health problems in late life, and conversely, health problems may initiate or exacerbate PTSD symptoms (Ladwig et al., 1999). Most studies in this area have used samples of men who were military veterans, former POWs, or Holocaust survivors. Veterans with PTSD have poorer self-rated physical health than those without PTSD (Schnurr & Spiro, 1999; Summers et al., 1996). In addition, Schnurr, Spiro, and Paris (2000) found that even after controlling for age, smoking, and body weight, older veterans with PTSD symptoms were more often diagnosed with arterial, gastrointestinal, dermatologic, and musculoskeletal disorders than those without PTSD. Lipton and Schaffer (1986, 1988) similarly noted that military veterans have high rates of cardiovascular disease (e.g., hypertension and myocardial infarctions requiring bypass surgeries), gastrointestinal disorders (e.g., stomach upset and pain, peptic ulcers, colitis, esophageal pain, and digestive problems), musculoskeletal problems (e.g., arthritis and other pains), and insomnia. Older men who had been POWs demonstrate high levels of negative health changes, somatization, cognitive deficits, and interpersonal problems in addition to PTSD symptomatology (Engdahl, Speed, Eberly, & Schwartz, 1991; Port, Engdahl, Frazier, & Eberly, 2002; Sutker, Winstead, Galina, & Allain, 1991). It is possible that some physical problems in former POWs may be caused by malnutrition and physical abuse rather than PTSD per se (Lipton & Shaffer, 1986). Nonetheless, adverse changes in health during old age (e.g., pain, difficulty sleeping, difficulty breathing) may evoke memories of POW traumatic experiences (Port et al., 2002).

Male and female Holocaust survivors have poorer self-reported and observed health and more pain than non-Holocaust survivors (Landau & Litwin, 2000; Stermer, Bar, & Levy, 1991; Yaari, Eisenberg, Adler, & Birkhan, 1999). Shmotkin and Barilan (2002) found that Holocaust survivors who reported frequent intrusive memories of Holocaust experiences had higher numbers of comorbid medical and mental health problems compared to survivors who were able to avoid preoccupation with these recollections. In addition, Higgins and Follette (2002) found that older women with histories of interpersonal trauma appear to have more health problems and take more medications than older women without such histories.

RISK FACTORS FOR POSTTRAUMATIC STRESS DISORDER

Individuals with PTSD, compared to those without the disorder, are more likely to have histories of a psychiatric illness, child abuse, and family adversity (Brewin, Andrews, & Valentine, 2000; Davidson et al., 1991). Predictors of a protracted course of PTSD and poor outcome include an intense physiologic response to the traumatic event, ongoing life stressors, dissociative phenomena, emotional constriction, and drug and alcohol abuse (Van der Kolk, 1987). Among older adults in the community, neuroticism and adverse events in childhood are significant vulnerability factors for full and subthreshold PTSD (Van Zelst et al., 2003b).

There are reasons to believe that the older adult population may be particularly vulnerable to PTSD. Older adults experience significant negative life events (Summers & Hyer, 1994), and the transitions associated with late life (e.g., retirement; widowhood; the loss of friends and family because of relocation, illness, and death) may combine with physical illness, cognitive decline, and functional problems to exacerbate the stress associated with negative events (Bonwick & Morris, 1996; Bossé, Spiro, & Levenson, 1997; Gatz, 1994; Green, Epstein, Krupnick, & Rowland, 1997; Schnurr, 1996).

ASSESSMENT IN OLDER ADULTS

Accurate diagnostic assessment is important for communication among clinicians and patients, for selecting treatments, for monitoring change over time, and for evaluating outcomes. There are several general issues to consider when assessing older adults (Thorp & Lynch, 2005). Many domains must be evaluated, including comorbid medical and psychiatric problems, medication adherence and tolerance, substance abuse and dependence, and past and current status of suicidal and parasuicidal behaviors. Cognitive status can vary considerably among older adults. Establishing a baseline for cognitive status can be useful during subsequent evaluations and it can help clinicians gauge the appropriateness of certain types of psychotherapy and medication regimens. Each of these areas can dramatically influence treatment implementation and outcome. Items that include slang or psychological jargon should be avoided. It is important to consider how social desirability of responses and differences among age cohorts may affect the expression of psychiatric symptoms. As noted, older adults may be hesitant to complain or discuss mental health issues related to themselves or their families. Questionnaires should be printed in large, bold fonts. This will likely reduce frustration about paperwork and the clinical process, but more importantly, there is some evidence that materials that are easier to read promote greater disclosure (Alter & Oppenheimer, 2009). Whenever possible, it is important to gather collateral data from family members, friends, or caregivers to augment self-report and observational methods.

ASSESSMENT OF POSTTRAUMATIC STRESS DISORDER IN OLDER ADULTS

Aging-related issues may affect the experience and expression of PTSD in older individuals and therefore tailored assessment and treatment for this age group is likely needed. Assessing PTSD in older adults presents numerous challenges. First, clinicians must remember to systematically ask older patients about exposure to past potentially traumatic events such as combat, accidents, sexual assault, or crime victimization. Many older adults present symptoms to primary care providers rather than mental health specialists, and because of time constraints, there may be a focus on current stressors rather than the historical context of symptoms. Asking about past traumatic events can normalize such events, encourage discussion, reduce stigma, and guide treatment decisions. Second, clinicians may recognize and treat some of the symptoms associated with PTSD (e.g., difficulty sleeping, hyperarousal) while neglecting the factors that maintain the global disorder (e.g., avoidance of stimuli, withdrawal from social support). Third, diagnostic assessment in older adults can be complicated by medical conditions and medications. There are many age-related changes that can affect the experience and expression of anxiety symptoms (Kogan, Edelstein, & McKee, 2000; Lau, Edelstein, & Larkin, 2001). For example, older adults may not display acute hyperarousal symptoms with the same intensity of younger adults, and the "sense of foreshortened future," which is a hallmark of PTSD, may not be as apparent when many milestones used to gauge this experience may have passed (e.g., marriage, birth of children, retirement).

As with younger adults, it is crucial that assessment of older adults includes the age of onset, severity, duration, and course of PTSD. It is particularly important to assess how these characteristics of the disorder are associated with changes in social support, mobility, self-care, employment, activity level, living situation, or health status. This can often be accomplished by constructing a visual time line of the disorder and important life events with the patient. It is also imperative to determine the meaning attributed to traumatic events and subsequent coping styles because there are some indications that these can influence the severity of the disorder (Averill & Beck, 2000). Other factors to assess include patients' level of motivation for treatment, prior treatment experiences (including psychotherapy and pharmacotherapy), and expectations for the current treatment. Finally, the use of more than one assessment measure is recommended because single measures are known to underestimate the prevalence of PTSD (Kulka et al., 1991). It is also good practice to use more than one method of assessment (e.g., self-report, observation, caregiver report, structured interviews). This is an important point, given that structured clinical interviews may yield higher prevalence rates than self-report questionnaires (Averill & Beck).

INSTRUMENTS FOR ASSESSING POSTTRAUMATIC STRESS DISORDER IN OLDER ADULTS

Table 7.1 provides a summary of PTSD instruments with established psychometrics using older adult samples. In regard to PTSD assessment, one of the most frequently used structured clinical interviews is the Clinician-Administered PTSD Scale (CAPS; Blake et al., 1995; Elhai, Gray, Kashdan, & Franklin, 2005). Since its introduction in 1990, the CAPS has become the "gold standard" for assessing PTSD in the general population because of its flexibility and excellent psychometric properties (Weathers, Keane, & Davidson, 2001). Hyer, Summers, Boyd, Litaker, and Boudewyns (1996) examined the use of the CAPS in a sample of older combat veterans and found that the scale was appropriate for use in this population based on its high internal consistency (alphas of 0.95 across the 17 core symptoms) and high validity (sensitivity, specificity, efficiency, and agreement) when compared to a computer-assisted version of the Structured Clinical Interview for *DSM-III-R* Decision Tree (First, Williams, & Spitzer, 1988).

Most studies on the applicability and accuracy of several self-report measures of PTSD in older adults have been conducted with older combat veterans and former POWs (for more detailed review, see Cook & O'Donnell, 2005). In brief, PTSD can be reliably and validly assessed in this population through various self-report measures: the Mississippi Scale for Combat-Related PTSD (Keane, Caddell, & Taylor, 1988), the Minnesota Multiphasic Personality Inventory PTSD Scale

TABLE 7.1   Summary of Assessment Instruments for Posttraumatic Stress Disorder in Older Adults

Scale	Type	Approximate Time Required	Notes
Clinician-Administered PTSD Scale (CAPS)	Interview	45 minutes	Provides both diagnostic status and a dimensional score (i.e., whether they have PTSD and how severe it is); requires training to administer reliably
PTSD Checklist (PCL)	Self-report	5 minutes	There are three versions: For military veterans (PCL-M), for the general population (PCL-C), and for a specific event (PCL-S)
Mississippi Scale for Combat-Related PTSD (M-PTSD)	Self-report	5 minutes	Designed to assess PTSD from combat
Impact of Event Scale (IES)	Self-report	5 minutes	Does not address all *DSM-IV* PTSD symptoms; a revised version (IES-R) is in wide use
Minnesota Multiphasic Personality Inventory (MMPI, includes PTSD Scale)	Self-report	60–120 minutes	Lengthy, but provides benefit of other MMPI scales; a revised version (MMPI-2) is in wide use
SCL 90-Revised (includes PTSD subscale)	Self-report	10–15 minutes	Longer than many self-report scales for PTSD, but provides information about other mental health and somatic symptoms
Self-Rating Inventory for Posttraumatic Stress Disorder (SRIP)	Self-report	5 minutes	Brief PTSD screening instrument; not ideal for determining diagnostic status

(MMPI-2 PTSD; Keane, Malloy, & Fairbank, 1984), the Impact of Event Scale (IES; Horowitz, Wilner, & Alvarez, 1979), the PTSD subscale from the Symptom Checklist (SCL) 90-Revised (Derogatis & Cleary, 1977), and the PTSD Checklist (PCL; Weathers, Litz, Herman, Huska, & Keane, 1993). In general, it has been recommended that lower cut-off scores be used on self-report measures of PTSD in the older adult population. For example, one of the most frequently used self-report instruments, the PCL, consists of 17 items on a 5-point Likert-type scale that correspond to the *DSM* criteria for PTSD. Although a score of 50 or greater typically designates a diagnosis of PTSD, a cutoff of 42 was found to optimally differentiate between older adults with and without PTSD (Cook, Thompson, Coyne, & Sheikh, 2003).

There is little information on PTSD assessment in community-dwelling, nonveteran older adults (Cook, Elhai, & Areán, 2005; Van Zelst et al., 2003a). In a sample of older, trauma-exposed primary care patients screened for psychiatric disorders (i.e., depression, other anxiety disorders, and alcohol abuse), the PCL demonstrated adequate internal consistency (Cronbach's alpha = 0.84; Cook et al., 2005). Van Zelst et al. (2003a) compared the Self-Rating Inventory for PTSD (SRIP) to the Composite International Diagnostic Interview (CIDI) in a large sample of adults aged 55 to 90 years. A cutoff score of 39 was selected to optimize the balance of sensitivity and specificity, but this score resulted in missed "true" diagnoses over one quarter of the time. Nonetheless, the SRIP may be useful as a brief screening instrument for older adults in the community.

COGNITIVE BEHAVIORAL INTERVENTIONS FOR POSTTRAUMATIC STRESS DISORDER IN THE GENERAL ADULT POPULATION

There have been several types of psychosocial interventions designed for the treatment of PTSD. Among these, cognitive behavioral therapy (CBT) has been tested most thoroughly, including more than two dozen rigorously controlled treatment outcome studies (Bradley, Greene, Russ, Dutra, & Westen, 2005; Cahill, Rothbaum, Resick, & Follette, 2009). CBT treatments are usually brief (5–20 weeks) and typically have moderate effect sizes when compared to psychological placebo conditions or wait-list controls (Van Etten & Taylor, 1998). Compared to pharmacotherapy, psychosocial interventions have lower attrition and appear to be more effective at symptom reduction with some evidence for decreased risk of relapse following treatment discontinuation (Van Etten & Taylor, 1998).

The most substantial support for psychotherapy approaches has emerged for exposure treatments, with variants including implosion therapy, systematic desensitization, prolonged exposure therapy, and flooding (Bradley et al., 2005). Exposure-based treatments have long been considered the psychosocial treatment of choice for other anxiety disorders (phobia, panic disorder, agoraphobia, and obsessive-compulsive disorder) and are now also considered one of the treatments of choice for PTSD (Keane & Barlow, 2002). Exposure therapies work by helping individuals to confront feared stimuli in their imagination (i.e., imaginal exposure) or in real life (i.e., in vivo exposure). Foa and Kozak (1986) proposed that therapeutic exposure leads to improvement in patients with fear responses (e.g., PTSD) when (a) there is evidence of arousal caused by the exposure (observed and reported by the individual), (b) the arousal habituates (decreases gradually) within therapy sessions, and (c) the arousal decreases across therapy sessions. More recent research has suggested that within-session habituation is not related to treatment response (Jaycox, Foa, & Morral, 1998), but arousal caused by the exposure and across-session habituation have consistently been related to treatment outcome and are central to the treatment model.

Empirical research also supports the use of anxiety management training (AMT; also known as stress management or stress inoculation training), cognitive therapy, and Eye Movement Desensitization and Reprocessing (EMDR) for the treatment of PTSD (Keane & Barlow, 2002). AMT emphasizes the acquisition of skills to bring relief from the symptoms of PTSD (particularly hyperarousal symptoms) and may include breathing retraining, relaxation, and education. Cognitive therapies, including Cognitive Processing Therapy (CPT; Resick & Schnicke, 1993), emphasize the tracking and alteration of maladaptive thoughts related to the trauma, current dangers, and one's ability to manage difficulties. EMDR includes cognitive and behavioral components and adds other stimuli such as bilateral stimulation or dual attention stimulus, which may include the therapist's fingers moving back and forth, in an effort to ameliorate PTSD symptoms (Shapiro, 2001).

Studies of hypnotherapy, assertiveness training, relaxation, biofeedback, and psychodynamic treatments have been hampered by methodological problems or inadequate evidence and have not received support as effective treatments. To date, there are no data to suggest that combining different types of cognitive behavioral techniques (e.g., CPT and Prolonged Exposure) results in outcomes that are superior to approaches that follow only one model of treatment (Keane & Barlow, 2002).

PSYCHOSOCIAL INTERVENTIONS FOR POSTTRAUMATIC STRESS DISORDER IN OLDER ADULTS

Although no randomized controlled treatment studies of PTSD in older adults have been conducted, several reports have been published describing psychotherapy for older adults with PTSD. Most are not empirically based, and those that have data are individual case studies.

Two studies, one with a 72-year-old woman (Hyer, 1995) and another with a 68-year-old Native American man (Thomas & Gafner, 1993), indicated significant decreases in PTSD symptoms after only a few sessions of EMDR. Russo, Hersen, and Van Hasselt (2001) described an exposure-based treatment for a 57-year-old White woman in which her PTSD related to two separate traumas (a transient ischemic attack and a rape during her adolescence) decreased significantly after imaginal exposure. These gains were maintained during the 2-year course of therapy. Two additional studies used less known treatment approaches, one including elements of EMDR (Hyer & Woods, 1998) and the other using life review (Maercker, 2002). Both reported general improvement in PTSD symptoms.

Foa and Meadows (1997) proposed seven "gold standards" for PTSD treatment outcome research. These include the following:

1. Clearly defined target symptoms;
2. Reliable and valid measures;
3. Blind assessors;
4. Stable and reliable assessors;
5. Manualized, replicable, specific treatment programs;
6. Unbiased assignment to treatment; and
7. Ratings of treatment adherence.

The five aforementioned reports of treatment of PTSD in older adults have not demonstrated a high level of quality according to these standards. The studies are underpowered because of the small sample sizes, and provide no control or comparison groups. If standardized measures are used at all, they are inconsistently used across studies and often the measures have not been validated for use in older adults. Additionally, many of these reports lack well-defined treatment procedures. Although exposure-based treatments have yielded the strongest empirical support in the general population, most of the studies attributed treatment success to other components of treatment (e.g., life review, group processing) even if exposure was implied in the treatment descriptions. In addition, longer term follow-up assessments are needed to determine how well treatment gains were maintained over time.

Many additional researchers have described psychosocial treatments for PTSD in older adults, but have not published empirical data supporting the efficacy of their interventions. The majority have described group interventions (i.e., Boehnlein & Sparr, 1993; Bonwick, 1998; Bonwick & Morris, 1996; Lipton & Schaffer, 1986, 1988; Molinari & Williams, 1995; Müller & Barash-Kishon, 1998; Snell & Padin-Rivera, 1997), many of which include techniques such as psychoeducation, relaxation training, social support building, and sharing of traumatic memories. Clower, Snell, Liebling, and Padin-Rivera (1996) developed a manual for their comprehensive treatment for PTSD in older veterans, which consists of psychoeducation, relaxation training, life review, cognitive restructuring, and behavioral activation components. Despite a lack of data on treatment efficacy, they suggest that the intervention is highly effective and efficient and that group therapy is the treatment of choice for older veterans (Snell & Padin-Rivera, 1997). Furthermore, some researchers have recommended family-based interventions for the treatment of late-life PTSD, such as involving children and grandchildren in therapy (Ginsberg-McEwan, 1987) and caring for grandchildren (Hierholzer, 2004). This is a promising avenue, given the disturbances in interpersonal relationships that are commonly observed in people with PTSD. Because of the lack of data in these studies, however, their efficacy cannot be determined.

GENERAL CONSIDERATIONS FOR PSYCHOTHERAPY WITH OLDER ADULTS

Some authors have suggested that standard psychotherapy may benefit from modifications for older adults. These could include progressing at a slower pace, providing opportunities for mastery early in treatment, using cognitive behavioral strategies, using a group format, providing more structure with more limited goals, and addressing issues of loss, death, dependency, and survivor guilt (Hyer et al., 1995). Weintraub and Ruskin (1999) have suggested that older adults require more time to recover from traumatic events, and they recommend (a) using name and proper titles when working with older adults, (b) acknowledging physical complaints, (c) providing more practical assistance, and (d) listening more and talking less. Bonwick and Morris (1996) recommended the inclusion of family members in treatment, and they note that compensation for psychiatric disability and military reunions may be therapeutic as well. When conducting cognitive behavioral therapy with cognitively impaired older adults, Koder (2007) encouraged therapists to use caregivers whenever possible for additional support and the reinforcement of materials presented in therapy. Koder also recommends simplifying material, using memory aids (e.g., lists, written summaries), and using structured behavioral techniques rather than cognitive methods. Although these modifications are intuitively appealing, it remains to be seen whether our standard interventions need modifications for older adults and whether each modification improves treatment outcomes.

PHARMACOTHERAPY FOR POSTTRAUMATIC STRESS DISORDER IN OLDER ADULTS

Selective serotonin reuptake inhibitors (SSRIs) have been recommended as a first-line pharmaceutical treatment for PTSD (Friedman, Davidson, Mellman, & Southwick, 2000). Their efficacy has been demonstrated in civilian PTSD (Brady et al., 2000; Connor, Sutherland, Tupler, Malik, & Davidson, 1999; Davidson, Rothbaum, van der Kolk, Sikes, & Farfel, 2001), although the evidence is not as strong for treating military veterans (e.g., Zohar et al., 2002). Overall, SSRIs appear to be effective in reducing all three clusters of PTSD symptoms as well as comorbid disorders and symptoms such as depression, panic, suicidality, obsessive-compulsive disorder, alcohol/substance dependence, and impulsivity (Friedman et al.; Sutherland & Davidson, 1994). Although insomnia, agitation, sexual dysfunction, and gastrointestinal symptoms are not uncommon side effects of SSRIs, this class of drugs is often tolerated better than other psychotropic medications (Friedman et al.). To date, sertraline and paroxetine are the only pharmaceutical agents that are FDA approved for the treatment of PTSD.

Most studies of medications for PTSD have not included older adults, and many of those that have included older adults have not analyzed results for this population separately. Only two pharmacotherapy studies have been conducted specifically with older adults, through which both prazosin (Peskind, Bonner, Hoff, & Raskind, 2003) and the atypical antipsychotic quetiapine (Hamner, Deitsch, Brodrick, Ulmer, & Lorberbaum, 2003) were found to reduce PTSD symptoms. Some researchers believe that more chronic PTSD, such as that often seen in older veterans, appears to respond better to tricyclic antidepressants (TCAs) than to SSRIs, although published clinical experience with chronic PTSD is limited (Friedman et al., 2000). TCAs and monoamine oxidase inhibitors (MAOIs) appear to reduce symptoms in the reexperiencing cluster of PTSD but have less of an effect on arousal or avoidant/numbing symptoms. Moreover, these classes of medications have side-effect profiles that are not optimal for older adults with medical issues such as hypertension or cardiac disease. Benzodiazepines have been shown to improve hyperarousal symptoms (including insomnia, anxiety, and irritability), but have not been linked to reductions in the reexperiencing, avoidant, or numbing symptom clusters of PTSD. Benzodiazepines should be used with caution in the older adult population because their use has been associated with cognitive impairment, excess sedation, respiratory problems, psychomotor impairment (with increased risk of falls), and risk of abuse and dependence (Sheikh & Cassidy, 2000).

GENERAL CONSIDERATIONS FOR PHARMACOTHERAPY WITH OLDER ADULTS

Although the parameters of treatment will differ for each patient and by settings, there are several general issues to consider that may inform the psychiatric care of older adults. Pharmacotherapy can be complicated by age-related changes in pharmacokinetics and pharmacodynamics. Older adults are often more sensitive to side effects, and the probability of side effects may be increased because medications remain in the body for longer periods due to changes in physiology associated with aging (Von Moltke, Greenblatt, Harmatz, & Shader, 1995). Medical comorbidity, especially diseases that affect the heart, liver, or kidney, may exacerbate the diminished metabolic efficiency and slower drug clearance demonstrated by many older adults (Sheikh & Cassidy, 2000).

Polypharmacy is also common among older adults. Complex drug regimens may confuse older adults and potentially lead to poor treatment adherence (Wetherell & Unützer, 2003). Moreover, polypharmacy compounds the risk of drug interactions and makes it difficult to determine the cause(s) of subsequent side effects. Given these considerations, it is advisable to consider the side-effect profiles of psychotropic medications, start with low dosage and increase levels slowly, and make single medication adjustments if possible so that responses can be interpreted more readily (Sheikh & Cassidy, 2000).

Although the combination of pharmacotherapy and psychotherapy are often promoted, there is little evidence to guide clinical decisions about when and how to make such combinations. Until more data are available, patient and provider preference for medications and psychotherapy should be considered. Patients with severe PTSD or comorbid psychiatric diagnoses that interfere with attending psychotherapy sessions may benefit from pharmacotherapy followed by a transition to psychotherapy. PTSD has been associated with nonadherence to medications and adverse outcomes among patients who have experienced an acute myocardial infarction (Shemesh et al., 2001). Psychotherapy could be applied for improving medication adherence in older adults with PTSD, as it has in other populations.

CASE EXAMPLE: AN OLDER VETERAN WITH POSTTRAUMATIC STRESS DISORDER

A fictitious case, based on a composite of older adults with PTSD that we have seen, can serve to illustrate some important points. Mr. Smith was a 66-year-old, married Vietnam War veteran. At his intake interview, Mr. Smith appeared forthright in sharing his psychosocial history, but when asked about his combat experiences he said, "I'd rather not talk about that." He entered the Army at the age of 17 (with his parents' permission), and said that he was motivated to serve his country as his father and grandfather had done. He said he was also interested in attending college after his service, and was drawn to the Army by the financial assistance he would receive for his education and for housing. He spent 4 years in the Army. He had a tour of duty in Vietnam in the infantry, and he acknowledged that he faced intense combat while he was there.

Mr. Smith reported that he was fundamentally changed by the experience. "When I was discharged and came home, my mom asked me what had happened to her son." He said that he had become irritable, had trouble sleeping, and avoided people (although he had been social before his combat experiences). He started drinking while he was in the military, and he said that it started to cause him problems within a year of his return to civilian life. He married his long-term girlfriend 1 month after he was discharged, but that marriage ended 2 years later. He said, "I didn't want to go out with our friends, and she was always walking on eggshells with me around our house. She just got fed up with my nasty mood and my drinking." His current marriage is his fourth, and he admits that the other marriages ended for similar reasons. He completed two semesters of college, but found that it was difficult for him to concentrate. He also complained that his college classmates were "young and stupid about the real world." He had lost many jobs over the years because of his "temper" and the complications of his alcohol use. He quit drinking on his own 6 years ago after he almost lost his job at the post office because of a physical altercation with a coworker. Mr. Smith is now retired, and he presents to the clinic stating, "I have too much time to think about the war now, and my wife wanted me to get fixed."

Early in the intake interview, Mr. Smith leaned toward the interviewer and appeared to favor his right ear. He acknowledged that he had had trouble hearing since he had returned from combat, and he accepted a referral to the audiology clinic. The interviewer made an effort to speak loudly and clearly, and encouraged Mr. Smith to stop her if he was having trouble understanding what was said. After the interview, the interviewer administered the PCL to Mr. Smith. To facilitate his completion of the form, she gave him a version that was printed in bold, large font and she explained the purpose of the assessment. She also reviewed the instructions and read the first few items with him to aid him in completing it. His responses yielded a score of 73, indicating probable PTSD. The diagnosis was confirmed by a CAPS interview.

When treatment options were discussed with Mr. Smith, he declined pharmacotherapy. He stated that he could not afford more medications and that he did not like to take pills. He was offered group therapy focused on psychoeducation and coping skills or individual exposure therapy. He said that he did not like groups of strangers and so declined group therapy, but said that he would consider the exposure therapy if it was with the interviewer (he said that he felt comfortable with her). He said, "Talking about what I saw over there is the last thing I want to do, but I know, after all of these years, I just have to face it and get it over with." He completed 12 sessions of exposure therapy. Initially, he reported higher levels of PTSD symptoms and said that the therapy was "stirring things up." He expressed embarrassment at being tearful when describing the death of his friends during combat. He was also concerned that the graphic nature of the events would upset the therapist. The therapist reassured him, normalized his responses, and encouraged him to keep attending sessions and doing homework outside of sessions. By the fifth session, he reported feeling better and his lower scores on the PCL reflected improvement. By the ninth session, he was smiling more in session and reported, "I think we've got this thing licked!" During the final session, Mr. Smith was engaged in many activities he had wanted to do but had avoided for years. He said that his wife was delighted that he would go to the beach with her and that they could have dinner with friends and family. He thanked the therapist, and said, "I feel like I've got my life back. I forgot how it felt to be me." Mr. Smith has left voice mail messages for the therapist in the 2 years following treatment, and he reports that he is feeling good despite financial concerns and that he continues to pursue new activities with his wife.

SUMMARY AND CONCLUSIONS

PTSD has emerged as a public health concern within the general population, particularly among those at higher risk for exposure to psychological trauma (e.g., combat veterans, emergency workers).

PTSD and trauma-related symptoms also affect a significant proportion of older adults, and the expression and experience of these symptoms may have some unique features in this population. PTSD may have initial onset in late life, or PTSD from early-life traumas may persist or reemerge in late life. Regardless of the duration of the disorder, PTSD has been linked to many detrimental problems in older adults, including distress and functional impairment, comorbid psychiatric disorders, and multiple health problems.

The challenges of assessing PTSD within the older adult population have been discussed, and recommendations for assessment were proposed. Foremost among the recommendations is for clinicians to ask older patients about exposure to past potential traumatic events such as combat, accidents, sexual assault, or crime victimization. This helps to normalize the events, reduce stigma, and aid interpretation of the clinical presentation. These past events are often neglected because of a focus on current symptoms.

The treatment literature for this population is in its infancy. It is known that people with PTSD cite more obstacles to psychiatric treatment than people with other anxiety disorders, including financial barriers, lack of knowledge about resources, and fear of stigma (Koenen, Goodwin, Struening, Hellman, & Guardino, 2003). Some of these barriers may be more pronounced in the older adult population, and additional research on treatment utilization and dissemination could help to augment the budding treatment literature. Clearly, there is a great need for randomized clinical trials of pharmacological and psychosocial treatments for PTSD in older adults. Although case studies are informative, they are limited by selection bias and it is not possible to determine how outcomes would compare to no treatment or alternative treatments. Randomized clinical trials can correct many of these problems. Although studies of pharmacotherapy for PTSD in older adults are slowly emerging, there are few studies that would lead us to recommend or discourage psychotherapy in this population.

Most studies with older adults have focused on White military veterans, and there is a great need for treatment outcome research that addresses the unique needs of women and ethnic minorities. It is also important to consider sociocultural responses to traumatic events. For example, it has been suggested that prevalence of PTSD is higher among Vietnam War veterans (as compared to World War II and Korean War veterans) in part because of the mixed response that soldiers received upon returning home from that unpopular conflict (Fontana & Rosenheck, 1994). It has also been shown that age-related differences in trauma response are tied to the cultural and economic factors that affect survivors (Glicksman & Van Haitsma, 2002; Norris, Kaniasty, Conrad, Inman, & Murphy, 2002).

Although the literature on PTSD in older adults is limited, there are signs that interest in this topic is growing. The necessity for adequate assessment and treatment methods for this population will become more apparent as the baby boomer cohort (including veterans of the Vietnam War) enters late life. The consequences of this disorder are substantial and potentially devastating to individuals, families, and society as a whole. Clinical researchers have an opportunity to alleviate a significant amount of suffering by testing established interventions in older adults and developing new methods if they are required. The future holds multiple challenges and significant promise for the study of PTSD in older adults.

ACKNOWLEDGMENTS

This work is supported by a Veterans Affairs (VA) Career Development Award (Dr. Thorp). Content does not necessarily represent the views of the Department of Veterans Affairs or the U.S. Government.

REFERENCES

Acierno, R., Brady, K. L., Gray, M., Kilpatrick, D. G., Resnick, H. S., & Best, C. L. (2002). Psychopathology following interpersonal violence: A comparison of risk factors in older and younger adults. *Journal of Clinical Geropsychology, 8*, 13–23.

Alter, A. L., & Oppenheimer, D. M. (2009). Suppressing secrecy through metacognitive ease: Cognitive fluency encourages self-disclosure. *Psychological Science, 20*, 1414–1420.

American Psychiatric Association. (2000). *Diagnostic and statistical manual of mental disorders* (4th ed., Text Revision). Washington, DC: Author.

Andrews, B., Brewin, C. R., Philpott, R., & Stewart, L. (2008). Delayed onset posttraumatic stress disorder: A systematic review of the evidence. *American Journal of Psychiatry, 164*, 1319–1326.

Averill, P. M., & Beck, J. G. (2000). Posttraumatic stress disorder in older adults: A conceptual review. *Journal of Anxiety Disorders, 14*, 133–156.

Blake, D. D., Weathers, F. W., Nagy, L. M., Kaloupek, D. G., Gusman, F. D., Charney, D. S., et al. (1995). The development of a clinician-administered PTSD scale. *Journal of Traumatic Stress, 8*, 75–90.

Boehnlein, J. K., & Sparr, L. F. (1993). Group therapy with WWII ex-POW's: Long-term posttraumatic adjustment in a geriatric population. *American Journal of Psychotherapy, 47*, 273–282.

Bonwick, R. (1998). Group treatment programme for elderly war veterans with PTSD. *International Journal of Geriatric Psychiatry, 13,* 64–65.

Bonwick, R. J., & Morris, P. L. P. (1996). Post-traumatic stress disorder in elderly war veterans. *International Journal of Geriatric Psychiatry, 11,* 1071–1076.

Bossé, R., Spiro, A., III, & Levenson, M. R. (1997). Retirement as a stressful life event. In T. W. Miller (Ed.), *Clinical disorders and stressful life events* (pp. 325–350). Madison, CT: International Universities Press.

Bradley, R., Greene, J., Russ, E., Dutra, L., & Westen, D. (2005). A multidimensional meta-analysis of psychotherapy for PTSD. *American Journal of Psychiatry, 162,* 214–227.

Brady, K. T. (1997). Posttraumatic stress disorder and comorbidity: Recognizing the many faces of PTSD. *Journal of Clinical Psychiatry, 58,* 12–15.

Brady, K., Pearlstein, T., Asnis, G. M., Baker, D., Rothbaum, B., Sikes, C. R., et al. (2000). Efficacy and safety of sertraline treatment of posttraumatic stress disorder: A randomized controlled trial. *Journal of the American Medical Association, 283,* 1837–1844.

Bramsen, I., & van der Ploeg, H. M. (1999). Fifty years later: The long-term psychological adjustment of ageing World War II survivors. *Acta Psychiatrica Scandinavica, 100,* 350–358.

Bremner, J. D., Southwick, S., Brett, E., Fontana, A., Rosenheck, R., & Charney, D. S. (1992). Dissociation and posttraumatic stress disorder in Vietnam combat veterans. *American Journal of Psychiatry, 149,* 328–332.

Breslau, N., & Davis, G. C. (1992). Posttraumatic stress disorder in an urban population of young adults: Risk factors for chronicity. *American Journal of Psychiatry, 149,* 671–675.

Brewin, C. R., Andrews, B., & Valentine, J. D. (2000). Meta-analysis of risk factors for posttraumatic stress disorder in trauma-exposed adults. *Journal of Consulting and Clinical Psychology, 68,* 748–766.

Brown, T. A., Campbell, L. A., Lehman, C. L., Grisham, J. R., & Mancil, R. B. (2001). Current and lifetime comorbidity of the DSM-IV anxiety and mood disorders in a large clinical sample. *Journal of Abnormal Psychology, 110,* 585–599.

Cahill, S. P., Rothbaum, B. O., Resick, P. A., & Follette, V. M. (2009). Cognitive-behavioral therapy for adults. In E. B. Foa, T. M. Keane, M. J. Friedman, & J. A. Cohen (Eds.), *Effective treatments for PTSD: Practice guidelines from the International Society for Traumatic Stress Studies* (2nd ed., pp. 139–222). New York, NY: Guilford Press.

Chilcoat, H. D., & Breslau, N. (1998). Posttraumatic stress disorder and drug disorders: Testing causal pathways. *Archives of General Psychiatry, 55,* 913–917.

Clower, M. W., Snell, F. I., Liebling, D. S., & Padin-Rivera, E. (1996). *Senior veterans program: A treatment program for elderly veterans with war-related post-traumatic stress disorder: Therapist notes.* Cleveland, OH: Department of Veterans Affairs.

Connor, K. M., Sutherland, S. M., Tupler, L. A., Malik, M. L., & Davidson, J. R. T. (1999). Fluoxetine in post-traumatic stress disorder: Randomised, double-blind study. *British Journal of Psychiatry, 175,* 17–22.

Cook, J. M., Areán, P. A., Schnurr, P. P., & Sheikh, J. (2001). Symptom differences of older depressed primary care patients with and without history of trauma. *International Journal of Psychiatry in Medicine, 31,* 415–428.

Cook, J. M., Elhai, J., & Areán, P. A. (2005). Psychometric properties of the PTSD Checklist with older primary care patients. *Journal of Traumatic Stress, 18,* 371–376.

Cook, J. M., & Elmore, D. L. (2009). Disaster mental health in older adults: Symptoms, policy and planning. In Y. Neria, S. Galea, & F. Norris (Eds.), *Mental health consequences of disasters* (pp. 233–263). New York, NY: Cambridge University Press.

Cook, J. M., & Niederehe, G. (2007). Trauma in older adults. In M. J. Friedman, T. M. Keane, & P. A. Resick (Eds.), *PTSD science and practice: A comprehensive handbook* (pp. 252–276). New York, NY: Guilford Press.

Cook, J. M., & O'Donnell, C. (2005). Assessment and psychological treatment of posttraumatic stress disorder in older adults. *Journal of Geriatric Psychiatry and Neurology, 18,* 61–71.

Cook, J. M., Thompson, R., Coyne, J. C., & Sheikh, J. (2003). Algorithm versus cutpoint derived PTSD in ex-prisoners of war. *Journal of Psychopathology and Behavioral Assessment, 25,* 267–271.

Creamer, M. C., & Parslow, R. A. (2008). Trauma exposure and posttraumatic stress disorder in the elderly: A community prevalence study. *American Journal of Geriatric Psychiatry, 16,* 853–856.

Davidson, J. R. T. (2000). Pharmacotherapy of posttraumatic stress disorder: Treatment options, long-term follow-up, and predictors of outcome. *Journal of Clinical Psychiatry, 61,* 52–59.

Davidson, J. R. T., Hughes, D., Blazer, D. G., & George, L. K. (1991). Post-traumatic stress disorder in the community: An epidemiological study. *Psychological Medicine, 21,* 713–721.

Davidson, J. R. T., Rothbaum, B. O., van der Kolk, B. A., Sikes, C. R., & Farfel, G. M. (2001). Multicenter, double-blind comparison of sertraline and placebo in the treatment of posttraumatic stress disorder. *Archives of General Psychiatry, 58,* 485–492.

Derogatis, L. R., & Cleary, P. A. (1977). Confirmation of the dimensional structure of the SCL-90: A study in construct validation. *Journal of Clinical Psychology, 33,* 981–989.

De Vries, G., & Olff, M. (2009). The lifetime prevalence of traumatic events and posttraumatic stress disorder in the Netherlands. *Journal of Traumatic Stress, 22,* 259–267.

Elhai, J. D., Gray, M. J., Kashdan, T. B., & Franklin, C. L. (2005). Which instruments are most commonly used to assess traumatic event exposure and posttraumatic effects?: A survey of traumatic stress professionals. *Journal of Traumatic Stress, 18,* 541–545.

Engdahl, B. E., Speed, N., Eberly, R. E., & Schwartz, J. (1991). Comorbidity of psychiatric disorders and personality profiles of American World War II prisoners of war. *Journal of Nervous and Mental Disease, 179,* 181–187.

First, M. B., Williams, J. B. W., & Spitzer, R. L. (1988). DTREE: Microcomputer-assisted teaching of psychiatric diagnosis using a decision tree model. In R. Greenes (Ed.), *Proceedings of the 12th annual symposium on computer applications in medical care* (pp. 377–381). Washington, DC: IEEE Computer Society Press.

Floyd, M., Rice, J., & Black, S. R. (2002). Recurrence of posttraumatic stress disorder in late life: A cognitive aging perspective. *Journal of Clinical Geropsychology, 8,* 303–311.

Foa, E. B., & Kozak, M. J. (1986). Emotional processing of fear: Exposure to corrective information. *Psychological Bulletin, 99,* 20–35.

Foa, E. B., & Meadows, E. A. (1997). Psychosocial treatments for posttraumatic stress disorder: A critical review. *Annual Review of Psychology, 48,* 449–480.

Fontana, A., & Rosenheck, R. (1994). Traumatic war stressors and psychiatric symptoms among World War II, Korean, and Vietnam War veterans. *Psychology and Aging, 9,* 27–33.

Friedman, M. J., Davidson, J. R. T., Mellman, T. A., & Southwick, S. M. (2000). Pharmacotherapy. In E. Foa, T. M. Keane, & M. J. Friedman (Eds.), *Effective treatments for PTSD: Practice guidelines from the International Society for Traumatic Stress Studies* (pp. 326–329). New York, NY: Guilford Press.

Frueh, B. C., Elhai, J. D., Hamner, M. B., Magruder K. M., Sauvageot, J. A., & Mintzer, J. (2004). Elderly veterans with combat-related posttraumatic stress disorder in specialty care. *Journal of Nervous and Mental Disease, 192,* 75–79.

Gatz, M. (1994). Application of assessment theory and intervention with older adults. In M. Storandt & G. R. VandenBos (Eds.), *Neuropsychological assessment of dementia and depression in older adults: A clinician's guide* (pp. 155–176). Washington, DC: American Psychological Association.

Ginsberg-McEwan, E. (1987). The whole grandfather: An intergenerational approach to family therapy. In J. Sadavoy & M. Leszcz (Eds.), *Treating the elderly with psychotherapy* (pp. 295–324). Madison, CT: International Universities Press.

Glicksman, A., & Van Haitsma, K. (2002). The social context of adaptation to traumatic events: Soviet Jews and the Holocaust. *Journal of Clinical Geropsychology, 8,* 227–237.

Goenjian, A. K., Najarian, L. M., Pynoos, R. S., Steinberg, A. M., Manoukian, G., Tavosian, A., et al. (1994). Posttraumatic stress disorder in elderly and younger adults after the 1988 earthquake in Armenia. *American Journal of Psychiatry, 151,* 895–901.

Green, B. L., Epstein, S. A., Krupnick, J. L., & Rowland, J. H. (1997). Trauma and medical illness: Assessing trauma-related disorders in medical settings. In J. P. Wilson & T. M. Keane (Eds.), *Assessing psychological trauma and PTSD* (pp. 160–191). New York, NY: Guilford Press.

Hagstrom, R. (1995). The acute psychological impact on survivors following a train accident. *Journal of Traumatic Stress, 8,* 391–402.

Hamner, M. B., Deitsch, S. E., Brodrick, P. S., Ulmer, H. G., & Lorberbaum, J. P. (2003). Quetiapine treatment in patients with posttraumatic stress disorder: An open trial of adjunctive therapy. *Journal of Clinical Psychopharmacology, 23,* 15–20.

Hankin, C. S., Abueg, F. R., Gallagher-Thompson, D., & Laws, A. (1996). Dimensions of PTSD among older veterans seeking outpatient medical care: A pilot study. *Journal of Clinical Geropsychology, 2,* 239–246.

Hierholzer, R. (2004). Improvement in PTSD patients who care for their grandchildren. *American Journal of Psychiatry, 161,* 176–177.

Higgins, A. B., & Follette, V. M. (2002). Frequency and impact of interpersonal trauma in older women. *Clinical Geropsychology, 8,* 215–226.

Hiskey, S., Luckie, M., Davies, S., & Brewin, C. R. (2008). The emergence of posttraumatic distress later in life: A review. *Journal of Geriatric Psychiatry, 21,* 232–241.

Horowitz, M., Wilner, N., & Alvarez, W. (1979). Impact of events scale: A measure of subjective stress. *Psychosomatic Medicine, 41,* 209–218.

Hyer, L. (1995). Use of EMDR in a "dementing" PTSD survivor. *Clinical Gerontologist, 16,* 70–73.

Hyer, L., Summers, M. N., Boyd, S., Litaker, M., & Boudewyns, P. (1996). Assessment of older combat veterans with the clinician-administered PTSD scale. *Journal of Traumatic Stress, 9,* 587–593.

Hyer, L., Summers, M. N., Braswell, L., & Boyd, S. (1995). Posttraumatic stress disorder: Silent problem among older combat veterans. *Psychotherapy, 32*, 348–364.

Hyer, L., & Woods, M. G. (1998). Phenomenology and treatment of trauma in later life. In V. M. Follette, J. I. Ruzek, & F. R. Abueg (Eds.), *Cognitive-behavioral therapies for trauma* (pp. 383–414). New York, NY: Guilford Press.

Jaycox, L. H., Foa, E. B., & Morral, A. R. (1998). Influence of emotional engagement and habituation on exposure therapy for PTSD. *Journal of Consulting and Clinical Psychology, 66*, 185–192.

Johnson, D. R., Fontana, A., Lubin, H., Corn, B., & Rosenheck, R. (2004). Long-term course of treatment-seeking Vietnam veterans with posttraumatic stress disorder: Mortality, clinical condition, and life satisfaction. *Journal of Nervous and Mental Disease, 192*, 35–41.

Keane, T. M., & Barlow, D. H. (2002). Posttraumatic stress disorder. In D. H. Barlow (Ed.), *Anxiety and its disorders* (pp. 418–453). New York, NY: Guilford Press.

Keane, T. M., Caddell, J. M., & Taylor, K. L. (1988). Mississippi Scale for Combat-Related Posttraumatic Stress Disorder: Three studies in reliability and validity. *Journal of Consulting and Clinical Psychology, 56*, 85–90.

Keane, T. M., Malloy, P. F., & Fairbank, J. A. (1984). Empirical development of an MMPI subscale for the assessment of combat-related posttraumatic stress disorder. *Journal of Consulting and Clinical Psychology, 52*, 888–891.

Kessler, R. C., Berglund, P., Demler, O., Jin, R., Merikangas, K. R., & Walters, E. E. (2005). Lifetime prevalence and age-of-onset distributions of DSM-IV disorders in the National Comorbidity Survey Replication. *Archives of General Psychiatry, 62*, 593–602.

Kessler, R. C., Sonnega, A., Bromet, E., Hughes, M., & Nelson, C. B. (1995). Posttraumatic stress disorder in the national comorbidity survey. *Archives of General Psychiatry, 52*, 1048–1060.

Kimerling, R., & Calhoun, K. S. (1994). Somatic symptoms, social support, and treatment seeking among sexual assault victims. *Journal of Consulting and Clinical Psychology, 62*, 333–340.

Kluznik, J. C., Speed, N., Van Valkenburg, C., & Magraw, R. (1986). Forty-year follow-up of United States prisoners of war. *American Journal of Psychiatry, 143*, 1443–1446.

Koder, D. A. (2007). Cognitive therapy with older adults: Are adaptations necessary? In D. A. Epstein (Ed.), *Innovations and advances in cognitive behavior therapy* (pp. 101–111). Bowen Hills, Queensland, Australia: Australian Academic Press.

Koenen, K. C., Goodwin, R., Struening, E., Hellman, F., & Guardino, M. (2003). Posttraumatic stress disorder and treatment seeking in a national screening sample. *Journal of Traumatic Stress, 16*, 5–16.

Kogan, J. N., Edelstein, B. A., & McKee, D. R. (2000). Assessment of anxiety in older adults: Current status. *Journal of Anxiety Disorder, 14*, 109–132.

Kulka, R. A., Schlenger, W. E., Fairbank, J. A., Hough, R. L., Jordan, B. K., Marmar, C. R., et al. (1990). *Trauma and the Vietnam War generation: Report of findings from the National Vietnam Veterans Readjustment Study.* New York, NY: Brunner/Mazel.

Kulka, R. A., Schlenger, W. E., Fairbank, J. A., Jordan, B. K., Hough, R. L., Marmar, C. R., et al. (1991). Assessment of posttraumatic stress disorder in the community: Prospects and pitfalls from recent studies of Vietnam veterans. *Psychological Assessment: A Journal of Consulting and Clinical Psychology, 3*, 547–560.

Ladwig, K. H., Schoefinius, A., Dammann, G., Danner, R., Gurtler, R., & Herrmann, R. (1999). Long-acting psychotraumatic properties of a cardiac arrest experience. *The American Journal of Psychiatry, 156,* 912–919.

Landau, R., & Litwin, H. (2000). The effects of extreme early stress in very old age. *Journal of Traumatic Stress, 13,* 473–487.

Lasoski, M. C. (1986). Reasons for low utilization of mental health services by the elderly. *Clinical Gerontologist, 5,* 1–18.

Lau, A. W., Edelstein, B. A., & Larkin, K. T. (2001). Psychophysiological arousal in older adults: A critical review. *Clinical Psychology Review, 21,* 609–630.

Lipton, M. I., & Schaffer, W. R. (1986). Post-traumatic stress disorder in the older veteran. *Military Medicine, 151,* 522–524.

Lipton, M. I., & Schaffer, W. R. (1988). Physical symptoms related to post-traumatic stress disorder (PTSD) in an aging population. *Military Medicine, 153,* 316–318.

Maercker, A. (2002). Life-review technique in the treatment of PTSD in elderly patients: Rationale and three single case studies. *Journal of Clinical Geropsychology, 8,* 239–249.

Mittal, D., Torres, R., Abashidze A., & Jimerson, N. (2001). Worsening of post-traumatic stress disorder symptoms with cognitive decline: Case series. *Journal of Geriatric Psychiatry and Neurology, 14,* 17–20.

Molinari, V., & Williams, W. (1995). An analysis of aging World War II POWs with PTSD: Implications for practice and research. *Journal of Geriatric Psychiatry, 28,* 99–114.

Müller, U., & Barash-Kishon, R. (1998). Psychodynamic-supportive group therapy model for elderly Holocaust survivors. *International Journal of Group Therapy, 48,* 461–475.

Nichols, B. L., & Czirr, R. (1986). Post-traumatic stress disorder: Hidden syndrome in elders. *Clinical Gerontologist, 5,* 417–433.

Norris, F. H. (1992). Epidemiology of trauma: Frequency and impact of different potentially traumatic events on different demographic groups. *Journal of Consulting and Clinical Psychology, 60,* 409–418.

Norris, F. H., Kaniasty, K. Z., Conrad, M. L., Inman, G. L., & Murphy, A. D. (2002). Placing age differences in cultural context: A comparison of the effects of age on PTSD after disasters in the United States, Mexico, and Poland. *Journal of Clinical Geropsychology, 8,* 153–173.

Norris, F. H., Kaniasty, K. Z., & Scheer, D. A. (1990). Use of mental health services among victims of crimes: Frequency, correlates, and subsequent recovery. *Journal of Consulting and Clinical Psychology, 58,* 538–547.

Otis, J. D., Keane, T. M., & Kerns, R. D. (2003). An examination of the relationship between chronic pain and post-traumatic stress disorder. *Journal of Rehabilitation Research and Development, 40,* 397–405.

Pary, R., Turns, D., & Tobias, C. R. (1986). A case of delayed recognition of post-traumatic stress disorder. *American Journal of Psychiatry, 143,* 941.

Peskind, E. R., Bonner, L. T., Hoff, D. J., & Raskind, M. A. (2003). Prazosin reduces trauma-related nightmares in older men with chronic posttraumatic stress disorder. *Journal of Geriatric Psychiatry and Neurology, 16,* 165–171.

Port, C. L., Engdahl, B., & Frazier, P. (2001). A longitudinal and retrospective study of PTSD among older prisoners of war. *American Journal of Psychiatry, 158,* 1474–1479.

Port, C. L., Engdahl, B. E., Frazier, P. A., & Eberly, R. E. (2002). Factors related to the long-term course of PTSD in older ex-prisoners of war. *Journal of Clinical Geropsychology, 8,* 203–214.

Resick, P. A., & Schnicke, M. K. (1993). *Cognitive processing therapy for rape victims: A treatment manual.* Newbury Park, CA: Sage Publications.

Reynolds, C. F., III, & Kupfer, D. J. (1999). Depression and aging: A look to the future. *Psychiatric Services, 50,* 1167–1172.

Rodgers, C. S., Norman, S. B., Thorp, S. R., Lebeck, M. M., & Lang, A. J. (2005). Trauma exposure, posttraumatic stress disorder and health behaviors: Impact on special populations. In T. A. Corales (Ed.), *Focus on posttraumatic stress disorder research* (pp. 203–224). Hauppauge, NY: Nova Science Publishers.

Ronis, D. L., Bates, E. W., Garfein, A. J., Buit, B. K., Falcon, S. P., & Liberson, I. (1996). Longitudinal patterns of care for parents with posttraumatic stress disorder. *Journal of Traumatic Stress, 9,* 763–781.

Russo, S. A., Hersen, M., & Van Hasselt, V. B. (2001). Treatment of reactivated posttraumatic stress disorder: Imaginal exposure in an older adult with multiple traumas. *Behavior Modification, 25,* 94–115.

Schnurr, P. P., Friedman, M. J., & Green, B. L. (1996). Post-traumatic stress disorder among World War II mustard gas test participants. *Military Medicine, 161,* 131–136.

Schnurr, P. P., & Spiro, A., III. (1999). Combat exposure, posttraumatic stress disorder symptoms, and health behaviors as predictors of self-reported physical health in older veterans. *Journal of Nervous and Mental Disease, 187,* 353–359.

Schnurr, P. P., Spiro, A., III, Aldwin, C. M., & Stukel, T. A. (1998). Physical symptom trajectories following trauma exposure: Longitudinal findings from the normative aging studies. *Journal of Nervous and Mental Disease, 186,* 522–528.

Schnurr, P. P., Spiro, A., III, & Paris, A. H. (2000). Physician-diagnosed medical disorders in relation to PTSD symptoms in older male military veterans. *Health Psychology, 19,* 91–97.

Shapiro, F. (2001). *Eye movement desensitization and reprocessing: Basic principles, protocols, and procedures* (2nd ed.). New York, NY: Guilford Press.

Sheikh, D. I., & Cassidy, E. L. (2000). Treatment of anxiety disorders in the elderly: Issues and strategies. *Journal of Anxiety Disorders, 14,* 173–190.

Shemesh, E., Rudnick, A., Kaluski, E., Milovanov, O., Salah, A., Alon, D., et al. (2001). A prospective study of posttraumatic stress symptoms and nonadherence in survivors of myocardial infarction (MI). *General Hospital Psychiatry, 23,* 215–222.

Shmotkin, D., & Barilan, Y. M. (2002). Expressions of Holocaust experience and their relationship to mental symptoms and physical morbidity among Holocaust survivor patients. *Journal of Behavioral Medicine, 25,* 115–134.

Snell, F. I., & Padin-Rivera, E. (1997). Group treatment for older veterans with post-traumatic stress disorder. *Journal of Psychosocial Nursing and Mental Health Services, 35,* 10–16.

Solomon, S. D., & Davidson, J. R. T. (1997). Trauma: Prevalence, impairment, service use, and cost. *Journal of Clinical Psychiatry, 58,* 5–11.

Spiro, A., III, Schnurr, P. P., & Aldwin, C. M. (1994). Combat-related posttraumatic stress disorder symptoms in older men. *Psychology and Aging, 9,* 17–26.

Spitzer, C., Barnow, S., Völzke, H., John, U., Freyberger, H. J., & Grabe, H. J. (2008). Trauma and posttraumatic stress disorder in the elderly: Findings from a German community study. *Journal of Clinical Psychiatry, 69,* 693–700.

Stermer, E., Bar, H., & Levy, N. (1991). Chronic functional gastrointestinal symptoms in Holocaust survivors. *American Journal of Gastroenterology, 86,* 417–422.

Summers, M. N., & Hyer, L. (1994). PTSD among the elderly. In L. Hyer (Ed.), *Trauma victim: Theoretical issues and practical suggestions* (pp. 633–679). Muncie, IN: Accelerated Development.

Summers, M. N., Hyer, L., Boyd, S., & Boudewyns, P. A. (1996). Diagnosis of late-life PTSD among elderly combat veterans. *Journal of Clinical Geropsychology, 2,* 103–115.

Sutherland, S. M., & Davidson, J. R. T. (1994). Pharmacotherapy for post-traumatic stress disorder. *Psychiatric Clinics of North America, 17,* 409–423.

Sutker, P. B., Winstead, D. K., Galina, Z. H., & Allain, A. N. (1991). Cognitive deficits and psychopathology among former prisoners of war and combat veterans of the Korean conflict. *American Journal of Psychiatry, 148,* 67–72.

Thomas, R., & Gafner, G. (1993). PTSD in an elderly male: Treatment with eye movement desensitization and reprocessing (EMDR). *Clinical Gerontologist, 14,* 57–59.

Thorp, S. R., & Lynch, T. R. (2005). Depression and personality disorders—older adults. In A. Freeman (Ed. in Chief), S. H. Felgoise, A. M. Nezu, C. M. Nezu, & M. A. Reineke (Eds.), *Encyclopedia of cognitive behavior therapy* (pp. 155–158). New York, NY: Springer.

Thorp, S. R., & Stein, M. B. (2005). Posttraumatic stress disorder and functioning. *PTSD Research Quarterly, 16*(3), 1–7.

Thorp, S. R., & Stein, M. B. (2008). Occupational disability. In G. Reyes, J. Elhai, & J. Ford (Eds.), *Encyclopedia of psychological trauma* (p. 453). Hoboken, NJ: John Wiley & Sons, Inc.

U. S. Census Bureau. (2009). Census bureau reports world's older population projected to triple by 2050. Retrieved December 9, 2009, from http://www.census.gov/newsroom/releases/archives/international_population/cb09-97.html

Van der Kolk, B. A. (1987). The drug treatment of post-traumatic stress disorder. *Journal of Affective Disorders, 13,* 203–213.

Van Etten, M. L., & Taylor, S. (1998). Comparative efficacy of treatments for post-traumatic stress disorder: A meta-analysis. *Clinical Psychology and Psychotherapy, 5,* 126–144.

Van Zelst, W. H., de Beurs, E., Beekman, A. T. F., Deeg, D. J. H., & van Dyck, R. (2003a). Criterion validity of the Self-rating Inventory for Posttraumatic Stress Disorder (SRIP) in the community of older adults. *Journal of Affective Disorders, 76,* 229–235.

Van Zelst, W. H., de Beurs, E., Beekman, A. T. F., Deeg, D. J. H., & van Dyck, R. (2003b). Prevalence and risk factors of posttraumatic stress disorder in older adults. *Psychotherapy and Psychosomatics, 72,* 333–342.

Von Moltke, L. L., Greenblatt, D. J., Harmatz, J. S., & Shader, R. I. (1995). Psychotropic drug metabolism in old age: Principles and problems of assessment. In F. E. Bloom & D. J. Kupfer (Eds.), *Psychopharmacology: The fourth generation of progress* (pp. 1461–1469). New York, NY: Raven Press.

Warshaw, M. G., Fierman, E., Pratt, L., Hunt, M., Yonkers, K. A., Massion, A. O., et al. (1993). Quality of life and dissociation in anxiety disorder patients with histories of trauma or PTSD. *American Journal of Psychiatry, 150,* 1512–1516.

Weathers, F. W., Keane, T. M., & Davidson, J. R. T. (2001). Clinician-administered PTSD scale: A review of the first ten years of research. *Depression and Anxiety*, *13*, 132–156.

Weathers, F. W., Litz, B. T., Herman, D. S., Huska, J. A., & Keane, T. M. (1993, October). *The PTSD Checklist (PCL): Reliability, validity, and diagnostic utility.* Paper presented at the meeting of the International Society for Traumatic Stress Studies, San Antonio, TX.

Weintraub, D., & Ruskin, P. E. (1999). Posttraumatic stress disorder in the elderly: A review. *Harvard Review of Psychiatry*, *7*, 144–152.

Wetherell, J. L., & Unützer, J. (2003). Adherence to treatment for geriatric depression and anxiety. *CNS Spectrums*, *8*, 48–59.

Yaari, A., Eisenberg, E., Adler, R., & Birkhan, J. (1999). Chronic pain in Holocaust survivors. *Journal of Pain and Symptom Management*, *17*, 181–187.

Yehuda, R., Kahana, B., Southwick, S. M., & Giller, E. L., Jr. (1994). Depressive features in Holocaust survivors with post-traumatic stress disorder. *Journal of Traumatic Stress*, *7*, 699–704.

Zatzick, D. (2003). Collaborative care for injured victims of individual and mass trauma: A health services research approach to developing early interventions. In R. J. Ursano, C. S. Fullerton, & A. Norwood (Eds.), *Terrorism and disaster: Individual and community mental health interventions* (pp. 189–205). New York, NY: Cambridge University Press.

Zohar, J., Amital, D., Miodownik, C., Kotler, M., Bleich, A., Lane, R. M., et al. (2002). Double-blind placebo-controlled pilot study of sertraline in military veterans with posttraumatic stress disorder. *Journal of Clinical Psychopharmacology*, *22*, 190–195.

8

Assessment and Cognitive-Behaviorally Oriented Interventions for Older Adults With Dementia

Jocelyn Shealy McGee and Kristi L. Bratkovich

The first part of this chapter provides an overview of the most frequently encountered dementias associated with advancing years, including epidemiological data, characteristics, and diagnostic criteria. Also, a brief discussion of normal cognitive aging, mild cognitive impairment, delirium, and potentially treatable medical conditions are discussed as they relate to dementia. The second part of the chapter provides information on the fundamentals of dementia assessment, including suggested guidelines for dementia assessment, frequently used standardized measures for dementia assessment, and the importance of feedback as an extension of dementia assessment. The third part of the chapter presents the literature on cognitive and behaviorally oriented interventions useful for older adults with varying levels of dementia.

Notably, each of the topics covered could warrant an entire chapter. Therefore, we have attempted to distill key findings from the literature, as well as give strategies we have found useful in clinical practice. The chapter is not an advanced text on geriatric neuropsychological assessment or practice, but it does provide core information that may be used by a variety of health care professionals, such as nurses, physicians, psychologists, and social workers, who work with older adults. Likewise, it does not address topics related to the advances in the neurobiology of dementia, but instead focuses on the psychosocial aspects of dementia care.

OVERVIEW OF DEMENTIA

In order to be diagnosed with dementia, an individual must demonstrate multiple cognitive deficits, including memory impairment (impaired ability to learn new information or to recall previously

219

learned information) and one (or more) of the following disturbances in cognition: aphasia (language disturbance); apraxia (impaired ability to carry out motor activities despite intact motor functioning); agnosia (failure to recognize or identify objects despite intact sensory function); and/or disturbance in executive functioning (e.g., planning, organization, sequencing, or abstraction). These cognitive deficits must result in significant impairment in social or occupational functioning and represent a decline from previous levels of functioning and must not occur exclusively in the course of a delirium, or as a result of substance-induced condition or general medical condition (American Psychiatric Association, 2000).

Dementia is an umbrella term for a heterogeneous group of neurological diseases, which may be classified in a variety of ways, such as by longitudinal course or progression. For example, the neurodegenerative dementias—such as Alzheimer's disease (AD), frontotemporal dementia, and Lewy body dementia—are progressive and deleterious in nature. Vascular dementia, alcohol-induced persisting dementia, and dementia associated with traumatic brain injury (TBI) tend to be more variable in their course, and symptoms may remain stable over time.

AD and related dementias present a significant public health challenge. By mid-century, it is estimated that over 13.2 million individuals will be affected (Herbert et al., 2003). AD is the most frequent cause of late-life dementia, accounting for nearly half of all cases of dementia in epidemiological and case-based series (Breitner et al., 1999). Vascular dementia (VaD) is the second most frequent dementia, accounting for approximately 12%–20% of dementia (Bowler, 2002).

Alzheimer's Disease (AD)

AD is an aged-related, progressive neurological disease marked by impairment in multiple areas of cognitive functioning. Additionally, AD is also characterized by progressive changes in behavioral, affective, and self-care functioning. Until recently, AD was considered an exclusionary disorder, which meant that it was diagnosed after all other potential conditions had been excluded. Although generally acknowledged that conclusively diagnosed cases of AD cannot be made until postmortem by autopsy, some investigations suggest a thorough evaluation according to diagnostic standards of the National Institute of Neurological Disorders and Stroke/Alzheimer Disease and Related Disorders Association are accurate in most cases (90 out of 100; Rasmusson et al., 1996). Amyloids, in various forms, are believed to be the primary pathogenesis of AD (Klunk et al., 2004). The symptoms of

AD include deficits in memory for recent events, and impairments in judgment, visual-spatial skills, and language. Specific language deficits are recognized by impoverished speech, with word-finding difficulties and progressive difficulty producing narrative speech. The course of the disease moves from forgetfulness in the early stages to other impairments in cognitive abilities, such as with decision making and performing everyday tasks, as well as personality changes and other behavioral symptoms, and eventually death.

Vascular Dementia (VaD)

VaD is the result of cerebrovascular disease (CVD) and is manifested through cerebrovascular accidents (stroke), hemorrhaging, and/or ischemia of large or small vessels in the cortical or subcortical regions of the brain. A stroke is caused by an interruption in blood flow to the brain. This interruption in blood flow can be caused by an embolism (or a "clot," which can be either a blood clot that develops or a fatty deposit that breaks off, which then becomes lodged in the blood vessel), thrombosis (narrowing or blockage of the blood vessel due to cholesterol and fatty deposits), or hemorrhage (a rupture of the artery). Ischemia is a temporary loss of blood flow, typically restricted to a small region of the brain. In order to diagnose CVD, both brain imaging and neurological symptoms consistent with CVD need to be present. The symptoms of VaD are dependent upon the site of the stroke or ischemia and coincide with the functions of the area affected. The progression of large stroke VaD is distinct from the insidious onset of dementia associated with AD. Specifically, VaD is described as stepwise, with periods of impairment following a stroke, punctuated by periods of stability and some recovery. Subcortical ischemia and infarcts may have an insidious onset and gradual course with impairment following an accumulation of lesions. Although it appears that AD and large stroke VaD have distinctive courses, diagnosing VaD can be a challenging task because VaD can co-occur with degenerative dementia (see Cato & Crosson, 2006, for an excellent and concise review).

Typical Progression of Dementia Symptoms

During early stage dementia, those affected often have difficulty recalling recent events, making decisions, planning, thinking in flexible ways, and difficulty concentrating. They may experience feelings of sadness, anxiety, and confusion. When confronted by others about their errors, they are likely to become upset and angry as many have diminished insight into their cognitive impairments. Moderate dementia is characterized by severe memory problems pertaining to recent events, whereas early memories may remain intact. Persons with moderate dementia may not be oriented to date, day, time, or place. Word-finding difficulties become more prominent and hallucinations and delusions may also occur. Anxiety, agitation, sadness, and confusion are common. Those experiencing severe dementia may not recognize family members. They are likely to experience severe speech difficulties and may not be able to communicate. Their mood may vacillate from apathetic to agitated, and they may become physically and verbally aggressive. They may lose their ability to ambulate, feed themselves (they may find it difficult to swallow, for instance), and they may become incontinent (Prince, Acosta, Castro-Costa, Jackson, & Shaji, 2009).

BRIEF DEMENTIA ASSESSMENT

When assessing older adults for possible dementia, it is important to have a good appreciation of normal cognitive aging, mild cognitive impairment, delirium, and the range of potentially treatable etiologies of cognitive decline. Also, it is important to understand various biopsychosocial and environmental factors that may influence test performance. In this section, we will present such issues along with brief standardized cognitive assessment measures that can be used by health care providers. We also discuss strategies for providing an assessment feedback session.

Normal Cognitive Aging and Mild Cognitive Impairment

Changes that come with normal cognitive aging do not suggest dementia but typically involve a reduction in cognitive processing speed (Salthouse, 1996), which can lead to inefficiencies in attention, memory, language, and executive functioning (Meyerson, Adams, Hale, & Jenkins, 2003; Hertzog & Bleckley, 2001; Peterson et al., 2001; Zimprich, 2002). Likewise, dementia must be distinguished from mild cognitive impairment (MCI), which was originally adopted to describe a boundary condition where cognition was not consistent with age expectations but daily functioning was not reduced enough to warrant a diagnosis of dementia (Peterson, 1995). Three subtypes of MCIs have been suggested: amnestic MCI (aMCI), which includes a memory complaint and impaired memory for age; single nonmemory domain MCI (sMCI), which includes impaired attention/concentration, executive functioning, language, or visuospatial functioning; and multiple-domain MCI (mMCI), in which there are two or more impaired cognitive domains, often including memory (Peterson et al., 2001).

Delirium

Delirium is a condition that frequently occurs in medically ill, hospitalized older adults, including those who have a preexisting dementia. Although both delirium and dementia can result in global cognitive impairment, delirium is marked by prominent and rapidly evolving changes in attention and awareness, which wax and wane over time in terms of severity. The most frequent etiologies of delirium include metabolic disorders, infections, hypoxemia, dehydration, and the iatrogenic effects of medications (e.g., anticholinergics, sedative hypnotics, and opioids), all of which necessitate immediate medical intervention. The Confusional Assessment Method Diagnostic Algorithm (CAM) used in conjunction with associated assessment instruments, such as the Attention Screening Evaluation, is a useful tool in identifying delirium (Ely et al., 2001; see Table 8.1).

TABLE 8.1   Confusional Assessment Method Diagnostic Algorithm (CAM)

Delirium is Diagnosed With the Presence of *Both* Features 1 and 2, and *Either* 3 or 4:
Feature 1: Acute Onset and Fluctuating Course This information is usually obtained from a family member or caregiver and represents a rapid change from previous functioning. Cognitive functioning may fluctuate significantly throughout the day.
Feature 2: Inattention The individual has trouble with attention, is easily distracted, and/or has trouble keeping track of what is said.
Feature 3: Disorganized Thinking Rambling or irrelevant conversation, unclear or illogical flow of ideas, and/or unpredictable switching from subject to subject is present.
Feature 4: Altered Level of Consciousness Anything other than alert Normal = Alert Vigilant = Hyperalert Lethargic = Drowsy but equally aroused Stupor = Difficult to arouse Coma = Unarousable

Source: Ely et al., 2001.

Potentially Treatable Etiologies of Cognitive Decline

There are a myriad of potentially treatable medical conditions and other factors that can lead to cognitive changes in older adults. These conditions may occur during the course of dementia, making cognitive and/or behavioral symptoms more pronounced if left untreated. Likewise, they may lead to symptoms that are mistaken for dementia if undiagnosed. Some of the most frequently occurring conditions that should be taken into consideration when assessing for dementia include depression, normal pressure hydrocephalus, hypothyroidism, sleep disordered breathing, and vitamin deficiencies (such as B12 and thiamine). Although a detailed discussion of the prevalence, etiology, cognitive profile, and treatment of these medical conditions is beyond the scope of this chapter, Houston and Bondi (2006) offer several general conclusions that may be helpful for clinical practice. First, most of these conditions typically present with a few isolated deficits, which are often mild rather than severe, as opposed to the global cognitive decline that is characteristic of dementia. Second, cognitive changes stemming from these conditions often present in a "subcortical" pattern (e.g., problems with memory retrieval, executive functioning, and psychomotor and cognitive processing speed) and may be difficult to distinguish from normal cognitive aging. Third, it is rare for a complete reversal of these cognitive symptoms to occur even though there will likely be some improvement upon treatment. Fourth, early detection and treatment often leads to greater recovery, and the degree of cognitive improvement is linked to the condition's severity prior to treatment.

Examination Factors

There are a number of examination factors that need to be taken into consideration when assessing for dementia in older adults. These factors may serve as potential confounders to findings on standardized tests of cognitive functioning and should be explored and accounted for prior to test administration. Some of the physical factors that may influence performance include motor functioning, problems with vision or hearing, illness, fatigue, pain, or discomfort. Psychosocial factors include culture, literacy, rapport, motivation, and affective state. Environmental factors include the physical space in which the older adult is assessed (e.g., performance may be reduced if the environment is overwhelming, lacks stimulation, or is unfamiliar).

Older adults comprise a highly diverse population and are considered to be more heterogeneous than any other age group (Crowther

& Zeiss, 2003). Cultural considerations that may influence test performance include ethnic variations in cognitive testing, acculturation, educational factors (e.g., years of education, quality of education, and literacy), racial socialization, and linguistic variations (Manly, 2006). Furthermore, diversity consists not only of one's racial or ethnic background, but also of gender, age, socioeconomic status, sexual orientation, disability status, residence (i.e., rural or urban), education, religion, and transitions in social status and living situations (American Psychological Association [APA], 2003).

With regard to gender, the older adult population is comprised of a higher number of women than men, which results in several gender-related issues (Federal Interagency Forum on Aging-Related Statistics, 2000). The longevity of women means they will likely experience caring for a partner/spouse, widowhood or significant loss, and are at increased risk for developing chronic health conditions associated with age, such as dementia (APA, 2003). Older women are also more likely to have fewer economic resources than older men because they received unequal wages at work. There is a paucity of literature addressing special issues of older men.

Racial and ethnic diversity is also a critical factor to consider. Although Whites composes 80% of the older adult population by recent estimates, the number of older adults from diverse racial and ethnic backgrounds is rapidly growing and is expected to account for a larger proportion of the older adult population in the coming decades (Federal Interagency Forum on Aging-Related Statistics, 2010). Given the expanding diversity among older adults in the United States, it is critical to consider how racial and ethnic differences may be significant factors that affect older adults' access to physical and mental health services. Of concern, discrimination and racism may have been a component of older adults' life experiences, which likely has led to decreased opportunity and ability to find affordable but quality health care and housing. These factors may have resulted in diverse older adults' having fewer economic resources and more physical health problems compared to others. As such, diverse older adults may be more likely to delay or refrain from seeking physical and mental health services (Abramson, Trejo, & Lai, 2002).

Environmental factors also present a host of considerations that need to be taken into account when assessing older adults. For instance, whether an older adult resides in an urban or rural setting affects his or her ability to access resources such as transportation and health services. Older adults who live in rural settings have less access to resources compared to their urban or metropolitan counterparts (Coburn & Bolda, 1999).

Clearly, there are an array of factors that can influence older adults' performance on cognitive tests. One factor that can be easily overlooked is the clinician's own biases, attitudes, and knowledge in working with older adults. It is important to be aware of ageist biases that can lead to misdiagnosis due to misattribution of symptoms (e.g., attributing anxiety, confusion, and irritability to "old age"; Goodstein, 1985). Lower expectations for performance or improvement can result in providing fewer treatment options (James & Haley, 1995).

Furthermore, positive stereotypes (e.g., viewing older adults as "cute"), can result in higher estimates of older adults' abilities or skills, which can result in inappropriate interventions or interventions that do not meet older adults' needs (Braithwaite, 1986). Examining one's biases toward older adults and older adults from culturally diverse backgrounds and seeking consultation are strategies recommended by the APA (2003) in order to help develop more accurate perceptions of older adults and culturally diverse persons.

The following is based on Manly (2006) practical recommendations for increasing validity of cognitive assessment in culturally diverse older adults. Manley noted that there is a relative paucity of research in this area and that the following recommendations should be taken with caution: (a) ask for self-identification of race/ethnicity rather than making an assumption; (b) cultural experience may be gleaned by asking about community of origin as well as current community of residence; (c) evaluation of educational history should not only include highest grade achieved but also where schooling took place (primary, secondary, and postsecondary), segregation level of the school, student-teacher ratio, urbanicity, and number of years of compulsory education required in the elder's country of origin; and (c) reading level should be evaluated prior to cognitive testing. For English speakers, there are several adequate measures (e.g., Wide Range Achievement Test-4 [Wilkinson & Robertson, 2006] and the American National Adult Reading Test [Grober & Sliwinski, 1991]); whereas the Word Accentuation Test (Del Ser, Gonzáles-Montalvo, Martínez-Espinosa, Delgado-Villapalos, & Bermejo, 1997) is recommended for Spanish speakers. (d) Evaluate English language proficiency for bilingual and multilingual older adults if tests will be administered in English; (f) always attempt to use the best available norms from a culturally similar population to the elder you are testing; (g) when using published measures which have been translated into another language, make sure that the normative sample for these measures is culturally similar to the background of the older adult being assessed (e.g., published norms for older adults residing in Mexico may not be appropriate for a second-generation

Mexican American); and (h) there are many complex ethical considerations when it comes to testing of non-English and non-native English speakers by English-speaking clinicians (Harris, Cullum, Bush, & Drexler, 2002). Manly (2006) cautions that interpreters (trained or untrained) may not be familiar with translating and/or administering test items in another language.

Assessing Dementia in Older African Americans

Previous studies have found that although the Mini Mental State Exam (MMSE; Folstein, Folstein, & McHugh, 1975) is a robust measure to screen for cognitive impairment, its usefulness with older African Americans may be limited due to an increased number of false positives in persons with education levels lower than 8th grade (Baker, Robinson, & Stewart, 1993; Fillenbaum, Heyman, Williams, Prosnit, & Burchett, 1990). Due to years of discrimination and reduced access to resources, some older African Americans do not have education levels higher than 8th grade. A useful alternative to the MMSE that has been adjusted for race and education levels below the 8th grade is the Short Portable Mental Status Questionnaire (SPMSQ; Pfeiffer, 1975). The SPMSQ was specifically developed to screen for cognitive impairments in older African Americans who live in rural areas and has been found to be a helpful measure with this population (Fillenbaum et al., 1990). Many older African Americans may not regularly attend physical and mental health appointments due to living in a rural area and having fewer resources. Therefore, it is important to rule out medical issues, malnutrition, and depression when screening for cognitive impairment in this population (Baker et al., 1993; Baker, Velli, Friedman, & Wiley, 1995).

Assessing Dementia in Older Hispanic Adults

When assessing for dementia in older Hispanic adults, both cultural and linguistic factors need to be considered. The U.S. Census Bureau (2000) estimated that 18% of U.S. residents spoke a language other than English at home. In light of this information, many older Hispanic adults may be bilingual or may speak only Spanish. Evaluating an individual's preferred language will determine what battery of assessments should be utilized. Measures that have been identified as useful with the Hispanic population who speak Spanish include the *Batería III Woodcock-Munoz* (Spanish version of the Woodcock-Johnson III), *Batería Neuropsicológica en Español* (Artiola i Fortuny, Hermosillo-Roma,

Heaton, & Pardee (1999)), *NEUROPSI* (Ostrosky-Solis, Gomez-Perez, Matute, Rosselli, Ardila, & Pineda, 2007), the *Spanish and English Neuropsychological Assessment Scales* (SENAS; Mungas, Reed, Haan, & González, 2005), and the *Neuropsychological Screening Battery for Hispanics* (NeSBHIS; Pontón et al., 1996).

Individuals who report being bilingual will need to be asked which language they would like to be evaluated. Examining their level of U.S. acculturation can be helpful in this process. Individuals with low U.S. acculturation should be evaluated in Spanish, and those with high U.S. acculturation should be evaluated in English (Pontón, 2001). However, the ideal scenario for evaluating bilingual individuals is to have a bilingual examiner conduct the assessment in both languages (Paradis, 2008). Being able to conduct the evaluation in both languages for bilingual patients provides a more comprehensive understanding of patients' current levels of functioning. Another important factor in assessing individuals who are bilingual is assessing the examiner's linguistic proficiency and ability to examine the bilingual client (Pontón, 2001). If it is determined that the examiner is not proficient enough to provide the evaluation, the use of another bilingual examiner should be utilized whenever possible, and therefore, referring out to a bilingual examiner would be the next best option. However, depending on location, these services may not be available, at which time it is appropriate to use a professionally trained interpreter (Paradis, 2008).

Cultural Considerations When Working With Older Hispanic Adults

The term *Hispanic* refers to those individuals who are of Latin American origin. There are many Spanish speaking countries; therefore, the Hispanic culture is heterogeneous and the common traits that will be discussed next should be viewed with this in mind. The two factors that warrant the most attention are education and language. Level of education is a significant factor to take into account when assessing older Hispanic adults. Research indicates that Hispanic individuals with lower levels of education and who are considered to be functionally illiterate obtain scores on neuropsychological assessments that are similar to those of individuals who have brain injuries (Ardila, 1993; Ardila, Rosselli, & Puente, 1994). Given the diversity within the Hispanic culture, language poses another issue. The language used in the measures to assess cognitive impairments may be translated from English to Spanish, but can still remain culturally inappropriate. Similarly, measures that are developed specifically for Spanish speaking individuals may not use vocabulary or reflect cultural norms of that individual's cultural origin or age group

(Taussig & Ponton, 1996). Individuals with aphasia in Spanish, who are bilingual, will not present with issues with grammatical construction, but will present with problems in the semantic aspects of language in English due to the more rigid rules of English as compared to Spanish (Ardila et al., 1994). Bilingual individuals experiencing issues with aphasia may experience difficulty with mixing grammatical rules of the languages.

Cross-Cultural Testing

In an attempt to remedy the issues in assessing cognitive impairments in culturally diverse populations, researchers have developed the Cognitive Abilities Screening Instrument (CASI; Teng et al., 1994). The CASI was developed as a cross-cultural test for dementia to serve the increasing need of ethnic minorities in the United States and to assist in global health care planning (Teng, 1996). It was designed to compensate for language and education level differences, which have posed serious barriers to previous assessment measures. It was developed with the intention to be adaptable to meet the assessment needs of the individual. This measure is comprised of items that were either taken or adapted from the MMSE (Folstein et al., 1975), the Modified MMSE (3MS; Teng & Chui, 1987), and the Hasegawa Dementia Screening Scale (Hasegawa, 1983). Areas addressed by the CASI include attention, concentration, orientation, short-term memory, long-term memory, language abilities, constructional praxis, list-generating fluency, abstraction, and judgment (Teng, 1996). This measure can be used for various functions, such as screening for dementia, assessing individual strengths and weaknesses, and tracking an individual's cognitive changes over time.

Brief Dementia Assessment

At a minimum, a brief dementia assessment should include: (a) an interview with the individual and a knowledgeable collateral source (e.g., family member and health care team member); (b) a review of available data, including family history (e.g., medical records); (c) a thorough medical examination, laboratory tests, and neuroimaging; (d) a screening exam for primary psychiatric disorders (e.g., depression, anxiety); (e) an evaluation of everyday functioning such as activities of daily living/instrumental activities of daily living (ADLs/IADLs); (f) a screening exam for sensory difficulties (especially vision and hearing) before testing; and (g) the provision of measures of various cognitive domains including orientation, attention/concentration, learning and memory, executive functioning, and language.

Brief Standardized Cognitive Assessment Measures
A systematic review of standardized measures of cognitive functioning
was recently conducted by the Evidence-based Synthesis (ESP) Center
located at the Portland VA Medical Center (Kansagara & Freeman, 2010)
and included the six item Blessed-Orientation-Memory-Concentration
Test (BOMC; Blessed, Tomlinson, & Roth, 1968), the Mini-Cog (Borson,
Scanlan, Brush, Vitaliano, & Dokmak, 2000), the Montreal Cognitive
Assessment (MoCA; Nasreddine et al., 2005), the St. Louis University
Mental Status Examination (SLUMS; Tariq, Tumosa, Chibnall, Perry,
& Morley, 2006), and the Short Test of Mental Status (STMS; Kokmen,
Naessens, & Offord, 1987). These measures are reviewed along several
lines, including cognitive domains assessed, limitations, sensitivity,
specificity, and other characteristics. This review is briefly summa-
rized in Tables 8.2 and 8.3.

Feedback
Feedback is a critical phase in the overall process of dementia assessment in which findings/recommendations are shared with the patient,
his or her family, and/or health care team. Indeed, the APA asserts that
individuals receiving assessment have the right to receive prompt and
understandable feedback of their results (APA, 2002). Feedback can be
viewed as a therapeutic process and requires considerable skill to translate an evaluation into an effective treatment plan. Effective feedback

TABLE 8.2 Cognitive Domains Assessed By Brief Measures of Cognitive
Functioning

	BOMC	Mini-Cog	MoCA	SLUMS	STMS
Cognitive Domain					
Orientation	x		x	x	x
Recall	x	x	x	x	x
Remote memory				x	x
Visuospatial		x	x	x	x
Verbal Fluency			x	x	
Attention	x		x	x	x
Abstraction			x	x	x
Executive functioning		x	x	x	x

Note: BOMC, Blessed-Orientation-Memory-Concentration Test; MoCA, Montreal Cognitive
Assessment; SLUMS, St. Louis University Mental Status Examination; STMS, Short Test of
Mental Status
Source: Adapted from Kansagara and Freeman (2010).

TABLE 8.3 Psychometric Characteristics of Brief Measures of Cognitive Functioning

	BOMC	Mini-Cog	MoCA	SLUMS	STMS
Characteristic					
Administration Time (minutes)	4–6	2–4	10–15	7	5
Sensitivity	0.83	0.76	0.94	< HS: 1.0 > HS: 0.98	0.86
Specificity	0.77	0.89	0.5	< HS: 0.98 > HS: 1.0	0.935

Note. BOMC, Blessed-Orientation-Memory-Concentration Test; MoCA, Montreal Cognitive Assessment; SLUMS, St. Louis University Mental Status Examination; STMS, Short Test of Mental Status
Source: Adapted from Kansagara and Freeman (2010).

with older adults can be complex given some of the special issues they face. Therefore, making feedback understandable and interactive can increase the individual's ability to understand and utilize the feedback provided. This means that participants feel comfortable asking questions, voicing concerns, and responding to the evaluator's comments. It can be helpful to invite the patient and family to ask questions during the session to ensure information is being understood, to carefully listen, and to check in with participants. It is important to keep in mind that providing feedback is often emotionally charged for all involved (Green, 2006).

Clinical skills are critical to the success of the feedback in interacting with patients and their support systems. Maintaining an alliance with the individual while concurrently working toward developing a positive rapport with those involved with the patient's care can be a balancing act, but a vital component of the feedback process. Assessing and maintaining sensitivity about the type and amount of information to be provided, as well as evaluating the participant's readiness to receive the information (e.g., diagnosis) will require the astute skills of the clinician (Green, 2006). Being sensitive to not leaving the individual and family feeling overwhelmed, hopeless, and powerless is critical during the process of providing feedback. Another aspect of clinical importance is addressing interpersonal, family systems, and team issues.

Prior to beginning the evaluation, discuss with the individual who they want to include in the feedback session. It is advisable to receive permission from the individual prior to initiating the assessment to include members of his or her support system (e.g., family, friends, and the team involved in care) (Green, 2006). Ideally, feedback is provided during an hour-long follow-up session, but could be incorporated into a patient-centered team meeting with the patient and family present. Some patients and their families may need further explanation and/or time to discuss alternative treatments, resident care, and follow-up services. Therefore, it is important to allow opportunities for additional sessions as needed.

An essential component of feedback is specifying the patient's cognitive strengths and limitations and providing an explanation of how these strengths/limitations contribute to the patient's behavior and/or changes in behavior. It is also a time to discuss compensatory strategies. In some cases it may appropriate to provide a summary of findings and recommendations to the patient and family. It is important to identify any follow-up evaluations needed for better identification of underlying disorders. Treatment recommendations such as pharmacological treatments and nonpharmacological treatments (such as cognitive training or therapy), which could contribute to the resident's health, independence, safety, and comfort, should be discussed with the patient and/or his or her family. It is important to discuss how the changes (e.g., possible pattern of decline, communication issues) can affect the individual and his or her family and provide support and assist in planning for the future (Green, 2006). Tables 8.4 and 8.5 summarize the objectives of a feedback session as well as include tips for conducting a successful feedback session.

TABLE 8.4 Objectives of Feedback Session

■ Detail an individual's cognitive strengths and limitations.

■ Explain how these strengths/limitations contribute to behavior.

■ Describe possible explanations for cognitive changes.

■ Identify any follow-up evaluations needed to further assess possible causes of disorder or impairments that may affect quality of life.

■ Discuss pharmacological treatments likely to be effective.

■ Discuss nonpharmacological treatments, such as cognitive training or psychotherapy, which can contribute to the older adult's quality of life.

■ Discuss how the changes can affect the individual and his or her family (e.g., possible pattern of decline, communication), and provide support.

■ Assist in planning for the future.

Source: Adapted from Green, 2006.

TABLE 8.5   Tips for Conducting a Successful Feedback Session

- Think of the feedback session as an interactive and therapeutic process.
- It is advisable to receive permission from older adults up front to include members of their support system (e.g., family, friends, team involved in care) in the feedback session.
- A feedback session is ideally provided during an hour-long session after an assessment.
- A feedback session can be provided for the individual who received the assessment, the family, and/or can be incorporated into a patient-centered team meeting.
- Strengths should be emphasized along with compensatory strategies for overcoming limitations.
- Treatment alternatives and follow-up services should be discussed.
- Encourage the older adult and others to ask questions and process information throughout the session.
- A written summary of findings and recommendations should be provided.
- Opportunities for additional sessions should be provided if needed. We have found that many older adults and families benefit from a series of 2–3 feedback sessions in order to fully understand results and recommendations.

Source: Adapted from Green, 2006.

COGNITIVE-BEHAVIORALLY ORIENTED INTERVENTIONS FOR DEMENTIA

In the first part of this section, an introduction to social contextual, peer group, and developmental factors that need to be considered when providing cognitive-behaviorally oriented interventions to older adults is provided. In the second section, an overview of cognitive-behaviorally-oriented interventions suitable for persons with dementia in the early, middle, and later stages is described.

Social Contextual Factors

Understanding the various social contextual factors that affect older adults is a vital component of developing and providing appropriate interventions. Such environmental factors include the rules and regulations inherent in the setting where the older adult receives care (e.g., nursing homes, home, aging services network, social and recreational centers, age-segregated housing). For example, if an older adult resides in a nursing home, he or she may be rewarded for taking a passive stance in their daily routine to comply with the facility's schedules and routines. This passivity could result in decreased activity levels, a sense of limited control, and depressive mood (Segal, 2005). Interventions may need to focus on the environment of care as well as the individual resident.

Peer Group Differences

Each generation is distinguished from others by different socialization processes that influence attitudes, beliefs, and, to some degree, personality features (Satre, Knight, & David, 2006). Social gerontology research reveals that some differences that have been attributed to the aging process are actually due to peer group effects. For instance, older adults who were born later in the last century in the United States have received more years of formal education in comparison to older adults who were born earlier in the century. This difference in years of formal education has resulted in intellectual aptitude differences. Older adults born earlier in the century demonstrate strong verbal fluency and arithmetic ability (Schaie, 1996), whereas older adults born later in the century tend to demonstrate relative strengths in spatial orientation, reasoning (Schaie, 1996), and vocabulary (Bowles, Grimm, & McArdle, 2005). Due to generational differences with regard to familiarity with psychotherapy, providing a detailed explanation of cognitive-behavioral therapy (CBT) can facilitate a health care professional's ability to develop positive rapport with older adults (Hyer, Kramer, & Sohnle, 2004). Specifically, describing CBT as a collaborative and structured process that is designed to provide individuals with practical life skills can be helpful (Knight & Satre, 1999).

Cognitive Factors and Aging

As people age, recognition memory remains relatively preserved, whereas word recall and working memory declines (Light, 2004). Older adults are better able to retain information that holds emotional significance, as opposed to neutral information, and positive rather than negative content. When working with older adults, it is helpful to use simple and concise phrasing. Material should be presented in a structured manner. When asking older adults to perform tasks pertaining to specific material, providing them with time to study the material, the ability to take notes, and cuing can increase their performance on these tasks. In therapy, it may be appropriate to lengthen the course of treatment in order to increase learning and retention. During a session, retention of information discussed may be increased by summarizing important information and repeating this information throughout the session. Also, having the older adult take notes at important times in the session can also help facilitate retention of the material being discussed. Furthermore, because homework is a critical component of CBT and can increase memory retention in older adults, using strategies to increase homework compliance is crucial. The provision of handouts, homework reminders, and trouble-shooting barriers can be helpful for enhancing treatment outcomes.

Cognitive-Behaviorally Oriented Interventions for Persons With Mild Dementia

In the early stages of dementia, people often experience frustration over cognitive changes, mood changes, and sleep disturbance. Problem-solving therapy focuses on reconceptualizing the individual's challenging experiences as problems with potential solutions and incorporating skills to test these possible solutions, which can be particularly helpful at this stage (Alexopoulos, Raue, & Arean, 2003).

To address cognitive impairment, the spaced-retrieval technique (SRT) focus on the activation of procedural motor memory and dual cognitive support by incorporating progressive and increasing time intervals between the presentation of material to be remembered and recall of that information (Acevedo & Loewenstein, 2007). During the intervals, individuals are engaged in activities to prevent rehearsal of the information presented (e.g., cognitive tasks, distracting conversation). Corrective feedback is provided if errors occur during the retrieval phase and the time interval between stimulus presentation and recall is reduced to the amount when recall is incorrect. The SRT is effective in teaching a number of skills, such as recalling personal information, object naming, and learning face-name and object-location associations (Camp, Bird, & Cherry, 2000; Clare, Wilson, Carter, Roth, & Hodges, 2002; Davis, Massman, & Doody; 2001). This technique appears to work by using a priming process that engages aspects of implicit memory, which is less affected by the AD process (Fleischman, Wilson, Gabrieli, Schneider, Bienias, & Bennet, 2005). Other approaches that have been found to be effective among patients with AD and that operate by engaging implicit memory are errorless learning and vanishing cues (Acevedo & Lowenstein, 2007).

Another approach that has been found to be effective with patients with AD, particularly when the information that is to be recalled is emotionally laden or is presented in a multimodal fashion, is the dual cognitive support approach. This approach emphasizes increased support during the encoding and retrieval stages of both learning and memory processes (Backman, 1992) through the use of stimuli that promote a high degree of organization, thus increasing the richness of stimuli, activating prior knowledge, or anchoring the material to be recalled to personal and salient life events (Backman, 1992).

In order to compensate for memory loss, various external memory aides have been found to be helpful. Memory books and timers can help in reducing behavioral excesses and repetitive questions as well as supporting daily functioning in very mild dementia (Bourgeois et al., 2003).

Several researchers have used multimodel approaches in the treatment of patients with mild-to-moderate AD (Spector et al., 2003; Zanetti, Rozzini, Bianchetti, & Trabucci, 1997; Zanetti et al., 2001). Two studies have shown promise in promoting generalization by using multimodal approaches in a group format. One study focused on ADL training. The intervention lasted 3 weeks, 5 days a week, for 1 hour each day. Participants with mild-to-moderate AD in this study were able to complete both trained and untrained tasks at a faster rate (Zanetti et al., 1997, 2001). Spector et al. (2003) used cognitive interventions, such as word games; discussing topics related to the current day, money, and famous faces; and the use of a reality orientation board. Their results suggested generalization of skills to untrained tasks. These results were comparable to the use of cholinesterase inhibitors.

Cognitive-Behaviorally Oriented Interventions for Persons with Moderate-to-Severe Dementia

Persons with moderate-to-severe dementia experience a complex constellation of mood, behavioral, cognitive, and perceptual changes, which tend to evolve over time and vary depending upon dementia type. These changes have been referred to as neuropsychiatric symptoms of dementia (Finkel, Silva, Cohen, Miller, & Sartorius, 1997), behaviors that challenges (National Institute for Health and Clinical Excellence, 2007), and behavioral and psychological symptoms of dementia (BPSD; Moniz Cook, De Vugt, Verhey, & James, 2009). Some of the most commonly experienced BPSD include agitation or aggression (physical or verbal), apathy, withdrawal, psychosis (delusions and/or hallucinations), and excessive motor activity (Kverno, Black, Blass, Geiger-Brown, & Rabins, 2008; Zuidema, de Jonghe, Verhey, & Koopmans, 2007). The majority of persons with advanced dementia experience at least one BPSD (Kverno, Black, Nolan, & Rabins, 2009).

There are currently three primary paradigms for understanding the etiology of BPSD, which serve as the basis for most psychosocial approaches to intervention in long-term care settings (O'Conner, Ames, Gardner, & King, 2009). According to the *unmet needs paradigm*, BPSD stems from the unmet physical, emotional, and social needs of persons with dementia (Cohen-Mansfield, 2001). These unmet needs may be related to physical and environmental factors (e.g., the need for reduced level of restraints, proper pain management, appropriate lighting) and psychosocial issues (e.g., loneliness, isolation, and boredom). The *learning/behavior paradigm* focuses on learned behaviors, desired or undesired, which may be inadvertently reinforced by family members or professional care staff. This approach teaches family and staff about the relationship between antecedents, specific behaviors, and consequences (e.g., ABC model). The *environmental vulnerability paradigm* is based on the assumption that as dementia progresses, there is a greater vulnerability to environmental stimuli and that adaptation of the environment to the individual (e.g., reducing or increasing the sensory demands of the person with dementia) may serve to decrease BPSD. In clinical practice, BPSD experienced by an older adult can have multiple overlapping etiologies, resulting in a complex clinical scenario. Likewise, when identifying appropriate ways of responding to BPSD, it is necessary that interventions be based on sound, multifactorial, interdisciplinary, and functional assessments, which take into consideration biological, emotional, social, and spiritual factors so that clinical interventions can be tailored to meet the needs of the person with dementia, their family, and the environment he or she is experiencing.

There are a number of ways to classify psychosocial interventions for addressing BPSD, and the list that follows is not mutually exclusive or exhaustive. Specific approaches can include: (a) sensory enhancement relaxation (e.g., massage/touch, listening to soothing music during meals and while bathing, white noise, sensory stimulation); (b) social contact, which may be real or simulated (e.g., animal companioning, one-on-one interaction, simulated interaction such as family videos); (c) family and staff training aimed at educating about BPSD and stress management; (d) structured activities (e.g., life enrichment, physical activities, and nature therapies); (e) environmental design (e.g., building wandering areas, natural/enhanced environments, and reduced stimulation); (f) medical/nursing care interventions (e.g., light therapy/sleep strategies, pain management, hearing/vision aids, restraint removal); (g) behavioral interventions, including differential reinforcement (e.g., reinforcing quiet behaviors), stimulus control (e.g., placing mirrors in front of doors to prevent exiting), and cognitive modalities (e.g. reality orientation); and (h) combination approaches that incorporate several of the strategies, usually in an individualized treatment plan.

Kasl-Godley and Gatz (2000) described and assessed a range of psychologically based interventions that have been used to assist persons with dementia, including psychodynamic approaches, reminiscence and life review, support groups, reality orientation, memory training, behavioral interventions, and cognitive-behavioral therapy. Behavioral interventions are based upon the principals of learning and seek to reduce frequency, duration, and intensity of an undesired behavior through functional analysis, which involves making detailed observations about the nature of the behavior, its antecedents, and its consequences. Behavioral interventions may include direct contingency principals (e.g., positive and negative reinforcement, schedules of reinforcement, stimulus control, cueing, shaping, extinction) and indirect contingency principals (e.g., verbal control, distraction, environmental modification, problem solving, behavioral rehearsal, relaxation training). Kasl-Godley and Gatz concluded that there was empirical evidence for using behavioral interventions to decrease BPSD. However, the majority of studies at the time of the review were case studies ($n = 1$) and many were not dementia specific and included both persons with dementia and chronic mental disorders. Kasl-Godley and Gatz did not discuss which types of behavioral interventions were most efficacious in addressing BPSD.

In 2001, Cohen-Mansfield conducted a literature review on non-pharmacological interventions for BPSD using more stringent criteria than Kasl-Godley and Gatz. Cohen-Mansfield's search yielded 83 studies that were categorized according to intervention type and included the following groupings: sensory, social contact (real or simulated), behavior therapy, staff training, structured activities, environmental interventions, medical/nursing care interventions, and combination interventions. The behavioral interventions category had the second largest number of studies, second only to sensory-based interventions, and included studies using differential reinforcement, cognitive rehabilitation, and stimulus control. The majority of these studies were case studies that used methods such as extinction (i.e., withholding positive reinforcement when attempting to eliminate a behavior), differential reinforcement (e.g., reinforcing either quiet behavior or behavior that was not congruent with the undesired behavior), and stimulus control (e.g., facilitating learning of an association between a stimulus/cue and behavior). There were mixed results regarding the efficacy of reviewed interventions. Cohen-Mansfield suggested the majority of interventions may have had a limited, but positive, effect and that better matching of the available interventions to residents' needs and capabilities would be critical to improving outcomes.

Livingston, Johnston, Katona, Paton, and Lyketsos (2005) used a systematic approach to review the literature on interventions derived from psychological/psychosocial models for treating BPSD, regardless of setting, with the aim of making evidence-based recommendations about interventions. The interventions included in their review were classified into the following categories: (a) reminiscence therapy, (b) validation therapy, (c) reality orientation, (d) cognitive stimulation therapy, (e) other dementia-specific therapies, (f) nondementia-specific therapies, (g) psychological interventions with caregivers, (h) psychosocial interventions (e.g., music, Snoezelen/multisensory stimulation, and other sensory stimulation), (i) structured activities, and (j) environmental manipulation/staff education. The majority of interventions discussed in this review targeted BPSD in the home rather than in long-term care settings. Although most of these studies were case reports and were conducted in the home setting, there were a few larger randomized controlled trials (RCTs) that were conducted in long-term care settings. Several investigations were identified which focused on staff education in managing BPSD, three of which were RCTs. The first study was an RCT of a manual-based communication skills training for nursing assistants, which found significant reductions in resident aggression at 3 months and reduction of depression at 6 months (McCallion, Toseland, Lacey, & Banks, 1999). The second RCT trained staff to implement an emotion-focused care program that entailed validation, reminiscence, and sensory stimulation, which was not effective in reducing BPRS (Schrijnemaekers et al., 2002). The third study was a staff education program that provided knowledge of dementia and potential management strategies. The results suggested a reduced use of physical restraints, but there was not a significant change in agitation score postintervention (Testad, Aasland, & Aarsland, 2005). Overall, Livingston and colleagues (2005) concluded that behavioral management interventions tailored to an individual patient's behavior are generally successful for reducing BPSD, even when qualitative differences were noted between studies, and that the effects of such interventions tend to last over time. They also concluded that staff education may lead to reductions in behavioral symptoms, use of restraints, and improved affect.

In another review, Spira and Edelstein (2006) evaluated over 20 studies that focused on *behavioral interventions for agitation* in older adults with dementia. The behaviors targeted in these studies included wandering, disruptive vocalizations, physical aggression, and other agitated behaviors. Well over half of the studies were case studies ($n = 1$) with the remaining using between groups designs entailing a comparison between an active treatment group and a group that received no intervention. Most of the studies were conducted in residential care settings. Spira and Edelstein concluded that behavioral interventions, based on functional assessment techniques, showed considerable promise, although the results of some of the studies were mixed and had several methodological shortcomings. Spira and Edelstein concluded the following: (a) wandering may be responsive to differential reinforcement of behavior (Hussian, 1981; Hussian & Brown, 1987; Mayer & Darby; 1991; Namazi, Rosner, & Calkins, 1989); (b) differential reinforcement for disruptive vocalizations produced mixed results (Birchmore & Clague, 1983; Bourgeois et al., 1997; Doyle, Zapperoni, O'Conner, & Runci, 1997); (c) use of functional analysis and noncontingent reinforcement decreased disruptive vocalizations in a preliminary investigation (Buchanan & Fisher, 2002); (d) differential reinforcement and cognitive behavioral interventions showed promise for reducing physical aggression (Lewin & Lundervold, 1987; Teri et al., 1998; Wisner & Green, 1986); and (e) a program that trained nursing assistants in behavior modification strategies resulted in modest reductions in agitation among nursing home residents (Burgio et al., 2002).

Logsdson, McCurry, and Teri (2007) reviewed the literature regarding evidence-based psychological treatments (EBTs) for BPSD in older adults using the APA's Committee on Science and Practice of the Society for Clinical Psychology criteria (Chambless & Hollon, 1998; Chambless & Oldendick, 2001). They defined "psychological treatments" as interventions formulated on the basis of psychological theories or models of behavior change and delivered or supervised by mental health professionals regardless of specific discipline. They broadly defined "behavioral disturbances" to include disruptive, distressing, and unsafe behaviors, as well as behaviors that interfere with care. They searched for prospective studies with pretreatment and posttreatment outcome measures, at least two supporting peer-reviewed publications, at least 30 participants randomly assigned to the same treatment condition, and adherence to a specific protocol or treatment manual. The studies included in this review were delivered at in home and residential care settings. Although 57 RCTs were reviewed for inclusion on the basis of titles or abstract information, 43 were excluded either because they did not meet EBT methodological criteria or because they involved environmental modification or psychoeducational nursing interventions in which the psychological component could not be separately evaluated. Fourteen studies were extensively reviewed. In six of the studies there were no significant differences between treatment and control groups. In eight of the studies, significantly different outcomes between treatment and control groups were noted. Only two of the studies were conducted in residential settings (Lichtenberg, Kemp-Havican, Macneill, & Schafer-Johnson, 2005; Proctor et al., 1999). Both of these interventions involved training professional caregivers to observe behaviors, identify antecedents, modify the physical environment, and schedule pleasant events or interpersonal interactions. Logsdson, McCurry, and Teri (2007) noted that behavioral problem solving appears to be most effective when it is provided by or supervised by clinicians who have expertise in dementia care and behavior therapy.

In their review of nonpharmacological interventions for BPSD in persons with *advanced dementia*, Kverno et al. (2009) identified and summarized the most relevant literature from 1998 through 2008. Out of 22 systematic reviews identified, which included 143 distinct intervention studies, only 11 studies (7.7%) described interventions for persons with advanced dementia and met the criteria for inclusion. The studies were divided into four broad intervention types: (a) *sensory-oriented interventions* that targeted withdrawal (e.g., apathy) and disruptive behaviors (e.g., agitation) through stimulating the senses (e.g., exercise, aromatherapy, listening to music); (b) *emotion-oriented intervention*s that focused on increasing pleasure or reducing distress (e.g., validation therapy and simulated presence); (c) *behavior-oriented interventions* that focused on creating a safe and positive environment (e.g., adequate space, low noise, special care units) and; (d) *cognitive-oriented interventions* (e.g., language-based interventions such as reality orientation, cognitive retraining, and skills training). Kverno and associates suggested that studies using sensory-focused interventions demonstrated limited moderate-to-high quality evidence of efficacy for persons with advanced dementia who were experiencing BPSD. Emotion-oriented interventions, such as simulated presence, were suggested to be more effective for individuals with preserved verbal interactive capacity; however, these did not appear efficacious for persons with advanced dementia. Kverno et al. emphasized the need for more research that takes severity of cognitive impairment into consideration.

Kong, Evans, and Guevara (2009) systematically reviewed the literature regarding the effectiveness of nonpharmacological interventions for *agitation in older adults with dementia* and conducted a meta-analysis based on their review. Studies that met criteria for inclusion were classified into seven types based on a classification scheme previously identified by Cohen-Mansfield (2001). Based on findings, Kong, Evans, and Guevara (2009) suggested that only sensory interventions (e.g., aromatherapy, thermal bath, calming music, hand massage) showed a statistically significant beneficial effect on reducing agitation in persons with dementia. No other type of nonpharmacological intervention (e.g., social contact, activities, environmental, caregiver training, combination therapy, behavioral therapy) showed overall efficacy in reducing agitation among older adults with dementia. Caution should be exercised when interpreting these results due to the small number of studies in each category; the small sample sizes in respective studies; the variability in the nature, frequency, and duration of the intervention programs; the inconsistent definitions of agitation and variability in outcome measures used; and the time of measurement.

O'Connor et al. (2009) conducted a systematic review of psychosocial interventions for BPSD that were derived from three psychologically oriented paradigms (learning theory, unmet needs, and altered stress thresholds). Primary interventions were music, professional caregiver education, sensory enrichment, simulated family presence, novel bathing techniques, aromatherapy, relaxation, and validation therapy. Interventions proved more effective than attention control conditions in reducing behavioral symptoms in only half of the 12 investigation, prompting O'Connor and colleagues to hypothesize that attentive, human interaction may be used to reduce BPSD in some older adults. Effect sizes could not be calculated for most studies due to methodological limitations and/or failure to report data needed for calculating effect sizes; however, O'Connor et al. found moderate effect sizes in studies using music during specific activities (e.g., meals, recreational activities).

Interventions for Wandering

Hussian (1981) found that the paths of those who wander can be modified by using simple antecedents, such as arrows or track lighting. In another study, Feliciano, Vore, LeBlanc, and Baker (2004) found that using a cloth barrier to keep people out of unsafe areas was effective. Beattie, Algase, and Song (2004) conducted a study that was implemented as a nursing intervention aimed at reducing wandering during mealtimes and increasing time spent sitting at the dining table and increasing food intake and body weight. The intervention required a trained interventionist to systematically reinforce the person with dementia sitting at the table by using two communication strategies: (a) focused conversation about the meal and eating, and social comments related to the mealtime experience; and (b) specific elements of social behavior (e.g., smiling, eye contact). The intervention was deemed successful in that participants were able to sit at the table longer and eat more food during the intervention. Body weight remained stable throughout the study.

Interventions for Disruptive Vocalizations

Buchanan and Fischer (2002) utilized functional analysis to address issues with disruptive vocalizations. First, variables that maintained vocalizations were identified. Subsequently, these stimuli were presented noncontingently. This combination of interventions resulted in substantial decreases in disruptive vocalization.

Agitation

Burgio et al. (2002) trained 85 care assistants in communication and behavior management skills over a 4-week period. Seventy-nine residents, who had at least mild BPSD, were targeted. Half of the care assistants received intensive continuing supervision with clinical monitoring, verbal and written feedback, and performance incentives to ensure that skills were maintained. The other half were monitored by senior nurses. At 6-month follow-up, the intensive supervision group showed greater skill retention; however, agitated behavior declined in both groups with no statistically significant differences between the groups. This finding suggests the need for follow-up during behavioral management skill training, but the intensity of follow-up that is necessary remains unclear.

Lichtenberg et al. (2005) conducted a clinical trial in a specialized dementia care nursing home and compared a behavioral intervention focused on increasing pleasant events in the usual care. After 3 months, both the "troublesomeness" and "dangerousness" of behavior problems declined for the treatment group, whereas they increased for the usual care group.

Cohen-Mansfield, Libin, and Marx (2007) conducted an RCT that included 11 suburban nursing home facilities. A variety of outcomes were assessed, but direction observation of agitation was primarily recorded by trained research assistants who observed participants for physically agitated (e.g. pacing, repetitive movements) and verbally agitated (e.g., screaming, complaining) behaviors. Specifically used in final analysis was an overall agitation score of all incidents of verbal and physically nonaggressive behaviors. The secondary outcome was the evaluation of positive and negative affect, which was also based on direct observation.

In this investigation (Cohen-Mansfield et al., 2007), control group nursing homes received staff training with regard to the causes of agitated behaviors and nonpharmacological interventions for such behaviors. Nursing home staff that received the active intervention education were provided training using Treatment Routes for Exploring Agitation (TREA). This intervention provides a systematic strategy for developing individualized, nonpharmacological care plans to address agitation in people with dementia. TREA incorporates information regarding older adults' unmet needs, intact capabilities, and preferences (e.g., past work, relationships, interests), which were identified by family members, professional caregivers, and direct observations. TREA can be conceptualized as a systematic decision-making process guiding professional caregivers to identify unmet needs that may be associated with agitated behaviors. TREA interventions are tailored to address specific agitated (e.g., verbally aggressive or physically nonaggressive) behaviors, as these are believed to be associated with specific correlates. TREA is based on Cohen-Mansfields' past research (e.g., Cohen-Mansfeld & Werner, 1999) identifying correlates of specific forms of agitated behaviors and is designed to use a variety of individualized activities (e.g., preferred music and simulated presence) to address agitated behaviors. Overall, Cohen-Mansfield and her colleagues (2007) found that nursing homes receiving the TREA intervention training were observed to have significantly fewer incidents of overall agitation compared to the control group nursing homes, which received training, but not TREA training. The TREA nursing home residents were reported to experience a statistically significant increase in pleasure and interest relative to residents in the control nursing homes. There was no statistically significant differences between nursing homes for negative affect.

Teri, Huda, Gibbons, Young, and van Leynseele (2005) developed a dementia-specific training program designed to teach direct care staff in assisted living residences to improve care and reduce problems in residents with dementia. Staff Training in Assisted Living Residence (STAR) provides staff training through a series of workshops covering a range of topics, including general information about dementia, communication strategies, pleasant event scheduling, changing ABCs of behavior, developing individualized care plans, team building, and effective communication with family members. In a small RCT, comparing assisted living facilities that received STAR training to those that did not, Teri et al. (2005) reported that residents in STAR training facilities experienced less BPSD compared to facilities that did not receive training. Staff receiving STAR training reported less adverse reactions to residents' BPSD than staff not receiving STAR training.

Identifying problematic behaviors and altering them have been shown to have a significant impact on reducing caregiver stress and can have a positive effect on the patient. The Functional Analytic (FA) model of behavior change (Austin & Carr, 2000; Sturmey, 2007) suggests that all behaviors are affected by the individual's current physical and social context as well as his or her physiological and psychological history. Therefore, the affective, behavioral, and cognitive changes that result from dementia are understood to result from or be exacerbated by interactions between the individual's personal characteristics, the environment, and social interactions. These can be exacerbated when interpersonal strife is experienced with a caregiver. The caregiver plays a critical role in the care of a person with dementia. The FA model is comprised of psychosocial and context-altering strategies.

Prior to beginning treatment, goals need to be identified and defined. This can be accomplished by determining what behavior(s) are to be targeted for intervention, identifying anticipated outcome, the setting where the behavior change is needed, and whose behavior needs to be altered. When assessing how to manage BPSD, there are three different approaches that can be used: (a) alter the antecedent situation or the situation that occurs prior to the target behavior, (b) alter the consequences or what happens after the target behavior that maintains the undesired behavior, and (c) reinforcing positive behavior or behaviors that need to increase in frequency.

In situations where a component of the contextual environment can be altered prior to a behavior problem occurring, or if the behavior occurs most often in a particular situation, altering or modifying the antecedent context might be most beneficial with these behaviors. Antecedent contexts can include an array of situations such as noise, inactivity, demands related to ADLs, and social demands. In situations in which a behavior occurs or behaviors occur across various settings, antecedent interventions can utilize the following techniques: discrimination training (entailing isolation of the occurrence of a desired behavior to specific settings) and/or generalization (increasing the occurrence of a behavior to various settings). The logic behind discrimination training is that if reinforcement is removed, the behavior will become less likely and/or occur less frequently (Hussian, 1981).

An example of generalization was demonstrated by Melin and Götestam (1981), who used antecedent techniques to increase communication between residents in a long-term care facility. In order to make the setting more conducive for communication, furniture was rearranged to be more conducive for conversations, the length of time allotted for meals was increased, and the food options were expanded. Results indicated that the frequency of communication increased. As this demonstrates, behavioral interventions may include direct contingency principals (e.g., positive and negative reinforcement, schedules of reinforcement, stimulus control, cueing, shaping, extinction) and indirect contingency principals (e.g., verbal control, distraction, environmental modification, problem solving, behavioral rehearsal, relaxation training).

Other approaches include altering or modifying consequences that maintain behavior and reinforcing desired behaviors. Behaviors can be reinforced by events that increase the likelihood of the behavior. Reinforcers can be positive or negative. Positive reinforcers are differentiated by the addition of events (e.g., attention, touching) or access to objects, events, or activities. Negative reinforcement occurs when events are removed or taken away and a particular behavior increases. Regardless if it is positive or negative, reinforcers always increase a behavior, whereas punishment decreases behaviors. Extinction is a cessation of a behavior resulting from lack of reinforcement. Using the process of extinction can result in highly variable behavior and therefore may not be appropriate intervention for persons with severe dementia. A combination of both antecedent and consequence interventions can be used to address problematic behaviors.

Often, caregivers spend the most time with a patient and can provide information regarding the antecedents and consequences of behavior problems. Educating caregivers with regard to effective communication and behavioral strategies for managing BPSD can be invaluable to increasing a caregiver's self-efficacy and reducing his or her reactions to BPSD, which can possible delay transition from the home setting to a skilled nursing setting.

Distraction can also be a highly valuable tool when working with persons with dementia. Various studies have used a combination of both antecedent and consequent interventions to manage behavior (Gwyther, 1994; Stokes, 2000). Distraction can be induced by presenting the care recipient with activities, events, topics, or materials that are of preference to him or her. When this occurs, the care recipient's behavior is then reinforced due to the addition of preferred stimuli.

CONCLUSIONS

Older adults are at increased risk for developing a number of dementing disorders, such as Alzheimer's disease and Vascular dementia. To establish a diagnosis for these conditions, a careful clinical interview and assessment is critical in order to distinguish dementias from other conditions, such as delirium and mild cognitive impairment. In the process of assessing cognitive functioning, clinicians must take in to account the older adults' racial, ethnic, and cultural background, as well as their educational history and language proficiency, so assessment results accurately reflect the older adults' cognitive functioning. A variety of brief screening measures, useful for assessing cognitive deficits with adequate psychometric properties, are available. Providing feedback that is responsive to patients' and caregivers' needs is also a critical part of the assessment process. It should incorporate not only a discussion of cognitive strengths and weaknesses, but also strategies for improving the quality of life over the long term. A variety of cognitive and behavioral interventions have evidence of addressing the cognitive impairments and behavioral symptoms often associated with MCI and dementia. Professional caregiver training has also been found to be potentially effective in addressing emotional and behavioral symptoms associated with dementia. Important factors to consider when implementing these approaches effectively are a careful overview of environmental and interpersonal triggers for behavioral problems, as well as a consideration of the patients' likes, dislikes, and personal history.

REFERENCES

Abramson, T. A., Trejo, L., & Lai, D. W. L. (2002). Culture and mental health: Providing appropriate services for a diverse older population. *Generations: Journal of the American Society on Aging, 26,* 21–27.

Acedvedo, A., & Lowenstein, D. A. (2007). Nonpharmacological cognitive interventions in aging and dementia. *Journal of Geriatric Psychiatry and Neurology, 20,* 239–249.

Alexopoulos, G. S., Raue, P., & Arean, P. (2003). Problem-solving therapy versus supportive therapy in geriatric major depression with executive dysfunction. *American Journal of Geriatric Psychiatry, 11,* 46–52.

American Psychiatric Association. (2000). *Diagnostic and statistical manual of mental disorders* (4th ed., Text revision). Washington, DC: Author.

American Psychological Association. (2002). *American Psychological Association ethical principles of psychologists and code of conduct.* Retrieved August 26, 2010, from http://www.apa.org/ethics/code2002.html

American Psychological Association (2003). *Guidelines for psychological practice with older adults.* Retrieved August 17, 2010, from http://www.apa.org/practice/guidelines/older-adults.pdf

Ardila, A. (1993). Future directions in the research and practice of cross-cultural neuropsychology. *Journal of Clinical and Experimental Neuropsychology, 15,* 1–19.

Ardila, A., Rosselli, M., & Puente, A. E., (1994). *Neuropsychological evaluation of the Spanish speaker.* New York, NY: Plenum Press.

Artiola i Fortuny, L., Hermosillo-Romo, D., Heaton, R. K., Pardee, R. E. (1999). Manual de normas y procedimientos para la Batería Neuropsicológica en Español. Brookfield, VT: Swets & Zeitlinger Publishers.

Austin, J., & Carr, J. E. (Eds.). (2000). *Handbook of applied behavior analysis.* Reno, NV: Context Press.

Backman, L. (1992). Memory training and memory improvement in Alzheimer's disease: Rules and exception. *Acta Neurologica Scandinavica, 139,* 84–89.

Baker, F. M., Robinson, B. H., & Stewart, B. (1993). Use of the Mini-Mental State Examination in African American elders. *Clinical Gerontologist, 14,* 5–13.

Baker, F. M., Velli, S. A., Friedman, J., & Wiley, C. (1995). Screening tests for depression in older Black and White patients. *American Journal of Geriatric Psychiatry, 3,* 43–51.

Beattie, E. R. A., Algase, D. L., & Song, J. (2004). Keeping wandering nursing home residents at the table: Improving food intake using a behavioural communication intervention. *Ageing and Mental Health, 8,* 109–116.

Birchmore, T., & Clague, S. (1983). A behavioural approach to reduce shouting. *Nursing Times, 79,* 37–39.

Blessed, G., Tomlinson, B. E., & Roth, M. (1968). The association between quantitative measures of dementia and of senile change in cerebral grey matter of elderly subjects. *British Journal of Psychiatry, 114*(512), 797–811.

Borson, S., Scanlan, J., Brush, M., Vitaliano, P., & Dokmak, A. (2000). The Mini-Cog: A cognitive 'vital signs' measure for dementia screening in multi-lingual elderly. *International Journal of Geriatric Psychiatry, 15,*1021–1027.

Bourgeois, M. S., Burgio, L. D., Schulz, R., Beach, S., & Palmer, B. (1997). Modifying repetitive verbalizations of community-dwelling patients with AD. *Gerontologist, 37,* 30–39.

Bourgeois, M. S., Camp, C., Rose, M., White, B., Malone, M., Carr, J., et al. (2003). A comparison of training strategies to enhance use of external aids by persons with dementia. *Journal of Communication Disorders, 36*(5), 361–378.

Bowler, J. V. (2002). The concept of vascular cognitive impairment. *Journal of Neurological Sciences, 203,* 11–15.

Bowles, R. P., Grimm, K. J., & McArdle, J. J. (2005). A structural factor analysis of vocabulary knowledge and relations to age. *Journals of Gerontology: Series B: Psychological Sciences and Social Sciences, 60,* 234–241.

Braithwaite, V. A. (1986). Old age stereotypes: Reconciling contradictions. *Journal of Gerontology, 41,* 353–360.

Breitner, J. C., Wyse, B. W., Anthony, J. C., Welsh-Bohmer, K. A., Steffens, D. C., Norton, M. C., Tschanz, J. T., Plassman, B. L., Meyer, M. R., Skoog, I., & Khachaturian, A. (1999). APOE-epsilon 4 count predicts age when prevalence of AD increases, then declines: The Cache County Study. *Neurology, 53,* 321–331.

Buchanan, J. A., & Fisher, J. E. (2002). Functional assessment and noncontingent reinforcement for the treatment of disruptive vocalization in dementia patients. *Journal of Applied Behavioral Analysis, 35,* 99–103.

Burgio, L. D., Stevens, A., Burgio, K. L., Roth, D. L., Paul, P., & Gerstle, J. (2002). Teaching and maintaining behavior management skills in the nursing home. *Gerontologist, 42,* 487–496.

Camp C. J., Bird, M. J., & Cherry, K. E. (2000). Retrieval strategies as a rehabilitation aid for cognitive loss in pathological aging. In R. D. Hill, A, Backman, N. Stigsdotter (Eds.), *Cognitive rehabilitation in old age.* (pp. 224–248). New York, NY: Oxford University Press.

Cato, M. A., & Crosson, B. A. (2006). Stable and slowly progressive dementias. In D. A. Attix and K. A., Welsh-Bohmer (Eds.), *Geriatric neuropsychology: Assessment and intervention* (pp. 89–102). New York, NY: Guilford Publishing.

Chambless, D. L., & Hollon, S. D. (1998). Defining empirically validated therapies. *Journal of Consulting and Clinical Psychology, 66,* 7–18.

Chambless, D. L., & Ollendick, T. H. (2001). Empirically supported psychological interventions: Controversies and evidence. *Annual Review of Psychology, 52,* 685–716.

Coburn, A., & Bolda, E. (1999). The rural elderly and long-term care. In T. C. Ricketts (Ed.), *Rural health in the United States* (pp. 179–189). New York, NY: Oxford University Press.

Clare, L., Wilson, B. A., Carter, G., Roth, I., & Hodges, J. R. (2002). Relearning face-name associations in early Alzheimer's disease. *Neuropsychology, 16,* 538–547.

Cohen-Mansfield, J. (2001). Nonpharmacologic interventions for inappropriate behaviors in dementia. *The American Journal of Geriatric Psychiatry, 9*(4), 361–381.

Cohen-Mansfield, J., Libin, A., & Marx, M.S. (2007). Nonpharmacological treatment of agitation: A controlled trial of systematic individualized intervention. *Journal of Gerontology: Medical Sciences, 62A*(8), 908–916.

Cohen-Mansfield, J., & Werner, P. (1999). Longitudinal predictors of non-aggressive agitated behaviors in the elderly. *International Journal of Geriatric Psychiatry, 14,* 831–844.

Crowther, M. R., & Zeiss, A. M. (2003). Aging and mental health. In J. S. Mio & G. Y. Iwamasa (Eds.), *Culturally diverse mental health: The challenge of research and resistance* (pp. 309–322). New York, NY: Brunner-Routledge.

Davis, R. N., Massman, P. J., & Doody, R. S. (2001). Cognitive intervention in Alzheimer disease: A randomized placebo-controlled study. *Alzheimer Disease Association Disorders, 15,* 1–9.

Del Ser T., González-Montalvo J. I., Martínez-Espinosa S., Delgado-Villapalos, C., & Bermejo, F. (1997). Estimation of premorbid intelligence in Spanish people with the Word Accentuation Test and its application to the diagnosis of dementia. *Brain Cognition, 33,* 343–356.

Doyle, C., Zapperoni, T., O'Conner, D., & Runci, S. (1997). Efficacy of psychosocial treatments for noisemaking in severe dementia. *International Psychogeriatrics, 9,* 405–422.

Ely, W. E., Margolin, R., Francis, J., May, L., Truman, B., Dittus, R, Speroff, T., Gautam, S., Bernard, G., & Inouye, S. (2001). Evaluation of delirium in critically ill patients: Validation of the Confusion Assessment Method for the Intensive Care Unit (CAM-ICU). *Critical Care Medicine, 29,* 1370–1379.

Feliciano, L., Vore, J., LeBlanc, L. A., & Baker, J. C. (2004). Decreasing entry into a restricted area using a visual barrier. *Journal of Applied Behavioral Analysis, 37,* 107–110.

Fillenbaum, G., Heyman, A., Williams, K., Prosnit, B., & Burchett, B. (1990). Sensitivity and specificity of standardized screens for cognitive impairment and dementia among elderly Black and White community residents. *Journal of Clinical Epidemiology, 43,* 651–660.

Finkel, S., Silva, J. C., Cohen, G., Miller, S., & Sartorius, N. (1997). Behavioral and psychological signs and symptoms of dementia: A consensus statement on current knowledge and implications for research and treatment. *International Journal of Geriatric Psychiatry, 12,* 1060–1061.

Fleischman, D. A., Wilson, R. S., Gabrieli, J. D., Schneider, J. A., Bienias, J. L., & Bennett, D. A. (2005). Implicit memory and Alzheimer's disease neuropathology. *Brain, 128,* 2006–2015.

Folstein, M. F., Folstein, S. E., McHugh, P. R. (1975). Mini-Mental State: A practical method for grading the cognitive state of patients for the clinician. *Journal of Psychiatric Research, 12,* 189–198.

Goodstein, R. K. (1985). Common clinical problems in the elderly: Camouflaged by ageism and atypical presentation. *Psychiatric Annals, 15,* 299–312.

Green, J. (2006). Feedback. In D. A. Attix & K. A. Welsh-Bohmer (Eds.) *Geriatric neuropsychology: Assessment and intervention* (pp. 223–236). Guilford Press: New York: NY.

Grober, E., & Sliwinski, M. (1991). Development and validation of a model for estimating premorbid verbal intelligence in the elderly. *Journal of Clinical and Experimental Neuropsychology, 13,* 933–949.

Gwyther, L. (1994). Managing challenging behaviors at home. *Alzheimer Disease and Associated Disorder, 8,* 110–112.

Harris, J. G., Cullum, C. M., Bush, S., & Drexler, M. (2002). *Ethical issues in clinical neuropsychology* (pp. 223–241). Lisse, The Netherlands: Swets & Zeitlinger.

Hasegawa, K. (1983). The clinical assessment of dementia in the aged: A dementia screening scale for psychogeriatric patients. In M. Bergener, U. Lehr, E., Lang, & R. Schmitz-Scherzer (Eds.), *Aging in the eighties and beyond* (pp. 207–218). New York, NY: Springer.

Herbert, L. E., Scherr, P. A., Bienias, J. L., Bennett, D. A., & Evans, D. A. (2003). Alzheimer's disease in the US population: Prevalence estimates using the 2000 census. *Journal of the American Medical Association, 60,* 1119–1122.

Hertzog, C., & Bleckley, M. K. (2001). Age differences in the structure of intelligence: Influences of information processing speed. *Intelligence, 29,* 191–217.

Houston, W., & Bondi, M. (2006). Potentially reversible cognitive symptoms in older adults. In D. K. Attix, & K. A. Welsh-Bohmer (Eds.), *Geriatric neuropsychology: Assessment and intervention.* New York, NY: The Guilford Press.

Hussian, R. A. (1981). *Geriatric psychology: A behavioral perspective.* New York, NY: Van Nostrand Reinhold.

Hussian, R. A., & Brown, D. C. (1987). Use of two-dimensional grid patterns to limit hazardous ambulation in demented patients. *Journal of Geronotology, 42,* 558–560.

Hyer, L., Kramer, D., & Sohnle, S. (2004). CBT with older people: Alterations and the value of the therapeutic alliance. *Psychotherapy: Theory, Research, Practice, Training, 41,* 276–291.

James, J. W., & Haley, W. E. (1995). Age and health bias in practicing clinical psychologists. *Psychology and Aging, 10,* 610–616.

Kansagara, D., & Freeman, M. (2010). *A systematic evidence review of the signs and symptoms of dementia and brief cognitive tests available in the VA.* VA-ESP Project #05-225. Washington, DC: Department of Veterans Affairs.

Kasl-Godley, J., & Gatz, M. (2000). Psychosocial interventions for individuals with dementia: An integration of theory, therapy, and a clinical understanding if dementia. *Clinical Psychology Review, 20*(6), 755–782.

Klunk, W. E., Engler, H., Nordberg, A., Wang, Y., Bloomqvist, G., Holt, D. P., et al. (2004). Imaging brain amyloid in Alzheimer's disease with Pittsburgh Compound-B. *Annals of Neurology, 55,* 306–319.

Knight, B. G., & Satre, D. D. (1999). Cognitive behavioral psychotherapy with older adults. *Clinical Psychology: Science and Practice, 6,* 188–203.

Kokmen, E., Naessens, J .M., Offord, K. P. (1987). A short test of mental status: description and preliminary results. *Mayo Clinical Proceedings, 62,* 281–288.

Kong, E. H., Evans, L. K., & Guevara, J. P. (2009). Nonpharmacological interventions for agitation in dementia: A systematic review and meta-analysis. *Aging and Mental Health, 13,* 512–520.

Kverno, K. S., Black, B. S., Blass, D. M., Geiger-Brown, J., & Rabins, P. V. (2008). Neuropsychiatric symptom patterns in hospice-eligible nursing home residents with advanced dementia. *Journal of the American Medical Directors Association, 9,* 509–515.

Kverno, K. S., Black, B. S., Nolan, M. T., & Rabins, P. V. (2009). Research on treating neuropsychiatric symptoms of advanced dementia with non-pharmacological strategies, 1998–2008: A systematic review. *International Psychogeriatrics, 21*(5), 825–843.

Lewin, L. M. & Lundervold, D. (1987). Behavioral treatment of elderly in foster care homes. *Adult Foster Care Journal, 1,* 238–249.

Lichtenberg, P. A., Kemp-Havican, J., Macneill, S. E., & Schafer-Johnson, A. (2005). Pilot study of behavioral treatment in dementia care units. *Gerontologist, 45,* 406–410.

Light, L. L. (2004). Commentary: Measures, constructs, models, and inferences about aging. In R. A. Dixon, L. G. Nilsson, & L. Backman (Eds.). *New frontiers in cognitive aging* (pp. 89–112). New York, NY: Oxford University Press.

Livingston, G., Johnston, K., Katona, C., Paton, J., & Lyketsos, C. (2005). Systematic Review of psychological approaches to the management of neuropsychiatric symptoms of dementia. *American Journal of Psychiatry, 162*(11), 1996–2021.

Logsdon, R. G., McCurry, S. M., & Teri, L. (2007). Evidence-based psychological treatments for disruptive behaviors in individuals with dementia. *Psychology and Aging, 22,* 28–36.

Manly, J. J. (2006). Cultural issues. In D. K. Attix & K. A. Welsh-Bohmer (Eds.) *Geriatric neuropsychology: Assessment and intervention* (pp. 198–222). New York, NY: Guilford Press.

Mayer, R., & Darby, S. J. (1991). Does a mirror deter wandering in demented older people? *International Journal of Geriatric Psychiatry, 6,* 607–609.

McCallion, P., Toseland, R. W., Lacey, D., & Banks, S. (1999). Educating nursing assistants to communicate more effectively with nursing home residents with dementia. *Gerontologist, 39,* 546–558.

Melin, L., & Götestam, K. G. (1981). The effects of rearranging ward routines on communication and eating behaviors of psychogeriatric patients. *Journal of Applied Behavior Analysis, 14,* 47–51.

Meyerson, J. Adams, D. R., Hale, S., & Jenkins, L. (2003). Analysis of group differences in processing speed: Brinley plots, Q-Q plots, and other conspiracies. *Psychometric Bulletin and Review, 10,* 224–237.

Moniz Cook, E., De Vugt, M., Verhey, F., & James, I. (2009). Functional analysis-based interventions for challenging behavior in dementia. *Cochrane Database of Systematic Reviews. 3,* 1–7.

Mungas, D., Reed, B. R., Haan, M. N., & González, H. (2005). Spanish and English neuropsychological assessment scales: Relationship to demographics, language, cognition, and independent functioning. *Neuropsychology, 19,* 466–475.

Namazi, K. H., Rosner, T. T., & Calkins, M. P. (1989). Visual barriers to prevent ambulatory Alzheimer's patients from exiting through an emergency door. *Gerontologist, 29,* 699–702.

Nasreddine, Z. S., Phillips, N. A., Bédirian, V., Charbonneau, S., Whitehead, V., Collin, I., Cummings, J. L., & Chertkow, H. (2005). The Montreal Cognitive Assessment (MoCA): A brief screening tool for mild cognitive impairment. *Journal of American Geriatric Society, 53,* 695–699.

National Institute for Health and Clinical Excellence (2007). *Dementia: The NICE-SCIE guideline on supporting people with dementia and their carers in health and social care* (National Clinical Practice Guideline No. 42). Retrieved from http://www.nice.org.uk/nicemedia/live/10998/30320/30320.pdf

O'Conner, D. W., Ames, D., Gardner, B., & King, M. (2009). Psychosocial treatments of behavior symptoms in dementia: A systematic review of reports meetings quality standards. *International Psychogeriatrics, 21*(2), 225–240.

Ostrosky-Solis, F.,Gomez-Perez, M., Matute, E., Rosselli, M., Ardila, A., & Pineda, D. (2007). Neuropsi attention and memory: A neuropsychological test battery in Spanish with norms by age and education level. *Applied Neuropsychology, 14,* 156–170.

Paradis, M. (2008). Bilingualism and neuropsychiatric disorders. *Journal of Neurolinguistics, 21,* 199–230.

Pfeiffer, E. (1975). A short portable mental status questionnaire for the assessment of organic brain deficits in elderly patients. *Journal of the American Geriatrics Society, 23,* 433–444.

Peterson, R. C. (1995). Normal aging, mild cognitive impairment, and early Alzheimer's disease. *The Neurologist, 1,* 326–344.

Peterson, R. C., Doody, R., Kurz, A., Mohs, R. C., Morris, J. C., & Rabins, P. V. (2001). Current concepts in mild cognitive impairment, *Archives of Neurology, 58,* 1985–1992.

Pontón, M. (2001). Research and assessment issues with Hispanic populations. In M. Pontón, J. León-Carrión, (Eds.), *Neuropsychology and the Hispanic patient: A clinical handbook.* Mahwah, NJ: Erlbaum.

Pontón, M. O., Satz, P., Herrera L., Ortiz F., Urrutia, C. P., Young, R., et al. (1996). Normative data stratified by age and education for the Neuropsychological Screening Battery for Hispanics (NeSBHIS): Initial report. *Journal of the International Neuropsychological Society, 2,* 96–104.

Prince, M. J., Acosta, D., Castro-Costa, E., Jackson, J., & Shaji, S. (2009). Packages of care for dementia in low- and middle- income countries. *PLOS Medicine, 6,* 1–9.

Proctor, R., Burns, A., Powell, H. S., Tarrier, N., Faragher, B., Richardson, G., et al. (1999). Behavioural management in nursing and residential homes: A randomized controlled trial. *Lancet, 354,* 26–29.

Rasmusson, D. X., Brandt, J., Steele, C., Hedreen, J. C., Troncoso, J. C., & Folstein, M. F. (1996). Accuracy of clinical diagnosis of Alzheimer disease and clinical features of patients with non-Alzheimer disease neuropathology. *Alzheimer Disease and Associated Disorders, 10,* 180–188.

Salthouse, T. A. (1996). The processing-speed theory of adult age differences in cognition. *Psychological Review, 103,* 403–428.

Satre, D. D., Knight, B. G., & David, S. (2006). Cognitive-behavioral interventions with older adults: Integrating clinical and gerontological research. *Professional Psychology: Research and Practice, 37,* 489–498.

Schaie, K. W. (1996). Intellectual development in adulthood. In J. E. Birren & K. W. Schaie (Eds.), *Handbook of the psychology of aging* (4th ed., pp. 266–286). San Diego, CA: Academic Press.

Schrijnemaekers, V., van Rossum, E., Candel, M., Frederiks, C., Derix, M., Sielhorst, H., van den Brandt, P. (2002). Effects of emotion-oriented care on elderly people with cognitive impairment and behavioral problems. *International Journal of Geriatric Psychiatry, 17*, 926–937.

Segal, D. L. (2005). Relationships of assertiveness, depression, and social support among nursing home residents. *Behavior Modification, 29*, 689–695.

Spector, A., Thorgrimsen, L., Woods, B., Royan, L., Davies, S., Butterworth, M., et al. (2003). Efficacy of an evidence-based cognitive stimulation therapy programme for people with dementia: randomized controlled trial. *British Journal of Psychiatry, 183*, 248–254.

Spira, A. P., & Edelstein, B. A. (2006). Behavioral interventions for agitation in older adults with dementia: An evaluative review. *International Psychogeriatrics, 18*(2), 195–225.

Stokes, G. (2000). *Challenging behaviour in dementia: A person-centered approach.* Bicester, United Kingdom: Speechmark.

Sturmey, P. (Ed.). (2007). *Functional analysis and clinical treatment.* San Diego, CA: Elsevier.

Tariq, S. H., Tumosa, N., Chibnall, J. T., Perry III, H. M., & Morley, J. E. (2006). The Saint Louis University Mental Status (SLUMS) Examination for detecting mild cognitive impairment and dementia is more sensitive than the Mini-Mental Status Examination (MMSE): A pilot study. *American Journal of Geriatric Psychiatry, 14*, 900–910.

Taussig, M., & Ponton, M. (1996). Issues in neuropsychological assessments for Hispanic older adults: Cultural and linguistic factors. In G. Yeo, & D. Gallagher-Thompson (Eds), *Ethnicity and the dementias.* Washington, DC; Taylor & Francis.

Teng, E. (1996). Cross-cultural testing and the cognitive abilities screening Instrument. In G. Yeo, & D. Gallagher-Thompson (Eds), *Ethnicity and the dementias* (pp. 77–85). Washington, DC: Taylor and Francis.

Teng, E. L., & Chui, H. C., (1987). The Modified Mini-Mental State (3MS) Examination. *Journal of Clinical Psychiatry, 48*, 314–318.

Teng, E. L., Hasegawa, K., Homma, A., Imai, Y., Larson, E., Graves, A., Sugimoto, K., Yamaguchi, T., Sasaki, H., Chiu, D., & White, L. R., (1994). The Cognitive Abilities Screening Instrument (CASI): A practical test for cross-cultural epidemiological studies of dementia. *International Psychogeriatrics, 6*, 45–58.

Teri, L., Huda, P., Gibbons, L., Young, H., & van Leynseele, J. (2005). STAR: A dementia-specific training program for staff in assisted living residences. *The Gerontologist, 45*, 686–693.

Teri, L., Logsdon, R. G., Whall, A. L., Weiner, M. F., Trimmer, C., Peskind, E., et al. (1998). Treatment of agitation in dementia patients: A behavior management approach. Psychotherapy, 35, 436–443.

Testad, I., Aasland, A. M., & Aarsland, D. (2005). The effect of staff training on the use of restraint in dementia: A single-blind randomised controlled trial. *International Journal of Geriatric Psychiatry, 20*, 587–590.

U.S. Census Bureau. (2003). *Language use and English-speaking ability: 2000.* Retrieved August 17, 2010, from http://www.census.gov/prod/2003pubs/c2kbr-29.pdf

Wilkinson G. S., & Robertson, G. J. (2006). *The Wide range achievement test: Professional manual* (4th ed.). Lutz, FL: Psychological Assessment Resources, Inc.

Wisner, E., & Green, M. (1986). Treatment of a demented patient's anger with cognitive-behavioral strategies. *Psychological Reports, 59,* 447–450.

Zanetti, O., Rozzini, M. E., Bianchetti, A., & Trabucci, M. (1997). Proceduralmemory stimulation in Alzheimer's disease: impact of a training programme. *Acta Neurologica Scandinavica, 95,* 152–157.

Zanetti, O., Zanieri, G., Di Giovanni, G., De Vreese, L. P., Pezzini, A., Metitieri, T., et al. (2001). Effectiveness of procedural memory stimulation in mild Alzheimer's disease patients: A controlled study. *Neuropsychology Rehabilitation, 11,* 263–272.

Zimprich, D. (2002). Cross-sectionally and longitudinally balanced effects of processing speed on intellectual abilities. *Experimental Aging Research, 28,* 231–251.

Zuidema, S. U., de Jonghe, J. F. M., Verhey, F. R. J., & Koopmans, R. T. C. M. (2007). Neuropsychiatric symptoms in nursing home patients: Factor structure invariance of the Dutch nursing home version of the Neuropsychiatric Inventory in different stages of dementia. *Dementia and Geriatric Cognitive Disorders, 24,* 169–176.

ONLINE RESOURCES FOR FAMILIES, CAREGIVERS, AND PERSONS WITH DEMENTIA

- **AARP Caregiving.** Contains articles, tools, and forums to assist caregivers in navigating the "labyrinth of caregiving." http://www.aarp.org/relationships/caregiving/
- **Alzheimer's Association.** This website provides information regarding AD, caregiving, research, and resources. http://www.alz.org/index.asp.
- **Alzheimer's Disease Centers (ADCs) Directory.** This National Institutes of Health website provides information on diagnosis and medical management; clinical research and drug trials; and information about the disease, services, and resources. http://www.nia.nih.gov/Alzheimers/ResearchInformation/ResearchCenters.
- **Alzheimer's Disease International (ADI).** ADI is an international membership group of Alzheimer's associations. This website provides information regarding worldwide statistics for AD, as well as implications for research. http://www.alz.co.uk/
- *Alzheimer's From the Inside Out.* This website was developed by Richard Taylor, a retired psychologist who was diagnosed with Alzheimer's-type dementia in 2001 at the age of 58. Now 65, he is a champion for individuals with early-stage and early-onset AD, and

author of the book *Alzheimer's from the Inside Out* (Health Professions Press, 2006). This website contains a thoughtful and personal perspective on living with AD. http://www.richardtaylorphd.com/

■ **Alzheimer Research Forum.** This website provides information regarding the latest research on AD. http://www.alzforum.org/

■ **Alzheimer Society of Canada.** This website is provides information regarding AD in Canada. http://www.alzheimer.ca/

■ **Alzheimer's Society UK.** This website provides information regarding AD in the United Kingdom. http://www.alzheimers.org.uk/site/index.php

■ **American Red Cross Family Caregiver Program.** This program offers caregivers a helping hand by providing a variety of information packed sessions covering topics such as home safety, healthy eating, bathing, legal and financial issues, and taking care of yourself. http://www.redcross.org/portal/site/en/menuitem.d229a5f06620c6052b1ecfbf43181aa0/?vgnextoid=58d2914124dbe110VgnVCM10000089f0870aRCRD&vgnextchannel=bf970c45f663b110VgnVCM10000089f0870aRCRD

■ **Caregiver.com.** Founded in 1995, Caregiver Media Group produces *Today's Caregiver* magazine, the Sharing Wisdom Caregivers Conferences, and this website, which includes topic-specific newsletters, online discussion lists, back issues of *Today's Caregiver* magazine, chat rooms, and an online store. http://www.caregiver.com/

■ *Caregiving in America.* Through a collaboration of experts and strategic partners who offer helpful services, information, and education, this new monthly magazine hopes to encourage, inspire, and uplift family caregivers nationwide. Each issue includes personal stories, professional articles, and other valuable resources. http://www.caregivinginamerica.com/

■ **Caring.com.** This website was created to help those caring for their aging parents and other loved ones. Their mission is to give caregivers information and other resources they need to make better decisions, save time, and feel more supported. Provides practical information, easy-to-use tools, and personal support needed during this challenging time. http://www.caring.com/

■ **Caring Today.** A leading provider of practical advice and knowledge for family caregivers since 2004, *Caring Today* has addressed the needs of America's 50 million caregivers with expertise, understanding, and answers through its quarterly national magazine and this website. http://www.caringtoday.com/

■ **Centers for Disease Control and Prevention (CDC) - Healthy Aging Program.** This program serves as the focal point for older adult health at the CDC, establishing programs, developing tools, and providing a comprehensive approach to helping older adults live longer, higher quality, more productive, and independent lives. Includes caregiving as a public health priority. http://www.cdc.gov/aging/caregiving/index.htm

- **eCare Diary.** Provides comprehensive information, tools, and resources to help those seeking and providing long-term care. A unique feature is the Care Diary, a set of online tools designed to make coordination of care and the sharing of information easy among family members and other caregivers. eCare Diary also has a comprehensive database of nursing home and home care services, guides on long-term care financing, and information on important health care documents everyone should have. http://www.ecarediary.com/
- **Family Caregiver Alliance.** Free reports, fact sheets, newsletters, support groups, and care advice for families, caregivers, policy makers, providers and the media. http://www.caregiver.org/caregiver/jsp/home.jsp
- **Family Caregiving eXtension.** Developed by the Cooperative Extension Services, this website is an interactive learning environment that strives to meet the educational and decision-making needs of family caregivers and the professionals who support them. Featuring articles, online educational sessions, and an "Ask the Expert" section, the website assists caregivers in finding and accessing local resources available to them. http://www.extension.org/family%20caregiving
- **Family Caregiving 101.** This site is designed to provide caregivers with the basic tools, skills, and information they need to protect their own physical and mental health while they provide high quality care for their loved one. http://www.familycaregiving101.org/
- **Fisher Center for Alzheimer's Research.** This website provides information for caregivers, family members, people living with AD, and the general public. http://www.alzinfo.org/
- **Medicare Caregiver Information.** Assistance for caregivers that includes help with understanding billing, navigating Medicare, financial and legal issues, and care options. Includes tools such as "Your Discharge Planning Checklist" for patients and their caregivers preparing to leave a hospital, nursing home, or other health care setting. http://www.medicare.gov/Caregivers/
- **National Alliance for Caregiving (NAC).** Established in 1996, NAC is a nonprofit coalition of national organizations focusing on issues of family caregiving. Alliance members include grassroots organizations, professional associations, service organizations, disease-specific organizations, a government agency, and corporations.

- **National Family Caregivers Association (NFCA).** NFCA educates, supports, empowers, and speaks up for the more than 50 million Americans who care for loved ones with a chronic illness or disability, or who suffer from the frailties of old age. NFCA reaches across the boundaries of diagnoses, relationships, and life stages to help transform family caregivers' lives by removing barriers to health and well-being. http://www.caregiving.org/
- **National Institute on Aging (NIA).** This website provides information regarding information and research, as well as federal government programs and resources. http://www.nia.nih.gov/alzheimers.
- **Next Step in Care.** Provides information and advice to help family caregivers and health care providers plan safe and smooth transitions for patients. Materials now available in Spanish and Chinese. http://www.nextstepincare.org/
- **Rosalynn Carter Institute for Caregiving (RCI).** The RCI provides caregiving agencies and organizations with the latest knowledge and practices relating to evidence-based caregiving. http://rosalynncarter.org/
- **Strength for Caring (SFC).** This comprehensive website is designed to provide family caregivers with a broad range of expert content and information, an emerging online community, daily inspiration, and much needed support. http://www.strengthforcaring.com/
- **This Caring Home.** This website provides tips and tools to enhance home safety for persons with AD and other forms of dementia. Highlights include a virtual home, product guides, videos, and animations. http://www.thiscaringhome.org/
- **Well Spouse Association.** A nonprofit membership organization that advocates for and addresses the needs of individuals caring for a chronically ill and/or disabled spouse/partner. Peer-to-peer support is available, along with education for health care professionals and the general public about the special challenges and unique issues "well" spouses face every day. http://www.wellspouse.org

Appendix A

BEHAVIOR OBSERVATION FORM

Behavior:
What is the behavior you are trying to target? (Describe in objective terms. Remember the target behavior may be demonstrated by the person with dementia, his or her caregiver(s), or others.)

Antecedent:

What happened immediately before the behavior?

When did the behavior happen?

Who was around?

What activity was occurring?

Where was the patient?

Describe the given information in terms of behavior. Do not try to guess emotions or thoughts.

Consequences:

What happened as a result of the behavior?

What did you do?

What did the patient do?

Were others involved?

Who?

What did they do?

Appendix B

TIP SHEET FOR DEMENTIA ASSESSMENT

Gain Rapport	Adjust the Environment
• Generally address older adults and their family members by their surnames. • Provide a clear explanation of the purpose of the assessment as well as the process. • Encourage the older adult, their family members, and staff to ask questions. • Consider interviewing older adults first and privately to denote respect and encourage expression. • Ask family members and staff for input in order to gain an accurate picture of the older adult's functioning and illicit cooperation with developing and implementing an intervention plan. • View the older adult and his or her family members as important members of the interdisciplinary team. • Provide overt expressions of concern for older or medically ill adults. They typically respond well to appropriate touching, offering water, etc. • Minimize use of psychological jargon.	• Prior to beginning the assessment, explain to family and/or staff that you will need some uninterrupted time with the older adult in a quiet space to conduct the assessment. • If needed, ask the older adult, family, or staff to turn off devices such as the TV or radio. • It can help to sit close to the older adult and to speak slowly, loudly, and concretely (but make sure not to shout). • Make sure the person uses their hearing aids, glasses, etc. • Make the sure room is adequately lit. • Use large print versions of tests for visual impairment if needed (or consider retyping to have larger fonts). • Oral administration of some self-report formats may be necessary. • Note any changes to standard testing in your report.

(Continued)

Adjust Typical Time Constraints	Develop Realistic Treatment Goals
• Allow sufficient time to complete the interview and assessment measures. • Do not rush the individual (this may result in decreased rapport, frustration, and inaccurate results). • Remember that less is often more; long, detailed interviews and testing batteries are typically not well tolerated by older adults. • Provide frequent breaks to decrease fatigue or consider conducting the assessment over more than one session if needed. • Many older adults perform better in the morning (rather than afternoon). Consider conducting the assessment in the morning.	• Collaborate with the older adult, family members, and staff when developing treatment goals. • Break down goals into simple and achievable steps. • Develop treatment goals that build on the older adult's strengths. • Discuss any potential barriers to achieving treatment goals. • Coordinate with family members and staff, as needed, to help the older adult achieve treatment goals. • Consider providing a written copy of mutually agreed upon treatment goals to the older adult, family, and staff. • Instill hope! Provide encouragement! Give compassion!

Appendix C

EXAMINATION FACTORS TO CONSIDER WHEN ASSESSING OLDER ADULTS FOR DEMENTIA

Physical	Psychosocial	Environmental
• Motor functions • Vision • Hearing • Acute illness • Chronic illness • Medication effects • Fatigue • Pain or discomfort	• Culture • Literacy • Rapport • Motivation • Depression • Anxiety	• Too large • Too small • Too much clutter • Too much stimulation • Too little stimulation • Unfamiliar environment

9

Sexual Health in Older Adults: Conceptualization and Treatment

Linda R. Mona, Maggie L. Syme, Gali Goldwaser,
Rebecca P. Cameron, Suzie Chen, Colleen Clemency,
Sarah S. Fraley, Dina O. Wirick, and Larry Lemos

As the population ages, sexual well-being is receiving more attention as an important factor in quality of life for older adults. In one study of older adult men and women who reported being sexually active, about half reported at least one sexual problem (Lindau et al., 2007). The most prevalent concerns reported among women included lower sexual desire, difficulty with vaginal lubrication, and inability to reach orgasm. Among men, erectile difficulties were the most commonly reported concern (Lindau et al.). Despite the relative frequency of sexual problems, few men, and even fewer women broach the topic of sexual health with a health professional (Laumann, Glasser, Neves, Moreira Jr., & Global Study of Sexual Attitudes and Behaviors [GSSAB] Investigators' Group, 2009). There is an increasing need for mental health providers to develop competence in working with older adults, specifically in being aware of and comfortable in addressing issues that are related to the sexual experiences and physical intimate relationships of these clients.

Working with older adults around issues of sexuality includes conducting appropriate assessment and providing targeted interventions when clinically indicated. In selecting treatment modalities, the American Psychological Association (APA) strongly supports evidence-based practice defined as "the integration of the best available research with clinical expertise in the context of patient characteristics, culture, and preferences" (APA, 2005, p. 5). Cognitive behavioral therapy (CBT) is an evidence-based, time-limited treatment that focuses on the role of cognitions in emotional and behavioral responses. CBT has demonstrated efficacy for many psychological problems (Butler, Chapman, Forman, & Beck, 2006), including sexual dysfunction (Wincze, Bach, & Barlow,

2008). In addition, it has been demonstrated that CBT can be modified to effectively treat psychological problems in older adults (Satre, Knight, & David, 2006).

This chapter is designed to assist clinicians in the assessment, case conceptualization, and treatment of sexual issues among older adults. We begin by addressing the importance of sexuality and intimacy among older adults, followed by an overview of common sexual problems experienced by this group. This chapter, then, focuses on the culture of older adults with an emphasis on considerations that may affect conceptualization and treatment. Also, given that treatment is often affected by the traditional pathology-focused and medicalized view of sexuality, we introduce the reader to a broadened conceptualization of sexual health and well-being of older adults that we hope will facilitate an affirming and flexible approach to treatment. Assessment will be addressed followed by a discussion of evidence-based approaches, including CBT and third-wave cognitive behavioral therapies (TWCBTs). We close the chapter with a case example describing common issues that may arise in working with older adults who have sexual health concerns and discuss treatment recommendations.

OLDER ADULT SEXUALITY

Most older adults are engaged in intimate relationships and appear to regard sexuality as an important part of life. According to the National Social Life, Health, and Aging Project (2007), 73% of participants between the ages of 57 and 64 years old reported engaging in sexual activity (Lindau et al., 2007). Data from this large scale study suggested that most older adults continue to be sexually active through the age of 74, with a significant decline in sexual activity between the ages of 75 and 85 years old. In addition to age, Kontula and Haavio-Mannila (2009) found that the best predictors of sexual activity were high sexual self-esteem, good health, active (and positive) sexual history, frequent alcohol use, and finding sex important in a relationship. Good general mental health, positive attitude toward sexual activity, and presence of a partner have also been found to be predictors of both sexual desire and activity (DeLamater & Sill, 2005; Kontula & Haavio-Mannila, 2009). Therefore, getting older and experiencing age-related physiological and biological changes does not necessarily equate with a decrease in sexual desire or activity. Instead, it appears that older adults are more motivated to continue enjoying their sexuality, and clinicians' efforts to address issues that interfere with their sexual functioning and intimacy may be of great consequence. CBT and TWCBT are ideal, in that they are structured and often are short-term therapies that nonetheless incorporate clients' culturally, generationally, and idiographically formed beliefs about sexuality, resulting in treatment that is both individually tailored and also efficiently delivered.

THE CULTURE OF THE OLDER ADULT

A Unique Generation

Older adults include persons aged 65 or older, born in 1945 or earlier. They include veterans of World War II, Korean Conflict, and Vietnam War, as well as those who were civilians during those eras. Integral experiences for this cohort include not only the Great Depression, Japanese internment camps, the Jim Crowe era, the polio epidemic, the Cultural Revolution, the Holocaust, and the Cold War, but also the development of the birth control pill, the sexual revolution, the feminist movement, and the beginnings of the gay civil rights movement. They have witnessed enormous population growth, technological advances, civil rights battles, and changes in family structure and societal mores. Additionally, many people from this cohort may have immigrated to the United States during their lives to be first generation Americans; thus, they may bring bicultural identities to important questions about how romantic and marital relationships are structured and nurtured, and to issues of what is valued, natural, shameful, or taboo about sexuality.

Health care providers need to be aware of their own limitations based on a lack of shared experience and lack of education about the historical events and realities that are of profound importance in the lives of their older adult clients. This may be particularly true with respect to episodes of political, religious, or economic oppression and strife that may have occurred in countries of origin other than the United States or to cultural groups within the United States whose histories are not part of the providers' own experience. Because these events may have shaped the cultural worldviews and belief systems of older adult clients, an awareness of clients' exposure to and participation in these historical events can be of central importance to a clinician developing a CBT conceptualization. Client histories may also yield critical examples of resourcefulness, creativity, and resilience that can be used by clinicians providing CBT in the service of current goals, for example, strategies used by marginalized groups to avoid oppression such as tactics lesbians and gay men used to appear heterosexual and avoid arrest, as described by Kimmel, Rose, Orel, and Greene (2006). The costs associated with surviving oppression are significant, but the ability to strategically adapt and cope is of consequence as well.

Among the changes that have occurred during the older adults' lifetime, two are of particular relevance to the topic of this chapter. One is the expansion of mental health care and increased openness about mental and physical health problems. Despite the increased availability of psychological and sexual health care, its level of empirical support, and its progress toward reducing stigma, older adults may continue to view these forms of care as shameful, inappropriate, or not applicable to their situation (Karlin, Duffy, & Gleaves, 2008), thereby missing opportunities for improved quality of life. CBT lends itself to the exploration of beliefs that interfere with self-care.

Another broad area in which tremendous change has occurred is sexuality. Formerly taboo behaviors are now seen by many as healthy and/or normative, including, for example, masturbation, premarital sexual activity, sexual activity initiated by women and distinct from reproductive goals, and the expression of same-gender sexual attractions by lesbian, gay, and bisexual people (Castelo-Branco, Huezo, & Lagarda, 2008; Smith, 1990). The invention of the birth control pill, the destructive consequences to sexual expression brought on by human immunodeficiency virus (HIV), and even more recently, the introduction of pharmaceutical treatments for erectile dysfunction have each altered the behavioral options available to people and the psychosocial meaning of those behaviors. CBT can be useful for clients who have witnessed a great deal of cultural change. It can be used to help clients examine meaning and coherence in their belief systems or to assist clients struggling with the behavioral, emotional, and relational consequences of rigid or negative beliefs about sexuality.

Diversity

As the baby boomer population ages, the older adult population is becoming more culturally diverse. According to the U.S. Census Bureau (2001), 35 million (12%) of Americans are older than the age of 65. It is anticipated that by 2030, this number will grow such that 20% of the population will be older than the age of 65 (Hinrichsen, 2006). In 2000, 84% of older adults were White, 8% were Black, 6% were Hispanic/ Latino, 2% were Asian, and 0.4% were American Indian (Federal Interagency Forum on Aging-Related Statistics, 2000). Comparably, by 2050, it is predicted that 64% of the older adult population will be White,

12% will be Black, 16% will be Hispanic/Latino, 7% will be Asian, and 0.6% will be American Indian (Federal Interagency Forum on Aging-Related Statistics).

Despite the increasing diversity of the population, culturally sensitive services for older adults has lagged behind the culturally sensitive services for their younger counterparts (Hinrichsen, 2006). In addition, clinicians' understanding of the cultural identities of sexual minorities and people with disabilities is often rudimentary, including the ability to effectively conceptualize multiple, intersecting minority identities (Hays, 2008). All too often, older adults are considered a homogenous group, and many clinicians hold stereotypic views of this population. Hinrichsen (2006) identifies multiple commonly held stereotypes about older adults, including that they are: (a) all alike; (b) alone and lonely; (c) sick, frail, and/or dependent; (d) depressed; (e) rigid in old age; and (f) unable to cope. Older adult sexuality also has been found to evoke stereotypic thinking in members of society, health professionals, and older adults themselves (Gott, Hinchliff, & Galena, 2004; Laumann et al., 2009). As a result, concerns about sexual functioning and sexual identity are often overlooked or ignored. Culturally responsive CBT encourages clinicians to examine their own biases and prejudices to better understand how these beliefs may impact the clinician's conceptualization of client concerns and the delivery of services (Hays, 2008).

Exploring the unique experiences of lesbian, gay, bisexual, and transgendered (LGBT) older adults illustrates the need for culturally responsive treatment. Prior to the gay and lesbian rights movement of the 1970s and 1980s, many members of the LGBT community were hesitant to disclose their sexual identity to family, friends, and coworkers (Johnson, Jackson, Arnette, & Koffman, 2005). In fact, gay older adults are less likely to be out to others than their younger counterparts (Sue & Sue, 2003). Older gay men and lesbians have often been ignored by researchers and helping professionals, perpetuating the stereotype that older members of the gay community are isolated, lonely, and unhappy (Johnson et al., 2005). Additionally, ageism may be internalized by a community, as with the focus on youthfulness and marginalization of older adults that has sometimes been described within LGBT communities (Kimmel et al., 2006). Also, the aging process may force people to face barriers related to heterosexist health care settings and put them into contact with health care providers who are prejudiced against them because of any one of the intersecting facets of their minority identities (Hinchliff, Gott, & Galena, 2005; Johnson et al.). For example, transgender clients may require care from providers who are either unprepared to accommodate their preferred gender presentation or who may even express judgment and hostility about their gender identity (Cook-Daniels, 2006). Clinicians working with LGBT older adults must be sensitive to how multiple minority statuses (sexual identity, age/generational factors, ethnicity) may interact in a complex manner; overlooking the significance of age and ethnicity for the gay older adult may lead to a failure to recognize central aspects of the client's overall experience.

Working with older adults on sexual issues is complex, particularly in the current era of tremendous heterogeneity among the older adult population. Increased awareness of the many contexts in which older adult clients exist, including social histories, economic realities, problematic health care systems, and diverse and multifaceted identities will promote high-quality mental health assessment, sensitive treatment planning, and appropriate advocacy for older adults wishing to enhance their sexual well-being.

CONCEPTUALIZATION OF SEXUAL HEALTH IN OLDER ADULTS

The model of sexual functioning that predominates in clinical training programs may inadvertently contribute to clinicians' difficulties in flexibly conceptualizing older adult sexuality and, therefore, limit the perspectives that clinicians can offer their clients in CBT. Historically, sexology has been dominated by a performance-oriented, penile–vaginal intercourse-focused, and medicalized version of sexuality. Initially, the field was greatly influenced by Masters and Johnson (1970), who posited that sexuality was a biological function and was subject to scientific principles, which has been criticized for "sacrificing the uniquely human dimension" of sexuality (Kleinplatz, 2001, p. xiv). The current approach to diagnosis of sexual dysfunction using the *Diagnostic and Statistical Manual- Fourth Edition-Text Revision* (APA, 2000) retains the pathology-focused model that has been prominent for more than 30 years. Additionally, the introduction and proliferation of medications intended to treat sexual disorders represents the continued view of sex as the response cycle of arousal, desire, orgasm, and resolution. These and many other current treatment options perpetuate the continued focus on physical symptoms in lieu of the social, emotional, cultural, and contextual factors that are inherent in sexuality (Tiefer, Hall, & Tavris, 2002).

Within the dominant conceptualization of sexuality, sexual well-being is often viewed in terms of the absence or presence of problematic sexual functioning. We propose a model that recognizes that the absence

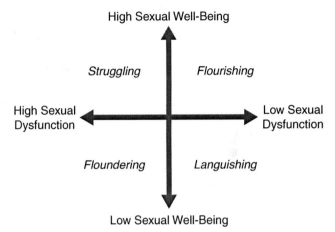

FIGURE 9.1   The Complete State of Sexual Health Model

Source: Adapted from Keyes, C. L. M. (2005). Mental illness and/or mental health? Investigating axioms of the complete state model of health. *Journal of Consulting and Clinical Psychology*, 73(3), 539–548.

of sexual dysfunction does not necessarily denote the presence of positive sexual functioning, or sexual well-being. In fact, in the proposed model, *sexual well-being* is a separate dimension than *sexual dysfunction* (see Figure 9.1). Notably, the conceptualization of sexual health, as illustrated in Figure 9.1, is a two-dimensional model based on the complete state model of mental health proposed by Corey Keyes and Shane Lopez (2002), which is a framework for general mental health (Keyes, 2005). We have applied this original idea to the conceptualization of sexuality with the hope that it will provide clinicians and researchers with a more comprehensive view of sexuality on which to base their assessment and treatment.

In the complete state of sexual health model, the two dimensions represented are *sexual well-being* and *sexual dysfunction,* each of which is on a continuum from low to high. This creates four quadrants designed to capture the sexual functioning of the client that are labeled as the following: (1) *Flourishing*—completely sexually healthy (high in sexual well-being and low in sexual dysfunction); (2) *Languishing*—incompletely sexually healthy (low in sexual well-being and low in sexual dysfunction); (3) *Floundering*—completely sexually unhealthy (low in sexual well-being and high in sexual dysfunction); and (4) *Struggling*—incompletely sexually unhealthy (high in sexual well-being and high in sexual dysfunction). This framework is an initial attempt to conceptualize sexual health in general, and older adult sexual health in specific, as more than the presence or absence of sexual dysfunction. Currently, it is a theoretical proposition and data is not available to test this model. Keyes (2005) has found replicated evidence that the complete state model of mental health is representative of adult mental health. Investigating the proposed model may provide us with a better understanding of sexual health in adult and older adult populations.

The complete state of sexual health model can be easily infused into a CBT treatment approach. The clinician can conceptualize the level of dysfunction and well-being by mapping the cognitive, behavioral, and emotional experiences of the client onto the model. For example, when identifying someone who is *flourishing*, they will not have behavioral difficulties with sex (low dysfunction)—such as avoidance, pain, or erectile dysfunction—and also will have flexible thinking about sex and will likely have positive attitudes and beliefs that facilitate satisfying sexual experiences (high sexual well-being). In contrast, when identifying a client who is *floundering*, they will likely have behavioral difficulties (high sexual dysfunction) such as impotence, pain, or intense anxiety during sex that may be connected to maladaptive and inflexible thinking/appraisals about sex ("sex is awful," "I can't perform well") that facilitate dissatisfying sexual experiences and avoidance (low sexual well-being). Through this mapping exercise, the clinician will have identified the levels of sexual well-being and functioning, and the cognitive, behavioral, and emotional symptoms to target during treatment planning to help enhance complete sexual health.

Approaching the assessment and treatment of sexuality in older adults requires the clinician to examine the process by which he or she is conceptualizing sexuality and incorporating the relevant biological, social, emotional, cultural, and contextual factors. Using the complete state of sexual health model as a tool for conceptualization is a step toward expanding sexuality to include both dysfunction and well-being with the hope that this framework will prompt clinicians to attend to both dimensions when treating older adults. In the following sections, we will outline assessment and treatment processes, keeping in mind the framework for the complete state of sexual health model.

ASSESSMENT OF SEXUAL HEALTH IN OLDER ADULTS

Prior to initiating a comprehensive sexual health assessment with an older adult, some important considerations that will influence the assessment approach must be taken into account. For example, the treatment setting in which the assessment will take place and the role of the clinician create a crucial context for the delivery of services.

Factors such as amount of existing privacy to establish a comfortable environment that promotes frank dialogue, available time with the client, type of provider conducting assessment and treatment, inpatient or outpatient status, and other factors all affect how a sexual health assessment may be conducted. Considering the multitude of health care access points (e.g., primary care, long-term care, community mental health) for the older adult population and the diversity of roles for clinicians, it is imperative to be aware that assessment, and subsequent treatment, may change as a function of the setting.

Additionally, the sexual beliefs and attitudes held by the client, as well as the staff providing care, should also be identified as these will be critical elements of any CBT intervention. Barriers to older adults broaching the subject of sexuality to their providers include a perception that decreasing sexuality is a normal part of aging, lack of knowledge about available treatment options, embarrassment about the topic, concerns about providers being disgusted and/or disinterested in their sexual functioning, and a perception that general practitioners hold negative attitudes toward older adult sexuality (Gott & Hinchliff, 2003; Laumann et al., 2009). Medical providers also report barriers to introducing the subject of sexuality, including time constraints, fear of opening the "floodgate" or offending the older adult, lack of training in sexual functioning assessment, and embarrassment (Bartlik, Rosenfeld, & Beaton, 2005; Gott et al., 2004). Such attitudes and beliefs, held by both clients and providers, may perpetuate the low identification rate of sexual health disorders in older adults who might otherwise benefit from treatment. Therefore, continued cognizance of these potential barriers on the part of the clinician, and other staff who have contact with the client, will aid in fostering successful sexual health treatment.

Lastly, the cognitive and functional status of the client should be taken into consideration given the influence it may have on sexual consent capacity, participation in a CBT treatment protocol, and the ability to engage in CBT-focused practice assignments. Clinicians will need to be especially sensitive to assessing sexual consent capacity (i.e., the ability to voluntarily make a reasoned decision whether or not to engage in sexual activity) when considering the high risk of dementing and cognitive disorders in the older adult population. Unfortunately, there is limited research in this area and uniform clinical and legal standards for use in this population are lacking, with few assessments for assessing sexual consent capacity in older adults (e.g., Lichtenberg & Strzepek, 1990). Thus, clinicians are encouraged to be aware of any legal and ethical standards governing sexual consent capacity and consult with a legal expert when needed (Mona et al., 2010).

Assessment Tools

The assessment of sexual functioning and sexual well-being among older adults requires the clinician to establish a relationship with sufficient rapport to explore sexuality and to create a nonthreatening therapeutic environment in which clients feel comfortable sharing with the clinician their thoughts, feelings, and behaviors about this especially personal topic (Mona, et al., 2010). A comprehensive sexual assessment necessitates the use of a semistructured interview and supplemental self-report measures (O'Connor et al., 2008). This is particularly true when considering CBT, as specific behaviors, thoughts, and feelings regarding sexuality will be targeted throughout treatment.

When feasible, the clinical interview should include both the patient and their partner to best understand the nature of the presenting concerns (Sbrocco, Weisberg, & Barlow, 1995; Zeiss, Zeiss, & Davies, 1999). The clinical interview also serves as an opportunity to teach positive sexual communication skills and provide education regarding normal sexual functioning and practice (Sbrocco et al., 1995). Psychoeducation that normalizes sexual practices that older adults may view as deviant (e.g., self-stimulation and masturbation practices) may place the client at ease to explore sexual well-being.

The semistructured interview developed by Zeiss, Zeiss, and Davies (1999) is recommended for establishing domains of inquiry for a sexual assessment. It is suggested that clinicians avoid the assumption of heterosexuality and communicate neutrality toward topics that are often considered socially taboo (e.g., use of prostitutes, sexual relationships outside of marriage, or other monogamous partnerships). Although this semistructured interview provides a framework for questioning, it is essential that clinicians are sensitive to often ignored diversity issues, sexual orientation, ethnicity, religion, and cultural factors that may or may not significantly influence sexual function and/or treatment options. Clinicians must also explore clients' experiences with pharmacotherapy and their willingness to explore alternative options (e.g., use of a penile vacuum pump for a male who has had limited success getting an erection through other means).

To date, few self-report measures of sexual behaviors, attitudes, or beliefs have been normed on older adults. The Sexual Beliefs and Information Questionnaire (SBIQ-R; Adams et al., 1996) is an example of a measure that was normed on older adults and developed to ascertain if misinformation about sexual functioning might impair functioning and satisfaction. In addition to the SBIQ-R, the Aging Sexual Knowledge and Attitudes Scale (ASKAS; White, 1982) may be a useful tool for clinicians who are interested in examining how beliefs and attitudes held by older adults may contribute to sexual function or dysfunction.

There are few standardized and valid measures of sexual well-being. Of the studies examining sexual well-being, questions related to judgment about satisfaction with physical and emotional pleasure, healthy sexual functioning, and positive attitudes toward sex are often used (Rosen & Bachmann, 2008). Clinicians may wish to use existing measures that incorporate sexual satisfaction after reviewing them for utility (e.g., Derogatis Sexual Functioning Interview—Derogatis & Melisaratos, 1979; Interpersonal Exchange Model of Sexual Satisfaction Questionnaire—Lawrence & Byers, 1998) to supplement clinical interview questions that capture sexual enhancement and well-being (e.g., What is most satisfying about sexuality/intimacy? What types of sexual activities do you enjoy? What areas of your intimate/sexual life would you like to enhance? In what ways would you like to enhance your intimacy/sexuality? Please describe your values about intimacy and sex.).

Overall, the assessment of sexual functioning and sexual well-being of the older adult should serve as a means to develop rapport, provide education, establish an initial diagnosis, and explore preliminary treatment options. Finally, of utmost importance in the assessment of sexual functioning and sexual well-being among older adults is that clinicians take the time to understand their clients in the context of their individual and cultural identities, personal and relationship history, and their presenting concerns.

COGNITIVE BEHAVIORAL TREATMENT APPROACHES FOR SEXUALITY IN OLDER ADULTS

Up until now, there has been no single model of psychotherapeutic treatment that is clearly articulated and sufficiently validated for promoting sexual adjustment and satisfaction among older women and men. Traditional CBT has a clearly established base of empirical support and serves as an effective therapy for the older adult population as its strengths include a collaborative and nonpathologizing approach that emphasizes identifying and alleviating focal areas of distress while addressing maladaptive beliefs about the self or others (Gallagher-Thompson & Thompson, 1996). Additionally, considerable evidence attests that CBT has great potential in promoting adjustment, well-being, and personal health behaviors among persons with disabling conditions that exist to a higher degree in the aging population (Chambless & Ollendick, 2001). Thus, the potential complexity involved in treating sexuality issues in older adults provides a superb opportunity for application of a range of CBT approaches. In this section, CBT and TWCBTs will be examined for their potential utility in treatment of sexuality issues in older adults. Additionally, practical and adaptive strategies for enhancing sexual expression and experience will be reviewed.

Current Literature on Cognitive Behavioral Treatments for Older Adults

There is now strong evidence for the efficacy of CBT for persons aged 65 years and older, with its components of client–clinician collaboration, flexibility, and empiricism being highly suitable for older adults (Laidlaw, Thompson, Dick-Siskin, & Gallagher-Thompson, 2003). Meta-analytic studies have supported the use of CBT as an efficacious treatment for older clients for various disorders, including depression (Engels & Vermey, 1997), generalized anxiety disorder (Stanley, Beck, & Glassco, 1996), panic disorder (Swales, Solfrin, & Sheikh, 1996), and insomnia (Morin, Kowatch, Barry, & Walton, 1993). More recent studies have also shown CBT to be at least as effective as antidepressant medication for this population (Thompson, Coon, Gallagher-Thompson, Sommer, & Koin, 2001).

As CBT was originally developed as a treatment for young and middle-aged adults, the application to the older adult population warrants consideration of different therapeutic approaches. Various studies have published recommendations on how to address concerns such as psychosocial issues, factors that may affect the therapeutic relationship, use of homework assignments, adjustment of behavioral modification strategies, and adaptation of therapy structure (Secker, Kazantzis, & Pachana, 2004). More specifically, some common issues that emerge while working with older adults include themes surrounding loss (e.g., declining health, changing roles, perception of decreased attractiveness, limited independence), the influence of the social aspect of a therapeutic relationship (i.e., how the relationship may facilitate outcomes or addressing ruptures therapeutic alliance), and the importance of induction into therapy so that the rationale for treatment is explained (e.g., overcoming "I'm too old to change"; Koder, 2007). The efficacy of the cognitive aspect of CBT may, in part, be caused by the ability to address these concerns.

Concrete CBT techniques that may be particularly helpful to older adults with potentially more complex issues (e.g., medical, cognitive, living situation) include clear establishment of homework guidelines, setting therapy and session goals and agendas, and adjusting therapy frequency and duration (e.g., increasing therapy frequency and decreasing duration of session; Kazantzis, Pachana, & Secker, 2003). Additionally, reinforcement strategies may also include linking content from one session to another and slowing the pace of therapy depending on the client's abilities and needs. Given the predominance of loss themes in older adults, it has also been recommended that sessions be gradually terminated with increasing intervals between sessions rather than an abrupt discontinuation of sessions (Koder, Brodaty, & Anstey, 1996). Consideration of physical disabilities (e.g., sensory, praxis deficits) or cognitive impairments is also crucial to the adaptation of these therapeutic approaches to older adults.

As described earlier, older adults are a heterogeneous group. And a culturally responsive CBT is called for to address the unique factors that comprise the culture of the individual older adult. Culturally responsive CBT requires that clinicians be sensitive to how the cultural environment shapes a client's emotions, behaviors, thoughts, and physical symptoms (Hays, 2008). The ADDRESSING model, as outlined by Pamela Hays (2008), provides a comprehensive framework for understanding how cultural identities interact to shape a client's worldview. This model encourages the examination of multiple minority statuses, including *A*ge and generational influences, *D*evelopmental disability, *D*isability acquired later in life, *R*eligion and spiritual orientation, *E*thnic and racial identity, *S*ocioeconomic status, *S*exual orientation, *I*ndigenous heritage, *N*ational origin, and *G*ender. Using the multifaceted ADDRESSING model decreases the likelihood that the clinician will make global assumptions about the client's experience. Cultural identities—particularly minority identities—often interact in a complex manner that makes each individual client unique. This is especially poignant given that the establishment of trust within therapeutic relationships becomes particularly salient when sensitive topics such as sexuality are broached.

Current Literature on Cognitive Behavioral Therapy for Sexuality Issues

Sexual expression and subjective sexual experiences include behavioral and experiential components, containing motivational, cognitive, and affective aspects for which CBT is a highly suitable treatment approach.

CBT treatments have been shown to exist for various sexual disorders, including orgasmic disorder in women (combination of psychoeducation and sexual skill training including directed masturbation exercises), erectile dysfunction (systematic desensitization), and premature ejaculation (gradual approximation of ejaculatory delay using stop-start exercises or the "squeeze technique"; Heiman, 2002; Heiman & Meston, 1997). For other sexual dysfunctions including vaginismus, dyspareunia, delayed male orgasm, and the sexual desire disorders, empirical support for CBT approaches was insufficient or poor (Heiman & Meston).

Other therapeutic approaches and techniques such as sensate focus (Masters & Johnson, 1970), disability affirmative therapy (DAT), a culturally centered and integrative framework that articulates an explicitly disability-positive orientation (Olkin, 1999), and bibliotherapy may be used adjunctively with CBT to successfully achieve therapeutic goals (Mona et al., 2009). Additionally, significant advances have been made in our understanding and effectiveness of pharmacotherapy options for sexual dysfunction, including PDE5 inhibitors. Treatments combining CBT with medications have been recently evaluated with the finding that the combination is more effective than medication alone in treating sexual disorders (Melnik, Soares, & Nasselo, 2008). Most of the research on pharmacological treatments has focused on males, although few studies have looked at the effects of PDE5 inhibitors for female sexual dysfunction. The evidence supporting unlicensed use of PDE5 inhibitors in women with sexual disorders remains inconclusive because of contradictory findings across studies (Foster, Mears, Goldmeier, 2009). As a result, there is the need for further research on the use of pharmacological agents to treat women with sexual dysfunction, particularly for postmenopausal women.

Specific goals and strategies for the treatment of sexuality issues employing CBT may include overcoming myths regarding sexuality via psychoeducation and bibliotherapy, decreasing performance anxiety using sensate focus, decreasing dysfunctional cognitions and maladaptive sexual self-schemas, and increasing stimulus control (Nezu, Nezu, & Lombardo, 2004). These strategies may be used to both decrease dysfunction and enhance well-being, allowing the clinician to target each of the quadrants of the complete state of sexual health model. With regard to decreasing dysfunctional cognitions, Barlow (1986) suggests that men and women with sexual disorders respond to sexual stimuli by focusing on negative self-statements and cognitions that distract from erotic cues, which interferes with sexual arousal. Thus, use of cognitive restructuring can help to replace maladaptive cognitions with more adaptive ones to facilitate sexual confidence and performance. Problem-solving therapy may also be used to address sexuality issues by changing cognitive factors that adversely influence problem orientation (general view of problems) and self-assessment of one's problem-solving ability (Nezu et al., 2004) to combat negative thinking about sexual issues. Improving stimulus control involves optimizing environmental (e.g., music, lighting), temporal (e.g., time of day sex is preferred), biological (e.g., fatigue, presence of medical conditions), psychological (e.g., mood), and interpersonal (e.g., level of attractiveness to partner) factors to further enhance aforementioned treatment strategies (Nezu et al.). Lastly, Wincze et al. (2008) suggested that goals addressing sexual relationships can help reduce performance pressure and anxiety.

Current Literature on Third-Wave Cognitive Behavioral Treatments for Sexual Issues

TWCBTs such as acceptance and commitment therapy (ACT) or mindfulness-based cognitive therapy have gained recent attention as effective treatments for various problems, including depression and anxiety. Although the distinctions between traditional CBT and ACT remain under debate, ACT also integrates cognitive and behavioral techniques that facilitate psychological flexibility. Distinguishing features of ACT that appear well suited for improving sexual health include mindfulness techniques, a present-focus orientation, and acceptance of emotional experiences that promotes the exploration of personal beliefs and core values. The emphasis on values clarification opens up the opportunity for persons with sexual issues to generate questions about how beliefs and values may be affecting their experiences of sexuality and intimate relationships (Mona et al., 2009). A client may benefit from contemplating his or her values underlying sexuality (e.g., how important is sex in my life), relationships (e.g., what do relationships mean to me), and beliefs (e.g., what exactly do I believe sex and intimacy to be like at this age).

Integrating What We Know About Cognitive Behavioral Therapy and Third-Wave Cognitive Behavioral Therapy for Older Adults With Sexual Issues

Many older adults feel that continued sexual relations provide a highly important source of psychological reinforcement and helps maintain feelings of physical and psychological well-being (Lindau et al., 2007).

CBT may be particularly effective in empowering older adults to address their sexuality with more cognitive flexibility and creativity to enhance sexual satisfaction and relational intimacy. However, support for CBT in the treatment of sexuality issues in the aging population is an area that remains sparsely developed for various reasons, including social stereotypes about older adult sexuality (Gott et al., 2004; Laumann et al., 2009), problematic research methodology, and difficulties in the definition of emotionally laden constructs (e.g., What is "old age"? [Libman, 1989]).

Given the limited empirical evidence pertaining to CBT or TWCBT as interventions for sexual concerns among older adults, the modification of previously established techniques such as sensate focus, can be customized to include the concept and practice of cognitive restructuring and mindfulness. More specifically, a sensual mindfulness approach would not only include the traditional sensate focus techniques, but would also emphasize explicitly the goal of accepting any uncomfortable feelings or thoughts that might arise during intimacy, remaining in the present moment and focusing on present-moment sensations. Additionally, careful attention must be paid to addressing attitudes and beliefs regarding sexuality that may reflect childhood teachings and that may interfere with optimal sexual functioning (e.g., "sex is a reproductive act," "masturbation is bad," "aging people are asexual"), negative self-statements (e.g., "I'm not as attractive as younger women," "My penis doesn't get as hard as it used to, so I might not be able to please my partner"), and making appropriate adaptations to CBT approaches (e.g., emphasizing rationale of therapeutic process, slowing session pace). Evidence-based CBTs that can accommodate sex therapy for older men and women are part of a shift in our understanding that departs from conventional conceptualizations of sexuality and sexual expression to promoting increasingly more sex-positive education and interventions.

The effect of age on sexual functioning is complex and involves comprehensive assessment to accurately inform treatment approach and planning. Appropriate medical evaluation, considerations regarding medications, comorbid mental health disturbance, marital distress/relationship conflict, cultural and religious factors, living situation (e.g., home, nursing facility) and current or history of sexual abuse may need to be considered. Understanding a client's attitudes is critically important to treatment planning because interventions may involve prescribing behaviors that are outside the client's comfort zone. It is also important to keep in mind that although consideration of age-related changes is important in addressing sexual health, these changes should not automatically be viewed as the "cause" of sexual functioning issues.

ADDITIONAL TREATMENT CONSIDERATIONS FOR OLDER ADULTS

As we move from consideration of maladaptive beliefs about self or others related to sexuality to more practical cognitive behavioral/ experiential interventions, it is important to consider the degree to which a decline in physical functioning, partner availability, and alternative sexual practices may affect the sexual expression of older adults. Relevant issues include the practical aspects of sexual positioning and the use of sexual enhancement products.

The use of sexual enhancement products or "sex toys" has gained popularity across generations for the past 15 years (Michael, Gangon, Laumann, & Kolata, 1994). For this population, sexual products that provide for better and safer positioning (e.g., sex cushions), increased lubrication for women (e.g., lubricating gels), or increased genital or other erogenous zone stimulation (e.g., ergonomically-designed vibrators) may be useful. However, it is important to understand that this may not be an acceptable option for all and to approach this topic with sensitivity. Also, people who are unfamiliar with the use of sexual aids may initially need education about safety and structured behavioral goals for use.

Self-stimulation may also be a positive way of expressing sexuality that is less likely to be impeded by physical and social limitations (Fraley, Mona, & Theodore, 2007). Many older adults may be in a position of desiring increased sexual expression and sexual well-being, but have no current intimate partner (either by choice or for lack of options). Depending on individual values, beliefs, and goals, self-stimulation may be an appropriate behavioral intervention, which should also be approached with sensitivity. When considering the topic of self-stimulation with the older adult, intervention strategies may include exploring core beliefs about solitary and coupled sexual behaviors, increasing cognitive flexibility about stimulation activities, and behavioral goals/homework, including stimulation exercises that incorporate mindfulness.

For those who are uncomfortable with self-stimulation (e.g., for religious or cultural reasons) or those who simply prefer a goal of seeking a romantic relationship for sexual expression, identifying opportunities for meeting people may become the primary goal of treatment.

Many older adults return to dating after divorce or death of a spouse, sometimes after a long period of being single or not sexually active, and may be hesitant or anxious about the prospect of dating. Interventions here may include increasing awareness of thoughts related to body image and self-esteem, identifying beliefs that may facilitate avoidance behaviors about dating, and implementing behavioral goals to address maladaptive cognitive and behavioral patterns, such as encouraging the individual to strategize physical locations to meet potential partners and exploring on-line dating resources.

CASE EXAMPLE

Cognitive behavioral therapists are able to draw on a range of techniques and strategies to intervene with older adult clients (e.g., collaborative goal setting, cognitive restructuring, stimulus control, increasing behavioral repertoires via homework, and mindfulness techniques). The following is an example of how CBT can be applied to enhance sexual well-being.

> Helen is a 72-year-old White lesbian who has been with her significant other, Elizabeth, for more than 20 years. They are very happy together and have always been comfortable and open with one another about their sexual intimacy. Helen has two adult daughters from an earlier relationship with a man. Both children are aware of her relationship with Elizabeth and they have been wonderfully supportive. However, Helen has not talked about her relationship with Elizabeth with many of her friends, feeling it is a private issue.
>
> Helen recently moved into a long-term care facility because medical issues prompted a need for more assistance with ADLs. Elizabeth has visited her 2 to 3 times per week. They usually spend their time talking, watching TV, or playing card games. They have little privacy because Helen shares a room with another female resident and staff performs regular rounds. When Helen initially moved into the center, she and Elizabeth discussed with one another their desire for privacy and more sexual connection. However, Helen feels intimidated and awkward in her new living situation and has not disclosed her sexual orientation or relationship with Elizabeth to the staff. Over the subsequent weeks, Elizabeth noticed Helen's hesitancy to ask for privacy and her unwillingness to tell others about their relationship, and she feels hurt by this. Also, Helen has begun showing less interest in affection and intimacy in the past few weeks, and this has put additional strain on their relationship.

The staff becomes concerned when they observe that Helen has "not been herself" and has been "feeling down." They approach Helen to tell her that they have noticed a difference in her over the past few weeks, and they ask her if she would like to talk to a psychologist. She appreciates their concern but wonders whether she will feel comfortable talking to anyone about this topic.

After talking with the staff about their concerns, the psychologist understood that a gentle and thoughtful approach was needed. The psychologist worked to establish a safe and comfortable environment for rapport building, which included directly addressing issues of confidentiality in the therapeutic relationship, making the processes and expectations of assessment and treatment transparent and collaborating with her to form the goals of treatment. Also, it was integral for the psychologist to normalize both older adult sexuality and Helen's personal experiences and provide her with education about sexual functioning across the lifespan, including cultural and generational factors.

As Helen began to trust the clinician, she opened up about her feelings and the distress related to her current situation. The psychologist decided to move toward a more comprehensive assessment of her sexual and psychological functioning and invited Helen to share her personal history of sex and intimacy. The semistructured interview outlined by Zeiss and colleagues (1999) was selected to aid with this process as it covers several important domains: psychological, medical, social, and cognitive factors in sexual function and dysfunction.

The comprehensive assessment was expanded to include measures of sexual well-being (satisfaction, enjoyment), psychological distress (depression, anxiety), and cognitive and behavioral concepts (attitudes and beliefs about sex and intimacy, sexual behaviors, avoidance behaviors, maladaptive thoughts). Helen was encouraged to explore her own values related to sexuality such as the importance of sex, how much sexual intimacy is right for her, the meaning of an intimate relationship, and what she believes sex and intimacy to look like.

Given Helen's age and recent change in daily functioning, it was essential to incorporate basic memory and thought processing questions within the context of the intake. Cognitive functioning was explored first with brief questions such as, "Have you noticed that you have been forgetting things that you would usually remember?" Helen did not endorse any cognitive functioning issues; however, if she had, it would have been imperative to pursue this further with screenings and potentially further testing to address issues related to capacity to consent to sexual activities.

The clinician began to map Helen's experience onto the complete state of sexual health model, noting that she was low in sexual dysfunction; however, Helen was also low in sexual well-being, which indicated that she may be *languishing*. The psychologist formulated the treatment plan to include directly addressing issues of sexual well-being and emotional well-being with a cognitive behavioral approach.

Helen was initially provided a rationale for treatment, including the connection between thoughts, feelings, and behaviors. The subsequent few sessions were aimed at identifying her thoughts and beliefs about intimacy in her current situation. Helen became aware of her own maladaptive thinking patterns about physical intimacy through Socratic questioning and reflections, realizing that she began to believe it was shameful and inappropriate given her age and setting. She was also able to connect these thoughts to her interactions with her significant other and her overall emotional well-being. Helen elucidated the value she put on closeness with her significant other and decided to share her concerns with Elizabeth in a joint session. Elizabeth was very supportive, reinforced Helen's value of closeness, and they agreed to take things slowly as Helen continued to work in therapy.

Through additional sessions, Helen became aware that her automatic thoughts were leading her to believe that the staff and other patients would not be receptive of her relationship and intimacy needs, misinterpreting their actions and interactions with her in this way. To help Helen become more aware and in tune with her subjective experience, mindfulness concepts and experiential exercises were employed, which helped Helen to distinguish her "self" from her thoughts, become an observer of her cognitions, and take a nonjudgmental stance about her thoughts and experiences. These cognitive techniques helped her to test the assumptions she had developed about the staff and led to increased trust and more positive interactions. This helped facilitate the behavioral goal of asking the staff for increased privacy (e.g., room, time), which was well-accepted. Between sessions, the psychologist encouraged Helen to use her flexible and creative thinking as she began to reengage in affectionate acts with her significant other Elizabeth, which ultimately helped her challenge her maladaptive beliefs about intimacy in her current situation. Helen also worked on integrating mindfulness techniques during physically intimate situations, including remaining nonjudgmental of the situation, accepting whatever feelings arise, and making an effort to remain in the present moment.

Helen began to feel more comfortable with physical intimacy in her current living situation and reported increased sexual and emotional well-being. Overall, Helen benefited from a therapeutic approach that included a collaborative therapeutic relationship; values clarification; an opportunity to explore her beliefs, emotions and behaviors; behavioral homework; and training in mindfulness strategies.

SUMMARY

Sexual well-being remains an integral part of the quality of life across adulthood for many people. Given the multifaceted nature of sexual well-being and the prevalence of sexual dysfunction in the older adult population, clinicians need effective and flexible treatments for sexual functioning in older adults. CBT is well suited to address the treatment issues related to sexual health in older adults by using a collaborative and nonpathologizing approach that emphasizes flexible and creative thinking. It provides the clinician with the tools to decrease maladaptive thoughts behaviors and feelings as well as enhance positive behaviors that facilitate sexual health and well-being. Understanding the practical issues of sexuality and aging and using enhancing tools and strategies to supplement a CBT approach will help to further enhance older adults' sexual experiences.

REFERENCES

Adams, S. G. Jr., Dubbert, P. M., Chupurdia, K. M., Jones, A., Jr., Lofland, K. R., and Leermakers, E. (1996). Assessment of Sexual Beliefs and Information in Aging. Couples with Sexual Dysfunction. *Archives of Sexual Behavior, 25*(3), 249–260.

American Psychiatric Association. (2000). *Diagnostic and statistical manual of mental disorders* (4th ed., text rev.). Washington, DC: Author.

American Psychological Association, Presidential Task Force on Evidence-Based Practice. (2005). *Report of the Presidential Task Force on Evidence-Based Practice.* Retrieved from http.//www.apa.org/practice/resources/evidence/evidence-based-report.pdf

Barlow, D. H. (1986). Causes of sexual dysfunction: The role of anxiety and cognitive interference. *Journal of Consulting and Clinical Psychology, 54*(2), 140–148.

Bartlik, B. D., Rosenfeld, S., & Beaton, C. (2005). Assessment of sexual functioning: Sexual history taking for health care practitioners. *Epilepsy and Behavior, 7,* S15–S21.

Butler, A. C., Chapman, J. E., Forman, E. M., & Beck, A. T. (2006). The empirical status of cognitive behavioral therapy: A review of meta-analyses. *Clinical Psychology Review, 26*(1), 17–31.

Castelo-Branco, C., Huezo, M. L., & Lagarda, J. L. (2008). Definition and diagnosis of sexuality in the XXI century. *Maturitas, 60,* 50–58.

Chambless, D. L., & Ollendick, T. H. (2001). Empirically supported psychological interventions: Controversies and evidence. *Annual Review of Psychology, 52,* 685–716.

Cook-Daniels, L. (2006). Trans aging. In D. Kimmel, T. Rose, & S. David (Eds.), *Lesbian, gay, bisexual, and transgender aging* (pp. 20–35). New York, NY: Columbia University Press.

DeLamater, J. D., & Sill, M. (2005). Sexual desire in later life. *Journal of Sex Research, 42*(2), 138–149.

Derogatis, L. R., & Melisaratos, N. (1979). The DSFI: A multidimensional measure of sexual functioning. *Journal of Sex & Marital Therapy, 5*(3), 244–281.

Engels, G. I., & Vermey, M. (1997). Efficacy of nonmedical treatments of depression in elders: A quantitative analysis. *Journal of Clinical Geropsychology, 3,* 17–35.

Federal Interagency Forum on Aging-Related Statistics. (2000). *Older Americans 2000: Key indicators of well-being.* Washington, DC: U.S. Government Printing Offices.

Foster, R., Mears, A., & Goldmeier, D. (2009). A literature review and case reports series on the use of phosphodiesterase inhibitors in the treatment of female sexual dysfunction. *International Journal of STD and Aids, 20*(3), 152–157.

Fraley, S. S., Mona, L. R., & Theodore, P. S. (2007). The sexual lives of lesbian, gay, and bisexual people with disabilities: Psychological perspectives. *Sexuality Research and Social Policy: Journal of NSRC, 4*(1), 15–26.

Gallagher-Thompson, D., & Thompson, L. W. (1996). Applying cognitive behavioral therapy to the psychological problems of later life. In S. H. Zarit & B. G. Knight (Eds.), *A guide to psychotherapy and aging: Effective clinical interventions in a life-stage context* (pp. 61–82). Washington, DC: American Psychological Association.

Gott, M., & Hinchliff, S. (2003). Barriers to seeking treatment for sexual problems in primary care: A qualitative study with older people. *Family Practice, 20*(6), 690–695.

Gott, M., Hinchliff, S., & Galena, E. (2004). General practitioner attitudes to discussing sexual health issues with older people. *Social Science and Medicine, 58*(11), 2093–2103.

Hays, P. A. (2008). *Addressing cultural complexities in practice: Assessment, diagnosis, and therapy* (2nd ed.). Washington, DC: American Psychological Association.

Heiman, J. R. (2002). Psychologic treatments for female sexual dysfunction: Are they effective and do we need them? *Archives of Sexual Behavior, 31*(5), 445–450.

Heiman, J. R., & Meston, C. M. (1997). Empirically validated treatment for sexual dysfunction. *Annual Review of Sex Research, 8,* 148–194.

Hinchliff, S., Gott, M., & Galena, E. (2005). 'I daresay I might find it embarrassing': General practitioners' perspectives on discussing sexual health issues with lesbian and gay patients. *Health & Social Care in the Community, 13*(4), 345–353.

Hinrichsen, G. A. (2006). Why multicultural issues matter for practitioners working with older adults. *Professional Psychology: Research and Practice, 37*(1), 29–35.

Johnson, M. J., Jackson, N. C., Arnette, J. K., & Koffman, S. D. (2005). Gay and lesbian perceptions of discrimination in retirement care facilities. *Journal of Homosexuality, 49*(2), 83–102.

Karlin, B. E., Duffy, M., & Gleaves, D. H. (2008). Patterns and predictors of mental health service use and mental illness among older and younger adults in the United States. *Psychological Services, 5*(3), 275–294.

Kazantzis, N., Pachana, N. A., & Secker, D. L. (2003). Cognitive behavioral therapy for older adults: Practical guidelines for the use of homework assignments. *Cognitive and Behavioral Practice, 10*, 324–332.

Keyes, C. L. M. (2005). Mental illness and/or mental health? Investigating axioms of the complete state model of health. *Journal of Consulting and Clinical Psychology, 73*(3), 539–548.

Keyes, C. L. M., & Lopez, S. J. (2002). Toward a science of mental health: Positive directions in diagnosis and intervention. In C. R. Snyder and S. J. Lopez (Eds.), *Handbook of positive psychology* (pp. 45–59). New York, NY: McGraw-Hill.

Kimmel, D., Rose, T., Orel, N., & Greene, B. (2006). Historical context for research on lesbian, gay, bisexual, and transgender aging. In D. Kimmel, T. Rose, & S. David (Eds.), *Lesbian, gay, bisexual, and transgender aging: Research and clinical perspectives* (pp. 1–19). New York, NY: Columbia University Press.

Kleinplatz, P. J. (2001). A critical evaluation of sex therapy: Room for improvement. In P. J. Kleinplatz (Ed.), *New directions in sex therapy: Innovations and alterations* (pp xi–xxxiii). Philadelphia, PA: Taylor & Francis.

Koder, D. (2007). Cognitive behavior therapy for older adults: Practical guidelines for adaptive therapy structure. In D. A. Einstein (Ed.), *Innovations and advances in cognitive behaviour therapy* (pp. 101–111). Bowen Hills, Queensland, Australia Academic Press.

Koder, D. A., Brodaty, H., & Anstey, K. J. (1996). Cognitive therapy for depression in the elderly. *International Journal of Geriatric Psychiatry, 11*, 97–108.

Kontula, O., & Haavio-Mannila, E. (2009). The impact of aging on human sexual activity and sexual desire. *Journal of Sex Research, 46*, 46–56.

Laidlaw, K., Thompson, L. W., Dick-Siskin, L., & Gallagher-Thompson, D. (2003). *Cognitive behaviour therapy with older people.* United Kingdom: John Wiley & Sons.

Laumann, E. O., Glasser, D. B., Neves, R. C. S., Moreira Jr., E. D., & Global Study of Sexual Attitudes and Behaviors (GSSAB) Investigators' Group. (2009). A population-based survey of sexual activity, sexual problems, and associated help-seeking behavior patterns in mature adults in the United States of America. *International Journal of Impotence Research, 21*, 171–178.

Lawrence, K., & Byers, E. S. (1998). Interpersonal exchange model of sexual satisfaction questionnaire. In C. M. Davis, W. L. Yarber, R. Bauserman, G. Schreer, & S. L. Davis (Eds.), *Sexuality-related measures: A compendium* (2nd ed., pp. 514–519). Thousand Oaks, CA: Sage Publications.

Libman, E. (1989). Sociocultural and cognitive factors in aging and sexual expression: Conceptual and research issues. *Canadian Psychology, 30*(3), 560–567.

Lichtenberg, P. A., & Strzepek, D. M. (1990). Assessments of institutionalized dementia patients' competencies to participate in intimate relationships. *Gerontologist, 30*(1), 117–120.

Lindau, S. T., Schumm, L. P. Laumann, E. O., Levinson, W., O'Muircheartaigh, C. A., & Waite, L. J. (2007). A study of sexuality and health among older adults in the United States. *New England Journal of Medicine, 357*, 762–774.

Masters, W., & Johnson, V. (1970). *Human sexual inadequacy.* Boston, MA: Little, Brown, & Co.

Melnik, T., Soares, B. G. O., & Nasello, A. G. (2008). The effectiveness of psychological interventions for the treatment of erectile dysfunction: Systematic review and meta-analysis, including comparisons to sildenafil treatment, intracavernosal injection, and vacuum devices. *Journal of Sexual Medicine, 5*(11), 2562–2574.

Michael, R. T., Gangon, J. H., Laumann, E. O., & Kolata, G. (1994). *Sex in America: A definitive survey.* New York, NY: Warner Books.

Mona, L. R., Cameron, R. P., Goldwaser, G., Miller, A. R., Syme, M. L., & Fraley, S. S. (2009). Prescription for pleasure: Exploring sex positive approaches in women with spinal cord injury. *Topics in Spinal Cord Injury Rehabilitation, 15,* 15–29.

Mona, L. R., Goldwaser, G., Syme, M. L., Cameron, R. P., Clemency, C., Miller, A. R., et al. (in press). Assessment and conceptualization of sexuality among older adults. In P. A. Lichtenberg (Ed.), *Handbook of assessment in clinical gerontology,* 2nd Ed and (pp. 331–356), New York, NY: Elsevier Publishers.

Morin, C. M., Kowatch, R. A., Barry, T., & Walton, E. (1993). Cognitive-behavior therapy for late-life insomnia. *Journal of Consulting & Clinical Psychology, 61*(1), 137–146.

Nezu, A. M., Nezu, C. M., & Lombardo, E. R. (2004). *Cognitive-behavioral case formulation and treatment design: A problem-solving approach.* New York, NY: Springer Publishing Company.

O'Connor, D. B., Corona, G., Forti, G., Tajar, A., Lee, D. M., Finn, J. D., et al. (2008). Assessment of sexual health in aging men in Europe: Development and validation of the European Male Ageing Study Sexual Function Questionnaire. *Journal of Sexual Medicine, 5,* 1374–1385.

Olkin, R. (1999). *What psychotherapists should know about disability.* New York, NY: Guilford Press.

Rosen, R. C., & Bachmann, G. A. (2008). Sexual well-being, happiness, and satisfaction in women: The case for a new conceptual paradigm. *Journal of Sex & Marital Therapy, 34,* 291–297.

Satre, D. D., Knight, B. G., & David, S. (2006). Cognitive behavioral interventions with older adults: Integrating clinical and gerontological research. *Professional Psychology: Research and Practice, 37,* 489–498.

Sbrocco, T., Weisberg, R. B., & Barlow, D. H. (1995). Sexual dysfunction in the older adult: Assessment of psychological factors. *Sexuality and Disability, 13,* 201–218.

Secker, D. L., Kazantzis, N., & Pachana, N. A. (2004). Cognitive behavior therapy for older adults: Practical guidelines for adaptive therapy structure. *Journal of Rational-Emotive & Cognitive-Behavior Therapy, 22*(2), 93–109.

Smith, T. (1990). The polls-a report: The sexual revolution? *Public Opinion Quarterly, 54*(3), 415–435.

Stanley, M. A., Beck, J. G., & Glassco, J. D. (1996). Treatment of generalized anxiety disorder in older adults: A preliminary comparison of cognitive-behavioral and supportive approaches. *Behavior Therapy, 27,* 565–581.

Sue, D. W., & Sue, D. (2003). *Counseling the culturally diverse: Theory and practice* (4th ed.). New York, NY: John Wiley & Sons.

Swales, P., Solfrin, J., & Sheikh, J. (1996). Cognitive behavioral therapy in older panic disorder patients. *American Journal of Geriatric Psychiatry, 4,* 46–60.

Thompson, L. W., Coon, D., Gallagher-Thompson, D., Sommer, B., & Koin, D. (2001). Comparison of desipramine and cognitive behavioral therapy in the treatment of elderly outpatients with mild-to-moderate depression. *American Journal of Geriatric Psychiatry, 9,* 225–240.

Tiefer, L., Hall, M., & Tavris, C. (2002). Beyond dysfunction: A new view of women's sexual problems. *Journal of Sex & Marital Therapy, 28*, 225–232.

U.S. Census Bureau. (2001). *Age: 2000.* Retrieved from http://www.census.gov/prod/2001pubs/c2kbr01-12.pdf

White, C. B. (1982). A scale for the assessment of attitudes and knowledge regarding sexuality in the aged. *Archives of Sexual Behavior, 11*(6), 491–502.

Wincze, J., Bach, A., & Barlow, D. H. (2008). Sexual dysfunction. In D. H. Barlow (Ed.), *Clinical handbook of psychological disorders: A Step-by-Step Treatment Manual* (4th ed. pp. 615–661). New York, NY: Guilford Press.

Zeiss, A. M., Zeiss, R. A., & Davies, H. (1999). Assessment of sexual function and dysfunction in older adults. In P. Lichtenberg (Ed.), *Handbook of assessment in clinical gerontology* (pp. 270–296). New York, NY: John Wiley & Sons, Inc.

II

Innovations Across
Care Settings

10

Cognitive Behavioral Therapy for Older Adults in the Primary Care Setting

John Paul Jameson and Jeffrey A. Cully

Providing mental health care to older adults in primary care settings presents a unique set of opportunities and challenges. In addition to providing effective care, a mental health provider in primary care must be prepared to work with patients suffering from debilitating chronic physical conditions, build relationships with providers across disciplines, engage patients who are sometimes reluctant to participate in treatment, and navigate competing practice demands. The foundational components of cognitive behavioral therapy (CBT) are consistent with the needs of primary care patients and hold the potential to be adapted into highly effective techniques for older adults with emotional and/or physical health difficulties. In this chapter, we present an overview of the mental health issues in the primary care setting and popular models of primary care/mental health integration. We also review evidence suggesting that CBT may be an effective treatment for older primary care patients. In the last section, we outline common pragmatic concerns and offer recommendations for adapting CBT-based interventions to primary care practice, and provide suggestions for future research directions.

PREVALENCE AND RECOGNITION OF MENTAL HEALTH CONDITIONS IN PRIMARY CARE

Epidemiological studies have consistently found higher prevalence rates for common mental disorders in primary care settings than in the general population. Point prevalence rates among primary care patients have been estimated at 10% to 29% for depression (McQuaid, Stein, Laffaye, & McCahill, 1999; Spitzer et al., 1994) and 13% to 20% for anxiety disorders (Kroenke, Spitzer, Williams, Monahan, & Lowe, 2007; Philbrick, Connelly, & Wofford, 1996). Prevalence among older

291

adults may even exceed these estimates; in a study of adults aged 65 years and older, Watts and colleagues (2002) found significant psychological distress in 48% of patients screened in primary care settings. Mental health concerns likely affect millions of older adults using primary care, and this number can be expected to grow significantly with the aging of the "baby boomer" generation.

Although prevalence rates in primary care settings are consistently high, primary care providers (PCPs) struggle to detect mental illness in their practices. A recent examination of a nationally representative dataset suggested that patients are diagnosed with depression or anxiety in only 1% to 4% of primary care visits (Jameson & Blank, 2010). Past findings suggest that diagnostic rates may be even lower among older adults (Stanley, Roberts, Bourland, & Novy, 2001). The low rates of mental illness detection in primary care settings may be attributed to short consultation times, focus on physical conditions, limited knowledge of diagnostic criteria and clinical indicators of mental health issues, limited resources for specialty referral or consultation, and nondisclosure of mental health symptomatology by patients (Geller, 1999; O'Connor, Rosewarne, & Bruce, 2001; Watts et al., 2002).

TREATMENT OF MENTAL HEALTH CONDITIONS IN PRIMARY CARE: A HEALTH SERVICES PERSPECTIVE

Unfortunately, research has demonstrated that detection of mental illness in primary care does not necessarily equate to adequate treatment for patients. A study of mixed-age adult primary care patients diagnosed with a depressive disorder revealed that less than half received treatment that met basic guidelines for quality care (Wells, Schoenbaum, Unützer, Lagomasino, & Rubenstein, 1999). These findings have been replicated by others (e.g., Jameson & Blank, 2010; Wang et al., 2005). Studies examining the treatment of anxiety in primary care have consistently shown that more than two-thirds of patients do not receive quality care (Jameson & Blank, 2010; Stein et al., 2004; Young, Klap, Sherbourne, & Wells, 2001). Taken as a whole, the findings suggest that current mental health treatment approaches in primary care are inadequate for most patients, and new approaches are necessary to successfully meet the needs of primary care patients.

In spite of the limited capacity to detect and treat mental illness in primary care settings, many older adults rely on primary care for mental health services. Older primary care patients often prefer mental health treatment in the primary care setting rather than receiving specialty care services (Bartels et al., 2004). Wang and colleagues (2005) found that adults aged 60 years and older were less likely to receive treatment through specialty mental health services, but treatment rates in primary care did not differ between older adults and their younger counterparts. Similarly, older Medicare recipients who received treatment for an anxiety disorder were much more likely to use services in primary care than specialty services (Ettner & Hermann, 1997). The tendency for older adults to use mental health treatment in primary care may reflect disparities in the availability, accessibility, and acceptability of specialty mental health care among this population. That is, older adults tend to be poorer and live in underserved areas (e.g., rural areas) and, therefore, may have more limited options for specialty mental health care services (Hanrahan & Sullivan-Marx, 2005). Moreover, the perceived stigma regarding specialty mental health care service use and negative treatment expectations may be more pronounced among older adults, particularly men and African Americans (Conner et al., 2010; Gum et al., 2006; Mackenzie, Gekoski, & Knox, 2006).

Most older individuals in primary care may prefer psychotherapy more than pharmacotherapy for the treatment of mental illness. In a large study of depressed older adults, 51% reported a preference for psychotherapy and 38% reported a preference for antidepressant medication (Unützer et al., 2003). Despite this preference, only 8% of those surveyed had received therapy in the past 3 months, and only 1% reported participation in 4 or more sessions in the past 3 months. The authors of this study cite access to mental health professionals trained in psychotherapy, high Medicare copayment rates for psychotherapy, and practical issues (e.g., the need for multiple in-person visits) as potential reasons for the mismatch between preference for and use of psychotherapy.

Older Adults and Chronic Illness

As medical technologies continue to advance life expectancy, older adults are increasingly facing chronic health conditions, which impact functional abilities and overall quality of life. These medical advances have shifted the leading causes of death from infectious diseases to chronic and degenerative diseases (e.g., heart disease, cancer, and stroke; Centers for Disease Control and Prevention [CDC] and The Merck Company Foundation, 2007). Almost 80% of older Americans are living with at least one chronic health condition and 50% have at least two more (CDC and The Merck Company Foundation). The impact of chronic health conditions has lead to an increase in the number of older adults who report being disabled due to physical or mental health difficulties (CDC).

The primary care setting represents the frontline of care for patients with these chronic health conditions. PCPs who treat the chronically ill often target the reduction of physical symptoms rather than "curing" the chronic disease itself. As such, guideline-recommended care for many chronic diseases runs contrary to the traditional "medical model" where patients are provided with medicine or surgical intervention to eliminate the problem. Because chronic diseases often have no cure, patient and providers are often left to negotiate symptom-based medication management with a heavy emphasis on lifestyle and behavioral health changes to reduce the impact of the chronic disease. Unfortunately, PCPs often are unable to provide the level of care necessary to aid patients in attaining lifestyle and behavioral health changes. Furthermore, patients are frequently unaccustomed to or uncomfortable with assuming an active role in treatment, and they may lack understanding of the behaviors necessary to "self-manage" their health conditions.

Facing a chronic illness often means that patients will struggle in multiple life domains. The cascading effects of a chronic health condition may lead to early retirement because of disability, dramatic changes in physical ability (decreased stamina, increased fatigue, increased pain), financial stress, strained family relationships, reduced ability to engage in prior hobbies or pleasant activities, and reduced social support networks. Ultimately, these changes may impact the patient's self-identity where the individual feels as though they are no longer the person they were prior to their illness.

The stress associated with a chronic illness places patients at increased risk for depression, anxiety, and physical health exacerbations. These stressors may manifest as diagnosable depression (major depressive disorder; dysthymia) or anxiety (e.g., generalized anxiety disorder, panic disorder), as subsyndromal depression or anxiety with significant symptom distress, or as physical health difficulties such as uncontrollable pain, physical symptoms, or reduced functional abilities. Notably, although the chronic disease itself may have no "cure," mental health treatments have the potential to address the emotional difficulties associated with a chronic disease and may, in fact, improve physical health and functioning (Cully, Paukert, Falco, & Stanley, 2009). Important mental health constructs for addressing the emotional and physical health needs of the medically ill include dealing with loss, increasing perceptions of control and predictability, and decreasing negative thinking related to self-identity and illness attributions.

COGNITIVE BEHAVIORAL THERAPY IN THE MEDICAL CARE SETTING

Evidence Base for Cognitive Behavioral Therapy in the Primary Care Setting

Surprisingly, few high-quality primary care CBT studies exist and even fewer trials have targeted older adults. Given the paucity of data on primary care CBT for older adults, the following section will not only examine the geriatric primary care CBT literature but will also broadly review the nongeriatric evidence for CBT in the primary care setting as well as CBT for specific medically ill patient populations.

Primary Care Cognitive Behavioral Therapy for Older Adults
Recent evidence suggests that CBT is an effective treatment for older primary care patients with depression (Laidlaw et al., 2008; Serfaty et al., 2009) and generalized anxiety disorder (Stanley et al., 2009; Wetherell et al., 2009).

Laidlaw et al. (2008) conducted a randomized controlled trial (RCT) of 44 older adult primary care patients recruited from multiple U.K. primary care settings. Enrolled patients met diagnostic criteria for mild-to-moderate major depressive disorder and were randomly assigned to either a treatment as usual (TAU) condition or CBT. CBT consisted of (on average) 8 sessions and was based on depression symptom reduction using problem-solving strategies. Outcomes suggested that fewer CBT patients met diagnostic criteria for depression at 3 months. Serfaty et al. (2009) enlisted 204 older adults with depression from the primary care setting and randomized participants to TAU, TAU plus talking control (TC), and TAU plus CBT. CBT was offered over a 4-month period and included, on average, 7 sessions. Depression symptoms at follow up favored CBT vs. TAU and TC. Lastly, Stanley et al. (2009) used 10 sessions of individual CBT to treat older adults from the primary care setting meeting diagnostic criteria for primary generalized anxiety disorder. In this large and well-controlled randomized trial, the authors found that CBT was superior to an enhanced usual care condition in terms of worry, severity, depression, and mental health quality of life.

Nongeriatric Primary Care Cognitive Behavioral Therapy Studies
Additional primary care-based studies have targeted depression and anxiety using large-scale collaborative care interventions where CBT (among other psychotherapy modalities such as problem solving therapy)

are embedded within a comprehensive mental health treatment approach. Frequently, CBT is paired with psychotropic medications and case management support services (Roy-Byrne et al., 2005). However, few of these trials have used CBT specifically and the contributions of the psychotherapeutic interventions are often difficult to determine from these multimodal treatment trials. In addition, none of these larger CBT collaborative trials have focused on the specific needs of older adults.

Results from these collaborative care intervention trials suggest strong support for the use of CBT in combination with psychotropic medications for conditions such as panic disorder and generalized anxiety disorder (Rollman et al., 2005; Roy-Byrne et al., 2005) as well as depression (Gaynes et al., 2009). Recent collaborative care efforts are expanding traditional face-to-face approaches and finding evidence for the efficacy of CBT using telephone (Ludman, Simon, Tutty, & Von Korff, 2007) and computer-assisted (Craske et al., 2009; Proudfoot et al., 2004) delivery methods.

Cognitive Behavioral Therapy in the Medically Ill

Preliminary evidence suggests that CBT is a potentially efficacious treatment for depression and anxiety in patients suffering from several common conditions, including diabetes mellitus, chronic lung disease (e.g., chronic obstructive pulmonary disease [COPD], bronchitis, emphysema, and asthma), gastrointestinal disorders (irritable bowel syndrome [IBS] and functional dyspepsia), cardiovascular conditions (e.g., acute coronary conditions and congestive heart failure), and chronic pain disorders (e.g., arthritis). Although an abundance of psychotherapy research exists within each of these broad medical domains, the number of high-quality, large-scale CBT trials is limited, and relatively no focused attention has been given to older adult patient populations.

However, because many older adults are afflicted with chronic health conditions, some studies included a high percentage of older adults and, therefore, the results may generalize to this population. Table 10.1 provides a listing of representative CBT studies by common health conditions and clinical foci, as well as a study design, a brief description of the CBT practices employed, and the general conclusions reached for each study.

Collectively, these clinical trials suggest the general utility of CBT for depression, anxiety, and pain within various medically ill patient populations. However, the impact of these CBT interventions on medical outcomes (e.g., physical health and overall quality of life)

TABLE 10.1   Cognitive Behavioral Therapy in the Medically Ill

Authors	Patients	Clinical Focus	Study Design	CBT Intervention	Main Outcomes
Lustman, Griffith, Freedland, Kissel, & Clouse, 1998	Diabetes ($n = 51$)	Depression	RCT; CBT plus education vs. usual care	Weekly group CBT with supportive diabetes education; 10 weeks	CBT achieved greater remission in depression relative to usual care
Snoek et al., 2008	Diabetes ($n = 86$)	Blood sugar control and depression	RCT; CBT vs. blood glucose awareness training	Six weekly group sessions	CBT lowered depression and improved HbA(1c) levels
Kunik et al., 2008	COPD ($n = 238$)	Depression, anxiety, and quality of life	RCT; CBT vs. education	Group CBT; eight sessions	CBT and education groups improved depression, anxiety and disease, and quality of life
Sharpe et al., 2001	Arthritis ($n = 53$)	Depression and others	RCT; CBT vs. usual care	Eight individual therapy sessions	CBT out-performed usual care for depression
Evers et al., 2002	Arthritis ($n = 64$)	Pain and disease impact	RCT; CBT vs. control condition	Tailored CBT; patient choice of modules; 10 bi-weekly sessions	CBT out-performed control condition on physical, emotional, and social functioning
Boyce, Talley, Balaam, Koloski, & Truman, 2003	IBS ($n = 105$)	IBS symptom severity	RCT; CBT vs. relaxation training vs. usual care	Weekly CBT; eight sessions	CBT and relaxation superior to usual care for IBS symptoms

(Continued)

TABLE 10.1   Cognitive Behavioral Therapy in the Medically Ill *(Continued)*

Authors	Patients	Clinical Focus	Study Design	CBT Intervention	Main Outcomes
Kennedy et al., 2005	IBS primary care (*n* = 149)	IBS symptom severity	RCT; CBT plus meds vs. meds alone	Six individual sessions	CBT plus meds better than meds alone at 6 months
Drossman et al., 2003	Functional bowel (*n* = 431)	Multiple measures—primary physical/ functional	RCT; CBT vs. education	12 weekly individual sessions	CBT outperformed usual care on composite score
Berkman et al., 2003	Myocardial infarction (*n* = 2481)	Depression	RCT; CBT plus SSRI vs. usual care	Individual; 11 sessions; 6 months	CBT outperformed usual care for depression

Note. CBT = cognitive behavioral therapy; COPD = chronic obstructive pulmonary disease; HbA(1c) = hemoglobin A1c; IBS = irritable bowel syndrome; meds = medicines; *n* = sample size with illness; RCT = randomized controlled trial; SSRI = selective serotonin reuptake inhibitor.

remains unclear. Additionally, many of these trials have applied traditional CBT procedures with limited or no modification to the unique needs of the medically ill patients investigated. Preliminary data from studies of specifically adapted CBT procedures (e.g., protocols with attention to physical health functioning and self-management) suggest that such adaptations may lead to improvements in both mental and physical functioning (Cully et al., 2009; Evers, Kraaimaat, van Riel, & de Jong, 2002). Additional high-quality RCTs are indicated, and focused adaptations for older adults may be required.

MODELS OF PRIMARY CARE INTEGRATION

Expectations of the mental health care provider in primary care can vary widely, depending on the integration model implemented. Zeiss and Karlin (2008) describe three models of mental health/primary care integration: the collaborative care/colocated model, the care management model, and the blended model.

The *collaborative care* (or colocated) *model* is characterized by the physical presence of a mental health provider, often a psychologist or social worker, within the primary care clinic who actively works with medical professionals on issues of patient care. In addition to providing short-term psychotherapies such as CBT, the mental health provider may be expected to provide "curbside" consults to PCPs (i.e., meet with providers and/or patients during a primary care visit to discuss mental and behavioral health issues), follow up with patients who screen positive for mental health concerns, and provide brief assessments and mental health triage for patients.

In the *care management model,* mental health providers (often registered nurses with specialized mental health training) designated as "care managers" assess and triage patients referred by PCPs. If the decision is made to treat the patient within the primary care setting, a treatment plan is formulated by the PCP. The care manager follows up with the patient regularly, often by phone, to support adherence, provide psychoeducation and problem-solving therapy, and monitor symptom severity and medication tolerance. If the patient does not improve or worsens, the care manager re-refers the patient to the PCP for adjustment of the treatment plan. The care management model is often implemented to improve treatment for a specific disorder such as depression (e.g., the TIDES program; Felker et al., 2006).

The *blended model* combines features of both the collaborative care model and the care management model. Such models often include immediate access to mental health providers (as in the collaborative care model) as well as enhanced follow up and monitoring of pharmacotherapy (as in the care management model). The VA health system is currently working to implement the blended model of care in a large number of its medical centers (Zeiss & Karlin, 2008).

The models described by Zeiss and Karlin (2008) differ in their emphases on CBT-based treatment (i.e., whether CBT is offered and within what capacity it is delivered). Although the care management model often incorporates elements of CBT into typical practice patterns, individual psychotherapy is not a primary focus of care. The collaborative care model of integration may offer a broader range of opportunities to practice CBT with various older patients. However, the emphasis on the provision of individual psychotherapy can vary widely between primary care practices operating under the same model as well (Robinson & Strosahl, 2009). It is notable that even within a treatment model, CBT providers may vary markedly in the types of services they render. For example, CBT providers may spend much of their time working closely with PCPs to manage difficult patients and help with lifestyle or behavioral health changes. In contrast, others may focus on traditional ambulatory mental health care via time-limited treatments for depression, anxiety, and substance abuse. Still others may spend most of their time performing assessments and triaging patients. To establish an effective practice, CBT providers must understand the mission or goals of the treatment program they work in and adapt their practice patterns accordingly.

Another factor which may affect emphasis on the delivery of CBT is the funding source for the practitioner's salary. Practitioner salaries that come from a medicine or primary care source may be more accepting of a health or medical approach, whereas salary support from a mental health service may lead to implementation of more traditional ambulatory mental health services (e.g., colocated care rather than fully integrated collaborative care models). Finally, obtaining reimbursement for activities other than therapy can present a serious challenge (Robinson & Strosahl, 2009). Practitioners are advised to understand the reimbursement rates and the details associated with their "deliverables" to effectively meet the mission and care expectations of the clinic.

Finally, the type of patients seen within primary care is directly related to the model and referral sources. As such, practitioners specializing in geriatric patient populations who wish to generate referrals would be encouraged to cultivate good working relationships with PCPs and other frontline providers with similar interests. When cultivating such referral networks, practitioners would be advised to explicitly state what services they can offer and to ensure that the referring provider is given regular updates on the patient's progress. Effective communication between the PCP and mental health provider are likely to produce more focused referrals and positive treatment outcomes, and can help to maintain relationships over the long term.

ADAPTING COGNITIVE BEHAVIORAL THERAPY TO THE PRIMARY CARE SETTING

Overview of Cognitive Behavioral Therapy in Primary Care

CBT as practiced in primary care is typically shorter in duration (i.e., 1–8 sessions) than in traditional practice. Given the short duration of contact, goals of treatment often center on symptom relief through the development of *self-management skills*: skills to effectively manage symptoms of psychological distress and/or medical conditions independently. These characteristics lend themselves to a modularized structure of treatment (e.g., Cully et al., 2009; Stanley et al., 2009), in which the patient and therapist work together to select several potential skill sets to meet the individual needs of the patient.

Techniques for teaching self-management skills are commonly included in CBT treatment protocols in more traditional mental health settings. However, the brevity of the treatment, patient characteristics, and demands of the setting often require that these techniques be adapted. The following section is intended to provide an overview of some of the issues encountered in primary care that encourage the adaptation of "standard" CBT techniques. Furthermore, because of the paucity of research on the use of CBT with older primary care patients, the succeeding recommendations are largely based on the nongeriatric studies and the clinical and research experiences of the authors.

Engaging Primary Care Patients in Cognitive Behavioral Therapy

Engaging patients in treatment is an especially important consideration in the primary care environment, as patients often do not expect to be referred to a mental health professional during a primary care visit. Patients may interpret a referral to a psychologist or social worker to imply that "my doctor thinks my condition is all in my head," or provide a response such as, "I'm not crazy." Such assumptions may be especially common among older patients who may be less accustomed to seeing a mental health presence in a medical setting, and may lead patients to resist participation in CBT-based interventions.

Demonstrating an established relationship between the PCP and mental health provider can help to allay patients' reservations regarding CBT. Therefore, "cold hand-offs" (i.e., referral with no further explanation or support from the PCP) should be avoided to the extent possible. Ideally, the mental health provider is given the opportunity to initially meet with the PCP and patient jointly to discuss presenting problems and treatment options (i.e., a "warm hand-off"). However, given the busy environment of most primary care practices, this is often not possible. A less time-intensive approach is to provide referring PCPs with "talking points" to encourage patients to consider CBT. Patients may feel more comfortable using a referral if the PCP describes his or her past experiences with the provider, outlines the typical focus of treatment, and discusses the treatment in terms of benefits in physical and mental functioning and symptom reduction. PCPs who provide detailed information about the available treatment options may help to normalize the use of mental health services and provide hope and encouragement to their patients.

Additionally, mental health providers should exercise caution in the choice of language used to introduce the available services and ask their PCP counterparts to do the same. A focus on overall wellness (rather than mental illness) can be seen as more palatable to older patients who might be suspicious of a mental health referral. Moreover, CBT often involves the development of skills to cope with physical health issues in addition to mental health difficulties. Emphasizing a broader approach to self-management skill development may help patients view mental health services as part of their broader care management plan.

Case Conceptualization and Goal Setting

Case conceptualization is a framework that is used to:

1. Understand the patient and his/her current problems;
2. Inform treatment and intervention techniques; and
3. Serves as a foundation to assess patient change/progress.

Case conceptualization also aids in establishing rapport and a sense of hope for patients entering therapy and, therefore, may be particularly important to allay the concerns of older primary care patients. Effective case conceptualization aids the therapist and patient in the establishment of collaborative treatment goals, and can also serve to maintain a therapeutic focus and provide allowances for the therapist to redirect patients when ancillary problems arise that distract from the core goals.

Developing a case conceptualization in the primary care setting is much the same as it is for CBT in other settings. However, constraints of the primary care setting require slight modifications. For example, because many CBT treatments in the primary care setting are brief in duration, case conceptualization becomes even more important earlier in the course of a treatment. Therefore, rapid conceptualization is often necessary and clinicians may feel particularly pressed to form clinical hypotheses with limited information. This necessitates brief accurate assessment of presenting problems with attention to symptomatology related to the presenting problem, comorbid medical conditions, and environmental stressors. An example of a template for a brief assessment is provided in the Appendix to this chapter.

Practitioners are encouraged to set preliminary goals as early as possible (during sessions 1 or 2) and subsequently modify goals when additional information becomes available throughout the course of treatment. Because of the abbreviated nature of treatment, goals should be reasonable, measurable, and as simple as possible. Often, this means a symptom reduction approach (as opposed to a curative approach), which works well within the general milieu of primary care. Brief self-report measures completed as part of each session can aid in the ongoing assessment functioning and therapeutic progress. Table 10.2 provides examples of brief self-report measures that may be helpful in the primary care setting.

TABLE 10.2 Examples of Self-Report Measures for Use With Older Primary Care Patients

Scale Name	Author	Description
Patient Health Questionnaire-9 (PHQ-9)	Kroenke, Spitzer, & Williams, 2001	Nine-item measure of depressive symptomatology and severity designed for use in primary care settings; based on *DSM-IV* criteria for major depressive disorder.
The Alcohol Use Disorders Identification Test (AUDIT)	Saunders, Aasland, Babor, de la Fuente, & Grant, 1993	Ten-item measure designed to detect harmful alcohol use in primary care settings.
Generalized Anxiety Disorder Scale (GAD-7)	Spitzer, Kroenke, Williams, & Löwe, 2006	Seven-item measure of generalized anxiety disorder (GAD) symptomatology and severity; based on *DSM-IV* criteria for GAD.
Penn State Worry Questionnaire-Abbreviated (PSWQ-A)	Hopko et al., 2003	Eight-item measure of pathological worry; has been validated in samples of older adults (Crittendon & Hopko, 2006).
Numeric Rating Scale (NRS-11)	Price, Bush, Long, & Harkins, 1994	One-item subjective measure of pain, rated on a 0–10 numeric rating scale.
Geriatric Depression Scale (GDS-15)	D'Ath, Katona, Mullan, Evans, & Katona, 1994	Fifteen-item measure of depressive symptomatology developed for use with geriatric patients in primary care; uses a dichotomous (yes/no) response scale.
Geriatric Anxiety Inventory (GAI)	Pachana et al., 2007	Twenty-item measure of dimensional anxiety developed for use in older adults; uses dichotomous (yes/no) response scale.
The Pittsburgh Sleep Quality Index (PSQI)	Buysse, Reynolds, Monk, Berman, & Kupfer, 1989	Nineteen-item measure of sleep quality over the prior month; has been used with older primary care patients (Stanley et al., 2003b).
Panic Disorder Self-Report (PDSR)	Newman, Holmes, Zuellig, Kachin, & Behar, 2006	Twenty-item measure of panic disorder symptomatology based on *DSM-IV* criteria; uses dichotomous (yes/no) response scale.

Note. DSM-IV = Diagnostic and Statistical Manual of Mental Disorders, 4th edition.

The use of case conceptualization with older adults requires additional modifications, depending on the specific needs of the patient. For example, some older adults may be therapy naïve and, therefore, require the use of simple, wellness-focused, nonmental health language. Multiple methods of instruction (e.g., verbal and written) on the principles of CBT and the conceptualization from the therapist may also help patients understand the treatment model and rationale.

Most patients will present with multiple symptoms and/or difficulties. CBT therapists are encouraged to obtain as complete a list from the patient as possible and then work with the patient to prioritize their concerns for treatment. As a general rule, the provision of CBT in the primary care setting should be restricted to intrapersonal patient issues and avoid interpersonal issues that often require prolonged treatment. In addition, patients with serious mental illness (e.g., schizophrenia, bipolar, dementia, etc.) and patients with long-standing mental health issues such as posttraumatic stress disorder and/or recurrent moderate/severe major depression are likely most appropriately treated within a specialty mental health treatment program.

Behavioral Interventions

Behavioral Activation
Behavioral activation includes a set of procedures and techniques aimed at increasing patient activity and access to reinforcing situations that improve mood and functioning. From this behavioral standpoint, depression, for example, contains a host of characteristics that function to maintain depressive affect (e.g., passivity, fatigue, feelings of hopelessness) and decrease chances of adaptive coping by increasing avoidance. Further, severe limitation of physical activity is often a by-product of avoidance, and may have negative consequences on health status. Reintroducing pleasant events (one form of behavioral activation) can serve to improve mood in many different ways: (a) reversing avoidance, (b) increasing physical activity and thus, physical health, (c) increasing self-confidence, and (d) increasing feelings of usefulness and purpose. Recent empirical evidence suggests that behavioral interventions improve mood symptoms but also reduce maladaptive thought patterns (Jacobson, Martell, & Dimidjian, 2001).

Given these benefits, behavioral activation can be a very useful tool in the primary care setting. However, because of the poor physical health of many older primary care patients, behavioral activation may require adaptation. Patients may focus on activities that they used to enjoy, but are no longer able to engage in because of physical disability. Such focus can have a deleterious effect on the patient's sense of control and self-confidence. Activities should be structured in such a way that they are enjoyable to the patient, but avoid exacerbation of physical conditions. Incorporating pacing skills into behavioral activation assignments can accomplish this in many situations (e.g., asking a patient to plant a single flower bed rather than all of the beds in the yard). Additionally, patients may receive an added benefit by generalizing the pacing skills to other areas of functioning. In other situations, behavioral activation may require engagement in new activities altogether. Brainstorming new activities based on existing interests can often yield appealing activities for behavioral activation assignments. For example, a jogger who is no longer able to run may be able to discern meaning from participating as a trainer or coach for other joggers to remain active in the sport. It is also important to plan behavioral activation assignments carefully. Identifying physical and environmental barriers and generating possible solutions in the session can help patients avoid frustration as they attempt to complete homework assignments. Enlisting the support of others and/or identifying facilitators can also improve the chances of treatment success while reducing isolation and stress.

Relaxation

Relaxation techniques consist of a collection of psychotherapeutic techniques designed to reduce tension, stress, worry, and/or anxiety. Relaxation techniques vary in their focus (e.g., physical sensations or changes in cognition/thoughts) and can be selected based on presenting difficulties, as well as patient preferences. Relaxation techniques are important for brief therapy for several reasons. First, they focus on skills that alleviate stress, anxiety, worry, and tension that are often debilitating and interfere with patient functioning. Second, stress, anxiety, worry, and tension are often very uncomfortable for patients, and providing help to alleviate their distress can go a long way toward increasing positive treatment expectations and rapport. Relaxation techniques are easily conveyed as a method of increasing control and often do not include a direct discussion of mental health difficulties, which can be important for some patients who are concerned about mental health stigma. Finally, relaxation techniques are generally easy to teach and learn. For these reasons, it is often advantageous to teach these techniques early in the treatment to give patients an easy-to-learn, yet highly effective, skill set.

Selection of appropriate relaxation requires knowledge of the patient's physical conditions. Because relaxation techniques such as progressive muscle relaxation and deep breathing exercises have a physical component, they may be contraindicated for patients with some conditions. Patients are often asked to tense and release muscle groups during progressive muscle relaxation, which could cause pain in individuals with arthritis or back pain. Older adults are also particularly susceptible to muscle cramping especially when tensing muscles such as toes, calves, and hands. Likewise, deep breathing exercises may exacerbate pulmonary conditions such as asthma, emphysema, or chronic obstructive pulmonary disorder. Although these dangers may be readily apparent to the therapist, patients may not understand these risks or may decide to complete the exercise to appease the therapist. Therefore, it is suggested that patients are directly asked about conditions that may be worsened by relaxation exercises. The therapist may modify relaxation techniques (e.g., omitting certain muscle groups from progressive muscle relaxation), reduce the length or pacing of deep breathing, or select alternative techniques using more cognitive methods (e.g., guided imagery, grounding exercises) based on this information.

Cognitive Interventions

Identifying and modifying maladaptive thoughts and beliefs are core skills for cognitive behavioral therapists. The cognitive model posits that the following three layers of cognitive dysfunction exist in individuals struggling with psychological problems:

1. Automatic thoughts,
2. Intermediate beliefs, and
3. Core beliefs (Beck, 1995).

Automatic thoughts often reflect immediate evaluations of a specific situation and may occur below the level of conscious awareness. *Intermediate beliefs* reflect more general rules and attitudes that influence our evaluation of specific situations. *Core beliefs* are more global beliefs about the self, and generally reflect broad views of self-efficacy (e.g., "I'm incompetent") and relationships with others (e.g., "I'm unlovable"). These core beliefs are often long standing, rigid, and difficult to modify.

In more traditional applications of CBT, the therapist often works toward uncovering and modifying maladaptive core beliefs. Core beliefs can be revealed through the identification of patterns of automatic thoughts and intermediate beliefs. However, the time-limited nature of the work often means that the depth of the cognitive interventions must be restricted. For example, within brief treatments, it is unlikely that patient core beliefs can be modified in 4 to 8 sessions of treatment. Targeting more surface-level automatic thoughts and possibly intermediate beliefs may serve as viable and meaningful goals. From our experiences, effective CBT, which addresses automatic thoughts and intermediate dysfunctional thinking can significantly improve core beliefs (but may not necessarily completely remove the core dysfunctional thinking).

Cognitive interventions in the primary care settings often focus on maladaptive automatic thoughts and intermediate beliefs related to the relationship between the patient's health conditions and psychological distress. Patients may view psychological distress as inseparable from a physical health condition and, therefore, the outcome may be believed to be completely dependent on the course of the physical illness. Moreover, they may not understand the impact that psychological distress may have on physical functioning and symptom severity. These external attributions of control often result in feelings of hopelessness and helplessness and may be reflected in beliefs such as, "I will only feel better if my medical condition improves," or, "How can I feel better when I am in this much pain?" Other patients may have maladaptive attributions related to the causes of their medical illness (e.g., "God is punishing me for not taking better care of my body."). And because the impact of a chronic physical condition can be far-reaching, patients may also generate problematic thoughts about their core sense of self (e.g., "I am no longer the person I used to be. I am a burden on my family.").

Identifying and challenging cognitive distortions regarding the relationship between physical and mental health as well as the patient's personal meaning of a physical health condition is often necessary to effectively treat older adults in the primary care setting. Highlighting evidence that the patient's mood fluctuates in spite of the consistent presence of physical symptomatology can help patients to rethink the relationship between mood and physical functioning. Further, demonstrating the influence of cognition on the experience of pain or illness (i.e., that this relationship is bidirectional) may also help to challenge this relationship. Homework assignments that encourage behavioral activation can help support these aims by providing concrete, experiential evidence for accurate beliefs regarding the mental–physical health relationship, and may be especially productive for patients struggling with concepts related to identity and feelings of usefulness.

When attempting cognitive interventions with medically ill primary care patients, it is helpful to obtain a basic understanding of the physical condition before active treatment is started. Knowledge of the course and symptoms, as well as the patient's personal experiences and prognosis, can help distinguish symptoms of the condition from psychopathological sequelae, as these sometimes overlap (e.g., fatigue in depression and diabetes mellitus). Such information can help the provider to establish realistic goals for treatment and distinguish realistic beliefs from maladaptive, inaccurate beliefs about the condition.

CASE EXAMPLE

Dana, a 68-year-old retired elementary school teacher, was diagnosed with Type II diabetes 4 years ago and has had difficulties maintaining her health since that time. She has suffered bouts of severe fatigue and dizziness. Dana says that she was "a born teacher," but her worsening health forced her to retire 2 years ago. Since this time, she has become increasingly inactive because "there's no longer any point to getting out of bed in the morning." Dana says that she was a very avid gardener but has lost the interest and energy to maintain her garden. She says that her depression has been worsened by her deteriorating health recently.

Dana was referred by her primary care provider, who informed her that a health psychologist was available to help her cope with the stress of retirement and manage the symptoms of her diabetes. She reluctantly agreed to meet with the psychologist. During the first session, the psychologist highlighted experiences that illustrated the relationship between psychological health, physical functioning, and overall wellness. Short-term CBT was presented as a skills-based approach to managing her diabetes more effectively and improving her mood and functioning. Preliminary goals for the treatment were outlined, and included the improved blood glucose monitoring (to avoid marked fluctuations in her blood glucose levels) and the reduction of depressive symptomatology as rated on the Geriatric Depression Scale (GDS). Depressive symptoms were also to be monitored based on the patient's positive mood and level of engagement in daily and pleasurable activities. Dana agreed to participate in the treatment, and appeared more hopeful about her ability to cope with her situation. She was interested in "getting her life back" and feeling a renewed "sense of purpose and hope."

The psychologist conceptualized Dana's depression as a response to the lifestyle changes brought about by her diabetes including her recent retirement. Dana also appeared to struggle with how to change her thoughts and behaviors to adjust to her new medical condition and retirement status. She appeared to have little belief that she had any control over her health and her ability to find meaning in her life. A treatment plan was designed to aid her adjustment by targeting dysfunctional thoughts about losing meaning in her life and exploring and increasing the things that she enjoyed. Further, the treatment plan included problem-solving skills to help her manage diabetes.

Dana participated in 6 sessions of therapy. The first two sessions were used to plan behavioral activation exercises, with a focus on preparing her garden for spring planting. Given her poor physical health, special attention was paid to the pacing of these activities; she was provided with techniques to monitor her physical functioning and fatigue level. She was able to complete most of the behavioral goals that she set for the exercise. In subsequent discussions of her experiences, her therapist pointed out that Dana often employed all-or-nothing thinking when she considered taking on new activities. Often, these manifested in automatic thoughts such as, "I can't do any work because of my diabetes." The following two sessions were spent teaching Dana to identify and challenge these beliefs, with moderately successful results. Additionally, it was revealed that she had difficulty following a diet that promoted healthy blood glucose levels, often indulging in sweets before bed. The final sessions were spent educating Dana on the effects of this behavior on her health and helping her to consider the advantages and disadvantages of these behaviors. She came to realize that indulging in sweets was costing her more than she realized in terms of functioning and health. With the help of the therapist, she was able to identify triggers for indulging in sweets (loneliness, boredom) and develop alternative plans of action (calling a friend, eating a piece of fruit).

By the end of the treatment, Dana's GDS score indicated a mild/moderate level of depression, down from a moderate/severe level. She reported a noticeable increase in her energy level and feeling more satisfied with her life. She also reported feeling that she had better control of her diabetes. She was encouraged to continue looking for ways to apply the skills discussed in therapy to other areas of her life (e.g., finding opportunities to teach in local community centers, identifying and challenging automatic thoughts related to loneliness).

CONCLUSIONS

Significant psychological distress is very common among older adults in the primary care setting, and often, these individuals suffer from one or more medical conditions adding complexity to the assessment of treatment of these patients. Unfortunately, common psychological disorders such as depression and anxiety are infrequently recognized, and detection often does not lead to effective treatment for older adults. Additionally, many chronic medical conditions require significant lifestyle changes to manage effectively, and the behavioral components of these lifestyle changes are often not adequately addressed in routine primary care. From a health services perspective, the integration of cognitive behavioral practice into primary care settings represents an opportunity to improve the accessibility, acceptability, and quality of mental health services for older patients, as well as improve their physical functioning and quality of life for many older adults.

Although some foundation has been laid for the use of CBT interventions in older primary care patients, a tremendous amount of work remains if the CBT's utility is to be fully realized in the primary care setting. Extent literature suggests that CBT has the potential to be a highly effective treatment for older adults in the primary care setting suffering from depression, anxiety, and/or health-related distress. However, much of this work has examined traditional CBT approaches that have been transported to primary care settings. Sustainable utilization of CBT in primary care will require significant adaptation to fit with the demands of the setting and the characteristics of older patients. Particular attention needs to be paid to these aspects of practice if CBT is to be effectively delivered to older patients in primary care. Modularized approaches to CBT are amenable to such adaptations, but more systematic investigations are needed. There is also a need for additional research and implementation studies, which target the use of CBT for the medically ill. Further, studies employing dismantling designs would be helpful in determining the "active ingredients" of CBT as applied to older primary care patients and would inform the design of short-term interventions suitable for primary care practice. Effectiveness trials are also needed to ensure that CBT can be adapted successfully to nonacademic primary care settings. Finally, future studies of all stripes should strive to evaluate not only improvement on mental health indicators, but also the impact CBT may have on medical issues such as physical symptoms and quality of life.

REFERENCES

Bartels, S. J., Coakley, E. H., Zubritsky, C., Ware, J. H., Miles, K. M., Areán, P. A., et al. (2004). Improving access to geriatric mental health services: A randomized trial comparing treatment engagement with integrated versus enhanced referral care for depression, anxiety, and at-risk alcohol use. *American Journal of Psychiatry, 161,* 1455–1462.

Beck, J. S. (1995). *Cognitive therapy: Basics and beyond.* New York, NY: Guilford Press.

Berkman, L. F., Blumenthal, J., Burg, M., Carney R. M., Catellier, D., Cowan, M. J., et al. (2003). Effects of treating depression and low perceived social support on clinical events after myocardial infarction: The Enhancing Recovery in Coronary Heart Disease Patients (ENRICHD) randomized trial. *Journal of the American Medical Association, 289,* 3106–3116.

Boyce, P. M., Talley, N. J., Balaam, B., Koloski, N. A., & Truman, G. (2003). A randomized controlled trial of cognitive behavior therapy, relaxation training, and routine clinical care for the irritable bowel syndrome. *The American Journal of Gastroenterology, 98,* 2209–2218.

Buysse, D. J., Reynolds, C. F. III, Monk, T. H., Berman, S. R., & Kupfer, D. J. (1989). The Pittsburgh Sleep Quality Index: A new instrument for psychiatric practice and research. *Psychiatry Research, 28,* 193–213.

Centers for Disease Control and Prevention and The Merck Company Foundation. (2007). The State of Aging and Health in America 2007. Whitehouse Station, NJ: The Merck Company Foundation. Available at http://www.cdc.gov/aging/pdf/saha_2007.pdf

Conner K. O., Copeland, V. C., Grote, N. K., Koeske, G., Rosen, D., Reynolds, C. F., et al. (2010). Mental health treatment seeking among older adults with depression: The impact of stigma and race. *American Journal of Geriatric Psychiatry, 18*(6), 531–543.

Craske, M. G., Rose, R. D., Lang, A., Welch, S. S., Campbell-Sills, L., Sullivan, G., et al. (2009). Computer-assisted delivery of cognitive behavioral therapy for anxiety disorders in primary care settings. *Depression and Anxiety, 26,* 235–242.

Crittendon, J. & Hopko, D. R. (2006). Assessing worry in older and younger adults: Psychometric properties of an abbreviated Penn State Worry Questionnaire (PSWQ-A). *Journal of Anxiety Disorders, 20,* 1036–1054.

Cully, J. A., Paukert, A., Falco, J., & Stanley, M. A. (2009). Cognitive behavioral therapy: Innovations for cardiopulmonary patients with depression and anxiety. *Cognitive Behavioral Practice, 16,* 394–407.

D'Ath, P., Katona, P., Mullan, E., Evans, S., & Katona, C. (1994) Screening, detection, and management of depression in elderly primary care attenders. I: The acceptability and performance of the 15 item Geriatric Depression Scale (GDS15) and the development of short versions. *Family Practice, 11,* 260–266.

Drossman, D. A., Toner, B. B., Whitehead, W. E., Diamant, N. E., Dalton, C. B., Duncan, S., et al. (2003). Cognitive behavioral therapy versus education and desipramine versus placebo for moderate to severe functional bowel disorders. *Gastroenterology, 125,* 19–31.

Ettner, S. L., & Hermann R. C. (1997). Provider specialty choice among Medicare beneficiaries treated for psychiatric disorders. *Health Care Financing Review, 18*, 43–59.

Evers, A. W. M., Kraaimaat, F. W., van Riel, P., & de Jong, A. J. L. (2002). Tailored cognitive behavioral therapy in early rheumatoid arthritis for patients at risk: A randomized controlled trial. *Pain, 100*, 141–153.

Felker, B. L., Chaney, E., Rubenstein, L. V., Bonner, L. M., Yano, E. M., Parker, L. E., et al. (2006). Developing effective collaboration between primary care and mental health providers. *Primary Care Companion to the Journal of Clinical Psychiatry, 8*, 12–16.

Gaynes, B. N., Warden, D., Trivedi, M. H., Wisniewski, S. R., Fava, M., & Rush, A. J. (2009). What did STAR*D teach us? Results from a large-scale, practical, clinical trial for patients with depression. *Psychiatric Services, 60*, 1439–1445.

Geller, J. M. (1999). Rural primary care providers' perceptions of their roles in the provision of mental health services: Voices from the plains. *Journal of Rural Health, 15*, 326–334.

Gum, A. M., Areán, P. A., Hunkeler, E., Tang, L., Katon, W., Hitchcock, P., et al. (2006). Depression treatment preferences in older primary care patients. *The Gerontologist, 46*, 14–22.

Hanrahan, N. P., & Sullivan-Marx, E. M. (2005). Practice patterns and potential solutions to the shortage of providers of older adult mental health services. *Policy, Politics, and Nursing Practice, 6*, 236–245.

Hopko, D. R., Stanley, M. A., Reas, D. L., Wetherell, J. L., Beck, J. G., Novy, D. M. et al. (2003). Assessing worry in older adults: Confirmatory factor analysis of the Penn State Worry Questionnaire and psychometric properties of an abbreviated model. *Psychological Assessment, 15*, 173–183.

Jacobson, N. S., Martell, C. R., & Dimidjian, S. (2001). Behavioral activation treatment for depression: Returning to contextual roots. *Clinical Psychology: Science and Practice, 8*, 255–270.

Jameson, J. P., & Blank, M. B. (2010). Diagnosis and treatment of depression and anxiety in rural and nonrural primary care: National Survey Results. *Psychiatric Services, 61*(6), 624–627.

Kennedy, T., Jones, R., Darnley, S., Seed, P., Wessely, S., & Chandler, T. (2005). Cognitive behavior therapy in addition to antispasmodic treatment for irritable bowel syndrome in primary care: A randomised controlled trial. *British Medical Journal, 331*, 435.

Kroenke, K., Spitzer, R. L., & Williams, J. B. (2001). The PHQ-9: Validity of a brief depression severity measure. *Journal of General Internal Medicine, 16*, 606–613.

Kroenke, K., Spitzer, R. L., Williams, J. B., Monahan, P. O., & Lowe, B. (2007). Anxiety disorders in primary care: Prevalence, impairment, comorbidity, and detection. *Annals of Internal Medicine, 146*, 317–325.

Kunik, M. E., Veazey, C., Cully, J. A., Souchek, J., Graham, D. P., Hopko, D., et al. (2008). COPD education and cognitive behavioral therapy group treatment for clinically significant symptoms of depression and anxiety in COPD patients: A randomized controlled trial. *Psychological Medicine, 38*, 385–396.

Laidlaw, K., Davidson, K., Toner, H., Jackson, G., Clark, S., Law, J., et al. (2008). A randomised controlled trial of cognitive behaviour therapy vs. treatment as usual in the treatment of mild to moderate late life depression. *International Journal of Geriatric Psychiatry, 23,* 843–850.

Ludman, E. J., Simon, G. E., Tutty, S., & Von Korff, M. (2007). A randomized trial of telephone psychotherapy and pharmacotherapy for depression: Continuation and durability of effects. *Journal of Consulting and Clinical Psychology, 75,* 257–266.

Lustman, P. J., Griffith, L. S., Freedland, K. E., Kissel, S. S., & Clouse, R. E. (1998). Cognitive behavior therapy for depression in type 2 diabetes mellitus: A randomized, controlled trial. *Annals of Internal Medicine, 129,* 613–621.

Mackenzie, C. S., Gekoski, W. L., & Knox, V. J. (2006). Age, gender, and the underutilization of mental health services: The influence of help-seeking attitudes. *Aging and Mental Health, 10,* 574–582.

McQuaid, J. R., Stein, M. B., Laffaye, C., & McCahill, M. E. (1999). Depression in a primary care clinic: The prevalence and impact of an unrecognized disorder. *Journal of Affective Disorders, 55,* 1–10.

Newman, M. G., Holmes, M., Zuellig, A. R., Kachin, K. E., & Behar, E. (2006). The reliability and validity of the panic disorder self-report: A new diagnostic screening measure of panic disorder. *Psychological Assessment, 18,* 49–61.

O'Connor, D. W., Rosewarne, R., & Bruce, A. (2001). Depression in primary care 1: Elderly patients' disclosure of depressive symptoms to their doctors. *International Psychogeriatrics, 13,* 359–365.

Pachana, N. A., Byrne, G. J., Siddle, H., Koloski, N., Harley, E., & Arnold, E. (2007). Development and validation of the Geriatric Anxiety Inventory. *International Psychogeriatrics, 19,* 103–114.

Philbrick, J. T., Connelly, J. E., & Wofford, A. B. (1996). The prevalence of mental disorders in rural office practice. *Journal of General Internal Medicine, 11,* 9–15.

Price, D. D., Bush, F. M., Long, S., & Harkins, S. W. (1994). A comparison of pain measurement characteristics of mechanical visual analogue and simple numerical rating scales. *Pain, 56,* 217–226.

Proudfoot, J., Ryden, C., Everitt, B., Shapiro, D. A., Goldberg, D., Mann, A., et.al. (2004). Clinical efficacy of computerised cognitive behavioural therapy for anxiety and depression in primary care: Randomised controlled trial. *British Journal of Psychiatry, 185,* 46–54.

Robinson, P. J., & Strosahl, K. D. (2009). Behavioral health consultation and primary care: Lessons learned. *Journal of Clinical Psychology in Medical Settings, 16,* 58–71.

Rollman, B. L., Belnap, B. H., Mazumdar, S., Houck, P. R., Zhu, F., Gardner, W., et al. (2005). A randomized trial to improve the quality of treatment for panic and generalized anxiety disorders in primary care. *Archives of General Psychiatry, 62,* 1332–1341.

Roy-Byrne, P. P., Craske, M. G., Stein, M. B., Sullivan, G., Bystritsky, A., Katon, W., et al. (2005). A randomized effectiveness trial of cognitive behavioral therapy and medication for primary care panic disorder. *Archives of General Psychiatry, 62,* 290–298.

Saunders, J. B., Aasland, O. G., Babor, T. F., de la Fuente, J. R., & Grant, M. (1993). Development of the Alcohol Use Disorders Identification Test (AUDIT): WHO collaborative project on early detection of persons with harmful alcohol consumption. II. *Addiction, 88,* 791–804.

Serfaty, M. A., Haworth, D., Blanchard, M., Buszewicz, M., Murad, S., & King, M. (2009). Clinical effectiveness of individual cognitive behavioral therapy for depressed older people in primary care: A randomized controlled trial. *Archives of General Psychiatry, 66,* 1332–1340.

Sharpe, L., Sensky, T., Timberlake, N., Ryan, B., Brewin, C. R., & Allard, S. (2001). A blind, randomized, controlled trial of cognitive behavioural intervention for patients with recent onset rheumatoid arthritis: Preventing psychological and physical morbidity. *Pain, 89,* 275–283.

Snoek, F. J., van der Ven, N. C., Twisk, J. W., Hogenelst, M. H., Tromp-Wever, A. M., van der Ploeg, H. M., Heine, R. J. (2008). Cognitive behavioral therapy (CBT) compared with blood glucose awareness training (BGAT) in poorly controlled Type 1 diabetic patients: Long-term effects on HbA moderated by depression. A randomized controlled trial. *Diabetic Medicine, 25,* 1337–1342.

Spitzer, R. L., Kroenke, K., Williams, J. B., & Löwe, B. (2006). A brief measure for assessing generalized anxiety disorder: The GAD-7. *Archives of Internal Medicine, 166,* 1092–1097.

Spitzer, R. L., Williams, J. B., Kroenke, K., Linzer, M., deGruy, F. V. III, Hahn, S. R., et al. (1994). Utility of a new procedure for diagnosing mental disorders in primary care: The PRIME-MD 1000 study. *Journal of the American Medical Association, 272,* 1749–1756.

Stanley, M. A., Diefenbach, G. J., Hopko, D. R., Novy, D. M., Kunik, M. E., Wilson, N. L. et al. (2003b). The nature of generalized anxiety in older primary care patients: Preliminary findings. *Journal of Psychopathology and Behavioral Assessment, 25,* 273–280.

Stanley, M. A., Roberts, R. E., Bourland, S. L., & Novy, D. M. (2001). Anxiety disorders among older primary care patients. *Journal of Clinical Geropsychology, 7,* 105–116.

Stanley, M. A., Wilson, N. L., Novy, D. M., Rhoades, H. M., Wagener, P. D., Greisinger, A. J., et al. (2009). Cognitive behavior therapy for generalized anxiety disorder among older adults in primary care: A randomized clinical trial. *Journal of the American Medical Association, 301,* 1460–1467.

Stein M. B., Sherbourne, C. D., Craske, M. G., Means-Christensen, A., Bystritsky, A., Katon, W., et al. (2004). Quality of care for primary care patients with anxiety disorders. *American Journal of Psychiatry, 161,* 2230–2237.

Unützer, J., Katon, W., Callahan, C. M., Williams, J. W., Hunkeler, E., Harpole, L., et al. (2003). Depression treatment in a sample of 1,801 depressed older adults in primary care. *Journal of the American Geriatrics Society, 51,* 505–514.

Wang, P. S., Lane, M., Olfson, M., Pincus, H. A., Wells, K. B., & Kessler, R. C. (2005). Twelve-month use of mental health services in the United States. *Archives of General Psychiatry, 62,* 629–640.

Watts, S. C., Bhutani, G. E., Stout, I. H., Ducker, G. M., Cleator, P. J., McGarry, J., et al. (2002). Mental health in older adult recipients of primary care services: Is depression the key issue? Identification, treatment, and the general practitioner. *International Journal of Geriatric Psychiatry, 17,* 427–437.

Wells, K. B., Schoenbaum, M., Unützer, J., Lagomasino, I. T., & Rubenstein, L. V. (1999). Quality of care for depressed primary care patients with depression in managed care. *Archives of Family Medicine, 8,* 529–536.

Wetherell, J. L., Ayers, C. R., Sorrell, J. T., Thorp, S. R., Nuevo, R., Belding, W., et al. (2009). Modular psychotherapy for anxiety in older primary care patients. *American Journal of Geriatric Psychiatry, 17,* 483–492.
Young, A. S., Klap, R., Sherbourne, C. D., & Wells, K. B. (2001). The quality of care for depressive and anxiety disorders in the United States. *Archives of General Psychiatry, 58,* 55–61.
Zeiss, A. M., & Karlin, B. E. (2008). Integrating mental health and primary care services in the Department of Veterans Affairs health care system. *Journal of Clinical Psychology in Medical Settings, 15,* 73–78.

ADDITIONAL RESOURCES

1. Belar, C. D., & Deardorff, W. W. (1995). *Clinical health psychology in medical settings: A practitioner's guidebook.* Washington, DC: American Psychological Association.
   - An excellent resource that examines psychology practice in medical settings, including primary care. Topics include basics of assessment and intervention, as well as the development of core competencies for practitioners, ethical issues, establishing an effective practice, and issues of malpractice in the medical setting.
2. Cully, J. A., & Teten, A. L. (2008). *A therapist's guide to brief cognitive behavioral therapy.* Houston, TX: Department of Veterans Affairs South Central MIRECC.
   - This manual provides an overview of the structure and techniques used in brief CBT, making it highly applicable to primary care practice. The manual is available free online at http://www.mirecc.va.gov/visn16/docs/Therapists_Guide_to_Brief_CBTManual.pdf
3. Cully, J. A., Paukert, A., Falco, J., & Stanley, M. A. (2009). Cognitive behavioral therapy: Innovations for cardiopulmonary patients with depression and anxiety. *Cognitive Behavioral Practice, 16,* 394–407.
   - This article presents an overview of ACCESS (Adjusting to Chronic Conditions using Education, Support, and Skills), a CBT-based intervention that targets anxiety and depression symptoms and provides skills for self-management of chronic medical conditions. The components of the intervention are described, and three case examples involving older male veterans are presented.

Appendix: Assessment Template

Referring provider:
Reason for referral:
Presenting problem and most distressing symptoms:
Depressive symptomatology:
☐ Dep. mood ☐ Anhedonia ☐ Weight loss/gain ☐ Insomnia/
Hypersomnia ☐ Agitation/Retardation ☐ Fatigue ☐ Worthlessness
☐ Difficulty concentrating
Notes:
Suicidality/Homicidality (describe):
☐ Ideation:
☐ Plan:
☐ Means:
☐ Intent:
Anxiety symptomatology:
☐ Excessive worry ☐ Restlessness ☐ Muscle tension ☐ Concentration
problems ☐ Irritability ☐ Sleep disturbance ☐ Panic attacks
☐ Agoraphobia ☐ Social phobia symptoms
Trauma-related symptoms:
☐ Avoidance ☐ Arousal ☐ Reexperiencing
Notes:
Substance Use:
    Alcohol use:
    Other substances:
Hallucinations/delusions/mania:
Other relevant psychopathological symptomatology:
**Medical conditions and limits on functioning (include pain
assessment):**
Current medications:
History of mental health treatment:
Current living situation/social support system:
Employment history/recreational interests:
Evidence for cognitive impairment:
Provisional 5-axis diagnosis:
Axis I:
Axis II:
Axis III:
Axis IV:
Axis V:
Treatment plan:

11

Integrating Neuropsychological Functioning Into Cognitive Behavioral Therapy: Implications for Older Adults

Laura E. Dreer, Jacquelynn N. Copeland, and Jennifer S. Cheavens

Cognitive behavioral therapy (CBT) is an effective treatment for mental health problems in late life including depression and anxiety (Alexopoulos, Raue, Kanellopoulos, Mackin, & Areán, 2008; Barrowclough et al., 2001; Schuurmans et al., 2006; Serfaty et al., 2009; Stanley et al., 2009; Wetherell, Lenze, & Stanley, 2005; Wilkinson et al., 2009). CBT has also been found effective for treating mental health complications resulting from neurological diseases as well (Dobkin, Allen, & Menza, 2006; Julian & Mohr, 2006; Mohr et al., 2005; Teri, Logsdon, Uomoto, & McCurry, 1997). Participation in CBT-related activities relies heavily on several neurocognitive abilities including attention (e.g., to new information, skills), executive functioning (e.g., hypothesis generation, problem solving, challenging thoughts), learning and memory (e.g., consolidation of new concepts, practicing skills in and between sessions, remembering to complete homework assignments), language (communication; naming emotions, thoughts, or feelings; comprehending concepts), motor functioning (recording homework assignments, self-monitoring), and ongoing information processing. Because older adults are at greater risk for some degree of neurocognitive dysfunction caused by either cognitive changes associated with normal aging, side effects from several medications, psychiatric disorders, or neurological diseases compared to younger adults, these factors may negatively influence psychotherapeutic outcomes and contribute to nonresponse or early attrition from treatment (Alexopoulos, Kiosses, Murphy, & Heo, 2004; Alexopoulos et al., 2000; Caudle et al., 2007; Dew et al., 2007; Driscoll, Karp, Dew, & Reynolds, 2007; Mohlman, 2005; Mohlman & Gorman, 2005; Scogin & McElreath, 1994). Even undetected subtle effects in neurocognitive functioning may serve as moderators for CBT efficacy with older adults. Thus, adapting traditional

CBT to the level of a client's neurocognitive functioning may serve to enhance outcomes in psychotherapy, minimize the potential for drop-out, and possibly minimize risk for institutionalization among older adults referred for mental health treatment.

Unfortunately, standardized CBT approaches have not tradition-ally focused on integrating neurocognitive functioning into clinical or research efforts. In fact, much of what we already know about the success of CBT is based largely on healthy, cognitively intact adults from randomized clinical trials (RCTs), leaving those with less than optimal functioning screened out from inclusion. This selection bias may, in part, explain the negative influence on psychotherapeutic out-comes observed among older adults when these types of standardized, evidence-based approaches are translated into everyday practice. This issue is only likely to increase over the next several decades as the population continues to age, resulting in an increased demand of older adults seeking effective mental health services.

Innovative interventions designed to integrate neuropsychologi-cal functioning into CBT may help address this problem (Post et al., 2000). In fact, several new contemporary CBT approaches have shown promising results when CBT is modified for neurocognitive function-ing (Mackin, Areán, & Elite-Marcandonatou, 2006; Mohlman, 2008). Therefore, the focus of this chapter is to provide an overview of (a) basic brain organization, geography, and domains of neurocognitive func-tioning; (b) existing evidence supporting a relationship between neu-ropsychiatric disorders and brain functioning; (c) evidence linking neurocognitive functioning and CBT outcomes; (d) assessment and therapeutic strategies for integrating neuropsychological function-ing into CBT within geriatric populations; (e) identification of barri-ers associated with integrating neuropsychological functioning; and finally (f) practical strategies for overcoming such obstacles.

BRAIN ORGANIZATION, GEOGRAPHY, AND DOMAINS OF NEUROCOGNITIVE FUNCTIONING

Over the past decade, significant strides have been made regarding the link between brain regions, structures, neurocognitive domains, and associated behaviors. Much of this understanding can be attrib-uted to advancements in the fields of neuroscience, neuropsychology, psychiatry, medical technology, and genetics (Grawe, 2007; Smith, Gunning-Dixon, Lotrich, Taylor, & Evans, 2007). In a sense, the brain can be considered analogous to computer operating systems (Lezak, Loring, Howieson, Fischer, & Hannay, 2004). For example, outside information (auditory, visual, and tactile) needs to be encoded, registered, processed, manipulated, stored, and made available for retrieval. Information that enters the senses is transmitted quickly among complex brain interconnections (i.e., synaptic transmission between vast neuronal networks). Although it is beyond the scope of this chapter to provide a detailed description of all brain structures, their functions, and intricate pathways or circuitry, a brief review is included to appreciate the complexity of brain functioning. Additionally, this review will enable readers without prior knowledge in this area to understand subsequent sections. This foundation is particularly important for practitioners and researchers working with geriatric populations given (a) the prevalence of age-related changes in neurocognitive functioning that occur in late life; (b) that all mental processes (how we think, feel, or when we do something) are grounded in neural processes associated with brain functioning; (c) the accumulating translational research documenting an association between brain structures, late-life neuropsychiatric disorders, and behavior; and (d) the fact that the success of CBT relies heavily on adequate brain functioning in various cognitive domains (i.e., attention, memory and learning, processing speed, language).

Organization and Geography

The brain is essentially the most powerful organ, yet weighs only about 3 lbs consisting of three major anatomical divisions: *the hindbrain* (brain stem), *the midbrain,* and *the forebrain* (cerebrum; Cummings & Trimble, 2002; Lezak et al., 2004). The *hindbrain* represents the lowest part of the brain stem (*medulla oblongata*) and is located beneath the cerebrum in front of the cerebellum. It connects the brain to the spinal cord and controls automatic functions such as breathing, digestion, heart rate, and blood pressure. The *reticular formation* is also located within this region and responsible for arousal, wakefulness, and alertness. Another structure higher in the *hindbrain* is the *pons,* which contains pathways connecting fibers running between the cerebral cortex and the *cerebellum,* which is located at the posterior base of the brain and mostly controls coordination, movement, and balance (Lezak et al.). The *midbrain* is essentially a small area just forward of the *hindbrain* and includes a major portion of the *reticular activating system.*

The *forebrain* is the most forward part of the brain and has two subdivisions (*diencephalic structures* and the *cerebrum*; Lezak et al., 2004). The *diencephalon* ("between-brain") consists of a set of structures that evolved at the anterior (most forward) part of the brain stem. The most important *diencephalic* structures are the *thalamus* (relays sensations;

sends motor signals to the cerebral cortex; regulates consciousness, sleep, alertness—surrounds the third ventricle) and *hypothalamus* (regulates basic drives such as appetite, sexual arousal, and thirst). The *cerebrum* represents the largest brain structure and most evolved part of the brain. It fills up most of the skull, is involved in remembering, problem solving, thinking, and feeling and also controls movement. The cerebrum contains two hemispheres. Within each cerebral hemisphere at its base are several nuclear masses known as the *basal ganglia* (*caudate, putamen,* and *globus pallidus*). In some references, the basal ganglia also include the *amygdala, subthalamic nucleus, substantia nigra,* and other *subcortical structures* (Lezak et al.). The cerebral cortex projects directly to the caudate and putamen, and the globus pallidus and substantia nigra project back to the cerebral cortex through the thalamus. In addition to the motor cortex, the basal ganglia are interconnected with several other cortical areas including subdivisions of the premotor, oculomotor, prefrontal (dorsolateral and orbitofrontal), and inferotemporal cortices (Cummings & Trimble, 2002).

The *limbic system* includes structures such as the *amygdala,* the *cingulate gyrus,* and the *hippocampus* (Lezak et al., 2004). Broadly speaking, these structures play important roles in emotion, motivation, and memory, and its integrity is responsible for emotional well-being (Cummings & Trimble, 2002). The *amygdala* is a small structure located deep in the anterior part of the temporal lobe and, in general, is important for emotional processing and learning as well as attention. The *cingulate gyrus* is located in the medial parts of the hemispheres above the *corpus callosum* (mass of fibers connecting the two hemispheres) and has been implicated in influencing attention, response selection, and emotional behavior. For example, together with the lateral prefrontal cortex, the *anterior cingulate cortex* is responsible for controlling behavior by deciphering errors and alerting the occurrence of conflict during the processing of information. This is important for the regulation of behavior and self-directed intentions. The *hippocampus* is a major structure for memory and learning and runs inside the fold of the temporal lobe (Lezak et al., 2004).

Most of the cerebral hemisphere is made up of *white matter,* which consists of densely packed conduction fibers that transmit neural impulses between cortical points within a hemisphere (association fibers), between hemispheres (commissural fibers), or between the cerebral cortex and lower centers (projection fibers; Lezak et al., 2004). The corpus callosum is a band of commissural fibers that connect the two hemispheres and maintain hemisphere connections. Damage or lesions in white matter sever connections between lower and higher centers or cortical regions, which interrupts critical circuitry. Evidence implicating damage in white matter and late-life psychiatric disorders will be discussed in greater detail later in this chapter.

The outer layer of the cerebrum, the *cerebral cortex*, consists of *gray matter* (i.e., wrinkled surface) composed of nerve cell bodies and their synaptic connections. This area represents the most highly organized center of the brain. Specific regions of the cortex interpret sensory information from the body and the outside world, generate thoughts, solve problems, make plans, form and store memories, and control voluntary movement.

The brain is further organized into right and left hemispheres (i.e., *lateralization*; Cummings & Trimble, 2002). In general, the left hemisphere is mostly responsible for speech, language, writing, reasoning, and controls the right side of the body. The right hemisphere is largely responsible for insight, imagination, creativity, spatial construction, nonverbal ideation, and controls the left side of the body.

The brain communicates information through a complex internal organization of neurons and transmission of action potentials (Grawe, 2007). Nerve signals are responsible for carrying electrical messages across synapses, which may trigger the release of chemicals at synapses. Neurotransmitters travel across the synapse carrying signals to other cells. In a sense, patterns of signals at the cellular level explain how the brain codes thoughts, memories, and skills. The degree of interconnectedness forms the basis for an unlimited number of communication patterns among neurons, which are the basis for an individual's experience and behavior.

Lastly, the brain can also be further divided into four *lobes*: *frontal*, *temporal*, *parietal*, and *occipital*. The *frontal lobes* are located in front of the central sulcus and are, in general, concerned with reasoning, planning, organization, parts of speech and movement (motor cortex), emotions, and problem solving. Thus, in a sense, the frontal lobe has been referred to as the "CEO" of the brain. The prefrontal cortex consists of subregions based on neuroanatomic markers (Lezak et al., 2004). The prefrontal cortex and underlying white matter of the frontal lobes is also the site of interconnections and feedback loops between major sensory and motor systems, linking and integrating all components of behaviors at the highest level. The frontal lobes can be further subdivided into five subregions (i.e., superior, middle, inferior, orbital, and cingulate; López-Larson, DelBello, Zimmerman, Schwiers, & Strakowski, 2002). Distinct subcortical regions project to regions in the striatum to initiate the prefrontal-striatal-thalamic loops (i.e., amygdala, hypothalamus, dorsomedial nucleus of the thalamus) that modulate human emotional, cognitive, and social behavior (Strakowski, DelBello, & Adler, 2004). The prefrontal cortex has an important role in modulating activity in the basal ganglia and limbic regions, and there are extensive cortical-subcortical interconnections (Sheline, 2003). A limbic-thalamic-cortical branch consisting of the amygdala and hippocampus, mediodorsal nucleus of the thalamus, and medial and ventrolateral prefrontal cortex is known to be involved in emotion regulation. In addition, the primary motor cortex is part of the frontal lobe and lies in the first two ridges in front of the central sulcus and mediates movement.

The *parietal lobe* is located behind the central sulcus and is involved in perception of stimuli related to touch, pressure, temperature and pain, integration of sensory information from various senses, and manipulation of objects (Lezak et al., 2004). Below the lateral fissure is the *temporal lobe*, which is concerned with perception and recognition of auditory stimuli (hearing) and memory (hippocampus). Lastly, the *occipital lobe* is located at the back of the brain, behind the parietal lobe and temporal lobe and is primarily concerned with vision.

Neurocognitive Domains

Distinct neurocognitive domains correspond to different brain regions and thus translate brain–behavior relationships. Table 11.1 provides a detailed overview of the primary neurocognitive domains along with their general locations and functions. The primary domains include *sensory/perception, motor functioning, attention, processing speed, executive functioning, learning and memory,* and *language functioning.* Given the intricate neurocircuitry of the brain, these domains often interact together when an individual perceives information and performs tasks in everyday living (e.g., noticing a piece of paper, picking it up, holding it while reading, comprehending information, and thinking about what was read involves communication between several areas such as sensory/perception, motor functioning, language, and executive functioning). As information enters the brain, it is processed through sensory stimulation and perception (*sensory/perception*). *Attention* often involves the ability to attend to information (i.e., auditory, visual) and maintain a focus. As illustrated in Table 11.1, attention can be further subdivided into components such as *selective attention, sustained attention, divided attention,* and *alternating attention. Speed of processing* refers to the ability to efficiently process information (verbal/nonverbal). Generally speaking, the ability to absorb and interpret information, problem solve, make decisions, demonstrate mental flexibility, organize, plan, and inhibit impulses is associated with complex aspects of *executive functioning* and represents what is considered higher order processing of information. Whereas the ability

TABLE 11.1 Neurocognitive Domains, Primary Brain Regions, and Associated Functions

Neurocognitive Domain	Primary Brain Region	General Purpose/Functions and Components
Sensory/ perception	Parietal lobe	■ Receive and process sensory information from the environment (vision, hearing, touch, taste, smell) ■ Dysfunction in sensory/perception may include problems interpreting or perceiving outside information through the senses, which may ultimately impact other areas of functioning (e.g., communication, walking).
Motor	Primary motor cortex	■ *Gross motor functioning*: execute gross, purposeful movement (e.g., walking) ■ *Fine motor functioning*: perform fine and detailed movement (e.g., picking up small objects, writing) ■ *Praxia*: ability to perform learned voluntary acts ■ Dysfunction may include *apraxia* (difficulty with movement), *dystonia* (sustained, involuntary muscle contraction), tremor, gait disturbance, and problems with posture.
Attention	Frontal lobe	■ *Verbal attention*: attention to auditory information ■ *Visual attention*: attention to visual information ■ *Sustained attention*: sustained control; during prolonged tasks, more effort is exerted to stay focused ■ *Divided attention*: splitting attention between two sources of input or performance on two subtasks ■ *Selective attention*: allowing one source of information to be processed from among many ■ *Alternating attention*: refers to the capacity for mental flexibility that allows individuals to shift their focus of attention and move between tasks having different cognitive requirements ■ Dysfunction in various aspects of attention may be evidenced by difficulty with concentration and distraction specific to the attention component function (i.e., ability to sustain prolonged concentration).
Executive function	Frontal lobe	■ Ability to absorb and interpret information, demonstrate flexibility in thinking, problem solving, reasoning, organizing and planning, initiating and monitoring behaviors, making decisions, and inhibiting responses

(Continued)

TABLE 11.1 Neurocognitive Domains, Primary Brain Regions, and Associated Functions *(Continued)*

Neurocognitive Domain	Primary Brain Region	General Purpose/Functions and Components
Executive function *(continued)*	Frontal lobe *(continued)*	■ This area is considered "the CEO" of the brain. ■ Dysfunction in this area may be evidenced by poor flexibility in thinking, reasoning, organizing, and planning; socially inappropriate behavior; lack of awareness or insight (*anosognosia*); perseveration (behaviors, thoughts); difficulty initiating behaviors or speech; apathy; disinhibition; and/or impulsivity.
Processing speed	Frontal lobe	■ Ability to efficiently and quickly process information ■ Dysfunction in processing speed may result in increased time to complete various tasks; slowed processing.
Visuospatial	Parietal lobe	■ Ability to manipulate visual objects in the environment; recognize objects ■ Dysfunction in this area may include problems such as *constructional praxis* (problems assembling, joining, or separating parts to form a unitary whole) or *prosopagnosia* (inability to recognize familiar faces).

Memory and learning	Temporal lobe	■ *Verbal memory*: encoding, registering, and retrieval (free recall versus recognition) of auditory information
		■ *Visual memory*: encoding, registering, and retrieval (free recall versus recognition) of visual information
		■ *Iconic and echoic memory*: first traces of a stimulus-fleeting visual image or auditory replay
		■ *Short-term memory or immediate memory*
		  ■ Temporarily holds information immediately after presentation retained from the registration process
		  ■ Rehearsal (repetitive mental process): can be used to lengthen duration of memory trace to last for hours
		  ■ *Working memory*: temporarily access and utilize information
		  ■ Limited capacity
		  ■ Rapid decay
		■ *Long-term memory or secondary memory*
		  ■ Ability to store information
		  ■ Process of storing information as long-term memory; involves consolidation (*learning*) of information

(Continued)

TABLE 11.1 Neurocognitive Domains, Primary Brain Regions, and Associated Functions *(Continued)*

Neurocognitive Domain	Primary Brain Region	General Purpose/Functions and Components
Memory and learning *(continued)*	Temporal lobe *(continued)*	■ *Learning* refers to effortful, attentive activities or incidental learning ■ Unlimited capacity ■ *Recent and remote memory* 　■ Refers to autobiographical memories stored within the last few hours, days, weeks, or even months 　■ *Amnesia* refers to periods of no recall *Elements of Declarative Memory (Memory for Facts)* ■ *Recall versus. recognition*: remembering 　■ *Recall*: ability to use an active, complex search process to remember previously learned information 　■ *Recognition*: ability to identify previously learned information ■ *Episodic or event memory*: memories of one's own experiences that can be localized in time and space; memory for ongoing autobiographical events ■ *Semantic memory*: learned knowledge without the significance of time/space (i.e., alphabet, historical information) ■ *Effortful versus automatic memory*: effortful processing of information versus passive acquisition *Elements of Nondeclarative (Implicit) Memory* ■ *Procedural memory*: skill memory; "how-to" memory; spared in amnesia ■ *Priming*: form of cued recall in which prior exposure facilitates the response without the person's awareness; classical conditioning *Other Aspects of Memory* ■ *Source/contextual memory*: knowledge of where or when something is learned; incidental memory ■ *Prospective memory* 　■ Ability to remember to do something at a particular time (i.e., appointments, homework assignments) 　■ Self-initiated; remembering to perform an intended action 　■ Requires both "what" knowledge of declarative memory and executive functioning

(Continued)

TABLE 11.1 Neurocognitive Domains, Primary Brain Regions, and Associated Functions *(Continued)*

Neurocognitive Domain	Primary Brain Region	General Purpose/Functions and Components
Memory and learning *(continued)*	Temporal lobe *(continued)*	■ Dysfunction in aspects of memory can cause difficulty with encoding information, the ability later to retrieve information, or in some cases, *amnesia* (an acquired disturbance of memory in which new information is not stored by long-term memory). ■ Dysfunction in learning can cause problems with the amount of information that can be stored over time.
Language	Frontal temporal lobe	■ Ability to produce and/or comprehend speech, read, write, and make purposeful expressive functions ■ Engage in speech (fluency, comprehension, repeat, name) ■ *Receptive language*: ability to understand information (problems with comprehending associated with Wernicke's aphasia) ■ *Expressive language*: ability to produce sounds (problems producing speech associated with Broca's aphasia) ■ Dysfunction in aspects of language can cause problems with word selection, language production, and language comprehension (*aphasia* is an impairment in linguistic communication; fluent versus nonfluent); articulation and motor aspects of speech (*dysarthria*); difficulty reading (*alexia*), naming (*anomia*), writing (*agraphia*), reading (*alexia*); and problems with *prosody* (melodic, intonational, and inflectional aspects of speech).

to encode, register, learn, retain, and later retrieve information represents another complex process that is referred to as *learning and memory functioning*. As can be seen in Table 11.1, understanding potential deficits in specific components of memory is critical for informing CBT modifications (e.g., retrieval versus storage problems). In general, *language functioning*, another complex neurocognitive domain, corresponds to the ability to produce speech, read, write, draw, (expressive language) and comprehend information (receptive language). Lastly, *motor functioning* includes the ability to execute fine motor movements (e.g., writing) and/or gross motor movements (e.g., walking). Most of these domains, some more than others, play a critical role in the success of CBT. Many of these domains such as executive functioning, learning and memory, and language functioning represent fairly complex brain processes with various components involved in successfully solving life's problems. Dysfunction in a particular domain may have mild to significant implications when implementing CBT. Thus, knowledge regarding these heterogeneous processes and wide-ranging sets of cognitive operations is imperative.

Age-Related Changes in Neurocognitive Functioning

Changes in neurocognitive functioning associated with aging are normal and often benign (Smith, 2006). The most apparent change observed in normal aging is a reduction in speed of processing or cognitive efficiency (Salthouse, 1996; Smith, 2006), as well as the amount of information that can be processed at one time. Compared to younger adults, older adults are less efficient at processing information. Changes in memory (Reuter-Lorenz & Sylvester, 2003) and other alterations in aspects of executive functioning have also been documented. These types of subtle changes are common in late life regardless of a psychiatric disorder or neurological disease and are universal. Although inevitable, there is considerable variability in the nature, degree, and timing of cognitive decline. Age-related cognitive changes can also be influenced by changes in other body systems and health conditions. Changes in anatomical, physical, physiological, and chemical brain functioning associated with normal aging have been well documented in the literature (Bussiere & Hoff, 2000; Magistretti, Joray, & Pellvin, 2000; Raz, 2000). Generally speaking, these types of changes reflect the following: (a) neurons and the strengths and richness of their interconnections progressively atrophy as individuals age; (b) the deteriorating brain connections and functioning includes cortical areas and subcortical nuclei that are related to sensation, cognition, memory, and motor control; (c) the metabolic decline and downregulation of key neuronal populations commonly precede cell death; (d) many aspects of physical and neurochemical deterioration and emergent neuropathology are correlated with general and specific behavioral losses; and (e) these changes are universal despite variability in onset, course, and magnitude.

EVIDENCE SUPPORTING A CONNECTION BETWEEN NEUROPSYCHIATRIC DISORDERS AND NEUROCOGNITIVE DYSFUNCTION

Much of the evidence supporting a link between neuropsychiatric disorders, brain structures, and neurocognitive functioning comes from investigations drawing on either *biological-based approaches* (i.e., neuroimaging: computed tomography [CT], magnetic resonance imaging [MRI], functional magnetic resonance imaging [fMRI]; positron emission tomography [PET]; single photon emission computed tomography [SPECT]; diffusion tensor imaging [DTI]; morphometric studies voxel-based morphometry [VBM]; postmortem studies) or *behavioral approaches* (i.e., neuropsychological testing), or some combination of the two. Neuropsychological tests, which are performance-based tests, have informed the design of neuroimaging studies to visualize the neuroanatomical changes in neural circuitry associated with neurocognitive deficits (Smith et al., 2007). This revolution of more sophisticated multimodal techniques, representing a clinical neuroscientific approach, has led to significant strides in our understanding of the neurocognitive concomitants in late-life psychiatric disorders (Beaudreau & O'Hara, 2008; Hoptman, Gunning-Dixon, Murphy, Lim, & Alexopoulos, 2006; Kumar, Aizenstein, & Ballmaier, 2008). However, this area of research is not well delineated in the literature and merits greater attention, particularly in terms of understanding dysfunction in neuroanatomic networks, which underlie pathophysiology of late-life mood disorders. This represents a challenge because depression and other common psychiatric disorders consist of complex and heterogeneous behaviors that are unlikely to follow a simple, single brain lesion–syndrome relationship (Hoptman et al., 2006; McClintock, Husain, Greer, & Cullum, 2010). Much of the research, which will be reviewed in the following section, will illustrate evidence that abnormalities in specific brain structures and their interconnections are related to late-life psychiatric disorders along with psychiatric complications resulting from neurological diseases as well.

MOOD DISORDERS

The most commonly studied mood disorder among geriatric populations is late-life depression. Evidence of brain correlates and neurocognitive functioning associated with late-life depression has increased substantially over the last decade. Neuroimaging studies have implicated several region-specific brain areas associated with late-life depression. In particular, involvement of multiple areas of the prefrontal cortex including the limbic and subcortical regions such as the anterior cingulate gyrus, neostriatum, and the hippocampus have been well documented (Goldapple et al., 2004; Kumar et al., 2004; Mayberg, Lewis, Regenold, & Wagner, 1994), especially because this region of the brain is associated with emotion regulation (Raz et al., 1997). Evidence from MRI scans of deep white matter hyperintensities involving frontal-subcortical pathways has also shown a relationship for both chronicity and cognitive impairment in late-life depression, along with hyperintense areas in subcortical gray matter structures in the prefrontal anterior cingulate and orbiofrontal cortex hippocampus, amygdala, and basal ganglia (Kohler et al., 2010; Krishnan, Hays, George, & Blazer, 1998; Murphy & Alexopoulos, 2006; O'Brien, Loyd, McKeith, Gholkar, & Ferrier, 2004; Steffens, MacFall, Payne, Welsh-Boehmer, & Krishnan, 2000; Tupler et al., 2002). Some of the evidence also supports associations between (a) whole brain white matter hyperintensities and neuropsychological measures assessing executive functioning; (b) whole brain white matter and episodic memory, processing speed, executive functioning, and some aspects of language functioning (Kramer-Ginsberg et al., 1999); and (c) whole brain gray matter with processing speed (Sheline et al., 2008). Deep white matter contains the long association and projection tracts that connect the dorsolateral prefrontal cortex to limbic nuclei and to other cortices (Filley, 2001). Disruption of these complex subcortical and medial temporal structure pathways/circuitry between the frontal lobe and other distant brain regions is hypothesized to underlie the emotional and cognitive abnormalities observed in certain psychiatric disorders (Phillips, Drevets, Rauch, & Lane, 2003). In other studies using proton magnetic resonance spectroscopy, Chen et al. (2009) also found biochemical abnormalities on the left side of frontal white matter and the basal ganglia when studying brain abnormalities in late-life depression, thus suggesting that neuron degeneration in the frontal white matter and second messenger system dysfunction or glial dysfunction in the basal ganglia are associated with late-life depression (Chen et al., 2009). Alternatively, Venkatraman, Krishnan, Steffens, Song, and Taylor (2009), using single-voxel 1H magnetic resonance spectroscopy, found biochemical abnormalities related to late-life depression in the medial prefrontal cortex and medial temporal lobe (Venkatraman et al., 2009).

Other biological-based approaches have examined changes in brain volume. For example, studies using PET scans have shown decreases in focal brain activation such as hypometabolism in areas that mediate executive functioning including the dorsolateral prefrontal cortex (Mann et al., 1996), medial frontal cortex (Bench et al., 1992), temporal lobe structures (Sheline, Sanghavi, Mintun, & Gado, 1999), orbitofrontal cortex (Ring et al., 1994), anterior cingulate, basal ganglia, and hippocampus among persons with late-life depression (Buchsbaum et al., 1986; Drevets et al., 1997; Lampe et al., 2003; Shah, Glabus, Goodwin, & Ebmeier, 2002). Another subset of studies have documented enlargement of the lateral and third ventricles or increased sulcal prominence in depressed patients (Elkis et al., 1996; Videbech et al., 2001) and volume reductions in specific frontal (cingulate gyrus orbitofrontal cortex) and temporal (left temporal lobe) brain regions (Dotson, Davatzikos, Kraut, & Resnick, 2009). Lastly, recent morphometric studies have found 11% to 30% decreases in cell-packing densities in both regions in persons with depression (Cotter, Mackay, Landau, Kerwin, & Everall, 2001), alterations in neuron and glial cell populations in the frontal and subcortical circuitry associated with major depression (Khundakar, Morris, Oakley, McMeekin, & Thomas, 2009), and significant gray matter volume reduction in the bilateral limbic system, especially in the hippocampus (Zou et al., 2010).

In general, results from neuropsychological testing are consistent with neuroimaging findings in relation to depression (Sheline et al., 2010). For example, investigations using neuropsychological tests implicate prefrontal/executive dysfunction in clients with late-life depression, which is associated with treatment resistance. (Alexopoulos et al., 2000; Kalayam & Alexopoulos, 1999; Lockwood, Alexopoulos, & van Gorp, 2002). There is, however, inconclusive evidence that executive dysfunction may mediate verbal memory deficits, thereby implicating a compromised frontostriatal neural pathway (Elderkin-Thompson, Mintz, Haroon, Lavretsky, & Kumar, 2006). Research appears to differentiate verbal perseveration from verbal initiation as the cognitive process most associated with poor treatment response for late-life depression, thereby suggesting that the orbitofrontal prefrontal cortex may also play a role in sustaining perseverative processing (Potter, Kittinger, Wagner, Steffens, & Krishnan, 2004). Deficits in other neurocognitive domains using neuropsychological test data with depressed older adults are evident in slowed processing speed, implicating frontostriatal dysfunction (Butters et al., 2004; Douglas & Porter, 2009; Herrmann, Goodwin, & Ebmeier, 2007; Sheline et al., 2006), set shifting and perseveration (Austin et al., 1999), verbal fluency (Lockwood et al., 2002), initiation (Alexopoulos, Kiosses, Klimstra, Kalayam, & Bruce, 2002), episodic and working memory (Hart, Kwentus, Taylor, & Hawkins, 1987; Kramer-Ginsberg et al., 1999; Nebes et al., 2000), verbal learning and memory (Elderkin-Thompson et al., 2006), visual-spatial function (Boone et al., 1995), slowed psychomotor functioning (Hart et al., 1987; Lockwood et al., 2002), and/or a combination of these types of deficits (Butters et al., 2004). Other studies support a global relationship between late-life depression and incident cognitive impairment (Rosenberg, Mielke, Xue, & Carlson, 2010). The extent to which deficits in one neurocognitive domain (i.e., processing speed) may mediate other domains is speculative at this point (Sheline et al., 2006). Lastly, treatment with antidepressant medications for late-life depression has also been shown to have a deleterious effect on some aspects of cognitive functioning (Culang et al., 2009; Raskin et al., 2007).

Other variants of late-life depression and brain lesions involving the frontal, basal ganglia, and subcortical white matter have also been supported in the literature. One variant, referred to as *depression-executive*

dysfunction syndrome (Alexopoulos, 2005; Krishnan, 2002), is characterized by psychomotor retardation and reduced interest in activities but a
less pronounced vegetative syndrome than in depressed clients without
significant dysfunction (Alexopoulos et al., 1996). More recently, there
has also been wide speculation of a vascular depression hypothesis,
which suggests that vascular diseases might place older individuals at
risk for depression due to small vessel disease in the frontal and subcortical regions of the brain. Support for this theory has substantially
accumulated in the past several years (Krishnan et al., 2004; Mast et al.,
2008; Sheline et al., 2010). There is also some evidence suggesting a
genetic link between late-life depression and neurocognitive dysfunction. For example, apolipoprotein E-e4 (APOE-e4) allele has been found
to be related to poorer cognitive functioning (Krishnan et al., 1996),
and serum anticholinergic burden has been found to negatively affect
neurocognitive functioning, especially memory, in late-life depression
(Mulsant et al., 2003; Nebes et al., 1997).

In summary, converging evidence from neuroimaging, neuropsychological, and neuropathological studies suggests that biological
susceptibility to late-life mood disorders is likely mediated by compromise in frontal-striatal-thalamic-limbic functions with contributions
from vascular, genetic, neurochemical, neurodegenerative, and other
age-related factors. Evidence also supports the role of the prefrontal
cortex, the anterior cingulate cortex, hippocampus, and amygdala in
late-life depression. Unfortunately, the benefits of this knowledge of a
relationship between psychiatric disorders and neurocognitive functioning has been slow to impact treatment efforts for late-life depression (Jaeger & Douglas, 1992).

ANXIETY DISORDERS

To a much lesser extent, the link between late-life anxiety disorders
and structural changes in the brain has also received some attention over the past decade. In particular, generalized anxiety disorder
(GAD) has received the greatest amount of attention of the anxiety
disorders in late life. Only a few neuroimaging studies have examined
late-life GAD. Of the studies to date, most implicate functional impairments in the dorsolateral region of the prefrontal cortex for worry
(Mathew et al., 2004) and the medial orbital cortex (Mohlman et al.,
2009), areas that strongly influence diverse neurocognitive functions
such as executive functioning. The medial orbital cortex is involved
in emotional decision making under uncertain conditions and has
the ability to suppress the amygdala, which is a suspected function

of worry (Mohlman et al., 2009). A review of the evidence examining GAD and obsessive-compulsive disorder (OCD), which both involve rumination and worry, has also been characterized by overactivity of the prefrontal cortex (Berkowitz, Coplan, Reddy, & Gorman, 2007). In contrast, anxiety disorders such as posttraumatic stress disorder (PTSD), panic, and phobias are characterized by an underactivity of the prefrontal cortex and thereby disinhibit the amygdala. Reduced neurotransmitter function has also been implicated in late-life anxiety disorders and neuropsychiatric dysfunction. For example, serotonin age-related alterations have been suggested to directly influence the emergence of behavioral symptoms such as problems with sleep and psychiatric disturbance (i.e., depression; Beaudreau & O'Hara, 2008). Evidence for serotonergic dysfunction affecting both hippocampal and frontal regions has also been found in GAD (Graeff, Guimaraes, De Andrade, & Deakin, 1996). Research is also growing in terms of genetic vulnerability and markers (i.e., short allele of the 5HTTLPR and APOE-e4; Serretti, Calati, Mandelli, & De Ronchi, 2006).

Evidence for late-life anxiety–related disorders and neurocognitive dysfunction on neuropsychological tests are also noted in the literature. For example, several studies using a range of different neuropsychological test batteries have found support for a link between anxiety and episodic memory (Bierman, Comijs, Jonker, & Beekman, 2005; Booth, Schinka, Brown, Mortimer, & Borenstein, 2006; Mantella et al., 2007), selective and divided attention (Hogan, 2003), and global cognitive functioning (Caudle et al., 2007; DeLuca et al., 2005). Although there is a slowly evolving body of studies examining anxiety disorders in late life, which have shown an association between brain–behavior relationships primarily in the prefrontal cortex, data should be considered speculative and inconclusive at this point given the limited research studies to date. A much larger body of research supports links between structural brain changes and anxiety disorders in younger adults with OCD, PTSD, panic disorders, and specific phobias.

NEUROLOGICAL-BASED DISEASES AND PSYCHIATRIC SYMPTOMS

Depression and other psychiatric symptoms often accompany neurological diseases as well and have been found to be associated with both cortical and subcortical atrophy (i.e., stroke, multiple sclerosis, dementia of the Alzheimer's type, Parkinson's disease; Burns, Jacoby, & Levey, 1990; Cummings, 1992; Cummings & Trimble, 2002; Dobkin et al., 2006;

Ghaffar & Feinstein, 2007; Minden & Schiffer, 1990). The link between depression and white matter changes has also been found among persons with neurological diseases (Feinstein et al., 2004). Neurological diseases often involve damage, as part of the disease process, to brain regions that are vital in emotional functioning, primarily the frontal cortex, hippocampus, thalamus, amygdala, and basal ganglia. Treating depression and other psychiatric correlates associated with these diseases is particularly important because these symptoms, if left untreated, often lead to an increased progression of physical symptoms, cognitive decline, poor quality of life, decrements in self-care, and institutionalization (McGuigan & Hutchinson, 2006; Starkstein, Mayberg, Leiguarda, Preziosi, & Robinson, 1992). Unfortunately, in neurological-based diseases, these symptoms are more often underrecognized and thus undertreated (McGuigan & Hutchinson, 2006), or treatments are less likely to be offered for psychiatric problems given some of the progressive nature of certain diseases (e.g., Alzheimer's disease, Parkinson's disease).

NEUROCOGNITIVE FUNCTIONING AND COGNITIVE BEHAVIORAL THERAPY APPROACHES

CBT emphasizes cognition in mediating psychological disorders. Efforts are aimed at alleviating distress by modifying cognitive content and processes and realigning thinking with more adaptive thinking (Longmore & Worrell, 2007). CBT-based approaches for late-life neuropsychiatric disorders (i.e., cognitive therapy, problem-solving therapy, behavioral activation, dialectical behavior therapy) rely heavily on several neurocognitive abilities. These abilities include attention, information processing, memory (homework assignments, concepts), learning (consolidation of concepts and skills), executive functioning (identification of maladaptive thoughts, modification of the meaning of thoughts, hypothesis generation, problem solving, reasoning, self-awareness, generalizing concepts to everyday situations), language functioning (comprehension, production of speech, communication, naming thoughts and feelings), and motor and sensory functioning (completion of homework assignments, self-monitoring; Hunt, Baker, Michie, & Kavanagh, 2009; Oathamshaw & Haddock, 2006). Columns 1 and 2 in Table 11.2 outline neurocognitive domains and their corresponding demands on the client required for CBT in greater detail. As is illustrated in the Table, many of the CBT-based approaches and techniques draw on a combination of these abilities. For example, completing homework assignments demands adequate memory functioning

TABLE 11.2 Examples of Neurocognitive Demands on Older Adults During Cognitive Behavioral Therapy and Potential Therapeutic Strategies to Maximize Treatment Success

Neurocognitive Domain	Examples of Neurocognitive Demands on Older Adults During CBT	Potential Therapeutic Strategies to Maximize Success With CBT
Sensory/perceptual functioning (vision, hearing)	■ Need to see/hear new information (e.g., concepts, skills, models; client worksheets and homework assignments). ■ Complete homework assignments (e.g., requires good vision for recording information on homework forms or on the computer; hearing and speech for participating in in-session discussions and/or for recording homework on external devices or on automated telephone services). ■ Use cognitive behavioral therapy (CBT)-based technology approaches (i.e., sensory input needed for CBT tasks involving virtual reality, biofeedback, voice recorders, DVD or CDs for computers).	■ Enlarge therapeutic materials for deficits in vision (e.g., adjust font to bold to increase contrast sensitivity or increase size of font). ■ Increase lighting in the office/setting for vision deficits. ■ Increase volume and pitch of speech for hearing deficits. ■ Use alternative devices depending on the sensory mode deficit (e.g., voice/tape recorders, podcasts of materials, video projector to enlarge presentation of CBT concepts). ■ Sit closer to clients with hearing difficulties or hearing aids; continually check for understanding. ■ Present information using multiple modalities when possible to reinforce learning; maximize learning by presenting information in terms of client's primary sensory modality strength (e.g., above average on visual attention visual memory, then consider relying more on symbols or designs illustrating CBT concepts).
Motor functioning (fine and gross motor functioning)	■ Manipulate client worksheets/handouts (gross motor functioning). ■ Record/track homework assignments (fine motor functioning). ■ Perform activities related to behavioral activation/scheduling pleasurable activities.	■ Use alternative strategies to record homework, depending on the extent and type of motor deficits (i.e., voice/tape recorders, automated telephone call-in services to record homework on voice mail system, family member to record information).

(Continued)

TABLE 11.2   Examples of Neurocognitive Demands on Older Adults During Cognitive Behavioral Therapy and Potential Therapeutic Strategies to Maximize Treatment Success *(Continued)*

Neurocognitive Domain	Examples of Neurocognitive Demands on Older Adults During CBT	Potential Therapeutic Strategies to Maximize Success With CBT
Attention and concentration (verbal/visual; sustained, selective, divided, alternating attention)	■ Attend to new information and materials (verbal, written). ■ Sustain attention during the discussion of materials/concepts and implementation of homework assignments; maintain train of thought. ■ Concentrate on thoughts, behaviors, and emotions while also self-monitoring. ■ Divide attention when thinking about and actually applying concepts/skills during real-life situations.	■ Break CBT concepts into simple, concrete steps. ■ Simplify treatment materials (e.g., handouts, worksheets, homework assignments, and instructions). ■ Provide greater structure for sessions (e.g., provide written session objectives to the client to help keep him or her focused and on task). ■ Arrange for shorter yet more frequent sessions; consider modifying the traditional session length and amount of contact time to enhance sustained attention deficits (e.g., 2–3 sessions per week versus once a week or shorter session intervals—30-minute session versus standard 50- to 60-minute sessions). ■ Schedule brief breaks in between concepts. ■ Check for understanding in between presentation of concepts, prior to moving onto new concepts/skills, and again at the end of session. ■ Address fewer topics in each session. ■ Use handouts/flipcharts/dry-erase boards to illustrate concepts for clients with verbal attention problems or those with strengths in visual attention.

(Continued)

TABLE 11.2   Examples of Neurocognitive Demands on Older Adults During
Cognitive Behavioral Therapy and Potential Therapeutic Strategies to Maximize
Treatment Success *(Continued)*

Neurocognitive Domain	Examples of Neurocognitive Demands on Older Adults During CBT	Potential Therapeutic Strategies to Maximize Success With CBT
Attention and concentration (verbal/visual; sustained, selective, divided, alternating attention) *(continued)*		■ Minimize distractions in and outside of the office area (e.g., turn off office telephone and ask client to also turn off his or her cell phone as well; turn on white noise machine to drown out outside noise). ■ Minimize external distractions/overstimulation. ■ Assign brief homework assignments with concrete instructions.
Executive functioning (mental flexibility, set shifting, reasoning, problem solving, abstract thinking, inhibition, planning, organizing, inhibition)	■ Identify maladaptive thoughts and core beliefs. ■ Restructure thinking and challenge catastrophic thoughts, beliefs, and assumptions. ■ Engage in mental flexibility in terms of thinking about life problems/solutions, CBT concepts, perspective taking, identifying alternative solutions, transferring skills acquired in CBT to everyday life, and adapting alternative beliefs. ■ Challenge thinking by treating thoughts as hypotheses; hypothesis generation and testing. ■ Inhibit automatic reactions, impulsive behaviors, or thoughts. ■ Organize thoughts, feelings, and behaviors. ■ Plan and execute application of CBT concepts to homework assignments or in-session discussions. ■ Think about own thinking (*metacognition*).	■ Structure session content to model organization and planning. ■ Use concrete examples versus metaphors or abstract examples to illustrate CBT concepts. ■ Simplify presentation of information (concepts, examples) and selection of CBT approach. ■ Reassess for understanding and learning in between presentation of concepts. ■ Encourage practice of the application of CBT concepts in session to better identify how specific deficits in executive functioning are interfering with the client's ability to successfully solve problems (e.g., perseverating on one solution, problems with perspective taking, difficulty inhibiting impulses or automatic reactions).

(Continued)

TABLE 11.2 Examples of Neurocognitive Demands on Older Adults During Cognitive Behavioral Therapy and Potential Therapeutic Strategies to Maximize Treatment Success *(Continued)*

Neurocognitive Domain	Examples of Neurocognitive Demands on Older Adults During CBT	Potential Therapeutic Strategies to Maximize Success With CBT
Executive functioning (mental flexibility, set shifting, reasoning, problem solving, abstract thinking, inhibition, planning, organizing, inhibition) *(continued)*	■ Engage in self-awareness to identify erroneous thoughts. ■ Plan and execute homework assignments. ■ Implement the sequence of skills for certain CBT approaches (i.e., stages of the problem-solving model, identification of problem, generation of alternatives, decision making [pros and cons, short- and long-term consequences, personal/social], and solution verification/implementation). ■ Regulate emotions and actions. ■ Construct personal narratives. ■ Generalize issues discussed in therapy to specific instances in everyday living.	■ Create structured homework assignment forms with concrete instructions; include examples from in session to help generalize practice of concepts outside of sessions. ■ Place a greater emphasis on self-monitoring to increase self-awareness of connections between thoughts, behaviors, and emotions; integrate feedback from others (i.e., family members). ■ Encourage the client to use voice recorders when doing homework assignments to review in session and understand the client's process of solving problems; how he or she organizes, plans, and implements solutions to solving distressing problems. ■ Provide coaching telephone calls in between sessions to help generalize concepts to situations in everyday living.
Speed of processing (verbal/visual information)	■ Efficiently process new information. ■ Quickly apply skills to problems. ■ Thoughtfully slow down thinking to recognize and dispute automatic processing of thoughts.	■ Allow for more time to learn new information and implement strategies. ■ Slow down the pace of introducing concepts and materials. ■ Simplify concepts, materials, and homework assignments ■ Check for understanding in-between concepts and session objectives. ■ Provide more time explaining concepts and reviewing homework.

(Continued)

TABLE 11.2 Examples of Neurocognitive Demands on Older Adults During Cognitive Behavioral Therapy and Potential Therapeutic Strategies to Maximize Treatment Success *(Continued)*

Neurocognitive Domain	Examples of Neurocognitive Demands on Older Adults During CBT	Potential Therapeutic Strategies to Maximize Success With CBT
Learning and Memory (verbal/visual information, encoding, registration, immediate recall, delayed recall, recognition, learning)	■ Learn new concepts; acquisition of new skills. ■ Encode, register, and consolidate new CBT-related concepts. ■ Recognize and recall concepts during and in-between sessions (i.e., thinking errors, automatic thoughts). ■ Remember what happens both within sessions and between sessions to build on learning skills and connecting concepts. ■ Recall life examples and connected emotions, thoughts, and behaviors for in-session practice and/or homework. ■ Remember homework assignments, instructions, and be able to locate assignment materials (worksheets/workbooks). ■ Utilize working memory to role-play application of concepts to actual problems. ■ Remember to continually self-monitor behaviors, thoughts, and emotions.	■ Modify traditional session length and amount of contact time to enhance learning (e.g., 2–3 sessions per week versus once a week; shorter session intervals—30 minutes versus standard 50- to 60-minute sessions). ■ Graph or chart client progress in learning concepts/skills over several sessions to reinforce learning/progress (graphs made in PowerPoint presentation or Excel to provide visual feedback). ■ Repeat information (e.g., increase practice and repetition of concepts, homework assignments); overlearn information. ■ Train client to use mnemonic strategies (e.g., method of loci) to remember concepts and/or homework assignments. ■ Use of a dry-erase board or flipchart in session to enhance verbal and visual repetition of concepts as well as learning. ■ Role-play to reinforce learning session material and content. ■ Use cross-modal repetition of information to enhance learning. ■ Summarize frequently in-between concepts. ■ Continually check for understanding and learning.

(Continued)

TABLE 11.2   Examples of Neurocognitive Demands on Older Adults During Cognitive Behavioral Therapy and Potential Therapeutic Strategies to Maximize Treatment Success *(Continued)*

Neurocognitive Domain	Examples of Neurocognitive Demands on Older Adults During CBT	Potential Therapeutic Strategies to Maximize Success With CBT
Learning and Memory (verbal/visual information, encoding, registration, immediate recall, delayed recall, recognition, learning) *(continued)*		■ Chunk information and teach mnemonic strategies to better remember concepts during and outside of sessions. ■ Conduct coaching calls to reinforce ongoing learning in between sessions and generalization of concepts. ■ Use priming or cueing to aid in remembering when discussing concepts/skills/emotions/thoughts in session. ■ Give reminder telephone calls to review homework assignments, review concepts, and answer questions, or use automated telephone systems to cue client. ■ Provide supplemental materials (notebook to record session notes, index cards, handouts, CDs, podcasts, DVDs illustrating CBT concepts). ■ Provide prompts/cueing to complete homework (i.e., alarm clocks, timers, automated telephone calls, family members). ■ Instruct homework to be completed at same time of the day to get into a habit/routine and minimize forgetting.
Language functioning (comprehension, speech production, verbal fluency, naming)	■ Comprehend verbal information; modify the meaning of thoughts. ■ Understand link between events, cognitions, and emotions. ■ Communicate in session (e.g., speak; discuss problems, concepts, and homework; find words to express thoughts, feelings, and behaviors).	■ Frequently check for understanding in between concepts. ■ Use visual icons/pictures to demonstrate session concepts and identify feelings, thoughts, and behaviors. ■ Provide cues to help elicit responses.

(Continued)

TABLE 11.2   Examples of Neurocognitive Demands on Older Adults During Cognitive Behavioral Therapy and Potential Therapeutic Strategies to Maximize Treatment Success *(Continued)*

Neurocognitive Domain	Examples of Neurocognitive Demands on Older Adults During CBT	Potential Therapeutic Strategies to Maximize Success With CBT
Language functioning (comprehension, speech production, verbal fluency, naming) *(continued)*	■ Language abilities needed to engage in active social, communication, and assertiveness skills training.	■ Allow client to communicate via alternative methods (i.e., drawing, symbols, communication board). ■ Provide cueing or priming for persons with problems in verbal initiation/fluency.
Intellectual functioning	■ Understand and grasp concepts, links between thoughts, emotions, and behaviors. ■ Identify and challenge thoughts.	■ Modify presentation of information and materials to level of client's overall intellectual functioning. ■ Match information to client education level and reading level. ■ Use symbols or icons. ■ Rely on using more simplified examples/metaphors to illustrate concepts.

(remembering the assignment instructions), executing functioning abilities (thinking about and challenging thoughts), language functioning (naming thoughts and feelings, changing communication patterns with others, speech, writing), and motor functioning (recording the assignment on paper). Requirements for tasks associated with CBT are often complex and demand adequate cognitive functioning to be successful. Such techniques are fairly sophisticated and require dismantling strings of thoughts into units (Mohlman, 2005). Furthermore, clients are then asked to generate evidence that either supports or refutes each individual thought, to then replace negative thoughts, and plan for the future. Thus, participation in CBT demands a higher order level of processing. In a sense, the practitioner's task is to facilitate the occurrence of new learning experiences that are likely to exert a positive influence on an individual's problems and the neural structures underlying those problems (Grawe, 2007). However, dysfunction in neurocognition may reduce existing coping strategies, ability to learn new skills, and impact adversely on treatment adherence and relapse. Without understanding possible deficits and making accommodations to standardized CBT techniques, lack of success in therapy may be misinterpreted as lack of motivation on the part of the client. Thus, an evaluation of the client's capacity to participate in CBT and/or benefit from strategies that may enhance participation in CBT is warranted.

Theoretical models demonstrating a link between CBT and neurocognitive functioning are limited but on the rise. For example, one model for CBT action in the treatment of depression generally implicates top-down neural mechanisms given the premise of such approaches on modifying attention and memory functions involved in the meditation of depression-relevant cognitions, affective bias, and maladaptive processing of information (DeRubeis et al., 1990; Simons, Garfield, & Murphy, 1984). Additionally, the time course of changes in symptoms resulting from CBT also supports an initial cortical site of action as hopelessness and perceptions of self, others, and mood typically precede changes in motivational symptoms. Brain correlates of this type and chronology have been largely understudied. Recent evidence by Goldapple and colleagues found that CBT appears to affect clinical recovery by modulating the functioning of specific sites in limbic and cortical regions (Goldapple et al., 2004). Treatment response was associated with significant metabolic changes in hippocampus and dorsal cingulate as well as decreases in dorsal, ventral, and medial frontal cortex.

Others hypothesize that the efficacy of CBT is partly dependent on the older adult's use of heterogeneous sets of executive functions (i.e. hypothesis testing, problem solving, inhibitory control), which are governed by the prefrontal cortex (Mohlman, 2005; Mohlman & Gorman, 2005). Intact executive functioning is implicated in facilitating the successful use of CBT (Hariri, Bookheimer, & Mazziotta, 2000). As stated previously, many of the CBT concepts are heavily dependent on multiple aspects of higher order executive functioning including identification and restructuring of thoughts, hypothesis generation, and problem solving. Additionally, CBT exercises require active participation and rely largely on role-playing, homework assignments, behavioral plans, and instruction from client handouts and workbooks (Craske, Barlow, & O'Leary, 1991; Greenberger & Padesky, 1995). These activities demand ongoing use of thought-restructuring exercises designed to train clients to practice, learn, and implement more adaptive thoughts based on evidence (D'Zurilla & Nezu, 2007). Another important aspect of CBT associated with executive functioning abilities is self-monitoring, which requires self-awareness, insight, and metacognition as clients are required to evaluate their thoughts, behaviors, and emotions and record their daily ratings of mood. Recent support for the connection between executive functioning and CBT among older adults using neuropsychological testing indicates that intact executive functioning predicts favorable responses to CBT for GAD compared to those with executive dysfunction, thereby supporting the assumption that adequate executive functioning is necessary for CBT (Mohlman & Gorman, 2005).

The exact neural substrates, neural networks, and domains involved with CBT have yet to be fully identified, much less is understood empirically (Grawe, 2007). An understanding of the mechanisms of change associated with CBT on brain functioning is insufficient at this point. If therapeutic changes achieve their effects via learning new skills and these skills are practiced intensely and maintained over an extended period, then they may be effective and may perhaps translate into changes in brain functioning (i.e., brain plasticity, reorganization, new neural activation patterns). Executive function deficits are far more common among older adults than younger adults and can occur because of processes of normal aging in the absence of injury, neurological disease, trauma, or neurotoxic events. For example, several researchers have proposed a circuit involving the anterior cingulate cortex and other medial prefrontal areas (LeDoux, 1996) and that CBT works by strengthening descending cortical pathways from the prefrontal cortex to the amygdala (Gorman, Kent, Sullivan, & Coplan, 1999). Evidence supporting this speculation has been supported by preliminary neuroimaging (fMRI) data, which implicate the prefrontal cortex in the intentional regulation and management of mood (Beauregard, Levelque, & Bourgouin, 2000; Hariri et al., 2000).

However, it is certainly plausible that in addition to executive functioning, other important neurocognitive domains are also critical to the success in CBT (see columns 1 and 2 of Table 11.2). For instance, clients need to attend to CBT concepts (attention), comprehend and communicate about information presented in and between sessions (language), name and label thoughts and emotions (executive as well as language functioning), quickly think about concepts/skills and immediately apply them to problems/situations (processing speed and working memory), communicate about concepts during role-playing/ homework assignments (language), encode/register and recall information presented from previous sessions (memory), consolidate concepts and skills across sessions (learning), physically record information as part of homework assignments (fine motor functioning and language functioning), hear concepts being presented and see information and material (sensory perceptual), and read and understand therapy materials (language functioning and general intelligence, literacy). Thus, in addition to executive functioning abilities, CBT-based approaches demand adequate functioning in other important aspects of brain functioning, some of which require interaction between domains to successfully carry out various techniques and activities.

Innovation: Integrating Neuropsychological Functioning Into Cognitive Behavioral Therapy

Contemporary approaches aimed at enhancing CBT for older adult clients who present for mental health services even with minimal neurocognitive dysfunction in one or more areas of functioning may serve to enhance outcomes and minimize dropout. Bridging knowledge from neurosciences and psychotherapy represents a more informed approach and has even been referred to as *neuropsychotherapy* in some instances (Grawe, 2007). Emerging research on adapted or enhanced CBT approaches for late-life psychiatric disorders and neurological diseases has shown promising results. For example, enhanced CBT incorporating an executive skills training program/attention process training (Mohlman, 2008) and/or learning and memory aids for late-life anxiety has proven effective (Mohlman et al., 2003). Thus, modifying CBT activities to account for a client's unique areas of cognitive dysfunction may enhance treatment success, even for older adults with psychiatric complications secondary to neurological diseases (Tompkins, 2004). In the following sections, we describe a framework for integrating neuropsychological functioning into CBT for older adults presenting for mental health services. In some instances, only minor modifications may be necessary given the subtle changes associated with normal aging. In other cases, CBT may not be appropriate and alternative strategies should be taken into consideration (i.e., pharmacological treatments, family-centered approaches, and/or behavioral approaches).

Step 1: Neurocognitive Assessment to Evaluate Capacity for Cognitive Behavioral Therapy and Treatment Planning

Understanding whether an older adult has the skills required to undertake CBT requires knowledge of neurocognitive functioning in late life (normal age-related changes, psychiatric disorders associated with late life, and neurological disease processes) as well as familiarity and training with commonly used neuropsychological tests and norms appropriate for older adults. A critical element of CBT treatment planning evolves during the initial evaluation through consideration of treatment capacity and/or goals. Neuropsychological evaluations often provide guidance regarding various capacity determinations (i.e., capacity to make medical decisions, manage finances, live independently, work, fitness to drive; Dreer et al., 2008; Marson & Dreer, 2007; Marson et al., 2005). Thus, this type of an assessment may also help in determinations for the capacity to participate in and potential to benefit from CBT.

When older adults are referred for treatment, the initial evaluation is the most important source of data from which a treatment plan
is generated (Attix, 2006). The success of treatment is often contin-
gent on data obtained from this source. During the initial evaluation,
capacity for CBT, insight, motivation to actively participate, selection
of feasible treatment goals, and targets of change are all taken into
consideration. A comprehensive neuropsychological evaluation incorporating an assessment of multiple neurocognitive domains is critical
because it addresses concerns surrounding the client's level of cognitive functioning in domain-specific areas, the presence of neurocognitive dysfunction, the type of diagnosis supported by the data and
prognosis over time, domains of strengths and weaknesses that may
guide therapeutic strategies to enhance CBT efficacy, and the development of realistic goals for the greatest gains (Attix, 2006). Even with
some level of neurocognitive dysfunction, clients can benefit from
CBT via therapeutic modifications and/or learn compensatory strategies to draw from their residual abilities. If practitioners do not have
training or expertise in neuropsychological testing and interpretation,
it is recommended that the therapist develop partnerships with local
neuropsychologists who also have backgrounds in CBT to help assess
their referred client's neurocognitive abilities and help with determining a client's capacity for CBT. Therapists should indicate that they are
looking for specific recommendations related to capacity to participate
in CBT, identification of areas of strengths and weaknesses for treatment planning, and any areas involved with CBT that might require
modification based on the client's results.

It is recommended that practitioners working with geriatric populations are familiar with commonly used standardized, neuropsychological tests. Table 11.3 provides a general overview of commonly used
neuropsychological measures and their corresponding domains. For a
more detailed explanation of these as well as other measures associated
with various domains of neurocognitive functioning, please refer to the
following resources: Lezak et al., 2004; Mitrushina, Boone, Razani, and
D'Elia, 2005; and Strauss, Sherman, and Spreen, 2006. Familiarity with
the administration and interpretation of these measures, along with
other cognitive tests for geriatric assessment, is critical to treatment planning. Although it is heavily recommended that a neuropsychological
evaluation include a comprehensive approach (i.e., multiple tests that tap
various aspects of neurocognition) versus a global screening approach
(i.e., Mini-Mental Status Examination [MMSE]), there are some instances
in which a full battery is precluded (i.e., inpatient hospitalization, time
constraints). Observation of a client's level of motivation and effort

TABLE 11.3 Commonly Used Neuropsychological Measures

Neurocognitive Domain	Name and Brief Description
Global orientation/ mental status	◾ **RBANS:** A short neurocognitive battery assessing immediate and delayed memory, attention, language, and visuospatial skills; assists with detecting overall neurocognitive dysfunction ◾ **MMSE:** A brief measure to evaluate overall global, cognitive functioning (i.e., orientation, immediate and delayed episodic memory, calculation/working memory, visuospatial ability, and language); unidimensional measure ◾ **Cognistat:** Assesses global functioning as well as profile of scores for each domain assessed, including level of consciousness, orientation, attention, comprehension, naming, repetition, construction, memory, calculation, and reasoning (similarities and judgment) ◾ **DRS-2:** Short test battery designed to globally assess adults with suspected dementia in areas such as attention, initiation/perseveration, visuospatial construction, conceptualization, and memory ◾ **CERAD:** Brief test battery designed to evaluate aspects of neurocognitive functioning associated with Alzheimer's disease; the core battery consists of well-recognized seven tests ◾ **Clock Drawing Test:** Quick screen for dementia as well as for visual-spatial, constructional, and executive abilities; requires the participant to draw a clock face with all the numbers on it and to set the time to 10 after 11
Sensory/perceptual functioning	◾ **Sensory-Perceptual Examination:** Gross screening measure that evaluates different aspects of senses ◾ **TPT:** Assesses tactile form recognition, incidental memory for shapes, and spatial location (dominant hand only, nondominant hand only, both hands)
Motor Functioning	◾ **Grooved Pegboard:** Measure of dexterity and fine motor functioning; requires clients to quickly place 25 pegs into designated holes with randomly positioned slots on a pegboard on three separate trials (dominant hand only, nondominant hand only, both hands); pegs with a key along one side must be rotated to match the hole before they can be inserted ◾ **Purdue Pegboard:** Measures unimanual and bimanual finger and hand dexterity; participant is required to take the pins with the preferred hand from the preferred hand cup and place them as quickly as possible in the right or left column of holes during a 30-second period; procedure is repeated with the nonpreferred hand; then pins are removed from both columns and repeated with both hands

(Continued)

TABLE 11.3 Commonly Used Neuropsychological Measures *(Continued)*

Neurocognitive Domain	Name and Brief Description
Motor Functioning *(continued)*	■ **Finger-Tapping Test:** Evaluates fine motor functioning; clients are asked to place their dominant hand palm down, fingers extended, with the index finger resting on a lever that is attached to a counting device in which clients tap their index finger as quickly as possible for 10 seconds, keeping the hand and arm stationary; trial is performed several times until examiner collects counts for five consecutive trials that are within five taps of each other; continued for the nondominant hand ■ **Grip Strength:** Assesses gross motor functioning; participants are instructed to grip a device on two separate trials (dominant hand only, nondominant hand) to measure the force applied by each hand to grip the device
Attention and Concentration	■ **Trail-Making Test A:** Assesses visual search, sequencing, switching, attention, processing speed, and concentration; participant is instructed to quickly draw a continuous line between circled numbers in ascending order ■ **WAIS-IV Digit Span subtest:** A quick auditory test of attention, mental control, and working memory; the client is asked to repeat a series of numbers forward and backward (i.e., in reverse order) ■ **SDMT:** Nonverbal measure of divided attention, visual scanning, tracking, and motor speed of processing; a coding key is presented consisting of nine abstract symbols, each paired with a number and the respondent is required to scan the key and write down the number corresponding to each symbol as rapidly as possible ■ **PASAT:** Measures aspects of divided attention, sustained attention, auditory information processing speed, working memory, and flexibility as well as calculation ability; test of timed attention; a serial-addition test; random series of numbers from 1 to 9 are presented on audiotape, and the person is instructed to consecutively add pairs of numbers such that each number is added to the one that immediately preceded it; the response requirement is sustained over numerous items until the end of the trial, and the interstimulus interval is then decreased, and the same process repeated ■ **Digit/Letter Cancellation Test:** Timed measure of concentration and neglect; client is asked to, as quickly as he or she can, cross out one or two-letter (E and A's) rows of distracter letters (B, S, C, F, H, etc.)
Language functioning	■ **BNT:** Designed to measure object naming from line drawings; client is presented with drawings and asked to name each drawing; if participant cannot freely name the object, a cue is given (i.e., phonemic, semantic, and multiple choice)

(Continued)

TABLE 11.3 Commonly Used Neuropsychological Measures *(Continued)*

Neurocognitive Domain	Name and Brief Description of Neuropsychological Measures
Language functioning *(continued)*	■ **COWAT (FAS/CFL):** Evaluates phonemic fluency and initiation to three different phonemic letter cues in a 60-second period per each letter cue; participant is asked to say as many words as possible as quickly as he or she can from a designated letter (i.e., "F," "A," "S") ■ **Animals:** Assesses semantic fluency and initiation; the participant is required to say as many words as possible from a designated category ■ **BDAE-3:** Provides a full assessment of an aphasic patient's language functioning with specific reference to the classic, anatomically based aphasia syndromes; participant is asked to complete a series of several subtests based on conversational and expository speech, auditory comprehension, oral expression, reading, and writing
Speed of processing	■ **Trail-Making Test A:** Provides a measure of attention, visuomotor processing speed, and visual scanning by requiring the participant to draw lines sequentially connecting 25 encircled numbers distributed on a sheet of paper ■ **WAIS-IV Coding subtest:** Test of visual-motor coordination and motor and mental speed ■ **WAIS-IV Symbol Search subtest:** Assesses visuomotor functioning and speed of processing; participant is required to quickly determine whether certain symbols are among distracter symbols
Executive functioning	■ **WCST:** Assesses one's ability to respond to changing contingencies by shifting cognitive problem-solving strategies, demonstrate mental flexibility in thinking, inhibition; requires that participants sort each stimulus card to one of four target cards, based on various attributes that are not explicitly stated by the tester (i.e., color, form, or number of stimuli) ■ **Trail-Making Test B:** Evaluates aspects such as visuomotor processing speed, set shifting, mental flexibility, and divided attention by requiring the participant to draw a continuous line alternating between numbers and letters in ascending order (1, a, 2, b, 3, c, etc.) ■ **COWAT (FAS/CFL):** Evaluates phonemic fluency and initiation to three different phonemic letter cues in a 60-second period per each letter cue; participant is asked to say as many words as possible as quickly as he or she can from a designated letter (e.g., "F," "A," "S") ■ **Animals:** Measures semantic fluency and initiation by instructing clients to quickly generate as many words as possible to a specific category (i.e., animals) in a 60-second period ■ **Stroop Color and Word Test:** A measure to assess inhibitory control; client is instructed to inhibit a well-learned response (word reading) and instead implement a novel response (text color naming)

(Continued)

TABLE 11.3   Commonly Used Neuropsychological Measures *(Continued)*

Neurocognitive Domain	Name and Brief Description
Executive functioning *(continued)*	■ **WAIS-IV Similarities subtest**: Assesses abstract verbal reasoning by asking the client to identify how two words are similar or alike ■ **WAIS-IV Comprehension subtest:** Evaluates judgment, rules and expressions, and social reasoning by having the client provide responses to social situations ■ **D-KEFS:** Evaluates multiple aspects of executive functioning abilities (e.g., set shifting, mental flexibility) using several subtests
Visuospatial abilities	■ **Clock-Drawing Test:** Quick screen for dementia as well as for visual-spatial, constructional, and executive abilities; requires the participant to draw a clock face with all the numbers on it and to set the time to 10 after 11 ■ **WAIS-IV Block Design subtest:** Evaluates spatial perception and visuospatial abstract processing by copying designs using several blocks with different colors on each side
Learning and memory	■ **CVLT-II:** Measures ability to encode, recall, and recognize verbal information (designated number of words) across five consecutive learning trials; after each trial, the client is prompted to recall as many words as he or she can from the list, thus providing information on immediate/short-term recall and verbal learning; approximately 20–30 minutes later, the client is asked to recall as many words as possible (free recall) and then given semantic cues and asked to discriminate previously learned words from distracter words (recognition) ■ **WMS-IV Logical Memory (LM I & II, recognition):** Evaluates ability to encode, recall, and recognize verbal semantic information; client is read a brief story and asked to recall the content of the story (immediate and delayed recall) as well as later recognize information from the story against distracter information (recognition) ■ **WMS-IV Visual Reproduction (VR I & II):** Assesses ability to encode, recall, and recognize visual designs; client is briefly shown a design(s) for 10 seconds and asked to remember the design and then copy the design on a blank piece of paper as best he or she can; the client is asked to draw each of the designs from memory (free recall/delayed memory) ■ **WMS-IV Visual Reproduction recognition:** Assesses recognition of previously learned visual designs against distracter designs (recognition) ■ **WAIS-IV Arithmetic subtest:** Measures working memory and concentration while verbally manipulating mental mathematical problems; client is instructed to perform various arithmetic problems ranging in difficulty

(Continued)

TABLE 11.3 Commonly Used Neuropsychological Measures *(Continued)*

Neurocognitive Domain	Name and Brief Description
General intelligence	■ **WAIS-IV:** Overall intellectual functioning based on various cognitive subtests resulting in Verbal IQ, Performance IQ, and Full Scale IQ and four index scores (Verbal Comprehension Index, Perceptual Reasoning Index, Working Memory Index, Processing Speed Index) ■ **WAIS-IV Vocabulary subtest:** Estimate of premorbid functioning and overall knowledge for school-learned information; participant is instructed to read and explain the meaning of a list of words ■ **AMNART:** Assesses reading ability; participants are asked to read a list of words aloud and is given points for each correctly pronounced word

Note: AMNART = American National Adult Reading Test (Grober & Sliwinski, 1991; Schwartz & Saffran, 1987); Animals (Goodglass & Kaplan, 1983); BDAE = Boston Diagnostic Aphasia Examination-Third Edition (Goodglass, Kaplan, & Barresi, 2001); BNT = Boston Naming Test (Kaplan, Goodglass, & Weintraub, 1983); CERAD = Consortium to Establish a Registry for Alzheimer's Disease (Morris et al., 1989); COWAT = Controlled Oral Word Association Test (Benton & Hamsher, 1978); CVLT-II = California Verbal Learning Test-Second Edition (Delis, Kramer, Kaplan, & Ober, 2000); Digit/Letter Cancellation Test (Diller et al., 1974); D-KEFS = Delis-Kaplan Executive Functioning System (Delis, Kaplan, & Kramer, 2001); DRS-2 = The Mattis Dementia Rating Scale-2 (Jurica & Leitten, 2001); Finger-Tapping Test (Reitan & Wolfson, 1993); Grip Strength (Reitan & Wolfson, 1993); Grooved Pegboard (Matthews, 1964 (Tiffin, 1968); MMSE = Mini-Mental State Exam (Folstein, Folstein, & McHugh, 1975); PASAT = Paced Serial Addition Test (Gronwall, 1977); RBANS = Repeatable Battery for the Assessment of Neuropsychological Status (Randolph, 1998); SDMT = Symbol Digit Modalities Test (Smith, 1982); Sensory Perceptual Examination (Reitan & Wolfson, 1993); Stroop Color and Word Test (Golden, 1978); TPT = Tactile Performance Test (Reitan & Wolfson, 1993); Trail Making Test A, (Reitan & Wolfson, 1993); Trail Making Test B (Reitan & Wolfson, 1993); WAIS-IV = Wechsler Adult Intelligence Scale-Fourth Edition (Wechsler, 2008); WCST = Wisconsin Card Sorting Test (Heaton, 1981); WMS-IV = Wechsler Memory Scale-Fourth Edition (Wechsler, 2009).

during screening and/or a comprehensive neuropsychological evaluation will provide important information regarding treatment planning, specifically the client's capacity to actively participate in traditional 50- to 60-minute sessions. A comprehensive assessment approach will provide the most detailed information to better inform areas, which may require modification for CBT and/or inform other potentially more appropriate approaches (i.e., behavior therapy, cognitive remediation interventions, family-based approaches). There is no consensus for determination of neurocognitive dysfunction or explicit cut-off scores for CBT. However, most clinicians have used statistical deviations from the normal mean of healthy adults incorporating age, education, and race as a criterion (Mitrushina et al., 2005) to guide the interpretation of a client's performance compared to his or her peers with similar backgrounds. As part of a neuropsychological evaluation, it is also critical to attempt to obtain informant/family reports and/or direct observations of real-world behaviors when possible. Obtaining premorbid information, types of current problems (psychosocial and/or cognitive), sudden/gradual changes, list of current medications, substance use/abuse, other health conditions, medical records, level of education, social support, impressions from neuroimaging findings, if warranted, and employment history are all important areas for CBT treatment planning, as well as understanding a person's neuropsychological functioning.

Other areas critical for understanding feasibility for treatment include an assessment of an older adult's level of insight, affective status, personal and environmental factors, and current emotional and cognitive compensatory strategies (Attix, 2006). Poor insight (anosognosia) can significantly influence treatment outcome. Consideration as to an older adult's level of insight in relationship to other deficits in judgment and reasoning, other cognitive deficits, and/or motivation is particularly important prior to initiating treatment because insight is critical for many CBT techniques and exercises.

Consideration of affective status is also important. Determination of cognitive deficits attributable to a late-life psychiatric problem versus an underlying neurological disease may affect treatment approaches (CBT versus cognitive interventions). A recommended first-line approach is to manage the emotional distress regardless of the etiology. Another consideration is related to factors unique to the client or his or her situation (i.e., family support, involvement, access to services, living alone, personality traits). Understanding of the types of strategies the client has previously attempted to use to help manage his or her cognitive and/or emotional dysfunction is also important. Awareness of previous attempts may assist with understanding what worked and what did not work and may require only slight modification. Reviewing these strategies with clients will help the practitioner decide how to best select therapeutic strategies to enhance CBT.

After this information is taken into consideration and a determination is made that the client does not have the capacity to participate in CBT (i.e., deficits that preclude the use of strategies requiring effortful, higher order processing; poor insight and/or motivation), a referral for alternative treatments for emotional distress might be more appropriate. For example, pharmacological treatment may be more effective in managing the emotional distress than CBT, along with efforts that focus more on behavior therapy (a more concrete approach) and/or consideration of family-based efforts. In cases in which an older adult has significant neurocognitive compromise resulting from a psychiatric disorder, this approach might help better manage the distress initially, thereby enhancing the potential for later participation in CBT. Depending on the nature of the cognitive deficits, the client may also benefit from cognitive remediation therapy or cognitive interventions designed to specifically improve neurocognitive abilities such as attention, memory, and executive functioning (Attix & Welsh-Boehmer, 2006; Penades et al., 2006; Sohlberg & Mateer, 2001). However, in cases in which the compromise is resulting from a progressive neurological disease (e.g., moderate-to-severe stages of Alzheimer's disease), a different approach targeting family members may more effectively help older adult clients, particularly during the middle-to-late phase of the disease process. Family members may benefit from training in strategies related to helping their loved one more effectively manage his or her stress and in making environmental modifications that may subsequently minimize their loved one's stress and enhance his or her quality of life. Family preparation and training may also help reduce and/or prevent caregivers' own level of distress.

Step 2: Augmenting Cognitive Behavioral Therapy for Neurocognitive Dysfunction: Therapeutic Strategies

If a determination is made that the older adult *does* have the capacity to participate in CBT with at least marginal-to-adequate neurocognitive functioning, then the next step is to identify specific areas of neurocognitive dysfunction in order to consider potential modifications to CBT and/or incorporation of cognitive rehabilitation interventions targeting improvement in these areas. Similar to the notion that CBT approaches are more likely effective when concepts and skills are applied to the unique problems facing clients, tailoring CBT to a client's unique level of neurocognitive functioning is equally important. Careful examination of the neuropsychological profile can contribute to both appropriate goal selection and type(s) of therapeutic strategies, which might best maximize areas of strength and compensate for weaknesses (Cicerone, 2005). To do so, the clinician should first determine the nature of dysfunction in different neurocognitive domains. For example, does a memory deficit reflect a problem with storage versus retrieval? If the deficit is related to a problem with retrieval, search strategies, which may provide cueing for the client in and between sessions, might enhance this aspect of memory (i.e., handouts, CD/DVD, podcasts, reminder calls to complete homework assignments, pagers). On the other hand, if the memory deficit is storage based, effortful processing strategies may be more beneficial and may include supplemental training in association techniques, visual association methods (i.e., stop-sign symbol for thought-stopping concept), story methods, coaching calls to reinforce learning, and subsequent long-term memory storage of CBT concepts and skills in and between sessions. Thus, it is merely not enough to randomly implement therapeutic strategies without evidence of domain-specific deficits (e.g., prescribing that the patient use post-it notes to help with "memory problems," specific components of memory need to be identified). Targeting domain-specific deficits informed by data is likely to yield more meaningful changes and subsequent therapeutic results. Likewise, determining the client's sensory modality preference (i.e., verbal versus visual processing) may also assist with the selection of therapeutic strategies.

Depending on the diagnosis (e.g., late-life depression, stroke) and nature of neurocognitive dysfunction, selection of the approach(es) to enhance CBT may rely on therapist adaptations (i.e., modification of protocols, worksheets, presentation of information), client adaptations (i.e., use of practical/external aids or cognitive training strategies to enhance cognitive abilities), or a combination of these approaches. Examples of such strategies are detailed in column 3 of Table 11.2 in which general therapeutic strategies are associated with their corresponding neurocognitive domains. Various strategies can be used to enhance CBT and may include mnemonic strategies, which refer to mental memory or learning aids (i.e., a method of loci—visually associating target items along a fixed visual route), or external aids/devices (e.g., reminder calls for homework, CBT concept reminder post-it notes for the refrigerator, voice recorders). Mnemonic strategies rely on associations between easy-to-remember constructs, which can be related in some way back to the information that is to be remembered. This approach is based on the premise that the human mind more easily remembers spatial, humorous, personal, or otherwise meaningful information than arbitrary sequences of simple to complex information. Mnemonic and external aids are strategies in which therapists can train clients to better remember information. There are also therapeutic strategies that rely on therapist initiation (i.e., reminder calls, creating session agenda/handouts, modifying materials, simplifying concepts). Understanding of the appropriateness of certain therapeutic strategies or techniques is crucial (Koltai & Branch, 1999), particularly when selecting a strategy to enhance CBT. In some instances, only minor modifications are needed (e.g., reminder calls to complete homework and reinforce learning). In other cases, it may be determined that based on neuropsychological test results, significant modifications are needed, which may require greater structure in and between sessions (e.g., use of flipcharts, simplified worksheets and handouts, written objectives, frequent checking for understanding) and/or assistance from involvement of family members. It should be noted that a random approach process of implementing therapeutic strategies is not likely to enhance outcomes. For example, an older adult with memory problems will not benefit from being told to use external aids such as post-it notes to help remember concepts and exercises. It should be emphasized that, as discussed earlier, selection of specific therapeutic strategies to enhance CBT should be informed by the evidence or data produced from the neuropsychological evaluation (i.e., memory problems specific to storage versus retrieval). This chapter was not intended to provide detailed descriptions of some of the more cognitive-based interventions. However, for a more detailed description of these types of interventions (spaced retrieval, face–name technique, verbal elaboration (story method), retrieval search techniques, and overt/covert repetition), recommended resources include the following: Attix and Welsh-Boehmer (2006); Halligan and Wade (2005); and Sohlberg and Mateer (2001).

Results from neuropsychological assessment should inform the practitioner's understanding of which aspects of CBT might require greater augmentation over others. Given that some of the training associated with CBT is dependent on multiple areas of neurocognitive functioning (i.e., executive, language, attention, learning, and memory), several therapeutic strategies may need to be considered. For example, a client who performs poorly on tests assessing attention (sustained attention), processing speed (verbal), and memory (retrieval deficits) may benefit from multiple strategies that involve breaking information down into small and concrete chunks, minimizing the amount of material covered in session, providing a client agenda list for each session to help stay focused, presentation of concepts using symbols, checking for understanding after concepts are presented prior to moving on to new material, slowing down the presentation of concepts, reducing environmental distractions, providing handouts to remember concepts in between sessions along with written instructions for homework, and conducting coaching calls in between sessions to prompt recall of concepts and remind the client to complete homework assignments. Conversely, maximizing strengths may also enhance treatment. For instance, if the same individual demonstrated strengths in areas of visual attention and visual memory, he or she may more likely benefit from therapeutic concepts that are presented using symbols or designs (e.g., a red stop sign next to a person standing and thinking to illustrate thought stopping or challenging of thoughts).

When a client's neurocognitive functioning is questionable or borderline in terms of the capacity to benefit from CBT, it may be helpful to incorporate family members as a supplement to the client's individual therapy or as the sole focus of therapy. Because family members often bring or accompany older adults to treatment, the role of the family should not be underestimated. Incorporation of family members into sessions can help to provide education regarding psychiatric disorders and/or neurological diseases seen in late life, as well as strategies for responding to their loved one's negative and pessimistic thoughts or behaviors in a more constructive manner and for implementing and reinforcing behavioral-based interventions. Family members may also benefit from learning strategies to reinforce their loved one's application of CBT strategies at home. They may also assist their loved one with generalizing concepts in their home environment along with the application of relevant external aids to enhance learning and memory. Again, the amount of emphasis placed on the family will depend largely on the nature and extent of their loved one's neurocognitive dysfunction. Incorporation of family members can serve to provide the family unit with ongoing emotional support and education in addition to training. The key to success is building a quality working alliance with the family and client to foster a successful collaboration.

Step 3: Treatment Monitoring and Evaluation

Once the treatment plan and therapeutic strategies have been implemented, similar to most CBT approaches, treatment progress should be closely monitored to make any necessary adjustments. This is critical in order to maintain client motivation for treatment and maximize gains. Evaluation of CBT might incorporate traditional, standardized measures of distress as well as client- and family-perceived gains, subjective well-being, limitations, activity level, problem-solving abilities, and/or participation in everyday activities of daily living. Neuropsychological assessments are not designed to evaluate the impact of CBT and thus are not recommended solely as a source of outcome data. However, such measures do serve the purpose of evaluating neurocognitive functioning for baseline and serial assessments, which help to provide information on potential changes in cognitive functioning. These types of assessments should be spaced out to minimize the potential for practice effects.

Barriers and Facilitators to Integrating Neuropsychological Functioning Into Cognitive Behavioral Therapy

Traditionally, this type of proposed framework, which incorporates a neuropsychological-informed approach, has not been routinely incorporated into CBT assessment or treatments for that matter. Several reasons have contributed to the lack of integration including concerns regarding (a) time restrictions, (b) competency in neuropsychological assessment and understanding regarding brain functioning, (c) misperception that neuropsychological functioning does not influence CBT, or (d) a lack of understanding/appreciation regarding the connection between brain–behavior relationships (i.e., "It doesn't impact what I'm doing. I only see older adult clients with depression or anxiety. I don't treat clients with brain damage."). Although these may be legitimate concerns in some respects, practitioners working with geriatric populations should be familiar, if not well versed, in terms of the growing research linking brain functioning to behavior. These relationships have implications for success in mental health treatment. Additionally, given the neurocognitive changes associated with normal aging, along with the increased risk for neurological changes or changes in cognitive functioning associated with aging and psychiatric disorders, practitioners need to be aware of these types of issues and their impact on CBT success. As previously discussed in this chapter, neglecting to understand an older client's level of neurocognitive functioning may lead to early attrition on the part of the client and/or therapist frustration due to a misattribution regarding client motivation.

There are several strategies that practitioners should consider for overcoming these types of barriers related to incorporating neuropsychological functioning into everyday practice with older adults. For example, continued education and training (workshops, conferences) serve as an educational opportunity for practitioners to gain hands-on experience to improve their knowledge and understanding regarding neuropsychological functioning, assessment, and interpretation. Although one is not expected to become an expert by attending a workshop, this type of opportunity can certainly enhance one's understanding. Additionally, readings, coursework, and/or grand rounds may serve as other educational opportunities to build on one's knowledge base. Another strategy is to make a referral for such an assessment to a qualified neuropsychologist. The obtained feedback can greatly assist with identifying areas of strengths and weakness as well as capacity for CBT. As discussed earlier, this may require practitioners to develop partnerships with local area neuropsychologists who may help with interpreting neuropsychological information and learning how to administer an unfamiliar but newly developed, evidence-based neuropsychological test. Consulting with other professionals working with geriatric populations may also be helpful because multidisciplinary approaches are vital to working with geriatric populations. Thus, establishing partnerships with geriatric practitioners from various fields may be helpful if/when additional consultation is needed (e.g., referral to a neurologist to rule out dementia).

CONCLUSIONS

In summary, this chapter proposes an innovative framework for incorporating neuropsychological functioning into CBT for older adults. The link between brain–behavior relationships has been well documented. CBT tasks demand efficient neurocognitive functioning, thus understanding a client's level of cognitive abilities and capacity for treatment will help to inform areas in need of potential modification when working with adult populations. Neuropsychological evaluations will help provide rich data for practitioners to make empirically informed choices about areas requiring modification for CBT. Therapeutic strategies outlined in this chapter may also serve to enhance outcomes and minimize early dropout. Thus, this type of contemporary approach may prove particularly beneficial in the treatment of psychiatric problems encountered in late life.

REFERENCES

Alexopoulos, G. (2005). Depression in the elderly. *Lancet, 365*, 1961–1970.

Alexopoulos, G., Kiosses, D., Klimstra, S., Kalayam, B., & Bruce, M. L. (2002). Clinical presentation of the "depression-executive dysfunction syndrome" of late life. *American Journal of Geriatric Psychiatry, 10*, 98–106.

Alexopoulos, G., Kiosses, D., Murphy, C., & Heo, M. (2004). Executive dysfunction, heart disease burden and remission of geriatric depression. *Neuropsychopharmacology, 29*, 2278–2284.

Alexopoulos, G., Meyers, B., Young, R., Kalayam, B., Kakuma, T., Gabrielle, M., et al. (2000). Executive dysfunction and long-term outcomes of geriatric depression. *Archives of General Psychiatry, 57*, 285–290.

Alexopoulos, G., Raue, P., Kanellopoulos, D., Mackin, S., & Areán, P. (2008). Problem solving therapy for the depression-executive dysfunction syndrome of late life. *International Journal of Geriatric Psychiatry, 23*(8), 782–788.

Alexopoulos, G., Vrontou, C., Kakuma, T., Meyers, B., Young, R., Klausner, E., et al. (1996). Disability in geriatric depression. *American Journal of Psychiatry, 153*, 877–885.

Attix, D. (2006). An integrated model for geriatric neuropsychological intervention. In D. Attix & K. Welsh-Boehmer (Eds.), *Geriatric neuropsychology: Assessment and intervention*. New York, NY: Guilford Press.

Attix, D., & Welsh-Boehmer, K. (Eds.). (2006). *Geriatric neuropsychology: Assessment and intervention*. New York, NY: Guilford Press.

Austin, M., Mitchell, P., Wilhelm, K., Parker, G., Hickie, I., Brodaty, H., et al. (1999). Cognitive function in depression: A distinct pattern of frontal impairment in melancholia? *Psychological Medicine, 29*, 73–85.

Barrowclough, C., King, P., Colville, J., Russell, E., Burns, A., & Tarrier, N. (2001). A randomized trial of the effectiveness of cognitive behavioral therapy and supportive counseling for anxiety symptoms in older adults. *Journal of Consulting and Clinical Psychology, 69*, 756–762.

Beaudreau, S., & O'Hara, R. (2008). Late-life anxiety and cognitive impairment: A review. *American Journal of Geriatric Psychiatry, 16*(10), 790–803.

Beauregard, M., Levelque, J., & Bourgouin, P. (2000). Neural correlates of conscious self-regulation of emotion. *Journal of Neuroscience, 21,* 1–6.

Bench, C., Friston, K., Brown, R., Scott, L., Frackowiak, R., & Dolan, R. (1992). The anatomy of melancholia: Focal abnormalities of cerebral blood flow in major depression. *Psychological Medicine, 22,* 607–617.

Benton, A., & Hamsher, K. (1978). *Multilingual aphasia examination.* Iowa City, IA: The University of Iowa.

Berkowitz, R., Coplan, J., Reddy, D., & Gorman, J. M. (2007). The human dimension: How the prefrontal cortex modulates the subcortical fear response. *Review of Neuroscience, 18,* 191–207.

Bierman, E., Comijs, H., Jonker, C., & Beekman, A. T. (2005). Effects of anxiety versus depression on cognition in later life. *American Journal of Geriatric Psychiatry, 13,* 686–693.

Boone, K., Lesser, I., Miller, B., Wohl, M., Berman, N., Lee, A., et al. (1995). Cognitive functioning in older depressed outpatients: Relationship of presence and severity of depression to neuropsychological test scores. *Neuropsychology, 9,* 390–398.

Booth, J., Schinka, J., Brown, L., Mortimer, J. A., & Borenstein, A. R. (2006). Five-factor personality dimensions, mood states, and cognitive performance in older adults. *Journal of Clinical & Experimental Neuropsychology, 28,* 676–683.

Buchsbaum, M., Wu, J., DeLisi, L., Holcomb, H., Kessler, R., Johnson, J., et al. (1986). Frontal cortex and basal ganglia metabolic rates assessed by positron emission tomography with [18F]2-deoxyglucose in affective illness. *Journal of Affective Disorders, 10,* 137–152.

Burns, A., Jacoby, R., & Levey, R. (1990). Psychiatric phenomena in Alzheimer's disease. III: Disorders of mood. *British Journal of Psychiatry, 157,* 81–86.

Bussiere, T., & Hoff, P. (2000). Morphological changes in human cerebral cortex during normal aging. In P. Hof & C. Mobbs (Eds.), *Functional neurobiology of aging* (pp. 77–84). San Diego, CA: Academic Press.

Butters, M. A., Whyte, E. M., Nebes, R. D., Begley, A. E., Dew, M. A., Mulsant, B. H., et al. (2004). The nature and determinants of neuropsychological functioning in late-life depression. *Archives of General Psychiatry, 61*(6), 587–595.

Caudle, D., Senior, A., Wetherell, J., Rhoades, H., Beck, J., Kunik, M., et al. (2007). Cognitive errors, symptoms severity, and response to cognitive behavior therapy in older adults with generalized anxiety disorder. *American Journal of Geriatric Psychiatry, 15,* 680–689.

Chen, C. S., Chiang, I. C., Li, C. W., Lin, W. C., Lu, C. Y., Hsieh, T. J., et al. (2009). Proton magnetic resonance spectroscopy of late-life major depressive disorder. *Psychiatry Research: Neuroimaging, 172*(3), 210–214.

Cicerone, K. (2005). Methodological issues in evaluating the effectiveness of cognitive rehabilitation. In P. Halligan & D. Wade (Eds.), *Effectiveness of rehabilitation for cognitive deficits.* New York, NY: Oxford University Press.

Cotter, D., Mackay, D., Landau, S., Kerwin, R., & Everall, I. (2001). Reduced glial density and neuronal size in the anterior cingulate cortex in major depressive disorder. *Archives of General Psychiatry, 58,* 545–553.

Craske, M., Barlow, D., & O'Leary, T. (1991). *Mastery of your anxiety and worry (MAW): Client workbook (treatments that work).* New York, NY: Oxford University Press.

Culang, M. E., Sneed, J. R., Keilp, J. G., Rutherford, B. R., Pelton, G., Devanand, D. P., et al. (2009). Change in cognitive functioning following acute antidepressant treatment in late-life depression. *American Journal of Geriatric Psychiatry, 17*(10), 881–888.

Cummings, J. (1992). Depression and Parkinson's disease: A review. *American Journal of Psychiatry, 149,* 443–454.

Cummings, J., & Trimble, M. (2002). *A concise guide to neuropsychiatry and behavioral neurology* (2nd ed.). Washington, DC: American Psychiatric Publishing, Inc.

Delis, D., Kaplan, E., & Kramer, J. (2001). *Delis-Kaplan Executive Function System (D-KEFS).* San Antonio, TX: The Psychological Corporation.

Delis, D., Kramer, J., Kaplan, E., & Ober, B. (2000). *CVLT-II California Verbal Learning Test.* San Antonio, TX: The Psychological Corporation.

DeLuca, A., Lenze, E., Mulsant, B. H., Butters, M. A., Karp, J. F., Dew, M. A., et al. (2005). Comorbid anxiety disorder in late-life depression: Association with memory decline over four years. *International Journal of Geriatric Psychiatry, 20,* 848–854.

DeRubeis, R., Evans, M., Hollon, S., Garvey, M., Grove, W., & Tuason, V. (1990). How does cognitive therapy work? Cognitive change and symptom change in cognitive therapy and pharmacotherapy for depression. *Journal of Consulting and Clinical Psychology, 58,* 862–869.

Dew, M. A., Whyte, E. M., Lenze, E. J., Houck, P. R., Mulsant, B. H., Pollock, B. G., et al. (2007). Recovery from major depression in older adults receiving augmentation of antidepressant pharmacotherapy. *American Journal of Psychiatry, 164*(6), 892–899.

Diller, L., Ben-Yishay, Y., Gertman, L., Goodkin, R., Gordon, W., & Weinberg, J. (1974). *Studies in cognition and rehabilitation in hemiplegia: Rehabilitation Monograph 50.* New York, NY: New York University Medical Center Institute of Rehabilitation Medicine.

Dobkin, R., Allen, L., & Menza, M. (2006). A cognitive-behavioral treatment package for depression in Parkinson's disease. *Psychosomatics, 47*(3), 259–263.

Dotson, V., Davatzikos, C., Kraut, M., & Resnick, S. (2009). Depressive symptoms and brain volumes in older adults: A longitudinal magnetic resonance imaging study. *Journal of Psychiatry Neuroscience, 34*(5), 367–375.

Douglas, K. M., & Porter, R. J. (2009). Longitudinal assessment of neuropsychological function in major depression. *Australian and New Zealand Journal of Psychiatry, 43*(12), 1105–1117.

Dreer, L., Krzywanski, S., Huthwaite, J., DeVivo, M., Novack, T., & Marson, D. (2008). Neurocognitive predictors of medical decision-making capacity in patients with traumatic brain injury. *Rehabilitation Psychology, 53,* 486–497.

Drevets, W., Price, J., Simpson, J. T., Reich, T., Vannier, M., & Raichle, M. (1997). Subgenual prefrontal cortex abnormalities in mood disorders. *Nature, 386,* 824–827.

Driscoll, H. C., Karp, J. F., Dew, M. A., & Reynolds, C. F., III. (2007). Getting better, getting well: Understanding and managing partial and nonresponse to pharmacological treatment of nonpsychotic major depression in old age. *Drugs & Aging, 24*(10), 801–814.

D'Zurilla, T., & Nezu, A. (2007). *Problem-solving therapy: A positive approach to clinical intervention* (3rd ed.). New York, NY: Springer Publishing Company.

Elderkin-Thompson, V., Mintz, J., Haroon, E., Lavretsky, H., & Kumar, A. (2006). Executive dysfunction and memory in older patients with major and minor depression. *Archives of Clinical Neuropsychology, 21*(7), 669–676.

Elkis, H., Friedman, L., Buckley, P., Lee, H., Lys, C., Kaufman, B., et al. (1996). Increased prefrontal sulcal prominence in relatively young patients with unipolar major depression. *Psychiatry Research, 67*, 123–134.

Feinstein, A., Roy, P., Lobaugh, N., Feinstein, K., O'Connor, P., & Black, S. (2004). Structural brain abnormalities in multiple sclerosis patients with major depression. *Neurology, 62*, 586–590.

Filley, C. (2001). *The behavioral neurology of white matter.* New York, NY: Oxford University Press.

Folstein, M., Folstein, S., & McHugh, P. (1975). "Mini-mental state." A practical method for grading the cognitive state of patients for the clinician. *Journal of Psychiatric Research, 12*, 189–198.

Ghaffar, O., & Feinstein, A. (2007). The neuropsychiatry of multiple sclerosis: A review of recent developments. *Current Opinion in Psychiatry, 20*(3), 278–285.

Goldapple, K., Segal, Z., Garson, C., Lau, M., Bieling, P., Kennedy, S., et al. (2004). Modulation of cortical-limbic pathways in major depression: Treatment-specific effects of cognitive behavior therapy. *Archives of General Psychiatry, 61*(1), 34–41.

Golden, C. (1978). *Stroop Color and Word Test: A manual for clinical and experimental uses.* Chicago, IL: Stoelting.

Goodglass, H., & Kaplan, E. (1983). *The assessment of aphasia and related disorders* (2nd ed.). Philadelphia, PA: Lea & Febiger.

Goodglass, H., Kaplan, E., & Barresi, B. (2001). *Boston Diagnostic Aphasia Examination* (3rd ed.). Philadelphia, PA: Lippincott Williams & Wilkins.

Gorman, J., Kent, J., Sullivan, G., & Coplan, J. (1999). Neuroanatomical hypothesis of panic disorder, revised. *American Journal of Psychiatry, 157*, 493–505.

Graeff, F., Guimaraes, F., De Andrade, T., & Deakin, J. F. (1996). Role of 5-HT in stress, anxiety, and depression. *Pharmacological Biochemistry and Behaviors, 54*, 129–141.

Grawe, K. (2007). *Neuropsychotherapy: How the neurosciences inform psychotherapy.* Mahwah, NJ: Lawrence Erlbaum Associates.

Greenberger, D., & Padesky, C. (1995). *Mind over mood: Change how you feel by changing the way you think.* New York, NY: Guilford Press.

Grober, E., & Sliwinski, M. (1991). Development and validation of a model for estimating premorbid intelligence in the elderly. *Journal of Clinical and Experimental Neuropsychology, 13*, 933–949.

Gronwall, D. M. A. (1977). Paced auditory serial-addition task: A measure of recovery from concussion. *Perceptual and Motor Skills, 44*, 367–373.

Halligan, P., & Wade, D. (2005). *Effectiveness of rehabilitation for cognitive deficits.* New York, NY: Oxford University Press.

Hariri, A., Bookheimer, S., & Mazziotta, J. (2000). Modulating emotional responses: Effects of a neocortical network on the limbic system. *Neuroreport, 11*, 43–48.

Hart, R., Kwentus, J., Taylor, J., & Hawkins, S. (1987). Rate of forgetting in dementia and depression. *Journal of Consulting and Clinical Psychology, 55*, 101–105.

Heaton, R. (1981). *Wisconsin card sorting test manual.* Odessa, FL: Psychological Assessment Resources.

Herrmann, L., Goodwin, G., & Ebmeier, K. (2007). The cognitive neuropsychology of depression in the elderly. *Psychological Medicine, 37,* 1693–1702.

Hogan, M. (2003). Divided attention in older but not younger adults is impaired by anxiety. *Experimental Aging and Research, 29,* 111–136.

Hoptman, M., Gunning-Dixon, F., Murphy, C., Lim, K., & Alexopoulos, G. (2006). Structural neuroimaging research methods in geriatric depression. *American Journal of Geriatric Psychiatry, 14,* 812–822.

Hunt, S., Baker, A., Michie, P., & Kavanagh, D. (2009). Neurocognitive profiles of people with comorbid depression and alcohol use: Implications for psychological interventions. *Addictive Behaviors, 34,* 878–886.

Jaeger, J., & Douglas, E. (1992). Neuropsychiatric rehabilitation for persistent mental illness. *Psychiatric Quarterly, 63,* 71–94.

Julian, L., & Mohr, D. (2006). Cognitive predictors of response to treatment for depression in multiple sclerosis. *Journal of Neuropsychiatry and Clinical Neurosciences, 18*(3), 356–363.

Jurica, P., & Leitten, C. M. S. (2001). *Dementia Rating Scale-2 (DRS-2): Professional manual.* Odessa, FL: Psychological Assessment Resources.

Kalayam, B., & Alexopoulos, G. (1999). Prefrontal dysfunction and treatment response in geriatric depression. *Archives of General Psychiatry, 56,* 713–718.

Kaplan, E., Goodglass, H., & Weintraub, S. (1983). *Boston Naming Test.* Philadelphia, PA: Lea & Febiger.

Khundakar, A., Morris, C., Oakley, A., McMeekin, W., & Thomas, A. J. (2009). Morphometric analysis of neuronal and glial cell pathology in the dorsolateral prefrontal cortex in late-life depression. *The British Journal of Psychiatry, 195*(2), 163–169.

Kohler, S., Thomas, A. J., Lloyd, A., Barber, R., Almeida, O. P., & O'Brien, J. T. (2010). White- matter hyperintensities, cortisol levels, brain atrophy and continuing cognitive deficits in late-life depression. *The British Journal of Psychiatry, 196*(2), 143–149.

Koltai, D., & Branch, L. (1999). Cognitive and affective interventions to maximize abilities and adjustment in dementia. *Annals of Psychiatry: Basic and Clinical Neurosciences, 7,* 241–255.

Kramer-Ginsberg, E., Greenwald, B. S., Krishnan, K. R. R., Christiansen, B., Hu, J., Ashtari, M., et al. (1999). Neuropsychological functioning and MRI signal hyperintensities in geriatric depression. *The American Journal Psychiatry, 156*(3), 438–444.

Krishnan, K. (2002). Biological risk factors in late life depression. *Biological Psychiatry, 52,* 185–192.

Krishnan, K., Hays, J., George, L., & Blazer, D. (1998). Six-month outcomes for MRI-related vascular depression. *Depression and Anxiety, 8,* 142–146.

Krishnan, K., Tupler, L., Ritchie, J., McDonald, W., Knight, D., Nemeroff, C., et al. (1996). Apolipoprotein E-epsilon 4 frequency in geriatric depression. *Biological Psychiatry, 40,* 69–71.

Krishnan, K. R. R., Taylor, W. D., McQuoid, D. R., MacFall, J. R., Payne, M. E., Provenzale, J. M., et al. (2004). Clinical characteristics of magnetic resonance imaging-defined subcortical ischemic depression. *Biological Psychiatry, 55*(4), 390–397.

Kumar, A., Aizenstein, H. M., & Ballmaier, M. M. (2008). Multimodal neuroimaging in late-life mental disorders: Entering a more mature phase of clinical neuroscience research. *American Journal of Geriatric Psychiatry, 16*(4), 251–254.

Kumar, A., Gupta, R. C., Albert Thomas, M., Alger, J., Wyckoff, N., & Hwang, S. (2004). Biophysical changes in normal-appearing white matter and subcortical nuclei in late-life major depression detected using magnetization transfer. *Psychiatry Research, 130*(2), 131–140.

Lampe, I. K., Hulshoff, P., Janssen, J., Schnack, H. G., Kahn, R. S., & Heeren, T. J. (2003). Association of depression duration with reduction of global cerebral gray matter volume in female patients with recurrent major depressive disorder. *American Journal of Psychiatry, 160,* 2052–2054.

LeDoux, J. (1996). *The emotional brain.* New York, NY: Simon and Schuster.

Lezak, M., Loring, D., Howieson, D., Fischer, J., & Hannay, H. (2004). *Neuropsychological assessment* (4th ed.). New York, NY: Oxford University Press.

Lockwood, K. A., Alexopoulos, G. S., & van Gorp, W. G. (2002). Executive dysfunction in geriatric depression. *American Journal of Psychiatry, 159*(7), 1119–1126.

Longmore, R. J., & Worrell, M. (2007). Do we need to challenge thoughts in cognitive behavior therapy? *Clinical Psychology Review, 27*(2), 173–187.

López-Larson, M., DelBello, M., Zimmerman, M., Schwiers, M., & Strakowski, S. (2002). Regional prefrontal gray and white matter abnormalities in bipolar disorder. *Biological Psychiatry, 52,* 93–100.

Mackin, R. S., Areán, P., & Elite-Marcandonatou, A. (2006). Problem solving therapy for the treatment of depression for a patient with Parkinson's disease and mild cognitive impairment: A case study. *Neuropsychiatric Disease and Treatment, 2*(3), 375–379.

Magistretti, S., Joray, S., & Pellvin, L. (2000). Brain energy metabolism: Cellular aspects and relevance to functional brain imaging. In P. Hof & C. Mobbs (Eds.), *Functional neurobiology of aging* (pp. 203–209). San Diego, CA: Academic Press.

Mann, J., Malone, K., Diehl, D., Perel, J., Cooper, T., & Mintun, M. (1996). Demonstration of vivo of reduced serotonin responsivity in the brain of untreated depressed patients. *American Journal of Psychiatry, 153,* 174–182.

Mantella, R., Butters, M., Dew, M., Mulsant, B. H., Begley, A. E., Tracey, B., et al. (2007). Cognitive impairment in late-life generalized anxiety disorder. *American Journal of Geriatric Psychiatry, 15,* 1–7.

Marson, D., & Dreer, L. (2007). Competence. In S. Gauthier (Ed.), *Clinical diagnosis and management of Alzheimer's Disease* (3rd ed., pp. 323–338). Oxon, United Kingdom: Informa Healthcare.

Marson, D., Dreer, L., Krzywanski, S., Huthwaite, J., DeVivo, M., & Novack, T. (2005). Impairment and partial recovery of medical decision making capacity in traumatic brain injury: A six month longitudinal study. *Archives of Physical Medicine and Rehabilitation, 86*(5), 889–895.

Mast, B. T., Miles, T., Penninx, B. W., Yaffe, K., Rosano, C., Satterfield, S., et al. (2008). Vascular disease and future risk of depressive symptomatology in older adults: Findings from the Health, Aging, and Body Composition study. *Biological Psychiatry, 64*(4), 320–326.

Mathew, S., Mao, X., Coplan, J. D., Smith, E. L., Sackeim, H. A., Gorman, J. M., et al. (2004). Dorsolateral prefrontal cortical pathology in generalized anxiety disorder: A proton magnetic resonance spectroscopic imaging study. *American Journal of Psychiatry, 161,* 1119–1121.

Mayberg, H., Lewis, P., Regenold, W. T., & Wagner, H. (1994). Paralimbic hypoperfusion in unipolar depression. *Journal of Nuclear Medicine, 35,* 929–934.

McClintock, S., Husain, M., Greer, T., & Cullum, C. (2010). Association between depression severity and neurocognitive function in major depressive disorder: A review and synthesis. *Neuropsychology, 24*, 9–34.

McGuigan, C., & Hutchinson, M. (2006). Unrecognized symptoms of depression in a community-based population with multiple sclerosis. *Journal of Neurology, 253*, 219–223.

Minden, S., & Schiffer, R. (1990). Affective disorders in multiple sclerosis: Review and recommendations for clinical research. *Archives of Neurology, 47*, 98–104.

Mitrushina, M., Boone, K., Razani, J., & D'Elia, L. (Eds.). (2005). *Handbook of normative data for neuropsychological assessment* (2nd ed.). New York, NY: Oxford University Press.

Mohlman, J. (2005). Does executive dysfunction affect treatment outcome in late-life mood and anxiety disorders. *Journal of Geriatric Psychiatry and Neurology, 18*, 97–108.

Mohlman, J. (2008). More power to the executive? A preliminary test of CBT plus executive skills training for treatment of late-life GAD. *Cognitive and Behavioral Practice, 15*, 306–316.

Mohlman, J., Gorenstein, E., Kleber, M., de Jesus, M., Gorman, J., & Papp, L. (2003). Standard and enhanced cognitive-behavior therapy for late-life generalized anxiety disorder: Two pilot investigations. *American Journal of Geriatric Psychiatry, 11*(1), 24–32.

Mohlman, J., & Gorman, J. (2005). The role of executive functioning in CBT: A pilot study with anxious older adults. *Behaviour Research and Therapy, 43*(4), 447–465.

Mohlman, J., Price, R. B., Eldreth, D. A., Chazin, D., Glover, D. M., & Kates, W. R. (2009). The relation of worry to prefrontal cortex volume in older adults with and without generalized anxiety disorder. *Psychiatry Research: Neuroimaging, 173*(2), 121–127.

Mohr, D., Hart, S., Julian, L., Catledge, C., Honos-Webb, L, Vella, L., & Tasch, E. T. (2005). Telephone-administered psychotherapy for depression. *Archives of General Psychiatry, 62*, 1007–1014.

Morris, J. C., Heyman, A., Mohs, R. C., Hughes, J. P., van Belle, G., Fillenbaum, G., et al. (1989). The Consortium to Establish a Registry for Alzheimer's Disease (CERAD). Part I. Clinical and neuropsychological assessment of Alzheimer's disease. *Neurology, 39*(9), 1159–1165.

Mulsant, B., Pollock, B., Kirshner, M., Shen, C., Dodge, H., & Ganguli, M. (2003). Serum anticholinergic activity in a community-based sample of older adults: Relationship with cognitive performance. *Archives of General Psychiatry, 60*(2), 198–203.

Murphy, C., & Alexopoulos, G. (2006). Attention network dysfunction and treatment response of geriatric depression. *Journal of Clinical & Experimental Neuropsychology, 25*, 866–877.

Nebes, R. D., Butters, M. A., Mulsant, B. H., Pollock, B. G., Zmuda, M. D., Houck, P. R., et al. (2000). Decreased working memory and processing speed mediate cognitive impairment in geriatric depression. *Psychological Medicine, 30*, 679–691.

Nebes, R., Pollock, B., Mulsant, B., Kirshner, M., Halligan, E., Zmuda, M. D., et al. (1997). Low-level serum anticholinergicity as a source of baseline cognitive heterogeneity in geriatric depressed patients. *Psychopharmacological Bulletin, 33*, 715–720.

Oathamshaw, S., & Haddock, G. (2006). Do people with intellectual disabilities and psychosis have the cognitive skills required to undertake cognitive behavioural therapy? *Journal of Applied Research in Intellectual Disabilities, 19*(1), 35–46.

O'Brien, J., Loyd, A., McKeith, I., Gholkar, A., & Ferrier, N. (2004). A longitudinal study of hippocampal volume, cortisol levels, and cognition in older depressed subjects. *American Journal of Psychiatry, 161,* 2081–2090.

Penades, R., Catalan, R., Salamero, M., Boget, T., Puig, O., Guarch, J., et al. (2006). Cognitive remediation therapy for outpatients with chronic schizophrenia: A controlled and randomized study. *Schizophrenia Research, 87,* 323–331.

Phillips, M., Drevets, W., Rauch, S., & Lane, R. (2003). Neurobiology of emotion perception II: Implications for major psychiatric disorders. *Biological Psychiatry, 54,* 515–528.

Post, R., Denicoff, K., Leverich, G., Huggins, T., Post, S., & Luckenbaugh, D. (2000). Neuropsychological deficits of primary affective illness: Implications for therapy. *Psychiatric Annals, 30*(7), 485–494.

Potter, G. G., Kittinger, J. D., Wagner, H. R., Steffens, D. C., & Krishnan, R. (2004). Prefrontal neuropsychological predictors of treatment remission in late-life depression. *Neuropsychopharmacology, 29*(12), 2266–2271.

Randolph, C. (1998). *RBANS manual.* San Antonio, TX: The Psychological Corporation.

Raskin, J., Wiltse, C., Siegal, A., Sheikh, J., Xu, J., Dinkel, J. J., et al. (2007). Efficacy of duloxetine on cognition, depression, and pain in elderly patients with major depressive disorder: An 8-week, double-blind, placebo-controlled trial. *American Journal of Psychiatry, 164,* 900–909.

Raz, N. (2000). Aging of the brain and its impact on cognitive performance: Integration of structural and functional findings. In F. Craik & T. Salthouse (Eds.), *Handbook of aging and cognition* (pp. 1–90). Mahwah, NJ: Lawrence Erlbaum Associates.

Raz, N., Gunning, F. M., Dupuis, J. H., McQuain, J., Briggs, S. D., Loken, W. J., et al. (1997). Selective aging of the human cortex in vivo: Differential vulnerability of the prefrontal gray matter. *Cerebral Cortex, 7,* 268–282.

Reitan, R., & Wolfson, D. (1993). *The Halstead-Reitan Neuropsychological Test Battery: Theory and clinical interpretation.* Tucson, AZ: Neuropsychology Press.

Reuter-Lorenz, P., & Sylvester, C. (2003). The cognitive neuroscience of working memory and aging. In R. Cabeza, L. Nyberg, & D. Park (Eds.), *Cognitive neuroscience of aging: Linking cognitive and cerebral aging* (pp. 186–217). New York, NY: Oxford University Press.

Ring, H., Bench, C., Trimble, M., Brooks, D., Frackowiak, R., & Dolan, R. (1994). Depression in Parkinson's disease. A positron emission study. *British Journal of Psychiatry, 165,* 333–339.

Rosenberg, P. B., Mielke, M. M., Xue, Q. L., & Carlson, M. C. (2010). Depressive symptoms predict incident cognitive impairment in cognitive healthy older women. *American Journal of Geriatric Psychiatry, 18*(3), 204–211.

Salthouse, T. (1996). The processing speed theory of adult age differences in cognition. *Psychological Review, 103,* 403–428.

Schuurmans, J., Comijs, H., Emmelkamp, P., Gundy, C., Weijnen, I., van den Hout, M., et al. (2006). A randomized, controlled trial of the effectiveness of cognitive-behavioral therapy and sertraline versus a waitlist control group for anxiety disorders in older adults. *American Journal of Geriatric Psychiatry, 14*(3), 255–263.

Schwartz, M. L., & Saffran, E. (1987). *The American NART: Replication and extension of the British findings on the persistence of word pronunciation skills in patients with dementia.* (Unpublished manuscript)

Scogin, F., & McElreath, L. (1994). Efficacy of psychosocial treatments for geriatric depression: A quantitative review. *Journal of Consulting and Clinical Psychology, 62,* 69–74.

Serfaty, M. A., Haworth, D., Blanchard, M., Buszewicz, M., Murad, S., & King, M. (2009). Clinical effectiveness of individual cognitive behavioral therapy for depressed older people in primary care: A randomized controlled trial. *Archives of General Psychiatry, 66*(12), 1332–1340.

Serretti, A., Calati, R., Mandelli, L., & De Ronchi, D. (2006). Serotonin transporter gene variants and behavior: A comprehensive review. *Current Drug Targets, 7,* 1659–1669.

Shah, P., Glabus, M., Goodwin, G., & Ebmeier, K. (2002). Chronic, treatment-resistant depression and right fronto-striatal atrophy. *British Journal of Psychiatry, 180,* 434–440.

Sheline, Y. I. (2003). Neuroimaging studies of mood disorder effects on the brain. *Biological Psychiatry, 54*(3), 338–352.

Sheline, Y. I., Barch, D. M., Garcia, K., Gersing, K., Pieper, C., Welsh-Bohmer, K., et al. (2006). Cognitive function in late life depression: Relationships to depression severity, cerebrovascular risk factors, and processing speed. *Biological Psychiatry, 60*(1), 58–65.

Sheline, Y. I., Pieper, C. F., Barch, D. M., Welsh-Boehmer, K., McKinstry, R. C., MacFall, J. R., et al. (2010). Support for the vascular depression hypothesis in late-life depression: Results of a 2-site, prospective, antidepressant treatment trial. *Archives of General Psychiatry, 67*(3), 277–285.

Sheline, Y. I., Price, J. L., Vaishnavi, S. N., Mintun, M. A., Barch, D. M., Epstein, A. A., et al. (2008). Regional white matter hyperintensity burden in automated segmentation distinguishes late-life depressed subjects from comparison subjects matched for vascular risk factors. *American Journal of Psychiatry, 165*(4), 524–532.

Sheline, Y. I., Sanghavi, M., Mintun, M. A., & Gado, M. (1999). Depression duration but not age predicts hippocampal volume loss in medically healthy women with recurrent major depression. *Journal of Neuroscience, 19,* 5034–5043.

Simons, A., Garfield, S., & Murphy, G. (1984). The process of change in cognitive therapy and pharmacotherapy for depression: Changes in mood and cognition. *Archives of General Psychiatry 41,* 45–51.

Smith, A. (1982). *Symbol Digit Modalities Test (SDMT). Manual (Revised).* Los Angeles, CA: Western Psychological Services.

Smith, G. (2006). Normal aging and mild cognitive impairment. In D. Attix & K. Welsh-Bohmer (Eds.), *Geriatric neuropsychology: Assessment and intervention.* New York, NY: Guilford Press.

Smith, G. S., Gunning-Dixon, F. M., Lotrich, F. E., Taylor, W. D., & Evans, J. D. (2007). Translational research in late-life mood disorders: Implications for future intervention and prevention research. *Neuropsychopharmacology, 32*(9), 1857–1875.

Sohlberg, M., & Mateer, C. (2001). *Cognitive rehabilitation: An integrative neuropsychological approach.* New York, NY: Guilford Press.

Stanley, M., Wilson, N., Novy, D., Rhoades, H., Wagener, P., Greisinger, A., et al. (2009). Cognitive behavior therapy for generalized anxiety disorder among older adults in primary care: A randomized clinical trial. *Journal of the American Medical Association, 301*(14), 1460–1467.

Starkstein, S., Mayberg, H., Leiguarda, R., Preziosi, T., & Robinson, R. (1992). A prospective longitudinal study depression, cognitive decline, and physical impairments in patients with Parkinson's disease. *Journal of Neurology, Neurosurgery, and Psychiatry, 55*(5), 377–382.

Steffens, D., MacFall, J., Payne, M., Welsh-Boehmer, K., & Krishnan, K. (2000). Grey-matter lesions and dementia. *Lancet, 356,* 1686–1687.

Strakowski, S. M., DelBello, M. P., & Adler, C. M. (2004). The functional neuroanatomy of bipolar disorder: A review of neuroimaging findings. *Molecular Psychiatry, 10*(1), 105–116.

Strauss, E., Sherman, E., & Spreen, O. (Eds.). (2006). *A compendium of neuropsychological tests* (3rd ed.). New York, NY: Oxford University Press.

Teri, L., Logsdon, R., Uomoto, J., & McCurry, S. (1997). Behavioral treatment of depression in dementia patients: A controlled clinical trial. *Journal of Gerontology: Series B: Psychological Sciences and Social Sciences, 52B*(4), P159–166.

Tiffin, J. (1968). *Purdue Pegboard examiner's manual.* Rosemont, IL: London House.

Tompkins, M. (2004). *Using homework in psychotherapy: Strategies, guidelines, and forms.* New York, NY: Guilford Press.

Tupler, L., Krishnan, K., McDonald, W., Dombeck, C., D'Souza, S., & Steffens, D. (2002). Anatomic location and laterality of MRI signal hyperintensities in late-life depression. *Acta Psychiatrica Scandinavica, 103,* 282–286.

Venkatraman, T. N., Krishnan, R. R., Steffens, D. C., Song, A. W., & Taylor, W. D. (2009). Biochemical abnormalities of the medial temporal lobe and medial prefrontal cortex in late-life depression. *Psychiatry Research: Neuroimaging, 172*(1), 49–54.

Videbech, P., Ravnkilde, B., Fiigaard, B., Clemmensen, K., Egander, A., Rasmussen, N., et al. (2001). Structural brain abnormalities in unselected in-patients with major depression. *Acta Psychiatrica Scandinavica, 103,* 282–286.

Wechsler, D. (2008). *Wechsler Adult Intelligence Scale-Fourth Edition (WAIS-IV).* San Antonio, TX: The Psychological Corporation.

Wechsler, D. (2009). *Wechsler Memory Scale-Fourth Edition (WMS-IV).* San Antonio, TX: The Psychological Corporation.

Wetherell, J., Lenze, E., & Stanley, M. (2005). Evidence-based treatment of geriatric anxiety disorders. *Psychiatric Clinic North America, 28,* 871–896.

Wilkinson, P., Alder, N., Juszczak, E., Matthews, H., Merritt, C., Montgomery, H., et al. (2009). A pilot randomized controlled trial of a brief cognitive behavioral group intervention to reduce recurrence rates in late life depression. *International Journal of Geriatric Psychiatry, 24,* 68–75.

Zou, K., Deng, W., Li, T., Zhang, B., Jiang, L., Huang, C., et al. (2010). Changes of brain morphometry in first-episode, drug-naïve, non-late-life adult patients with major depression: An optimized voxel-based morphometry study. *Biological Psychiatry, 67*(2), 186–188.

12

Cognitive Behavioral Therapy Within the Palliative Care Setting

Sharon Morgillo Freeman

Those who have the strength and the love to sit with a dying patient in the silence that goes beyond words will know that this moment is neither frightening nor painful, but a peaceful cessation of the functioning of the body.

—Elizabeth Kubler-Ross

Patients who have been deemed by their medical team to have serious diseases that are resistant, nonresponsive, or have failed reasonable treatments are often referred to specialists for "comfort measures." According to the World Health Organization (WHO, 1990):

> Palliative care is the active total care of patients whose disease is not responsive to curative treatment. Control of pain, of other symptoms, and of psychological, social, and spiritual problems is paramount. The goal of palliative care is the achievement of the best possible quality of life for patients and their families. (p. 11)

The National Center for Health Statistics ([NCHS], 1996) estimated that 20% of all deaths and 30% of the deaths of older adults occurred in extended care facilities. Extended care facilities are but one place where end-of-life issues are a common fact of daily life. However, regardless of the setting, each person faces the end of life with his or her own view of life, death, and the dying process.

The estimated number of patients in palliative care varies because of the difficulty in capturing the actual numbers from hospitals, primary care practitioners, families, and emergency rooms. The estimate of patients receiving the Medicare benefit for hospice and palliative care is approximately half a million, and it is estimated that, in 2000, approximately 20% of patients dying in the United States received hospice or palliative care services. It should be noted that although many, if not most, patients in hospice/palliative care settings are aged 85 years or older, this level of care is not limited to older adults. Motor vehicle accidents, posttraumatic incidents, drug overdoses, and other physiologically devastating disorders may result in permanent damage to the younger body as well. It is estimated that by 2030, more than 15 million older adults will experience a mental illness and many of these individuals will be living in long term care facilities (Jeste, D. V., et al, 1999).

This chapter will focus on the reduction or modification of autonomic, psychiatric, or sensory symptom experience of these patients through the use of cognitive behavioral therapy (CBT). CBT uses a structured and collaborative approach while helping patients to recognize, evaluate, and restructure the relationships between their thoughts, feelings, and behaviors. Through a process of targeted interventions, the therapist assists patients in identifying, monitoring, and cognitively restructuring the dysfunctional thoughts and/or modifying behaviors that are maladaptive, useless, or even harmful (Beck, 1976; Freeman & Freeman, 2005; Turk, Meichenbaum, & Genest, 1987). CBT includes a range of both cognitive and behavioral techniques such as relaxation, guided imagery/visualization, biofeedback, behavioral experiments, guided discovery, stress management, training in pain or stress management strategies, and cognitive restructuring for dysfunctional thinking, and many others. Although there is a paucity of research on the use of CBT in palliative care settings, CBT is effective for many of the psychological issues that are prevalent in palliative care, including depression, anxiety, pain management, and insomnia. The purpose of this chapter is to provide an overview on the use of CBT for assessment and treatment of psychological distress in palliative care settings.

ASSESSMENT OF EMOTIONAL FUNCTIONING IN PALLIATIVE CARE

There are many challenges to the assessment of mood disorders in palliative care settings. An initial challenge is the myth that psychological distress is a normal reaction to end of life. Despite expectations, most patients in palliative care settings do not have symptoms of anxiety, depression, or dementia. Many patients arrive at this stage of their lives or illnesses with a sense of calm resignation, if not expectations of relief and of "going home" to God, heaven, or family members waiting for them in the hereafter. Therefore, those patients who are experiencing symptoms that require intervention may achieve significant benefit from the interventions. The most common presentations are those of depression, anxiety, pain management failures with exhaustion and anguish, and sleep disorders. The health care provider requires tools necessary to differentiate major depression from anger, sadness, and anxiety associated with the symptoms of an untreatable or chronic illness.

Assessment of Preparatory Grief and Depression

Another obstacle to the assessment process is simply overcoming the challenges of differentiating symptoms from normal grief of the illness itself. Differentiating between preparatory grief and depression is a key component to the proper assessment of depression in palliative care and has important treatment implications. *Preparatory grief* can be defined as what a patient must "undergo to prepare himself or herself for his or her final separation from this world" (Kubler-Ross, 1997). Symptoms of preparatory grief include (a) mood waxes and wanes with time, (b) normal self-esteem, (c) occasional fleeting thoughts of suicide, and (d) worries about separations from loved ones (Periyakoil & Hallenbeck, 2002). Preparatory grief is a normal, nonpathological life-cycle event (Axtell, 2008; Periyakoil & Hallenbeck, 2002).

Major depression is defined as five or more of the following symptoms during the same 2-week period:

1. Depressed mood,
2. Marked diminish in pleasure,
3. Weight loss or gain,
4. Insomnia or hypersomnia,
5. Psychomotor agitation/retardation,
6. Fatigue/loss of energy,
7. Feelings of worthlessness or inappropriate guilt,
8. Lack of concentration/indecisiveness, and
9. Recurrent thoughts of death and suicidal thoughts or plans (American Psychiatric Association [APA], 1994).

Table 12.1 provides a symptom list. The list is not intended to be all inclusive; however, it gives the clinician an overall view of symptoms that may be observed in the individual dealing with depression in a palliative care setting.

TABLE 12.1 Signs and Symptoms of Depression

- Sadness
- Hopelessness
- Feelings of worthlessness or being a burden
- Decreased interest in visitors or activities
- Change in appetite (usually decreased appetite)
- Anergia or fatigue
- Feeling overwhelmed
- Difficulty articulating thoughts and/or less talkative
- Inability to experience pleasure (anhedonia)
- Sleep disturbance: hypersomnia or insomnia with early morning awakening
- Inability to concentrate or pay attention
- Focus on death or suicidal thoughts
- Withdrawal from family and friends
- Tearfulness
- Expressed grief over impending death

Source: Adapted from Hospice and Palliative Nurses Association Patient and Family Teaching Sheets.

Although some symptoms of grief and depression overlap, there are ways to distinguish between grief and depression. Table 12.2 summarizes the ways to differentiate symptoms of grief versus depression according to temporal variation, self-image, hope, anhedonia, response to support, and active desire for an early death (Periyakoil & Hallenbeck, 2002).

TABLE 12.2 Symptoms of Preparatory Grief Versus Depression

Grief	Depression
Mixture of good and bad days	Persistent flat affect or dysphoria
Self-image intact	Disturbed self-image
Hope shifts, but is not lost	Sense of hopeless and helplessness
Able to feel pleasure	Anhedonia
Responds to social support	Social support alone is not enough to resolve depression
No active desire for an early death	May experience a persistent, active desire for an early death

Source: Periyakoil, V. S., & Hallenbeck, J. (2002). Identifying and managing preparatory grief and depression at the end of life. *American Family Physician, 65*, 883–890.

The first step to proper recognition of depression involves the identification of possible risk factors (Wilson, Chochinov, de Faye, & Breitbart, 2000). Certain demographic characteristics such as younger age, poor social support, limited financial resources, and family history of a mood disorder as well as a personal history of previous mood disorders place patients at a greater risk for developing depression or anxiety in end-of-life situations. Risk for developing a mood disorder also is elevated with certain types of diagnoses, including pancreatic cancer and brain tumors, and particular medical interventions such as radiation therapy. Symptoms of the illness, including poor symptom control, physical disability, and malnutrition also place patients at higher risk.

The second step to the proper assessment of depression includes the use of appropriate assessment tools. Many times, it is the degree and persistence of symptoms that provide the information necessary when considering major depression. Major depression, which is estimated to occur in fewer than 25% of patients in end-of-life care, may be best screened with targeted questions such as "How much of the time do you feel depressed?" In addition, for those patients who have a difficult time describing their symptoms or history, asking family members to provide information about a previous history of depression or a family history can be very useful.

Although studies validating assessment tools vary greatly, many of the self-report measures have been shown to be effective in palliative care patients. The most commonly used tools in palliative care settings tend to omit somatic symptoms of depression because many of these symptoms overlap with the terminal disease process. Examples of self-report measures that omit somatic symptoms include the Beck Depression Inventory (BDI-II; Beck, Steer, & Brown, 1996), Hospital Anxiety and Depression Inventory (HADS; Zigmond & Snaith, 1983), and the Geriatric Depression Scale (GDS; Yesavage et al., 1983). The Hayes and Lohse Non-Verbal Depression Scale (NVDS; Hayes, Lohse, & Bernstein, 1991) is a third party observational measure that can be completed by staff, family, or friends to assist with the diagnostic process. The Terminally Ill Grief or Depression Scale (TIGDS), comprising of grief and depression subscales, is the first self-report measure designed and validated to differentiate between preparatory grief and depression in adult inpatients (Periyakoil et al., 2005).

Assessment of Anxiety

The symptoms of anxiety may differ in patients in the palliative care environment. Many times, symptoms of anxiety have a physiological component. For example, in those patients with chronic obstructive

TABLE 12.3   Anxiety Symptoms in Palliative Care Patients

■ Increased pulse, respirations, and blood pressure
■ Expressions of fearfulness
■ Obsessing or worrying
■ Difficulty sleeping
■ Onset of or increased confusion
■ General tense appearance with muscle aches
■ Tremors (shaking)
■ Complaints of an inability to relax or get comfortable
■ Difficulty concentrating or paying attention
■ Feeling uncomfortably warm or sweating

Source: Adapted from Hospice and Palliative Nurses Association Patient and Family Teaching Sheets.

pulmonary diseases (COPD), difficulty in breathing, low oxygen levels, and overall compromised respiratory function causes "air hunger," which is experienced as anxiety and even panic. Table 12.3 lists some of the common anxiety symptoms seen in this population.

Family members are often at a loss as to what they can do to assist their loved one who is experiencing anxiety and especially fear. It is often useful to provide significant others with a checklist of items that are important to report to the health care provider. Involving the family has the benefit of giving them a structured guide for response, which reduces their own anxiety in response to the patient. In addition, the patient may relax more knowing that a family member is involved with his or her care in an approved, helpful manner. An example of a list of items for family members to watch for and report to the health care team is listed in Appendix A.

COGNITIVE BEHAVIORAL INTERVENTIONS IN PALLIATIVE CARE

Psychological intervention in the palliative care setting includes those aspects of treatment that would provide relief from emotional distress when an individual is dying. Often, this time period includes depression, anxiety, grief, and organic brain dysfunctions such as dementia and/or cerebral vascular diseases. Patients and their family members are both considered "the patient" during these times. Many of these patients are suffering from chronic, unremitting pain conditions, which negatively affect their emotional health. Treatments for pain and chronic conditions also play a part in the individual's mental status. The use of CBT is extremely useful for these patients. CBT has the strongest empirical support of any psychological intervention for the management of symptoms typically seen in a palliative care setting.

The most common presentations of psychological distress in the dying patient include anxiety, depression, hopelessness, guilt over perceived life failures, and remorse. Persistence of these thoughts and feelings interfere with functioning, makes the person generally miserable as well as those around them, and can severely affect his or her quality of life. Medical treatments such as antidepressants, anxiolytics, and cholinesterase inhibitors exist for these problems; however, supportive psychotherapy such as relaxation training, imagery, distraction, skills training, and negative thought restructuring improves the possibility of remission. CBT can also improve the symptoms of spiritual distress that may include feelings of disappointment, guilt, loss of hope, remorse, and loss of identity.

Cognitive Behavioral Therapy for Depression

Symptoms of depression are common in end-of-life care. It can be one of the most distressing groups of symptoms an individual can experience and may interfere significantly with daily tasks of life. Some experts have estimated that up to 75% of patients with terminal illnesses experience symptoms of depression. Amelioration of some of the symptoms of depression can increase the amount of pleasure and meaning in life as well as add hope and peace. Treatment for depression can reduce the experience of physical pain as well as general misery and suffering. In addition, reduction of the symptoms of depression may improve the treatment of coexisting illnesses more effective. Most importantly, given that one of the most serious symptoms of depression is suicidal ideation, it makes sense to treat depression to prevent successful suicidal outcomes.

There is a paucity of literature in the area of the use of CBT with depression in palliative care because of the high attrition rate resulting from physical morbidity and mortality (Moorey et al., 2009). Therefore, these factors pose significant barriers to conducting randomized clinical trials (RCT) in palliative care to address these components. The following is a review of the sparse literature on CBT in palliative care with depression.

In an attempt to address this problem, Moorey et al. (2009) conducted a cluster RCT to determine if it was possible to teach nurses CBT techniques to reduce anxiety and depression symptoms in patients with advanced cancer. Eight nurses were trained in CBT by attending several 1- and 2-day workshops and then were rated on the Cognitive Therapy First Aid Rating Scale (CTFARS) for CBT competence. Seven nurses did not receive training and served in the control group. Eighty home care patients entered the trial; however, most of these participants were excluded because of being too ill to participate. Sixteen patients were in the CBT group and 18 patients were in the control group. The participants received home care nursing visits in which assessments were conducted at 6-, 10-, and 16-week intervals. The patients who received CBT reported lower anxiety scores over time, but no effect of the training was found regarding depression. It was noted that both groups experienced lower rates of depression over the course of the study. The authors noted the heterogeneity of the sample and the high attrition rate because physical morbidity and mortality presented several barriers to conducting the study and may have played in a role in the findings (Moorey et al., 2009).

Cole and Vaughan (2005), in their review on the feasibility of using CBT for depression associated with Parkinson's disease (PD), found that it is a promising option. The authors noted that patients with depression and PD experienced a significant reduction in depressive symptoms and negative cognitions, and an increased perception of social support over the course of treatment (Cole & Vaughan, 2005). The recommended course of action for patients in this setting included (a) stress management training, (b) behavioral modification techniques for sleep hygiene, (c) relaxation training, and (d) cognitive restructuring. Modification of life stressors contributing to depressed mood should be identified and plans made to minimize stress and maximize quality of life. In addition, patients use thought restructuring to maintain a sense of purpose and fulfillment through the use of meaningful activity and adjustment of the expectations of themselves and others. Patients are also encouraged to do what they found to be enjoyable to maximize feelings of pleasure and happiness. Through systematic defocusing on physical conditions, a person is able to experience more pleasant activities, which are also encouraged.

Similarly, Dobkin, Allen, and Menza (2007) conducted a study, which explored the effects of modified CBT for depressed patients with PD, in conjunction with a separate social support intervention for caregivers. The patients received 10–14 sessions of modified CBT whereas caregivers attended three to four separate psychoeducational classes. The modified CBT sessions were comprised of the same components of the previous Cole and Vaughan (2005) study such as stress management training, behavioral modification techniques for sleep hygiene, relaxation training, cognitive restructuring, modification of life stressors, and increasing engagement in pleasurable activities. The classes were targeted at providing caregivers with ways to respond to the patients' negative thoughts and beliefs, as well as strategies to offer appropriate support. The modified CBT sessions were comprised of training in stress management, behavioral modification, sleep hygiene, relaxation techniques, and cognitive restructuring. Patients reported a significant reduction in their depressive symptoms and cognitions and increased perception of social support. These gains were maintained at a month's follow up.

Cognitive Behavioral Therapy for Anxiety

Along with depression, anxiety is a common mental health problem in palliative care settings and also appears to be alleviated with CBT interventions. In a small feasibility study, examining the use of CBT techniques from mild-to-moderate anxiety and depression in hospice patients, 4 sessions of CBT techniques were found to significantly reduce anxiety and depression in most patients (Anderson, Watson, & Davidson, 2008). Overall, participants in the study found the CBT techniques acceptable, helpful, and qualitatively reported improved mood. A significant reduction in anxiety symptoms also was seen in a randomized controlled trial (RCT) of CBT administered by home care nurses in patients with advanced cancer (Moorey et al., 2009).

CBT techniques are particularly effective to assist with the management of anxiety related to breathing difficulties commonly seen with pulmonary diseases such as COPD. In a group of patients with COPD, six sessions of guided imagery, a CBT relaxation technique, was found to significantly increase the partial percentage of oxygen saturation, which is a physiological indicator signaling more effective breathing (Louie, 2004). In another study, as little as 2 hours of CBT group therapy yielded a decrease in depression and anxiety among older adults with COPD, but there was no change in physical functioning (Kunik et al., 2001).

Cognitive Behavioral Therapy for Pain Management

Pain is not simply a biological response to unpleasant stimuli. It is a complex phenomenon that includes biological, psychological behavior, and social factors that interact in complex ways to influence the pain experience. Some of the factors that can influence a person's experience of pain include (a) previous pain experiences, (b) biologic and genetic predispositions, (c) mood disorders such as anxiety and depression, (d) beliefs about pain, (e) fear about the pain experience, (f) individual pain threshold and pain tolerance level, and (g) skill with coping methods. CBT has the most empirical support for the management of chronic pain especially when used as part of an interdisciplinary treatment approach to manage pain symptoms (Turk, Swanson, & Tunks, 2008).

Cognitive behavioral techniques can be used independently to assist with pain management or integrated into a comprehensive cognitive behavioral case conceptualization framework to address pain (Turk, Swanson, & Tunks, 2008). The three components to CBT for pain management are the following:

1. Education and rationale for the use of CBT,
2. Coping skills training, and
3. Application and maintenance of CBT skills (Keefe, 1996).

Useful behavioral interventions to assist with pain management include goal setting, relaxation strategies such as deep breathing and guided imagery, and activities scheduling. Cognitive interventions would include increasing problem-solving skills and addressing an individual's maladaptive thoughts related to pain management. Examples of maladaptive thoughts include the following:

1. I have tried every pain management intervention with no success.
2. I cannot do any of the things that I used to do.
3. Nothing will help manage my pain.

CBT for pain management has demonstrated efficacy in various diagnoses often addressed in palliative care. CBT has been found to be efficacious in the management of cancer-related pain in single studies (Syrjala, Donaldson, Davis, Kippes, & Carr, 1995) as well as in systematic reviews (Abernethy, Keefe, McCrory, Scipio, & Matchar, 2006).

Cognitive Behavioral Therapy for Sleep Hygiene

Insomnia, sleep duration, and quality are major concerns for people with pain disorders such as osteoarthritis (Vitiello, 2009). Approximately 60% of patients with chronic pain disorders report frequent nighttime awakening because of pain during the night. Disrupted sleep patterns exacerbate chronic pain intensity and experience which, in turn, causes more disturbance of the sleep/wake cycle. Successful treatment of interrupted sleep may reduce the pain experience as well as improve the overall quality of life for these patients. Psychotherapeutic techniques that target sleep disturbances are easily incorporated within behavioral and cognitive management of other co-occurring disorders as well.

Sleep disorders are common in patients who suffer from diagnoses that often benefit from palliative care such as Parkinson's Disease. (Stocchi, Barbato, Nordera, Berardelli, & Ruggieri, 1998). Specifically, insomnia, nightmares, REM sleep behavior disorder (RBD), sleep attacks, sleep apnea syndrome, excessive daytime sleepiness, and periodic limb movement in sleep result from changes in sleep structure, movement disturbances in sleep, disturbances in neurotransmission, and medications. Patients who are sleep deprived are at risk to develop infections, cardiovascular disease, hypertension, diabetes, depression, and require increased time to recover from stress (Schutte-Rodin, Broch, Buysse, Dorsey, & Sateia, 2008). CBT improves sleep by addressing unhelpful beliefs regarding sleep and misperceptions about the amount of sleep that one obtains. Many misperceive the amount of time they are actually asleep. People who suffer from insomnia actually sleep more than they are aware of because they are only attentive when they are awake. Furthermore, many people believe that they require 8 hours of sleep to be able to function during the day and any amount of sleep that is less is insufficient and will result in reduced ability to function during the day. Therefore, these beliefs and misperceptions can increase one's stress level about sleep and a stress response may result when one thinks about going to sleep. Clearly, a heightened stress response is not conducive to sleeping. CBT increases one's control over his or her unhelpful and inaccurate beliefs and enables him or her to replace them with more helpful and accurate beliefs (Whitworth, Crownover, & Nichols, 2007).

CBT also addresses the behavioral components of one's sleep routine or patterns that interfere with one's ability to obtain restful sleep. Exercising, smoking, or drinking caffeinated drinks just before bedtime can interfere with one's sleep. All of these activities are stimulants that energize the body. In addition, not having a bedtime routine, a regular sleep–wake pattern, or taking naps may interfere with one's ability to get restful sleep. Increasing one's sleep hygiene by developing positive habits that influence sleep such as having a bedtime routine to prepare one's mind and body for sleep, regular exercise several hours before one intends to prepare for sleep, and avoiding coffee, alcohol, and smoking in the evening as well as increasing activities that produce relaxation (e.g., taking a hot bath 1 to 2 hours before going to bed, meditation, deep breathing, or muscle relaxation) can increase the likelihood of obtaining restful sleep. Another behavioral strategy used in CBT is sleep restriction. This technique attempts to match one's actual sleep requirement with the amount of time one spends in his or her bed. The theory behind this approach is that reducing the amount of time spent in bed without sleep will increase one's desire to sleep (Harvey, Ree, Sharpley, Stinson, & Clark, 2007).

Results of a study made by Vitiello (2009) showed that treatment improves both immediate and long-term self-reported sleep and pain in older patients with osteoarthritis and comorbid insomnia without directly addressing pain control. This study included 23 patients with a mean age of 69 years who were randomly assigned to CBT, whereas 28 patients with a mean age of 66.5 years were assigned to a stress management and wellness control group. Participants in the control group reported no significant improvements in any measure although patients treated with CBT reported significantly decreased sleep latency (onset of sleep) by an average of 16.9 minutes and 11 minutes a year after treatment. Interruptions in sleep after sleep onset decreased from an initial average of 47 minutes to an average of 21 minutes after a year. Pain symptoms improved from 9.7 points initially to 4.7 points. Sleep efficacy (how rested does the person feel upon awakening) initially increased by 13% and 8% a year after treatment. The improvements remained robust in 19 of 23 patients within a year of follow-up visit.

Furthermore, while many older adults experience insomnia, it is reported that up to two-thirds of those who experience these symptoms have limited knowledge regarding available treatment options. Sivertsen et al. (2006) conducted RCT to compare the efficacy of non-benzodiazepine sleep medications with CBT. This study included 46 patients with a mean age of 60.8 years who were diagnosed with chronic primary insomnia. Participants were randomly assigned to either the CBT intervention (information on sleep hygiene, sleep restriction, stimulus control, cognitive therapy, and progressive relaxation), sleep medication (7.5 mg zopiclone each night), or placebo medication. Treatment lasted 6 weeks and the CBT intervention and sleep medication treatments were followed up at 6 months. Data regarding total wake time, total sleep time, sleep efficiency, and slow-wave sleep was collected using sleep diaries, and polysomnography (PSG; monitors physiologic activity during sleep). Results revealed that the total time spent awake improved significantly more for those in the CBT group compared to the placebo group at 6 weeks and the zopiclone group at both 6 weeks and 6 months. In comparison, the zopiclone group did not reveal significant results from the placebo group. The CBT group experienced a 52% reduction in total wake time at 6 weeks compared with 4% and 16% in the zopiclone and placebo groups, respectively. A statistically and clinically significant finding was that participants receiving CBT improved their PSG-registered sleep efficiency by 9% at posttreatment, as opposed to a decline of 1% in the zopiclone group. Total sleep time increased significantly between 6 weeks and 6 months for the CBT group. The zopiclone group showed improvements at 6 weeks and maintained these improvements at 6 months, but did not show further improvements. The CBT group showed significant improvements compared to the zopiclone group in total wake time, sleep efficiency, and slow-wave sleep; total sleep was the only area that did not yield a significant difference.

ADAPTING COGNITIVE BEHAVIORAL THERAPY TO THE PALLIATIVE CARE SETTING

Overview of Cognitive Behavioral Therapy in Palliative Care

CBT is effective for many of common mental health issues seen in palliative care and often augments the success of pharmacological interventions. In addition to the patients with the terminal illness, their family members, as well as multiple health providers are considered integral members to the success of the collaborative relationship. Use of a CBT case conceptualization framework and various components offer flexibility, which makes the CBT approach feasible to implement within a palliative care setting. The following section provides an overview of the components of CBT and necessary adaptations to palliative care settings.

Collaborative Relationship

As mentioned in the previous chapters of this book, a collaborative relationship is a core component of an effective cognitive behavioral intervention. In a palliative care setting, the collaborative relationship often involves more than just the client and the therapist. The interdisciplinary treatment team works with the individual to develop an individualized treatment plan that is central to the case conceptualization and goal setting of CBT. Various disciplines, such as nursing and social work use CBT techniques in palliative care settings. Patients receiving palliative care often need assistance with CBT interventions as their illness progresses. Patients receiving palliative care often need assistance from the treatment team with practicing skills such as relaxation techniques, and adapting CBT interventions as goals of care change.

Some patients in the palliative care setting may not be facing death in the near future, and if they are facing impending death, they may not be aware of it. In these cases, the primary patient may be the family member or significant other. It is also common practice for most patients to seek help concerning mental health problems from their family practitioner, even though the typical family practitioner has very little training in psychiatric/mental health assessment, diagnosis, and treatment. In cases where the family is relying on an undertrained health care provider, it may be incumbent on the mental health provider to negotiate the gap between family and medical care.

Case Conceptualization and Goal Setting

Therapy with the dying person should begin with having the person identify, explore, and determine outcome goals regarding the issues at hand. Similar to the primary care setting, case conceptualization and goal setting need to occur almost immediately. The therapist uses the socratic dialogue to explore the person's concerns and worries. This gives the person more of a sense of control over what will be happening in the therapy session. Once this sense of control is established, it becomes easier to explore other more emotion-laden topics.

Goals should be small, obtainable, and proximal to the session to be most effective. For example, "Mrs. Jones, I will be back to see you tomorrow. One of the things you have decided to practice is your deep breathing at least twice tonight and again in the morning. When I return, I will check with you to see how you are doing with the practice." In a palliative care setting, it may be necessary to discuss how other people involved in care can assist with reaching goals. For example, nurses might remind patients to practice relaxation strategies during wakeful periods as well as talk them through the relaxation technique when experiencing a high level of pain.

Behavioral Interventions

Pleasant Events Scheduling
Activities scheduling is a useful intervention to assist with mood disorders, pain management, and sleep hygiene issues seen in a palliative care setting. Engaging in pleasant events distracts an individual from negative thoughts and provides experimental evidence to support

more adaptive thinking styles. Often in palliative care, the first barrier to overcome is identifying pleasant events that can occur in a palliative care setting because of health limitations. Pleasant events need to be person-centered, meaningful, and feasible activities that can be built into a daily routine.

Meaningful pleasant events can be identified through both clinical interview and self-report methods. Clinical interview queries should include taking a history of a patient's daily schedule and identifying activities the patient enjoyed while engaging in on a routine basis prior to their illness. From the generated list of previously enjoyed pleasant events, it needs to be determined which activities the patient can continue to engage in or how can these activities be modified due to functional limitations.

Assessment tools that assist with identifying pleasant events include a weekly activity chart and a pleasant events inventory. An activity chart has an individual list of activities from waking up to bedtime on an hourly basis. Each activity is then rated in terms of sense of accomplishment, enjoyment/pleasure, or pain on a scale of 0–10 (Winterowd, Beck, & Gruener, 2003). Activity monitoring provides the patient with the terminal illness and the therapist with critical information regarding activity levels, types of activities, and the roles particular activities play in the patient's degree of psychological distress. For example, a patient may not be able to independently engage in an activity he or she previously enjoyed, adding to depressive symptoms, but may be able to continue to enjoy routine activities with assistance. In addition to activity monitoring, there are several pleasant events inventories well suited to patients seen within a palliative care setting. For example, the Pleasant Events Schedule (MacPhillamy & Lewinsohn, 1982), the California Older Adult's Pleasant Events Schedule (COPPES; Gallagher-Thompson, Thompson, and Rider, 2004), and the Pleasant Events Preference Inventory (PEPI; Van Haitsma, 1999), which was developed for patients with dementia.

Relaxation Techniques

Both deep breathing and guided imagery have been found to be efficacious in palliative care settings. Breathing is an essential component of life. As described in Cully and Teten (2008), when people become stressed or anxious, their breathing gets rapid and shallow, this can lead to feeling dizzy, lightheaded, or they may hyperventilate. Experiencing these symptoms produce feelings of anxiety, which, in turn, increase the physical signs, creating a negative cycle. This cycle can be stopped or interrupted by attending to one's breathing. Changing the rate and way in which one breathes can actually make one's body more "relaxed" and function more effectively, which is essential in palliative care where comfort is a primary goal of care. Adapted from Cully and Teten (2008), the following are steps for deep breathing:

1. Put one hand on your abdomen, with your little finger about 1 inch above your navel and place one hand on your chest.
2. Begin to notice your breathing (pause for several seconds)—which hand is doing more of the moving? The goal is to move the stomach and not the upper chest area.
3. Breathe slow and deep so that your stomach goes in and out when you breathe while your other hand on your chest stays as still as possible. *Your hand on your diaphragm should move out as you inhale and in as you exhale* (Acknowledge if the patient has COPD—lung capacity might be reduced, but reassure them of the benefits of practicing deep breathing).
4. Continue to take slow, even, deep breaths. *Breathe in to the count of 3, 4, or 5 depending on what is comfortable for you and then breathe out to the same number. It is okay to start breathing to the count of 2 or 3. You may be able to work up to a larger number, but...if the smaller interval works, remain there with benefits. Do not pause at the top of each breath* (please refer to Appendix B, which provides a pocket card for deep breathing).

The primary goal of guided imagery is to distract the patient from aversive stimuli such as pain or maladaptive thoughts, redirecting his or her focus to relaxing scenes and adaptive thinking styles. The intervention is based on the mind–body connection. There are several Web sites listed in the electronic Appendix that offer several free relaxation scripts such as beach and forest visualizations as well as scripts depicting a peaceful meadow and floating on a cloud. Patients receiving palliative care also may benefit from creating a personal script based on their life experiences. Steps to assist with developing a personally meaningful script include the following:

1. Identify a setting and time in life when he or she experienced relaxation.
2. Determine what about this setting and time was found to be relaxing.
3. Next, have him or her vividly describe the details of that setting, focusing on sensory experiences including sights, sounds, smells, and textures.

Cognitive Interventions

The basic premise of CBT is that beliefs about self, others, and the world significantly impact our psychological responses. These belief systems are comprised of multiple layers ranging from adaptive thinking patterns to maladaptive dysfunctional thoughts (e.g., cognitive distortions). Some of these thoughts are well ingrained, if not completely ossified into ways of thinking of self, the future, or the world around us (e.g., core beliefs). Research has shown us that persons with neutral or positive core beliefs respond to life situations in more adaptive ways whereas persons with negative core beliefs tend to respond to situations in an anxious or depressed way (Carr, 1974; Foa & Kozak, 1986; Obsessive Compulsive Cognitions Working Group, 1997; Salkovskis, 1985; Salkovskis, Shafran, Rachman, & Freeston, 1999).

As in most setting where CBT is used, patients progress faster in therapy through the use of dysfunctional thought records (DTRs). Throughout the course of treatment, patients are asked to monitor the thoughts and feelings that they have in response to specific stressful situations during the day. The therapist reviews the patients' automatic thoughts and assists them in challenging the dysfunctional thoughts, in creating logical and reasonable (fact based) responses, and in identifying those aspects of thoughts and behavior over which they have control. The DTR is an excellent tool for patients with depression or anxiety (along with many other mood symptoms). An example of a DTR for a patient with anxiety as his or her presenting problem is included in Table 12.4.

TABLE 12.4   Dysfunctional Thought Record Example: Anxiety

Situation/ Trigger	Immediate Response	Feeling	Automatic Thoughts	Rational or Logical Responses	Feeling Rating after Rational Response
I was told my doctor was coming in today for an extra visit.	"Oh no! This is something bad!"	Anxiety Fear Dread	He is going to tell me that what I have is going to cause more pain! He is sending me home and no one will be available to help me. He has bad news.	He has extra time today so he is making his rounds early. He might have some good news for me and wants to tell me in person—he has done that before.	Less anxious Not fearful

Source: From Gilson, M., Freeman, A., Yates, J. & Morgillo Freeman, S. (2009) *Overcoming Depression: A Cognitive Therapy Approach Therapist Guide (Treatments That Work Series).* Oxford University Press. Pg. 179. Reproduced with permission of the authors.

CONCLUSION AND SUMMARY

There are multiple issues and multiple changes associated with the dying process. Loss of living in the home situation, loss of control over the physical body, pain, loss of daily routines, loss of friends, and loss of activities are but a few. CBT can have numerous benefits for patients including (a) decreased psychological distress, (b) improved pain management, (c) increased *self-efficacy* (the belief in one's capability to organize and execute the sources of action required to manage prospective situations), and (d) better quality of life and function. In addition, patients treated with CBT may have fewer visits to other health care providers and fewer hospital admissions. Patients can be treated with CBT over a period of weeks or months, giving it significant utility as a psychotherapeutic model.

REFERENCES

Abernethy, A. P., Keefe, F. J., McCrory, D. C., Scipio, C. D., & Matchar, D. B. (2006). Behavioral therapies for the management of cancer pain: A systematic review. In H. Flor, E. Kalso, & J. O. Dostrovsky (Eds.). *Proceedings of the 11th World Congress on Pain* (pp. 789–798). Seattle, WA: IASP Press.

American Psychiatric Association. (1994). *Diagnostic and statistical manual of mental disorders* (4th ed.). Washington, DC: Author.

Anderson, T., Watson, M., & Davidson, R. (2008). The use of cognitive behavioural therapy techniques for anxiety and depression in hospice patients: A feasibility study. *Palliative Medicine, 22*, 814–821.

Axtell, A. (2008). Depression in palliative care. *Journal of Palliative Medicine, 11*(3), 529–530.

Beck, A. T. (1976). *Cognitive therapy and the emotional disorders.* New York, NY: International Universities Press.

Beck, J. S. (1995). *Cognitive therapy: Basics and beyond.* New York, NY: The Guilford Press.

Carr, A. T. (1974). Compulsive neurosis: A review of the literature. *Psychological Bulletin, 81*, 311–318.

Chochinov, H. M., Wilson, K. G., Enns, M., Mowchun, N., Lander, S., Levitt, M., et al. (1995). Desire for death in the terminally ill. *American Journal of Psychiatry, 152*, 1185–1191.

Cole, K., & Vaughan, F. L. (2005). The feasibility of using cognitive behavior therapy for depression associated with Parkinson's disease: A literature review. *Parkinsonism Related Disorders, 11*, 269–276.

Cully, J. A., & Teten, A. L. (2008). *A therapist's guide to brief cognitive behavioral therapy.* Houston, TX: Department of Veterans Affairs South Central MIRECC.

Dobkin, R. D., Allen, L. A., & Menza, M. (2007). Cognitive-behavioral therapy for depression in Parkinson's disease: A pilot study. *Movement Disorders, 22*, 946–952.

Dobkin, R. D., Menza, M., & Bienfait, K. L. (2008). CBT for the treatment of depression in Parkinson's disease: A promising nonpharmacological approach. *Expert Reviews of Neurotherapy, 8,* 27–35.

Foa, E. B., & Kozak, M. J. (1986). Emotional processing of fear: Exposure to corrective information. *Psychological Bulletin, 99,* 20–35.

Freeman & Freeman. (2005)

Gallagher-Thompson, D., Thompson, L., & Rider, K. L. (2004). *California older person's pleasant events schedule.* Unpublished Self-Report and Manual. PaloAlto, CA: Standford School of Medicine: Older Adult and Family Center.

Gilson, M., Freeman, A., Yates, J. & Morgillo Freeman, S. (2009) Overcoming Depression: A Cognitive Therapy Approach Therapist Guide (Treatments That Work Series). New York, NY: Oxford University Press.

Harvey, A. G., Ree, M. J., Sharpley, A. J., Stinson, K., & Clark, D. M. (2007). An open trial of cognitive therapy for chronic insomnia. *Behaviour Research and Therapy, 45,* 2491–2501.

Hayes, P. M., Lohse, D., & Bernstein, I. (1991). The development and testing of the Hayes and Lohse non-verbal depression scale. *Clinical Gerontologist, 10*(3), 3–13.

Hospice and Palliative Nurses Association Patient and Family Teaching Sheets, accessed 1/8/2011 http://www.hpna.org/DisplayPage.aspx?Title=Patient/Family Teaching Sheets

Jeste, D. V., Alexopoulos, G. S., Bartels, S. J., Cummings, J. L., Gallo, J. J., Gottlieb, G. L., et al. (1999). Consensus statement on the upcoming crisis in geriatric mental health: Research agenda for the next 2 decades. *Archives of General Psychiatry, 56,* 848-853.

Keefe, F. J. (1996). Cognitive behavioral therapy for managing pain. *The Clinical Psychologist, 49*(3), 4–5.

Kubler-Ross, E. (1997). *On death and dying: What the dying have to teach doctors, nurses, clergy, and their families* (1st ed.). New York, NY: Simon and Schuster.

Kunik, M. E., Braun, U., Stanley, M. A., Wristers, K., Molinari, V., Stoebner, D., et al. (2001). One session cognitive behavioural therapy for elderly patients with chronic obstructive pulmonary disease. *Psychological Medicine, 31,* 717–723.

Louie, S. W. (2004). The effects of guided imagery relaxation in people with COPD. *Occupational Therapy International, 11*(3), 145–159.

MacPhillamy, D. J., & Lewinsohn, P. M. (1982). The pleasant events schedule: Studies on reliability, validity, and scale intercorrelation. *Journal of Consulting and Clinical Psychology, 50*(3), 363–380.

Miller, K. E., Adams, S. M., & Miller, M. M. (2006). Antidepressant medication use in palliative care. *American Journal of Hospice Palliative Care, 23,* 127–133.

Moorey, S., Cort, E., Kapari, M., Monroe, B., Hansford, P., Mannix, K., et al. (2009). A cluster randomized controlled trial of cognitive behavior therapy for common mental disorders in patients with advanced cancer. *Psychological Medicine, 39,* 713–723.

Morgillo Freeman, S. & DuBry Morgillo, M. (2005). *End-of-Life Issues,* in Freeman SM, & Freeman A, eds. *Cognitive Behavior Therapy in Nursing Practice.* New York, NY: Springer Publishing Company; 2005:221–238.

National Center for Health Statistics. (1996).

Noorani, N. H., & Montagini, M. (2007). Recognizing depression in palliative care patients. *Journal of Palliative Care Medicine, 10,* 458–464.

Periyakoil, V. S., & Hallenbeck, J. (2002). Identifying and managing preparatory grief and depression at the end of life. *American Family Physician, 65*, 883–890.

Periyakoil, V. S., Kraemer, H. C., Noda, A., Moos, R., Hallenbeck, J., Webster, M., et al. (2005). The development and initial validation of the Terminally Ill Grief or Depression Scale (TIGDS). *International Journal of Methods in Psychiatric Research, 14*(4), 202–212.

Salkovskis, P. M. (1985). Obsessional-compulsive problems: A cognitive behavioural analysis. *Behaviour Research and Therapy, 23*, 571–583.

Salkovskis, P. M., Shafran, R., Rachman, S., & Freeston, M. H. (1999). Multiple pathways to inflated responsibility beliefs in obsessional problems: Possible origins and implications for therapy and research. *Behaviour Research and Therapy, 37*, 1055–1072.

Substance Abuse and Mental Health Services Administration. (2004).

Schutte-Rodin, S., Broch, L., Buysse, D., Dorsey, C., & Sateia, M. (2008). Clinical guideline for the evaluation and management of chronic insomnia in adults. *Journal of Clinical Sleep Medicine, 4*, 487–493.

Sivertsen, B., Omvik, S., Pallesen, S., Bjorvatn, B., Havik, O. E., Kvale, G., et al. (2006). Cognitive behavioral therapy vs zopiclone for treatment of chronic primary insomnia in older adults: A randomized controlled trial. *Journal of American Medical Association, 295*, 2851–2858.

Stocchi, R., Barbato, L., Nordera, G., Berardelli, A., & Ruggieri, S. (1998). Sleep disorders in Parkinson's disease. *Journal of Neurology, 245*, S15-S18.

Syrjala, K. L., Donaldson, G. W., Davis, M. W., Kippes, M. E., & Carr, J. E. (1995). Relaxation and imagery and cognitive-behavioral training reduce pain during cancer treatment: A controlled clinical trial. *Pain, 63*(2), 189–198.

Turk, Meichenbaum, & Genest. (1987).

Turk, D. C., Swanson, K. S., & Tunks, E. R. (2008). Psychological approaches in the treatment of chronic pain patients—when pills, scalpels, and needles are not enough. *The Canadian Journal of Psychiatry, 53*(4), 213–223.

Van Haitsma, K. (1999). *The assessment and integration of preferences into care practices for persons with dementia residing in the nursing home.* Unpublished manuscript. Philadelphia, PA: Philadelphia Geriatric Center.

Vitiello, M. V. (2009, September 7). Cognitive behavioral therapy improves sleep and pain in people with osteoarthritis. *ScienceDaily.*

Whitworth, J. D., Crownover, B. K., & Nichols, W. (2007). Which nondrug alternatives can help with insomnia? *Journal of Family Practice, 56*, 836–838.

Wilson, K. G., Chochinov, H. M., de Faye, B. J., & Breitbart, W. (2000). Diagnosis and management of depression in palliative care. In H. M. Chochinov & W. Breitbart (Eds.), *Handbook of psychiatry in palliative medicine* (pp. 25–49). New York, NY: Oxford University Press.

Winterowd, C., Beck, A. T., & Gruener, D. (2003). *Cognitive therapy with chronic pain patients.* New York, NY: Springer Publishing Company.

World Health Organization. (1990). *Technical report series 804, cancer pain and palliative care* (p. 11). Geneva, Switzerland: Author.

Yesavage, J. A., Brink, T. L., Rose, T. L., Lum, O., Huang, V., Adey, M., et al. (1983). Development and validation of a geriatric depression screening scale: A preliminary report. *Journal of Psychiatric Research, 17*(1), 37–49.

Zigmond, A. S., & Snaith, R. P. (1983). The hospital anxiety and depression scale. *Acta Psychiatrica Scandinavica, 67*, 361–370.

RECOMMENDED RESOURCES

Chronic Pain

Byock, I. (1997). Dying Well: Peace and Possibilities at the End of Life. New York, NY: Riverhead Books.

Kubler-Ross, E. (1969). On Death and Dying. New York, NY: Scribner.

Qualls, S.H. & Kasl-Godley, J.E. (2010). End-of-Life Issues, Grief, and Bereavement: What Clinicians Need to Know. Hoboken, NJ: John Wiley & Sons, Inc.

Sage, N., Sowden, M., Chorlton, E., & Edeleanu, A. (2008). CBT for Chronic Illness and Palliative Care. West Sussex, Enland: John Wiley & Sons Ltd.

Satterfield, J.M. (2008). A Cognitive-Behavioral Approach to the Beginning of the End of Life: Minding the Body Facilitator Guide. New York, NY: Oxford.

Winterowd, C., Beck, A. T., & Gruener, D. (2003). Cognitive therapy with chronic pain patients. New York, NY: Springer Publishing Company.

Appendix A: Symptoms to Report to the Health Care Team

- Change in skin color to a more dusky appearance if respirations are increasing in frequency
- Your own concerns about your loved ones illness or concerns your loved one has about their illness
- Worries that increase your loved ones fears (such as financial ability to pay for care, lack of medication resources, fear that they won't be able to get to the hospital in time if there is an emergency for example)
- Problems with the family, friends or family relationships
- Signs or symptoms that indicate the anxiety is worsening
- Changes in personality that are abrupt or unusual
- Changes in physical condition that causes your loved one to become frightened or more anxious.
- Lack of sleep, increased interruption in sleep
- Medication control of pain symptoms is no longer working

Source: From Hospice and Palliative Nurses Association Patient and Family Teaching Sheets, accessed 1/8/2011 http://www.hpna.org/DisplayPage.aspx?Title=Patient/FamilyTeachingSheets

Appendix B: Deep Breathing Techniques Pocket Card

Introduction:
When people become stressed or anxious, their breathing gets rapid and shallow, this can lead to feeling dizzy or lightheaded, or hyperventilating. Experiencing these symptoms produces feelings of anxiety, which in turn increase the physical signs, producing a negative cycle. This cycle can be stopped by attending to your breathing. Changing the rate and way you breathe can actually make your body more "relaxed" and function more effectively. The following are steps for deep breathing:

1. Put one hand on your abdomen, with your little finger about 1 inch above your navel and place one hand on your chest.

2. Begin to notice your breathing (pause for several seconds). Which hand is doing more of the moving? The goal is to move the stomach and not the upper chest area.

3. Breathe slow and deep so that your stomach goes in and out when you breathe while your other hand on your chest stays as still as possible. *Your hand on your diaphragm should move out as you inhale and in as you exhale* (Acknowledge if the patient has COPD—lung capacity might be reduced, but reassure them of the benefits of practicing deep breathing).

4. Continue to take slow, even, deep breaths. *Breathe in to the count of 3, 4, or 5 depending on what is comfortable for you and then breathe out to the same number. It is okay to start breathing to the count of 2 or 3. You may be able to work up to a larger number if the smaller interval works, remain there with benefits. Do not pause at the top of each breath.*

Guiding a patient through Deep Breathing:

I want you to breathe more slowly, evenly, and deeply. **Inhale through your nose and exhale through your mouth. As you exhale, purse your lips** *(like you are blowing on hot soup). As soon as you finish inhaling, begin to exhale—***do not pause at the "top" of your breathing cycle.** *The duration of inhaling should take approximately the same amount of time as your exhaling.*

Now I'd like you to **close your eyes and breathe with me as I count**—*counting to 5 to inhale and again to 5 to exhale. "Inhale—2–3. Exhale—2–3." Good. Let's try again. You can attempt to gradually build up to counting to 4 or even 5 if you feel capable of this. Repeat the same procedure about 3 times.*

Source: Cully, J. A., & Teten, A. L. (2008). *A therapist's guide to brief cognitive behavioral therapy.* Houston, TX: Department of Veterans Affairs South Central MIRECC. Adapted with permission of the authors.

13

Integrated Depression Care for Homebound Medically Ill Older Adults: Using Evidence-Based Problem-Solving Therapy

Zvi D. Gellis and Arthur M. Nezu

The shift in demographics of American society has received a great deal of attention in recent years. Where once they reflected a small percentage of the census, older adults are now the fastest growing sector of the population in the United States. Older adults are likely to have relatively longer life spans given advances in medical treatments and public health efforts for healthier aging lifestyles. Consequently, the health and mental health care systems of care will be especially relied on by current and future older generations. This will place increased stress on such services. With the aging-boom effect, the overall number of older persons with mental disorders, particularly mood disorders, will also increase. With a dearth of geriatric professionals, a public health crisis looms. It is estimated that 60,000 to 70,000 geriatric social workers will be needed by 2020, yet less than 10% of that projected number is now available (Council on Social Work Education, 2001). Geriatric mental health problems will also demand more attention from service providers to minimize their effects on disability, health care utilization, and quality of life of older adults and their caregivers. As such, the need for accessible and quality mental health care for medically ill and disabled older persons is and will continue to be significant.

Policy initiatives for home and community-based services (HCBS) have expanded over the past decade because of the need for care coordination (American Association of Retired Persons [AARP], 2009). Such initiatives are established because older adults are challenged by the co-occurrence of health and mental health problems. The provision of effective HCBS has enabled many older people to remain in their home rather than be admitted to institutions. In fact, most older adults age 50 and older wish to remain in their own homes and not transition to a care facility (AARP). Home-based services can contribute to improve quality of life by providing health and mental health services, and assistance with activities of daily living and other supportive services. There is evidence that HCBS can contain institutional costs, moderate the growth of Medicaid spending, and reduce nursing home facility admissions (Cheh, 2001; Federal Register, 2000; Government Accountability Office, 1994; Medicare Payment Advisory Commission, 2003; Mollica & Kassner, 2009). One such example of home-based services for older adults is the home health care (HHC) sector.

SIGNIFICANCE OF DEPRESSION IN MEDICALLY ILL OLDER ADULTS

The 2008 Institute of Medicine report, "Retooling for an Aging America," noted that for the older adult population, depression was identified as one of the priority conditions requiring substantial improvements in quality care based on its prevalence, expense, and policy relevance (Institute of Medicine, 2008). The 1999 Surgeon General's mental health report also noted that "depression in older adults not only causes distress and suffering but also leads to impairments in physical, mental, and social functioning" (U.S. Department of Health and Human Services, 1999, Chapter 5, p. 1).

Prevalence estimates of current major depression in elderly community range from 1% to 3% (Kessler et al., 2003). However, the prevalence is much higher in medical and treatment settings: 5% to 10% in primary care (Hybels & Blazer, 2003; Tai-Seale, et al., 2005), 14% in HHC (Bruce et al., 2002), and 24% in long-term care (Hyer, Carpenter, Bishmann, & Wu, 2005). Moreover, depression is twice as prevalent in the HHC setting as in primary care (Brown, Kaiser, & Gellis, 2008) and disproportionally higher than reported prevalence studies of community-dwelling older adults (Kessler et al.). Despite these high rates, evidence suggests that few depressed home care older adults receive adequate treatment, even though effective treatment options for depression exist (Brown, McAvay, Raue, Moses, & Bruce, 2003; Gellis, 2009).

Subthreshold depression (SD) is even more prevalent than major depression and ranges from 16% to 28% depending on the definition (SD) and the number of symptoms (Lyness, 2008). Our research group has estimated a prevalence rate of SD at 16% in a sample

(N = 289) of older adults (age ≥65) receiving skilled nursing care from an acute HHC agency in New York state (Gellis, 2010). Among these medically ill older patients, depression was also characterized by symptoms (e.g., anhedonia and suicidal ideation) associated with negative outcomes. Given the expected growth of older adults coping with chronic illness and disability, the consequences of late-life depression and low rates of treatment (Wei, Sambamoorthi, Olfson, Walkup, & Crystal, 2005), improving the mental health care of homebound older adults is a priority.

A core service strategy in response to this challenge is the identification and implementation of effective interventions to enhance depression care and treatment for older adults (National Institute of Mental Health, 2006). The U.S. Preventive Services Task Force recommends screening for depression in adults if there is a mechanism in place for adequate assessment, treatment, and follow-up (Pignone et al., 2002). Home care is well positioned to provide such a system because of its mission of community-based health care to medically ill older patients.

BARRIERS TO DEPRESSION CARE FOR MEDICALLY ILL OLDER ADULTS

HHC serves some of the oldest and most isolated medically ill patients in the community. Studies have found that mobility limitations along with other disabilities are significant predictors of depressive symptoms (Beekman, Deeg, Braam, Smit, & van Tilburg, 1997; Raue et al., 2003). During medical appointments, primary care physicians (PCP) spend little time discussing or detecting mental health problems with their older patients and rarely refer them to a mental health specialist even if they exhibit symptoms of depression (Tai-Seale, McGuire, Colenda, Rosen, & Cook, 2007). HHC nurses who are responsible for the initial patient assessment may not have the formal training needed to accurately identify depression (Brown, Kaiser, & Gellis, 2008), and without recognizing depression, nurses will not be able to make appropriate referrals to home care social workers, PCPs, or external mental health services, thus depriving older patients of access to needed treatment services. Interviews with home care nurses and social workers and review of medical records indicate that depression is frequently undetected, placing the depressed medically ill home care older adult at high risk for negative mental and physical outcomes (Bruce et al., 2002; Gellis, McGinty, Horowitz, Bruce, & Misener, 2007).

FACTORS ASSOCIATED WITH POOR ACCESS TO GERIATRIC DEPRESSION TREATMENT

The problem of inadequate detection and treatment for depression in medically ill older adult is compounded by several sets of factors. First, patient factors include behaviors resulting from symptoms of depressive illness. Older home care patients often have intricate medical needs that may obscure depression detection. In addition, stigma, amotivation and pessimism, distrust, avolition, financial worries, and fear of losing independence may reduce an older person's willingness to seek mental health care when depression is detected. Finally, for homebound medically ill older persons, a lack of social support and transportation may also impede access to mental health care.

Second, provider factors are known to create barriers to effective mental health care and lead to underdetection and/or undertreatment of depressed medically ill older adult (Zeltzer & Kohn, 2006). HHC workers are constrained by time-consuming mandated assessment forms and may not be able or willing to devote additional time needed to gather appropriate history for older depressed patients. Knowledge and skill deficits in mental health care frequently discourage home care workers from assessing depression. Providers may also be uncomfortable in dealing with depressed patients because of preconceptions and biases about mental illness (Brown et al., 2003).

Finally, organizational factors may impede appropriate depression care. In HHC agencies, patient care is typically conducted without on-site supervision by PCPs. Likewise, home care nurses have little direct contact with patients' physicians. Sometimes, older adults do not receive appropriate depression care even when they are positively screened or do seek help (Gellis, 2010; Wei et al., 2005). PCPs often report feeling pressured for time to investigate all medical problems (Adelman, Greene, Friedmann, & Cook, 2008). In primary care, financial constraints of managed care are increasingly restricting the time spent with older patients, forcing psychiatric concerns to compete with comorbid medical conditions (Gallo et al., 2002).

COMMUNITY-BASED HOME CARE SERVICE DELIVERY OF INTEGRATED DEPRESSION CARE

HHC is a diverse and dynamic health service industry that annually serves approximately 7.6 million individuals by 83,000 providers, for acute illness, chronic medical conditions, and disability (U.S. Census

Bureau, 2004). Of these recipients, 86% are 65 years or older and approximately 64% are female (Center for Medicare & Medicaid Services, 2008). Medicare is the largest single payer of the annual $57.6 billion in HHC services and is a key component of the Medicare wellness agenda because it significantly lowers overall health care costs by treating patients in the community rather than more expensive venues like hospitals, emergency departments, or nursing homes (Center for Medicare & Medicaid Services, 2008; Marmor, 2000).

HHC agencies use a structured and centralized organizational system to support the provision of Medicare-certified skilled nursing care and ancillary services in the patient's home, including social work, physical, occupational and speech therapies, nutrition, and home aides. Usually, patients are discharged from acute care hospital or referred by primary care to home health. The responsibility for care, however, is highly decentralized and remains with the patient's physician who often does not meet with the home care nurse or other providers and has never been to the agency (Figure 13.1). PCPs refer patients needing HHC to an agency that assigns a nurse who travels to the patient's home, completes a Medicare (Outcomes Assessment and Information Set) form, and develops a plan of care. Based on the intake assessment, the home care nurse can recommend internal home care social work services for depression treatment, patient or family/caregiver counseling, financial and housing issues, and services information and referral. Most patients (85%) are referred to home care for medical or

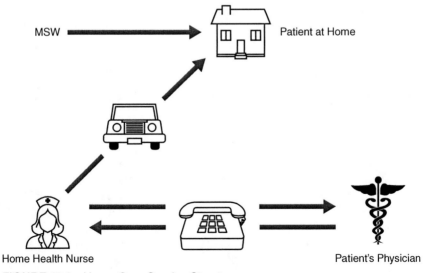

MSW   Patient at Home

Home Health Nurse   Patient's Physician

FIGURE 13.1   Home Care Service Structure

postsurgical needs for which they receive skilled nursing care. Mental health services are rarely provided to medically ill older adults identified with depression while receiving care (Brown et al., 2003, 2008). Home care nurses frequently do not refer depressed patients to primary care, but when they do, there is little to no further contact with the physician about the patient's clinical status or antidepressant treatment monitoring.

CLINICAL SOCIAL WORK ROLE FOR GERIATRIC DEPRESSION TREATMENT

Clinical social workers play a critical role in the HHC system by providing expertise in navigating complex systems of care—be those psychological, social, medical, or economic. Within home care settings, social workers provide brief psychotherapy, care coordination, family and caregiver counseling, information and referral for community social services, and financial and housing issues. Effective evidence-based social work practice that expedites the mental health care of home care patients and reduces negative outcomes is highly valued in the managed-care context. Our teams' problem-solving therapy (PST) research focus is targeted to integrating the depression care functions in home health and using the varied skills of the clinical social worker within the HHC organization to create a more synergistic and effective system of depression care that is sustainable. With additional training in PST as a depression treatment, home care social workers are uniquely positioned to provide depression care for medically ill older adults and thus bridge the divide between patient, home health, and primary care settings.

PSYCHOTHERAPY IS A VIABLE DEPRESSION TREATMENT FOR OLDER ADULTS

Psychosocial treatments, including problem-solving, cognitive behavioral, and interpersonal therapies, have demonstrated effectiveness among depressed older adults, particularly those who reject medication or who are not managing their daily living problems, not coping well with chronic medical conditions, or who are experiencing limited social support (Areán, Alvidrez, Barrera, Robinson, & Hicks, 2002; Gellis & Bruce, 2009; Gellis & Kenaley, 2008). PCPs, who are often the principal source of medical care for depressed older adults, tend to rely on antidepressant medications as the main treatment for late-life depression and are significantly less likely to refer older patients to specialty mental health services (Crystal, Sambamoorthi, Walkup, & Akincigil, 2003; Wei et al., 2005). However, older adults have reported a preference of psychotherapy over pharmacotherapy for their depression treatment (Gum et al., 2006; Landreville, Landry, Baillargeon, Guerette, & Matteau, 2001; Lundervold & Lewin, 1990). Our research group uses a home-based brief therapy—PST—as a key component of depression care for medically ill older adults because of the fast-paced nature of acute HHC service delivery. Based on our research, brief PST is feasible and acceptable to depressed older adults who are recipients of home care services (Gellis et al., 2007, 2008; Gellis & Bruce).

PROBLEM-SOLVING THERAPY MODEL FOR MEDICALLY ILL HOME HEALTH CARE OLDER ADULTS

PST is an evidenced-based, cognitive-behavioral clinical intervention, based on research demonstrating a strong link between social problem solving (SPS) and psychopathology (Nezu, 2004). The overarching treatment goal of PST is to foster adoption and implementation of adaptive problem-solving attitudes and behaviors as a means of decreasing emotional distress and improving overall quality of life (D'Zurilla & Nezu, 2007; Nezu, Nezu, & D'Zurilla, 2007). Originally developed by D'Zurilla and Goldfried (1971), Nezu and his colleagues (Nezu, 1987; Nezu, Nezu, & Perri, 1989) revised and adapted PST for the treatment of major depression. Early studies by Nezu and colleagues (e.g., Nezu, 1986; Nezu & Perri, 1989) established PST as an effective approach for the treatment of major depressive disorder (MDD). Subsequent research has found PST to be effective for the treatment of MDD in primary care settings (e.g., Mynors-Wallis, Gath, Davies, Gray, & Barbour, 1997), as well as for individuals with a medical illness, such as cancer (e.g., Nezu, Nezu, Felgoise, McClure, & Houts, 2003) or diabetes (e.g., Williams et al., 2004) that was concomitant with clinical depression. In fact, two recent meta-analyses provide significant quantitative support for the efficacy of this approach for reducing depression (Bell & D'Zurilla, 2009; Cuijpers, van Straten, & Warmerdam, 2007). With specific relevance to this chapter, PST has also been adapted to treat depression among older adults (e.g., Areán et al., 1993) and has consistently found to be effective for this population (e.g., Ciechanowski et al., 2004), including depressed older adult patients with executive functioning difficulties (Alexopoulus, Raue, & Areán, 2003).

PST helps to reduce depression by increasing an individual's optimism, self-efficacy, and skill levels in effectively coping with stressful problems. In addition, it focuses on a more realistic (as compared to catastrophic) appraisal and evaluation of specific daily living problems linked to depression, as well as developing and choosing the best possible solution alternatives and implementing such action plans to solve these problems. PST can also address anhedonia and psychomotor retardation through increased exposure to daily pleasurable activities (behavioral activation). Scheduling and implementation of daily pleasurable activities can be used as a pathway to problem-solving strategies and skills. PST that is integrated into routine home care practice and delivered by staff social workers is a practical option in the treatment of moderate-to-severe depression in older adults. Within our integrated depression care model, it is imperative to coordinate depression care management with PCPs to facilitate assessment of the older patient for antidepressant therapy because medication is known to be an effective treatment for depression.

Thus, we use PST depression treatment because of its conceptual relevance to medically ill older adults, its robust evidence base (Cuijpers, van Straten, & Smit, 2006; D'Zurilla & Nezu, 2001; Gellis & Kenaley, 2008) including our empirical work with community-dwelling and medically ill older adults, its brevity, and its acceptability to depressed patients and to HHC agencies.

PROBLEM-SOLVING CONCEPTUAL FRAMEWORK

PST for depression is based on a model of depression that characterizes SPS as serving both mediating (e.g., Kant, D'Zurilla, & Maydeu-Olivares, 1997; Nezu & Ronan, 1985) and moderating (e.g., Nezu, Nezu, Saraydarian, Kalmar, & Ronan, 1986; Nezu & Ronan, 1988) roles regarding the relationship between stressful life events and depression. SPS is the multidimensional psychosocial variable that has been repeatedly identified as an important factor in the pathogenesis of both mental health and health problems resulting from poor adaptation to stress (Elliott, Grant, & Miller, 2004; Nezu, 2004). More specifically, SPS has been defined as the cognitive-behavioral process by which a person attempts to identify or discover effective or adaptive means of coping with stressful problems encountered during the course of everyday living (D'Zurilla & Nezu, 2007). In this context, it involves the process whereby individuals attempt to direct their coping efforts at altering the problematic nature of a stressful situation itself, their reactions to such situations, or both. SPS refers more to the meta-process of understanding, appraising, and adapting to stressful life events, such as those related to the experience of a chronic illness, rather than representing a singular coping strategy or activity (Nezu & Nezu, 2010).

Contemporary models of SPS indicate that it is comprised of two general, but partially independent, processes: problem orientation and problem-solving style (D'Zurilla, Nezu, & Maydeu-Olivares, 2004). *Problem orientation* involves the set of generalized appraisals and emotional reactions concerning problems in living, as well as one's ability to successfully resolve them. It can either be *positive* (e.g., viewing problems as opportunities to benefit in some way, perceiving oneself as able to solve problems effectively), which serves to enhance subsequent problem-solving efforts, or *negative* (e.g., viewing problems as a major threat to one's well-being, overreacting emotionally when problems occur), which functions to inhibit attempts to solve problems.

Problem-solving style refers to specific cognitive-behavioral activities aimed at coping with stressful problems. It can be either adaptive, leading to successful problem resolution, or dysfunctional, leading to negative consequences, such as emotional distress. *Rational problem solving* is the constructive style geared to identify an effective solution to the problem and involves the systematic application of various specific problem-solving tasks. It includes accurately identifying obstacles that need to be overcome to achieve reasonable goals, generating alternative solutions to cope with such difficult problems, making effective decisions regarding which coping strategies to engage in, and monitoring the consequences of one's coping attempts to determine the need to engage in additional problem solving. Dysfunctional problem-solving styles include (a) *impulsivity/carelessness* (i.e., the tendency to engage in impulsive, hurried, and/or incomplete attempts to solve a problem); and (b) *avoidance* (i.e., the tendency to avoid problems, procrastinate, and/or depend on others to solve one's problems).

This problem-solving conceptualization suggests that depression can result as a function of deficiencies, or decreased effectiveness, in these problem orientation and problem-solving style dimensions (Nezu, 1987, 2004; Nezu & Nezu, in press). For example, depressed individuals are often characterized by a strong negative orientation, having little faith in their ability to cope with stressful problems, often believing that problems are catastrophes, frequently blaming themselves for causing the problem, and becoming distressed when problems occur. Collectively, negative beliefs decrease one's desire or motivation to engage in any meaningful coping attempts. One's ability to effectively define and formulate problems and to set realistic goals is also decreased when depressed, thus making it very difficult to identify effective solutions. Often, depressed individuals set unrealistically high goals—when not achieved, self-blame, frustration, and decreased motivation are likely to occur. Depressed individuals also tend to generate both fewer and less effective alternatives to problem situations. A negative problem orientation and lack of alternatives biases the depressed person to selectively attend to negative versus positive events and to immediate versus long-term consequences. The depressed individual may also have difficulty actually carrying out his or her plan because of specific behavioral and social skill deficits. Further, a negative problem orientation may impact on an individual's ability to be objective about the outcome of solution implementation. Thus, the depressed individual is unsatisfied with the coping attempt and may feel that the goals have not been achieved. In addition, poor problem solving has been found to be related to feelings of hopelessness and suicidal intent (D'Zurilla, Chang, Nottingham, & Faccini, 1998; Rudd, Rajab, & Dahm, 1994).

PST, then, is geared to teach older adults specific skills to (a) enhance their positive problem orientation, (b) decrease their negative orientation, (c) improve their rational problem-solving ability, (d) decrease their tendency to be avoidant, and (e) minimize their tendency to be impulsive and careless when attempting to cope with stressful problems in living. In addition, we believe that the PST model works for medically ill older adults because it specifically targets the skills of solving daily living problems and self-efficacy. Through modeling and reinforcement of cognitive and behavioral skills, PST can also increase older adults' sense of self-competence and self-efficacy in taking responsibility for day-to-day management of their illnesses and for reducing and minimizing the negative emotional and physical effects of their medical problems. Improved problem-solving and coping skills along with resulting self-efficacy are potential active components thus likely to buffer against the effect of risk factors on depression. Strengthening self-efficacy by allowing older individuals the experience of successfully dealing with and thus overcoming specific problems can be a primary strategy for preventing and reducing late-life depression.

PROBLEM-SOLVING THERAPY IN HOME CARE INTERVENTION COMPONENTS

PST in Home Care (PST-HC) is based on PST procedures for depression recently revised and updated (e.g., Nezu et al., 2007) and conducted by master of social work (MSW)-level clinical social workers (Gellis et al.,

2007, 2008). Standard PST (i.e., Attitude, Define, Alternatives, Predict, Try out [ADAPT] model of Nezu et al., 2007) was modified in several ways to increase its feasibility for homebound patients and to meet their needs living with one or more medical illnesses. First, treatment was provided in the patient's home. Second, PST was provided in six weekly 1-hour sessions conducted usually over an 8-week period. The clinical social work PST therapists were directed to ensure that the intervention protocol be made brief and relevant to the specific life circumstances of each homebound medically ill older adult patient. Educational brochures on the topics of "late-life depression" and "improving one's quality of life" were used in the PST sessions.

PST-HC involved teaching depressed older adults to (a) clearly define the nature of their daily living problem and develop a realistic goal to improve coping ability, (b) generate a wide range of alternative solutions, (c) systematically evaluate the potential consequences of each solution examining the advantages and disadvantages of each potential solution option, (d) select the optimal one to implement based on decision criteria (effort, realistic, cost, achievability), and (e) monitor and evaluate an actual solution outcome after its implementation. Table 13.1 provides an outline of the PST-HC therapy session skills sets and content for medically ill home care older adults.

An important component of PST is preparing the older adult for depression treatment. The PST therapist advocates with the older person for a positive optimistic outlook or attitude toward solving daily stressful problems (cf. Nezu & D'Zurilla, 1989). As PST is a brief treatment for depression, patients are also informed that they are being referred, when warranted, to their PCPs for antidepressant medication assessment. Psychoeducation on depression and the basics of solving daily problems are provided in the initial session but may also be reviewed over the duration of therapy as needed. Synthesized research data are provided by the therapist to inform the patient on what is known about the causes of depression, depressive symptom profiles, effective treatments, and its links to problem solving and behavioral activation.

Sessions 1 and 2 involve a general introduction, structure, and orientation to the PST therapy that includes developing a positive attitude toward solving one's problems, problem identification and establishing a realistic measurable goal, brainstorming and evaluating solution options, and trying out a solution. Sessions 3 and 4 involve continued psychoeducation and practice in the problem-solving skills. The last two sessions provide for an applied integration of the PST model, as well as for continued practice in the various problem-solving

TABLE 13.1   Problem-Solving Therapy in Home Care (PST-HC)

Session	Content
1 Adopt Positive Attitude *Skill Set:* Identify problems Develop goals	Orient and introduce problem-solving therapy for depression in home care (adopt positive attitude toward problem solving); explain connections between daily problems, stress, mood, and pleasurable events; review causes, symptoms, medications, and treatments for depression; identify and define nature of stressful problems in daily living; identify patient-coping responses; set realistic goal for relief of problem; orient to choose two pleasurable activities (daily scheduling); set homework activity; obtain permission to contact and update primary care physician; have a brief telephone contact with the patient during the week as a reminder to complete homework and pleasurable activities.
2 *Skill Set:* Brainstorm alternative solutions	Review homework; review log of pleasurable activities; review symptoms; review coping responses to problem; identify problem-solving style; review goals; generate many alternative solutions; identify/choose one or two solutions based on the following criteria: realistic, achievable, cost, effort (predict outcome effectiveness and consequences); instruct patient to try out chosen solutions with action plan and monitor outcome; troubleshoot any difficulties; set homework; choose/schedule two pleasurable activities each day; have a brief telephone contact during the week as a reminder to complete homework and pleasurable activities.
3 *Skill Set:* Review advantages (pros) and disadvantages (cons)	Review homework; review performance outcome for chosen solution; teach patient to reward self for efforts in attempted problem solving; review log of pleasurable activities; review symptoms; review goal and alternative solutions if solution was less than successful, or examine new problem and renew goals; brainstorm alternative solutions; choose one or two solutions (predict consequences: pros/cons); try solutions with action plan, monitor, and evaluate outcome; troubleshoot any difficulties; set homework; choose two pleasurable activities; have a brief telephone contact during the week for homework reminder; review patient progress with assigned home care provider.
4 *Skill Set:* Decide and choose solution(s)	Review homework; review performance outcome for chosen solution; patient rewards self for efforts in attempted problem solving; review log of pleasurable activities; review symptoms; review goal if solution was less than successful, or examine new problem and renew goals; generate alternative solutions; choose a solution (predict consequences) based on the following criteria: realistic, achievable, cost, effort; try solution with action plan; monitor and evaluate outcome; set homework; troubleshoot any difficulties; choose two pleasurable activities; have a brief telephone contact during the week as a reminder to complete homework and pleasurable activities.

(Continued)

TABLE 13.1 Problem-Solving Therapy in Home Care (PST-HC) *(Continued)*

Session	Content
5 *Skill Set:* Try out chosen solution(s) action plan monitor	Review homework; review performance outcome for chosen solution; patient rewards self for efforts in attempted problem solving; review log of pleasurable activities; review symptoms; review goal if solution was less than successful, or examine new problem and renew goals; generate alternative solutions; choose a solution (predict consequences); try solution with action plan, monitor, and evaluate outcome; set homework; troubleshoot any difficulties; choose two pleasurable activities; prepare patient for clinical termination; review PST-HC steps; have a brief telephone contact during the week for homework reminder; review patient progress with home care provider
6 *Skill Set:* Evaluate review skills closure	Review homework; review performance outcome for chosen solution; patient rewards self for efforts; review log of pleasurable activities; review symptoms; review goal if solution was less than successful, or examine new problem and renew goals; generate alternative solutions; choose a solution (predict consequences); try solution with action plan; monitor and evaluate outcome; set homework; troubleshoot any difficulties; choose two pleasurable activities; clinical termination with patient; review PST-HC steps and wrap-up; review progress with patient and home care provider

skill components. The PST therapist uses a PST worksheet in each session as a guide to cover the problem-solving skills sets delineated in Table 13.1 with the older patient. The PST therapist completes the worksheet based on the patient's assessed needs for the week. Interviews with PST therapists in training indicate that the worksheet helped the trainee to maintain session structure and as a way for the older patient to learn the problem-solving steps needed to try out identified realistic solutions on a weekly basis.

CASE EXAMPLE 1: MRS. MARGOLIS

Mrs. Margolis, age 77, has lived alone in her own home for 4 years since her husband's death. She has diabetes and osteoarthritis. Recently, she was hospitalized for a fall. She has in-home nursing for diabetes disease management, and physical therapy for balance and walking exercise. She spends most of her time in her bedroom or in front of the TV, and most days, her only human contact is the home care service. She has a daughter in another city who calls her a couple of times a month. Mrs. M. says she is lonely, but does not initiate any contact with her family or neighbors. Mrs. M is aware that she needs a homemaker service for house cleaning and meal preparation; she talks with a home care nurse about her needs. However, Mrs. M. comes up with many reasons not to follow through. Her primary concern is money. She believes that her depressed mood and lack of interest is caused by her health problems, and she refuses to take medication. She is inclined, though, to try to talk with a social worker for her depression, but does not want to be in a group with older people and does not have means of transportation to get to therapy.

To identify stressful life problems, the PST therapist uses a *Problem List Form*, adapted for HHC older adult patients. For example, in Case 1, numerous problems are identified and the PST therapist uses the problem list form (see sample in Table 13.2) and prioritizes which problem to start with based on current expressed needs. This form delineates various older patient problem domains: (a) personal health, health care system/ providers; (b) emotional or psychological; (c) finances; (d) living arrangements; (e) transportation; (f) relationships; (g) activities of daily living; (h) house management; and (i) socialization. Sufficient time is offered by the PST therapist to uncover the patient's problems and to develop a priority list (based on the older adult's needs) of problems to tackle and solve over six sessions. One important issue is that PST therapists are taught to distinguish between short- and long-term problems and concomitant solutions that may start to be used in therapy and continued posttherapy. One of the primary goals of the therapy is to teach the older person the necessary problem-solving skills to deal with daily life stresses in a rational and planned way to prevent depressive symptoms from reoccurring.

As mentioned, the PST therapist uses the *Problem List Form* to identify all current problems experienced by the older patient and the reason for referral. The therapist itemizes the type of problems reported by the older patient into identified life stress domains (described earlier). Many of the problems identified by older adults are related to their chronic medical conditions and symptoms of depression. The PST therapist uses a reflective nondirective style to engage the older patient and develop therapeutic alliance as well as a directive approach to engage in problem resolution. To ascertain the nature and extent of the problems identified, the therapist orients the older patient to the importance of developing a positive attitude toward solving his or her problems. The therapist gains insight into the problems identified by asking the five W questions (who, what, where, when, and why) for the older patient to gain awareness of why a certain problem persists. The PST therapist identifies the patient's problem-solving coping style using items from the Social Problem

TABLE 13.2   PENN-PST Problem List Form

Case Example: Mrs. Margolis   *TIP: This worksheet is for the therapist to use during assessment.*
Problems With Health Problems, Health Care, Obstacles: Patient is concerned about falling, has numerous health problems, and refuses to take antidepressant medication.
Problems With Emotional/Psychological, Loneliness, Isolation, etc.: Patient has little contact with others; isolated.
Problems With Money And Finances: Patient stated that she is worried about her financial status.
Problems With Living Arrangements: She is living alone while her daughter lives in another city; they have some telephone contact.
Problems With Transportation: None, according to the patient.
Problems With Relationships: ■ Spouse or partner: ■ Family members: children, grandchildren, other family members ■ Friends, Other: Unknown
Problems With Doing Activities Around The House: The patient needs assistance with house cleaning.
Problems With ADLs: Shopping, Cooking, Bathing, Taking Meds, Grooming, Dressing, Walking, etc. The patient needs assistance with meal preparation.
Problems In Coping With Stress

Note. ADLs = activities of daily living.

Solving Inventory (SPSI; D'Zurilla, Nezu, & Maydeu-Olivares, 2002) to understand past coping attempts to resolve problems that may have been ineffective.

The PST therapist uses the *Session Worksheet* (Figure 13.2) for every session to document the steps that the patient is learning to use in solving problems. The PST therapist helps the older patient rate problems from highest to lowest priority. The patient is then asked to choose a priority problem that he or she would like to solve, and then a short-term goal is developed with the provision that it must be realistic and measurable. Once these tasks are completed, the older patient is oriented to the skill of freely "brainstorming" alternative solutions to solve the identified problem without judging each solution option during this phase. Once the older patient has completed this phase, the PST therapist directs the patient to examine each potential solution

Name:	**Homework Review from Previous Session**	
Date:	**Depression Score:**	**Pleasant Activity Level Score (PALS):**
Session #:	20–27 ... 15–19 . . . 10–14 . . . 5–9 . . . . . 1–4 . . . . . 3	Severe HOW PLEASANT, ENJOYABLE, OR REWARDING was the activity? Moderately severe Moderate 0 This was not pleasurable. Mild 1 This was somewhat pleasurable. Minimal 2 This was pleasurable. This was very pleasurable.

PENN-PST SESSION WORKSHEET

S1. **Socialize and orient to problem solving (positive attitude)**

S2. **Problem identified in session**:

S2a. **Specify goal** (realistic, measurable):

S3. **Brainstorm solutions** (to the identified problem below)	S4a. **Evaluate each solution option** (based on effort, time needed, achievable, etc.)

	Pros ☑ (advantages)	Cons ☒ (disadvantages)
1. Solution Option 1	1	1
2. Solution Option 2	2	2
3. Solution Option 3	3	3
4. Solution Option 4	4	4
5. Solution Option 5 etc.	5	5

S4b. **Choose Solution** (based on S4a evaluation)	S5. **Steps To Achieve Solution** (reduce barriers)	**Try Out Solution/ Evaluate Outcome**

Homework/Activity Schedule for the Week:

Pleasant activities:

Solution(s) to try out:

Use of coping cards, positive statements, stop-and-think rule, and so forth, as examples

FIGURE 13.2 PENN-PST Session Worksheet

option for its advantages (Pros) and disadvantages (Cons) on the PST worksheet. This process assists the patient in shaping decisions about the solution options based on several decision-making criteria: (a) Is the solution option realistic? (b) Is the solution option achievable (i.e., Can I do it?)? (c) How much effort do I have to expend? and (d) Is there an emotional or time cost? Based on the older patient's responses in the decision-making process, the patient can make an effective solution choice from the options list as an attempt to reach his or her goal and solve the identified problem.

During treatment sessions, emphasis is placed on psychoeducation about depression and scheduling pleasurable activities chosen from a list adapted for older adults based on the Pleasurable Events Schedule (MacPhillamy & Lewinsohn, 1982). Together, the PST therapist and the older patient develop a personal tailored list of pleasurable activities in each session as part of the weekly homework activity. The PST therapist encourages the older person to choose and complete one or two pleasurable activities each day until the next PST session. The pleasant activity scheduling builds on simple and graduated activities that target depressive symptoms.

The older patient is provided with a pleasant activities weekly scheduling form to keep track of type and frequency of activities. The older patient is asked to rate each completed activity using (developed for our studies) the PALS on a scale from 0 (*this was not pleasurable*) to 3 (*this was very pleasurable*) to reinforce behavioral activation. The PST therapist monitors and reviews the pleasant activity schedule in each session as part of the homework phase.

Finally, between-session homework assignments relevant to each problem-solving step are included as part of the therapeutic process. The older patient is encouraged to choose and try out a selected solution predicted to be realistic and achievable. A brief telephone call to the older patient in-between sessions is completed to support the therapeutic alliance and serves as a reminder to complete the homework—that is, trying out the chosen solution option and completing daily pleasurable activities itemized in the previous session.

PST therapists assess for late-life depressive symptoms at each session by administering the Patient Health Questionnaire-9 (PHQ-9) items (Spitzer, Kroenke, & Williams, 1999). The PST therapist completes this process because (a) it assists the therapist in tracking the treatment progress of the older patient; (b) it helps older patients monitor their own symptoms each week; (c) it provides a connection between how they feel and their level of pleasurable activity, thus counteracting anhedonia; (d) the PHQ-9 outcomes can be visually illustrated to the client to interpret and explain progress; and (e) the process provides a way for older patients to take more control of their mood and engage in their recovery from depression.

PST therapists are asked to administer the interventions in a flexible manner, reviewing all skills for each patient but allocating different amounts of time, depending on the older person's needs. Flexibility is recommended in the use of terminology, mode of presentation, and homework format to fit individual difference in educational background, cognitive skills, and sensory capacity. PST therapists are encouraged to be flexible with the schedule of sessions to accommodate individual patient needs. Sessions are shortened or lengthened and scheduled around medical appointments based on patient needs and preferences.

COMMON PROBLEM-SOLVING THERAPY CHALLENGES

First Session: There are times when older patients pose challenges for the PST therapist, particularly in the first session. Older patients may deny the existence of depressive symptoms, suggest that the experienced symptoms are of a physical nature and caused by their illnesses, and they may not be able to see the interrelatedness of their physical and psychological symptoms. First, it is important to spend sufficient time in the first session to provide a rationale for PST and delineate the connections between the depressive symptoms, how one copes with daily stressors, and solving daily problems. It is important to spend sufficient time with the older patient listening to his or her issues and related daily problems while building therapeutic alliance. In addition, the therapist needs to expose the patient to the process of positive problem solving as part of developing a positive attitude toward problem resolution. This process is a component of the socialization of the patient to PST and attempts to instill hope in gaining control over one's quality of life. The therapist can also assess the patient's problem-solving coping skills using the revised SPSI. This will provide an understanding of the patient's problem-solving style and previous coping attempts of current and past daily problems.

Homework Compliance: Another problem that may arise is the completion of homework assignments. Tasks are provided to the patient at the end of the session as part of homework. PST therapists request that specific homework tasks be completed by the patient including (a) attempting a chosen solution to implement in real life, (b) evaluating the outcome, and (c) choosing and completing two pleasurable activities daily until the next session. At times, patients will forget or lack the motivation to write down their evaluation of the outcome of their attempt at solving a problem, and instead, provide only oral feedback during a session on the outcome of the solution. Sometimes, assignments are unclear or are not sufficiently specific. There may also be unanticipated obstacles for the patient. At other times, the older patient may require assistance in reconfiguring the environment or arranging time to make it more favorable for homework completion. Telephone reminders between sessions are built into the therapy for maximum adherence. At other times, the therapist may be inconsistent in reviewing homework assignments. The review of previous homework should occur at the beginning of each session following the initial assessment session. In this way, the patient receives a message that adherence to homework completion is important to overall success in therapy and problem resolution. In such cases, it is recommended that the PST therapist spend sufficient time on the homework assignment and ask the patients to review and repeat their task prior to session termination. To increase homework adherence, the PST therapist or the patient can write down the tasks on a weekly homework form as a reminder. The forms should be in large print, identifying the steps to be taken for assessing the solution outcome, that is, (a) When and where will you try the solution? (b) How will you prepare yourself? (c) Will you need someone's help in completing the solution task? (d) Did the solution work in reaching the identified goal? (e) What do you think worked? (f) What didn't work? (g) What obstacles did you experience if any? (h) Was is difficult? (i) Did it require a lot of effort? In this way, the PST therapist helps the older patient to break down the components of the homework into manageable parts, and the patient has been empowered to help in the development and implementation of the homework task. The PST therapist can offer guidance in starting with small modest steps for success in reaching the stated goal. As the patient gains confidence in using the problem-solving steps, the PST therapist can adjust the pace to complement patient progress, thus reducing patient burden.

PROBLEM-SOLVING TREATMENT FIDELITY

Fidelity can assist to ascertain whether PST with depressed older adults can be provided as intended, and if increased treatment adherence to the procedures is related to a decrease in depressive symptoms. Our

PST training team collects information on treatment fidelity through various means, including audiotapes and live observations of sessions. We have developed a PST Therapist Fidelity Scale (PSTTFS) based on the work of Nezu et al. (2007) as seen in Figure 13.3. The fidelity scale covers all five components of the PST process and specific therapist tasks subsumed under each that would generally make for a high-quality session. Each component is observed and rated on a fidelity scale from 0 (*almost never*) to 4 (*almost always*), resulting in a global treatment fidelity score.

RESEARCH ON PROBLEM-SOLVING THERAPY FOR LATE-LIFE DEPRESSION IN MEDICALLY ILL OLDER PATIENTS

Several randomized controlled trials (RCTs) have tested PST on late-life depression outcomes among medically ill older adult recipients of HHC services. The first RCT in HHC compared the impact of PST-HC to usual care (UC) on outcomes of depression and secondary outcomes of problem-solving skills and quality of life (Gellis et al., 2007). Participants ($n = 40$) were older medically ill HHC patients receiving skilled nursing care in their homes because of various medical conditions (e.g., cardiovascular disease [CVD], diabetes, chronic obstructive pulmonary disease, cancer, hip replacement).

Our research team examined the feasibility, acceptability, and efficacy of PST-HC among isolated medically ill home care older adults. We trained home care nurses in depression screening, assessment, and referral of appropriate cases to an independent MSW-level social worker (i.e., PST therapist). The clinical social worker was trained and supervised in PST but not employed by the HHC agency. The PST therapist worked alongside a home care team comprised of nurses, social workers, physical therapists, and nurse supervisor. Communication with the PCP about the patient's depression level was provided by the assigned home care nurse.

PST treatment was provided to the experimental condition participants for 6 weeks as an augmentation to UC services, and included approximately 1 hour per session per week in the patient's home, plus a midweek telephone call for homework reminder. Participants in the UC condition were told that they would receive standard acute HHC services based on their primary medical diagnoses and a referral for antidepressant medication assessment to their PCP. The UC group also received literature on facts about depression and its treatment and was encouraged to review the material with the home care social

PENN - *Problem-Solving Therapy Training Institute*

PST Therapist Fidelity Scale

PST Session # □ 1 □ 2 □ 3 □ 4 □ 5 □ 6 □ **Booster**

PST Therapist trainee ID Code:_____ Agency Site:_____

Client ID Code:_____ Date of PST Session: ____/____/____ Date of Rating: ____/____/____

For each item, assess the PST therapist's fidelity level on a scale from 0 to 4

0	1	2	3	4
Never (almost never)	Rarely	Sometimes	Frequently	Always (almost always)

PST Components: **A.D.A.P.T.**

Notes

1. ATTITUDE   (Adopt a positive optimistic attitude towards solving problems)

_____Socialize client/patient to PST: Problem Orientation
_____Provide introductory statements
_____Provide definition of problem solving, coping with life stresses
_____Provide rationale for PST & depression
_____Review depression symptoms (PHQ-9) [Form]
_____Review depression brochure and pleasurable activity rationale

2.   DEFINE--the problem

_____Develop a "Problem List" [Form]
_____Get facts about problem, ask W5 questions (what when where who why & how) in clear concrete terms
_____Identify 1-2 problem(s) to work on from problem list
_____Ask about past coping attempts
_____Determine Problem Solving style: rationale, impulsive/carelessness, avoidance

Establish a Realistic Goal

_____Specify realistic, rational goal-determined by client/patient
_____Describe in objective, behavioral, measurable terms
_____Goal is achievable
_____Goal follows directly from identified problem

FIGURE 13.3 Problem-Solving Therapist Fidelity Scale

Notes

3.   ALTERNATIVES (generate alternative solution options)

_____Prepare client for brainstorming technique [Form]
_____Generate alternative options list for solving problem
_____Withhold judgment now

4.   PREDICT (predict the +ve and -ve consequences)

_____Evaluate list of solution alternatives: [Form]
            Consider Pros [+] (advantages) & Cons [-] (disadvantages)
            for self/others on following criteria:
□realistic?   □time   □effort   □emotional cost   □effects on family or friends

_____Choose solution option(s) that has the <u>best chance of achieving the
        desired goal</u> while minimizing the costs and maximizing benefits

5.   TRY OUT (implement chosen solution)

_____instruct client to try out solution in real life
_____develop action plan to evaluate the outcome
_____review homework tasks (write down homework) [Form]
            (a) Go over client's list of pleasant activities
            (b) Plan pleasant activity schedule for the week
            (c) Action plan to implement & evaluate solution

Homework Tasks
_____ Identify pleasant activities [Form]
_____ Schedule Daily Activity Planning
_____ Identify and Review Homework tasks [Form]
_____ Review last session homework; solution(s); activities

Therapy Process Tasks
_____ Summarize process at end of session
_____ Ask client about their homework tasks
_____ Remind client about homework
_____ Remind client about telephone call during week

Non-Therapeutic Factors
_____empathic, caring, confident, professional
_____clear & positive communication
_____builds therapeutic alliance   **PST Session Fidelity Rating_____**
_____uses reflective/directive style

NOTES / QUESTIONS / SUGGESTIONS FOR DISCUSSION

FIGURE 13.3   Problem-Solving Therapist Fidelity Scale _(Continued)_

worker during a standard planned home care visit. To ensure patient safety, each UC participant was contacted by telephone during the first 2 weeks to assess the need for crisis management or a referral outside the protocol. No direct counseling was provided during these telephone calls, only minimal information. All PCPs involved, by virtue of their connection to older patients, received a study letter informing them that their patient was receiving PST psychosocial treatment for depression and that they were being referred for antidepressant assessment. Our study team also provided each patient's physician with American Psychiatric Association treatment guidelines for geriatric depression. All patients who completed PST-HC did so in six sessions, with an average duration of 7.1 weeks (SD: 0.71). All follow-up interviews were completed in the patient's home. PST interventionists received 2 weeks of PST training and weekly PST supervision.

Data were obtained at baseline, posttreatment, and 3 and 6 months on all 40 participants. Of the 40 patients, most were Whites (80%), female (85%), living alone in an apartment or their own home (60%), and most had at least three diagnosed medical conditions (55%). At baseline, patients had moderate-to-severe levels of depression (BDI: 29.85 ± 6.3; GDS: 14.27 ± 5.9). There was also no difference at baseline between the groups in functioning as measured by the Quality of Life Index (QoLI: 8.30 ± 1.92) or in problem-solving abilities (SPSI-R: 8.86 ± 1.70). Participants in the PST-HC condition reported significantly lower levels of depressive symptoms compared with UC participants as measured by the Beck Depression Inventory (BDI) and the Geriatric Depression Scale (GDS), significantly higher quality of life scores, and significantly higher problem-solving ability scores as measured by the Social Problem Solving Inventory-Revised (SPSI-R) version. The PST-HC treatment group improved on the BDI scores with no advantage for the UC group, reflecting an effect size in the large range ($d = 2.7$).

Comparison of PST-HC and UC conditions on treatment satisfaction indicated that PST-HC scores were significantly greater than the UC group. Participants in UC and PST-HC conditions reported receiving similar types of home care services over the study period. There were no significant differences in the number of home visits, number of patients receiving mental health referrals, new psychotropic medications, or total number of primary care visits over the treatment period.

A second randomized trial tested the impact of PST in the HHC setting among 62 homebound medically ill older adults diagnosed with minor depression (Gellis et al., 2008). Although the level of depressive symptomatology is less than that for major depression, minor depression is serious, accompanied by significant functional decline, increased health care use, and a risk factor for mortality from medical conditions as well as suicide (Horowitz, Reinhardt, & Kennedy, 2005).

To address the lack of evidence on psychosocial treatments for minor depression among acute home care patients, we conducted a 6-week RCT. Eligible older participants met *Diagnostic and Statistical Manual for Mental Disorders, Revised, 4th edition (DSM-IV)* criteria for minor depression and scored 11 or higher on the 17-item Hamilton Depression Rating Scale (HRSD; Hamilton, 1967). Criteria for minor depression were based on the *DSM-IV* research indicators, which included patient reports of two to four symptoms for at least 2 weeks. We compared treatment-as-usual (TAU) in acute home care, augmented with education on depression, to PST-HC added to TAU in home care. Sixty-two participants completed the protocol and provided baseline, posttreatment, and 3- and 6-month follow-up data. All patients who completed PST-HC did so in six sessions, with an average duration of 7.1 weeks. Patients in TAU were contacted weekly by phone over an average of 7.0 weeks to assess the need for crisis management or a referral outside the protocol. No direct counseling was provided during these phone calls, only minimal information.

The mean age for the study sample was 77.6 years and mean education level was 11 years. Of the 62 patients, most were Whites (85%), female (88%), living alone in an apartment or their own home (80%), and had at least three diagnosed chronic medical conditions (55%). Participants in the PST-HC condition were found to report significantly lower levels of depressive symptoms compared with TAU participants as measured by the HAM-D and GDS, and significantly higher problem-solving ability scores on the SPSI-R, but not significantly higher quality of life scores. Further, patients in the TAU condition did not experience any significant changes on any measure from baseline to posttreatment. Patients receiving PST-HC depression treatment reported significantly lower levels of depressive symptoms at 3- and 6-month follow-up points as assessed by the two indices: HAM-D and GDS depression measures. This suggests that the positive effects of the original PST-HC intervention were maintained 6 months following treatment.

In the previous RCTs, we discovered that a large percentage of home care patients (44%) had a primary diagnosis of CVD, a leading cause of death in older adults. Thus, we completed a small pilot trial comparing tailored home-based PST-HC and UC enhanced with depression education among depressed homebound older adults with CVD (Gellis & Bruce, 2009). Results indicated that the PST-HC depression intervention group reported more favorable treatment satisfaction than controls and demonstrated significant improvement in depression scores. Most participants (63%) reported that they preferred talking to a depression therapist about their mental health symptoms rather than receive antidepressant medication.

These studies demonstrated the following: (a) PST significantly reduced depression scores relative to controls; (b) depression assessment and treatment is feasible in home care; (c) treatment is acceptable to older adults; and (d) integrating depression care in home health is acceptable to home care nurses and social workers. Through extensive qualitative interviews with home care workers and managers, we learned that the following required components were needed for "real world" integrated depression service delivery: (a) home care nurses need comprehensive training in depression screening, assessment, and referral; (b) home care social workers need training in evidence-based PST depression treatment; (c) training in appropriate communication about depression within home care and with primary care; and (d) a structured internal referral and follow-up mechanism within the agency for depression care. Home care nurses reported that they could improve their skills in screening and referral of appropriate depressed patients, but they stated that the home care social worker was the most appropriate staff within the home care organization to provide brief depression treatment in the patient's home (Gellis et al., 2007, 2008).

SUMMARY

In summary, the observation that PST-HC intervention is effective in reducing depressive symptoms in later life is encouraging for several reasons. First, from the patient perspective, these findings suggest that despite the complexity and magnitude of chronic medical and of physical disability in the average older adult receiving home care services, clinically significant depressive symptoms can be alleviated and quality of life improved with a brief and manualized psychotherapy. Psychosocial interventions such as PST, which are based on cognitive and behavioral theory principles, have also been found effective in the treatment of older primary care patients with major and minor depression. The mechanism by which the intervention reduces depressive symptoms involves, to some extent, improvement in the participant's ability to solve problems by generating new options, evaluating the solution options, and making realistic decisions about solving life stressors.

Second, from a community-based service delivery perspective, our empirical work suggests the feasibility of providing home-based psychotherapy in the context of routine HHC services. The effective use of clinical social workers is especially relevant because the cost of independent social work home visits for Medicare patients is a reimbursable service. The data also suggest that modifications made to traditional PST to increase its feasibility in HHC (e.g., six session, problem-solving skill development, flexible scheduling, and home visits) do not undermine its potential effectiveness.

Third, the brevity of PST-HC is also advantageous relative to the typical 12 to 16 sessions used for cognitive or interpersonal therapy. This line of research demonstrates home and community-based "real world" rigorous research applications of a potentially feasible and replicable depression intervention for homebound medically ill acute home care patients. The PST depression intervention is theoretically driven, empirically supported, manualized, brief, and can be provided by integrated home care clinical social workers in the patient's home.

REFERENCES

American Association of Retired Persons. (2009). American Association of Retired Persons Public Policy Report. Fact Sheet. Providing more long-term support and services at home: Why it's critical for health reform. Washington, DC: AARP Public Policy Institute.

Adelman, R., Greene, M., Friedmann, E., & Cook, M. (2008). Discussion of depression in follow-up medical visits with older patients. *Journal of the American Geriatrics Society, 56,* 16–22.

Alexopoulos, G. S., Raue, P., & Areán, P. A. (2003). Problem-solving therapy versus supportive therapy in geriatric major depression with executive dysfunction. *American Journal of Geriatric Psychiatry, 11,* 46–52.

Areán, P. A., Alvidrez, J., Barrera, A., Robinson, G. S., & Hicks, S. (2002). Would older medical patients use psychological services? *The Gerontologist, 42,* 392–398.

Areán, P. A., Perri, M. G., Nezu, A. M., Schein, R. L., Christopher, F., & Joseph, T. X. (1993). Comparative effectiveness of social problem-solving therapy and reminiscence therapy as treatments for depression in older adults. *Journal of Consulting and Clinical Psychology, 61,* 1003–1010.

Beekman, A., Deeg, D., Braam, A., Smit, J., & van Tilburg, W. (1997). Consequences of major and minor depression in later life: A study of disability, well-being and service utilization. *Psychological Medicine, 27,* 1397–1409.

Bell, A. C., & D'Zurilla, T. J. (2009). Problem-solving therapy for depression: A meta-analysis. *Clinical Psychology Review, 29,* 348–353.

Brown, E., Kaiser, R., & Gellis, Z. D. (2008). Screening and assessment of late-life depression in home health care: Issues and challenges. *Annals of Long Term Care, 15*(1), 27–32.

Brown, E. L., McAvay, G. J., Raue, P. J., Moses, S., & Bruce, M. L. (2003). Recognition of depression in the elderly receiving homecare services. *Psychiatric Services, 54*(2), 208–213.

Bruce, M. L., McAvay, G. J., Raue, P. J., Brown, E. L., Meyers, B. S., Keohane, D. J., et al. (2002). Major depression in elderly home health care patients. *American Journal of Psychiatry, 159,* 1367–1374.

Centers for Medicare & Medicaid Services. (2008). *National health expenditures projections, 2007–2017.* Retrieved June 14, 2010, from www.cms.hhs.gov

Cheh, V. (2001). *The final evaluation report on the National Home Health Perspective Payment Demonstration: Agencies reduce visits while preserving quality.* Princeton, NJ: Mathematica Policy Research, Inc.

Ciechanowski, P., Wagner, E., Schmaling, K., Schwartz, S., Williams, B., Diehr, P., et al. (2004). Community-integrated home-based depression treatment in older adults: A randomized controlled trial. *Journal of the American Medical Association, 291,* 1569–1577.

Council on Social Work Education. (2001). *Executive summary: Strengthening the impact of social work to improve the quality of life for older adults and their families: A blueprint for the new millennium.* Washington, DC: Sage-SW.

Crystal, S., Sambamoorthi, U., Walkup, J., & Akincigil, A. (2003). Diagnosis and treatment of depression in the elderly Medicare population: Predictors, disparities, and trends. *Journal of the American Geriatrics Society, 51,* 1718–1728.

Cuijpers, P., van Straten, A., & Smit, F. (2006). Psychological treatment of late-life depression: A meta-analysis of randomized controlled trial. *International Journal of Geriatric Psychiatry, 21,* 1139–1149.

Cuijpers, P., van Straten, A., & Warmerdam, L. (2007). Problem solving therapies for depression: A meta-analysis. *European Psychiatry, 22,* 9–15.

D'Zurilla, T. J., Chang, E. C., Nottingham, E. J., IV, & Faccini, L. (1998). Social problem-solving deficits and hopelessness, depression, and suicidal risk in college students and psychiatric inpatients. *Journal of Clinical Psychology, 54,* 1–17.

D'Zurilla, T. J., & Goldfried, M. R. (1971). Problem solving and behavior modification. *Journal of Abnormal Psychology, 78,* 107–126.

D'Zurilla, T. J., & Nezu, A. M. (2001). Problem-solving therapies. In K. S. Dobson (Ed.), *Handbook of cognitive-behavioral therapies* (2nd ed.). New York, NY: Guilford Press.

D'Zurilla, T. J., & Nezu, A. M. (2007). *Problem-solving therapy: A positive approach to clinical intervention* (3rd ed.). New York, NY: Springer Publishing Company.

D'Zurilla, T. J., Nezu, A. M., & Maydeu-Olivares, C. (2002). *Social problem-solving inventory revised (SPSI-R): Manual.* North Tonawanda, NY: Multi-Health Systems.

D'Zurilla, T. J., Nezu, A. M., & Maydeu-Olivares, A. (2004). Social problem solving: Theory and assessment. In E. C. Chang, T. J. D'Zurilla, & L. J. Sanna (Eds.), *Social problem solving: Theory, research, and training* (pp. 11–27). Washington, DC: American Psychological Association.

Elliott, T. R., Grant, J. S., & Miller, D. M. (2004). Social problem-solving abilities and behavioral health. In E. C. Chang, T. J. D'Zurilla, & L. J. Sanna (Eds.), *Social problem solving: Theory, research, and training* (pp. 117–133). Washington, DC: American Psychological Association.

Federal Register (2000). Medicare program; prospective payment system for home health agencies. Health Care Financing Administration (HCFA), HHS. Final rule. *Federal Register, 65*(128), 41128–41214.

Gallo, J. J., Meredith, L., Gonzales, J., Cooper, L., Nutting, P., Ford, D., et al. (2002). Do family physicians and internists differ in knowledge, attitudes, and self-reported approaches for depression? *International Journal of Psychiatry in Medicine, 32,* 1–20.

Gellis, Z. D. (2009). Evidence based practice in older adults with mental health disorders. In Roberts, A. R. (Ed.), *Social Workers' Desk Reference.* London: Oxford University Press.

Gellis, Z. D. (2010). Depression screening in medically ill home healthcare elderly. *Best Practices in Mental Health: An International Journal, 6*(1), 1–16.

Gellis, Z.D., & Bruce, M.L. (2009). Problem solving therapy for depression among home health care patients with cardiovascular disease. *American Journal of Geriatric Psychiatry* (published ahead of print). DOI: 10.1097/JGP.0b013e3181b21442.

Gellis, Z. D., & Kenaley, B. (2008). Problem solving therapy for depression in adults: A systematic review. *Research on Social Work Practice, 18,* 117–131.

Gellis, Z. D., McGinty, J., Horowitz, A., Bruce, M., & Misener, E. (2007). Problem-solving therapy for late-life depression in home care: A randomized field trial. *American Journal of Geriatric Psychiatry, 15*(11), 968–978.

Gellis, Z. D., McGinty, J., Tierney, L., Burton, J., Jordan, C., & Misener, E. (2008). Randomized controlled trial of problem-solving therapy for minor depression in home care. *Research on Social Work Practice, 18*(6), 596–606.

Government Accountability Office. (1994). *Successful state efforts to expand home services while limiting costs* (GAO-HEHS-94-167). Washington, DC: Author.

Gum, A. M., Areán, P. A., Hunkeler, E., Tang, L., Katon, W., Hitchcock, P., et al. (2006). Depression treatment preferences in older primary care patients. *The Gerontologist, 46*(1), 14–22.

Hamilton, M. (1967). Development of a rating scale for primary depressive illness. *British Journal of Social and Clinical Psychology, 6*(4), 278–296.

Horowitz, A., Reinhardt, J., & Kennedy, G. (2005). Major and subthreshold depression among older adults seeking vision rehabilitation services. *American Journal of Geriatric Psychiatry, 13,* 180–187.

Hybels, C., & Blazer, D. (2003). Epidemiology of late-life mental disorders. *Clinics in Geriatric Medicine, 19,* 663–696.

Hyer, L., Carpenter, B., Bishmann, D., & Wu, H. S. (2005). Depression in long-term care. *Clinical Psychology: Science and Practice, 12*(3), 280–299.

Institute of Medicine. (2008). *Retooling for an aging America: Building the health care workforce.* National Academy of Sciences, Washington, DC: The National Academies Press.

Kant, G. L., D'Zurilla, T. J., & Maydeu-Olivares, A. (1997). Social problem solving as a mediator of stress-related depression and anxiety in middle-aged and elderly community residents. *Cognitive Therapy and Research, 21,* 73–96.

Kessler, R., Berglund, P., Demler, O., Jin, R., Koretz, D., Merikangas, K., et al. (2003). The epidemiology of major depressive disorder. Results from the national comorbidity survey replication. *Journal of the American Medical Association, 289*(23), 3095–3105.

Landreville, P., Landry, J., Baillargeon, L., Guerette, A., & Matteau, E. (2001). Older adults' acceptance of psychological and pharmacological treatments for depression. *Journal of Gerontology, 50B*, P285–P291.

Lundervold, D., & Lewin, L. M. (1990). Older adults' acceptability of pharmacotherapy and behavior therapy for depression: Initial results. *Journal of Applied Gerontology, 9*, 211–215.

Lyness, J. M. (2008). Naturalistic outcomes of minor and subsyndromal depression in older primary care patients. *International Journal of Geriatric Psychiatry, 23*, 773–781.

MacPhillamy, D., & Lewinsohn, P. (1982). The pleasant events schedule: Studies on reliability, validity, and scale intercorrelation. *Journal of Consulting and Clinical Psychology, 50*, 363–380.

Marmor, T. (2000). *The politics of Medicare* (2nd ed.). Hawthorne, NY: Aldine de Guyter.

Medicare Payment Advisory Commission (2003, June). *Report to the Congress: Variation and innovation in Medicare.* Retrieved June 14, 2010, from http://www.medpac.gov/documents/June03_Entire_Report.pdf

Mollica, R. L., & Kassner, E. (2009). Taking the long view: Investing in Medicaid home and community-based services is cost-effective. AARP Public Policy Institute. *Insight on the Issues, 26*, 1–8.

Mynors-Wallis, L. M., Gath, D., Davies, I., Gray, A., & Barbour, F. (1997). Randomized controlled trial and cost analysis of problem-solving treatment given by community nurses for emotional disorders in primary care. *British Journal of Psychiatry, 170*, 113–119.

National Institute of Mental Health. (2006). *Special meeting on current research in psychosocial interventions for late-life mental disorders.* Arlington, VA: Geriatrics Research Branch, Division of Adult Translational Research and Treatment Development.

Nezu, A. M. (1986). Efficacy of a social problem-solving therapy approach for unipolar depression. *Journal of Consulting and Clinical Psychology, 54*, 196–202.

Nezu, A. M. (1987). A problem-solving formulation of depression: A literature review and proposal of a pluralistic model. *Clinical Psychology Review, 7*, 122–144.

Nezu, A. M. (2004). Problem solving and behavior therapy revisited. *Behavior Therapy, 35*, 1–33.

Nezu, A. M., & Nezu, C. M. (2010). Problem-solving therapy for relapse prevention in depression. In S. Richards & M. G. Perri (Eds.), *Relapse prevention for depression.* Washington, DC: American Psychological Association.

Nezu, A. M., Nezu, C. M., & D'Zurilla, T. J. (2007). *Solving life's problems: A 5-step guide to enhanced well-being.* New York, NY: Springer Publishing Company.

Nezu, A. M., Nezu, C. M., Felgoise, S. H., McClure, K. S., & Houts, P. S. (2003). Project Genesis: Assessing the efficacy of problem-solving therapy for distressed adult cancer patients. *Journal of Consulting and Clinical Psychology, 71*, 1036–1048.

Nezu, A. M., Nezu, C. M., & Perri, M. G. (1989). *Problem-solving therapy for depression: Therapy, research, and clinical guidelines.* New York, NY: John Wiley & Sons, Inc.

Nezu, A. M., Nezu, C. M., Saraydarian, L., Kalmar, K., & Ronan, G. F. (1986). Social problem solving as a moderator variable between negative life stress and depressive symptoms. *Cognitive Therapy and Research, 10,* 489–498.

Nezu, A. M., & Perri, M. G. (1989). Social problem solving therapy for unipolar depression: An initial dismantling investigation. *Journal of Consulting and Clinical Psychology, 57,* 408–413.

Nezu, A. M., & Ronan, G. F. (1985). Life stress, current problems, problem solving, and depressive symptomatology: An integrative model. *Journal of Consulting and Clinical Psychology, 53,* 693–697.

Nezu, A. M., & Ronan, G. F. (1988). Stressful life events, problem solving, and depressive symptoms among university students: A prospective analysis. *Journal of Counseling Psychology, 35,* 134–138.

Pignone, M. P., Gaynes, B. N., Rushton, J. L., Burchell, C. M., Orleans, C. T., Mulrow, C. D., et al. (2002). Screening for depression in adults: A summary of the evidence for the U.S. Preventative Services Task Force. *Annals of Internal Medicine, 136*(10), 765–776.

Raue, P., Meyers, B., McAvay, G., Brown, E., Keohane, D., & Bruce, M. (2003). One-month stability of depression among elderly home-care patients. *American Journal of Geriatric Psychiatry, 11,* 543–550.

Rudd, M. D., Rajab, M. H., & Dahm, P. F. (1994). Problem-solving appraisal in suicide ideators and attempters. *American Journal of Orthopsychiatry, 64,* 136–149.

Spitzer, R. L., Kroenke, K., & Williams, J. B. (1999). Validation and utility of a self-report version of PRIME-MD: The PHQ primary care study. Primary care evaluation of mental disorders. Patient Health Questionnaire. *Journal of the American Medical Association, 282,* 1737–1744.

Tai-Seale, M., Bramson, R., Drukker, D., Hurwics, M. L., Ory, M., Tai-Seale, T., et al. (2005). Understanding primary care physicians' propensity to assess elderly patients for depression using interaction and survey data. *Medical Care, 43*(12), 1217–1224.

Tai-Seale, M., McGuire, T., Colenda, C., Rosen, D., & Cook, M. (2007). Two-minute mental health care for elderly patients: Inside primary care visits. *Journal of the American Geriatrics Society, 55,* 1903–1911.

U.S. Census Bureau. (2004). *Economic census.* Retrieved October 2002, from http://www.census.gov

U.S. Department of Health and Human Services. (1999). *Mental health: A report of the Surgeon General. [Chapter 5].* Washington, DC: U.S. Government Printing Office.

Wei, W., Sambamoorthi, U., Olfson, M., Walkup, J., & Crystal, S. (2005). Use of psychotherapy for depression in older adults. *American Journal of Psychiatry, 162,* 711–717.

Williams, J. W., Katon, W., Lin, E. H. B., Nöel, P. H., Worchel, J., Cornell, J., et al. (2004). The effectiveness of depression care management on diabetes-related outcomes in older patients. *Annals of Internal Medicine, 140,* 1015–1024.

Zeltzer, B., & Kohn, R. (2006). Mental health services for homebound elders from home health nursing agencies and home care agencies. *Psychiatric Services, 57*(4), 567–569.

14

Prolonged Exposure Therapy for Older Combat Veterans in the Veterans Affairs Health Care System

Steven R. Thorp, Heather M. Sones, and Joan M. Cook

Most of the 24 million living U.S. military veterans have served during times of war (National Center for Veterans Analysis and Statistics, 2008), and over one-third of these veterans received benefits or services from the Department of Veterans Affairs (VA) in fiscal year 2008. In the VA system, 44% of veterans were aged 65 years or older (National Center for Veterans Analysis and Statistics, Office of Policy and Planning, 2009) and many more Vietnam veterans are entering older age. With the aging of the population, there has been increased interest in how trauma affects the physical and mental health of veterans in later life (Chatterjee, Spiro, King, King, & Davison, 2009; Rodgers, Norman, Thorp, Lebeck, & Lang, 2005). Data from the Normative Aging Study (NAS), a large longitudinal cohort study of community-residing male U.S. veterans, many of whom were highly educated and had relatively high socioeconomic levels, suggest that many older veterans have been exposed to traumatic events; some (less than 1%) met the criteria for current posttraumatic stress disorder (PTSD), while many more (nearly 10%) met the criteria for partial PTSD (Schnurr, Spiro, Vielhauer, Findler, & Hamblen, 2002). Other research has found rates of significant PTSD in nearly 40% of older veterans (Cassels, 2009). PTSD symptoms are known to interfere with social, recreational, and occupational functioning (Thorp & Stein, 2005). Older adults with PTSD may experience symptoms somewhat differently than younger adults, and little is known about treatments for older adults with PTSD (see Thorp, Sones, & Cook, 2011, [Chapter 7 in this volume]).

The purpose of this chapter is to describe an evidence-based psychotherapy—prolonged exposure therapy (PE)—for older veterans within the VA health care system. General information on VA outpatient care for PTSD is presented, followed by the theory and practice of PE, and then the challenges and promise of implementing PE for older veterans in the VA system. Common concerns of therapists and veterans as well as recommended strategies for addressing concerns are provided. A case example is also presented to illustrate the typical experiences of a therapist and a veteran as they learn about PE.

OUTPATIENT POSTTRAUMATIC STRESS DISORDER CARE IN THE VETERANS AFFAIRS HEALTH CARE SYSTEM

The assessment and treatment of war-related PTSD, caused by combat exposure or internment, is a major focus of the clinical, research, and educational resources within the VA health care system (Desai, Rosenheck, Spencer, & Gray, 2008). In addition to inpatient and residential care, the VA has developed Specialized Outpatient PTSD Programs (SOPPs). Many of these programs are interdisciplinary and can include psychologists, psychiatrists, social workers, nurses, chaplains, and pharmacists. Duties of the team members include case management (periodic "check-ins" for treatment planning and coordination of care); administration of psychotherapy in individual, couple, family, or group formats; medication management; spiritual guidance; and assistance in accessing additional resources. Teams typically meet weekly to develop assessment, treatment, and consultation plans for veterans.

The Long Journey Home is an annual report on PTSD services within the VA system. The most recent report (Desai et al., 2008) reveals that in fiscal year 2008, over 120,000 veterans received services in the SOPPs. The report also details the demographics of veterans in the SOPPs. The mean age of veterans was 47.9 years, and 92% of the veterans were male; 65% were White, 21% were Black, 9% were Hispanic/Latino, and 6% were identified as other racial or ethnic background. The veterans were well educated, as 95% had a high school education or beyond, and most (54%) were married (17% had never married). Only 42% were working when they entered the SOPP. Forty-six percent of veterans seen in the SOPPs served during the Persian Gulf era, 45% during the Vietnam War era, 2% during the Korean Conflict era, and 1% during the World War II era (the remainder served during other eras). Regarding traumatic events, 82% had been fired up on during their service, and 1% were former prisoners of war. Upon entry to the SOPP, 65% of veterans had received prior psychiatric treatment and 61% had been prescribed with psychotropic medications.

PROLONGED EXPOSURE THERAPY

Exposure therapies like PE have generated more empirical support than any other type of treatment for PTSD (Bradley, Greene, Russ, Dutra, & Westen, 2005). The Institute of Medicine of the National Academies Committee on Treatment of Posttraumatic Stress Disorder (2007) established that exposure therapies, and not pharmacotherapies or other types of psychotherapy, have demonstrated efficacy in treating PTSD. PE has proven effective at reducing the severity of PTSD symptoms resulting from various traumatic events (e.g., sexual assault, combat, torture, traffic accidents), and has been shown to work for both men and women (Foa, Hembree, & Rothbaum, 2007). The VA Office of Mental Health Services has started to disseminate PE information throughout the VA health care system to meet a requirement that all veterans shall have access to PE or cognitive processing therapy (CPT; Resick & Schnicke, 1993) at each VA health care facility.

PE has been applied in slightly different formats across studies, but it typically involves 8 to 15 individual (one-on-one) 90-minute sessions. Sessions are usually conducted weekly or twice weekly and they are audio recorded so that clients can listen to the sessions after they leave the therapist's office. Following are the four primary components of PE:

1. *Psychoeducation* about PTSD, the treatment rationale, and common reactions to trauma;
2. *Breathing retraining* that serves as a method of reducing anxiety in the short term to manage necessary tasks;
3. *In vivo exposure* between sessions in which the therapist asks the client to engage in safe activities, be in safe situations or places, or come into contact with safe objects that have been avoided since the traumatic event; and
4. *Imaginal exposure*, wherein clients repeat the details of their most upsetting traumatic event aloud, many times during sessions with the therapist.

The rationale behind PE is guided by emotional processing theory (EPT; Foa & Kozak, 1985, 1986). This theory postulates that fear is represented in memory as a structure that includes the feared stimuli (e.g., man with a gun), feared responses (e.g., breathing faster), and interpretations of meaning about the stimuli and responses (e.g., I am in danger). This fear structure can guide adaptive responses to dangers, but it is less useful, and possibly even pathological, if stimuli are inaccurately perceived as dangerous, if responses are overly intense and interfere with daily functioning, or if the meaning of stimuli or responses are inaccurately associated with threat. Foa and Rothbaum (1998) suggested that PTSD may result from fears generalizing too many stimuli (e.g., all men, rather than only men with guns) and responses (e.g., breathing faster always indicates a threat) that combine to support a view that one is incompetent in a dangerous world.

Foa and Kozak (1985, 1986) argued that maladaptive fear structures can be modified through emotional processing. This involves activation of the fear structure through the presentation of the feared stimulus and elicitation of the feared responses. After the fear structure is activated, incompatible information that challenges the client's maladaptive fear structure is introduced. The introduction of this information leads to habituation, the final step in emotional processing. *Habituation* is the "dissociation of response elements from the stimulus elements of the fear structure" (Foa & Kozak, 1986, pg. 29), which allows for the incorporation of the corrective information into the fear structure. For example, a person may learn that an image of a man with a gun on television is not dangerous, although it may remind the person of a dangerous event, and rapid breathing does not necessarily indicate excessive fear (e.g., it could indicate excitement or physical exertion). In PE, the fear structure is activated through therapeutic exposure to trauma-related memories (imaginal exposure) and other stimuli (in vivo exposure). Emotional processing occurs as a result of feared stimuli being presented and responses elicited repeatedly without the feared consequences.

Comparison of Prolonged Exposure Therapy to Other Approaches for Posttraumatic Stress Disorder

Despite the growing body of empirical literature demonstrating the effectiveness of exposure therapy for the treatment of PTSD, Rosen et al. (2004) found that fewer than 10% of VA PTSD specialists were routinely providing repeated exposure (for memories or other stimuli) to veterans with PTSD. PE, as an exposure therapy, guides clients in confronting feared stimuli with the expectation that anxiety may increase during the initial phase of therapy, but will decrease with repeated exposures. Another approach, known as anxiety management techniques (AMT; which includes stress inoculation models), aims to decrease anxiety directly through the use of relaxation training, guided imagery, and breathing exercises. Cognitive therapies focus less, if at all, on exposure to memories or other stimuli, and instead target monitoring and restructuring distorted thought processes.

Eye Movement Desensitization and Reprocessing (EMDR; Shapiro, 1995) includes exposure to images, affect, and sensations associated with the traumatic memory and adds other stimulation such as the movement of therapist's fingers or alternating tones or hand taps. EMDR has demonstrated empirical support for the treatment of PTSD, although there is some controversy about the theoretical rationale and mechanisms for the treatment (O'Donohue & Thorp, 1996).

Is Exposure Therapy Contraindicated for Older Adults?

As previously stated, the exposure-based treatments have enjoyed the most empirical support for the general population with PTSD. In regards to the aging population, however, few quantitative studies of psychotherapies for older adults with PTSD have been conducted (Thorp et al., 2009; see also Thorp, Sones, & Cook, 2011 [chapter 7 in this volume] for a review). Valid arguments exist both for and against the use of exposure-based therapies in older adults.

Some researchers have suggested that intense exposure therapy should not be used with older adults (Boudewyns, Hyer, Klein, Nichols, & Sperr, 1997; Coleman, 1999; Hankin, 1997; Hyer & Woods, 1998; Kruse & Schmitt, 1999). Boudewyns et al. (1997) argued that although exposure therapy may be appropriate for individuals with nonchronic PTSD, those with chronic PTSD may have "widespread defensive blocks" to exposure and may lack the "emotional control or energy" (p. 363) to obtain benefit from this type of therapy. These authors, therefore, discourage exposure early in the treatment of chronic PTSD, although they allow that exposure may be helpful when the individual is "ready." Hyer and Woods (1998) and Hyer et al. (1995) state that intensive exposure methods are undesirable and counterproductive for older victims of trauma because they lead to increased autonomic arousal and decreased cognitive performance. These authors do not state whether they think these changes are temporary or permanent and they provide no evidence to justify their claim aside from a report on resilience and vulnerability factors in the general population (i.e., McFarlane & Yehuda, 1996).

It is reasonable to assume that exposure results in temporary increased arousal (by definition) and that this would result in a temporary physiological and cognitive change. Indeed, increased physiological arousal, as one indicator of emotional engagement, has been cited as a requirement for successful exposure (Jaycox, Foa, & Morral, 1998). It is also known that excessive physiological activity can result in misinterpretations and lapses in attention and logic that could limit emotional processing in the general population (Foa, Steketee, & Rothbaum, 1989). McCarthy, Katz, and Foa (1991) argued that AMT; e.g., progressive muscle relaxation and controlled breathing) should be used instead of exposure-based treatments for late-life anxiety. Although they cited no evidence comparing the two types of treatment for older adults, they stated: "Though they are highly effective in younger patients, forms of exposure that produce high levels of arousal may be less effective for the treatment of anxiety in the older adults" (McCarthy et al., 1991, p. 207).

In contrast, many researchers advocate the use of exposure-based therapies for PTSD in older adults. These researchers agree that increased physiological arousal is expected, but is an integral component of treatment that can be tolerated by older adults. In fact, as Keane et al. (1989) noted in an early report of exposure therapy of Vietnam combat veterans, older adults with PTSD tolerated many unintended "exposures" outside of treatment because of the symptoms (e.g., intrusive thoughts, flashbacks, and nightmares) they frequently reexperience about aspects of their trauma. Because increased arousal is expected, it is reasonable to closely monitor individuals who are at great risk from high arousal such as patients with serious cardiac or respiratory problems. When we have done PE with veterans with these problems in the past, we have sought consultation from veterans' primary care physicians and have asked them to alert us if the experience is physically uncomfortable. Although increased arousal may be worth monitoring in the beginning for some veterans, its function in treatment is to help move toward the long-term goal of decreased hyperarousal when unintentionally exposed to triggers. Several factors are believed to reduce the effectiveness of exposure-based interventions, including thoughts of mental defeat, permanent change, or alienation related to the trauma; dissociative behaviors (which interfere with emotional processing); and extreme guilt, anger, depression, or anxiety (Ehlers et al., 1998; Hembree & Foa, 2000; Pitman et al., 1991). Mental defeat refers to a perception by the trauma survivor that he or she "gave up," wished for death, or had been completely psychologically defeated during the traumatic event. None of these factors are known to be more prevalent among older adults.

Self-management strategies, such as the previously mentioned AMT, may be challenging for older adults who have cognitive deficits because they demand the retention of information about PTSD and coping skills (Cook, Ruzek, & Cassidy, 2003), and thus behavioral techniques (such as exposure) may be more suitable (Pontillo, Lang, & Stein, 2002). A comparison of AMT, imagery-based exposure therapy, and a wait-list control condition for (non-older adults) combat veterans with chronic PTSD revealed that the exposure therapy (flooding) showed significant improvements in PTSD symptoms at posttreatment and 6-month follow up (Keane, Fairbank, Caddell, & Zimering, 1989). In this study, there were no adverse outcomes for the participants in the exposure condition, but there were insufficient data for analyses from participants assigned to AMT because of the high number of treatment dropouts in that condition. The authors argued that attrition might in fact be higher if exposure-based treatments are not used to treat PTSD because patients may be disillusioned by ineffective treatments and terminate prematurely. In any case, there do not appear to be differences in drop-out rates among different psychotherapy approaches (e.g., exposure-based behavior therapies versus other types of treatment) for PTSD in the general population based on a meta-analysis of relevant studies (Hembree et al., 2003).

There is evidence that exposure-based treatments are tolerated well by older adults. Swales, Solfvin, and Sheikh (1996) used an exposure-based intervention for the treatment of 20 older adults with panic disorder and found that 15 participants completed the protocol with statistically significant improvements in cognitive, behavioral, affective, physiological, and global domains at posttreatment and a 3-month follow-up. No adverse cognitive or other events were reported. The researchers reported that in vivo exposure was "instrumental in treatment of anxiety with avoidance behaviors" (Swales et al., 1996, p. 57). Exposure treatments have also been successful and well-tolerated for older adults with phobias (Thyer, 1981) and chronic obsessive-compulsive disorder (Rowan, Holburn, Walker, & Siddiqui, 1984). There are some data suggesting that PE works well in older veterans with PTSD (Nierengarten, 2009).

Implementing Prolonged Exposure in the Veterans Affairs Health Care System

Traditional Structure of Veterans Affairs Outpatient Care

Most VA PTSD clinical teams treat hundreds of veterans each year, and the demand for services increased 40% from fiscal year 2004 to 2008 (Desai et al., 2008). VA providers have traditionally met this demand by offering group-based psychotherapy augmented with case management meetings or individual sessions. Group therapy purportedly has several advantages, including cost effectiveness, an efficient use of therapists' time (one therapist can meet with 10 to 20 veterans at the same time), social interactions for veterans, peer feedback, and accountability (Foy et al., 2000). When individual therapy had been offered in PTSD clinics in the past, it was not usually manualized or exposure-based (Rosen et al., 2004). Generally, supportive therapy may be beneficial, but it does not have the robust scientific support of exposure therapy. In recent years, the VA health care system has endorsed PE as a first-line treatment for PTSD and has trained hundreds of VA clinicians in the treatment.

Transition to Prolonged Exposure for Older Veterans Within the Veterans Affairs System

Although the use of PE for older veterans in the VA health care system holds great promise, mental health providers and veterans have concerns about the treatment. Some common concerns are noted in this section, along with ways of addressing concerns and some helpful resources.

Veteran Concerns

Veterans' concerns about PE often revolve around the rationale, intensity, and confidentiality of treatment. Some older veterans who have been treated for PTSD in the past were taught that PTSD was a chronic illness. These veterans may have learned that AMT and distraction could help them cope with their symptoms in the short term. A transition to PE, using a recovery model (emphasizing a return to normal functioning in as many domains as possible such as work and social activities), may be challenging because it offers a contrasting view.

Older veterans may also be concerned about the intensity of PE. Older veterans with PTSD may have avoided thoughts and cues related to traumatic events for 50 years or more in an unsuccessful effort to decrease PTSD symptoms. They may worry that they will not be able to tolerate actively facing the memories and reminders. Some veterans worry that they will "go crazy" or become permanently and intensely upset if they are confronted with memories and situations associated with the traumatic events. Veterans may also worry about the confidentiality of sessions and how they are documented and recorded. They may wonder about privacy because the sessions are audio recorded.

Addressing Veteran Concerns

PE therapists can effectively address many concerns at the onset of treatment. Veterans will likely question the rationale for purposefully remembering a traumatic event and engaging in feared activities; and throughout the treatment, providers will validate the urge to avoid while reminding the veteran that avoidance has not worked in the long run (evidenced by their current PTSD). Providers teach veterans that exposure, though uncomfortable at first, does work in the long run by helping the veteran to do the following:

1. Discriminate true threats from perceived threats;
2. Realize that distress will not last forever or lead to permanent dysfunction;
3. Understand that he or she will habituate to safe stimuli over time; and
4. Gain mastery over previously avoided situations and memories.

Regarding the intensity of treatment, we recommend telling veterans that we expect they might feel uncomfortable doing previously avoided activities or remembering the traumatic event because that is a natural response. A therapist can normalize veteran's concerns by sharing stories about other veterans with similar symptoms or concerns (without giving identifying information), and viewing Web sites about PE can help give veterans a better understanding of what is done in therapy. The U.S. VA Web site contains information about PE, which can be found at http://www.ptsd.va.gov/public/pages/prolonged-exposure-therapy.asp. It is often helpful to remind veterans that the therapist will be supporting them throughout treatment. A common mistake is to emphasize the intensity or "scariness" of the treatment too early in the description rather than recommending the treatment and highlighting the potential benefits (and the immediate benefit of individual attention from an expert therapist). Many veterans with PTSD do not like group therapy; and PE, because it is provided individually, may be an attractive option. Veterans with a significant decrease in PTSD symptoms often discover a richer life, and will have the flexibility to be more active outside of the health care system.

We recommend telling veterans how sessions are documented (including showing them a note template), and we work with veterans to help maintain their privacy. It is usually reassuring to veterans when they see that great detail about traumatic events is not needed in notes, especially if they feel guilt or shame about the event. We ask veterans to treat audio recordings as they would their wallet, and to not play the recordings for others. Although veterans may see the value in sharing their experience with loved ones, we remind them that their loved ones do not need to hear the details of traumatic events to understand that the veteran experienced combat, an assault, or an accident, as examples. We remind veterans that audio recordings are for their use, and that at each new session we record over the previous session.

Provider Concerns

Many PTSD specialists within the VA have cared for veterans for years, and some are hesitant to disrupt the status quo to begin a new treatment such as PE. With long experience offering other treatments to older veterans, providers may be confident that the approaches they have used are working well. They may express concern that new treatments constitute a temporary trend or that veterans will be uncomfortable adjusting to a new approach. Providers may also be concerned that PE will be too intense for older veterans and that a "softer" approach may work better.

Time management may also be a concern. In recent years, perhaps because of "triggers" (cues) in the environment such as news coverage of the September 11th attacks and the current wars in Iraq and Afghanistan, larger numbers of veterans with PTSD have been seeking treatment in VA hospitals (Desai et al., 2008). Providers who face the challenge of growing caseloads may wonder how they will integrate PE into their usual schedule. Although some studies are underway to test PE in a group format, it is currently recommended only for individual sessions. Individual therapy in VA SOPPs has traditionally been done in 45- to 60-minute sessions. It can, therefore, be challenging to implement PE because it requires 90-minute sessions. In other words, therapists may be concerned that in the time required for a PE session, they could have completed (and had formally recognized) two regular psychotherapy sessions or an intake interview. Providers may also be concerned that PE requires more time for preparation before sessions and more documentation after sessions.

Addressing Provider Concerns

For both providers and veterans, it is useful to give a quick description of PE when first introducing the therapy. One summary version of PE is as follows: 'We ask veterans to revisit one traumatic memory many times and help them to do things they have wanted to do since the trauma but felt uncomfortable doing.' Some staff may understandably be wary of a new and manualized treatment because they are concerned about the extra time and effort involved, or because they worry that it implies that the treatments they have been doing for years are being undervalued. It is critical to validate the work providers have done to care for our veterans and to make it clear that those clinical skills are still needed. Providers may think that a manualized treatment will deprive them of their strengths as therapists, when in fact, the semi-structured manual for PE encourages individual wording and therapeutic styles while adhering to the structure of the treatment. It is also important to convey understanding regarding the challenges to start any new treatment process, especially given other VA mandates for assessments, treatment, and documentation. In that context, it is useful to share stories about the rewards of watching veterans improve after completing a course of PE. Although practice guidelines and randomized clinical trials may convince some people about the importance of PE, others may be more swayed by anecdotes about veterans who are thriving after treatment (especially if the veteran is from the same clinic; Cook, Schnurr, Biyanova, & Coyne, 2009). The strongest endorsement of the PE model may come from fellow providers who describe the satisfying final sessions of a successful PE case, coupled with an honest appraisal of the challenges of PE. A Web site with a PE provider video is located at http://vawww.infoshare.va.gov/sites/pe/videos/videos.aspx. Note that this Web site is only accessible from VA computers.

Providers may worry that it appears as if their productivity is lower if they are conducting longer PE sessions with individual veterans. It is important to educate the staff about the effectiveness of PE to help them realize the greater return on the investment of time when using such a treatment. For example, a therapist could spend only 60 minutes with a veteran using supportive therapy, but that treatment might last for a year or more because it is not significantly reducing the veteran's PTSD symptoms. PE, on the other hand, often works in as little as 10 sessions (only 5 weeks if two sessions per week or 10 weeks if one session per week), which frees the remainder of the year for providers to do other tasks (including psychotherapy for other veterans with PTSD). Moreover, it has been shown that the beneficial effects of PE can last for years, which improves the lives of those treated and reduces the demands on SOPPs. As stated earlier, a VA mandate requires that all veterans with PTSD are offered either PE or CPT. Program directors and clinical supervisors are aware of this mandate and will work with providers to ensure that these treatments are available. There is some evidence that among women who had PTSD because of sexual assault, older subjects in PE had better outcomes than younger subjects (Rizvi, Vogt, & Resick, 2009).

PE can be intense for both veterans and providers. Provider concerns about the intensity of the treatment, or the veterans' potential discomfort with PE may be allayed after the provider completes one or two full courses of PE with a veteran(s) because most often, PE successfully reduces PTSD symptoms and the manualized treatment becomes more familiar with use. Our experience is that the more exposure therapy gets much easier for veterans and providers, the more it is done. Some experienced therapists will be comfortable seeing up to four PE sessions per day, but others may want to have a smaller limit on PE cases done each day or week depending on other time commitments, energy levels, and concurrent clinic demands.

Support Teams
We recommend having a local partner or team to consult with about PE cases, and using national VA PE consultants as needed. The local team is very helpful to share information and resources about clinic logistic issues and for guidance when cases are not "textbook" in terms of symptoms or treatment response. Partners or teams can also provide support and validation when cases are particularly challenging and can help celebrate successes. The Web site that offers the provider video on VA computers also provides general information and resources for implementing PE in the VA health care system:

http://vaww.infoshare.va.gov/sites/pe/default.aspx

Shared Preparation of Resources
One of the challenges with cognitive behavioral therapies like PE is that they demand preparation on the part of the therapist before each session. The time required can be considerably lessened if the clinic can pool resources (therapists and VA support staff working together) to prepare therapists' paperwork, handouts for veterans, questionnaires, and homework forms ahead of time. This blank paperwork can be stored in a public area (like a bookshelf or file cabinet) and shared, and replenished as needed. Similarly, the clinic can consolidate and organize recording devices (audio recorders), media (tapes), and playback devices (audio players) to facilitate therapy sessions and consultation. Older veterans may have vision problems, and the paperwork should be printed in clear, large fonts (see Thorp & Lynch, 2005). Like all psychotherapy sessions, PE sessions should be documented. As noted, we recommend broad summaries of traumatic events because the specific details are unnecessary for progress notes. Progress notes for PE often reflect the standardized nature of the treatment, and thus, note templates can be created in the VA's computerized record system (and modified as needed) to increase efficiency.

Other Issues to Consider

Signs of "Good Fit" With Prolonged Exposure
Older veterans with PTSD from any traumatic event are likely to be good candidates for PE. To date, there is no evidence to suggest that either older age or time since trauma interferes with veterans' response to PE. As with younger adults, individuals with unmanaged mania or psychosis and/or alcohol or substance dependence should not be treated with PE because these comorbid issues have not been included in previous

studies. Moreover, the candidate for PE should have a clear and time-limited memory of a traumatic event. Many older veterans with PTSD will report gaps in their memories, and that is common and acceptable. However, they must have some recollection of the traumatic event to do the imaginal exposure in PE. The memory should be episodic versus generic. That is, it should be of a particular event (e.g., the worst day they remember from childhood abuse) rather than a general summary of past traumas (e.g., description of how childhood abuse often happened). Veterans must be willing to commit to time outside of sessions, generally about 1 hour per day for homework. Older veterans who are retired or unemployed because of disability will have fewer scheduling issues related to work, but they may be reluctant to commit time to homework given the demands of medical appointments and complications from comorbid physical and psychological problems. Veterans who do not appear to be a good fit for PE should be offered other treatments (ideally other therapies with empirical support for PTSD). Lastly, occasionally, the timing for PE is not optimal (e.g., acute suicidality, housing problems, current domestic violence, upcoming surgeries, and recovery time), and a veteran may benefit from postponing or discontinuing therapy for months or even years.

Nonresponders or Under-responders
In some cases, the results of PE may be disappointing for the therapist or the veteran. In those cases, it is often helpful for the therapist and the veteran to have an open and honest discussion about what appeared to be helpful and what appeared to inhibit improvements. This may include issues particular to the treatment, or the clinic, or the veteran (e.g., other life crises interfering with treatment; repeated lateness or missed sessions; nonadherence to homework).

CASE EXAMPLE: A VETERANS AFFAIRS THERAPIST NEW TO PROLONGED EXPOSURE AND HER FIRST VETERAN TREATED WITH PROLONGED EXPOSURE

A fictitious example is provided to illustrate a typical experience of a VA therapist new to PE and her first PE case.

The Therapist
Dr. Maria Hernandez is a 52-year-old psychologist who has worked in the VA health care system for 13 years. She enjoys working with military veterans and takes pride in her work. She wants to provide the best treatments she can, and she believes she has done so because she started

working in the PTSD clinic 9 years ago. In recent months, she learned that she is encouraged to learn a treatment called prolonged exposure therapy, or PE. She thinks that psychotherapy researchers often "cherry pick" their subjects so that only relatively easy and healthy patients are included. She also wonders whether it is a good idea to expose veterans to the things that frighten them the most. Dr. Hernandez has heard many stories of veterans who were greatly upset when someone would mention combat or when they would have involuntary memories of the horrific events they saw in combat. She has been exposed to numerous new psychotherapies over the years and feels that she has been able to take the best elements of these without being tied down to any particular technique. Despite her reservations, Dr. Hernandez signed up for a 4-day PE workshop with a fellow therapist from the VA.

The workshop was facilitated by two VA therapists who knew PE well. They began by reviewing the diagnosis and course of PTSD. Although Dr. Hernandez thought she knew the diagnosis well, she learned some knew facts about how PTSD progressed and what helped initiate and maintain the disorder (i.e., avoidance behaviors and maladaptive thoughts). The facilitators reviewed the PTSD treatment literature as well as taught how to implement PE. They emphasized the importance of teaching patients the rationale for the treatment because patients may be tempted to avoid reminders again without a good understanding of why they were confronting the upsetting cues. Dr. Hernandez learned that while about 1 in 10 patients will experience a brief worsening of PTSD symptoms between the initial sessions of imaginal exposure in PE, most have a strong emotional response to the initial imaginal exposure (by design) and then show a steady improvement in subsequent sessions. She also learned that even those with the temporary worsening do as well as everyone else by the end of treatment. She learned that what she feared most, that veterans would "over-engage" by dissociating or rushing from the room distraught, was relatively rare. Dr. Hernandez was told that PE patients are often appropriately engaged, meaning, that they had strong emotions but were able to participate successfully, although sometimes they were "underengaged" and would benefit from giving a "richer" account of the traumatic event or participating more fully in activities outside of therapy sessions. She learned strategies for addressing all levels of engagement and was assigned a consultant to guide her through her early PE cases. She also learned who would make good training cases as she learned the therapy. She and her colleague left the workshop reassured by the information they received and felt excited about trying PE. Dr. Hernandez made herself a reminder of the goals during the different stages of treatment, which looked like Table 14.1.

TABLE 14.1 Summary of Therapeutic Goals for Prolonged Exposure

Phase	Goals
Earlier Sessions	■ Orient patient to structure of therapy, including how many sessions and the planned duration of therapy. ■ Introduce veteran to questionnaires, forms, and recording equipment. ■ Orient veteran to PTSD symptoms and related problems. ■ Instruct veteran in breathing retraining. ■ Discuss how avoidance and negative thoughts about the world (and one's ability to be competent in the world) help maintain PTSD. ■ Present the rationale and procedures for in vivo exposure and imaginal exposure. ■ Develop a list of desired in vivo activities and situations and identify the worst traumatic event experienced by the veteran.
Middle Sessions	■ Guide the veteran in completing in vivo exposures (mostly outside of sessions). ■ Guide the veteran in revisiting the traumatic memory by narrating what happened repeatedly in sessions and listening to audio recordings of the narration outside of sessions. ■ "Process" the experience of the imaginal exposures with the veteran, eliciting their thoughts and feelings and sharing the therapist's observations. ■ Focus the imaginal exposure on one or two particularly upsetting "scenes" in the memory ("hot spots"). ■ Monitor progress through veteran's report, affect, and questionnaires.
Later Sessions	■ Encourage veteran to identify additional in vivo exercises or ways of completing the exercises. ■ Encourage greater independence from the therapist in exposures. ■ Review progress with veteran, noting challenges and successes. ■ Illustrate treatment gains by sharing improvements in veteran's scores and ratings. ■ Aid relapse prevention by predicting that in times of stress some PTSD symptoms may reemerge, along with urges to avoid; veteran can maintain gains by continuing exposure. ■ Plan for booster sessions, as needed, or direct to alternative treatments if indicated.

The Veteran

Ms. Jones was a surgical nurse in Vietnam in 1970. She was only 25 years old when she served in the war, but she reports that she felt much older because most of the soldiers and Marines she saw there were younger. She went to the VA when she was discharged from the military in the early 1970s because she was haunted by the anguished face and piercing cries of a soldier she had known well. This soldier friend was brought in with severe injuries to his head and neck and ultimately died on the operating table while she tried to stop his blood loss. Ms. Jones was not satisfied with her initial experience at the VA, but she has returned now at the age of 65 because her PTSD symptoms were interfering with the life she planned to have in retirement. She hoped to enjoy time with her husband of 44 years and her grandchildren, but found that she could not sleep or concentrate. She felt irritable and jumpy, especially when she heard friends discussing the war in Iraq.

Ms. Jones was referred to the PTSD clinical team by her primary care doctor when she briefly described her nightmares and the traumatic event she endured. She received a phone call from a therapist who told her that they could meet to discuss a treatment called prolonged exposure therapy. She understood from this therapist, Dr. Hernandez, that she might be asked to face her fears if she decided to do the treatment.

Before Ms. Jones met with Dr. Hernandez, she was concerned that the therapist would not understand her experience. She was unsure about how she herself would respond when discussing her trauma, fearing that she would "break down" and embarrass herself. She also wondered whether Dr. Hernandez would be able to tolerate her description of the soldier as he died. Lastly, she wondered whether this therapist would force her to reveal aspects of the trauma she did not want to share. She realized that her PTSD symptoms were making her miserable and that her avoidance was a "bargain with the devil" because it did not actually make the PTSD stop. However, she also did not want things to get worse.

When Ms. Jones met with Dr. Hernandez, she learned that this therapist had worked with trauma survivors for many years. She learned that this was an informational meeting and that she would never be asked to do anything against her will. Dr. Hernandez asked her about her symptoms and she made her reactions seem normal after what she had experienced. After learning more about Ms. Jones, the therapist said she was confident that PE would be helpful to her. Ms. Jones felt comfortable with the therapist and they made a plan to begin PE the following week.

The Prolonged Exposure Sessions

Dr. Hernandez used the first few sessions to learn more about Ms. Jones and to explain what to expect from the therapy. She helped Ms. Jones understand why avoidance works for many things in life, although it does not work well for PTSD. She also explained that exposure counteracts avoidance and helps most people who have PTSD feel much better. Ms. Jones liked the fact that she could meet alone with her therapist because she felt guilty about not doing more for her friend who died and she did not want to share her perceived failure with others. She also appreciated that they planned only 10 weeks of therapy because she was afraid she would have to continue therapy for years. Ms. Jones learned more about PTSD and she felt like Dr. Hernandez knew her before she walked in from the symptoms she described. She learned that her occasional discomfort when being intimate with her husband might be caused by feelings of vulnerability linked to PTSD.

Ms. Jones and Dr. Hernandez made a list together. They wrote down things Ms. Jones had used to enjoy before her experiences in Vietnam and things that now frightened her, although her friends and family did them. Ms. Jones began to do these activities, starting with easier tasks accompanied by her husband. She also started to describe the death of her soldier friend in detail when she met with Dr. Hernandez. She sobbed the first four times she told the story, but eventually she could describe it without feeling the intense loss (although it was always unpleasant). She discovered she could remember even small details of her experience and was surprised when she could ultimately describe the event without the strong emotion she expected. By the end of the treatment, Ms. Jones was able to recall the things she liked best about her friend who died. She felt like she was able to honor him by remembering these details and sharing them with someone who did not get to meet him. In the 10th and final session, Dr. Hernandez showed her the list of things she was now able to do with little difficulty. They discussed how to continue doing exposure after treatment ended, and Dr. Hernandez invited Ms. Jones to call if she ever needed a "tune up" of the skills she had learned. Ms. Jones told Dr. Hernandez that both her husband and her grandchildren had noticed how much happier she seemed, and her husband wanted to share his thanks with the therapist for helping "get his wife back."

Potential Benefits of Prolonged Exposure for Older Veterans

Although many VA administrators and providers are excited about implementing PE and other empirically-based treatments, a slow transition may prove most beneficial. Because many clinics have a strong tradition of group therapies and supportive therapies, it will take time to integrate PE into existing treatment formats. It is important to provide adequate time for early PE cases so that clinicians feel supported, and to highlight and share successes. It is also helpful to work as a team to help determine factors that may interfere with PE for veterans who have an insufficient response to the treatment.

In VA SOPPs, we see many older veterans with challenging backgrounds and comorbid health and mental health symptoms. PE provides hope for veterans who may have suffered from PTSD for decades. Many of our older veterans who have completed PE say that they feel that they have their lives back, and only wish that they had started treatment sooner. We see emotional and sometimes physical transformations in our veterans as they realize that through facing temporary discomfort, they can feel joy and love again. Veterans we have treated have spoken about the satisfaction in returning to previously enjoyed pastimes and in initiating or renewing valued relationships after successful completion of PE. PE therapists have reported the great reward of observing these positive changes and knowing that such changes directly benefit veterans and their loved ones. Therapists have also noted that PE is efficient and can help bring relatively quick relief to veterans who have faced the torment of PTSD for years.

ACKNOWLEDGEMENTS

This work is supported by a VA Career Development Award (Dr. Thorp). Content does not necessarily represent the views of the Department of Veterans Affairs or the U.S. Government.

REFERENCES

Boudewyns, P. A., Hyer, L. A., Klein, D. S., Nichols, C. W., & Sperr, E. V. (1997). Lessons learned in the treatment of chronic, complicated posttraumatic stress disorder. In T. W. Miller (Ed.), *Clinical disorders and stressful life events* (pp. 353–378). Madison, CT: International Universities Press, Inc.

Bradley, R., Greene, J., Russ, E., Dutra, L., & Westen, D. (2005). A multidimensional meta-analysis of psychotherapy for PTSD. *American Journal of Psychiatry, 162,* 214–227.

Cassels, C. (2009). AAGP 2009: High prevalence of PTSD among older veterans. Findings suggest PTSD may be undertreated, underdiagnosed. *Medscape Today.* Retrieved February 23, 2010 from http://www.medscape.com/viewarticle/590037?src=rss

Chatterjee, S., Spiro, A., King, L., King, D., & Davison, E. (2009). Research on aging military veterans: Lifespan implications of military service. *PTSD Research Quarterly, 20*(3), 1–7.

Coleman, P. G. (1999). Creating a life story: The task of reconciliation. *The Gerontologist, 39*, 133–139.

Cook, J. M., Ruzek, J. I., & Cassidy, E. L. (2003). Posttraumatic stress disorder and cognitive impairment in older adults: Awareness and recognition of a possible association. *Psychiatric Services, 54*, 1223–1225.

Cook, J. M., Schnurr, P., Biyanova, T., & Coyne, J. C. (2009). Apples don't fall far from the trees: An internet survey of influences on psychotherapists' adoption and sustained use of new therapies. *Psychiatric Services, 60*, 671–676.

Desai, R., Rosenheck, R. A., Spencer, H., & Gray, S. (2008). *The long journey home XVII: Treatment of posttraumatic stress disorder in the Department of Veterans Affairs: Fiscal year 2008 service delivery and performance.* West Haven, CT: Department of Veterans Affairs, Northeast Program Evaluation Center.

Ehlers, A., Clark, D. M., Dunmore, E., Jaycox, L. H., Meadows, E. A., & Foa, E. B. (1998). Predicting response to exposure treatment in PTSD: The role of mental defeat and alienation. *Journal of Traumatic Stress, 11*, 457–471.

Foa, E. B., Hembree, E. A., & Rothbaum, B. O. (2007). *Prolonged exposure therapy for PTSD: Emotional processing of traumatic experiences - therapist guide.* New York, NY: Oxford University Press.

Foa, E. B., & Kozak, M. J. (1985). Treatment of anxiety disorders: Implications for psychopathology. In A. H. Tuma & J. D. Maser (Eds.), *Anxiety and the anxiety disorders* (pp. 421–452). Hillsdale, NJ: Lawrence Erlbaum Associates.

Foa, E. B., & Kozak, M. J. (1986). Emotional processing of fear: Exposure to corrective information. *Psychological Bulletin, 99*, 20–35.

Foa E. B., & Rothbaum B. O. (1998). *Treating the trauma of rape: Cognitive behavioral therapy for PTSD.* New York, NY: Guilford Press.

Foa, E. B., Steketee, G., & Rothbaum, B. O. (1989). Behavioral/cognitive conceptualization of posttraumatic stress disorder. *Behavior Therapy, 20*, 155–176.

Foy, D. W., Glynn, S. M., Schnurr, P. P., Jankowski, M. K., Wattenberg, M. S., Weiss, D. S., et al. (2000). Group therapy. In E. B. Foa, T. M. Keane, & M. J. Friedman (Eds.), *Effective treatments for PTSD: Practice guidelines from the International Society for Traumatic Stress Studies* (pp. 155–175). New York, NY: Guilford Press.

Hankin, C. S. (1997). Treatment of older adults with posttraumatic stress disorder. In A. Maercker (Ed.), *Treatment of PTSD* (pp. 357–384). New York, NY: Springer Press.

Hembree, E. A., & Foa, E. B. (2000). Posttraumatic stress disorder: Psychological factors and psychosocial interventions. *Journal of Clinical Psychiatry, 61*, 33–39.

Hembree, E. A., Foa, E. B., Dorfan, N. M., Street, G. P., Kowalski, J., & Tu, X. (2003). Do patients drop out prematurely from exposure therapy for PTSD? *Journal of Traumatic Stress, 16*, 555–562.

Hyer, L. A., & Woods, M. G. (1998). Phenomenology and treatment of trauma in later life. In V. M. Follette, J. I. Ruzek, & F. R. Abueg (Eds.), *Cognitive-behavioral therapies for trauma* (pp. 383–414). New York, NY: Guilford Press.

Hyer, L. A., Summers, M. N., Braswell, L. C., & Boyd, S. (1995). Posttraumatic stress disorder: Silent problem among older combat veterans. *Psychotherapy, 32*, 348–364.

Institute of Medicine of the National Academies Committee on Treatment of Posttraumatic Stress Disorder. (2007). *Treatment of posttraumatic stress disorder: An assessment of the evidence.* Washington, DC: The National Academies Press.

Jaycox, L. H., Foa, E. B., & Morral, A. R. (1998). Influence of emotional engagement and habituation on exposure therapy for PTSD. *Journal of Consulting and Clinical Psychology, 66,* 185–192.

Keane, T. M., Fairbank, J. A., Caddell, J. M., & Zimering, R. T. (1989). Implosive (flooding) therapy reduces symptoms of PTSD in Vietnam combat veterans. *Behavior Therapy, 20,* 245–260.

Keane, T. M., Fairbank, J. A., Caddell, J. M., Zimering, R. T., Taylor, K. L., & Mora, C. A. (1989). Clinical evaluation of a measure to assess combat exposure. *Psychological Assessment: A Journal of Consulting and Clinical Psychology, 1,* 53–55.

Kruse, A., & Schmitt, E. (1999). Reminiscence of traumatic experiences in (former) Jewish emigrants and extermination camp survivors. In A. Maercker, M. Schützwohl, & Z. Solomon (Eds.), *Posttraumatic stress disorder: A lifespan developmental perspective.* Seattle, WA: Hogrefe & Huber.

McCarthy, P. R., Katz, I. R., & Foa, E. B. (1991). Cognitive-behavioral treatment of anxiety in the elderly: A proposed model. In C. Salzman & B. D. Lebowitz (Eds.), *Anxiety in the elderly: Treatment and research.* New York, NY: Springer Publishing.

McFarlane, A. C., & Yehuda, R. (1996). Resilience, vulnerability, and the course of posttraumatic reactions. In B. A. van der Kolk, A. C. McFarlane, & L. Weisaeth (Eds.), *Traumatic stress: The effects of overwhelming experience on mind, body, and society* (pp. 155–181). New York, NY: Guilford Press.

National Center for Veterans Analysis and Statistics. (2008). *FY07 Annual VA information pamphlet (February 2008).* Retrieved December 29, 2009 from http://www1.va.gov/VETDATA/docs/SpecialReports/uniqueveteransMay.pdf

National Center for Veterans Analysis and Statistics, Office of Policy and Planning. (2009). *Analysis of unique veterans utilization of VA benefits & services (April 29, 2009).* Retrieved December 29, 2009 from http://www1.va.gov/VETDATA/docs/SpecialReports/uniqueveteransMay.pdf

Nierengarten, M. B. (2009). ADAA 2009: Exposure therapy for PTSD may benefit older veterans: Pilot study results show promise. *Medscape Medical News.* Retrieved February 23, 2010 from http://www.medscape.com/viewarticle/589792

O'Donohue, W. T., & Thorp, S. R. (1996). EMDR as marginal science. [Review of the book *Eye movement desensitization and reprocessing: Basic principles, protocols, and procedures*]. *The Scientist Practitioner, 5,* 17–19.

Pitman, R. K., Altman, B., Greenwald, E., Longpre, R. E., Macklin, M. L., Poire, R. E., et al. (1991). Psychiatric complications during flooding therapy for posttraumatic stress disorder. *Journal of Clinical Psychiatry, 52,* 17–20.

Pontillo, D. C., Lang, A. J., & Stein, M. B. (2002). Management and treatment of anxiety disorders in the older patient. *Journal of Clinical Geriatrics, 10,* 38–49.

Resick, P. A., & Schnicke, M. K. (1993). *Cognitive processing therapy for rape victims: A treatment manual.* Newbury Park, CA: Sage Publications.

Rizvi, S. L., Vogt, D. S., & Resick, P. A. (2009). Cognitive and affective predictors of treatment outcome in cognitive processing therapy and prolonged exposure for posttraumatic stress disorder. *Behaviour Research and Therapy, 47,* 737–743.

Rodgers, C. S., Norman, S. B., Thorp, S. R., Lebeck, M. M., & Lang, A. J. (2005). Trauma exposure, posttraumatic stress disorder and health behaviors: Impact on special populations. In T. A. Corales (Ed.), *Focus on posttraumatic stress disorder research* (pp. 203–224). Hauppauge, NY: Nova Science Publishers, Inc.

Rosen, C. S., Chow, H. C., Finney, J. F., Greenbaum, M. A., Moos, R. H., Sheikh, J. I., et al. (2004). VA practice patterns and practice guidelines for treating posttraumatic stress disorder. *Journal of Traumatic Stress, 17*, 213–222.

Rowan, V. C., Holburn, S. W., Walker, J. R., & Siddiqui, A. (1984). A rapid multicomponent treatment for an obsessive-compulsive disorder. *Journal of Behavior Therapy and Experimental Psychiatry, 15*, 347–352.

Schnurr, P. P., Spiro, A., III, Vielhauer, M. J., Findler, M. N., & Hamblen, J. L. (2002). Trauma in the lives of older men: Findings from the normative aging study. *Journal of Clinical Geropsychology, 8*, 175–187.

Shapiro, F. (1995). *Eye movement desensitization and reprocessing: Basic principles, protocols, and procedures.* New York, NY: Guilford Press.

Swales, P. J., Solfvin, J. F., & Sheikh, J. I. (1996). Cognitive-behavioral therapy in older panic disorder patients. *American Journal of Geriatric Psychiatry, 4*, 46–60.

Thorp, S. R., Ayers, C. R., Nuevo, R., Stoddard, J. A., Sorrell, J. T., & Wetherell, J. L. (2009). Meta-analysis comparing different behavioral treatments for late-life anxiety. *American Journal of Geriatric Psychiatry, 17*, 105–115.

Thorp, S. R., & Lynch, T. R. (2005). Depression and personality disorders–older adults. In A. Freeman (Ed. in Chief), S. H. Felgoise, A. M. Nezu, C. M. Nezu, & M. A. Reineke (Eds), *Encyclopedia of cognitive behavior therapy* (pp. 155–158). New York, NY: Springer Publishing Company.

Thorp, S. R., & Stein, M. B. (2005). Posttraumatic stress disorder and functioning. *PTSD Research Quarterly, 16*(3), 1–7.

Thyer, B. A. (1981) Prolonged in vivo exposure therapy with a 70-year-old woman. *Journal of Behavior Therapy and Experimental Psychiatry, 12*, 69–71.

OTHER INTERNET RESOURCES

The following list provides additional Internet resources that may be useful for therapists and veterans:

- U.S. Department of Veterans Affairs: General services for veterans: http://www.va.gov/landing2_vetsrv.htm
- Physical and mental health resources at the VA: http://www.myhealth.va.gov/
- Aging veterans and PTSD: http://www.ptsd.va.gov/public/pages/ptsd-older-vets.asp
- National Center for PTSD: http://www.ptsd.va.gov/
- National Suicide Prevention Lifeline for veterans: 1-800-273-8255, http://www.suicidepreventionlifeline.org/Veterans/Default.aspx
- National Institute of Mental Health: http://www.nimh.nih.gov/index.shtml
- National Alliance on Mental Illness: http://www.nami.org/Home template.cfm

- Site for connecting with military members and general resources for each branch of the service: http://www.military.com/Page/0,12170, 1-OO-0,00.htm
- Support for veterans by veterans: http://www.vets4vets.us/
- A veterans-only online network: http://communityofveterans.org/? gclid=CJWP5tKsyJcCFQQRswodtgVGSg
- PTSD-related resources for veterans who are reintegrating into civilian life: https://www.woundedwarriorproject.org/content/view/479/940/
- Site for injured veterans: http://www.acenet.edu/Content/Navigation Menu/ProgramsServices/MilitaryPrograms/veterans/index.htm
- Resources for veterans and families: http://web.welcomebackveterans .org/resources_for_veterans/
- Resources for veterans and families: http://swords-to-plowshares.org/
- Resources for veterans and families: http://supportyourvet.org/
- Job bank for veterans: http://helmetstohardhats.com/
- Job bank for spouses of veterans: http://jobsearch.spouse.military.com/
- Guidance about military terminology: http://www.dtic.mil/doctrine/ jel/doddict/acronym_index.html
- Guidance about military terminology: http://www.militarywords.com/
- A free 16-page booklet to check out is *Post Deployment Stress: What Families Should Know, What Families Can Do* http://www.rand.org/ pubs/corporate_pubs/CP535-2008-03/
- The companion volume for veterans is *Post Deployment Stress: What You Should Know, What You Can Do* http://www.rand.org/pubs/ corporate_pubs/CP534-2008-03/

15

The Stress-Busting Program: The Evolution and Implementation of a Self-Help Program for Family Caregivers

Denise Miner-Williams and Sharon Lewis

COGNITIVE BEHAVIORAL THERAPY–BASED EMPIRICALLY SUPPORTED TREATMENTS FOR FAMILY CAREGIVERS

Cognitive behavioral therapy (CBT) has been used extensively with family caregivers of people with Alzheimer's disease and related disorders (ADRD) and caregivers of older adults with physical limitations. However, the diversity of CBT delivery to family caregivers transcends the "typical" CBT format of individual or group psychotherapy. As with other patient groups, such as depressed young and older adults, CBT has been found to be effective in reducing psychological distress experienced by family caregivers. Indeed, in their comprehensive review of the literature, Gallagher-Thompson and Coon (2007) found that individual psychotherapy and psychoeducational groups met criteria for evidence-based treatments for family caregivers.

The earliest reported investigation assessing CBT for depressed caregivers was developed by Gallagher-Thompson and Steffen (1994). In this investigation, depressed family caregivers of physical and cognitively compromised older adults received individual CBT for depression, which included a unique focus on challenging and changing caregivers' negative thoughts about caregiving through cognitive restructuring and problem solving. Gallagher-Thompson and Steffen also integrated behavioral strategies such as pleasant event scheduling to address depressed mood and enhance self-efficacy. Over time, Gallagher-Thompson et al. (2003) provided CBT for family caregivers in psychoeducational groups to address depression. The most comprehensive CBT-based psychoeducational group intervention developed by Gallagher-Thompson et al. (2003)

443

was formulated for the Resources for Enhancing Alzheimer's Caregiver Health (REACH) project, a multisite initiative funded by the National Institutes of Health (NIH) to evaluate various interventions for caregivers of people with ADRD using randomized controlled trial methodology.

In the REACH protocol, Gallagher-Thompsons et al.'s (2003) CBT-based psychoeducational group intervention relied on various psychoeducation, cognitive, and behavioral strategies to address symptoms of depression in family caregivers of people with ADRD. Through didactic presentation and guided discussion, caregivers were provided information about dementia, the emotional and physical toll associated with caregiving, and strategies for planning for future care (e.g., end-of-life care). Participants were also taught common causes of behavioral problems in people with ADRD, how to track behavioral problems over time using a daily diary method, as well as developing appropriate behavioral goals and plans for achieving behavioral goals (e.g., removing triggers and/or reinforcing alternative behaviors). For example, if a caregiver reported that his or her care receiver was wandering the house at night, possible causes for wandering would be reviewed. In addition, strategies for tracking, assessing, and addressing wandering would be developed and monitored for the duration of the group.

Caregivers were also introduced to the elements commonly associated with traditional CBT interventions (Gallagher-Thompson et al., 2003). For example, caregivers were taught that feeling stressed, overwhelmed, and depressed was associated with potentially maladaptive beliefs associated with caregiving, which is a core conceptualization associated with cognitive therapy in general. To address these negative emotional reactions, caregivers were presented with a three-step strategy entailing identification of maladaptive beliefs, modification or replacement of these beliefs, and observation of resulting changes in emotions as a function of cognitive restructuring. To facilitate recognition of maladaptive beliefs, caregivers were introduced and instructed in the use of a three-column thought record. Specifically, caregivers were assisted in monitoring changes in mood and identifying specific incidents and thoughts associated with these changes. In following sessions, caregivers were introduced to a five-column thought record, which added the steps of challenging maladaptive thoughts and monitoring emotions associated with these thoughts. Caregivers were taught specific strategies for challenging maladaptive thoughts, such as taking another's perspective, asking others for advice, and developing behavioral experiments to test assumptions and beliefs. Throughout the intervention, time in the group was used to demonstrate and apply these strategies. Intersession assignments (e.g., therapeutic homework) and monitoring assignment completion were also used to facilitate skill acquisition and generalization.

Behaviorally, participants were taught effective communication strategies, pleasant event scheduling, and various relaxation exercises (Gallagher-Thompson et al., 2003). For pleasant event scheduling, specific strategies that were used included education regarding the effects of pleasurable and negative events on mood, identifying pleasant events, as well as implementing pleasant events and tracking mood. In subsequent sessions, caregivers were taught strategies to cope with obstacles to completing pleasant events and incorporating their care receiver into pleasant events, which has been found to be an effective behavioral strategy to reduce caregiver and care-receiver depression in previous investigations (e.g., Teri, Logsdon, Uomoto, & McCurry, 1997). In their comparison to an enhanced support group, the CBT-based psychoeducational group produced greater decrements in depression, frequency of negative interactions with the care receiver, and emotional distress–associated problem behaviors as well as increased positive coping for White and Latina caregivers (Gallagher-Thompson et al., 2003).

The general structure of Gallagher-Thompson et al.'s (2003) psychoeducational CBT-based intervention developed over several iterations and has demonstrated surprising flexibility for addressing a range of distressing emotions associated with caregiving. For example, Coon, Thompson, Steffen, Sorocco, and Gallagher-Thompson (2003) used the CBT-based psychoeducational model to address anger in women caregivers of people with ADRD. A series of investigations using a CBT-based intervention delivered via DVD and telephone coaching by researchers have found this a useful method to address emotional distress experienced by White and Black family caregivers (Steffen, 2000), caregiving men (Gant, Steffen, & Lauderdale, 2007), and Chinese American caregivers (Gallagher-Thompson et al., 2010). Similar investigations have suggested that CBT-based interventions may be effective for addressing caregiver emotional distress (Marriott, Donaldson, Tarrier, & Burns, 2000) and anxiety (Akkerman & Ostwald, 2004) experienced by family caregivers. In summary, based on this short review, it seems clear that a CBT-based intervention, whether delivered in an individual or group format, is an effective choice for addressing emotional distress experienced by family caregivers of people with ADRD.

SELECTING A CAREGIVER PROGRAM

Given the benefits of CBT for caregivers, offering a program incorporating CBT is a reasonable way to assist caregivers. There are many factors to consider in the selection of an effective caregiver program to implement in a particular setting (Toseland, 2004). The first major factor to consider is the characteristics of the population to be served. Demographic characteristics such as the caregiver's relationship to the care recipient, the care recipient's degree of disability, and the type of illness all need to be considered when choosing a program (Toseland, 2004). Once the characteristics of the population have been identified, the goals of a program can be defined and existing programs identified or new programs developed. The second major factor to consider is empirical support for the program (Toseland, 2004). Any program considered should include basic program evaluation, such as instructor effectiveness, satisfaction with the program, elements that were helpful or not helpful, and areas of need that were not addressed during the program.

As noted earlier, there are several empirically supported CBT interventions for caregivers of individuals with dementia; however, little is written on the experience of implementing a caregiving program. The purpose of the remaining portion of this chapter is to provide a detailed case example on key aspects to consider when implementing a caregiver program. In the next section, we describe the development of a caregiver intervention based on the research of Sharon Lewis, PhD, RN. After describing the program, attention is devoted to issues related to program implementation and elements to consider when implementing a new caregiver program.

PROGRAM DEVELOPMENT

Evolution of the Stress-Busting Program

In 1995, Sharon Lewis, PhD, RN, was engaged in immunology research investigating the causes of altered host defenses in dialysis patients. Being interested in the field of psychoneuroimmunology and the relationship between mind and body, she started to refocus her research on investigating the effects of stress and relaxation on the immune system. Although many populations would benefit from examining the effects of stress and relaxation on the immune system, caregivers of patients with dementia were identified as the target population.

This evolved into the first phase of an intervention study, the Stress-Busting Program (SBP) for family caregivers. It consisted of working on an individual basis with spouses and adult children who were primary caregivers of patients with Alzheimer's disease. The intervention used was teaching simple relaxation strategies (relaxation breathing, guided imagery). The effectiveness of the intervention was assessed using self-report measures of quality of life, immune parameters, and biofeedback monitoring.

The results indicated that relaxation therapy can be an effective intervention in decreasing perceived stress and depression and enhancing quality of life (Lewis et al., 2002a, 2002b). However, caregivers wanted more educational information on stress management, preferably done in the setting of a small support group. This led to the development and implementation of the second phase of SBP. The intervention of this phase involved psychoeducational groups of up to eight caregivers that met for 9 weeks for 1 hour 30 minutes per week. The primary goal was to determine the effectiveness of a multicomponent SBP for caregivers of patients with ADRD (Lewis et al., 2009).

Word of the program spread among the caregiver community. We received numerous calls from family caregivers of persons with Parkinson's disease requesting to be in a "group," as each iteration of the intervention was called. Phase 3 was then devised, which entailed modification of some of the materials to be pertinent to Parkinson's disease. In addition, more extensive relaxation techniques were included. After pilot work to validate the changes, the program got underway.

Funding

This intervention work has been funded with NIH grants since 1995. In 2002, a 4-year grant was obtained from the US Department of Veterans Affairs (VA) to adapt the program to caregivers of patients with Parkinson's disease. In total, more than $6 million of funding has been provided for the duration of these studies.

Description of Program

The mission of the Stress-Busting Program is to provide family caregivers of persons with Alzheimer's and Parkinson's diseases education on the recognition and management of stress in their lives. Led by two facilitators, SBP takes place in a support group setting with no more than eight caregivers in a group, with each group meeting once a week for 90 minutes for 9 weeks. The program content is structured for an 8-week program. However, as we recognized the importance of encouraging interaction among the caregivers and giving each participant time to share his or her story, we added the extra meeting and found this to be beneficial and appreciated by the group participants. Because active participation and sharing can sometimes get very emotional, small group guidelines of confidentiality and respect are also addressed in the introductory session.

The overarching goal of the program is to assist caregivers by giving them the skills and permission to take proper care of themselves. The content of the program focuses on the identification of stress in one's life and how to cope with it. Topics for each week are found in Table 15.1. Theory and information are intermingled with personal and practical application. We begin with illuminating the relationships of perception, coping abilities, and balance with stress and then stress the importance of mind–body–spirit integration. We work with the caregivers in recognizing the specific stressors in their lives and discuss how to choose an appropriate coping strategy. Coping strategies include engaging resources from physical, social, cognitive, emotional, and spiritual realms. Each week at least one relaxation technique is discussed and, when appropriate, practiced. Although the program is designed to address stress management and self-care rather than specific caregiving skills, it is clearly recognized that the disease process itself is a stressor. Therefore, one of the weekly topics is devoted to knowledge about the disease process itself. Handouts include reading material on the disease as well as a book on caregiver tips. The course is succinctly described in the summary handout given to caregivers at the last meeting (see the Appendix at the end of this chapter).

We have found that very frequently caregivers need to overcome an emotional hurdle that prevents them from caring for themselves. Sometimes this can be done by simply giving them permission to do things for themselves; for other caregivers, a stronger message needs to be given. The message is that caring for oneself is not a luxury, but a necessity because self-neglect can result in a lessened ability to provide good care for their loved one. Over the 2 months of meeting with caregivers the changes in how they deal with the stress in their lives is often very evident.

An important aspect of the program was that its implementation be in keeping with the high regard the Stress-Busting team accorded to caregivers. This was made manifest in a welcoming and comforting atmosphere for the caregiver-participants. Snacks and drinks were provided at each group session and personal and individual attention

TABLE 15.1   Title and Content of Sessions and Stress Management Techniques

Session	Title and Content	Stress Management Technique
1	*Group Introductions and Guidelines* ■ *Focus:* Group introductions, purpose and expectations of group; handouts for participants (Appendix 1)	Relaxation, breathing
2	*Stress and Relaxation—Part 1* ■ *Focus:* Causes of stress, unique caregiver stressors, mind–body–spirit connections to stress	Meditation
3	*Stress and Relaxation—Part 2* ■ *Focus:* Effects of stress, positive aspects of caregiving, relaxation response, creating a relaxation environment; given meditation/relaxation CD and stress-busting for caregivers DVDs; CD and DVD guide them in learning relaxation breathing, meditation, imagery, and muscle relaxation	Progressive muscle relaxation and guided imagery
4	*Reactions to Grief and Loss* ■ *Focus:* Grieving process and losses; understanding the relationships among loss, grief, and depression	Art therapy
5	*Coping Skills* ■ *Focus:* Self-assessment to assist caregivers to identify their coping strategies; discussion of self-focused and environment-focused coping strategies; use of humor as a stress reliever; changing roles and relationships	Aromatherapy
6	*Challenges* ■ *Focus:* Understanding and managing difficult and challenging behaviors commonly exhibited by people with ADRD. Strategies to manage these behaviors are discussed. Self-assessment assists caregivers to identify these behaviors and the effect they have on their lives.	Massage
7	*Positive Thinking* ■ *Focus:* Changing the way one can think (cognitive restructuring) and how to view situations in a more positive framework; twisted thinking is discussed	Journaling
8	*Taking Care of Yourself: Healthy Living* ■ *Focus:* Integrating the strategies learned in earlier sessions to help develop a healthier lifestyle; emphasis on incorporating good nutrition and exercise into daily routines, prevention of burnout, and good sleep habits	Music therapy
9	*Choosing a Path to Wellness* ■ *Focus:* Final integration of the first seven sessions and applying it so the caregivers will be empowered to take care of themselves; caregivers create a plan to do this and focus on healthy living; discuss assertiveness skills; given "graduation" certificates	

was accorded each caregiver. During the last 5 years of the program, an annual caregiver luncheon, which was a formal and festive event with entertainment, was provided for all program "graduates."

CASE STUDY

It is not always easy to predict which caregivers need and accept assistance. One caregiver had heard of SBP from other caregivers and asked to join a group. This came as a bit of a surprise for the team as this caregiver, whose spouse had an early-onset disease and who had required assistance for many years, was active in the city and national disease organization group. She sported the reputation of someone who was knowledgeable about caregiving and was in control. However, it was clear from her comments at the introductory session that she had much to vent about and needed assistance with coping with her stressors. Each week when the participants began with sharing events in their lives, this caregiver would mention her struggle with a lack of patience. One week she came in all excited to communicate her success story of an incident where she was able to use the technique of humor to override her impatience. She gave an account of how her husband that week had asked for scrambled eggs for a meal. As she was preparing it, she dropped the eggs all over the floor. She described the look of horror on his face when he saw that, expecting her to get angry. "Instead," she said, "I paused and took a slow deep breath. Then I looked at him and said, 'Well, you said you wanted them scrambled!'" She recounted with pride how that episode, which formerly would have darkened both of their days, was a time of enjoyment for them both as they were able to laugh about it.

Shortly after completing the program, her husband died unexpectedly from an accident. The caregiver wrote to us after the funeral stating that she would never have been able to survive that whole experience without the skills she had acquired during the SBP.

Conceptual Framework

Although the program always maintained the focus of facilitating stress reduction through the use of relaxation therapy and information, the manner and techniques in which the information was presented evolved over time. The changes were based on reflective program review by the staff using both the feedback of the caregivers in the program and the use of the bourgeoning literature on the concept of stress management.

The format readjustment and the ongoing analysis of the content, process, and outcomes of the SBP resulted in an understanding of the change in the underlying theoretical framework. Initially, the program was based on the Folkman and Lazarus (1984) model of coping and the appraisal and coping model (Folkman et al., 1991), which both use a rational approach to distinguish two styles of coping: problem-focused and emotion-focused. It involved appraising the events or problems that cause the distress, identifying and using the appropriate coping approach, and reappraising the situation (see Figure 15.1).

Although teaching about deep breathing was always a part of the program, an increasing importance on the physical component of relaxation evolved. In addition to the didactic and group discussion, each session involves the experience and/or discussion of a physical relaxation technique. One such example was the elicitation of Herbert Benson's (1975) relaxation response. Other physical relaxation methods were massage, passive muscle relaxation, soothing baths, and physical exercise. Hands-on participation in the technique was encouraged when appropriate, such as bringing in a massage therapist to instruct the caregivers on the benefits of massage, give them hand massages, as well as to show them how to administer hand massage to another.

With the addition of staff attaining certification in holistic stress management instruction and a background in holistic nursing, the course content matured to include an emphasis on mind–body connections. The spiritual aspect of the person and its role in stress were emphasized more. Relaxation techniques of meditation, imagery, journaling, art therapy, and music therapy were incorporated. Caregiver participant response to this material was very positive.

Program Monitoring

The SBP staff held team meetings to discuss the progress of the study. Meeting topics included such areas as data collection status (number of groups, recruitment, scheduling of biofeedback data, etc.), review of current groups and caregiver needs, and manuscript and conference presentations. At one point, we decided to convert the handouts that we gave out weekly and create a printed handbook into a textbook. This entailed a more in-depth review of the program to ensure the best organization for a printed handbook. We realized that some of the course content no longer fit in the framework. The Folkman and Lazarus model, which addresses cognitive and affective means of coping, does not lend itself to accommodating spiritual and physical coping methods. It became evident that SBP had grown out of the Folkman and Lazarus rational model into a more holistic model (see Figure 15.2).

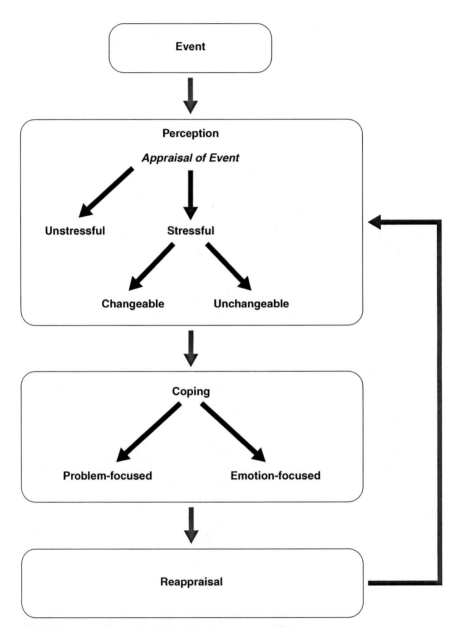

FIGURE 15.1 Framework Used by Lazarus and Folkman

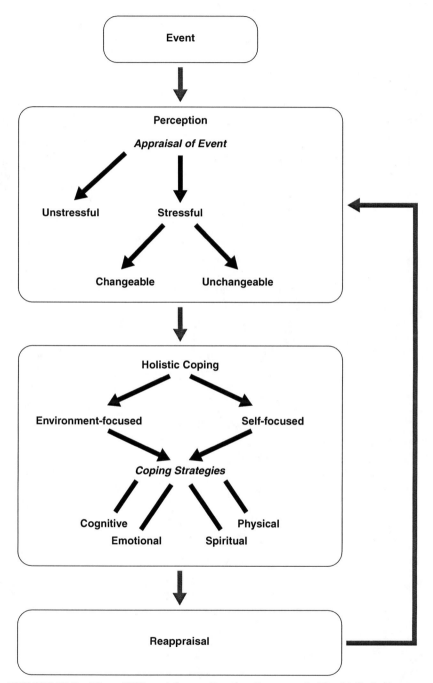

FIGURE 15.2   Miner-Williams' Stress-Busting Framework: The Holistic Framework Used for Stress-Busting Program

With the holistic stress-busting model of coping, we maintain the Folkman et al. (1980) initial appraisal aspect of identifying the global stressor and specific stressors, and clarifying the changeable and unchangeable conditions. However, coping strategies, instead of being emotion-focused and problem-focused, are identified as environment-focused and self-focused. Using an environment-focused approach, the SBP addresses the stressors themselves. This requires awareness of the situation as well as information processing of the problems at hand and using problem-solving methods. Some of the problem-solving methods, such as organizing a family meeting, might incorporate spiritual, social, and physical coping skills, in addition to cognitive problem solving.

A self-focused approach to coping involves managing one's personal perception and response to events. It includes understanding one's values and beliefs system, and addresses spiritual and physical realms of being, as well as emotional and cognitive realms. Emphasis is placed on the conceptual approach that events in life are emotion-neutral, with one's perception of the event defining whether it is stressful for the individual.

Our Holistic Framework model maintained the concept of the Folkman et al (1991) model which indicates that whether a stressor is changeable or unchangeable can influence which coping strategy is most predominantly used. Environment-focused coping is very helpful in stressful events or situations that can be changed. One may choose a self-focused approach with situations that are less receptive to change. Ideally, a combination of strategies will be used. Techniques for coping also can be cognitive, emotional, spiritual, and/or physical. We emphasize that these categories are not always clear-cut. Being only academic distinctions of a holistic approach, they melt together in many ways, with change in any one area affecting the others.

Program Implementation

Implementation of intervention research involves recruitment of participants, provision of the intervention, and supporting logistics. Two areas that are of particular interest in the implementation of this program were the recruitment and the interdisciplinary composition of the staff.

Recruitment
Recruiting caregivers for an intervention program can be challenging. We began the process of recruitment with recruiting procedures such as coordinating with the staff of adult daycare facilities and the local Alzheimer's and Parkinson's associations, distributing flyers, having

a table at Alzheimer's and Parkinson's disease events, and offering presentations for both lay people and healthcare providers on stress management. The longer the program was offered, however, the less active recruiting was needed as the adulation of program participants reverberated throughout the caregiving community. In addition, this program was a referral resource that those in the community who work with caregivers frequently used.

However, as self-identified names of interested caregivers were collected, it became evident that convincing the caregivers to commit to the 9-week program even after they expressed interest in the program was not always easy. Interacting with these caregivers led to a great deal of insight into the worldview of overwhelmed, highly-stressed, and self-neglecting family caregivers; and acquiring an understanding of this worldview led to refinement of strategies on how best to reach out to them to help them to agree to participate.

We learned several lessons from this study about caregivers and their willingness to participate in a self-help program, from both observation and through interviews conducted after completion of the program. The first lesson learned was that caregivers must first recognize their need for help. They may do this on their own or with a nudge from a healthcare provider or family or friend, but at some point, they need to admit that the demands of caregiving are greater than their coping skills. Secondly, the participants had to come to recognize their own worth as caregivers. Often, caregivers would ask about the program but then would initially back off, as they would question whether they would be able to take the time away from their family member to engage in the program. It would be only when they recognized the importance of themselves as people and as caregivers that they would sign on.

A third important insight was to recognize that the timing had to be right for the caregiver. It was very helpful to have recurrent groups. Once a person indicated an interest but would not commit to participate, we would continue to call and invite him or her each time a new group was being formed. For some caregivers, this could take multiple calls over the course of a year. The perceived benefit by the participant was another impacting element. Although we were very clear that we would be collecting data through multiple questionnaires and through blood draws and time-consuming biofeedback, we were also very clear about what caregivers would gain from the program. We described this as being the group support; the resources of the take-home book, DVD, and CD; and mostly the information and techniques on how better to take care of themselves so that they could better take care of their loved ones. Lastly, the manner in which the research staff approached the caregiver who indicated interest in the program was an important factor in participation. Many caregivers indicated that the caring interest of the staff in hearing their stories was a determining factor in participating.

An exemplar story of recruitment of one caregiver was a woman who had left her name with us at a table at a caregiver workshop where we were displaying information on the program. When I called her, she talked for a long time of all that was going on in her life. This included stressors that were beyond caring for her husband. When I offered information on the 9-week program, her immediate response was to say that she did not have the time each week to attend the sessions. And then she would continue to discuss her frustrations with her life. I offered her the thought that this program could be of benefit to her and she again backed away from committing, but continued to talk. She displayed paradoxical behavior of sharing about her life, refusal of help from the program saying she did not have time to come to it, and yet continuing to talk about her difficult life. I sensed that she not only needed to be given permission that it was permissible to take the time, but also wanted to be told to do it. And yet, I realized that I had to be careful not to bully her. After each episode of her story I would quietly make comments like, "I think this program could help you." She finally heard the message and signed up for the next available group. This woman became one of our biggest self-designated recruiters for the program, telling caregivers how much this program could help them. She often joked how she had to be "strong-armed" into coming and how glad she was when she was finally convinced.

Interdisciplinary Approach

A strength of this program as perceived by the staff providing it was the multidisciplinary input on the development and implementation of the program. Through serendipity, professionals from different disciplines interested in working with caregivers joined the team. Eventually, nursing, family counseling, and clinical psychology came together with complementary input into this program. Each group was facilitated by two professionals of different disciplines. Frequently after each group, a debriefing session was held between the facilitators to cross-check how the session went and to discuss concerns presented by the caregiver group members. Although this was a spontaneous effort that was not incorporated into the research plan, it contributed greatly to understanding and dealing with both the individual caregivers and the dynamics within the groups. Having the perspectives of different disciplines was very helpful in responding to the complex issues caregivers brought up during group sessions.

Program Evaluation

The results of the SBP, from both quantitative and qualitative measurement, indicate that caregivers who completed the SBP showed meaningful improvement in their ability to relax and manage stress. The SBP has also resulted in significant decreases in stress, depression, and anxiety, as well as enhanced quality of life and general health. Caregivers report that the program was very effective in helping them to increase their sense of self-control and giving them permission to take care of themselves (Lewis et al., 2009). Some of the qualitative data regarding the perceived value of the program by participants include the following:

- "I was at a very low point in my life. The program saved me from going into a deep depression . . . it saved my life."
- "The program was a turning point in my being able to cope."
- "The descent into my husband's Alzheimer's accelerated for both of us. I thought my life had ended, that I would be nothing more than an empty shell forever. The stress-busting program gave me a safety net when I most needed it, and gave me the impetus to live richly."

Stress-Busting Program as a Resource Center

An interesting development of this program was how the administrative office of the program became a resource for caregivers. It began partly as a means to strengthen the data collection, with calls to remind participants about completing questionnaires. But this also evolved in response to the earnest concern on the part of the team members for the individual caregivers because the reminder calls also became check-in calls to ask how the caregivers were doing. When some caregivers would have questions or would be in crisis, the SBP office was a place they could depend on for resource referral, objective advice, and/or a comforting ear.

Dissemination Challenges

Intervention research such as the SBP has an important challenge once efficacy is established; that is, to disseminate the program into public domain that it may benefit those for whom it is intended. One might argue that it is also an ethical responsibility. However, that is not easily accomplished. There are many issues that must be considered in this phase that initially may be answered with funding to explore dissemination concerns of converting the program to a community setting. Some questions include: Who should best facilitate the program (professionals or lay involvement)? What type of setting will support it (faith-based, healthcare, government programs, etc.)? The program, as intervention research, has initially operated on research grants. How will it now be funded? A great deal of coordination is involved in getting buy-in from different private and governmental organizations to adopt the program. Should the program be copyrighted? Are the researchers willing to enter into business enterprise to do this? What are the legal concerns involved?

There are several challenges to overcome when disseminating a new program; however, once the challenges are identified, solutions can be generated, permitting successful program implementation at other sites (Hepburn, Lewis, Sherman, & Tornatore, 2003). Similar to our concerns regarding the "how" of program implementation, Hepburn and colleagues (2003) identified four major challenges to transporting The Savvy Caregiver Program:

1. Translating the expertise
2. Transporting the content
3. Maintaining program integrity
4. Obtaining unique aspects of the program that might not be offered routinely at other sites.

The results of dissemination study of the The Savvy Caregiver Program across multiple states suggested that it was feasible to implement a research-based caregiver intervention without direct involvement of the program initiators. Program integrity and evaluation measures were similar to findings obtained at the original site of program development (Hepburn et al., 2003).

In May 2010, the Military Stress-Busting Program, another adaptation of the original SBP, was implemented. With funding from the Department of Defense Triservice Nursing Research Program, a 2-year feasibility study will address the needs of family caregivers of wounded warriors.

In October 2010, the Administration on Aging funded the Community Stress-Busting Program for Family Caregivers, which is another adaptation of the original SBP. Using a master trainer–lay facilitator model, the SBP will be disseminated in various areas of south Texas together with our partners at the South Texas Veterans Health Care System, Area Agencies on Aging, Well-Med Charitable Foundation, and Leeza's Places.

REFERENCES

Akkerman, R. L., & Ostwald, S. K. (2004). Reducing anxiety in Alzheimer's disease family caregivers: The effectiveness of a nine-week cognitive-behavioral intervention. *American Journal of Alzheimer's Disease and Other Dementias, 19*(2), 117–123.

Coon, D. W., Thompson, L., Steffen, A., Sorocco, K., & Gallagher-Thompson, D. (2003). Anger and depression management: Psychoeducational skill training interventions for women caregivers of a relative with dementia. *Gerontologist, 43*(5), 678–689.

Folkman, S., Chesney, M., McDusick, L., Ironson, G., Johnson, D. S., & Coates, T. J. (1991). Translating coping theory into an intervention. In J. Eckenrode (Ed.), *The social context of coping* (pp. 239–260). New York: Plenum Press.

Gallagher-Thompson, D., & Coon, D. W. (2007). Evidence-based psychological treatments for distress in family caregivers of older adults. *Psychology and Aging, 22*(1), 37–51.

Gallagher-Thompson, D., Coon, D. W., Solano, N., Ambler, C., Rabinowitz, Y., & Thompson, L. W. (2003). Change in indices of distress among Latino and Anglo female caregivers of elderly relatives with dementia: Site-specific results from the REACH national collaborative study. *Gerontologist, 43*(4), 580–591.

Gallagher-Thompson, D., & Steffen, A. M. (1994). Comparative effects of cognitive-behavioral and brief psychodynamic psychotherapies for depressed family caregivers. *Journal of Consulting and Clinical Psychology, 62*(3), 543–549.

Gallagher-Thompson, D., Wang, P. C., Liu, W., Cheung, V., Peng, R., China, D., et al. (2010). Effectiveness of a psychoeducational skill training DVD program to reduce stress in Chinese American dementia caregivers: Results of a preliminary study. *Aging and Mental Health, 14,* 263–273.

Gant, J. R., Steffen, A. M., & Lauderdale, S. A. (2007). Comparative outcomes of two distance-based interventions for male caregivers of family members with dementia. *American Journal of Alzheimer's Disease and other Dementias, 22*(2), 120–128.

Hepburn, K. W., Lewis, M., Wexler Sherman, C., Tornatore, J. (2003). The Savvy Caregiver program: Developing and testing a transportable dementia family caregiver training program. *The Gerontologist, 43*(6), 908–915.

Lazarus, R. S., & Folkman, S. (1984). *Stress, appraisal, and coping.* New York: Springer Publishing Company.

Lewis, S. L., Clough, D. H., Hale, J. M., Blackwell, P. H., Murphy, M. R., & Bonner, P. N. (2002a). Comparison of the emotional and immunological impact of relaxation therapy for male and female caregivers. *Psychosomatic Medicine, 64,* 131.

Lewis, S. L., Clough, D. H., Hale, J. M., Blackwell, P. H., & Bonner, P. N. (2002b). Comparison of stress reactivity and recovery in spousal and children caregivers following relaxation therapy. *Applied Psychophysiology and Biofeedback, 27,* 304–305.

Lewis, S. L., Miner-Williams, D., Novian, A., Escamilla, M. I., Blackwell, P. H., Kretzschmar, J. H., et al. (2009). A stress-busting program for family caregivers. *Rehabilitation Nursing, 34*(4), 151–159.

Marriott, A., Donaldson, C., Tarrier, N., & Burns, A. (2000). Effectiveness of cognitive-behavioural family intervention in reducing the burden of care in carers of patients with Alzheimer's disease. *The British Journal of Psychiatry, 176,* 557–562.

Steffen, A. M. (2000). Anger management for dementia caregivers: A preliminary study using video and telephone interventions. *Behavior Therapy, 31,* 281–299.

Teri, L., Logsdon, R. G., Uomoto, J., & McCurry, S. M. (1997). Behavioral treatment of depression in dementia patients: A controlled clinical trial. *The Journals of Gerontology. Series B, Psychological Sciences and Social Sciences, 52*(4), 159–166.

Toseland, R.W. (2004). Caregiver Education and Support Program: Best Practice Models. Family Caregiver Alliance National Center on Caregiving. www.caregiver .org/caregiver/jsp/content/pdfs/Education_Monograph_01-20-05.pdf

Appendix

SUMMARY OF STRESS-BUSTING PROGRAM: PULLING IT ALL TOGETHER

Stress involves *perception* and *balance*. Awareness of your perception of life events and how well you balance the demands of these life events (stressors) with your coping skills will determine how stressful you allow your life to be. Relaxation is the opposite of stress.

Human beings may be thought of as various "parts" or aspects of body, mind, emotion, and spirit, but in reality they are all one. Therefore, how well one part or aspect "functions" affects the other parts or aspects. When the mind is stressed, the body, spirit, and emotions will be stressed. Conversely, when you are stressed and you work to achieve relaxation in one aspect, such as the spirit, you will be lessening the stress on the rest of you—your body, mind, and emotions.

In the Stress-Busting Program, you were given ideas on how to reduce your stress. These included:

Identify Your Perception of Stressors

- Identify your stressors.
  - Break each major stressor down into smaller parts, from a global perspective to more concrete (e.g., global stressor = my husband has dementia; concrete stressors might be the repetition of questions, never having time to myself, the kids cannot deal with his changes and will not visit, etc.).
- Distinguish each stressor whether it is changeable or unchangeable.

Choose the Most Effective Coping Strategy to Match the Stressor

- Changeable: If the stressor has aspects where you are able to influence some change, an environment-focused (problem-solving) approach is helpful.
- Unchangeable: If the situation is unchangeable, focus on your own response (physical, mental, emotional, and spiritual) to the stressor to promote relaxation.
- The combination of environment-focused and self-focused coping is often the most effective.

Stress Management Techniques

- Many of these techniques overlap into the "different" categories but are listed in only one.
- Cognitive
  - Use "cognitive restructuring": Challenge your perception or understanding of the stressor. Am I helping myself by thinking this way? Could I see things differently? What is the evidence on which I base this way of thinking? What more helpful thoughts might replace my current way of thinking?
  - Use visualization.
  - Recognize and avoid "twisted thinking."
- Physical
  - Use relaxation breathing: This is the easiest, fastest, and most effective method and should be used for most situations.
  - Use passive muscle relaxation.
  - Exercise.
  - Follow good nutrition.
  - Use aromatherapy.
  - Use massage therapy.
  - Get adequate rest.
- Emotional
  - Deliberately use and develop humor.
  - Maintain a social network—somehow.
  - Use respite—time alone or away—as a regular and *mandatory* part of your life.
  - Use journaling.
  - Use art therapy.
- Spiritual
  - Become aware of your personal spirituality and develop your "muscles of the soul" (e.g., hope, forgiveness, resilience, joy, patience, perseverance).
  - Use meditation.
  - Practice mindfulness.

Social Support

- Get help from friends and family.
- Identify your needs.
- Allow yourself to accept offered help.
- Know how to ask for help—overcome any reluctance to ask for or accept help.
- Know and use community resources.

Important Points to Remember

- *Taking care of yourself (including occasional pampering) is not a luxury; it is a necessity.*
- Give yourself credit for the good you do, not blame for what you do not do!
- Your emotions and your actions are your own choice. No one can *make* you feel anything; only overpowering physical force can make you do anything not of your choosing.
- *Never* underestimate the power of your mind and your belief.

Index

Note: Page numbers followed by *f* indicate figures, and *t* indicate tables.

older adult sexuality, 264–265
third-wave CBT, 277–279
third-wave CBT literature, 277
sexual well-being, 269, 269*f*
sexuality, older adults and, 264–265
Short Portable Mental Status Questionnaire (SPMSQ), 227
Short Test of Mental Status (STMS), 230
SIGN. *See* Scottish Intercollegiate Guidelines Network
single nonmemory domain MCI (sMCI), 223
sleep architecture, 129
sleep disorders
CBT, in palliative care, 376–379
course, 132–133
depression and, 132–133
prevalence, assessment, 129–132, 131*t*
treatment considerations, 133–138, 135–136*t*
SLUMS. *See* St. Louis University Mental Status Examination
sMCI. *See* Single nonmemory domain MCI
social contextual factors, 233–234
social factors, MDD and, 37–38
social problem solving (SPS), 397–399
Social Problem Solving Inventory-Revised (SPSI-R), 413
Social Rhythm Metric (SRM), 75
Society of Clinical Psychology, 70
SOPPS. *See* Specialized Outpatient PTSD Programs
spaced-retrieval technique (SRT), 235
Spanish and English Neuropsychological Assessment Scales (Mungas, Reed, Haan, & González), 228
Specialized Outpatient PTSD Programs (SOPPS), 422
SPMSQ. *See* Short Portable Mental Status Questionnaire
SPS. *See* Social problem solving
SPSI-R. *See* Social Problem Solving Inventory-Revised

SRIP. *See* Self-Rating Inventory for PTSD
SRM. *See* Social Rhythm Metric
SRT. *See* Spaced-retrieval technique
SSRIs. *See* Selective serotonin reuptake inhibitors
St. Louis University Mental Status Examination (SLUMS), 230
Staff Training in Assisted Living Residence (STAR), 244
State-Trait Anxiety Inventory (STAI), 163
STEP. *See* Systematic Treatment Enhancement Program
stereotypes, dementia and, 225
STMS. *See* Short Test of Mental Status
stress inoculation training, PTSD and, 201
stress management, PTSD and, 201
stress-busting program (SBP)
description of, 447–450, 449*t*, 460–462
dissemination challenges, 457–458
funding, 447
interdisciplinary approach, 456–457
program evaluation, 457
program monitoring, 451–454, 453*f*
recruitment, 454–456
Structured Clinical Interview for DSM-IV-TR Axis I Disorders (SCID), 45–46
subcortical structures, 320
substance abuse
CAGE questionnaire, 142–143, 143–144*f*
course, 145
depression and, 145
future directions, 148–149
physical symptom screening, 143*t*
prevalence, assessment, 141–145
treatment considerations, 146–148
Substance Abuse and Mental Health Services Administration (SAMHSA), 142
Substance Abuse Profile for the Elderly (SAPE), 145